HANDBOOK ON HUMAN SECURITY, BORDERS AND MIGRATION

Peace does not mean an absence of conflicts; differences will always be there. Peace means solving these differences through peaceful means; through dialogue, education, knowledge, and through humane ways.
Dalai Lama XIV

For those who dedicate their lives to better borders, through peaceful dialogue and determined human ways.

Handbook on Human Security, Borders and Migration

Edited by

Natalia Ribas-Mateos

Universitat Autònoma de Barcelona, Spain

Timothy J. Dunn

Salisbury University, USA

Edward Elgar
PUBLISHING

Cheltenham, UK • Northampton, MA, USA

© Natalia Ribas-Mateos and Timothy J. Dunn 2021

Cover artwork: © Ralph Bernabei 2020.

All rights reserved. No part of this publication may be reproduced, stored in a retrieval system or transmitted in any form or by any means, electronic, mechanical or photocopying, recording, or otherwise without the prior permission of the publisher.

Published by
Edward Elgar Publishing Limited
The Lypiatts
15 Lansdown Road
Cheltenham
Glos GL50 2JA
UK

Edward Elgar Publishing, Inc.
William Pratt House
9 Dewey Court
Northampton
Massachusetts 01060
USA

A catalogue record for this book
is available from the British Library

Library of Congress Control Number: 2020952074

This book is available electronically in the Elgaronline
Sociology, Social Policy and Education subject collection
http://dx.doi.org/10.4337/9781839108907

Printed on elemental chlorine free (ECF)
recycled paper containing 30% Post-Consumer Waste

ISBN 978 1 83910 889 1 (cased)
ISBN 978 1 83910 890 7 (eBook)

Printed and bound in the USA

Contents

List of contributors   viii

Introduction to the *Handbook on Human Security, Borders and Migration*   1
Natalia Ribas-Mateos and Timothy J. Dunn

PART I   THE ICONIC US–MEXICO BORDER REGION

1   The militarization of the US–Mexico border in the twenty-first century and implications for human rights   35
Timothy J. Dunn

2   The U.S.–Mexico border since 2014: overt migration contention and normalized violence   54
Josiah Heyman

3   The mantling and dismantling of a tent city at the U.S.–Mexico border   71
Cynthia Bejarano and Ma. Eugenia Hernández Sánchez

4   *Undo/redo* the violent wall: border-crossing practices and multi-territoriality   90
Marlene Solís

PART II   ON THE WAY TO THE US

5   The predatory character of today's economies: a focus on borders and migrations   102
Saskia Sassen

6   New security: threat landscape and the emerging market for force   111
Blanca Camps-Febrer and John Andrew Carter, Jr.

7   An anti-Latin@ policing machine: enforcing the U.S.–Mexico border along the Great Lakes and the 49th Parallel   125
Geoff Boyce and Todd Miller

8   The invisible dimension of institutional violence and the political construction of impunity: necropopulism and the averted medicolegal gaze   137
Bilgesu Sümer

9   'Migrant trash' or humanitarian responsibility? Central American government state responses to deported nationals   148
Isabel Rosales Sandoval

vi *Handbook on human security, borders and migration*

10   Biopolitical governmentality at Chile's northern border (Arica–Tacna)   165
     Luis Iturra Valenzuela

PART III   CHALLENGING MEDITERRANEAN BORDERS

11   Major changes in "migrations and borders" after the "revolution" of
     globalized liberalism   177
     Salvatore Palidda

12   Documenting and denouncing violence at eastern European borders:
     the socio-legal relevance of refugee voices through the production of
     audio-visual material   189
     Chiara Denaro

13   Transnational humanitarianism: blurring the boundaries of the
     Mediterranean in Libya   210
     Natalia Ribas-Mateos

14   Migration policies at the Spanish border in Southern Europe: between
     'welfare chauvinism', hate discourse and policies of compassion   225
     Belén Fernández-Suárez

15   The wall and the tunnels: crossings and separation at the border
     between Egypt, Israel and the Gaza Strip   239
     Lorenzo Navone

16   Spanish–Algerian border relations: tensions between bilateral policies
     and population mobilities   253
     *María-Jesús Cabezón-Fernández, Juan-David Sempere-Souvannavong and
     Arslan Mazouni*

17   Neighbour or stranger? Bordering practices in a small Catalan town   269
     Martin Lundsteen

PART IV   REGIONS, PARTITIONS AND EDGES

18   Border regions, migrations and the proliferation of violent expulsions   285
     Saskia Sassen

19   Borders and violence in Burundi: regional responses, global responsibilities   300
     Niamh Gaynor

20   Blood, smoke and cocaine? Reflections on the governance of the
     Amazonian border in contemporary Brazil   312
     José Miguel Nieto Olivar, Flávia Melo and Marco Tobón

21   The borders of Macau in a geohistorical perspective: political dispute,
     (non)definition of limits and migratory phenomena in an original *border-city*   328
     Alfredo Gomes Dias and Jorge Macaísta Malheiros

Contents vii

22	The Crimean borderscape: a changing landscape of political compassion and care *Greta Lynn Uehling*	345
23	The Irish border as sign and source of British–Irish tensions *Katy Hayward, Peter Leary and Milena Komarova*	357

PART V VIOLENCE AND CONTAINMENT: APPROACHES TO YOUTH AND GENDER

24	African women on the road to Europe: violence and resilience in border zones *Kristin Kastner*	373
25	Impact of the permanent crisis in the Central African Republic on Cameroonian return migrants *Henri Yambene Bomono*	384
26	From Afghanistan border to Iranian cities: the case of migrant children in Tehran *Pooya Alaedini and Ameneh Mirzaei*	399
27	Adolescent mobilities and border regimes in the western Mediterranean *Mercedes G. Jiménez-Álvarez*	412

Afterword: a brief mapping on borders   421
Marcos Correia

Index   427

Contributors

Pooya Alaedini, Universtiy of Tehran, Tehran, Iran.

Cynthia Bejarano, New Mexico State University, USA.

Geoff Boyce, Earlham College, USA.

María-Jesús Cabezón-Fernández, Center for the Study of Migrations and Intercultural Relations (CEMyRI), University of Almería, Spain.

Blanca Camps-Febrer, Universitat Autònoma de Barcelona, Catalonia.

John Andrew Carter, Jr., Universitat Autònoma de Barcelona, Catalonia.

Marcos Correia, IGOT – University of Lisbon, Portugal.

Chiara Denaro, Università di Trento, Italy.

Timothy J. Dunn, Salisbury University, USA.

Belén Fernández-Suárez, University of A Coruña, Spain.

Niamh Gaynor, Dublin City University, Dublin, Ireland.

Alfredo Gomes Dias, Polytechnic of Lisbon and Centre of Geographical Studies of the Institute of Geography and Spatial Planning of the University of Lisbon, Portugal.

Katy Hayward, Queen's University, Belfast, Northern Ireland.

Ma. Eugenia Hernández Sánchez, Art Department, Universidad Autónoma de Ciudad Juárez, Mexico.

Josiah Heyman, Center for Inter-American and Border Studies, University of Texas at El Paso, USA.

Luis Iturra Valenzuela, Universidad Arturo Prat, Iquique, Chile.

Mercedes G. Jiménez-Álvarez, Universidad Complutense de Madrid, Spain and ACRES, Tangiers, Morocco.

Kristin Kastner, Ludwig-Maximilian University, Munich, Germany.

Milena Komarova, Queens University, Belfast, Northern Ireland.

Peter Leary, Oxford Brookes University, UK.

Martin Lundsteen, Pompeu Fabra University (UPF), Spain.

Jorge Macaísta Malheiros, Centre of Geographical Studies (CEG) and Institute of Geography and Spatial Planning of the University of Lisbon, Portugal.

Arslan Mazouni, Independent researcher, big data analyst, France.

Flávia Melo, Federal University of Amazonas, Brazil.

Todd Miller, independent journalist, USA.

Ameneh Mirzaei, independent scholar, Tehran, Iran.

Lorenzo Navone, University of Strasbourg, France.

José Miguel Nieto Olivar, University of São Paulo, School of Public Health, Brazil.

Salvatore Palidda, University of Genoa, Italy.

Natalia Ribas-Mateos, Universitat Autònoma de Barcelona, Spain.

Isabel Rosales Sandoval, Facultad de Ciencias Políticas y Sociales, Universidad Rafael Landívar, Guatemala.

Saskia Sassen, Columbia University, New York, USA.

Juan-David Sempere-Souvannavong, University of Alicante, Spain.

Marlene Solís, El Colegio de la Frontera Norte, Tijuana, Mexico.

Bilgesu Sümer, University of Massachusetts Amherst, USA.

Marco Tobón, State University of Campinas, Brazil.

Greta Lynn Uehling, University of Michigan in Ann Arbor, USA.

Henri Yambene Bomono, Ethnologist/Geographer, Senior research officer at National Centre for Education, Ministry of Scientific Research and Innovation, Cameroon.

Introduction to the *Handbook on Human Security, Borders and Migration*
Natalia Ribas-Mateos and Timothy J. Dunn

We are intrigued about world borders, their history and their spatial representation. We are interested in rediscovering the importance of spatial structure shaping globalization, which has deeply challenged geographic borders that were once "fixed" historical divisions of sovereignty and citizenship. This is why we are attentive to the changing role of borders in the twenty-first century. We are interested in researching how border zones are made up of assemblages of capital, objects, people, information and different contradictory and violent policies.

We are also intrigued with the logistics and designs of global borders. Furthermore, we see border zones as blockades to mobility or the slow-down of the mobility of people. How do different types of cross-border mobility reflect classic personhood in light of the contemporary understanding of humanitarianism and compassion? We consider the concept of classic personhood understood as the status of human beings having individual and social human rights.

The present era is marked by expanding state restrictions to the cross-border mobility of certain types of international migrants, particularly refugees and low-income labor migrants. This especially manifests in the Mediterranean and US–Mexico border regions, sites of contact between developed and developing nations and the movement of people from the Global South to the Global North. It is also exemplified in many other different areas of the world. In turn, we are witnessing the expansion of manifold forms of migrant humanitarian assistance and solidarity across these contested border zones. This type of solidarity is connected to a progressive form of activism, using transparency and sharing information in different scales and territories. Thus, the challenge is to carefully piece together the different blurred pieces of given information through a long-term empirical and theoretical examination. This is displayed by most of the contributors to this handbook,[1] who cumulatively cover a very diverse array of borders throughout the world.

Drawing on the concept of the "politics of compassion", the book begins with the premise that persistent violence in border areas needs further investigation. More specifically, individual chapters of this edited volume provide different analyses in case studies in a wide variety of border areas which vividly describe the lived experiences of people. By doing this, the chapters in this book raise important research and theoretical questions regarding contemporary forms of border violence (Jones 2016); they interrogate the political, geopolitical, social and anthropological processes in the contemporary global moment we live in. The chapters of the book map different aspects of structural violence in specific border zones, forms and practices which connect with labor exploitation, legal exclusion and a severe absence of human rights. However, they also consider the possible resistance to the proliferation of such violence, by taking into account remarkable efforts that communities and activists put forth to survive and challenge these oppressive arrangements. This volume highlights the dynamic, asymmetric relationship between the social structure of border enforcement and the human agency of migrants and activists.

Given that the lack of human security is a principal cause of migration, we also contemplate how advocates and activists attempt to provide this to migrants. Human security is a framework that shifts the focus of security from nation-states to people.[2] It consists of a broad array of characteristics rooted in human rights that impact the well-being of people everywhere, but especially those most vulnerable, and includes the following types: personal security, economic security, food security, health security, political security, environmental security, and community security (United Nations (UN) Human Security Unit 2009). Migrants are typically fleeing the lack of economic and personal security, conditions that are often exacerbated by financial, corporate, and coercive foreign policies of wealthy core nations (Graham and Poku 2000; Edwards and Ferstman 2010; Vietti and Scribner 2013; Purkayastha 2018).[3] Further, the exclusionary border securitization policies of core nations have also increasingly undermined migrant human security, while doing little to boost the actual human security of receiving country populations.[4] The security of one group cannot be built successfully on denying the security and humanity of others, which is implicitly recognized by migrant/gender activists and advocates.

Lastly, this handbook highlights key influential topics in the social sciences today: the structure–agency link, the human security[5] and human rights nexus within global border conditions. The border site represents then the materialized contradiction between national sovereignty (the power of the nation-state) and the degrading of human rights of migrants. The state uses its hard-security arm to territorialize and protect its sovereignty, creating ripe conditions for violence and human rights abuses in border zones.

These themes are shown through a diversity of cases and topics outlining the plan of the book, which is divided into five sections: (I) The Iconic US–Mexico Border Region; (II) On the Way to the US; (III) Challenging Mediterranean Borders; (IV) Regions, Partitions, and Edges; and (V) Violence and Containment: Approaches to Youth and Gender. Each part presents an interesting array of case studies from the world, and that is the real innovation of the book; there is certainly no other work that challenges contemporary border conditions through research from a human security and politics of compassion perspective.

1. STATE OF THE ART

Since the beginning of the twenty-first century we have witnessed a proliferation of scholarly works which have sought to identify and interpret the relationship between socioeconomic and broader social problems in border regions, principally related to constructing different forms of new identities in different border regions of the world (Ribas-Mateos 2011). A range of parallel social processes – based in the movement of capital as well as people[6] – are taking place at global borders in relation to mobility and the different cultures of humanitarianism in the twenty-first century. The border site not only represents the materialized contradiction between national sovereignty (the power of nation-state) and the degrading human rights of migrants (Dunn 2014), but also the clash between the humanitarian projects and neoliberal logics overpassing the state boundaries.

For this shared venture, in this handbook, we will focus largely (but not exclusively) on two paradigmatic cases, the borders of Mexico and the United States and different regions of the European Union (EU) and the Mediterranean. We also examine other world cases through involving the different regional cases (as there is a part on regional cases outside those main regions), as well as a final part focusing on specific approaches to youth and gender.

Most border regions feature militarized border enforcement as well as similar (un)humanitarian policies, directed at asylum seekers and irregular migration.[7] The humanitarian/unhumanitarian focus is considered from different angles. The state policies are generally increasingly inhumane. The humanitarianism is in principle provided by advocates and activists but also by the welfare state and by international institutions.

Nevertheless, more complex mobility occurs at these borders, including privileged (by class, race, and gender) and other differentiated and sorted types (e.g. by visa and commerce). The iconic US–Mexico border region and the contemporary transformations of the Mediterranean Sea as a region are key sites for the fraught relationship between global wealth and global poverty as well as coercive control of human mobility and humanitarian action. In the former region, Dunn contrasts the importance of immigration enforcement and its human rights problems (2009, 2014), which builds on previous works on border militarization (Dunn 1996, 2001). Human rights implications are here manifold, including continually high border-crossing deaths, widespread racial–ethnic profiling, denial of due process, and the use of increasingly widespread punitive detention measures. Furthermore, it is now well recognized that the US model of border militarization has been exported to many other border zones (Miller 2019).

According to Heyman and Ribas-Mateos (2019), three key kinds of relationship are involved in such a border regional context: (i) Militarized barriers (combined natural and human-made) that prevent the entry of peasant-workers and working classes from the Global South. This includes both uninspected entry of unauthorized workers and asylum-seeker attempts. But mixed with official rejection is humanitarianism of various kinds, both state management of migrant bodies to avoid bad political publicity, as well as resistant humanitarianism from below by activists and organizations. (ii) A permeable membrane (a system of entry inspections) that allows a range of other people to enter the space of relative wealth, including elites, tourists and shoppers, non-immigrant temporary laborers, some family members, etc., as well as massive flows of commercial goods. These are crucial to global alliances of economic, political, and intellectual elites. (iii) However, not all labor crosses the border; indeed most does not. Border enforcement reinforces a global division of labor which often places low wage production sites in the Global South and prosperous consumption sites mostly in the North (ibid.)

The challenge for empirical research in the Mediterranean, as well as for other regions in the world, is that they are often contrasted with more paradigmatic ones, such as the US–Mexico case (Ribas-Mateos 2011, 2015). Therefore, one of the main problems of "the universality of the US–Mexico border" is that it creates a "new ethnocentrism" implying that other borders will resemble it. Of course, the history and the culture are not the same in such distant regions, nor are the problems surrounding cross-border dialogue (e.g. US–Mexico, Southern Europe with the Maghreb). Differences are also constructed in welfare regimes, migration regimes, types of circulation, type of closure, and so forth. We argue that the Mediterranean setting is key for observing cross-border mobility historically and in the present moment. Here, borders are intertwined with mobility filters that differentiate people according to social categories in a place that is today one of the most militarized and heavily patrolled areas in the world, and, in the last decade, the most lethal border region in the world. In addition, this Mediterranean setting – beset by conditions of socioeconomic crisis, weak social policies, restricted borders, and multiple forms of mobility – exceeds rigid, established area studies and spills over into examining the interrelations between the EU, Southern Europe, North Africa, the Arab/Berber North Africa, the Middle East (also including Iran, Turkey, and Kurdistan), the Balkans, etc. In contrast, US–Mexico border studies are built on a more unified view of North and Latin America, while Mediterranean migration studies would be more fragmented and diverse. Over the last ten years the production of research and studies on border conflicts in the Mediterranean has increased dramatically – (over-production of publications in that sense), especially after the biggest tragic shipwrecks in the island of Lampedusa in 2013.

Indeed, there are many European borders related to mobility restriction that are not located on the classical sites of geopolitical conflict of the 1990s, such as the Strait of Gibraltar or the Otranto Channel. Today, the list of sites reflects more the tensions of migration across boundaries of wealth and poverty. We can illustrate it as: the Strait of Gibraltar and the Canary Islands, Lesbos, Greece; Malta; Lampedusa island, Italy (especially after the 2013 tragedy); the Sicilian Channel and other borders of Southern Italy (the route through Libya/Tunisia); Calais–Dover (with a Schengen border); the borders of the East, etc. Even if highly exposed in the media and more well researched in recent years (compared to the 1990s), the Mediterranean model needs to be understood in a *long durée* perspective of policies in the changing construction of "Fortress Europe." In the Mediterranean (also including here the Middle East), border transformation is accompanied by severe social inequalities expressed in different ways: increasing limitations placed on the mobility of refugees[8] and migrants, yet decreasing limitations on the cross-border flow of goods; the proliferation of refugee encampments and settlements (formal and informal); human vulnerability and rights violations; and expanded border securitization. How do we understand such changes in the formation and proliferation of the world's borders – from the notion of the strict classic border defined by geopolitical lines to the complex meaning of intensified conflict and contention of migration in the era of globalization?

These more recent trends in the Mediterranean have long been present in the US–Mexico border. They have played out in especially stark fashion in major cities and border sites, most notably in Southern Europe and also the US–Mexico border, especially during the Trump era. In these sites the contradictions are stronger between ordinary cross-border mobility for most people versus the reinforcement of border closures for other specific people on the move, particularly migrants and refugees, and an acute deterioration in their human rights and human security. It is here that we locate the revival of ancient political questions regarding the "rights to have rights" and the role of human rights defenders in border zones.

Undeniably, camps of all sorts are becoming a central step in refugees' journeys, as they structure their mobility and drastically limit their access to human and social rights (see the concept of "encampment of the world" in Agier 2014; Lagarde 2016). A case in point is the situation of the "migrants trapped in Libya" where UN institutions, European actors, national actors, multiple militias, non-governmental organizations (NGOs), hegemonic media, and independent media all play an important role in creating and revealing a complex situation of multiple forms and sources of violence[9] – particularly sexual and gender-based violence and other extreme violence[10] – and eliciting a politics of compassion and mobility in the Mediterranean (forthcoming, Ribas-Mateos 2021).

While this regional comparative border research has been a breakthrough in the study of migration in relation to their effects on spatial and social parameters, we believe that new emerging issues require a thorough analysis in order to better understand the contemporary reality of international borders. Issues such as the securitization of borders, humanitarian intervention in border areas, and the analysis of the conditions of violence exercised on people in transit (taking a careful gender perspective on such mobilities) reveal a changing, urgent reality that needs to be studied in detail by academics, border activists and policy-makers. In order to respond to this new reality centered on the clash between border security and humanitarian policies, the chapters in this handbook converge in these types of responses:

(i) They review the existing forms of conditions of vulnerability to violence in border areas and the policies of compassion that are put in place in response, beyond the classic paradigms of the "victim/survivor" (for example, sea victims in the Mediterranean). Such policies can be understood as humanitarian contradictions in the studies of violence and protection.[11] Do vulnerability and agency engender new notions of humanitarianism within global networks? How do migrants and refugees shape the complex understanding of borders in different parts of the world?

(ii) They emphasize the emergence of new forms of transnational solidarity within a framework of feminist solidarity (for example, anti-*feminicidios* networks in El Paso Juárez on the US–Mexico border). Such aims are inserted in the interest of the politics of compassion in both regions and beyond. We understand the politics of compassion as the moral–political dimension of humanitarianism set in a complex social process that is contradictory and constrained by unequal and authoritarian political contexts (Ticktin 2012).

1.1 The Politics of Compassion

In the twenty-first century, humanitarian responses to challenging crisis (such as Covid) are emergent preoccupations for most societies which are still using humanitarian tools conceptualized during the mid-twentieth century. In practice, humanitarian aid aims to save lives and alleviate suffering, but it is normally less concerned with upholding human dignity. In other words, humanitarian aid, through assistance and the growing spectrum of protection activities, aims primarily to tackle the effects on human beings of extraordinary circumstances as in contemporary border crossing. Through our view a context in which to first locate how to think such politics of compassion in border areas would especially find its roots in the concepts of human suffering, politicized pity (as referred to by Arendt 1973[12]), and the concept of compassion itself.[13]

Much of the core of such debates is present today when solving the contradictions between those who help and those who are helped, which displays the main contradictions of humanitarism in social environment relationships. According to Fassin (2012b), the emphasis is between solidarity and structural inequality between the helper and the helped, between the compassion fatigue of the helper and the tension of the asymmetry of the helped.[14] Therefore, this opens up an unsolved paradox emerging in this handbook as a contradiction in border politics: in other words, the transformation of the political on the moral terms (for example, in a compassion form). Or as Fassin (2007) recalls – the transformation of the political milieu into a moral, medical, and psychological profile of the victim. Put differently, the clash is placed between national sovereignty (political) and the human rights and human security of migrants (moral).

In general, the wide gap between the protection migrants formally enjoy under international law, and even under national laws, versus the actual experiences of individuals, reveals a severe absence of human rights, as states tend to distance themselves from state-based obligations towards migrants and refugees, not only in wealthy countries but also in other regions like the Middle East. In that region, exile, statelessness,[15] and refugee crisis have been the result of the state-building process.

In this glaring contradiction, we also see many of the main issues related to global borders: securitization, the constant search for re-routing, the importance of irregular migration, entangled forms of legal and institutional racism, complex gender issues in mobility trends, the increasing autonomous migration of minors, different forms of human trafficking, globally networked surveillance, etc. At these border sites we also witness humanitarian aid – as well as the varying other reactions of civil society in border regions.

Together with the moral–political dimension added earlier by Ticktin, we understand the politics of compassion as the moral–political manifestation of humanitarianism present among the different social actors in a particular global border. In studying this phenomenon, we draw, in part, on the work of Luc Boltanski (in the "distant suffering," 1999) and his framework of "pragmatique." This framework takes an inductive approach of observing actors in order to discern the principles of their actions and contradictions – and by extension in our handbook, observing multiple actors dealing with borderlanders and border communities in a wide range of border and migration contexts.

We can review the politics of compassion here at least in three clarifying examples, the first, located in the US–Mexico border, the second located in Morocco, and the third located in the Central Mediterranean migrant route. They are key examples to elaborate the politics of compassion; however, we will cover other Mediterranean cases in a more general way.

Generally speaking, we could take as illustrations many examples regarding such contradicting policies. First, when considering migration to the US, Uehling (2008) addresses the politics of compassion on the case of the 100,000 children apprehended in the US as unaccompanied minors, plus the number of children who escape detention measures. In such policies of compassion, Uehling examines the robust national and ethnic hierarchies which are used in the policies and practices of children's detention by US administrations. These hierarchies are manifest not only in the likelihood that a child will be sent back to a country of origin (rather than reunited with family in the US), but also in the type of attention that a child receives from the time of their apprehension until their release. The image used here is the classic "the hand that rocks the cradle" used as a protection image for migrant children in the US.

Ultimately, the politics of compassion have created an uneven terrain of protection for children. Such inconsistencies involve, on one side, protection to the innocent, and, on the other, discrimination against children by country of origin, creating a tension in the framework guiding care.[16] Children, therefore, throw into bold relief two contradictory impulses in immigration policy and discourse: an impulse to protect them as vulnerable persons (generating politics of compassion), and an impulse to "protect" and barricade borders. Since 2018 the Trump administration has opted strongly for a punitive child migrant detention policy marked by extreme overcrowding and unsafe conditions as well as family separation, intentionally constructed to attempt to deter future migration.

A second example is Jiménez's (2019) illustration of how the politics of compassion are shown in the processes of European externalization of borders in the Western Mediterranean region. Through politics of migrant control, a victimization process is developed by counting, researching, and assisting them. According to her view, these practices of humanitarianism position the migrants as passive and "compassionated" objects, while mediators such as cooperation workers, doctors, translators, etc. are the active subjects and recipients of funds dedicated to migration policies. However, counting, researching, and assisting migrants in border areas are much less severe forms of victimization than the strict, punitive border enforcement by nation-states. However, one might argue that paternalism is preferable to direct repression.

The third example is the theoretical–empirical work of Poguisch (2018) in the Central Mediterranean route. She analyzes such politics especially after 2013 connected to the Mare Nostrum Operation, where "saving lives was put on the European Agenda," and later on with treaties between Italy and Libya. These treaties tried to synthesize humanitarian rhetoric with governmental policies of migration management. However, she points out the ambiguity of such humanizing policies was expressed in multiple ways – for example, the contradiction between border control and humanitarian rescue prevents many migrants from reaching Europe.

1.2 The Changing Twenty-First-Century Borders

Borders usually contain a strong visual component, most dramatically symbolized in the idea of a wall. However, even in these physical expressions of border-as-restriction or closure, border spaces are inherently partial, selective, and opportunistic in their presentation as well as in the interests they serve. For instance, they simultaneously exclude and facilitate the mobility of other subjects and objects. Recognizing the multifaceted, contradictory nature of borders challenges conventional thinking and practices about problems that are non-linear, diffused, and simultaneous.

Reflecting this perspective, we draw upon a wide range of disciplines, methodologies, and concepts from ethnographic vocabularies to view the border as the embodiment of mobility and globalization. Therefore, based on the evidence of our collective experiences in the field (of all contributors) as well as existing research, we argue that the border is a key place of contemporary global construction, as globalization questions border capacity; borders are a clear expression of empirical global contradictions, a key empirical research site, and for such reasons it is our main focus of analysis.

Correspondingly, there are different types of academic literature on borders. For example, there is great deal from the US devoted to borders as metaphors for hybridization, creolization, multiculturalism and post-colonialism. Our approach is different, as we visualize borders as empirical realities that reflect intricate global socioeconomic processes, wherein borders act as frames (contexts) instead of objects (they are socially embedded relations), from which we can observe border filters, processes of space deterritorialization,[17] and processes of industrial outsourcing in the same manner as Sassen (2014) has analyzed.

About what kind of borders are we talking about? As mentioned earlier, cartography has offered fertile ground upon which to stress border changes throughout history (frontier, boundary, border, etc.). But this handbook is focused on a more complex understanding of such concepts, with a special emphasis on the dynamic, interactive, multilayered nature of border relations entangled with different mobilities which open up important questions on human rights and vulnerability.

In several of the past works previously carried out by the contributors, they shed light on what "the vulnerability of human rights" means today, by researching the experiences of vulnerable populations in border regions. They are impacted by the relocation of the industry and services industry (as care work) (see Oso and Ribas-Mateos 2013, among an extensive already published literature), and its effect on the labor market, gender and class inequality, extreme violence, as well as forms of resistance against human rights abuses that occur especially in diverse border areas. Thus, the contributors also address the issues of solidarity, humanitarianism, and border activism as a global action in these specific sites as key ways of analyzing contemporary violence.

Additionally, we refer here to a theme very present in border literature of the "fabrication of corpses," which in the book covers at least four different contributions. This can be clearly associated with "the manufacture of corpses" that Arendt (1973) pointed out as the characteristic of a totalitarian regime, wherein one can analyze the limits of human experience. She referred to the fabrication of corpses or the factories of destruction that the totalitarianism of the holocaust developed. They are zones of oblivion, where rights are annihilated and forgotten, and as Jacques Rancière (2003) adds, where not even humanitarianism is enough. Many independent journalists and many activists are working on these issues located in the Central Mediterranean route where such parallelism can be made, even using the concept of "genocide" (forthcoming, Ribas-Mateos 2021). Others might think that such parallelism can be far too extreme. Regardless, it is clear that powerful organizations are undermining human rights and actively neglecting the protection and well-being of the "truly disadvantaged," highly vulnerable migrants and other outsiders in a process of "social triage"[18] (Sjoberg 1999: 54–55, see also Sjoberg et al. 2001). This author gives us here a setting to understand how powerful bureaucracies tend to harm disadvantaged groups and are rarely held accountable.

2. OUR PURPOSE

With these theoretical approaches emphasized, our general purpose is to analyze the changes and the challenges of the impacts of globalization on borders, without ever forgetting the past (the history, see Sahlins 1990)), the present moment and the future challenge, and without forgetting the spatial fix as also going beyond such spatial mapping (externalization of borders, internal borders, deterritorialization). The contributors offer a solid theoretical framework (based on long-term research practices), and address public policy and institutions (governments, independent associations, universities), in the US–Mexico region, the Mediterranean region as well in other areas of the world: Latin America, Africa, Asia.

The general themes more fully specified are:

> First, to reveal the contradictions between border security and humanitarianism, paying special attention to discourses of compassion, which offer a more humane and egalitarian response to migration in contrast to more common racially and ethnically biased policies. And to analyze the practices and policies which are structurally connected to such discourses of compassion.
> Second, to analyze the dynamics of solidarity in border regions that respond to the challenges of securitization and the different forms of violence suffered by migrants in transit across borders, and violence to borderlanders, etc.

Those themes are connected with several more specific focal points of analysis in this handbook:

(a) **Analysis of the concepts of violence, compassion, and mobility in different humanitarian border environments**. Through these three ideas, we will review the logics of border governance in Morocco (Jiménez's chapter), applicable throughout the Southern Mediterranean and other borders in the world. We will analyze the structural and daily violence faced by migrants in their transit towards Europe (outsourcing processes and the so-called "war against migrants") within the framework of a new European rhetoric of human rights as a part of border enforcement policies. In this we underline the reconstruction of human testimony – for example, in the cases of extreme violence – by using very careful interviews with witnesses.

(b) **Analysis of the transit of recently arrived Latin American migrants in the El Paso–Texas area and the reproduction of border restrictions, as well as the forms of solidarity to people in transit**. See, for example, the works of Heyman or Bejarano and Hernández Sánchez in the handbook. On the US–Mexico border, the traditional migration of Mexican laborers has declined drastically, now largely replaced by Central American families and unaccompanied minors, many of them asylum seekers. Using the concepts of violence, compassion, and mobility in a multiplicity of border spaces, we can see a national political response of incitement to moral panic towards asylum seekers, including coercive "prevention policies" (before the physical blockade at the border) and the punitive treatment of those who do not manage to enter (family detention, family separation). This harsh process is countered by a response of growing compassion and care from the border population and compassion towards migrants in transit.

(c) **Analysis of the forms of transnational feminist solidarity as a form of solidarity in humanitarian work**. Dramatic changes in immigration, migration and refugee policies, as well as the exaggerated security measures such as "building a wall," have resulted in new patterns of forced diaspora from Central America, various parts of Latin America and the Caribbean (including Haiti), Africa, and migrants from untypical countries arriving at the US–Mexico border. Bejarano and Hernández Sánchez (in this book) explore these migration patterns towards the US–Mexico border from the feminist perspective by emphasizing an analysis of this new mobility and the intersection with gender, sexuality race, ethnicity, and other cultural images.

(d) **Analyzing how a gender perspective interrogates cross-border geographies in different humanitarian border settings**, particularly under circumstances marked by the conditions of extreme border violence. The project also investigates complex mobility and geographies of resistance from a cross-border feminist perspective.

The handbook coverage also addresses: population displacement, migration policies, the responsibility to protect the vulnerable, the analysis of the culture of violence, the transnational and local dynamics of violence, as well as new social practices around border phenomena. Moreover, this handbook also aims to rethink borders from a critical position, shed light on the dynamics of solidarity in response to violence, and analyze the different discourses built upon the politics of compassion.

3. WAYS OF APPROACHING BORDER FIELDWORK

Many case studies shown in the book are observed from the forces of economic neoliberalism placed in borders. But, of course, not all results are the same. Each case has roots in its own history; the contextual history of the site also shapes the neoliberal logic. Therefore each case, even with rampant communalities, displays a diversity of rhythms, dynamics, and variety of social practices.

Despite the increasing number of case studies on different borders across the world and the deepening of theoretical and conceptual thoughts on borders and bordering in global regions, there is a significant lack of systematic and comparative reflections on the methodological foundations and consequences of border studies, going beyond the limitations of border scholars' research circumstances. In our understanding, methodologies link theoretical and empirical research accounts as they gather the relationship of the heuristic use of theories, epistemological perspectives, choice of different research methods, reflections on the research process and the role of the researcher, and the use of different types of data and forms of interpretation. We will focus below in a specific methodological set:

(a) The general methodology is based upon the elaboration of the research that most of the participating researchers have been working on for at least the last ten years. We base our work in a *long durée* involvement.

(b) The theoretical framework in which many cases are inserted are in a way a continuation of the collective works carried out in the past (see, for example: the 2011 book (in Spanish) *The Rio Bravo Mediterráneo. Border regions in the era of globalization*, by Ribas-Mateos). The theoretical–empirical viability of this work is justified by the internal coherence of the joint efforts conducted by researchers over the last ten years as well as incorporating new young authors and researchers from other parts of the world into the collective project. Since that publication, authors have added the complexity of economic global processes, forms of resistance to anti-Trump cultural assumptions, and the emergence of transborder activist feminism.

(c) Action research methods in social sciences are applied, within a human rights perspective, particularly in the study of violation and support of human rights in border areas. Such action research also includes: the direct consequences towards the population in contexts of armed conflict or serious social conflict; forced displacement of the population and economic immigration; and criminalization of the resistance.

(d) Grounded theory: We use comparative methods and emergent theorizing, based upon grounded theory as a powerful tool for linking research-to-practice across disciplines. This can be particularly effective for practitioner-driven border issues, regarding:

- Conflicts and human rights, for example, through the analysis of the involvement of the actors that operate in situations of armed conflict or serious social conflict and their impacts on people, human rights and the general protection of universal rights.
- The identification of best practices and lessons in border areas through actions directed by different border networks that respond to different aspects of border violence.

Within this grounded theory more inductive approach, various texts do inform us on the effects of capitalism, the concentration of settlement around border sites of global production and exchange, which is an important traditional focus of border ethnography (Heyman and

Ribas-Mateos 2019). In many chapters there is a background of border ethnography: they include border narratives, identifications and political movements that speak to resistance and reinforcement. Therefore, the book also develops a critical stance regarding border theory, which has become very important in the last decades in several academic circles, not only in the United States but also in Latin America and in the Mediterranean region. Most ethnographic inquires of the book are also theoretically laden. Such border perspectives are also very related to the new anthropology, which is often mobile and multi-sited as well as implying complex forms of activism. The new racism that arises in multicultural late global capitalism splits the other into halves in order to celebrate one of those halves while demonizing the other [...]. But other aspects are framed as "fundamentalism" and rejected (Mexican machismo, fatalism, violence, etc.). This is precisely the "trick" global capitalism performs to guarantee its world expansion.

As Vila (2000, 2003) gives us some notes on how to conduct ethnographic work in the US–Mexico border, in the Mediterranean region the asymmetries are put in a different context. Through his work *Le proche et le lointain*, Rachik (2012) shows us the axis which can be underlined in a ethnographic border situation. Through a cognitive axis – based on theory construction – with an endo–exo (inside–outside) articulation which can cover all the distinct categories of the fieldwork in Moroccan colonial ethnography, the "beldi" and the "roumi", the foreigner and the outsider. However, he underlines how important it is to overcome the binaries of the fieldwork encounter: the civilized/the savage, the Christian/the Muslim, the colonizer/the colonized. He insists in taking into account the subjective, relational dynamic of the fieldwork.

4. THE HANDBOOK CHALLENGES

This handbook is innovative in its topic and framing, range, and combination of issues addressed, multi-continent research collaboration, and multiple research methodology employed. We detail below the most innovative aspects which the different authors deliver in this common production.

4.1 A New Research Field?

Until recently, in the countries at the center of capitalism, labor supply and demand were more balanced; there was also, more or less, a "freedom of relative circulation of labor" (or pushed to underground/undocumented migration in some regions, like the US–Mexico case). Currently, we are in the presence of a strong "mismatch," or imbalance in the labor market demand–supply, compared, for example, with the high-labor demanding situation in Western Europe in the 1970s when migration was openly needed and requested. In addition to this dilemma of an over-supply of labor, there are a number of other problems: the coarsening of the social climate between communities, the use of xenophobia as a political argument, a highly securitized model of border area management (especially after September 11), and the general impact of immigration restrictionist policies (in the US, Europe, and transit countries).

Within this current background, Heyman (in this book) shows how the border between Mexico and the US is one of the places, par excellence, where the processes of "globalization" are concentrated and expressed openly. On one hand, some 13 million people live within a region of what can be perceived as a successful example of economic, social, and cultural integration of a binational society. On the other, however, this same border area is also the site of rigorous instruments of control of migratory flows from Mexico and other Latin American countries, based on a security model stressing "national sovereignty." This security policy has several perverse effects, such as the risks, often fatal, to which migrants are exposed, and the reinforcement of criminal groups that organize clandestine passage to the US.

The main contribution of the research in this handbook is to demonstrate the contemporary importance of mobility – of the mobility of people both inside and outside the two selected regions as the contemporary understanding of humanitarianism and compassion in the design of global borders. The Euro-Mediterranean group, on the one hand, and the American–Mexican border zone, on the other, are configured as regional cases, and, in each of them, we can observe similar phenomena that are often described in diffuse and general ways, such as border restrictions in mobility filters, proliferation of the *maquila*[19] export-assembly industry, the existences of a binational community, and humanitarian action.

Nevertheless, the originality of the book goes beyond these two selected border regions and beyond such issues as shown in Part IV, Regions, Partitions, and Edges, and Part V, Violence and Containment: Approaches to Youth and Gender. These include borders and violence in Burundi, the migration crisis of the Cameroon–Central African Republic border, governance of the vast Amazonian borders in Brazil, Brexit and the Irish border, the civilian blockade in the Crimea Ukraine–Russia border, the agency of West African women en route to Europe, Afghan children migrants in Iran, Moroccan children in Europe, racial profiling on the US–Canadian border, and the smuggling regimes on the Gaza–Egyptian border.

4.2   An Innovative Analysis of Border Filters

According to Heyman (2011), an important quality of contemporary borders is that they classify or filter the mobility of different types of people and goods, based on a complex set of social, cultural, and economic inequalities.

Mobility has always been important in cross-border relationships and is even more crucial in the present era of the "compression of time and space" (as the interpretation of globalization implies). However, borders have increasingly broad roles in the control of people and goods. An example given by both Dunn and Heyman (in this book) is the patrolling of the 3,200 kilometers of land border between the US and Mexico by about 20,000 officers, hundreds of helicopters and fixed-wing aircraft, sophisticated cameras and motion detectors, hundreds of kilometers of wall, and so on. They make the crossing dangerous, but they do not deter it or stop it. Mobility control at legal entry points is also extensive and complicated, both from its conceptual form and from its practical application. Another current way of labeling this phenomenon theoretically, according to Adey (2004), is "*sorting*," or the "classification and separation" of different flows or groups of people.

While asylum seekers and unauthorized migrants receive the most attention from media, activists, and scholars, it is important to examine borders in terms of unequal mobility that includes millions of legal entries (see Heyman and Ribas-Mateos 2019). A diverse and complex range of people pass through the Mediterranean and US–Mexico borders, making a complete account unrealistic here, but there is a scattering of ethnographies of privileged crossers and the kinds of visas they hold (managers, shoppers, students, legal border commuting laborers, etc.), while others have looked at the differential inspections process by state officers at borders that sort out such crossers. More needs to be done, but we are beginning to understand borders as differentiating filters linking and managing stratified components of the world system. For this task, we need an ethnography of privilege and normalization as well as the reduction to "bare life" and risks in crossing, and humanitarian action at borders (see Heyman and Ribas-Mateos 2019). Ethnography then seeks to make connections between close-ups and extreme long shots. This ethnographic look allows different scalar views, thus allowing us how to see the way the macro situation connects with cases of local human rights violations, which connects together border political conditions with individual cases.

4.3   Humanitarian Challenges to Borders

Borders attract a variety of activists both from outside and within the border region. Activists include people broadly supportive of state enforcement, including those who play-act enforcement at borders (such as militia groups), and also pro-immigrant activists who provide humanitarian aid and advocate for migrants and asylum seekers. In the last decade much important work has been done on activism in the Mediterranean, especially since 2015, and particularly regarding displacement and camps, research on the forms of mobility and violence in border areas, and also regarding the politics of compassion. This work highlights the contradictions inherent between border security and humanitarian policies as well as the politics of compassion, moving beyond the classic paradigms of victimhood,[20] which mostly refer to women and children.

Many authors have considered this humanitarian work during their different fieldwork projects. One classic example in the Middle East is the humanitarian pictures that politically position the concepts of "refugee" and "camp" as moral indictments of the states and agencies that impact refugees' lives (see the case of the Bekaa in Lebanon, Ribas-Mateos, ongoing research, forthcoming 2021). In the past and continuing case of the Palestinian camps, the idea of not settling into new countries has been seen as a form of agency, with the refugees focused instead on their return and economic survival. They were normally seen as revolutionaries rather than recipients of international aid or subjects of humanitarian crises (Marron 2016). However, from the perspective of the NGOs in the Mediterranean today there is a new form of humanitarism that is both rational and emotional, containing a fraternal spirit and a concern for the situation of other human beings, by expressing compassion and solidarity. This has arisen along with the new displacement of millions of additional persons in a brief time, stemming from multiple conflicts – many of which are tied to disastrous foreign policy and coercive interventions in the Middle East and North Africa by the US and major European powers. This highlights how humanitarianism is a response that is embedded in politics, as seen in the moral need to save lives.[21] In this respect, there is a need to make clear that the receiving countries do play a major role in creating or worsening the conditions that many refugees are fleeing. They are the product, in part, of failed foreign policies and armed interventions.

This failure is very clear in the Mediterranean. The Mediterranean setting is constructed by a scenario which includes: socioeconomic changes in Southern European countries, mobility changes impacted by the Arab Spring, shipwreck events in the Mediterranean, EU emergency policies, proliferation of push backs, etc. They have all pushed an externalization of borders towards the South, towards Sub-Saharan Africa, especially from 2011 – the time of the Arab Spring – to 2015, and from 2015 until now, creating a crisis of border externalization and paired with a new phase of turbulence at the maritime frontier. In the aftermath of a major shipwreck involving a migrant boat and the loss of many lives on the Central Mediterranean route (April 2015), the Council of the EU launched "Operation Sophia," which was mandated to undertake systematic efforts to identify, capture, and dispose of vessels as well as enabling assets used or suspected of being used by migrant smugglers or traffickers – as a part of wider EU efforts to block south–north migration. Its justification is to disrupt the business model of human smuggling and trafficking networks in the Southern Central Mediterranean and prevent the further loss of life at sea.

One key aspect of these complex policies of compassion is the case of the re-imposed border externalization in Libya and closing off of the Central Mediterranean route by driving rescue NGOs out of the area and by expanding Libyan coast guard interceptions under EU coordination, and *refoulement/migrant return* southward. These EU policies are implemented mainly via Italy, to stem migration across the Central Mediterranean deployed as a strategy of delegitimizing and criminalizing migrant rescue operations by NGOs.

In the case of the "migrants trapped in Libya" (forthcoming, Ribas-Mateos 2021), the methodology involves a focus on human rights violations and defenses and a gender perspective. The work has particularly focused on the conditions of gender vulnerability and extreme violence. The general background is the articulation of the triangle: spaces of violence, politics of border compassion and mobilities.

4.4 Emerging Forms of Resistance

According to Bejarano and Hernández Sánchez (in this book) through necessity, vulnerable communities embark on strategies of resistance and challenge the blockades of the nation-state through the border regions. One can also add the use of the concept of "morality of risk," where norms of reciprocity and moral duties strengthen community networks despite the individual risk present at the border. Consequently, offering food, transportation, or lodging for migrants in the border regions are forms of defiance and resistance on the US–Mexico border.

On the other hand, this handbook is also novel in making scientific knowledge on these volatile topics available to society. The current reality – with the increase in hostility towards migrant populations, the increase of Islamophobia in Europe, or the closing of borders and heightening conditions of vulnerability to violence – highlights the need to provide society with new tools for analyzing the migratory reality and borders, which move away from misinformed rhetoric and discourse common in politics.

5. STRUCTURE OF THE BOOK

5.1 Part I: The Iconic US–Mexico Border Region

The first part starts with the base of the book, the iconic US–Mexico border region. **Dunn** provides an overview of the history and conceptualization of militarization in US border enforcement efforts along the US–Mexico border since 2000, focusing primarily on immigration enforcement, and some attention to the human rights problems accompanying this. His main finding is that contemporary militarization has increased through greater presence of military troops, military equipment, and a much expanded para-military Border Patrol force. The human rights implications are manifold, including continually high border-crossing deaths, widespread racial–ethnic profiling, denial of due process, and the use of increasingly widespread punitive detention measures. This constitutes an expanding, coercive form of organizational power directed against subordinate and vulnerable groups. Ultimately, for Dunn, human rights should retain a primary position, for although they are admittedly imperfect, they provide a more universal moral framework that is much less subject to the whims and destructive machinations of nation-states (and corporations) than are national laws (and corporate policies) and are more adaptable to diverse human agents and their struggles for dignity.

Heyman presents a very ambitious tour de force of a chapter on a complex multiplicity of violence, direct and structural, faced by migrants and residents also in the case of Mexicans. This chapter seems to be shaped by the reality of the wide range of violence (direct and indirect) trauma – after the horror and suffering that the region and many people have faced. This is a violent border, one of many in the world, with open violence from Mexico and hidden violence from the US. By violence he implies: both direct physical violence, including mental health and so-called structural violence. The border is here also an import symbol in enacting xenophobia, and the most violence engendering processes are enacted in this region. In El Paso, along with the Lower Rio Grande Valley, the border as field of contention between state agencies (US and Mexican) and voluntary humanitarians, another important domain of violence and suffering continues in the same space: the repressive drug war and small arms trade into Mexico. Homicides, disappearances, kidnappings, extortion, and physical and sexual assault are directed at Mexican-side border populations and migrants at extraordinary levels. While the logic of violence largely spares settled populations in the United States (though migrants in passage remain vulnerable), the total field of social life in the region is extensively subject to violence and victimization. The migration debates are well-publicized but the worlds of violence at the border are largely unremarked and normalized.

Bejarano and Hernández Sánchez examine the practice of migrants creating a "tent city within a city," one tent at a time, or one shelter at a time, transforming the urban scapes, political economy, and social relations of the border metropolis of Ciudad Juárez, Chihuahua, Mexico, as a phenomenon of being both displaced and disposable interlocks with ideologies of racism, classism, nativism, and sexism, formed in an *intersectional vulnerability*. They explore the tent city/settlement phenomenon via the interconnecting concepts of displacement, disposability, debordering, and re-bordering (within the modes of survival of different border populations, with reference to a "Border Tuner" project, which allowed people across borders to literally hear each other's heartbeats and to speak to one another without limits).

They describe tent cities as a system of symbolic *basurization* where both the US and Mexico profit ideologically from the construction of disposable people. For that they use ethnographic work on a tent city, through a system of border dialogues in order to do justice to our representations. They focus on the ethnography of displacement, analyzed as a previous experience of dispossession, as well as oppressive mechanism while appropriated as resistance. They view how tent city/ies, as small settlements appeared and disappeared suddenly. Thus, the contrast of human mobility of Central American migrants as forced migration clashes with a city facing at least three decades of violence.

Solís analyzes the different ways of crossing the border and its effects on bordering processes between Mexico and the US. She considers the Trump era as strengthening previous restrictive border policies within a network territory characterized by circularity, virtuality, instability, and conflict operating under a global context, which is not about the end of the states but the dispute over hegemonic power, where the nation-state becomes a strategic actor with new functions. Globalization entails then the "disassembly" of the nation-states in territory, authority, and rights, always within a capitalist logic that privileges capital.

Solis' chapter's main idea is that contemporary multi-territoriality is recreated by different populations in this context, generating a heterogeneous and complex landscape that allows the border to be thought of as a mobile and flexible device, which is built on territorial violence but also by resistance and by confluence. There are many types of border-crossing practices and experiences along the US–Mexico border, especially among residents in the region, which illustrate the complex nature of a border as both a point of contact and exchange as well as a barrier and exclusion. Further, these varied practices and experiences lead to a wide range of subjective understandings and views of the border among the diverse types of crossers and residents. This heterogeneity of border-crossing practices and subjectivities is very important to consider and is a good counter to both the common political view of the border as a security problem and crossers as threats as well as to the typical economic view of the border as a zone of international trade and commercial exchange. Much of the public and many policy-makers outside the region fail to keep in mind this vast volume of many different types of crossers and crossings (the overwhelming majority of which are legal), but instead see them as some sort of threat through a lens of illegality.

5.2   Part II: On the Way to the US

Expulsions on the way to the US originate in soaring income inequality and unemployment, expanding populations of the displaced and imprisoned, and accelerating destruction of land and water bodies. **Sassen** recalls how today's socioeconomic and environmental dislocations cannot be fully understood in the usual terms of poverty and injustice. Different examples in the US–Mexico–Central American region connections illuminate the systemic logic of these expulsions. The sophisticated knowledge that created today's financial "instruments" is paralleled by the engineering expertise that enables exploitation of the environment, and by the legal expertise that allows the world's have-nations to acquire vast stretches of territory from the have-nots. *Expulsions* lays bare the extent to which the sheer complexity of the global economy makes it hard to trace lines of responsibility for the displacements, evictions, and eradications it produces – and equally hard for those who benefit from the system to feel responsible for its depredations.

Camps-Febrer and Carter provide us with many important concepts and theoretical insights focused on the privatization of security and the state's receding monopoly on the use of force, with some attention to political economy but more to discourse and narrative concepts. However, private security provision is only a small portion of state-funded security – outsourcing, while troubling, is still a relatively small portion of total state-funded military and security activities in the world. Further, the state may have retreated from economic matters (deregulation of global economy, etc.), but it has emerged strongly to address immigration and border issues especially, not to mention foreign military engagements. It is not a simple either–or binary issue (strong state–weak state – it can be both depending on the issue, but is nearly always subservient to capital). The authors provide us with an original context in which to locate violence, regarding armed conflict and war (as social experiences), where violent experiences and traumatic events shape social action by work embedded in cultural coding.

Boyce and Miller explore the expansive nature of post 9/11 US border expansion, focusing on the US–Canada divide, and the increase in racial–ethnic profiling of Latinos, even in a region where there are relatively few, by the Border Patrol, illustrating its character as a national quasi-racial–ethnic police force. Over the past 20 years, the US has undertaken an unprecedented build-up of its enforcement capacity along the country's border with Canada. Officially, this enforcement build-up is justified with reference to the specter of terrorism and the kinds of security concerns that proliferated in the aftermath of the terror attacks of September 11, 2001. Although along the US/Mexico border agents arrest many more individuals actively seeking to enter the US, here too apprehension records reveal the arrest of hundreds of US citizens and thousands of individuals who are long-term US residents, through the very same kinds of practices – transit checks, roving patrol stops, highway checkpoints and third-party law enforcement custody-transfer – observed above in urban and rural areas across the southern US borderlands.

Sümer explores theoretically the invisible dimension of violence that goes in counterinsurgency operations, analyzing the cultural rationality and physiological effects arising from the use of dead bodies and human remains for sending political messages. He examines historical records as well as the everyday culture through the lens that ethnographic and geographic methods provide. Through necropopulism (using Mbebe's critique of Foucaldian bio-power) and the "averted medicolegal gaze," he compares Turkey and Mexico as nation-states whose governments make use of invisible violence through institutionalized mechanisms. By arguing that these mechanisms are created through a regime of counter-forensics and systematic impunity (examples of the political lives of slain insurgents and dead protestors), he defines necropopulism (in the period of resurgence of imperialism) represented as the discursive representation of the border, as a site of legitimate and expected violence: dying migrants as a spectacle of protected borders. He discusses the way in which political control attained through the use of dead bodies also applies to an understanding of the power configurations at the border crossings, where migrants often encounter violence in myriad forms.

Long before Central American migrants reach the US–Mexico border, they travel for weeks or months through some of the most impoverished regions of Mexico, some riding on the roofs of freight trains. It is a difficult journey even for those who make it to the US, because they sometimes face deportation. Each week a steady stream of migrants is arrested and deported from the US to El Salvador, Guatemala and Honduras, the Northern Triangle of Central America. In the last decade there has been an increase in the number of Central American migrant deportations; after the Mexicans, Northern Triangle emigrants are the most numerous. **Rosales Sandoval** examines how migrant-sending states are institutionalizing reception policies for deported migrants. These policies vary from country to country and can include the creation of institutions, programmes or statistical databases, or short-term actions such as providing snacks, phone calls and currency exchange to deported citizens. She asks which factors make some sending states reluctant to implement reception policies and argue that since deported migrants represent neither a political nor an economic gain, governments give limited attention to reception policies.

In the revival area of border studies of a Latin American tripartite border, **Iturra Valenzuela** focuses on Chile's extreme northern region, where borders have historically been highlighted by the migratory circularity between inhabitants of the surrounding countries. However, the current Colombian, Haitian and Venezuelan migration flow has caught the attention of social scientists and politicians. He details the 2018 Plan Frontera Segura. This logic of selection of trade and migration flows, between what is desired and the unwanted, is framed in the Foucauldian terms of a neoliberal governmentality and more precisely in an exercise of biopolitics where there is one desired migratory population and another unwanted. He underlines how the Tacna-Arica urban complex operates as an integration space but necessarily produces an asymmetry allowing, on the one hand, the exploitation of Peruvian migrants who insert themselves to work in the agricultural world of Arica, and, on the other, making public the discourses of President Piñera highlighting bilateral trade relations and promoting humanitarian aid for countries in conflict, but in turn denying the entry of poor Venezuelans in order to protect the border.

5.3 Part III: Challenging Mediterranean Borders

Part III on Mediterranean borders starts with the history of migration marked by periods of racism and violent rejection and also by periods of peaceful integration and assimilation in immigration countries. **Palidda** opens such a narrative with the understanding of the consequences of the economic neoliberal global "revolution," which have generated today's migrations in the transition from a more tolerant biopolitics of migrations favorable to the migrant integration into the receiving society to a more coercive thanatopolitics of death and exclusion. This is basically the radical shift in the meaning of migration policies: from *let live* to *let die*, especially in the Mediterranean. Therefore, migration and borders shift and the migrants become "wasted lives" or get trapped as "excess humanity." For Palidda, Pandemics are also part of the understanding of the migration paradigm and borders. Among the first measures adopted by nearly all governments in the Covid-19 crisis was the closure of borders (or large-scale restriction of migration), the abandonment of any duty to help refugees, which has resulted in the tragic aggravation of the situation of migrants located near borders, exemplified especially on the Turkish–Greek border zone.

Solidarity movements have had a particularly relevant role in the post-2011 period, which has been characterized by relevant changes in the Mediterranean space, both concerning migration routes and border management strategies. **Denaro** shows it particularly in the frame of Syrian migration to and throughout Europe, observing an increase of communication exchanges among refugees and a wide array of – old and new – listeners of such voices. The context is the insufficiency of the resettlement policies and the absence of humanitarian corridors to Europe that have forced people to challenge the European border regime. Bringing empirical references from the Greek–Turkish border, this chapter aims at analyzing how the individuals and associations performing solidarity with migrants on the move have been represented by the dominant narratives in the media (as key actors in humanitarian practices), and – in some cases – legally prosecuted for smuggling related accusations.

Ribas-Mateos covers a theoretical challenge set on a complex framework, considering the proliferation of spaces concerning the situation of migrants trapped in Libya and the proliferation of borders and actors when dealing with this topic. The research entails an action research (development of human rights) with a gender perspective. This perspective gives the reader a way into a complex understanding about existing extreme violence. Apart from extreme violence many other concepts end up making us reflect on the understanding of suffering, distant suffering (the view from a distance and the outsider view) when considering the answers to humanitarian crisis, as well as the question of humanitarian accountability and the NGOs' advocacy in cases of extreme violence.

Fernández-Suárez, focusing on the case of Spain, is able to unveil how in Western countries the political agenda on migration management has its main focus on migration control. Her arguments are based on the emergence and growth of xenophobic parties in Europe which have caused a rise in hate speech and this has been followed by "welfare chauvinist" policies and by emotional responses (in opposition to empathic and compassionate policies). In order to analyze the development of her research she also uses as references the context of restrictive liberalism in Western societies, the paradigm of late neoliberalism, populism, and necropolitics.

Navone shows the paradigmatic violent border in the case of Palestine as demonstrating all the elements needed to designate it as a case of "humanity in excess" using Pablo Vila's (2000, 2003) idea of borders reinforcing fractured identities between and among various ethnic communities. It is based on ethnographic materials collected during fieldwork on the borderland between Egypt, Israel, and the Gaza Strip, between 2009 and 2011. The chapter is based on participant observation and on several interviews conducted around the Rafah Border Crossing, on the Egyptian side. During the random and unpredictable openings of the border crossing, thousands of people stand in a queue in front of the terminal, waiting to cross the border. How does this "triangular" border work? When and where does it work? Who is allowed to cross it? Who is not? Can an adequate answer to all these questions be provided by interpreting the border as a membrane, compressed between opposing forces acting from either side – "border crossing" versus "border reinforcing," inside versus outside? What emerges from Navone's research is the widespread perception that the border, balanced unsteadily beneath the pressure of multiple forces, is not functioning. He focuses on the reconfiguration of the border system taken on following the Egyptian revolution. How does it function currently, and what are its effects on Palestinian mobility, and particularly the importance of vast smuggling efforts. The new *spatialization* of the border has broadened its magnitude, further complicating its identification, the understanding of its functioning, and its crossing as well as the policies directed to population on the move.

In a very little researched area of the Mediterranean borders, **Cabezón-Fernández**, **Sempere-Souvannavong** and **Mazouni** examine the movements of population between Spain and Algeria and the changes in control since the 1990s, when Spain became a member of the European Economic Community. Since then, the visa policy has been an unbreakable boundary for the political class whereas the population from both sides of the Mediterranean claim better conditions. Graphics are also attached to this chapter.

This section ends with a very local and grassroots context through an specific location in Catalonia. **Lundsteen**, inspired by the ideas of Yuval-Davis, et al. (2017), analyzes the everyday bordering practices in a small town as a paradigm of contemporary politics of belonging in Catalonia, in relation to the Spanish state. Through an approach close to a symbolic-interactionist approach and extensive use of qualitative data of close observations and interviews/conversations, he unveils how the fluid bordering process used by "locals" or white nationals in relation to immigrants is obviously relevant to our topic (immigrants and borders). However, it is more about the border as a metaphor than the geopolitical boundary, by arguing that, although Catalan ideas of belonging might be more open to other sociocultural expressions, they have their limits and inherent dominant ideas of what is more "at home" than others. On the other hand, nonetheless, attempts at constructing an urban belonging or citizenship has the same fate, as they often ignore the underlying socio-spatial inequalities.

5.4 Part IV: Regions, Partitions, and Edges

Sassen gives us a very interesting theoretical reflection on the predatory character of modern global capitalism, and how it has left populations behind, so tremendously shaping migration, and, moreover, it is in danger of extinguishing human life via climate change. Such predatory character includes mining, plantations, land grabs to expand cities or new built types of private enclaves for the rich, water grabs by the big bottlers, and more. These modes of development are typically registered as "economic development" and show up as growth in a country's gross domestic product (GDP). The fact that they expel millions of smallholders and often destroy small manufacturing and other local economic activities is not registered in those measures. The millions who have been expelled from their land (mostly in Africa, Asia, and Latin America) are invisible to these standard measures. The options they typically face are either to go to the slums of big cities in their own countries or try to emigrate. Confronted with this situation, can we develop a new legal regime that recognizes these outcomes and either condemns them or secures justice for the millions of people whose sources of livelihood are being summarily and often brutally destroyed?

In such extreme conditions, Sassen tries to de-stabilize the concept of the border in the context of predatory practices based on expulsions and extractive logics (see, for example, Chapter 20 on the Amazon in the handbook) in different regions of the Global South. This multi-decade history of destructions of rural economies and expulsions dressed in the clothing of "modernization and development" has reached extreme levels today: vast stretches of land and water bodies are now dead due to mining, plantations, and water extraction by the likes of Nestlé. At least some of today's localized wars and conflicts in Africa arise out of such destruction and loss of habitat; climate change further reduces livable ground. And access to Europe is no longer what it used to be. According to Sassen, this mix of conditions – wars, dead land, and expulsions of smallholders from their modest economies in the name of "development" – has produced a vast loss of life options for a growing number of people in more and more communities. We see this in areas as diverse as Africa, Central America, and parts of Asia, notably Myanmar.

Gaynor takes us to Burundi (ranking as one of the poorest countries in the world), situated within the volatile Great Lakes region of Africa, the country has suffered decades of violence, displacement, and re-displacement. As violence and insecurity continues, most notably following a third term bid in 2015 by the country's president, an estimated 400,000–500,000 have been re-displaced, mostly across regional borders into neighboring Tanzania, Rwanda, the Democratic Republic of the Congo, and Uganda. This chapter examines the reasons for this movement. Exploring the complex root causes of violence and instability, it moves beyond simplistic internal ethnic explanations and highlights the role of the global political economy in fomenting and sustaining insecurity, both within the country and on its borders. The chapter goes on to examine regional responses and policies to the ensuing displacement. Noting that the country continues to receive both the lowest level of international funding for refugees and relatively low levels of international aid, it makes the case for a globalized politics of compassion and responsibility in responding to and tackling the globalized root causes of structural violence in this border region. Thus, Gaynor gives an empirical account of the notion of a "globalized politics of responsibility" as key concept for the handbook.

Following on the regional scale focus we focus then on the Amazon, through a very interesting chapter, both conceptually (with a highly complex frame) and empirically. It is composed of different types of research conducted by **Nieto Olivar, Melo and Tobón** in a region divided between Brazil, Peru, Colombia, and Venezuela in the Northwest Amazon. Described within the vertices of a quadrangle of destruction that connects four cities of the Brazilian Amazon: Novo Progresso and Altamira in the state of Pará, and São Gabriel da Cachoeira and Tabatinga in the state of Amazonas. They research managing human (and non-human) insecurity and violence as a form of production, transformation, and governance in one of the most important transborder regions on the planet, in the Amazonian frontier, observed as a plural object being disputed by capitalist extractive forces. The contextual debates are: the *Anthropocene* and *Cosmopolitics*, articulating three axes through which the politics of violence, control, production, and destruction gain expression. These small Brazilian cities and the people who inhabit them have had their lives traversed by highly predatory "national defense," "regional development," "social," and "civilizational" policies based on the reckless exploitation of the much coveted Amazonian "natural wealth" and upon the "need" to guarantee national sovereignty. The necropolitical devices upon which this destruction is conducted also mark bodies, especially those of indigenous people, youth, and women, such as the hungry and drunken Hupd'ah bodies scattered in the camps of the "Beiradão," or the abused and abandoned bodies of indigenous girls in downtown São Gabriel da Cachoeira. From the Venezuelan border to the Peruvian–Colombian border, blood and smoke mingle with cocaine and the device of violence as a form of government materializes in militarized bodies that act together, extensively and intensively, on the territories of the upper Rio Solimões combating the "violence" of international drug trafficking with the "violence" of militarized forces.

We move again to the regional focus, this time towards Southeast Asia with the chapter on Macau (by **Gomes Dias and Macaísta Malheiros**). The focus is on the old colonial Portuguese territory within a historical perspective (from 1999). From its origins in the mid-sixteenth century to the founding of the Macao Special Administrative Region (MSAR) in 1999, the definition of the land and sea boundaries of Macao has always been an issue, assuming a character that can be analyzed in different dimensions. From the diplomatic point of view, the question of the boundaries of Macao remained a matter of dispute. In its political dimension, the option assumed was to maintain the status quo defined in the late nineteenth century as a way of preserving the economic and sociocultural characteristics of the city. At the social level, it has maintained its role as a port of entry and passage for various migratory movements, including not only commuting between Mainland China and Macao, but also the reception of refugees, Portuguese and Chinese, a particularly relevant phenomenon in the twentieth century. The uniqueness of the chapter on the "Macau case," from its historical perspective, makes it possible to understand today's reality, as a region with a special administrative status, preserving border control mechanisms and flexibility of labor mobility in a specific political and economic context, of progressive integration into the People's Republic of China.

Going back to Eastern Europe as an illustration of cases, **Uehling** explores what has been transpiring at the contested border between the Russian Federation and Ukraine over the disputed territory of Crimea. While it is well known that the Russian Federation annexed the territory in 2014, few know of the civilian blockade, which has been successful in modifying the flows of people, capital, and goods. Indigenous activists opposed to Russian rule stopped the illicit flow of goods, made Russian electricity more expensive to supply, and took on functions of the state in monitoring the human rights of border crossers. The differences that can be observed between this border and more paradigmatic examples trouble current theorizing on border regimes in two principal ways. First, it was indigenous activists, not the authorities of either state that imposed more rigorous filters. Second, the activists responded with counter-measures that expose the mirrored and performative nature of border security. The chapter contributes to the volume as a whole by vividly describing the lived experience inside the activists' armed compound, demonstrating how border restrictions are not the sole purview of state border and security services, and revealing the micro-solidarities and emotional resilience of people seeking to ameliorate the human rights situation in Crimea.

Next is the collective chapter by **Hayward, Leary and Komarova** on the Irish border, an empirical topic that is of great importance and likely to reveal much for the future. It shows the challenges of managing the Irish border after Brexit, the UK's decision to leave the EU centered on a campaign to "take back control" of its borders. This objective was largely assumed to mean controls on the movement of people through British sea and airports. The movement of goods and services across the UK's 500 kilometer land border with the EU was given scant consideration. Two and a half years on, it has proven to be the most complicated challenge for the Brexit process – and one that creates an incredibly complex case for future border management. The border that partitions Northern Ireland from the rest of the island of Ireland has been contested since it was drawn (what many expected to be a temporary measure) almost a century ago. While unionists have seen it as a vital means of preserving British culture and rule in Northern Ireland, Irish nationalists detest it as a lingering manifestation of British colonialism. This is a result of two key processes that fundamentally changed the relationship between the UK and Ireland. First, the peace process built on the 1998 Good Friday (Belfast) Agreement and, second, their common membership of the EU. In fact, the benefits of free movement of goods and services through the UK and Ireland's common membership of the EU's customs union and single market really couldn't be properly felt in the Irish border region until the peace process bore fruit. Apart from showing the big macro picture and the historical context in depth the authors also incorporate the micro community level with the Pettigo case study.

5.5 Part V: Violence and Containment – Approaches to Youth and Gender

Part V focuses especially on youth and gender, as the title suggests, first with the chapter by **Kastner**, who examines a harsh reality through a bodily migrant's experience of borders making clear empirically the asymmetrical and dynamic relationship between social structure and human agency, in this case the social structures impacting migrant women and the human agency of vulnerable, highly disadvantaged African undocumented/unauthorized migrants to Europe (the Western route to Spain). She offers us rich tools on border ethnography, where the body plays a crucial and ambivalent role as both an object of violence and a means of protection and capital.

Going South towards Cameroon, **Yambene Bomono** (also along the thematic line of Rosales Saldoval's chapter) show us how the state basically abdicated its role to care for the safety and well-being of its returning citizens. This is a very important finding when discussing the border implications for Cameroonian return migrants from the Central African Republic (CAR) that had previously been migrants in CAR. The context is long-term violence as, since the 1960s, the history of CAR is marked by political insecurity. Recurrent episodes of violence, banditry, rebellion, and successive overthrow of government can be observed. Today the country is mostly controlled by criminal armed groups struggling among themselves to appropriate the country's resources. This insecurity mainly affects the frontal areas and therefore neighboring countries. With CAR, Cameroon shares a long border of 797 kilometers. It is located in eastern Cameroon and west of CAR. Historical and geographical links unite the two countries. On both sides of the Cameroonian–CAR border, societal composition is almost identical. The two dominant ethnic groups are the Fulani and Gbaya. This means that in this neighboring region, inhabitants share the challenges of security and humanitarian crises due to CAR's troubled history. Because of countless government overthrows, rebellions, and mutinies in CAR, many CAR nationals and Cameroonian citizens have lost their lives and property. The 2013–2014 crisis is a perfect illustration. The March 2013 putsch of Michel Djotodia, supported by the Seleka militia composed mostly of Muslims, first led a population flow to Cameroon composed mostly of Gbaya suspected of being pro-Bozize, the deposed president. The chapter highlights the experiences of Cameroonian migrants during and after the CAR crisis of 2013–2014 with a focus on key actors that participated in the provision of evacuation, return and reintegration assistance and returnees' reintegration experiences in Cameroon. It is a case study to demonstrate how the repeated crises in CAR endanger the lives of many people on the border of this country. Insecurity on the border is a long-term issue and evolves according to the political context. The research demonstrates concrete ways in which migrants have adopted a range of strategies to flee the host country and also that crisis has long-lasting implications for the mental health of migrants. Discrimination, xenophobia, violence, harassment, beatings, as well as horrific scenes of people butchered with cutlasses, rape and torture were reported.

Not much research has covered the situation of minors and borders in Iran. Thanks to the chapter written by **Alaedini and Mirzaei** we can understand the situation of Afghans between the border and Teheran. The framework of analysis is the policies in Iran related to migration and borders, welfare and inequalities in urban neighborhoods. Of all of Afghanistan's lawless provinces, Nimruz border region is perhaps the rawest and most untamed of all, located in the desert in south-western Afghanistan, cornering up against Iran and Pakistan. The International Organization for Migration has already made various statements regarding how this border is a main gate for unaccompanied children and youth. Furthermore, the compulsory deportation of some Afghans has raised concerns for human and children's rights organizations and Afghan citizens, making new displaced families. How are these children connected with a wider framework of itineraries with families that have been concentrated in particular neighborhoods of Tehran in the recent period? These connections among youngsters between the border and the metropolis are a central issue of analysis in this chapter.

The notion of human agency in migration is vital, in the case of **Jiménez**, seen as a form of resistance to the international neoliberal economic policies and abusive policies, in her case applied to teenagers from Morocco migrating to Europe. She unveils her research through the context of the compassion industry. The context is a socio-anthropological interpretation on border policies and the process of securitization in southern borders of Europe, on the basis of the analysis of the functioning of border regimes (from the definition of a legal, technological, and ideological framework), constrained by forms of institutional abuse (arrest, reunification, expulsion, denial of rights, criminalization). In sum, Jiménez opens up many key issues on the research of migration and borders: what is the meaning for migrant and child human rights (not solely the treaties, but the broader ideals), the role of government policies, the role of humanitarian NGOs and social service providers, and the growing issue of unaccompanied minor migrants throughout the world? How is autonomy and agency useful in improving their lives, or are their lives just subject to the control of others?

Finally, **Correia** closes the handbook with the maps that accompany the 28 chapters which demonstrate the effect of borders on people's daily and ritual life, in their life transitions and travels, in their aspirations for a better life, and in their experience of violence and forms of compassion. They fundamentally show the interactions between migrants and borders (here represented by policies, politics, law enforcement agencies, and society) in different areas of the world and between and in different countries and regions: USA, Canada, Mexico, South America, Europe, North and Central Africa and Asia. The maps created in this book follow a non-traditional format. Still, they are accurate enough for one to easily understand where each chapter takes place. The style used was drawn from the abstract and fragment pieces from geography that are usually in our mind when we think about countries and the world's borders.

6. CONCLUSION: THE POWER OF PARADOX

> No es la geografía sola la que hace la historia; es el hombre que engendra la historia en la geografía.
> Jorge Mañach, 1961.

The contribution of the handbook suggests opening at least four different paradoxes which bind several of these chapters together.

6.1 The Paradox of Contemporary Mobility Itself

Mobilities are easier and simultaneously harder with emerging nationalism, populism and pandemic measures. In general, according to mobility filters (using long-running ethic and racial profiling), it gets particularly harder for asylum seekers, lower-class migrants and populations from the Global South.

Paradoxes can be reflected in many scales. Territorial subdivisions and geographic borders are essential for understanding phenomena in sociology, political science, geography, history, and economics. They influence the interregional flow of information and cross-border trade and affect the diffusion of innovation and technology. However, the analytical framework for spatially embedded multi-scale interaction is of fundamental consideration.

For our studies, we have selected regions, cities, neighborhoods, communities. Some regions have had a wide coverage, others less. In such an observance of scale we focus on regional patterns of migration, the triple borders (the case of Chile, the case of the Amazon), the colonial powers defining the border (the case of Macau), the Amazon as the configuration of the complex ecological border. Transformation and governance is shown in one of the most important transborder regions on the planet, the Amazon, the huge cosmopolitan frontier.

Such scale makes us also reflect the physicality of the borders: walls, tunnels (the Gaza Tunnel, tunnels for small goods, tunnels for larger goods, etc.), bridges (the international bridges) seas..., the mantling and dismantling of a Tent City (where one sees the clear connection between displacement, disposability and debordering), border and border cities, where port-cities constitute a particular space with specific dynamics within, which contractions driven by globalization appear in a very obvious manner.

Such scale makes us also think about communities, in how the separation between "the same people" is constructed: the cases of Ireland, Cameroon, or different in the case of anti-Latino policing along US borders with both Mexico and Canada or the construction of the foreign neighbour in a small Catalan town.

Who are the actors of mobilities? In many cases they have been minors and women. For example, with the youngster agency role in the Western Mediterranean, especially in the case of Morocco, the case of the Afghanistan Border to Iranian Cities, with the example in Chapter 26 of teenage children from Afghanistan working in solid ways recycling in Tehran, which follows the tale of large-scale migration traceable over four decades.

Other important actors are also returnees in Latino America and Western Africa. It is shown through the impact of the permanent crisis in the Central African Republic on Cameroonian return migrants. The children are especially selected as being those where the confusions around moral agency is more blatant: poor children, minority children, foreign children, children of immigrants. This is why their situation normally responds to advocacy interests.

Most ethnographic inquires of the handbook are also theoretically laden, mobile and multisided as well as implying complex forms of activism. As shown in Chapter 24, while on a conceptual level, postcolonial and transnational perspectives regarding border zones have contributed to overcoming methodologic nationalism to a remarkable extent, where the impact of borders and boundaries on migrant lives remains formidable.

6.2 The Paradox of Humanity and the Humanitarian

Human rights are also additionally precarious at the borders of a State, as this tends to be a space where the State sovereignty and security needs tend to trump civilian and individual rights and liberties – though many of the security concerns in the case of borders between rich and poor nations are largely specious. Humanitarian relief efforts and refugee-support services are also usually based at a border, and these create an entirely different form of cross-border networking and flow of people and goods. Within it, how does civil society organize complex responses? How does the State violate the right of migrants in the midst of pervasive border control and walls construction?

Is violence the paradigmatic concept in this second paradox? Such proliferation of expulsions and violence makes us go beyond the mere description of border violence. However, the real research task is to identify predatory formations which are dressed in pretty robes. The concept of violence (Chapter 2, throw two types of violence, open violence in Mexico, hidden one, in the US through an articulation of physical, mental and structural violence) but often we obscure what is behind violence (Chapters 5 and 18). This is put into context through the role of the US–Mexico border region as a boom region in international capitalism and staging point for contraband in both directions. However, observing violence is an isolated process, one that disrupts the seamless structures and systems of human life without acknowledging its joint causes and effects. There are ways to describe the violence, to replicate, to look for causes but also to obtain their answer through resilience: as with the case of African women on the road to Europe; violence and resilience in border zones. Furthermore, such deepening on violence takes us to another turn, the dispossession of humanity, the emergence of the Arendtian concept of the refugee. In short, many emerging terms that imply that the humanitarian understanding is essential in today's human mobility.

A second concept of this paradox is compassion. Exploring compassion provides insight into how some groups come to be included in circles of concern whilst others remain excluded. Why do good people turn a blind eye to the suffering of strangers? As Chapter 22 indicates, while some analysts argue that compassion is crucial for democratic politics and essential to humanitarian assistance, others are more sceptical, pointing out that compassion has a tendency to be capricious and often fails to deliver on its promises. Thus, compassion is necessary, but is not sufficient by itself.

Thirdly, the concept to consider is necropolitics. Mourning and death, death in the Mediterranean and horrorism... Necropolitics crosses many chapters of the book, by referring to the works of Mbembe 2003 (see, for example, Chapter 8) as having the sovereign right to kill. Horrorism is then what we find beyond violence, to underline the despersonification of victims, their vulnerability and their condition of being unarmed (see the reference to Cavarero in Chapter 8). We can see it in the case of Mexico, Turkey, Italy...

6.3   The Paradox of Border Control and Border Policies

These are expressed at different levels in how borders are applied. For example, by opening the doors to international students and closing them to others.

The first element here is security. Trafficking, militarization, enforcement, technological security, policing, spatial incarceration, confinement, securitization, many names that imply that migrants are invaders and human mobility is an aberration. Overall, the chapters in this volume emphasize just the opposite through the analysis of the diversity of origins, consequences and experiences of varied patterns of human mobility. Through militarization we have the example of the paradigmatic US–Mexico region, put into practice by border law enforcement agencies using all kinds of military equipment, troops, aerial reconnaissance/surveillance. What is more, this connection is even expressed more clearly in pandemic times as a secondary quotation of Chapter 7 mentions: "(...) the real threat to human beings is microbes and being able to control disease is to start controlling your borders".

One can also question what is new in this new security as a global market, like the chapter directed at new security, threat landscape and the emerging market for force. As the humanistic level, the use of force must be regarded as continuum where Foucaldian power is deployed through surveillance and technology in the name of "security and modernity" (Chapter 6), where private actors become today central together with the State security in border zones. Such reflections on security can connect again with drugs and violence as it is exposed through the reflections on the governance of the Amazonian border in contemporary Brazil.

6.4   The Paradox of Inequality

Such described inequality in border realities is linked with the discontinuity of geopolitical borders and the porous state: some borders are still weak, others experience a sudden intensified control, others continue the emergence of strict control since the implications of the policies on the "war on terror". How do such contemporary inequalities provoke numerous differentiated forms related to the "encampment of the world", the increase of expulsion, the proliferation of new transitory spaces? What is the impact of such inequalities? Inequalities palpable through human costs of current deportation regimes like in the cases of Guatemala, el Salvador, Cameroon, Central African Republic are the clearest expressions to the punishment to mobility.

What are the answers to them? Probably through global responsibilities which have to be undertaken considering the changes in "migrations and borders" after the "revolution" of globalized economic neoliberalism. From compassion to culpability, the case for a globalized politics of responsibility like in the case of Burundi-Tanzania border are shown in detail. There are ways to be found that are far from damaging through human aims, ways that are more equitable and economically sustainable, pathways to global peace and justice

Not only big macro global solutions are to be found, at a smaller scale, others find ways of documenting and denouncing violence at eastern European borders by using the socio-legal relevance of refugee voices through visual research. Last but not least the maps presented at the end of the book do not show the reticular dimensions of human and material movements; they do not show the temporality of circulation; they do not show geo-visualization, nor the "encampment of the world" or changing routes, but they reflect six different figures to think about the cases selected for the monograph. In this way the maps match with empirical analyses of critical border spaces. The book covers extensively the US–Mexico border region and border zones around the Mediterranean. Border issues in South and Central America, Eastern Europe, Northern Europe, the Middle East, Central Africa and South Eastern Asia are also discussed.

NOTES

1. We would like to thank the publishing team, who have helped us make this dream come true. For proofreading the book we would like also to thank Pamela Londe for linguistic services and the TRANSMENA Project at the UAB for their Scientific Support.
2. Human security is vital to an international migration and gender focus and is a relatively new concept for framing security, as the latter has historically been seen in terms of the nation-state. Ideally, national security promotes the safety and well-being of a nation's citizens, but it excludes immigrants and has often been used to rationalize all manner of repression and coercive policies against civilians to advance state power and elites (Commission on Human Security 2003; Edwards and Ferstman 2010).
3. For instance, neoliberal economic state and multinational corporate policies promote economic austerity and exploitation without benefiting (and often undermining) workers and most others. Meanwhile, military arms sales and interventionist policies by "great powers" are instrumental in much mass violence spurring mass migration (Boulby and Christie 2018).
4. Restrictionist immigration and border policies actually do little to promote security, because they often do not prevent migrants from entering, but only further push them into more risky underground arrangements. Further, migrants generally pose no physical threat (apart from a tiny minority) and immigration generally has positive economic benefits and makes for little competition with native workers (e.g. see NAS 2016).
5. We refer here to human security at borders when the most common way has been to refer to sites of security/insecurity. Many authors, referring to violence and conflict contexts, as expressed by Weizman (2007), use the Israel/Palestine conflict and Israel's conduct as a "laboratory of the extreme." In such an extreme, the site is related to perfecting the politics of fear, separation, seclusion, and visual control; the settlements, checkpoints, walls, and other security measures are also the last gesture in the hardening of enclaves, and the physical and virtual extension of borders in the context of the most recent "war on terror."
6. We have also managed to delineate a reinterpretation of social processes at particular border regions, considering the current dynamics of mobility and its representations in recent decades. In order to do so, the axis of the discussion has been located in the study of common phenomena in both regions of interest: transnational practices; relocation industry through the *maquiladoras*; the creation of "off-shore" zones; the emergence of transnational mobility; the increased passage of thousands of undocumented workers; the new role of women and border families' strategies; the representations and practices of these spaces; the global meaning of border control; the persistence of the multiple material and digital types of walls; the symbolism of death in border spaces; the social position of minors and their lack of rights – all while taking into account the sociocultural specificities of each region as a whole.

7. Cartography has offered fertile ground upon which to stress border changes throughout history. Throughout the nineteenth and twentieth centuries scholarly literature gradually made the distinction between boundaries and frontiers clearer by differentiating between a linear and a spatial concept. In the twentieth century, the lexical mismatch between English and Latin languages – as we shall see, 'frontier' always had military connotations – also played a role: where 'frontier' would refer more to a fuzzy border to a zone, in contrast, 'boundary' would refer to the linear legal division and would mostly be set in the context of the restrictive division of nation-states (Ribas-Mateos 2015). Nevertheless, today's tendency is to focus on a more complex understanding of such concepts, but with a special emphasis on the dynamic, interactive, multilayered nature of border relations. Thus, nowadays, we are witnessing a whole new approach to the study of borders and mobilities. We now have literature that covers a range of perspectives from trends in securitization, surveillance to digital borders, biometric borders, materialization of violence at borders, the environment of borders, the externalization of borders (especially by extending maritime boundaries) and the impact of EU enlargement on borders, particularly after the changes witnessed in Eastern Europe during the 1990s. Moreover, between 1989 and 1991, 14,000 km of new international borders were created (Foucher 2007).

8. Logically, a clear contemporary example is that of Syrian refugees. We can see this through the mapping research of Lagarde. He studies the movements of the population of Deir Mqaren – a Syrian village between Damascus and the Lebanese border – questioning the reticular dimension of human mobility. Through the life stories of the refugees and the analysis of their migration routes to Jordan and Germany, he deciphers the networks of places and actors often considered marginal, but nevertheless forming the backbone of the roads of exile linking Syria to the rest of the world. Different relational mechanisms allow access to resources (information, mobility, housing, employment) despite the structural constraints migrants continue to face in the mobile, unstable, and particularly labile nature of socio-spatial dynamics (Lagarde 2018).

9. Extreme is often used in humanitarian references or in violence references. Let's consider, for example, the work of war journalists as "in extremis": "It has always seemed to me that what I write is about humanity in extremis, pushed to the unendurable, and that it is important to tell people what really happens in wars" (journalist Marie Colvin in 2001, quoted in Hilsum 2018, p. 4). A second example is extreme violence. In Spring 2019, The MMSH in Paris (see http://www.fmsh.fr/en/research/30040 accessed 25/2/2020), organized a conference on the study of "extreme violence," reflecting on the cooperative approaches and practices of social scientists, humanitarian practitioners, and defenders of human rights in time of war, genocide, and mass crimes. Based on their experiences in Syria, Rwanda, and the Democratic Republic of Congo, they addressed: local determinants of mass killings; relief methodologies and their impacts; the actions of United Nations' multilateral agencies and of international criminal justice and national judicial institutions; and the engagement of human rights organizations. They also covered a collective reflection on the growing challenge of judicialization (recourse to the courts) that creates constraints and dangers for everyone – researchers, humanitarian actors, and human rights defenders – working on the problem of mass crimes. The possibility that they might be obliged to provide access to sources, informants, and testimonies creates situations of legal conflict, testing the professional secrecy by which researchers and practitioners consider themselves to be bound, particularly when such access may endanger witnesses and humanitarian staff members.

10. The use of such extreme violence that we all try to examine is found in many classic authors. For example, in Levi: "I would like to say a word, as an example of extreme violence, at the same time absurd and symbolic, about the use of sacrilege, not by accident but methodologically, of the human body considered as an object, as a thing not belonging to anybody, a thing one can dispose arbitrarily" (Levi 1986: 122, taken from the French version of the Italian book).

11. The concept of the responsibility to protect (R2P) which is assumed as a profound moral imperative in today's world (in the words of Ban-ki-Moon's discourses) has been criticized by some scholars on the grounds that it is incompatible with the principle of sovereignty (Glanville 2016). This implies protecting vulnerable populations from genocide, ethnic cleansing, war crimes and crimes against humanity, even implying military intervention. This idea followed that states had to be accountable to the international society, but at the same time threatens the supposed traditional rights to govern themselves and be free from external interference. At the same time, states have a responsibility to

protect their own populations from mass atrocities. When referring to the responsibility to protect, in border regions the clash between national sovereignty and human rights of migrants is especially visible (Dunn 2014).
12. "If compassion sets out to change worldly conditions in order to ease human suffering, it will shun the drawn-out wearisome processes of persuasion, negotiation and compromise, which are the processes of law and politics, and lend its voice to the suffering itself, which must claim for swift and direct action with the means of violence" (Arendt 1973: 86–87). "Pity taken as the spring of virtue, has proved to possess a greater capacity for cruelty than cruelty itself", and "politicised pity runs at cross-purposes to the liberal values of respect and tolerance " (idem: 88).
13. These are to be found in the paradoxes of compassion. We somehow touch the difficult emotional complexity of Zweig's novel (*Beware of Pity*, 2003 [1939]) on the two types of pity, distinguishing the sentimental kind (to fortify oneself against the suffering of another) from the unsentimental but creative kind that is determined to hold out, in patience and forbearance, to the very limit of its strength and even beyond. How do we feel compassion for others when they are considered weaker or less lucky than us? How is compassion a proof of our humanity looked at from the perspective of our relations to individual people or to groups considered as vulnerable? This classic book explores how good intentions do not always involve a positive impact and even the opposite: they can have devastating consequences. To see "the other" through the sentimental feeling, through the desire to protect "the other" from being hurt or to help out at a site of an unacceptable reality sometimes has opposite effects, offering the lies of denial. This is only a very brief comment on the concept of compassion, as we are very aware that there is a much larger and complex debate regarding the ethics of compassion today.
14. See the whole debate in "Ethnography and Theory with Didier Fassin – Conversations with History": https://www.youtube.com/watch?v=pNsG5wDWmhw (retrieved on 5 February 2020).
15. Examples of those conditions of lack of state protection are those of Palestinians living in Iraq in 2003 and Palestinians expelled from Libya in 1995.
16. Child welfare advocates typically take a human rights approach and contend that the children are largely akin to refugees as victims of abuse and economic circumstance. Under this argument, their care and treatment should correspond to the care and treatment of "national" children. Immigration security advocates, on the other hand, argue that unauthorized immigrants (including unaccompanied minors) are associated with increased community violence and illicit activities (such as gang memberships).
17. Even if state and territory continue to play an important role, state territorial power is re-articulated and reterritorialized in relation to both sub- and supra-state scales (Brenner 1998). Here, the nation-state reproduces both old and new roles for administrative forms, including categories and sub-categories of how nation-states classify mobilities and populations. In other words, one can appreciate that border places are configured as a highly complex variety of filtering effects. Such deterritorialization involves a simultaneous reterritorialization process. In order to illustrate this, we shall point to some instances of deterritorialization of border controls, in the sense that controls are now exercised by transportation companies and within the consulates of most countries. As Anderson points out, the controls that were formally concentrated at national border posts are now exercised by a variety of means (Anderson 2000: 25).
18. Sjoberg is making an analogy with medical triage in extreme circumstances, wherein some are "sacrificed" because treating them would take too many limited resources and thus be "inefficient," so that resources can be focused on those deemed more likely to survive with less treatment. Likewise, Sjoberg argues powerful bureaucracies disregard the well-being of the most disadvantaged groups (and at times repress them and/or dissidents advocating for them), because using extensive resources on them would be "inefficient" from the perspective of elites.
19. The US–Mexico border has provided the clearest illustration in sociology and anthropology, the *maquiladora* export assembly plants concentrated in Mexico's northern border zone.
20. See here other complex notions of this idea of victimhood. As the noted war historian John Keegan said in his recent study of military intelligence, "it is force not fraud or forethought, that counts in modern wars … the whole point of explaining clean techniques and their history is to demonstrate that there are painful coercive techniques and to alert others to the danger they represent. Until

recently, most people believed victims of these techniques suffered little or no discomfort" (Rejali 2007: 480).
21. For example in Helena Maleno's case. Maleno's book (2020) portrays a long reflection from the temporality of the 15 months duration of her judicial process (accused by the Spanish police of being a migrant smuggler in Tangiers). In the form of political ethnography she depicts the place of the protagonists on the migration path in the last 20 years, from the construction of the forest city next to Ceuta, the riots against the sub-Saharans in a Tangiers neighborhood, the helplessness of women in trafficking networks to the struggle for the right to life at sea and the lack of recognition of African lives. In all her activist journey she describes the situation of extreme humanity in her situation as a criminalized human rights defender, where a complex debate between the human, humanism, and the limitations of rights erupts. She also addresses persecution, the conception of protection and of suffering, and the understanding of suffering and self-compassion in human rights defenders.

BIBLIOGRAPHY

Adey, P. (2004) "Surveillance at the Airport: Surveilling Mobility/Mobilising Surveillance." *Environment and Planning A*, 36(8): 1365–1380.
Adey, P. (2019) "Evacuated to Death: The Lexicon, Concept, and Practice of Mobility in the Nazi Deportation and Killing Machine". *Annals of the American Association of Geographers*, DOI: 10.1080/24694452.2019.1633904.
Agamben, G. (2005) *Lo que queda de Auschwitz: El archivo y el testigo. Homo sacer III*. Valencia: Pre-textos.
Agier, M. (ed.) (2014) *Un Monde de camps*. Paris: La Découverte.
Alvarez, R.T. (2012) "Borders and Bridges: Exploring a New Conceptual Architecture for (US–Mexico) Border Studies." *Journal of Latin American and Caribbean Anthropology*, 17: 24–40.
Anderson, M. (2000) "The Transformation of Border Controls: A European Precedent?" In P. Andreas and T. Snyder (eds), *The Wall around the West: State Borders and Immigration Controls in North America and Europe*. Lanham, MD, Rowman & Littlefield Publishers, pp. 15–29.
Arendt, H. (1973) *On Revolution*. Harmondsworth: Penguin.
Arendt, H. (2006) "Nosotros, los refugiados." In M. Luise Knott (ed.), *Tiempos Presentes*. Barcelona: Editorial Gedisa.
Berumen, H.F. (2011) "Fronteras imaginadas. Diez notas y una postal." In N. Ribas-Mateos (ed.), *El Río Bravo Mediterráneo. Las Regiones Fronterizas en la época de la Globalización*. Barcelona: Edicions Bellaterra, pp. 225–238.
Boltanski, L. (1993) *La souffrance à distance*. Paris: Métailié.
Boltanski, L. (1999) *Distant Suffering: Morality, Media and Politics*. New York: Cambridge University Press.
Bornstein, E. and Redfield, P. (eds) (2011) *Forces of Compassion: Humanitarianism between Ethics and Politics*. Santa Fe, NM: School for Advanced Research Press.
Boulby, M. and Christie, K. (2018) *Migration, Refugees, and Human Security in the Mediterranean and MENA*. New York: Palgrave Macmillan.
Brenner, N. (1998) "Global Cities, 'Glocal' States: Global City Formation and State Territorial Restructuring in Contemporary Europe." *Review of International Political Economy*, 5(1): 1–37.
Commission on Human Security (2003) *Human Security Now*. New York: Commission on Human Security. https://reliefweb.int/sites/reliefweb.int/files/resources/91BAEEDBA50C6907C1256D19006A9353-chs-security-may03.pdf (retrieved on 6 June 2020).
Denaro, C. (2016) "The Reconfiguration of Mediterranean Migration Routes after the War in Syria: Narratives on the Egyptian Route to Italy and Beyond." In N. Ribas-Mateos (ed.), *Spaces of Refugee Flight: Migration and Mobilities after the Arab Spring in the Eastern Mediterranean*. Cheltenham, UK and Northampton, MA, USA: Edward Elgar Publishing, pp. 71–104.
Dinerstein, A. (2015) *The Politics of Autonomy in Latin America: The Art of Organising Hope*. Basingstoke, UK: Palgrave Macmillan.

Dunn, T. (1996) *The Militarization of the U.S.–Mexico Border, 1978–1992: Low Intensity Conflict Doctrine Comes Home*. Austin, TX: CMAS Books, Center for Mexican American Studies, University of Texas at Austin.

Dunn, T. (2001) "Border Militarization via Drug and Immigration Enforcement: Human Rights Implications." *Social Justice*, 28(2): 7–30.

Dunn, T. (2009) *Blockading the Border and Human Rights: The El Paso Operation that Remade Immigration Enforcement*. Austin, TX: University of Texas Press.

Dunn, T. (2014) "Immigration Enforcement at the U.S.–Mexico Border: Where Human Rights and Citizenship (& National Sovereignty) Collide." In C. Mueller and W. Simmons (eds.), *Binational Human Rights: The U.S.–Mexico Experience*. Philadelphia: University of Pennsylvania Press, pp. 68–87.

Edwards, A. and Ferstman, C. (2010) *Human Security and Non-Citizens: Law, Policy and International Affairs*. Cambridge: Cambridge University Press.

Fassin, D. (2007) "Humanitarianism as a Politics of Life." *Public Culture*, 19(3): 499–520.

Fassin, D. (2008) "The Humanitarian Politics of Testimony: Subjectification through Trauma in the Israeli–Palestinian Conflict." *Cultural Anthropology*, 23: 531–558.

Fassin, D. (2012a) *"Humanitarian Reason": A Moral History of the Present*. Berkeley: University of California Press.

Fassin, D. (2012b) *Moral Anthropology: A Companion*. Malden: Wiley-Blackwell.

Fassin, D. and Rechtman, R. (2009) *The Empire of Trauma: An Inquiry into the Condition of Victimhood*. Princeton, NJ: Princeton University Press.

Fernández-Kelly, M.P. (1983) *For We Are Sold, I and My People: Women and Industry in Mexico's Frontier*. Albany, NY: State University of New York Press.

Forensic Oceanography (2018) "MARE CLAUSUM Italy and the EU's Undeclared Operation to Stem Migration across the Mediterranean: A Report by Forensic Oceanography (Charles Heller and Lorenzo Pezzani), affiliated to the Forensic Architecture Agency", Goldsmiths, University of London, May.

Foucher, M. (2007) *L'obsession des frontières*. Paris: Libraire Académique Perrin.

Galván, R. (2014) "Chicana/Latin American Feminist Epistemologies of the Global South (Within and Outside the North): Decolonizing *El Conocimiento* and Creating Global Alliances." *Journal of Latino/Latin American Studies*, 6(2): 135–140.

Glanville, L. (2016) "Sovereignty." In A.J. Bellamy and T. Dunne (eds.), *The Oxford Handbook of the Responsibility to Protect*. Oxford: Oxford University Press, pp. 151–66.

Graham, D.T. and Poku, N.K. (2000) *Migration, Globalisation, and Human Security*. New York: Routledge.

Heyman, J. (2017) "Contributions of U.S.–Mexico Border Studies to Social Science Theory." In C. Vélez-Ibáñez and J. Heyman (eds.), *The U.S.–Mexico Transborder Region: Cultural Dynamics and Historical Interactions*, Tucson: University of Arizona Press, pp. 44–64.

Heyman, J. and Ribas-Mateos, N. (2019) "Borders of Wealth and Poverty: Ideas Stimulated by Comparing the Mediterranean and U.S.–Mexico." In C. Brambilla (ed.), *Guest Session on Anthropology and Critical Border Studies*. *Archivio antropologico mediterraneo* 21, no. 2.

Hilsum, L. (2018) *In Extremis: The Life and Death of the War Correspondent Marie Colvin*. New York: Farrar, Straus and Giroux.

Jiménez, M. (2019) "Externalización fronteriza en el Mediterráneo Occidental: movilidades, violencias y políticas de compasión." https://www.researchgate.net/publication/290212829_Externalizacion_fronteriza_en_el_Mediterraneo_Occidental_movilidades_violencias_y_politicas_de_compasion (retrieved on 2 March 2019).

Jones, R. (2016) *Violent Borders: Refugees and the Right to Move*. New York: Verso.

Lagarde, D. (2016) "Mapping the Encampment of the World and its Consequences on Refugees' Itineraries", paper presented at the Refugees on the Move Conference, CERMigracions, Barcelona, 21–22 April.

Lagarde, D. (2018) "De Damas à Dortmund, le parcours d'une famille syrienne." In V. Bontemps, C. Makaremi, and S. Mazouz (eds.), *Entre accueil et rejet: ce que les villes font aux migrants*. Paris: Le passager clandestin.

Levi. P. (1986) *Les naufragés et les rescapés. Quarante ans après Auschwitz*. Paris: Arcades Gallimard. Translated from Italian by André Maugé.

Maleno, H. (2020) *Mujer de Frontera*. Barcelona: Editorial Península.

Marcus, G. (1995) "Ethnography in/of the World System: The Emergence of Multi-Sited Ethnography." *Annual Review of Anthropology*, 24: 95–117.

Marron, R. (2016) "Introduction. On the Humanitarian Cause." In *Humanitarian Rackets and their Moral Hazards: The Case of the Palestinian Refugee Camps in Lebanon*. Abingdon and New York: Routledge, pp. 1–29.

Martínez, O.J. (1998) *Border People: Life and Society in the U.S.–Mexico Borderlands*. Tucson: University of Arizona Press.

Mezzadra, S. and Neilson, B. (2013) *Border as Method, or, the Multiplication of Labor*. Durham, NC: Duke University Press.

Miller, T. (2019) *Empire of Borders: The Expansion of the US Border Around the World*. London: Verso.

NAS (National Academies of Sciences, US) (2016) *The Economic and Fiscal Consequences of Immigration*. Washington: National Academies Press. https://www.nap.edu/download/23550 (retrieved on 1 November 2020).

Oso, L. and Ribas-Mateos, N. (2013) "An Introduction to a Global and Development Perspective: A Focus on Gender, Migration and Transnationalism." In L. Oso and N. Ribas-Mateos (eds.), *Gender, Migration and Transnationalism: Global and Development Perspectives*. Cheltenham, UK and Northampton, MA, USA: Edward Elgar Publishing, pp. 1–41.

Poguisch, T. (2018) "I Confini Fantasma dell'Europa." In T. Poguisch and T. Milano-Udine (eds.), *Decolonizzare le migrazioni. Razzismo, confini, marginalità*. Milan: Mimesis/Cartografie Sociale, pp. 41–60.

Purkayastha, B. (2018) "Migration, Migrants, and Human Security." *Current Sociology Monograph*, 66(2): 167–191.

Rachik, H. (2012) *Le proche et le lointain. Un siècle d'anthropologie au Maroc*. Marseille: Parenthèses/MaisonMéditerranéenne des Sciences de l'Homme.

Rancière, J. (2003) *El maestro ignorante*. Laertes: Barcelona.

Rejali, D. (2007) *Torture and Democracy*. Princeton: Princeton University Press.

Ribas-Mateos, N. (2005), *The Mediterranean in the Age of Globalization. Migration, Welfare and Borders*. New Brunswick: Transaction Publishers.

Ribas-Mateos, N. (ed.) (2011) *El Río Bravo Mediterráneo: Las Regiones Fronterizas en la Epoca de la Globalización*. Barcelona: Ediciòns Bellaterra.

Ribas-Mateos, N. (2015) *Border Shifts: New Mobilities from Europe and Beyond*. Frontiers of Globalization series. Basingstoke: Palgrave Macmillan.

Ribas-Mateos, N. (ed.) (2016) *Migration, Mobilities and the Arab Spring*. Cheltenham, UK and Northampton, MA, USA: Edward Elgar Publishing

Ribas-Mateos, N. (2019) "Migrants Trapped in Libya: Is Detention and Human Rights' Abuse the 'Solution'"? Seminar, Department of Social and Policy Sciences, University of Bath, March.

Ribas-Mateos, N. (2020) "Borders and Mobilities in the Middle East: Emerging Challenges for Syrian Refugees in 'Bilad Al-Sham'. In Z. Babar (ed.), *Mobility and Forced Displacement in the Middle East*. London: Hurst and Company, pp. 19–32.

Rossetto, T. (2015) "Performing the Nation between Us: Urban Photographic Sets with Young Migrants." *Fennia*, 193(2): 165–184.

Sahlins, P. (1990) *Boundaries: The Making of France and Spain in the Pyrenees*. Berkeley, Los Angeles and Oxford: University of California Press.

Sassen, S. (2014) "Migrants or Expelled? Beyond the 20th Century Migration Modes" (video-conference). Paper presented at the International Conference "Guests and Aliens. Re-configuring New Mobilities After 2011," IFEA Istanbul, 9–10 December.

Sheller, M. and Urry, J. (2006) "The New Mobilities Paradigm." *Environment and Planning A*, 38(2): 207–226.

Sjoberg, G. (1999) *Bureaucratic Capitalism and Human Rights' Sociology for the Twenty-first Century*. Chicago: University of Chicago Press.

Sjoberg, G., Gill, E. and Williams, N. (2001) "A Sociology of Human Rights." *Social Problems*, 48(1): 11–47.

Sontag, S. (2003) *Regarding the Pain of Others*. New York: Picador.

Ticktin, M. (2011a) *Casualties of Care: Immigration and the Politics of Humanitarianism in France.* Berkeley: University of California Press; Tucson: University of Arizona Press.

Ticktin, M. (2011b) "The Gendered Human of Humanitarianism: Medicalising and Politicising Sexual Violence." *Gender and History*, 23(2): 250–65.

Ticktin, M. (2012) *Casualties of Care: Immigration and the Politics of Humanitarianism in France.* Berkeley, CA: University of California Press.

Uehling, G.L. (2008) "The International Smuggling of Children: Coyotes, Snakeheads and the Politics of Compassion." *Anthropological Quarterly*, 81(4): 833–872.

UN Human Security Unit (2009) *Human Security in Theory and Practice.* New York: United Nations. https://www.unocha.org/sites/dms/HSU/Publications%20and%20Products/Human%20Security%20Tools/Human%20Security%20in%20Theory%20and%20Practice%20English.pdf (retrieved on 1 November 2020).

Velasco Ortiz, L., and Contreras, O.F. (2011) *Mexican Voices of the Border Region.* Philadelphia, PA: Temple University Press.

Vietti, F. and Scribner, T. (2013) "Human Insecurity: Understanding International Migration from a Human Security Perspective." *Journal on Migration and Human Security*, 1(1): 17–31.

Vila, P. (2000) *Crossing Borders, Reinforcing Borders: Social Categories and Narrative Identities on the US–Mexico Frontier.* Austin: University of Texas Press.

Vila, P. (2003) "Conclusion: The Limits of American Border Theory." *Ethnography at the Border.* Minneapolis and London: University of Minnesota Press, pp. 306–341.

Weizman, E. (2007) *Hollow Land: Israel's Architecture of Occupation.* London: Verso.

Yuval-Davis, N., Wemyss, G. and Cassidy, K. (2017) "Everyday Bordering, Belonging and the Reorientation of British Immigration Legislation." *Sociology*, 52(2): 1–17.

Zweig, S. (2003) [1939] *Beware of Pity* [Ungeduld des Herzens]. London: Pushkin Press.

PART I

THE ICONIC US–MEXICO BORDER REGION

1. The militarization of the US–Mexico border in the twenty-first century and implications for human rights

Timothy J. Dunn

The US–Mexico border was gradually militarized by US authorities through immigration and drug enforcement during the last decades of the twentieth century (Dunn 1996, 2001). (Mexican authorities have also engaged in border militarization measures to varying degrees, about which Heyman discusses the contemporary features in this volume.) Border militarization emerged after decades of relatively subdued border enforcement during mid-century, though there was massive border militarization in the early twentieth century (Hernández 2010; Levario 2012). The target of this control has long been Mexicans and more recently Central Americans (and other Latinos), wherein Latino US citizens and migrants have intermingled and frequently been mistaken by the authorities. And the adverse human rights impacts have fallen on these groups as well, with citizens more able to challenge it (Dunn 2009). The border militarization process has greatly expanded in the first two decades of the twenty-first century as well.

Border militarization as a concept merits elaboration. I define militarization as police acting like the military and the military acting like police as well as their mutual collaboration and integration, particularly military involvement in domestic law enforcement and security matters (Dunn 1996, 2001).[1] Though there are some important limitations on the domestic use of the US military – they are generally prohibited from arrest, search, and seizure activities – a wide range of other military support for police is allowed otherwise.[2] And much of this has been pioneered in border enforcement before being allowed more widely elsewhere (Correa and Thomas 2018). More specifically, I focus on the use of military-style equipment by police bodies as well as the use and integration of military, paramilitary, and police and other security forces to control targeted civilian populations – all of which is part of US military doctrines.[3] I also conceptualize a continuum of border militarization as a constructed typology based on US laws and actions dating back to 1982 through the 1990s, consisting of various forms and degrees of border militarization (Dunn 2001). This includes a broad array of military support for border law enforcement agencies (e.g., Border Patrol), from less to more severe, including: loaning or granting of military equipment, military construction and maintenance support, military troops providing training and advisors, military transport support, military aerial reconnaissance/surveillance, small-scale deployments of military ground troops near the border, integration of military and law enforcement efforts, large-scale military troop deployments near the border, and military troops granted authority to search, seize, and arrest civilians and property in the border region (generally prohibited for the military within the US with a few exceptions; see note 1). This process of US border militarization has now been exported abroad in a variety of settings within the US sphere of influence (Miller 2019a).

The dangers of border militarization were highlighted in the tragic 1997 shooting death of an innocent Mexican American teenager by US Marines in a rural area of border on a clandestine surveillance mission for the Border Patrol (Dunn 2001). This tragedy did significantly limit the use of armed ground troops on the border for several years, until after September 11, 2001. However, in the current century the border militarization has accelerated.

Several key concepts help us to better understand the broader implications of border militarization. One key theoretical idea is that powerful bureaucracies tend to undermine human rights, particularly those of disadvantaged groups, including most migrants, more often through malign neglect (i.e., structural violence) and sometimes repression (i.e., direct violence) (Sjoberg 1999). Bureaucracies (both governmental and corporate) are the chief organizational, structural means for exercising power in the modern world, and as such loom large in human rights problems, particularly as they often lack accountability, especially in their dealings with disadvantaged groups. At the same time, human agency can change bureaucratic structures, though this is an asymmetrical relationship weighted toward the latter (Sjoberg et al. 2001; Sjoberg 2009). This chapter is focused primarily on the bureaucratic structure element, but certainly migrants and many aid and solidarity workers exercise tremendous agency. And there is a clash in the main frameworks used for migrant rights, between the nation-state-bound citizenship framework and the international human rights view (Dunn 2009, 2014), with the former characterized by more enforcement power, and this is a more common if not dominant approach in immigration studies (e.g., see Nichols 2019; Nyers 2019; Díaz-Barriga and Dorsey 2020). Nonetheless, the rights of migrants as non-citizen border crossers fit better into the human rights perspective, and that is the view adopted in this chapter.

Another idea that aids our understanding of border militarization is that self-interested "political entrepreneurs have long constructed a political narrative of an 'immigration threat,'" which has driven the ever-increasing border immigration enforcement militarization process (Massey et al. 2016). This is despite the fact that immigration poses no significant threat – neither economic (NAS 2016a) nor physical, nor terrorist (Schmitt et al. 2019) nor elevated crime (Horton 2018; NAS 2016b; Light and Miller 2018) – while increased border enforcement has had little of the intended impact on migration.[4] Nonetheless, three important social actors have long projected xenophobic and racist fear onto border immigration, often in a sensationalistic manner as a "Latino threat," to advance their own agendas – i.e., politicians to mobilize votes, media pundits to generate viewers and readers, and border enforcement bureaucrats to secure larger budgets (Massey et al. 2016). Trump obviously fits this, but with much more openly racist demagoguery (e.g., he declared Mexican migrants to be rapists and drug dealers during the 2015 announcement of his presidential campaign [Lee 2015] and has frequently characterized Central American migrants as violent criminals and dangerous gang members); however, the process predates him.

I have conducted most of my research on border militarization over more than three decades based largely on government documents and other reports and press, though I have also periodically conducted field research in the border region, at times very extensive as a years-long resident, and including many in-depth interviews, most recently in 2017. The remainder of the chapter is organized chronologically for the 2000s, with the key break point being the Bush and Obama administrations – which exhibited much continuity – versus the Trump administration and its more extreme measures.

1. THE BUSH–OBAMA PERIOD, 2000–2016

While representing different political parties, the border enforcement policies of the Bush and Obama administrations share a good deal in common; the same bipartisan continuity in border militarization was present in the 1980s and 1990s as well (Dunn 1996). While there were some differences, they are relatively small compared to the more drastic expansion of border militarization under the Trump administration.

1.1 Equipment and Barriers

An enormous amount of sophisticated materials has been deployed to aid immigration enforcement along the US–Mexico border during the twenty-first century, fueled by ever expanding budgets, such that a Border Security Industrial Complex has emerged to provide them (Miller 2014), smaller and analogous to the massive Military Industrial Complex. This was fueled by explosive budget growth for the Customs and Border Protection (CBP) section of the Department of Homeland Security (DHS), which more than doubled from 2003 to 2016, reaching some $13.2 billion, while its Border Patrol unit nearly quadrupled to $3.8 billion from 2000 to 2016. The importance of this is underlined by research finding that an increase in military equipment has been found to increase police violence (Delehanty et al. 2017). The most obvious border enforcement measures in this regard are physical border barriers, such as fencing and walls. Though Trump has made this his signature issue, a great deal of this was built previously during the Bush and Obama administrations. Following the near unanimous passage of the "Secure Fence Act" in 2006, border fencing/wall was expanded nearly from approximately 100 miles to 700 miles (of the 1,900 mile border), approximately half of which was 10–15 feet high and the remainder lower-level vehicle barriers (Johnson 2015; see also Correa 2013; Maril 2011). This drastic fence expansion was very similar to that proposed in a 1993 report by Sandia National Laboratory at Kirkland Air Force base in Albuquerque, part of the nation's weapons security system (Nevins and Dunn 2008).

Accompanying the expansion in physical fencing/wall was a similar expansion of a "virtual wall" of electronic surveillance, most based on military-related technology. By 2015 this included ten military-grade (though unarmed) predator drones/unmanned aerial systems for surveillance (Munsil 2015), and some 119 other aircraft (including dozens of military-grade helicopters). A host of land-based surveillance systems drawing on the same type of specialized security technology often used by US military forces was also deployed on the border (some of which was military surplus, granted to the Border Patrol) – including some 11,863 underground sensors, 272 remote video surveillance systems (fixed to towers, etc.), 179 mobile video surveillance systems (Johnson 2015), 195 local video surveillance systems, and 261 Forward Looking Infrared Radars (Miller 2014: 39). The DHS attempted to construct an even more sophisticated, comprehensive "virtual wall" of near total border surveillance, termed the Secure Border Initiative (SBI), headed by the Boeing corporation, a leading military contractor. However, this failed to perform adequately and was discontinued in 2011, but a similar attempt was resumed in 2014 with the Israeli military surveillance corporation Elbit and continues into the present. Another obvious militaristic form of equipment used by the Border Patrol is some 16,000 M4 rifles, the same model widely used by the US military, which are essentially standard issue for most field agents (Chiaramonte 2014) along with side arms/pistols. Prior to 2000 M4 (or also M16 rifles) were not so widely issued to agents. The use of military rifles has been justified by the use of similar arms by Mexican drug smugglers in the border region; nonetheless, Border Patrol agents have long generally experienced far fewer assaults and agent deaths than do regular state and local police in the US (Frey 2013; Ortega 2018), as their principal focus is on typically non-resisting migrants. This use and sharing of military equipment by police agencies has become more visible and controversial in episodes of militarized police facing protestors in recent years, though its border roots go back to the early 1980s (Correa and Thomas 2018).[5]

1.2 Strategy and Tactics

During the 2000–2016 period border enforcement strategy and tactics became increasingly militarized, particularly after 9/11, although there was much continuity also with measures adopted during the 1990s (Dunn 2001, 2009). The primary strategy remained the Border Patrol's "prevention through deterrence" strategy, begun in 1994 (pioneered in El Paso, Texas in 1993) in the Border Patrol's first formal national strategy, written with the assistance of the Pentagon's Center for Low-Intensity Conflict (Dunn 1996, 2009; Andreas 2009). It consists of massing enforcement resources (agents, fencing, lighting, etc.) in border urban areas to deter (or greatly reduce) unauthorized immigration in these traditional and most convenient crossing areas (Maril 2004; Andreas 2009; Dunn 2009; Nevins 2010; Rosas 2012; De León 2015). Unauthorized border crossers were diverted to more difficult and dangerous rural border sections of deserts, mountains, and brush lands – with the thought that these "natural barriers" would reduce crossing (Dunn 2009; Nevins 2010; De León 2015). However, these measures did not reduce unauthorized crossing but only pushed it out of sight and also greatly increased the hardships and deaths of border crossers, roughly doubling annual bodies recovered to 300–500 per year, and especially focused in the desert of Southern Arizona, with untold more bodies unrecovered (De León 2015).[6] This selective "prevention through deterrence" doctrine remained the principal approach in the 2004 Border Patrol National Strategy, though with a new post-9/11 focus "[T]he Border Patrol has as its primary mission preventing terrorists and terrorist weapons from entering the United States" (Border Patrol 2004: 2). However, this would be accomplished mainly by focusing on unauthorized immigrants and their smugglers, and narcotics and other contraband, as these were seen as means for terrorist entry as well. As a part of this, the Border Patrol strategy came to focus more on Transnational Criminal Organizations (TCOs) involved in the smuggling of people, drugs, and other contraband (Border Patrol 2012), to which the "prevention through deterrence" strategy forced nearly all unauthorized migrants to turn for assistance in the now more difficult crossing process. While the Border Patrol likes to highlight its efforts against drug trafficking, it is important to note that its efforts are relatively modest, as 80–90 percent of drugs (except marijuana, the least dangerous and increasingly legal) seized near the border during recent years were discovered at official ports of entry (POEs)/crossing stations, not between POEs where the Border Patrol is the principal enforcement body (Isacson 2019a).

The selective "prevention through deterrence" strategy was supplemented with a new "Consequence Delivery System" (CDS) approach (Border Patrol 2012), which began in 2005 along the Arizona section of the border with the increasing formal criminal prosecution of unauthorized border crossers and jail time, a major departure from past practices.[7] By 2016 the CDS was operating along the entire border and was the main enforcement tactic (Slack 2019), placing deported migrants at serious risk from escalating drug cartel violence on the Mexican side of the border (Slack 2019). At the same time, the "prevention through deterrence" strategy also remained in place, though the Border Patrol also emphasized "managing risks" and "mobile response" based on intelligence about various "threats" (Border Patrol 2012). The Border Patrol also maintained a Special Coordination Center acting as a liaison with the Department of Defense and its Joint Task Force–North (JTF–N), with both units located on a border military base, Fort Bliss, in El Paso, Texas (Border Patrol 2012).

The other primary strategy that was greatly expanded during the 2000–2016 period was the supplemental use of the military to assist the Border Patrol primarily in immigration enforcement – a more obvious, direct form of border militarization. There were two primary vehicles for this, the previously noted JTF–N border military unit and two relatively large-scale (up to 6,000 troops) National Guard deployments for immigration enforcement: "Operation Jumpstart" from 2006 to 2008 and the smaller scale "Operation Phalanx" from 2010 to 2016 (Sliney 2016). JTF–N was formed in 2004 with a mission to support law enforcement agencies in the interdiction and disruption of "suspected transnational threats" such as "international terrorism, narco-trafficking, [and] alien smuggling" as well as "transnational criminal organizations" (JTF–N 2015). This mission is nearly identical to the Border Patrol's, which is the main law enforcement body with whom JFT-N worked, though data is limited due to the national security nature of the work. However, by 2015 JTF–N had completed over 6,000 missions since 1989 when its predecessor was formed, Joint Task-Force–6 (JTF–6) (JTF–N 2015) – an average of 230 missions per year, though at a slower pace since 2000.[8] The range of mission operations was quite vast, some 33 types of activities spread across four broad categories (JTF–N 2015):

1. *Operational Support* – including aerial reconnaissance and surveillance, ground surveillance and Listening Post/Observation Post [the latter involving deployment of armed ground troops].
2. *Intelligence Support* – mainly threat assessment and analysis.
3. *Engineering Support* on southwest border – mainly construction of barriers and roads.
4. *General Support* – mainly Mobile Training Teams of soldiers to teach everything from interview techniques to mission planning to tactical operations and marksmanship as well as "threat mitigation."

The Operational Support is the arguably most militaristic type offered to the Border Patrol by JTF–N, and constituted some 53 percent of their missions for 2011 (GAO 2011: 22).

However, the controversy surrounding a tragic 1997 shooting of an innocent 18-year-old, Esequiel Hernandez, in rural Redford, Texas (on the Rio Grande boundary area) by a US Marine on a JTF–6 covert Listening post/Observation post mission for the Border Patrol did somewhat restrict the use of armed ground troops along the border. The Pentagon suspended such for nearly two years after the incident and resumed them with closer supervision (Dunn 2001). As of 2011 they no longer allowed armed mobile patrols, but rather stationary and unarmed ground deployments (GAO 2011: 27). Other deployments, such as National Guard troops, however, were armed.

Nonetheless, by 2004 with the formation of JTF–N, the military resumed the use of ground forces along the border and now to explicitly aid immigration enforcement, as well as the previous focus on only drug enforcement (Dunn 2009). This included several hundred members of Army Stryker armored vehicle units (tank-like armored personnel carriers with heavy machine guns and sophisticated surveillance equipment) in the New Mexico/Arizona border area on at least three occasions from 2010 to 2013 (Isacson and Meyer 2012: 24–25; JTF–N 2015). In addition, a great deal of other less obvious military assistance has also gone on over the years across all the four types of support categories (particularly engineering and construction), with JTF–N typically having some 300–750 troops engaged in a wide range of support activities along the border at any one time.

The other principal strategy using the military has been the relatively large-scale deployment of National Guard troops to aid the Border Patrol in "Operation Jumpstart" from 2006 to 2008 and "Operation Phalanx" from 2010 to 2016. The first entailed the deployment of some 6,000 Guard troops and second some 1,200 and eventually decreased that to 300. Their main activities were to provide help with border surveillance (ground and aerial) as well as support roles behind the scenes such as maintenance and intelligence analysis (Dunn 2009: 218–219, 225–227; GAO 2011, Sliney 2016; National Border Patrol Council 2016). This was the first deployment of military troops explicitly designated to aid in immigration enforcement (rather than drugs, terrorism, or TCOs), and they aided in the apprehension of nearly 200,000 unauthorized immigrants. This was the largest deployment of military troops on the border by the US since the Mexican revolution, 90 years earlier, and resonated with the growing anti-immigration sentiment nationally. Both operations were intended as stop-gap measures to boost the Border Patrol while the unit was rapidly expanded from approximately 10,000 agents to 20,000, with special preference for military veterans (many returning from wars in the Middle East).

At the state level, Texas undertook a unique effort starting in 2006 through at least 2017 to direct a portion of the state's Department of Public Safety (DPS, like State Police) to patrol the border with military equipment and agents armed with military-grade weapons (M16 rifles, 30 caliber machine guns, and the like), from helicopter patrols to armored river boat patrols. The governor also ordered 1,000 Texas National Guard troops to the border to aid this effort. The rationale for this extreme approach was to meet the supposed threats of drugs and terrorism on the border (Del Bosque 2015; Sliney 2016). The border was treated as a "war zone," a fear fueled by increasing drug gang violence in northern Mexico, despite the fact that the violence has stayed on the Mexican side of the border, US border cities have some of the lowest violent crime rates in the country, and crime dropped 33 percent from 2009 to 2014 in the 12 border counties in South Texas (Rosenthal and Collette 2015). And bi-annual Texas state spending on border security doubled to some $800 million for 2016–2017 to "take down [border] crime cartels" (Kauffman 2015). This militarized approach at the state level led to a tragic incident in October 2012 in which a DPS officer accidently killed two unauthorized immigrants from Guatemala. The officer fired 18 high-powered rifle shots from a helicopter into the bed of a fleeing pick-up truck, which he thought contained drugs but turned out to hold a group of unauthorized immigrants (Del Bosque 2015).

Beyond government efforts, small private border militia vigilante groups emerged in the 2005–2006 period to monitor the border against immigrants, drug cartels and potential terrorists (Doty 2009; Shapira 2013). These non-state actors saw themselves as supporting and supplementing the supposedly under-staffed Border Patrol – and its state-led militarization – and many agents were sympathetic. The border militias were not large but more so symbolic performances amplified by the media that helped shape US immigration policy debates, though with some tragic results, and they largely disappeared by 2015.[9] They made a comeback during the Trump administration, however, though remained small in number.

It is important to recall the Border Patrol was the principal recipient of all of this border military (and militia) assistance, typically working in tandem and with close coordination with elements of the military. In addition, the Border Patrol considers itself a paramilitary force, something distinct from typical police units, as noted by a former agent (see Cantú 2018). And within it there are specialized more obviously militarized units, such as its Mobile Response Teams and Special Operations Group. Further, the unit had at least ten "forward operating bases" – a military tactic in wars in Middle East and elsewhere – among remote stretches of the border in New Mexico and Arizona and hoped to expand them (Santos 2015; Miller 2014).

Also noteworthy is that this massively expanded militarized border enforcement had little effect on unauthorized migration. While Border Patrol apprehensions fell sharply (roughly 60–70 percent) from the early 2000s to 2016, as noted earlier Massey and colleagues (2016) determined that the massive increase in border enforcement had little effect. Instead it was more affected by economic factors (e.g., recession and falling labor demand), demographic shifts (falling Mexican birthrates), and the proliferation of temporary worker visas for Mexicans (growing from some 100,000 to nearly 850,000 per year during this period). Further, the much increased and expensive formal criminal prosecution of unauthorized border crossers had only a very limited deterrent effect (Martinez et al. 2018). Meanwhile, starting in 2014 the now reduced unauthorized migration shifted to become a majority Central American issue for the first time, mostly refugees fleeing violence, including many children, who willingly turned themselves in to Border Patrol so they could apply for asylum. While overwhelming in a few areas, this was largely unaffected by border enforcement resources, but more so required social services. This refugee influx receded from 2015 to 2018, before a large increase in 2019 and much expanded border militarization.

2. THE TRUMP PERIOD, 2017–2020

The Trump administration with its hyperbolically racist view of migrants as extremely dangerous (even calling them "animals") has greatly amplified and expanded the pre-existing border militarization process, as much escalated and purposefully harsh and cruel border immigration enforcement has become a signature political issue for Trump, particularly the proposal to build a 30-foot-high wall for the entire 1,900 mile border. This was fueled in part with increased budgets for the CBP section of DHS and its Border Patrol unit, as their budgets rose approximately 25 percent over the first three years of the Trump administration, reaching $17.1 billion and $4.8 billion, respectively. While the border wall proposal has consistently been opposed by a majority of the public, including in border states such as Texas, and congress has consistently refused to fund it, the Trump administration has pushed ahead on the project (by using "emergency powers" to transfer funds from the Pentagon budget to the wall). By early 2020, the administration had constructed only 101 miles of new wall barriers, but very optimistically pledged to have some 450 miles completed by the end of the year, and has allocated some $18.4 billion, theoretically enough for 885 miles of border wall (Miroff 2020). Trump initially proposed a 30-foot-high concrete wall, but designs have shifted to 25-foot-high steel bollards (thick poles) placed very close together, which allow agents to see activity on the other side of the border, topped by five feet of thin, solid steel (to deter climbers), and with razor wire in some locations. This entire wall construction process, dating back to previous administrations but now much expanded, has been actively challenged for years by local activists and land owners, especially in South Texas, and particularly Hispanic residents (Díaz-Barriga and Dorsey 2020). Thus far, the wall has proven vulnerable to numerous efforts to cut holes to allow entry, and many climb it (some with ladders) – a practice that caused 64 cranial or spinal injuries from falls from the border wall/fence recorded by one border region Arizona hospital over five years through 2017 (Ramey et al. 2019).

Beyond the much-hyped border wall, the "virtual wall" of surveillance devices continues to be developed, as the Border Patrol has continued to acquire and deploy ever more sophisticated high-tech surveillance in the border region. The Elbit Corporation (Israel's largest military contractor) has continued to deploy an array of more advanced surveillance technology (cameras, radars, sensors, etc. tied to a specific tower) for the Border Patrol particularly in the Arizona section of the border region, and hopes to one day provide surveillance coverage for the entirety of the southern and northern land borders as well as ports and harbors along the coasts (Parrish 2019). Another technology long deployed but refined and advanced is the blimp-like (large balloon) aerostat outfitted with radar and posted along the border for aerial and ground surveillance, but it is limited in bad weather. All told a host of major security- and military-focused corporations competed for $5.6 billion in equipment and technology contracts from CBP (the Border Patrol's parent agency) during 2017–2018, approximately the same level for the prior decade, as the Border Security Complex continues unabated (Miller 2019b).

The border wall and plethora of expanded border surveillance equipment are a key feature of the Border Patrol's 2020 strategy as they expand their "zone of security" and strive to gain "Operational Control" of the border (Border Patrol 2020a). Much like previous versions, the highest priority is to prevent terrorism and the activities of "Transnational Criminal Organizations" engaged in various forms of smuggling (drugs and migrants). Beyond the physical barriers and hardware, the strategy is to "Strengthen Impedance and Denial," which means "Deterring cross-border illicit activity" (Border Patrol 2020a: 8) – i.e., essentially the same "prevention through deterrence" strategy in place since 1994, which in practice has not prevented illegal entry so much as push it out of urban areas and into more dangerous, remote desert and brush country areas and led to increased migrant costs, risks, injuries, and deaths. Another returning element from the 2012 strategy is an emphasis on supporting the "Consequence Delivery" system through "Detention and Prosecution Support" for partner agencies to discourage illegal entry via criminal prosecution and legal sanctions (jail time) for unauthorized border migrants (Border Patrol 2020a: 9). This is to be further buttressed by a "layered approach" of enforcement and "tactical mobility" throughout the border region, not only near the border.

The Border Patrol's strategy is largely a rehashing of its previous doctrine, but the Trump administration came into office with a particularly punitive view toward immigration and laid out a number of harsh, unprecedented measures right away, including several directly related to the border (in addition to the wall). Their strategy was laid out in a January 2017 memo from the Secretary of Homeland Security (the parent agency of the Border Patrol and other immigration enforcement units), himself a retired army general, and much of this has since been implemented. Many of the 16 key measures presented focused on expanded detention in the border region and more aggressive criminal prosecutions, deportations, and other removals of migrants, including of refugees to contiguous countries on their transit route – i.e., Mexico (as they awaited US decisions on their request for asylum) – with a special focus on unaccompanied minors (mainly Central Americans). Most relevant for border enforcement, beyond the wall expansion, was a call to increase the size of Border Patrol by 5,000 additional agents (to approximately 25,000 agents) as well as the expansion of the granting of federal immigration enforcement authority to state and local police agencies in border states (DHS 2017b) – which is otherwise handled by federal police typically, though there are many exceptions.

A much more extreme border militarization measure was proposed in an earlier draft of the DHS memo, to authorize "members of the State National Guard [in border states and adjacent states] … to perform functions of an immigration officer in relation to the investigation, apprehension, and detention of aliens in the United States" (DHS 2017a). This would have provided up to 100,000 National Guard troops to round up unauthorized immigrants in border states (Burke 2017). While this was removed from the final memo, it does provide a view of what key Trump policy makers desired to do, namely an unprecedented level of border militarization that very likely would have been directed at people of Latino appearance as suspected immigrants, who are the vast majority of the border region's residents and overwhelmingly US citizens.

A year later in the spring of 2018 the Trump administration began to deploy up to 4,000 National Guard soldiers to aid border enforcement, with duties very similar to prior similar National Guard border deployments under the Bush and Obama administrations, discussed previously – i.e., ground and aerial surveillance, construction, maintenance support, intelligence analysis, etc. This deployment occurred despite historically low levels of Border Patrol apprehensions of unauthorized border crossers in 2017 and slightly elevated but continuing low levels in 2018. However, it was part of a series of escalated harsh measures implemented in the border region in 2018, the most notorious of which was the family separation policy and drastic increase in migrant detention (discussed below).

In the fall of 2018 the Trump administration, just days before the mid-term congressional election, announced the deployment of up to 15,000 military troops, including active duty forces, on the US–Mexico border in response to caravans of several thousand Central Americans headed through Mexico to the border, which Trump portrayed in alarmist terms as threatening criminals and some sort of invasion (Sonne and Ryan 2018). This was dubbed "Operation Faithful Patriot," and ultimately led to approximately 6,000 active duty troops deployed along the border, but there was relatively little for them to do as a mass influx of migrants failed to materialize and they are prohibited from the most direct law enforcement (arrest, search, and seizure), as noted previously. However, active duty troops did set up 25 miles of dangerous razor wire on border fencing and walls. At the same time, there were several thousand National Guard troops on the border as well, making for approximately 8,000 to 10,000 troops deployed, though many of the active duty troops were removed in less than two months. Critics ridiculed it as an expensive, media attention stunt to turn the election in Trump's favor, but if so it failed, as his party lost dozens of seats and control of one House of Congress.

Nonetheless, it marked a period of increased military deployment along the border of 5,000–7,000 troops (active duty and National Guard combined) at any one time throughout 2019 and 2020. Much of this activity is similar to missions dating back nearly 30 years, discussed previously. However, a 2019 briefing by the commander of Northcom, the parent unit of the military's border coordinating unit, JTF–N, sheds new light on the military efforts to support the Border Patrol. At that point, JTF–N was overseeing some 2,500 troops engaged in 155 missions in the border region, primarily for the Border Patrol. Nearly all entailed some sort of ground surveillance, such as mobile surveillance camera units. Further, as a part of its "threat fusion running estimate" the military was monitoring and alert to not only criminal activity but also "Protests/Anarchists" and "Unregulated Militias" vigilante groups (US Army Northcom 2019: 7). Among the former the briefing specified were groups protesting the detention of children and families, including religious groups – i.e., legal activity protected by the constitution. To have the military engaged in monitoring such protest groups is extremely troubling, and certainly seems to come close to violating legal guidelines. By April 2020 the Trump administration was considering replacing the 2,500 active duty troops on the border with National Guard forces (Brown 2020).

As noted previously these border military deployments were part of a larger array of extremely punitive measures to restrict immigration from 2018 onward. Inadmissible entries and apprehensions more than doubled from 2018 reaching some 850,000 in 2019, but dropped sharply in the first six months of fiscal year 2020. During this period, the detention of migrants grew enormously and in a variety of locations (official detention centers, contract temporary facilities, child detention centers, family detention centers, etc.). At one time, some 4,000 children were held in tents in a temporary detention center in the desert near El Paso, and the government and its contractors held a record-level 70,000 children in total nationwide during 2019. The Border Patrol's role was primarily apprehension and transportation of unauthorized immigrants as well as those legally applying for political asylum, as there was a large influx of mainly Central American asylum seekers, mostly families and children. The Border Patrol wound up detaining far more people (many times their designed capacity, such as 50 people per room with one toilet) for far longer (months in some cases) in their temporary holding cells designed to hold people for a few days at most (Romero et al. 2019; OIG 2019). They even failed to provide soap and adequate food, claiming legal requirements to keep detained children in "safe and sanitary" conditions did not specify such items (Flynn 2019). This cruelty was intentional to deter further migration, and at least six children died (accidently or through negligence) in Border Patrol custody and several more in other detention settings from 2019 to 2020. Another move that caused massive outrage and protest was a draconian policy for several months in mid-2018 of family separation of children from parents and other adult family members, though it started earlier in 2017 and has since continued at a smaller scale, and which led to the infamous "kids in cages" in temporary detention centers and left untold thousands of families separated (most eventually reunited) (GAO 2020). The military was called upon to develop plans to hold up to 20,000 migrant families and children in the border region (McLaughlin 2018), but thus far has not been called upon to implement it. It is important to note border detention conditions under the Obama administration were also terrible and very overcrowded at times (and they even used a military base to briefly house and detain some child migrants, supervised by the Department of Health and Human Services). However, conditions have generally been much worse under the Trump administration and often made intentionally so by policy makers.

3. HUMAN RIGHTS IMPLICATIONS

Obviously, many of these border militarization and related enforcement actions entail a wide range of human rights abuses, some already noted (such as the horrid detention conditions). However, at least two additional features merit at least brief elaboration. The first is that border immigration enforcement has long been directed with little meaningful oversight and accountability, and not only toward immigrants but Latino residents suspected of being such, the vast majority of whom are citizens and legal residents, and has included the structural violence of substantial denials of due process and reduced access to basic rights. This constitutes long-running ethnic–racial profiling, which the federal government allows in border immigration enforcement, and also includes several state-level laws (in Arizona and Texas) that compel state and local police to engage in immigration questioning of suspects, again nearly always Latino, and collaborate with federal immigration enforcement. This is structural "legal violence" (Menjívar and Abrego 2012) and it has long also been accompanied by significant (typically extralegal) direct violence, such as a long history of questionable shooting and other deaths of suspects, including 33 deaths from 2010 to 2015 but only one criminal charge of an agent (Santos 2015) (later found not-guilty). In addition, a ground-breaking random survey of recently deported migrants in six Mexican border cities found that 11 percent reported being physically abused by US immigration authorities, mainly Border Patrol, and much higher proportions reported verbal abuse, lack of food, and lack of medical attention when needed (Slack et al. 2018).

The second big human rights issue is the structural violence of the never-ending deaths of unauthorized border crossers pushed by "prevention through deterrence" Border Patrol enforcement efforts to more remote, dangerous desert crossing areas (Martinez et al. 2014; De León 2015), with 250 to 500 human remains recovered annually through 2019 (Border Patrol 2019, 2020b), and untold thousands of others never recovered in the high traffic, dangerous rural deserts and dry brush country (De León 2015; Boyce et al. 2019). The American Public Health Association (APHA) in 2009 designated these mounting border crosser deaths as a formal "public health crisis" and called upon the Border Patrol to adopt "strategies that do not endanger the lives and health of migrants (APHA 2009). Activist groups have challenged these human rights crises for years, putting the Border Patrol on the defensive, and have won a few legal cases, but they continue nonetheless. During recent years the Trump administration has stepped up legal repression of such activists by prosecuting (for the first time in more than a decade) several humanitarian aid volunteers for providing assistance to unauthorized migrants crossing the dangerous deserts of Southern Arizona – while leaving private militia groups unmolested for their vigilante efforts – though the most high profile, felony case ended in acquittal for the accused.

Other more drastic human rights abuses have stemmed from the hyping by Trump and other conservative politicians and conservative media of the border as a site of "invasion" by immigrants falsely portrayed as overwhelmingly dangerous criminals. These alarmist portrayals led to two massacres by racist anti-immigrant murderers: one of 12 people at a Pittsburgh, PA synagogue in October 2018 (because of their supposed role in aiding refugees headed to the border that President Trump was villainizing) and another of 23 Latino people (US and Mexican citizens) at an El Paso, Texas store in August of 2019 by a white supremacist trying to prevent a "Hispanic invasion" of Texas (in a region where Hispanics have been the majority since before the establishment of the border in 1848).

Finally, in contrast to these tragedies and abuses, it should be noted that local migrant assistance groups in the border region during 2018–2019 undertook exceptional heroic efforts, especially in El Paso, Texas, and the Lower Rio Grande Valley of Texas, to house, feed, and otherwise assist tens of thousands of migrants dumped on their community streets after border enforcement authorities eventually released many from detention, often overwhelming predominantly low-income local communities (Isacson 2019b). And in contrast to the massively funded border enforcement agencies, no migrants have died in the volunteer humanitarian aid efforts despite the exhaustion (and secondary traumatization) and much fewer resources of those aid groups.

4. CONCLUSION

Border militarization has a long trajectory in the contemporary era, decades prior to Trump's bombastically xenophobic, openly racist escalations. While it began in earnest in the 1980s and expanded notably during the 1990s, both the Bush and Obama administrations (2001–2016) each further deepened border militarization by doubling the paramilitary Border Patrol, increasing its use of much sophisticated military technology and equipment (e.g., the "virtual wall" of surveillance equipment) as well as some less sophisticated (e.g., 700 miles of new border fencing/wall). Most notably, the Bush and Obama administrations both established the use of military forces along the border explicitly for immigration enforcement – in the Bush case up to 6,000 National Guard reserve troops. Previously military troops were technically only allowed to assist in border drug enforcement (generally with the Border Patrol), though in practice this typically aided immigration enforcement as a "side benefit." Both administrations pursued a legislative strategy for "comprehensive immigration reform" that proposed large-scale legalization programs for millions of undocumented immigrants residing in the US and expanded temporary worker visas in exchange for increased enforcement, especially border enforcement – e.g., the Obama administration backed a "compromise" that included $40 billion for border enforcement and another doubling of the Border Patrol to 40,000 agents. Both administrations failed to achieve the former (legalization and visas, though some of the latter), but they did both massively increase border enforcement resources and militarization.

Consequently the Trump administration inherited a massive border militarization apparatus, which was overwhelmingly aimed at Mexican and Central American immigrants – as well as US legal residents and citizens who might appear to be such (i.e., Latinos in the border region). Trump is an openly racist "political entrepreneur" who seized upon these powerful bureaucratic tools in implementing intentionally crueler, more openly xenophobic and racist immigration policies, particularly in the border region. This was based on Trump's fearful and false political framing of Mexican and Central immigrants as dangerous criminal invaders (e.g., claiming most were rapists, drug dealers, violent gang members, etc.). This approach helped him win the presidency, amplified by conservative (and sometimes mainstream) media in often dramatic fashion in their quest for viewers, and has been opportunistically used by border enforcement agency bureaucrats to secure more resources – the same tri-part constellation of politician–media–border bureaucrat that has driven escalated border militarization for decades (Massey et al. 2016), only now in more exaggeratedly racist fashion. Thus the Trump administration escalated the already existing border militarization process, most notably by proposing and beginning to build a much higher, more imposing border wall to eventually run the entire 1,900 mile length of the border, as well as continuing to expand the "virtual wall" of surveillance. The most extreme militarization, however, has been the deployment of up to 10,000 military troops along the border in 2018–2020, a majority of whom since late 2018 have been active duty forces supplemented by National Guard reserve forces, with upwards of 5,000 still in place as of mid-2020.

Two of the only remaining more extreme features of border militarization that have yet to be breached are (1) an even more massive deployment (e.g., tens of thousands) of troops to face the supposed (non-physical) threat of migrants at the border, and (2) the use of military troops in arrest, search, and seizure activities (legally prohibited for active duty troops outside mass civil unrest, but allowed for National Guard reserve troops). The latter is a key feature of authoritarian regimes and was briefly raised by Trump in June 2020, in response to massive largely peaceful (though with some violence against property) protests throughout the US against police violence against African Americans, but the current military leadership and many former military leaders have decidedly disagreed. In the meantime, state governors called up several thousand National Guard troops to help police.

The increasing use of the military during recent decades in border law enforcement against civilians has arguably paved the way for military involvement in civilian law enforcement more generally outside the border region. What was directed against the migrant "Other"/"Latino threat" in the border region (Massey et al. 2016) can be turned on US citizens in the interior, particularly racial and ethnic minorities (and to some extent has been by militarized police for years – see Kraska 2007; Balko 2013; Schrader 2019). This was made easier by the fact that migrants generally lack many rights in the dominant and more enforceable citizenship rights framework tied to the nation-state, resulting in less accountability and oversight of border police and militarization. Thus agents of bureaucratic power structures could treat migrants with less concern in a coercive border militarization immigration enforcement system laden with both substantial structural violence and significant direct violence (e.g., strategies that pushed unauthorized crossers into more dangerous desert crossings with increased injuries and mortalities, making asylum claims nearly impossible at the border, intentionally separating parent and child migrants, intentionally detaining them in horrifically overcrowded, dangerous conditions, otherwise physically abusing or mistreating migrants, etc.). Now some of those same militarization tools are being used (more widely) in civilian law enforcement in the interior (by militarized police and several thousand National Guard troops, and active duty troops perhaps) against citizens protesting racist police violence.[10]

In contrast, the international human rights framework views all people, citizens and migrants, as having basic civil, political, social, and economic rights. While these are much less enforceable than those in the more dominant citizenship framework commonly used to frame immigration studies (e.g., see Nichols 2019; Nyers 2019; Díaz-Barriga and Dorsey 2020), they do provide disadvantaged and repressed groups a well-recognized, non-nation-state-dependent moral basis for making claims against unjust bureaucratic power structures (state and corporate) to achieve fair, humane treatment and recognition (Sjoberg 1999, 2009; Sjoberg et al. 2001). As such this enables further human agency versus what is often overwhelming organizational and state power. Thus the tensions, injustice, and violence present in border militarization of immigration enforcement highlights the clash of the citizenship–national sovereignty view of rights versus the international human rights perspective (Dunn 2009, 2014). While less enforceable, the latter is an important, adaptable means for human agents to promote human dignity and fair, just treatment for all, citizens and migrants alike and not only in border regions, by powerful organizations. This is perhaps not an either/or dichotomy, as both rights frameworks are useful. Nonetheless human rights should retain a primary position, for although they are admittedly imperfect, they provide a more universal moral framework that is much less subject to the whims and destructive machinations of nation-states (and

48   *Handbook on human security, borders and migration*

corporations) than are national laws (and corporate policies) and are more adaptable to diverse human agents and their struggles for dignity.

NOTES

1. On police militarization more broadly, see Kraska (2007), Balko (2013), and Schrader (2019).
2. The 1878 *Posse Comitatus* law prohibits the military from engaging in arrests, searches, or seizures within the US, with the exception of times of insurrection or mass civil unrest (Dunn 1996: 105–108). Such uses of the military have been rare since the early twentieth century, the most recent being 1992 (Los Angeles riots following grave racial injustice by police). However, in June 2020 President Trump threatened mass deployment of military troops in the face of widespread peaceful protests and some violence (most against property) regarding (another) police death of an unarmed Black man in Minneapolis, MN, George Floyd, although such a move is opposed by the Secretary of Defense (Stewart and Ali 2020) and a number of high ranking ex-military officials. This law, however, does not limit the police use of National Guard reserve military troops under the control of state governors. Beyond this, the law allows a very wide range of other forms of military support for law enforcement (US Code, Title 10, Section 284 2020), many of which were first allowed in border drug, immigration, and customs enforcement dating back to 1982 (Dunn 1996) before being allowed and adopted by police throughout the US (Correa and Thomas 2018). The primary rationale for much of this was drug enforcement, but over time the focus broadened to include "transnational organized crime," a very broad category that includes migrant smuggling and thus allows military support explicitly for immigration enforcement. Previously, in the border region drug enforcement efforts typically overlapped with immigration enforcement to some degree, so military support for one also aided the other (Dunn 1996, 2001).
3. In conceptualizing this I have drawn on the Pentagon's low-intensity conflict (LIC) doctrine, developed in the 1980s to address political upheaval and instability in Central America, which focused on the social control of key segments of the civilian population through a variety of unconventional military activities, from counterinsurgency and anti-terrorism efforts, to suppressing civil unrest and conducting drug enforcement, to conducting military exercises among civilians and aid operations for civilians in emergencies – all with a strong emphasis on integrating military, paramilitary, and civilian police and other security agencies (Dunn 1996: 19–30). By the mid-1990s and early 2000s much of the less severe of these were incorporated into a new doctrine of military operations other than war (MOOTW) (Joint Chiefs of Staff 1995; Bonn and Baker 2000). Meanwhile counterinsurgency became the centerpiece of US wars in Iraq and Afghanistan and was revived in an updated doctrine (US Army 2007).
4. No terrorist coming to harm the US has ever been apprehended along the US–Mexico border and only a very few potential "suspects" are apprehended annually (Schmitt et al. 2019) and immigrant crime levels are significantly lower than those of natives (NAS 2016b; Light and Miller 2018), while border region crime levels are generally below national averages (Horton 2018). Further, border militarization has failed to have much impact on unauthorized Mexican migration (the largest source), which is instead tied to changing economic conditions and demography/falling birthrates (Massey et al. 2016). Meanwhile, the unauthorized immigrant population in the US more than tripled from 1993 to 2008, reaching an estimated 12 million. The increase in border enforcement greatly increased costs and risk, and therefore reduced circular unauthorized migration from Mexico and compelled many to remain in the US and bring family members.
5. The lending and giving of military equipment to the Border Patrol began with the 1982 Defense Authorization Act, ostensibly for drug enforcement by federal police, but also included were those with immigration enforcement authority (Dunn 1996). This practice was much expanded in 1990 with a new program allowing the Department of Defense to give old equipment to any police agency for drug enforcement and then further broadened in 1997 to be used for any type of law enforcement (not just drugs) – i.e., a border practice used against mainly non-citizens was brought to the interior and used disproportionately against minority citizens (Correa and Thomas 2018). This drew little attention until 2014 when protests to a police shooting of a local Black teen in Ferguson were

met with police outfitted with a variety of military equipment (armored vehicles, M4 rifles, etc.). The Obama administration subsequently put some modest limits on the program, but the Trump administration removed them. And in summer 2020 the issue arose again as militarized police faced a massive wave of protestors across the nation, sparked by another police killing of an unarmed Black man, George Floyd, in Minneapolis, MN (this time filmed and witnessed by bystanders).
6. Unauthorized border crossing remained at high levels until 2006, just before the recession, when it subsequently fell sharply, though it had been declining since 2000. Moreover, it was largely unaffected by enforcement efforts and instead was impacted by economic changes, demographic factors (e.g., declining birthrate in Mexico), and an increase in temporary worker visas (Massey et al. 2016). However, the strategy did greatly reduce previous patterns of circular migration between Mexico and the US, and compelled more migrants to remain in the US longer and bring their families, thereby tripling the unauthorized immigrant population by 2008.
7. Previously formal criminal prosecution of unauthorized border crossing was rare and unauthorized crossers were returned to home countries (Mexico for more than 90 percent) shortly after apprehension via "voluntary departure." Under the criminal approach, first offenses are misdemeanors but second offenses are felonies; as a result of the aggressive expansion of immigration prosecutions the federal court system has become devoted primarily to immigration offenses (Slack 2019).
8. JTF–6 (predecessor of JTF–N) conducted some 390 per year on average from 1989 to 2000 (based on 4,300 total missions during that time; Dunn 2001). From 2001 to 2015 JTF–6/JTF–N appears to have conducted an average of 113 missions per year. (The latter figure is based having completed at least 6,000 missions from 1989 to 2015 [JTF–N 2015] minus 4,300 missions from 1989 to 2000 [Dunn 2001], meaning approximately 1,700 missions [at least] from 2001 to 2015, for an annual average of 113.) This estimate of a slower pace of missions is consistent with a Government Accountability Office (GAO) report (2011: 21) that JTF–N conducted 79 missions along the border in 2010.
9. While not particularly menacing in general, in May 2009 several rouge elements did murder two Arivaca, Arizona border community residents, including a nine-year-old girl, in a horribly-gone-wrong home invasion robbery of a supposed drug trafficker (Smith 2011).
10. In Washington, DC during early June 2020 several hundred active duty troops were brought in and some were deployed on the streets. This was made possible by the fact that the federal government directly controls DC as a special federal district which is not a state. Local officials and much media loudly protested this use of military forces.

REFERENCES

Andreas, Peter. 2009 *Border Games: Policing the US–Mexico Divide*. Ithaca, NY: Cornell University Press. Second edition.

APHA (American Public Health Association). 2009 (November 10) "Border Crossing Deaths: A Public Health Crisis Along the US–Mexico Border." Policy Number: 20092. https://www.apha.org/policies-and-advocacy/public-health-policy-statements/policy-database/2014/07/24/08/56/border-crossing-deaths-a-public-health-crisis-along-the-us-mexico-border.

Balko, Radly. 2013 *Rise of the Warrior Cop: The Militarization of America's Police Forces*. New York: Public Affairs.

Bonn, Keith E. and Anthony E. Baker. 2000 *Guide to Military Operations Other Than War: Tactics, Techniques, and Procedures for Stability and Support Operations: Domestic and International*. Mechanicsburg, PA: Stackpole Books.

Border Patrol (US). 2004 (September) "National Border Patrol Strategy." US Customs and Border Protection, Department of Homeland Security. http://www.customs.gov/linkhandler/cgov/border_security/border_patrol/national_bp_strategy.ctt/national_bp_strategy.pdf.

Border Patrol (US). 2012 (September) "Border Patrol Strategic Plan." US Customs and Border Protection, Department of Homeland Security. http://www.cbp.gov/border-security/along-us-borders/strategic-plan.

Border Patrol (US). 2019 "Southwest Border Sectors: Southwest Border Deaths by Fiscal Year." US Customs and Border Protection. Department of Homeland Security. https://www.cbp.gov/sites/default/files/assets/documents/2019-Mar/bp-southwest-border-sector-deaths-fy1998-fy2018.pdf.

Border Patrol (US). 2020a "Border Patrol: 2020 Border Patrol Strategy." US Customs and Border Protection. Department of Homeland Security. https://www.cbp.gov/sites/default/files/assets/documents/2019-Sep/2020-USBP-Strategy.pdf.

Border Patrol (US). 2020b "United States Border Patrol Sector Profile – Fiscal Year 2019." US Customs and Border Protection. Department of Homeland Security. https://www.cbp.gov/sites/default/files/assets/documents/2020-Jan/U.S.%20Border%20Patrol%20Fiscal%20Year%202019%20Sector%20Profile_0.pdf.

Boyce, Geoffrey Alan, Samuel N. Chambers, and Sarah Launis. 2019 "Bodily Inertia and the Weaponization of the Sonoran Desert in US Boundary Enforcement: A GIS Modeling of Migration Routes through Arizona's Altar Valley." *Journal of Migration and Human Security*, vol. 7, no. 1, pp. 25–35.

Brown, Ryan. 2020 (April 28) "Pentagon Weighs Replacing Active Duty Troops on US–Mexico Border with National Guard." CNN. https://www.cnn.com/2020/04/28/politics/pentagon-national-guard-southern-border/index.html.

Burke, Garance. 2017 (February 18) "DHS Weighed Nat Guard for Immigration Round Ups." Associated Press. https://www.apnews.com/5508111d59554a33be8001bdac4ef830.

Cantú, Francisco. 2018 *The Lines Becomes a River: Dispatches from the Border*. New York: Riverhead Books.

Chiaramonte, Perry. 2014 (November 12) "Border Patrol agents say agency's gun recall puts them in danger." https://www.foxnews.com/politics/border-patrol-agents-say-agencys-gun-recall-puts-them-in-danger

Correa, Jennifer G. 2013 "'After 9/11 Everything Changed': Re-formations of State Violence in Everyday Life on the US–Mexico Border." *Cultural Dynamics*, vol. 25, no. 1, pp. 99–119.

Correa, Jennifer and James T. Thomas. 2018 "From the Border to the Core: A Thickening Military-Police Assemblage." *Critical Sociology*, vol. 45, no. 7–8, pp. 1133–1147.

De León, Jason. 2015 *The Land of Open Graves: Living and Dying on the Migrant Trail*. Oakland: University of California Press.

Del Bosque, Melissa. 2015 (March 2) "Death on Sevenmile Road: The Rush to Militarize the U.S.–Mexico Border has Tragic Consequences in Texas." *Texas Observer*. http://www.texasobserver.org/human-cost-border-security-build-up/.

Delehanty, Casey, Jack Mewhirter, Ryan Welch, and Jason Wilks. 2017 "Militarization and Police Violence: The Case of the 1033 Program." *Research and Politics*, vol. 4, no. 2, pp. 1–7. https://journals.sagepub.com/doi/pdf/10.1177/2053168017712885.

DHS (Department of Homeland Security). 2017a (January 25) "Implementing the President's Border Security and Immigration Enforcement Improvements Policies" [unsigned preliminary draft]. https://cdn2.vox-cdn.com/uploads/chorus_asset/file/8001743/Implementing_the_President_s_Border_Security_and_Immigration_Enforcement....0.pdf.

DHS (Department of Homeland Security). 2017b (February 20) "Implementing the President's Border Security and Immigration Enforcement Improvements Policies" [signed final draft]. https://www.hsdl.org/?view&did=799093.

Díaz-Barriga, Miguel and Margaret E. Dorsey. 2020 *Fencing in Democracy: Border Walls, Necrocitizenship, and the Security State*. Durham, NC: Duke University Press.

Doty, Roxanne. 2009 *The Law Into Their Own Hands: Immigration and the Politics of Exceptionalism*. Tucson, AZ: University of Arizona Press.

Dunn, Timothy J. 1996 *The Militarization of the U.S.–Mexico Border, 1978–1992: Low Intensity Conflict Doctrine Comes Home*. Austin, TX: CMAS Books, Center for Mexican American Studies, University of Texas at Austin.

Dunn, T. 2001 "Border Militarization via Drug and Immigration Enforcement: Human Rights Implications." *Social Justice*, vol. 28, no. 2, pp. 7–30.

Dunn, T. 2009 *Blockading the Border and Human Rights: The El Paso Operation that Remade Immigration Enforcement*. Austin, TX: University of Texas Press.

Dunn, T. 2014 "Immigration Enforcement at the U.S.–Mexico Border: Where Human Rights and National Sovereignty Collide," in *Binational Human Rights: The U.S.–Mexico Experience*. William Paul Simmons and Carol Mueller (editors). Philadelphia: University of Pennsylvania Press, pp. 68–87.

Flynn, Meagan. 2019 (June 21) "Detained Migrant Children Got No Toothbrush, No Soap, No Sleep. It's No Problem, Government." https://www.washingtonpost.com/nation/2019/06/21/detained-migrant-children-no-toothbrush-soap-sleep/.

Frey, John Carlos. 2013 (May/June) "Over the Line: Why are US Border Patrol Agents Shooting into Mexico and Killing Innocent Civilians." *Washington Monthly*. http://www.washingtonmonthly.com/magazine/may_june_2013/features/over_the_line044512.php?page=all.

GAO (Government Accountability Office). 2011 (September) "Observations on the Costs and Benefits of an Increased Department of Defense Role in Helping to Secure the Southwest Land Border." http://www.gao.gov/assets/100/97733.pdf.

GAO (Government Accountability Office). 2020 "Southwest Border: Actions Needed to Improve DHS Processing of Families and Coordination between DHS and HHS." GAO-20-245. https://www.gao.gov/assets/710/704683.pdf.

Hernández, Kelly Lytle. 2010 *Migra! A History of the U.S. Border Patrol*. Berkeley: University of California Press.

Horton, Alex. 2018 (January 20) "Trump Keeps Calling the Southern Border 'Very Dangerous'. It is – But Not for Americans." *Washington Post*. https://www.washingtonpost.com/news/politics/wp/2018/01/17/trump-calls-the-u-s-mexico-border-extremely-dangerous-it-is-but-not-for-americans/?utm_term=.cc1adf30e019.

Isacson, Adam. 2019a (March 6) "New Migration Numbers at U.S.-Mexico Border Show a Growing Humanitarian Crisis." Washington Office on Latin America. https://www.wola.org/analysis/new-migration-numbers-us-mexico-border-show-growing-humanitarian-crisis/

Isacson, Adam. 2019b (December 19) "'I Can't Believe What's Happening – What We're Becoming': A memo from El Paso and Ciudad Juárez." Washington Office on Latin America. https://www.wola.org/analysis/i-cant-believe-whats-happening-what-were-becoming-a-memo-from-el-paso-and-ciudad-juarez/#thebig.

Isacson, Adam and Maureen Meyer. 2012 (April) "Beyond the Border Buildup: Security and Migrants Along the U.S.–Mexico Border." Washington Office on Latin America and El Colegio de la Frontera Norte.

Johnson, Jeh Charles (Secretary of Homeland Security). 2015 (June 8) "Immigration: Perception versus Reality." James A. Baker III Institute for Public Policy, Rice University, Houston, Texas. http://www.dhs.gov/news/2015/06/08/remarks-secretary-johnson-immigration-perception-versus-reality.

Joint Chiefs of Staff. 1995 *Joint Doctrine for Military Operations Other Than War*, Joint Pub 3-07. US Department of Defense. http://smallwarsjournal.com/documents/jp3-07.pdf.

JTF–N (Joint Task Force–North). 2015 Website. http://www.jtfn.northcom.mil/.

Kauffman, Greg. 2015 (June 17) "Texas is Spending $800M to Increase Border Security. Is it Necessary?" *Christian Science Monitor*. http://www.csmonitor.com/USA/USA-Update/2015/0617/Texas-is-spending-800M-to-increase-border-security.-Is-it-necessary.

Kraska, Peter B. 2007 "Militarization and Policing – Its Relevance to 21st Century Policing." *Policing*, vol. 1, no. 4, pp. 501–513.

Lee, Michelle Ye Hee. 2015 (July 8) "Donald Trump's False Comments Connecting Mexican Immigrants and Crime." *Washington Post*. https://www.washingtonpost.com/news/fact-checker/wp/2015/07/08/donald-trumps-false-comments-connecting-mexican-immigrants-and-crime/.

Levario, Miguel Antonio. 2012 *Militarizing the Border: When Mexicans Became the Enemy*. College Station, TX: Texas A&M University Press.

Light, Michael T. and Ty Miller. 2018 "Does Undocumented Immigration Increase Violent Crime?" *Criminology*, vol. 56, no. 2, pp. 370–401. https://onlinelibrary.wiley.com/doi/epdf/10.1111/1745-9125.12175.

Maril, Robert Lee. 2004 *Patrolling Chaos: The US Border Patrol in Deep South Texas*. Lubbock, TX: Texas Tech University Press.

Maril, Robert Lee. 2011 *The Fence: National Security, Public Safety, and Illegal Immigration along the U.S.–Mexico Border*. Lubbock, TX: Texas Tech University Press.

Martinez, Daniel E., Robin C. Reineke, Raquel Rubio Goldsmith, and Bruce O. Parks. 2014 "Structural Violence and Migrant Deaths in Southern Arizona: Data from the Pima County Office of the Medical Examiner 1990–2013." *Journal of Migration and Security*, vol. 2, no. 4, pp. 257–286. http://jmhs.cmsny.org/index.php/jmhs/article/view/35.

Martinez, Daniel E., Jeremy Slack, and Ricardo Martinez-Schmidt. 2018 "Repeat Migration in the Age of the "Unauthorized Permanent Resident": A Quantitative Assessment of Migration Intentions Postdeportation." *International Migration Review*, vol. 52, no. 4, pp. 1186–1217.

Massey, Douglas A., Jorge Durand, and Karen A. Pren. 2016 "Why Border Enforcement Backfired." *American Journal of Sociology*, vol. 121, no. 5, pp. 1557–1600. https://www.journals.uchicago.edu/doi/10.1086/684200?mobileUi=0&.

McLaughlin, Elizabeth. 2018 "Homeland Security Eyeing 2 Military Bases to House Migrants Amid Child Separation Controversy." ABC. https://abcnews.go.com/US/homeland-security-eyeing-military-bases-house-migrants-amid/story?id=56146968.

Menjívar, Cecilia and Leisy J. Abrego. 2012 "Legal Violence: Immigration Law and the Lives of Central American Immigrants." *American Journal of Sociology*, vol. 117, no. 5, pp. 1380–1421.

Miller, Todd. 2014 *Border Patrol Nation: Dispatches from the Front Lines of Homeland Security*. San Francisco: City Lights Books.

Miller, Todd. 2019a *Empire of Borders: The Expansion of the US Border around the World*. New York: Verso.

Miller, Todd. 2019b "More than a Wall: Corporate Profiteering and the Militarization of US Borders." Transnational Institute. https://www.tni.org/files/publication-downloads/more-than-a-wall-report.pdf.

Miroff, Nick. 2020 (January 20) "Trump Planning to Divert Additional $7.2 billion in Pentagon Funds for Border Wall." *Washington Post*. https://www.washingtonpost.com/immigration/trump-planning-to-divert-additional-72-billion-in-pentagon-funds-for-border-wall/2020/01/13/59080a3a-363d-11ea-bb7b-265f4554af6d_story.html.

Munsil, Leigh. 2015 (July 23) "Skirmish over Drones on U.S.–Mexico Border." http://www.politico.com/story/2015/07/drone-maker-lawmakers-skirmish-border-mexico-120489.

NAS (National Academies of Sciences, US). 2016a *The Economic and Fiscal Consequences of Immigration*. Washington: National Academies Press. https://www.nap.edu/download/23550.

NAS (National Academies of Sciences, US). 2016b *The Integration of Immigrants into American Society: Issue Brief Crime*. Washington: National Academies Press. https://www.nap.edu/resource/21746/issue_brief_crime.pdf.

National Border Patrol Council. 2016 (December 20) "NBPC Press Statement on Operation Phalanx." https://bpunion.org/media-relations/press-releases/nbpc-press-statement-on-operation-phalanx/.

Nevins, Joseph. 2010 *Operation Gatekeeper and Beyond: The War on "Illegals" and the Remaking of the US–Mexico Boundary*. New York: Routledge. Second edition.

Nevins, Joseph and Timothy Dunn. 2008 (November/December) "Barricading the Border." *NACLA Report on the Americas*, vol. 41, no. 6, pp. 21–25.

Nichols, Walter J. 2019 *The Immigrant Rights Movement: The Battle over National Citizenship*. Stanford, CA: Stanford University Press.

Nyers, Peter. 2019 *Irregular Citizenship, Immigration, and Deportation*. New York: Routledge.

OIG (Office of Inspector General, Department of Homeland Security). 2019 (July 2) "Management Alert – DHS Needs to Address Dangerous Overcrowding and Prolonged Detention of Children and Adults in the Rio Grande Valley." https://www.oig.dhs.gov/sites/default/files/assets/2019-07/OIG-19-51-Jul19_.pdf.

Ortega, Bob. 2018 (May 1) " Is Border Patrol Work Dangerous? Not Compared to Being a Cop." https://www.cnn.com/2018/05/01/us/border-patrol-agent-less-dangerous-than-being-police-officer-invs/index.html.

Parrish, Will. 2019 (August 25) "The U.S. Border Patrol and an Israeli Military Contractor Are Putting a Native American Reservation Under 'Persistent Surveillance.'" https://theintercept.com/2019/08/25/border-patrol-israel-elbit-surveillance/?fbclid=IwAR2Nhd4xEFddAqPtc_aSSAL2sI6eoMT3K1doCWNrp1wR35Nw_24tuWUTHyk.

Ramey Wyatt L., Christina M. Walter, Jeffrey Zeller, Travis M. Dumont, G. Michael Lemole, and R. John Hurlbert. 2019 "Neurotrauma From Border Wall Jumping: 6 Years at the Mexican–American

Border Wall." *Neurosurgery*, vol. 85, no. 3, pp. E502–E508. doi:10.1093/neuros/nyz050. https://pubmed.ncbi.nlm.nih.gov/30873543/.

Romero, Simon, Zolan Kanno-Youngs, Manny Fernandez, Danile Borunda, Aaron Montes, and Caitlin Dickerson. 2019 (July 6) "Hungry, Scared and Sick: Inside the Migrant Detention Center in Clint, Tex." *New York Times*. https://www.nytimes.com/interactive/2019/07/06/us/migrants-border-patrol-clint.html?te=1&nl=morning-briefing&emc=edit_MBAE_p_20190707&section=topNews?campaign_id=7&instance_id=10744&segment_id=14995&user_id=4b3cd664ada25419ec6eb2765eaa437b&regi_id=60867007tion=topNews.

Rosas, Gilberto. 2012 *Barrio Libre: Criminalizing States and Delinquent Refusals of the New Frontier*. Durham, NC: Duke University Press.

Rosenthal, Brian M. and Mark Collette. 2015 (May 22) "Image of Violent Texas Border is False, Statistics Show." *Houston Chronicle*. http://www.houstonchronicle.com/news/houston-texas/houston/article/Image-of-violent-Texas-border-is-false-6282006.php.

Santos, Fernando. 2015 (October 14) "Drivers Report Gunplay, Profiling, and Abuse by Border Patrol." *New York Times*. http://www.nytimes.com/2015/10/15/us/aclu-accuses-border-patrol-of-underreporting-civil-rights-complaints.html?emc=eta1&_r=0.

Schmitt, Eric, David E. Sanger, and Glenn Thrush. 2019 "A Border Wall to Stop Terrorists? Experts Say That Makes Little Sense." *New York Times*. https://www.nytimes.com/2019/01/08/us/politics/trump-border-wall-terrorists.html?emc=edit_th_190109&nl=todaysheadlines&nlid=215203380109.

Schrader, Stuart. 2019 *Badges without Borders: How Global Counterinsurgency Transformed American Policing*. Oakland, CA: University of California Press.

Shapira, Harel. 2013 *Waiting for José: The Minutemen's Pursuit of America*. Princeton, NJ: Princeton University Press.

Sjoberg, Gideon. 1999 "Some Observation on Bureaucratic Capitalism: Knowledge about What and Why?," in *Sociology for the Twenty-first Century: Continuities and Cutting Edges*. Janet L. Abu-Lughod (editor). Chicago: University of Chicago Press, pp. 43–64.

Sjoberg, Gideon. 2009 "Corporations and Human Rights," in *Interpreting Human Rights: Social Science Perspectives*. Rhiannon Morgan and Bryan S. Turner (editors). New York: Routledge, pp. 157–176.

Sjoberg, Gideon, Elizabeth Gill, and Norma Williams. 2001 "A Sociology of Human Rights." *Social Problems*, vol. 48, no. 1, pp. 11–47.

Slack, Jeremy. 2019 *Deported to Death: How Drug Violence is Changing Migration on the US–Mexico Border*. Oakland: University of California Press.

Slack, Jeremy, Daniel E. Martinez, and Scott Whiteford. 2018 *The Shadow of the Wall: Violence and Migration at the U.S.–Mexico Border*. Tucson, AZ: University of Arizona Press.

Sliney, Samantha Arrington. 2016 "Use of the National Guard on the U.S.–Mexico Border to Quell Border Security Concerns: Increase Coordination Between Border States and Federal Government by Expanding 32 U.S.C. Section 112 to Encompass Immigration Issues." *Indiana Law Review*, vol. 49, no. 3, pp. 693–711.

Smith, Kim. 2011 (July 1) "Third Person Convicted in Killing of Arivaca Man,, Daughter." *Arizona Daily Star*. http://azstarnet.com/news/local/crime/article_618c7a50-a439-11e0-bc8e-001cc4c002e0.html.

Sonne, Paul and Missy Ryan. 2018 (October 31) "Trump Says He May Send 15,000 Troops to the US–Mexico Border." *Washington Post*. https://www.washingtonpost.com/world/national-security/ahead-of-midterm-elections-trump-says-he-may-send-15000-troops-to-us-mexico-border/2018/10/31/9e7740ec-dd4a-11e8-aa33-53bad9a881e8_story.html?utm_term=.dad533c98ab7.

Stewart, Phil and Idrees Ali. 2020 (June 3) "U.S. Shouldn't Invoke Insurrection Act, Defense Secretary Says." https://www.reuters.com/article/us-minneapolis-police-protests-pentagon/u-s-shouldnt-invoke-insurrection-act-defense-secretary-says-idUSKBN23A2BD.

US Army. 2007 *The US Army and Marine Corps Counterinsurgency Field Manual, No. 3–24*. Chicago: University of Chicago Press.

US Army Northcom. 2019 "Commander's Update Briefing" (unclassified). https://www.documentcloud.org/documents/6543793-Commander-Briefing-Metadata-Free-Final-3.html.

US Code. Title 10. Armed Forces. Section 284. 2020 "Support for Counterdrug Activities and Activities to Counter Transnational Organized Crime."

2. The U.S.–Mexico border since 2014: overt migration contention and normalized violence

Josiah Heyman

1. INTRODUCTION

In August 2019, a white nationalist drove 700 miles from a suburb of Dallas–Fort Worth to El Paso, on the Mexican border. He killed 22 people at a Walmart, from both countries. Influenced by the racist rhetoric of Texas Republican leaders, his goal was kill Mexicans, apparently making no distinction between Mexicans and Mexican Americans. El Pasoans argued, correctly, that this hatred came from outside the border region, and that El Paso is one of the safest cities in the United States. Indeed, I have made this very argument, characteristic of El Paso and other U.S. border advocates who are arguing against the escalation of coercive border enforcement, including the militarization that Dunn describes in his chapter of this book. However, this stance obscures the reality of violence on both sides of the U.S.–Mexico border.

My task here is to outline the major features of this violence.[1] It includes open violence in Mexico, and hidden violence in the United States. By violence I mean both direct physical violence, including mental health, and so-called structural violence (Galtung 1969). The latter term includes reduction of human capacity caused by broader societal conditions. For example, U.S. refusals of asylum-seekers make them wait in places where violent criminals victimize them; the violence is done by the U.S. government as well as the criminals in Mexico. As Slack et al. (2018: 85–87) point out, so-called U.S. border "security" policy actually makes many migrants insecure, to deadly effect. Here I build on that insight. I propose that it occurs through processes of hiding of violence in the United States and displacement of violence into Mexico. Both sides are thus implicated in violence. A central argument at the core of my work (Heyman 2017) has been that at the U.S.–Mexico border, safety and wealth accumulate on the U.S. side, and poverty, risk, and insecurity on the Mexican, but they constitute one dynamic whole. This unifying pattern of uneven and combined development (Smith 1984) cuts across specific phenomena: money, drugs, guns, migration, etc.

In the United States, violence is inflicted on people who are from some viewpoints seen as undeserving outsiders, it is rationalized by the allegedly legitimate application of law, and it occurs in locations that are marginal to the dominant society. These all hide violence. In Mexico, violence is outrageously open, but mostly conducted with impunity (over 90 percent of homicides in Mexico are unsolved or unprosecuted). Mexicans are themselves victims but subordinate non-Mexicans, such as Central American migrants, and devalued Mexicans, such as returned deportees, are even more likely to be victims. The United States displaces such stigmatized people into the maelstrom of violence in Mexico, either sending them back or blockading them, making them wait there. Likewise, the criminal business nexus of drugs–guns–money is conveniently silent and safe in the United States (even though important elements occur there) while openly, dangerously conducted on the Mexican side. While Mexican and U.S. activists, journalists, and scholars have done admirable work of documenting and publicizing Mexican realities in both countries, this displacement into Mexico unquestionably reduces attention to its horror.

Because the suffering imposed on migrants (asylum-seekers, unauthorized labor and family-reunification migrants) affects large numbers of people, often violating their basic human rights, and bringing about direct and indirect violence, this feature of the border justifiably garners the most attention from activists, journalists, and scholars. This distracts us from other processes that generate violence, which overlap in important ways. To speak of migration first, however, we must name U.S. racist xenophobia that drives an immigration policy (generous in some ways, for some people) that rejects most asylum-seekers and seriously reduces legal paths for migration for the others. The border is an important symbol in enacting xenophobia, and the most violence-engendering processes are enacted in this region. (It should be noted that there is widespread disagreement with and resistance to these politics, but here I will focus on what is being done by the U.S. federal government.) While rooted in U.S. xenophobia, violence against migrants extends deeply into Mexico (such as coercion against deportees), and Mexican xenophobia in turn is directed against Central Americans and other non-Mexicans. We will examine closely all the mechanisms used in the practice of xenophobia on both sides of the border. An important cause of violence against migrants is the overlap between migration and the illegalized drug business (Slack and Whiteford 2011; revised and reprinted in 2018).

Because drug trafficking is an illegalized business, coercion is central to its conduct. Secrets cannot be protected and contracts cannot be guarded through legal processes, so violence, threatened and actual, is essential. Drug markets are widespread in both the United States and Mexico, accompanied by violence, and the border has a central role as smuggling is a central point of profit over which extremely violent struggles occur.[2] (Local drug markets in Mexican northern border cities are also controlled by violence.) This is similar in Central America. The drug business is interlocked with the business in guns and munitions, and in money. Guns are widely available in the United States, while they are in law (but not in practice) illegalized in Mexico. As a result, arms and munitions from Mexico must be smuggled southward; they certainly are the deadliest border trade. Over 70 percent of guns seized in Mexico come from the United States, and much of the remainder are simply not traced, rather than known as coming through other routes (U.S. Department of Justice, Bureau of Alcohol, Tobacco, and Firearms 2019: 7). Gun smuggling from the United States to Mexico accounts for a significant part of the U.S. gun business, especially in border regions (McDougal et al. 2015). The U.S. gun business is sheltered quite effectively by the political power—the voices of an organized minority of voters, mobilized by the gun dealer lobby, the National Rifle Association. Guns are not the only cause of border violence—I will discuss Mexican politics shortly—but the high level of death and injury would not be possible without this important U.S. cause.

Money, meanwhile, has enormous legitimacy within capitalism (in all the countries concerned), but some is illegalized as profits of the drug business. Contraband money moves both north (capital flight from Mexico and Central America to the United States) and south (repatriated profits from the United States to drug and weapons operations south of the border). For example, "HSBC Holdings Plc agreed to pay a record $1.92 billion in fines to U.S. authorities for allowing itself to be used to launder a river of drug money flowing out of Mexico and other banking lapses" (Viswanatha and Wolf 2012).[3] While little violence directly surrounds the money flows (capitalism, again), they are the driving force of violence in all the other domains.

The armed agencies of the U.S. state, such as the Department of Homeland Security and the Department of Justice, and in more ambiguous ways those of Mexico and Central America, also profit from these conflicts. They profit from budgets and from increased employment (the aim largely of their worker unions). They also benefit extensively from asset seizure from wealthy criminals (cash, real estate, vehicles, etc.). The state agencies and the criminal organizations arguably are in a symbiotic relationship, even as they appear to be polar opposites. Together they amplify the climate of violence in the region. The result is, as Reece Jones points out (2017), a "violent border," one of many around the world.

2. CONTEXTUALIZING THE NEXUS OF VIOLENCE AT THE BORDER

The diverse, interacting patterns of violence at the border stem from deep historical patterns of interaction between the two countries, and relatedly inequalities inside each of them (Heyman 2017). A full historical account extends well beyond this chapter, but some basic points are worth reviewing. U.S. military conquest against Mexico established the border, and the expropriation of land and water involved a mixture of violence and legal chicanery. Military and police violence was often unrestrained when exercised against Mexican-origin people (Hernandez 2010; Levario 2012). Waves of mass expulsion (including against U.S. citizens) occurred at the 1930s and in 1954, with periods of "normal" enforcement in between. Mass arrests at the border started upward again in the late 1970s, intensifying from 1993 onward (Dunn 2010; Nevins 2010).

One cannot simply draw a straight line from the past to the present, but key patterns can be seen (Heyman 2012 discusses continuities and transformations in more depth).[4] Latin American peasant-workers often are welcomed as laborers, without legal rights or rights of settlement (de jure or de facto), but likewise they can be expelled with few or no rights of due process. Direct official violence is widely, if unofficially, tolerated, and structural violence by policy is openly embraced. The border is a symbol of imagined threats from Latin America (when the policing itself is the real threat), and domestic anxiety over global and domestic change often is channeled into racially coded fears about the Mexican border (Heyman 2012). Racist rhetoric, such as the interpretation of immigration as an invasion resulting in racial replacement of whites by non-whites (Abutaleb 2019), draws on the long-standing racialized justification of violent aggression and domination in U.S.–Mexico history (Levario 2012). While the ultimate analysis emphasizes racist symbolic politics (e.g., the pointless but highly visible border wall), the symbolism is materialized in massive border enforcement programs that generate violence directly and indirectly (Heyman 1999). The chronology of border enforcement initiatives and punitive immigration laws, which long predate Donald Trump's administration (see Dunn 2010; Nevins 2010; and Ngai 2004), clearly demonstrate the depth of these key patterns. Trump at his worst has been more open, more systematic, and a little less scrupled than previous administrations, but fundamentally continuous with them.

The politics and policies of the United States hold the main responsibility for death and suffering at the Mexican border, but the internal dynamics of Mexico also account for much violence. Mexico, for most of the twentieth century, had a unified political regime emanating from a powerful presidency; even as this has changed and fragmented in recent decades, basic patterns of conduct remain. Control is central, and involves a mixture of elite–criminal alliances, corruption, selective use of violence, unaccountable police and military operations, and toleration of particular criminal formations. As top-down control has weakened and fragmented (but not disappeared, for example with a growing military), regional and local political–criminal formations have grown larger and more autonomous, in a very dynamic and chaotic way. The border, a boom region in international capitalism and a staging point for contraband in both directions, has long been important to these processes (Boullosa and Wallace 2015). Because of this, various state and non-state actors vie for control of lucrative border smuggling corridors, engendering regional violence. Politicians are interwoven with criminals in a deeply rooted pattern of "authorized crime," notably at Mexico's northern border (Schmidt and Spector 2013).

"Internal" dynamics of Mexico of course are in causal relationship to the United States. Mexican authoritarianism and its increasingly violent and militarized collapse is supported by U.S. police and military aid (Boyce et al. 2015). Arguably more important, but poorly documented, is toleration of questionable money flows between the two countries (Kar 2012). The United States bullies Mexico, as can be seen in the policies recounted below, and in turn at the border it gets the kind of Mexico—violent, corrupt, pliable—that it has cultivated over the long run.

In summary, the border is a particular site for violence-generating processes: a political target of racist xenophobia and also a target of human rights activism (Heyman and Symons 2012), a site for the visible performance of state power on less powerful others (Andreas 2001), a crossing place for asylum-seekers and unauthorized family and labor migrants, a site of return and recovery—or victimization—for those pushed back (Slack 2019), a staging site for gun, drug, and human contraband, and a resource for politicians and state agencies to accumulate money and influence in both countries. Such actors and processes are not reducible to each other, but they do interact and reinforce each other. A diverse range of direct and structural violence is the product.

3. VIOLENCE AT THE BORDER: A SYSTEMATIC REVIEW

U.S. migration and drug enforcement policies, and the toleration of southbound weapons trafficking, have built up over many decades (Boullosa and Wallace 2015; Dunn 2010; Nevins 2010). While practically and rhetorically extreme, the Trump administration has mainly extended, deepened, and worsened long-accumulated policies. With the goal of changing the scene of widespread violation of human rights, including direct and indirect forms of violence, here I present a systematic survey of border violence as an interwoven, complex system.

The motives for people to leave northern Central America are diverse and often multiple. Violence by military, police, higher scale criminal organizations, and gangs is widespread; Honduras and El Salvador regularly vie for the worst civilian homicide rate in the world (discussed below). The track through Mexico likewise has widespread direct violence (kidnapping, for example) and structural violence, such as causes of injuries (París Pombo 2017; Vogt 2018). Mexico's subordinate role, for the United States, in enforcing migration blockades and deportation makes these people even more vulnerable, since they are easily exploited and deported by authorities. While the focus in this chapter is on the border region itself, the stunning dangers of the voyages back and forth are relevant. They render people poorer and more vulnerable when they do arrive at or near the border, and make their return once deported either more difficult or more desperate.

Due to U.S. escalation of enforcement against unauthorized border entry and movement north, most unauthorized migrants use smugglers. Non-Mexicans sometimes use smugglers, if they have the funds, to move quickly and safely through Mexico in the face of the above-mentioned risks. The cost of being smuggled can lead to various coercive situations, such as exploitation through the leverage of debt, carrying drugs into the United States to earn money, and being trafficked for work, commercial sex, etc.[5] There is an active debate about the character of smuggling (Izcara Palacios 2012, 2015; Sanchez 2014; Slack and Campbell 2018; Spener 2009), smuggling itself is diverse, and it has changed over time. It seems likely that criminal organizations based in violent coercion in Mexico, notably at the border, currently are not mostly involved directly in human smuggling (except labor in drug packaging and transportation); rather, they engage in a protection racket over human smugglers. This covert, unpredictable world of criminality pervades the border crossing staging areas and deportation-reception sites along Mexico's northern border. It makes human smuggling expensive, volatile, and dangerous for migrants.

Migrants may attempt to enter the United States in two ways (here I discuss just the southwestern border, and not the Caribbean, Canada, or airports). Entry with falsified documents or via bribed U.S. officers at ports of entry is safe but expensive (and has harsher legal penalties if caught). Little is known about it at this border. Entry without inspection—crossing rivers and/or walking across land—poses serious risks of physical suffering, injury, and death. As of 16 years ending September 2017, the Border Patrol reported almost 6,000 border crossing deaths,[6] and independent observers found at least another uncounted 564 deaths (Ortega 2018). Deaths in 2019 were 520 (Missing Migrants 2020). Clearly, this is a quintessential example of context-caused structural violence (Cornelius 2001; Martínez et al. 2014). Because their path into the United States is illegalized, they suffer these physical and mental traumas. These sorts of risks affect people who try to enter the United States without detection, such as former deportees. However, asylum-seekers aim to become known to officers of the government, in order to begin their asylum case, they typically enter in relatively simpler and less risky ways (sadly, some do drown in rivers and canals).

The safest and most readily managed way for asylum-seekers to present themselves is by going directly into legal ports of entry (the vast majority are still unauthorized, since they lack a visa to proceed through the port). They can request asylum there. However, since 2016 and widely since 2017 the United States has blocked most asylum-seekers from crossing the literal international boundary in ports. If they do not cross the line, they cannot be considered by the United States for asylum. A few people, sometimes zero, are admitted through this route each day; at the border, a long waiting line has formed. People put their names on a list, run by various actors like the migrants themselves, Mexican security guards, and Mexican government officials. This is called "metering." While waiting, they must find some way of surviving in the Mexican border city, to be discussed shortly. Cynically, the U.S. government tells asylum-seekers to go through ports, while mainly obstructing them. This sets up one experience of violence.

In the xenophobic framework that has dominated U.S. border immigration policy—against vigorous resistance—asylum-seekers must be physically prevented from entering the country, made to suffer in order to deter them, or denied asylum whatever their case.[7] U.S. policies have moved among these options in a chaotic and partial way. Some asylum-seekers have been put into mass detention centers and camps; some of these are specific for families (but never enough spaces), and some for children without parents (unaccompanied minors). As punitive as this is, most children are eventually released to sponsors (mainly their relatives). In 2018, the Trump administration attempted to punish children by holding them in improvised child prisons at the border and elsewhere; the specific tools were slowing down to a crawl their release paperwork and providing their sponsoring families' information to enforcement agents, frightening those families away from sponsorship. This exploded in the numbers of imprisoned children, costs, and terrible publicity. The arrest, processing, release flow for unaccompanied children has nearly resumed its previous pace.

Meanwhile, from 2015 onward, parents with children legally must be released, pending their immigration court case (in many cases, asylum case) after 20 days' imprisonment (a rule that is, however, often violated). There had been notable surges of asylum-seeking families and children in 2014 and 2016; in 2018 this picked up again. People arrived at the border, began an asylum process, were released to charitable organizations, contacted sponsors, quickly obtained transportation, and moved to be united with their relatives or compatriots—a process devoid of violence, but one vigorously opposed by the Trump administration, and essentially ended by late 2019 by returns to Mexico or Central America, as discussed below. While multi-billion dollar federal agencies like Customs and Border Protection (CBP) and Immigration and Customs Enforcement (ICE) failed to provide even minimal conditions for human life in their facilities, Annunciation House in El Paso, Catholic Charities in south Texas, and so forth rose to the occasion by housing and feeding waves of incoming refugees, at the peak over a thousand a night released by federal authorities (in some cases dumped in the streets). In some places municipal assistance was involved, but mostly charitable contributions and volunteer labor made this possible. The typical pattern, in which I participated, was a core organization giving instructions on how to organize a reception site (e.g., a church hall) and process the refugee flow in and out, enabling individual sites to emerge and replicate as needed. Volunteers came from both border communities and the national interior, and were motivated by a combination of deep religious values and secular humanism.

The United States has long aspired to imprison all the families, and this is still a disturbing possibility (plans for mass internment camps on military bases at and near the border, for reasons that are not clear, have been announced but never actualized [Baldor 2018; Sisk 2018; Jowers 2019]). Several thousand people at a time in family groups are imprisoned, mainly at two Texas ICE camps near the border. Beginning on a pilot basis in fall 2017, and conducted in mass along the border in summer 2018, over 5,400 children were forcibly separated from their families. While the mass policy ended in June 2018, due to an American Civil Liberties Union (ACLU) lawsuit, the practice continues at a lower rate. Children are still removed from caretakers who are not directly parents (e.g., older siblings). They also are sometimes taken away from parents that CBP officers at their discretion disapprove of, such as parents with tattoos. Separated children are handled as unaccompanied minors. Separation of children from trusted and loved caretakers is traumatic in the extreme (Physicians for Human Rights 2020).

Through this period of extensive family migration with limited returns to home countries or Mexico, CBP underwent a humanitarian crisis in its short-term detention system. The causes include numbers of people overwhelming spaces for imprisonment, ICE (the long-term imprisonment agency) slowly taking immigration detainees from CBP (the short-term processing and imprisonment agency) as spaces opened, deliberate preference in the Trump administration for imprisonment as deterrence (effectuated by reluctance to release people for later court dates), and desire to create a media spectacle of crisis. The effect was concentration of imprisoned migrants, both families and single adults, in CBP's short-term holding cells. These cells by policy should not hold people longer than three days (72 hours), and they are not designed for longer occupation or large numbers—but that is exactly what happened. Inspections mandated by law concerning conditions of imprisonment of immigrant children revealed horrendous conditions, juvenile and adult, forcing the government rapidly to ramp up temporary housing and services. A comparable story can be told about deaths of children and adults in short-term custody and transportation, involving neglect of basic medical checks and services. In a shocking example, six children died in government custody between September 2018 and May 2019, the first such deaths in a decade (Moore 2020).

During this real or constructed logistical crisis, CBP housed hundreds of families, children and adults, in a rocky open space under a bridge at the border in El Paso. It was during the late winter, cold season. They lived there only with mylar blankets for shelter. This outrageous episode culminated in a CBP Director press conference—emphasizing video—in front of the fenced-in crowd, in appearance dirty, pitiful, dark-skinned, and vaguely disturbing. A main theme of U.S. government actions in the 2017–summer 2019 period was the creation and publicity of "crisis" as a political move against immigration. Often, this was a failure (most notably with family separation), and the government, especially the Department of Homeland Security (DHS), shifted in early summer 2019 from dramatized crisis to processes of hiding by displacement and inaccessibility.

While U.S. policy, advocacy, and publicity has concentrated on family migration and not identically on asylum, large numbers of non-family adults (I crudely term them single adults) are arrested and processed, some but not all with asylum claims. There continues in particular to be substantial ongoing Mexican adult migration without asylum claims, as well as some Mexican asylum-seeking migration treated later. The U.S. border system aims to use extended imprisonment and criminalization to punish and ostensibly deter single adults. This includes the continuation of the Consequences Delivery System, formerly known as Operation Streamline, which involves criminal charges and almost always conviction of illegal entry. It also involves extremely high cost and difficult conditions for bonding out of immigration prison. The Attorney General implemented a policy of never bonding out asylum-seekers, but it was stayed in court. As a result, immigration prisons expand and expand, more and more people lasting longer and longer, despite explicit mandates by Congress to cap and reduce the immigration-imprisoned numbers.

Of course, the period of large-scale but mostly safe family migration (arrival, processing, and release) could not last; xenophobia requires suffering by and expulsion of the outsiders. The U.S. government threatened Mexico with economic devastation through tariffs and border closures/severe slowdowns, and Mexico is profoundly dependent on trade with the United States. Mexico then implemented a number of measures to slow down, detain, and expel migrants crossing through the country. They affected migrants along the length of Mexico, increasing their vulnerability, and at the border these measures included deployment of National Guard troops to obstruct physically access to the border. This restriction by Mexico appears to have reduced asylum-seeking migration at the U.S. southwestern border, but not completely ended it (this pattern of Mexico serving as a U.S. proxy also occurred in 2014 and 2016).

Also, starting in early 2019 but rolled out extensively along the border by May 2019, the United States has returned arriving non-Mexican asylum-seekers to Mexico while they wait for their immigration court cases (they briefly enter for proceedings, and then are returned) (American Immigration Council 2020). This has mostly been applied to family groups; single adults mainly are imprisoned in the United States. It also is applied only to non-Mexican, Spanish speakers; it clearly strikes at Central Americans. This is the Migrant Protection Protocol (MPP), a cynical name because returning people from the United States to Mexico moves them from a relatively safe space (with important exceptions), the U.S. side, to a very dangerous space, the northern Mexican border region (as detailed below). Being non-Mexican, with few or no protective networks, they are particularly vulnerable to victimization and exploitation. In addition to crime and direct violence, conditions of living in Mexico are structurally violent: people initially lack supplies more than they carry in, say, a backpack, lack places to live except mass shelters with dubious safety, have poor communications access, and have little or no money.[8] MPP also obstructs legal cases; few U.S. immigration lawyers meet with clients on the Mexican side, and documents needed for asylum cases are hard to gather. Somewhere between 57,000 and 62,000 people have been sent to Mexico so far under MPP; some abandon their quest but others (the proportion is unclear) remain in limbo (American Immigration Council 2020: 4, 6). Those who abandon their quest likely will return to the site of violent threats and other persecution. The MPP population is at serious risk of direct and indirect violence, but, except for advocates and service providers in the two countries, largely invisible because of displacement away from the United States and the marginality of the people involved.

The MPP is an extreme measure to delay and deter asylum-seekers. But it is not the most extreme measure. The U.S. government recently has made agreements to send asylum-seekers arriving at the border to other countries to apply for asylum (giving up their U.S. case). For example, Hondurans are sent to Guatemala or El Salvador, Salvadorans to Honduras or Guatemala, Guatemalans to Honduras or El Salvador, and most recently, Mexicans are proposed to be sent to Guatemala—or required to return to the country of their fear (American Immigration Council 2020). This policy is cynical in the extreme. These are tiny, poor countries with little or no capacity to serve asylum-seekers. And they are among the most dangerous places in the world.[9] The U.S. policy violates the international legal principle of non-refoulment (not sending a persecuted person back into danger).

Connected to this initiative is a proposed legal change in which people who enter the United States from another country—even one that is not a designated "first country of asylum," which required safety and adequate support for asylees—will be denied asylum if they have not already asked for asylum in that previous country. In other words, asylum across the land border with Mexico will be impossible.[10] This still is in court.

Mexicans still can seek asylum at the land border, but a new program, the Humanitarian Asylum Review Process (HARP), establishes a high-speed asylum review right at the border. For non-Mexicans, the Prompt Asylum Claim Review (PACR) does the same (American Immigration Council 2020). The problem with HARP and PACR is that imprisoned asylum claimants are given little time to contact legal representatives, with serious practical barriers actually to accomplish this, as well as continuing difficulties in gathering supporting materials. These concerns are now in court. The entire pattern in these procedural and policy details is that migrants as a whole, and in particular those fleeing persecution, are blockaded inside or returned to highly violent environments.

Beyond policy measures, the physical enforcement process embodies actual and potential violence. Over several decades, military units and resources have been deployed to support civilian law enforcement along the border, as well as diffusion of military tactics and technologies into the civilian law enforcement side (Dunn 1997). The military has firmly resisted actually carrying out direct arrests, and shooting cases have been accidental (if made possible by the wider deployment process). However, a subtle but profound legal line may have been crossed in early 2019 when Donald Trump declared a national emergency to use military money in wall construction at the border (also, military units again were deployed to the border).

The broader issues of the border wall surpass this chapter, but its violent quality is worth describing. The wall causes extensive injuries, as memorably documented by Ieva Jusionyte (an anthropologist who worked as a first responder at the border; 2018). These include complex fractures and shattering of bones as people fall from climbing over the wall in the process of unauthorized migration or small-scale drug smuggling. As the wall is built higher, it becomes more injurious or deadly. When military units were deployed in 2019, in a symbolic show of force, they occupied themselves in hanging vast amounts of razor concertina wire on the wall, border ports of entry, and other locations along the border. The concertina wire brutally slices people and animals that touch it.

Physical violence and verbal assault are an important feature of the U.S. immigration enforcement system. Twenty-three percent of deported Mexicans in a systematic random sample survey at the border reported verbal abuse by U.S. authorities (about three quarters of them Border Patrol), and 11 percent reported physical abuse (Martínez et al. 2013). Expressed attitudes of enforcers were shockingly abusive; to pick just one representative case, a migrant reported that "an immigration agent shouted we don't want you, go back to your country, and the agent in a green uniform [Border Patrol] took out his gun and threatened them, using bad words" (Heyman et al. 2019). While abuse does not occur in the majority of encounters, it is commonplace, not a rare deviation. These border reports confirm previous studies of Salvadorans in El Salvador immediately after deportation (Phillips et al., 2002, 2006; also see Chapters 9 and 10 of this book). Alongside abuse by officials are threats by self-appointed vigilantes at the border. Holding people at gunpoint for turnover to the Border Patrol, for example, is common; the border vigilantes cooperate with CBP and are closely connected to the Steve Bannon wing of the nationalist right (Devereaux 2019; Nathan 2019). The physical and symbolic violence pervading border passage, arrest, detention, and deportation is largely hidden, under cover of remote sites and secret police operations, applied to voiceless outsiders.

Some people who are deported have resources or supportive family and hometown connections to move back to places of origin in reasonably quick and safe ways. However, other deported people are raw materials for the hyper-violent drug business, as Jeremy Slack's (2019) important ethnography *Deported to Death* shows. Kidnapping is the most extreme manifestation of this coercive and exploitative process. Some kidnapping aims to get quick payments for release from family members, mostly in the United States. But kidnapping also serves to recruit workers in criminal businesses, such as packing and transporting drugs. And it sometime devolves into pointless torture and killing, as exemplified by the San Fernando massacre of 193 captive migrants in 2011, and the 2012 Cadeyreta massacre of another 49, both by the Zeta cartel. Post-deportation processes intersect the violent world of gun and drug trafficking, information that informs us about wider conditions also affecting arriving migrants coming northward into the border region and border region residents who slip into this domain.

The common narrative about drug business violence at the border is that U.S. demand for illegalized drugs causes competitive violence in Mexico. This is only partially true, and becoming more complicated today. In fact, there are large, lucrative markets for illegalized drugs in both countries, and bloody violence to control access to such markets and supply delivery activities in both sites. The fundamental challenge is the illegalization of the product. Illegality—especially of high value commerce—brings horror. Contracts and deals cannot be enforced in court. Instead, they are enforced by fear and violence. Information about illegal practices is communicated with blatant displays of wealth and impunity, and threats of force and torture. Because a lucrative business might bring detection, seizure, and arrest by state authorities, illegality requires cooptation, corruption, and intimidation of government and community. For these reasons, Mexico has paid an enormous toll for feeding its own and the U.S. appetite for illegalized drugs. With many tens of thousands of dead and disappeared, it is a tragedy of cataclysmic proportions.

Meanwhile, the tools of death, guns and munitions, move south. Killers worse than fentanyl,[11] weapons are widely available in the United States but tightly regulated in Mexico. The United States has become the world's leading "drug dealer" of guns; at least 70 percent of all Mexican homicides use U.S. weapons. Meanwhile, the illegalized drugs are produced in Mexico or transported through that country. For example, U.S. government data clearly show that most drugs are transported north via ports of entry alongside legitimate trade and travel, not covertly outside such ports (Finklea 2019: 7).[12] Flexible, advanced capitalists based in Mexico but operating across the world orchestrate the business. U.S. drug-war bureaucrats ostensibly fight these criminal businesses, but garner their budgets by failing just enough to maintain in place a visible problem and succeeding just enough to make profits for their "enemies."

Money ties this all together. The United States cajoles and pays Mexico to fight a war against the drug business itself, but winks and nods at the unaccountable money sloshing back and forth across the border. Wachovia Bank, later gobbled up by Bank of America, cheerfully washed the blood off Mexican criminal dollars (Vulliamy 2011). In the failed U.S. tactic of illegalization, the border is the single greatest barrier to the drug business, and thus the most important site to realize a profit or fear-monger a budget. Meanwhile, we are distracted from real corruption and low-level warfare by xenophobic fear of border refugee arrivals, people whose aspiration is to clean our offices and flee thugs with semi-automatics.

For most of the twentieth century, Mexico had a cynical one party state, dedicated above all to control: in the face of regular dissent and discontent, maintaining politicians in control, with access to the income streams of power (what follows is based on Astorga Almanza 1996; Boullosa and Wallace 2015; Flores Pérez 2013). Criminal enterprises, with unaccountable, liquid money, were crucial. The money enriched politicians and bribed others to maintain the peace (a peace with a brutal edge for dissidents). Drug corruption is absolutely essential to a main task of Mexican governance, which is keeping the military rich and happy, but out of politics (which has proven successful). Likewise, state governors and other regional political bosses often have fingers in the bloody money cake, to maintain control and to keep them fat and happy. A city like Ciudad Juárez on the border is absolutely vital to the drug and weapons business, and while the Municipal Presidents themselves may not be in the business, their acquiescence to a particular arrangement of flows and bribes (such as to state and municipal police) is crucial. For many decades under single-party rule these arrangements worked, with sporadic slippage and violence. The explosive potential of illegality—that rivalries and disagreements cannot be solved in court but only by killing—was kept within limits, as governors and generals assigned criminal territories, punished maverick bosses, and mediated disputes.

Beginning in 1968, Mexico's authoritarian political system slowly weakened, and finally broke down in 2000. One party rule shattered into multiple pieces, while old corruption hung on in many states and spread to new parties and governors. Indeed, at the present the old parties barely exist and politics centers on individual personalities. While this evolution has been a step forward for electoral democracy, the older single-party system of authoritarian management of criminal business gave way to open competition and uncontrolled conflicts. High-level drug trafficking organizations (misnamed "cartels" despite not monopolizing supplies) arose, attacked, shattered, and were replaced by new formations. These high-level organizations flexibly contract coercion out to hyper-violent cells, which produce fear-inspiring propaganda. Bloody competition occurs in many ways, by many units, and in many sites. Violence metastasizes across society.

In 1982, burdened by elite theft and a massive debt, Mexico's economy collapsed. It has never fully recovered. Steady growth spread across society has been replaced by widening inequality—now among the worst in the world—and an extreme commitment to free markets that has dissolved social bonds. Outrageous ostentation coexists with people's desperate search for income. In the 1990s and 2000s the United States was able to make Caribbean smuggling routes more difficult, thereby hurting Colombian criminal organizations; the path through Central America and Mexico, and the Mexican organizations, simply rose to the fore. This reinforced the Mexican drug business (as a way to survive or a way to pile up wealth) and drug trafficking culture (as a display of nouveau riche luxuries). Politicians have been among the worst offenders. With a fractured state and vastly increased profits, we may be witnessing a disturbing reversal in which criminals control politicians rather than the older pattern of politically managed illegal business.

In 2006, Felipe Calderón won a close and disputed presidential election. To make a dramatic move, and debatably to favor the Sinaloa faction, he dramatically ramped up a militaristic drug war. Recent court documentation shows that Calderón's security chief, Genaro García Luna, was in the pay of Sinaloa; possibly arrangements also assisted the election of Calderón's successor, Enrique Peña Nieto (La Política Online 2019). The period from 2007 to 2012 was filled with horrific official and unofficial slaughter, by some estimates, over 120,000 people. The United States flooded the country with police–military aid. Police have been deeply corrupt, but their replacement by the military worsened violence. Military bastions and convoys, while frightening, offer little law enforcement presence in reality, while police and military were freed to enforce the law by killing people they despised. While excused (inexcusably) as pragmatic killing of criminals, in fact there was extensive murder of social activists, journalists, and people with land and property that could be stolen by force (Molloy 2013). The mass firing of police and the killing of key criminals unleashed a wave of chaotic, competitive killing in society, especially by armed criminal enforcement cells. Even though murders and disappearances slowed somewhat after 2012, they have returned in force in the last two years (2018–2019).

Street shoot-outs, massacres, torture, and the display of dismembered bodies on a large scale has become in the last two decades a common and everyday manifestation of the conflict between and among Mexican cartels, between the government and cartels, and between myriad other actors involved in organized or simply street crime. What seemed new and unique about these horrific acts was not only their extreme cruelty and perversity—facilitated by the illegal U.S. weapons trade—but that they were designed for public distribution and consumption in the cyber-communication sphere, and they were part of a war *for* drugs and profit, not political gain or military victory per se. Moreover, they were meant to defeat and destroy an enemy in the criminal world but also to intimidate the government and civil society. The new drug cartels became essentially private business armies or narco-states within a state.

Additionally, the acts of macabre violence were not simply a way of maintaining control of the profits of the illicit drug business, but were a type of theatrical "performance violence" in Mark Juergensmeyer's terms (2017). They were carried out "to theatrically enact and communicate an imagined reality" (2017: 7). That imagined reality was one of a kind of Narco Kingdom in which omnipotent, charismatic drug barons ran entire states and regions and magically disposed of their enemies through unspeakable, spectacular brutality made almost cartoon-like in its repetitive display on videos, social media, blogs, television, and music videos.

Mexico's northern border is vital to the gun–drug–physical cash smuggling business, though not unique. In Mexico, the drugs are illegal, but well protected by political arrangements. In the United States, the drugs are much more vulnerable to seizure, though the presence of political cover is understudied. As a result, the Mexican side of the border is a crucial site in packaging and disguising drugs, and then crossing them into the United States. Likewise, guns are tightly limited in Mexico, and need to be smuggled south across the border. Physical cash is legal in both countries but monitored, above the amount of $10,000, when crossing from the United States into Mexico. All of these patterns amount to making the Mexican northern border region a site of violent contention in this criminal-political world.

The consequences are shocking. Tijuana, the largest Mexican northern border city, was the most homicidal large city in the world in 2018 at 138.26 homicides per 100,000 people and Ciudad Juárez, the second largest Mexican border city, was fifth at 85.56 per 100,000 (Seguridad, Justicia, y Paz 2019). Homicides in the extraordinarily dangerous northeastern border state of Tamaulipas may be underestimated due to the risk of gathering information. Border violence is exemplified by the Allende massacre. Allende, Coahuila, is a small city (around 20,000 population) near the U.S. border. A massacre in 2014 of at least 300 people (killed, dissolved in caustic soda, and lightly buried) was touched off by revenge for a U.S. Drug Enforcement Administration penetration of the secure phones of the leaders of the Zeta cartel (Thompson 2017). Border interactions caused this massacre. It is important to recognize, however, the movements to draw attention to the violence and demand safety and justice in the region (Durin 2019: 389–430). For example, an important social movement in Ciudad Juárez demanded visibility and accountability from the Mexican government, which had been trying to hide and excuse the violence, and a retreat from military occupation of the region (Staudt and Méndez 2015).

Northern border Mexico, it is important to remember, is home to millions of innocent people. It has seen widespread internal displacement of Mexicans, and some flight to the United States, as people flee actual and threatened violence (Durin 2019). The northern border cities are also places where non-Mexican migrants (and some displaced Mexicans) wait long periods on U.S. port of entry metering, and the place of return for MPP populations and deported Mexicans. (Others are being sent to unthinkably dangerous northern Central America.) Through such processes, violence is both pushed outside the United States, and intimately bound up in its processes of labor recruitment, white racist illusion, drug consumption, and weapon production and sale.

4. CONCLUSION

The increasing direct and indirect occurrence of harm to people in migration across the U.S.–Mexico border is a fundamental moral challenge that we must face. While it has deep historical roots, an important turning point was the early to mid-1990s (Abrego et al. 2017; Dunn 2010; Kerwin 2018; Nevins 2010). The long-standing pattern of cross-border migration had been toleration but subordination, though accompanied by barriers the overcoming of which present dangers and costs constituting structural violence. Migration for asylum, however, has been more often blockaded and refused at this border, though when accessed it sometimes is protected by the legal framework of asylum claims in immigration court. These deep-seated patterns have worsened under the Trump administration. Subordination after unauthorized entry has shifted to rejection, building on the longer history of treatment of asylum-seekers. Many examples can be adduced, but a telling one has been the refusal to bond out immigration prisoners and the accumulation of imprisoned adults in detention.

While previous practices were harmful, directly or indirectly, the various policies of rejection have greatly increased direct and structural violence toward migrants and Mexican border residents, occurring in a context of interacting migration and drug law enforcement, and criminal organizational conflict. The most important and morally repugnant action is returning incoming migrants, most of them asylum-seekers with reasonable claims (given the places they flee), to northern Mexican border cities, and recently to Guatemala, Honduras, and El Salvador. These are sites of widespread coercion, kidnapping, and killing.

Alongside this is the equally repugnant failure to curb the arms trade from the United States across the border, since these weapons are crucial in the conduct of violence. And many other items can be enumerated, all of them deserving moral scrutiny. But the process of rejection worsens an already existing moral veil that obscures these terrible processes. They are hidden by displacement into Mexico and Central America, by use of a largely secret, hidden, and unaccountable enforcement apparatus, and because of the racist devaluation of Latin American and Caribbean people, especially peasant-workers. Our task is both critical of the odious present, and visionary of a more fully inclusive future (Heyman 1998).

Harm-generating relations and processes have over historical time generated a large, dynamic, violent, and exploitative border. Morally repugnant policies and effects must be revealed, discussed publicly, and changed—not just specific to Trump (really, Stephen Miller), though those two are completely awful—but deep within U.S. and Mexican history and laws. For such matters, all Mexicans and United Statesians have moral agency and moral choice.

NOTES

1. My methods are fairly simple and unsophisticated. I use a combination of participant-observation in El Paso, United States, and to a lesser extent Ciudad Juárez, Mexico, and citation of secondary sources. As a researcher on U.S. border enforcement, policy advocacy, and voluntary services to migrants, and as a director of a scholarly center with active research programs on human rights and well-being of migrants in the current moment, I have a good ethnographic grounding in the region.
2. The illegalized drug business is partially politically tolerated in Mexico (it is deeply interwoven with power in the country), while it is not openly tolerated in the United States (the corruption comes more in toleration of arms and money). That makes the price much lower in Mexico than the United States, and creates a large increment of value and thus violence for border smuggling.

3. This is the tip of the iceberg of capital flows; almost a trillion dollars of capital flowed illegally out of Mexico from 1970 to 2010, mainly in deliberate mispricing of commercial trade, not money laundering from criminal activities (Kar 2012).
4. Mexicans are the model for U.S. xenophobia and racism, but such patterns are applied also to Central Americans; middle and upper class migrants have had a different trajectory.
5. Smuggling is a voluntary business transaction to be guided and transported across various barriers; trafficking is deceptive or involuntary migration or with coerced outcomes. But there is a gray zone in between; the need to get funds for smuggling and to subordinate oneself to smugglers can become trafficking.
6. The Border Patrol numbers are only of human remains recovered, and they are likely significantly less than the actual deaths, as many go unrecovered and are scattered by the elements, as noted by Jason De León (2015).
7. From Fiscal Year 2017 to Fiscal Year 2020 (up to January 2020), approximately the period of the Trump administration, 66 percent of asylum cases were denied in immigration court. Border immigration courts are notably harsh. Harlingen courts (in South Texas) denied 85 percent of asylum cases, El Paso non-detained 91 percent, El Paso detained 83 percent, and San Diego 84 percent (calculated by the author from TRAC Immigration 2020).
8. The Mexican government is giving short-term identification and work permits, but employment (such as maquiladora export assembly plants) is poorly paid. One single maquiladora income is not enough to survive in the border city.
9. El Salvador had the highest civilian homicide rate in the world (108.60 per 100,000), and Honduras was second in 2015 (63.80/100,000). Guatemala rounds out the top 10 (at 31.20/100,000). For comparison, criminally violent Mexico has a civilian homicide rate of 16.30/100,000 and the United States, by no means a peaceful country, has a rate of 4.90/100,000 (Index Mundi n.d.).
10. Arrivals by air and sea port are unaffected. Arrivals by land from Canada are already considered covered because Canada is a safe first country of asylum. And, Mexicans can still ask for asylum since they evidently are fleeing that country.
11. Fentanyl is an opioid anesthetic, also used as a drug of recreation/addiction, that is notably lethal.
12. CBP inspects only a small fraction of commercial shipments through ports (3.7 percent of all containers), which may encourage these specific flows (Kulisch 2016). This slightly dated figure, however, mixes seaports and land ports; we have no reason to think the land ports are different.

REFERENCES

Abrego, Leisy, Mat Coleman, Daniel E. Martínez, Cecilia Menjívar, and Jeremy Slack (2017), 'Making Immigrants into Criminals: Legal Processes of Criminalization in the Post-IIRIRA Era', *Journal on Migration and Human Security* 5(3): 694–715.

Abutaleb, Yasmeen (2019), 'What's Inside the Hate-filled Manifesto Linked to the Alleged El Paso Shooter', *Washington Post*, August 4, accessed March 12, 2020 at https://www.washingtonpost.com/politics/2019/08/04/whats-inside-hate-filled-manifesto-linked-el-paso-shooter/.

American Immigration Council (2020), 'Fact Sheet: Policies Affecting Asylum Seekers at the Border: The Migrant Protection Protocols, Prompt Asylum Claim Review, Humanitarian Asylum Review Process, Metering, Asylum Transit Ban, and How They Interact', accessed March 12, 2020 at https://www.americanimmigrationcouncil.org/research/policies-affecting-asylum-seekers-border.

Andreas, Peter (2001), *Border Games: Policing the U.S.–Mexico Divide*, Ithaca: Cornell University Press.

Astorga Almanza, Luis Alejandro (1996), *El siglo de las drogas*, México, DF: Espasa-Calpe Mexicana.

Baldor, Lolita C. (2018), 'Pentagon Says 2 Military Bases to House Immigrants', The Associated Press, June 25, accessed March 12, 2020 at https://www.military.com/daily-news/2018/06/25/pentagon-says-2-military-bases-house-immigrants.html.

Boullosa, Carmen, and Mike Wallace (2015), *A Narco History: How the United States and Mexico Jointly Created the 'Mexican Drug War'*, New York: OR Books.

Boyce, Geoffrey A., Jeffrey M. Banister, and Jeremy Slack (2015), 'You and What Army? Violence, the State, and Mexico's War on Drugs', *Territory, Politics, Governance* 3: 446–68.
Cornelius, Wayne A. (2001), 'Death at the Border: Efficacy and Unintended Consequences of US Immigration Control Policy', *Population and Development Review* 27: 661–85.
De León, Jason (2015), *The Land of Open Graves: Living and Dying on the Migrant Trail*, Oakland, CA: University of California Press.
Devereaux, Ryan (2019), 'The Bloody History of Border Militias Runs Deep—and Law Enforcement Is Part of It', *The Intercept*, April 23, accessed March 12, 2020 at https://theintercept.com/2019/04/23/border-militia-migrants/.
Dunn, Timothy J. (1997), *The Militarization of the U.S.–Mexico Border, 1978–1992: Low-Intensity Conflict Doctrine Comes Home*, Austin TX: CMAS Books, University of Texas at Austin.
Dunn, Timothy J. (2010), *Blockading the Border and Human Rights: The El Paso Operation that Remade Immigration Enforcement*, Austin, TX: University of Texas Press.
Durin, Séverine (2019), *¡Salvese quien pueda!: violencia generalizada y desplazamiento forzado en el noreste de México*, México, DF: Centro de Investigaciones y Estudios Superiores en Antropología Social.
Finklea, Kristen (2019), *Drug Flows and Seizures in the United States: What Do We [Not] Know?* Congressional Research Service, Report R45812, accessed March 12, 2020 at https://fas.org/sgp/crs/misc/R45812.pdf.
Flores Pérez, Carlos Antonio (2013), *Historias de polvo y sangre: Génesis y evolución del tráfico de drogas en el estado de Tamaulipas*, México: Centro de Investigaciones y Estudios Superiores en Antropología Social.
Galtung, Johan (1969), 'Violence, Peace, and Peace Research', *Journal of Peace Research* 6(3): 167–91.
Hernandez, Kelly Lytle (2010), *Migra! A History of the U.S. Border Patrol*, Berkeley, CA: University of California Press.
Heyman, Josiah McC. (1998), *Finding a Moral Heart for U.S. Immigration Policy: An Anthropological Perspective*, Washington, DC: American Anthropological Association.
Heyman, Josiah McC. (1999), 'State Escalation of Force: A Vietnam/US–Mexico Border Analogy', in Josiah McC. Heyman (ed.) *States and Illegal Practices*, Oxford: Berg Publishers, pp. 285–314.
Heyman, Josiah McC. (2012), 'Constructing a "Perfect" Wall: Race, Class, and Citizenship in US–Mexico Border Policing', in Pauline Gardiner Barber and Winnie Lem (eds) *Migration in the 21st Century: Political Economy and Ethnography*, New York and London: Routledge, pp. 153–74.
Heyman, Josiah McC. (2017), 'Contributions of U.S.–Mexico Border Studies to Social Science Theory', in Carlos Vélez-Ibáñez and Josiah Heyman (eds) *The U.S.–Mexico Transborder Region: Cultural Dynamics and Historical Interactions*, Tucson: University of Arizona Press, pp. 44–64.
Heyman, Josiah McC., and John Symons (2012), 'Borders', in Didier Fassin (ed.), *A Companion to Moral Anthropology*, Malden, MA: Wiley-Blackwell, pp. 540–557.
Heyman, Josiah McC., Jeremy Slack, and Daniel Martínez (2019), *Why Border Patrol Agents and CBP Officers Should Not Serve as Asylum Officers*, New York: Center for Migration Studies, Essays, accessed March 12, 2020 at https://cmsny.org/publications/heyman-slack-martinez-062119/.
Index Mundi (n.d.), *Intentional homicides (per 100,000 people)—Country Ranking*, accessed March 12, 2020 at https://www.indexmundi.com/facts/indicators/VC.IHR.PSRC.P5/rankings.
Izcara Palacios, Simon Pedro (2012), 'Coyotaje y grupos delictivos en Tamaulipas', *Latin American Research Review* 47(3): 41–61.
Izcara Palacios, Simon Pedro (2015), 'Coyotaje and Drugs: Two Different Businesses', *Bulletin of Latin American Research* 34: 324–39.
Jones, Reece (2017), *Violent Borders: Refugees and the Right to Move*, London: Verso.
Jowers, Karen (2019), 'These Three Military Bases May Soon House Unaccompanied Immigrant Children', *Military Times*, June 5, accessed March 12, 2020 at https://www.militarytimes.com/pay-benefits/2019/06/05/these-three-military-bases-may-soon-house-unaccompanied-immigrant-children/.
Juergensmeyer, Mark (2017), *Terror in the Mind of God: The Global Rise of Religious Violence*, Oakland, CA: University of California Press.
Jusionyte, Ieva (2018), *Threshold: Emergency Responders on the US–Mexico Border*, Oakland, CA: University of California Press.

Kar, Dev (2012), *Mexico: Illicit Financial Flows, Macroeconomic Imbalances, and the Underground Economy*, Global Financial Integrity, accessed March 12, 2020 at https://www.gfintegrity.org/wp-content/uploads/2014/05/gfi_mexico_report_english-web.pdf.

Kerwin, Donald (2018), 'From IIRIRA to Trump: Connecting the Dots to the Current US Immigration Policy Crisis', *Journal on Migration and Human Security* 6(3): 191–203.

Kulisch, Eric (2016), 'Special Coverage: U.S. Lawmakers Say with New Technology, It's Time to Inspect All Inbound Containers', *American Shipper*, August 18, accessed March 12, 2020 at https://www.freightwaves.com/news/special-coverage-u-s-lawmakers-say-with-new-technology-its-time-to-inspect-all-inbound-containers.

La Política Online (2019), 'Former Presidents Peña Nieto, Calderón Fear García Luna's Trial Revelations', *La Política Online*, December 19, accessed March 12, 2020 at https://www.lapoliticaonline.com/nota/123643-former-presidents-pena-nieto-calderon-fear-garcia-lunas-trial-revelations/.

Levario, Miguel Antonio (2012), *Militarizing the Border: When Mexicans Became the Enemy*, College Station, TX: Texas A&M Press.

Martínez, Daniel E., Jeremy Slack, and Josiah McC. Heyman (2013), *Bordering on Criminal: The Routine Abuse of Migrants in the Removal System, Part I: Migrant Mistreatment While in U.S. Custody*, Washington, DC: American Immigration Council, accessed March 12, 2020 at https://www.americanimmigrationcouncil.org/sites/default/files/research/bordering_on_criminal.pdf.

Martínez, Daniel E., Robin C. Reineke, Raquel Rubio-Goldsmith, and Bruce O. Parks (2014), 'Structural Violence and Migrant Deaths in Southern Arizona: Data from the Pima County Office of the Medical Examiner, 1990–2013', *Journal on Migration and Human Security* 2: 257–86.

McDougal, Topher L., David A. Shirk, Robert Muggah, and John H. Patterson (2015), 'The Way of the Gun: Estimating Firearms Trafficking across the US–Mexico Border', *Journal of Economic Geography*, 15(2): 297–327.

Missing Migrants (2020), 'Americas', *Missing Migrants Project*, the International Organization for Migration (IOM), accessed March 12, 2020 at https://missingmigrants.iom.int/region/americas?region=1422.

Molloy, Molly (2013), 'The Mexican Undead: Toward a New History of the "Drug War" Killing Fields', *Small Wars Journal*, accessed March 12, 2020 at https://smallwarsjournal.com/jrnl/art/the-mexican-undead-toward-a-new-history-of-the-%E2%80%9Cdrug-war%E2%80%9D-killing-fields.

Moore, Robert (2020), 'Six Children Died in Border Patrol Care. Democrats in Congress Want to Know Why', *ProPublica*, January 13, accessed March 12, 2020 at https://www.propublica.org/article/six-children-died-in-border-patrol-care-democrats-in-congress-want-to-know-why.

Nathan, Debbie (2019), 'Vigilantes Helped Steve Bannon's Group With Private Border Wall Near El Paso', *The Intercept*, May 31, accessed March 12, 2020 at https://theintercept.com/2019/05/31/private-border-wall/.

Nevins, Joseph (2010), *Operation Gatekeeper and Beyond: The War on 'Illegals' and the Remaking of the U.S.–Mexico Boundary*, New York and London: Routledge, 2nd ed.

Ngai, Mae M. (2004), *Impossible Subjects: Illegal Aliens and the Making of Modern America*, Princeton, NJ: Princeton University Press.

Ortega, Bob (2018), 'Border Patrol Failed to Count Hundreds of Migrant Deaths on US Soil', *CNN Investigates*, May 15, accessed March 12, 2020 at https://www.cnn.com/2018/05/14/us/border-patrol-migrant-death-count-invs/index.html.

París Pombo, María Dolores (2017), *Violencias y migraciones centroamericanas en México*, Tijuana, BCN, México: El Colegio de la Frontera Norte.

Phillips, Scott, Nestor Rodríguez, and Jacqueline Hagan (2002), 'Brutality at the Border? Use of Force in the Arrest of Immigrants in the United States', *International Journal of the Sociology of Law* 30: 285–306.

Phillips, Scott, Jacqueline Maria Hagan, and Nestor Rodríguez (2006), 'Brutal Borders? Examining the Treatment of Deportees during Arrest and Detention', *Social Forces* 85: 93–109.

Physicians for Human Rights (2020), '"You Will Never See Your Child Again": The Persistent Psychological Effects of Family Separation', accessed March 12, 2020 at https://phr.org/wp-content/uploads/2020/02/PHR-Report-2020-Family-Separation-Full-Report.pdf.

Sanchez, Gabriella (2014), *Human Smuggling and Border Crossings*, New York and London: Routledge.

Schmidt, Samuel, and Carlos Spector (2013), '"Authorized Crime" in Mexico: A Paradigm to Explain Violence', *Mexico and the World* 18(6), accessed March 12, 2020 at http://www.profmex.org/mexicoandtheworld/volume18/6fall2013/Authorized_Crime_in_Mexico.pdf.

Seguridad, Justicia, y Paz (2019), *Las 50 ciudades más violentas del mundo*, accessed March 12, 2020 at http://seguridadjusticiaypaz.org.mx/files/estudio.pdf.

Sisk, Richard (2018), 'Plan to House Migrant Children on Military Bases Shelved Indefinitely', Military.com, October 2, accessed March 12, 2020 at https://www.military.com/daily-news/2018/10/02/plan-house-migrant-children-military-bases-shelved-indefinitely.html.

Slack, Jeremy (2019), *Deported to Death: How Drug Violence is Changing Migration on the US–Mexico Border*, Oakland, CA: University of California Press.

Slack, Jeremy, and Howard Campbell (2018), 'On *Narco-Coyotaje*: Illicit Regimes and their Impacts on the U.S.–Mexico Border', in Jeremy Slack, Daniel E. Martínez, and Scott Whiteford (eds) *The Shadow of the Wall: Violence and Migration on the U.S.–Mexico Border*, Tucson: University of Arizona Press, pp. 166–89.

Slack, Jeremy, and Scott Whiteford (2011), 'Violence and Migration on the Arizona–Sonora Border', *Human Organization* 70: 11–21. Reprinted as: Slack, Jeremy, and Scott Whiteford (2018), 'Violence and Migration on the Arizona–Sonora Border', in Jeremy Slack, Daniel E. Martínez, and Scott Whiteford (eds) *The Shadow of the Wall: Violence and Migration on the U.S.–Mexico Border*, Tucson: University of Arizona Press, pp. 43–62.

Slack, Jeremy, Daniel E. Martínez, Scott Whiteford, and Emily Peiffer (2018), 'In Harm's Way: Family Separation, Immigration Enforcement Programs, and Security on the U.S.–Mexico Border', in Jeremy Slack, Daniel E. Martínez, and Scott Whiteford (eds) *The Shadow of the Wall: Violence and Migration on the U.S.–Mexico Border*, Tucson: University of Arizona Press, pp. 73–93.

Smith, Neil (1984), *Uneven Development: Nature, Capital, and the Production of Space*, Oxford, UK and New York, NY: Blackwell.

Spener, David (2009), *Clandestine Crossings: Migrants and Coyotes on the Texas–Mexico Border*, Ithaca: Cornell University Press.

Staudt, Kathleen A., and Zulma Y. Méndez (2015), *Courage, Resistance, and Women in Ciudad Juárez: Challenges to Militarization*, Austin: University of Texas Press.

Thompson, Ginger (2017), 'How the U.S. Triggered a Massacre in Mexico', *ProPublica*, June 12, accessed March 12, 2020 at https://www.propublica.org/article/allende-zetas-cartel-massacre-and-the-us-dea.

TRAC Immigration (2020), *Asylum Decisions by Custody, Representation, Nationality, Location, Month and Year, Outcome and more*, accessed March 12, 2020 at https://trac.syr.edu/phptools/immigration/asylum/.

U.S. Department of Justice, Bureau of Alcohol, Tobacco, and Firearms (2019), *Mexico: Data Source, Firearms Tracing System, January 1, 2013–December 31, 2018*, accessed March 12, 2020 at https://www.atf.gov/file/135106/download.

Viswanatha, Aruna, and Brett Wolf (2012), 'HSBC to Pay $1.9 Billion U.S. Fine in Money-laundering Case', *Reuters*, December 10, accessed March 12, 2020 at https://www.reuters.com/article/us-hsbc-probe/hsbc-to-pay-1-9-billion-u-s-fine-in-money-laundering-case-idUSBRE8BA05M20121211.

Vogt, Wendy A. (2018), *Lives in Transit: Violence and Intimacy on the Migrant Journey*, Oakland, CA: University of California Press.

Vulliamy, Ed (2011), 'How a Big US Bank Laundered Billions from Mexico's Murderous Drug Gangs', *The Guardian*, April 2, accessed March 12, 2020 at https://www.theguardian.com/world/2011/apr/03/us-bank-mexico-drug-gangs.

3. The mantling and dismantling of a tent city at the U.S.–Mexico border

Cynthia Bejarano and Ma. Eugenia Hernández Sánchez

1. INTRODUCTION: *DISPLACED PLÁTICAS, TU AQUÍ Y YO ALLÁ*

When people cross the borders between nation-states, regions, or even landscapes, they are changed by the experiences they endure. They in turn transform the places where they wait in anticipation of their next movement. Their language and accents, their social customs and beliefs shift as they adjust to the spaces and places around them, and the people they meet along the way. Networks are forged, lost, and reconfigured. People develop an aptitude for adaptation as their vulnerability intensifies. Migrants, like the sojourners that now gather at the northern Mexican border, were not only displaced from their home countries in Central and South America and Africa, they were forced to move across transborders for their survival. Mexican migrants became displaced within their country, living like nomads in what are popularly known as "tent cities."

Within these tent cities and shelters that grew in numbers, a gradual development among the enclaves of Central American refugees, were Mexican political asylum seekers, who became "*autoasilados*"[1] as they were transformed into internally displaced people moving from the interior of Mexico to the northern border. These burgeoning tent cities were mainly composed of Mexican "*autoasilados*," although all migrants struggled to be represented and seen by civil society organizations, law enforcement, and migration officials. Mexican *autoasilados* sought refuge within their own country, but their circumstances could not be understood with existing theoretical concepts, since their migration was a new phenomenon. For tent people, the future was either a tenuous and unpredictable one, or an assured death, if they remained in their hometowns. Suddenly, categories of citizenship were no longer solely assigned in accordance to the land one was from, or the land that emigrants traversed when crossing borders. Wingard (2013: 5) argues how, "immigrants as 'other' become both outsiders of community and insiders of economy." The practice of migrants creating a "tent city within a city," one tent at a time, or one shelter at a time, transformed the urbanscapes, political economy, and social relations of the border metropolis of Ciudad Juárez, Chihuahua, Mexico, where international bridges bind it to El Paso, Texas, U.S.; together, they share a population of over 2.0 million.[2]

The proliferation of tent cities across these urban international bridges linking Ciudad Juárez to El Paso uncovers competing discourses between groups of people that in turn represent geopolitical relations.[3] The phenomenon of being both displaced and disposable interlocks (Razack 2008) with ideologies of racism, classism, nativism, and sexism. The rhetoric of mass exoduses of migrant caravans—predominantly of women and children—in 2014, and in subsequent years, justified increased surveillance at the southern U.S. border. At international ports of entry, migration, inspection, and body scrutiny is part of a continuous formation that works to create a perpetual state of vigilance for Central American migrants in the area, for the growing number of internally displaced Mexican migrants from the interior, and the everyday

Mexican citizen and transnational migrants or binational citizens of Mexico and the U.S. that traverse the bridges linking the two nation-states.

In this chapter, we explore the tent city/settlement phenomenon via the interconnecting concepts of displacement, disposability, and debordering (Bejarano 2010). These practices foster what Hernández Sánchez calls a framework of *intersectional vulnerability* where we move from understanding specific identities, toward understanding specific practices of mobility in the Ciudad Juárez–El Paso border (2017). We explore how migrants shape the contours of a city through their modes of survival. We also describe the responses of locals and translocals who support them throughout their migrant journey, while others treat them like *disposable people*. We discuss the relationship between *displacement, disposability, and debordering* as interrelated concepts that help us establish the complex experience of migrants living in temporary tent settlements, while two neighboring and disparate countries argue over what to do with them. We next describe the inimitable project called Border Tuner (Lozano-Hemmer 2019), which allowed people across borders to literally hear each other's heartbeats and to speak to one another without limits (Figure 3.1). We end this chapter by discussing the ephemeral tent cities that disappeared without any knowledge of the tenants that lived in them.

Source: Google Maps, 2020.

Figure 3.1 U.S. and Mexico ports of entry, tent city locations and Border Tuner

Our intention with this chapter is to rescue the material experience as an axis to think of the border as a space of constant movement, which in turn generates long-term processes given the permanence (Giménez 1997) of that same movement. In Vogt's words, "Mobility is not an abstract process; it is a material and embodied one" (2018: 7). Displacement from one's own country while still living within one's country in tent settlements, thus, reveals the unavoidable materiality of mobility due to concrete situations of violence and unequal opportunities. There are no absolute numbers with this ephemeral settlement, but in September 2019, approximately 3,000 Mexican citizens from Mexican interior states like Guerrero, Michoacán, and Zacatecas arrived in Ciudad Juárez seeking refuge from drug violence (Isacson 2019).

The groups of tents were mainly settled by Mexican migrants, but some people from Central America also came to live there. Tent cities are visually interrupting urban landscapes and revealing a long-term process of marginalization.

According to Silva Santisteban (2008), mobility and its consequences for people of color, in this case internally displaced Mexican citizens and Central American migrants, is a process of othering through what or who is considered "disposable." Borrowing from Castillo (1999) the term "garbage," Silva Santisteban develops an interpretative analysis of garbage as a symbol, that we in turn, use to analyze the treatment of migrants as *displaced, disposable, and debordered*. *Basurización* turns garbage into a verb that explains how the image of garbage represents something "barbaric" or "exotic-hyperbolic" (in Silva Santisteban 2008):

> Garbage(ing)/basurización has a double meaning: the obscure and loathsome, which causes disgust and repulsiveness; and the strangely addictive side that, despite everything, invites us to search through it to uncover the footprints of previous enjoyment. (2008: 64)

The idea of displacement in relation to *basurización* acts as a global phenomenon which socially constructs migrants into what Silva Santisteban calls symbolic *basurización*, that comprises: "authoritarian discourses based on a patriarchal and colonial culture [which] operates through ... symbolic garbage/basurization ... a way of organizing the other as a leftover element of a symbolic system" (Silva Santisteban 2008: 18). This makes evident the challenges people face when forced to migrate, and the barriers to inclusion wherever they arrive. Migrants who formed tent cities near the international bridges with hopes of having their asylum cases heard in the U.S., became an exoticized spectacle as Silva Santisteban (2008) implies, for observers to gawk at or to pity, or, conversely, to empathize with and advocate for.

Pairing Silva Santisteban's ideas with what we have witnessed people in the U.S. and Mexico claim about migrants, we use the term *disposable people* to further articulate the ideas of displacement and disposability that migrants endure. In their spontaneous settlements (tent cities), the dominant societies treated migrants like *disposable people*, non-entities to be discarded or eventually removed from public spaces. Neither the U.S. nor Mexico (because of the U.S.'s inhumane response through the Remain in Mexico policy) knew what to do with the tent people that materialized. Critics of the tent cities eagerly demanded their dismantling. Perhaps more than interrupting a system, tent people made evident the system of exclusion shared by both Mexico and the U.S. That is, citizenship is a category that requires further exploration as a heterogenous one and not a fixed category. On one hand, Mexicans seeking refuge within Mexico makes evident the process of alienation by local communities. On the other hand, when Mexicans seek asylum in the United States, their process is not recognized, ergo, *Remain in Mexico* becomes an affirmation. The presence of the tents represented a nuisance for some, an eyesore for others, but all the while, tent people lived as outcasts in these outdoor shelters, as if they had committed a crime or societal infraction. Migrants were dehumanized, criminalized, and racialized (Vogt 2018; Bejarano and Morales 2011). Their displacement for weeks and even months signaled their disposability. Conversely, though, migrants resignifed and debordered the meaning of public spaces and rebordered heavily geopoliticized areas, like Mexican walkways near international bridges and the iconic Chamizal Federal Park in Ciudad Juárez to establish their settlements. Migrants refused to be rendered invisible; instead, they made claims to space where the busiest signs of commerce and capitalism took place—near the lines of vehicles moving in between two countries.

Walicki reminds us of other sites of resistance worldwide, where people experience a collective fatigue for being harassed and persecuted. Walicki (2009: 25) states, "A characteristic of long-term displacement in Europe is the disproportionate number of legal sentences against certain ethnic groups, tired of the[ir] sponsors and how the media addresses the topic and [in concreto] how the world contributes to forgetting those who remain displaced." Throughout this chapter, we will discuss a concept that we call "scales of humanity" to describe the vast range of responses toward migrants. Responses include the collective galvanization of civil society and everyday citizens across borders to work as volunteers, or who gave donations of time and resources, to the opposite range of extreme inhumanity witnessed when U.S. Customs and Border Protection agents were instructed by supervisors and Washington, DC to bar migrants entry into the U.S. who asserted their traumatic experiences for asylum. Others like vigilante, militia groups preyed on migrants as they attempted to cross the border, or when practicing racist rhetoric that portrayed or alluded to migrants as disposable people.[4]

In response to these reactions, migrants and their advocates debated lawmakers and law enforcers including nativists[5] locked in disputes on claims to rights-making and place-making as makeshift tent communities were temporarily constructed. While migrants were displaced and assessed as disposable, they lived as squatters pushing back by debordering and rebordering public spaces as a temporary claims-making assertion. They deterritorialized public places to create "in the moment" home spaces as they waited for their next upheaval.

2. *DISPLACED PLÁTICAS*: A METHODOLOGICAL APPROACH DURING URGENT TIMES

Our analysis is based on discussions we call *displaced pláticas*.[6] We write this work from Ciudad Juárez, Chihuahua, and Las Cruces, New Mexico just 45 miles away from each other, as we each bear witness to the movement and obstruction of migrants at the border, and the raging debates that occur about them across the region. We write to bear witness and to reveal stories that can easily be erased from public memory—like the ephemeral tent settlements in Ciudad Juárez that vanished as we completed this chapter.

We both have worked as volunteers with migrants in shelters and as interpreters, and have collected donations and provided other needs to migrants for several years. We each have visited or worked with migrant children, youth, and families in several capacities for over 20 years. We reflect on our conversations about migration as *displaced pláticas* because, as citizens from Mexico and the U.S., and as women born and raised at the border, we too cross borders to visit each other, to reflect and write together, and to advocate for migrants across borders.

As migrant defenders and feminista fronterizas that engage the topic of migration as scholars, activists, and border people, we refer to our dialogues as *displaced pláticas*. We try to listen and to commit our time and advocacy to migrants even though we recognize that we cannot completely understand or conceptualize, or count, or conclude people's experiences. As such, we are displaced in two ways. We are displaced from migrants in not sharing their experiences, because we are not fleeing our homes as migrants and are privileged in writing this chapter, as we write from the comfort of our homes. We are also displaced from each other because of nation-state boundaries that often make working, advocating, and visiting each other complicated and mitigated by hours' long wait lines at international border crossings and obtrusive scrutiny by customs border inspections. What we know is that people's experiences are key to thinking about borders, global processes and the meaning of our own work in and out of academia. As ethnographers, we know that we must leave our home in order to be critical of our own privileges. We talk, write and visit with each other often, but must cross international borders to do so. Our *displaced pláticas* are representative of our reflections, advocacy work, and solidarity praxis of crossing the same international bridges where migrants have established their settlements.

Our participation with other migrant advocates' engagement in the Border Tuner art installation, discussed later, as *platicadoras* talking back and forth to each other across the U.S. border wall apparatus is an example of how we re-interpret displacement. The main axis of our present work is to interrupt the way in which discourses on the border, migration, agency, academia, and advocacy are considered. We propose our *displaced pláticas* as a dialogue of transnational solidarity (Carastathis 2013; Galván 2014), understood as a process of separation, confrontation, mutual tensions, and critical friendships that channel solidarity in times of profound vigilance. In Mohanty's words, "home, community, and identity all fit somewhere between the histories and experiences we inherit and the political choices we make through alliances, solidarities and friendships" (2003: 136). This relational component is the principle we want to engage with.

3. DISPLACEMENT: RUPTURES OVER TERRITORIES, CLAIMS-MAKING, AND SURVIVAL

The establishment of spontaneous tent cities signaled an aesthetics of emergency and urgency that emerged as asylum seekers were stranded at the border. Laddaga introduces the concept of "emergency" to describe temporal experiences that cannot be explained with fixed categories (2006). These temporal experiences (i.e. border crossings and migration) are unique in time and space but are also prevalent for the masses who attempt to cross borders and endure a preponderance of global state and nation-state vigilance. Thus, we embody what Laddaga discusses as "disjunctive relations" (2006: 98) to describe the disjunctive features of international ports of entry and their surrounding areas, and what was understood as a rupture of territory and claims-making through tent cities.

As migration refers to the traditional movement of people from one country to another, our discussion of displacement involves both internal and external migration. We include the disjunctive relations that were forged between migrants who were foreign to each other vis-à-vis the unfamiliar spaces that they collectively came to inhabit. We also argue that displacement is rooted in the tension between having the "right" kind of citizenship/legal status and access to rights' claims-making or not. According to Bello et al. (n.d.), the U.S. has not signed many of the treaties to protect people based on their values within themselves (by being human), while Mexico has signed many treaties, yet the violence makes evident the lack of follow through with these human rights protocols. It is not our intention to compare human rights to citizenship claims, but to show that both nation-state(s) unlawfully implement mechanisms of control that have material consequences for thousands of people and society at large. This is the case for tent people that were not shown the degree of empathy needed.

Displacement also involves a relationship with territory and control over that territorial claim. Although our present analysis is based on the actual experience of people inhabiting and creating new spaces and places of survivability, Monje and Burin (2008: 41) recuperate the historical discussion of privatization of land as a system that organizes belonging, and challenges us to consider, "any dispute to recuperate land for collective untransferable use from a perspective that assigns such a use as a basic human right." Migrants inhabiting public spaces while living in tents along the sidewalks of side streets adjacent to Mexico's international bridges disrupt traditional uses of public spaces to make human rights claims to public land as sovereign, albeit, internally displaced Mexicans. Central American and other refugees also change the consumption of public use land, buildings, and local peoples by making assertions as migrants who have international and inalienable human rights to move freely and to live without violence.

Even though tent people move as the result of internal national conflicts and remain stagnated as a result of hyper U.S. surveillance, their autonomous agency is evident just by the presence of their tent cities along the three international bridges. Although it is important to stress that their places of settlement and their processes to have access to refugee status reveal an intention to enter through official state channels, their autonomous organization (internal system of organization) remains uniquely theirs. In Appadurai's words, "the smaller the number and the weaker the minority, the deeper the rage about its capacity to make a majority feel like a mere majority rather than like a whole and uncontested ethnos" (2006: 37). People migrate for their survival despite an intense vulnerability as they travel, but they also create a collective autonomous migration (Rodriguez 1996) process through caravans and temporary tent cities, that disrupts the governability of nation-states and the regularity of local systems and ordinances.

4. FROM MIGRANT CARAVANS TO REMAIN IN MEXICO POLICY

The relationship between nation-state empire building and the extreme enforcement of migration policies that build on historical patterns of exclusion and surveillance toward migrants, immigrants, and everyday people are central to this work. The emerging formations of even more restrictionist policies around migration are at the center of this chapter, as are the urgent responses to these policies by people balancing their survivability with experiences and feelings of "unknowing" waiting for permission to enter the U.S. from cities like Ciudad Juárez. "Migrants are caught up in what scholars have called 'regimes of mobility' and 'precarious transit zones' produced at the nexus of exclusionary state policies and increased circulation around the globe" (Vogt 2018: 7).

The most recent impetus for this exclusionary regime was triggered by the alarmist portrayals of caravans of women and children traveling en masse to the U.S. in 2014, as they escaped violence in their home countries. Women and children from the Northern Triangle (Honduras, Guatemala, and El Salvador) arrived at the U.S. border fleeing the gang violence, domestic violence, extreme poverty, food insecurities, and severe drought that contributed to their departures (Isacson 2019; Rosenblum and Ball 2016; Vogt 2018). In 2014, unaccompanied children and family units traveling together peaked at 27,000 in June, although the numbers dropped below 5,000 three months later (Rosenblum and Ball 2016). Subsequent numbers of migrants ebbed and flowed as nativists' anxieties fostered a hateful and racist rhetoric about the migrants leeching government resources, and bringing crime and violence to the U.S.—a nation already saturated with gun violence by its own citizens, and infamously having the highest rates of incarcerated people in the world (Alexander 2012). The migration from the Northern Triangle triggered the proliferation of the U.S. border enforcement apparatus, and the growth in public information campaigns that included the launching of the Plan for the

Alliance for Prosperity in Honduras, Guatemala, and El Salvador (Rosenblum and Ball 2016), which in theory would help curb the out-flow of migration from Central America.

These deterrent developments did not halt migrants from moving northward. Surviving violence, in all its iterations, is a surefire mechanism for movement. In efforts to avoid the well-documented abuse of traveling alone or in small groups atop *La Bestia*, the train system vertically snaking up the eastern coast of Mexico, migrants began to travel together in large groups called caravans.[7] The first caravan arrived at the Tijuana, Mexico border in November 2018, where people were met with a violent response by U.S. border agents who tear gassed migrants as they neared the U.S. international boundary in Tijuana, while U.S. President Trump ordered the U.S. military on standby (Fry 2019).

A year later, Mexico's national guard responded similarly to a caravan of 2,000 African migrants in southern Mexico (Fry 2019). Ensuing caravans received the same fate, gaining momentum as they began their journeys in Central America, and then gradually lost people along the way who tried their luck in Mexico or elsewhere. In January 2020, Mexican security forces used pepper spray on 4,000 Central Americans at its southern border with Guatemala, increasing their deterrence tactics and what some have referred to as the invisible border wall fostered by the Trump administration (Semple and McDonald 2020). These migrant caravans resulted in a more regimented and dangerous restrictionist era of migration policies including the Remain in Mexico policy innocuously dubbed the Migrant Protection Protocol (Isacson 2019).

5. REMAIN IN MEXICO POLICY

The Remain in Mexico policy implemented in January 2019 by the Trump administration is an example of emergent borders working to further dispossess and displace people beyond their original uprooting. The Remain in Mexico policy forces asylum seekers to remain in Mexico—typically migrants remain at the northern Mexican border with the U.S.—while they await court dates, making it seemingly impossible for them to meet with U.S.-based attorneys or other advocates; most migrants go without legal representation (Isacson 2019). This policy works to disrupt migratory flows and international protocols protecting migrants' rights to seek asylum in the U.S. and elsewhere. As of December 13, 2019, Mexico reported receiving over 60,000 non-Mexican migrants under this policy; nearly 18,000 people were sent to Ciudad Juárez to await their asylum hearing (Isacson 2019).

Through the Remain in Mexico policy, the U.S. has abandoned its adherence to international interventions and protocols to protect migrants in states of extreme vulnerability and emergency. The U.S. has ignored its commitments to the international community, instead helping to foster a predatory atmosphere at border transit zones (Bejarano and Morales 2011). "As a signatory to the 1967 Protocol, and through U.S. immigration law, the United States has legal obligations to provide protection to those who qualify as refugees. The Refugee Act established two paths to obtain refugee status—either from abroad as a resettled refugee or in the United States as an asylum seeker" (American Immigration Council 2020).

We argue that the Trump administration not only breaks with U.S. and international migrant/refugee/political asylum protection protocols, but it equally refuses to see Mexico as a sovereign nation. Instead, it views it as an occupied territory of the U.S. by demanding the execution of U.S. policies like Remain in Mexico to be implemented in Mexico, and an

Table 3.1   Tent city: between countries-within a city

U.S.	Tent city	MX
Metering: the process of vetting applications based on a fixed number allocated per day that can vary, and not specifically by specific asylum cases	Spontaneous settlements created in the contours of each of the main international bridges between Mexico and the U.S.	Remain in Mexico policy forced the hand of migrants to establish tent settlements
Metering occurs as a form of inspection of refugees at the middle of the international bridge	Autonomous organization of migrants established tent settlements	Violence forced internal displacement/ migration of Mexican citizens
Central Americans must return to Mexico after their application review	Migrants established a numerical system to present their cases in the U.S., although there were many lists kept by U.S. Customs and Border Protection and shelters, and by migrants themselves	Mexican government shelters were forced to respond to U.S. Remain in Mexico policy
Mexicans can apply for refugee status through the Humanitarian Asylum Review Process (HARP) applicable for Mexican citizens. They were also expected to wait out their asylum elsewhere through a "third safe country" agreement	Settlement locations near international bridges, were to keep migrants' place in line to have their asylum cases heard in the U.S.	Mexico responds by militarizing its Mexican borders, like the U.S., which increased militarization at the border

Source: Authors.

increase in ever growing policies and agreements to further convolute asylum protections and migrants' rights-based assertions and protocols. Ultimately, migrants in Mexico experience dispossession, displacement, and a debordering phenomenon where the U.S. overreaches into Mexico and Central America by extending its ideology of border walls into other sovereign nations.

Migrants in Ciudad Juárez and across the U.S.–Mexico borderlands remain cramped in shelters in need of support to care for so many people (Ortiz Uribe 2019), or migrants decide to take matters into their own hands by creating tent settlements. As earlier stated, about 3,000 Mexican citizens arrived in Ciudad Juárez in early fall 2019 (Isacson 2019). Mexican migrants comprised the bulk of tent residents establishing settlements near the international bridges. As governments construct more elaborate and vexing policies, migrants experience daily consequences of "regimes of mobility" (Vogt 2018) that fortify stringent practices like metering at the international boundary line—the center point of international bridges (Table 3.1).

6.   METERING PRACTICE AT THE INTERNATIONAL BRIDGES: THE PRICE OF ENTRY

The practice of metering at international ports of entry, where people are systematically categorized based on their documents and nationalities, is a recent development.[8] People seeking asylum in the U.S. are rejected by U.S. Customs and Border Protection agents as they are turned away by the practice of metering. This is the process in which agents screen documents at the middle of the international bridges, a hairline space that demarcates Mexico from the U.S. Since migrants began arriving in larger numbers at the U.S.–Mexico border seeking political asylum, this most recent encroachment began. A few people can cross into the U.S. daily, as they wait in pedestrian lines with other border crossers. This second, new inspection is another security apparatus coupled with concertina wire, large, orange jersey barriers, and even canopies meant to protect agents from the blazing sun. "A new rule would ban asylum for anyone who did not first seek it in a country through which he or she crossed en route to the U.S ... [Although] [i]t is illegal [process called refoulement] to knowingly send people back to countries where they're likely to be persecuted" (Isacson 2019: 4–5).[9] Since 2018, from one moment to the next, asylum processes can change, and laws or protocols can be dismissed or ignored.

Those with the most extreme and violent stories might have an opportunity to at least secure an audience with a U.S. immigration judge, but they are forced to wait in Mexican border cities like Ciudad Juárez. These unabashed practices of displacing people and creating socio-cultural conditions mimicking war-torn countries with refugees forced into a liminal and temporal, and in some ways a stateless, space is nothing short of torturous and violent. Migrants released from the U.S. as part of the Remain in Mexico policy are returned to the Paso del Norte bridge in Ciudad Juárez at 9:00am and 6:00pm respectively, leaving those who cross in the evening more vulnerable as dusk settles in the city metropolis (Isacson 2019). These practices foster the *intersectional vulnerability* that Hernández Sánchez calls the location where systems of oppression meet critical race theory (CRT) at the Ciudad Juárez–El Paso border (2017). Combined, these policies represent blatant racist and discriminatory policies like those of previous years, and we witness the worst rungs of what we call scales of humanity. Hence, the criminalization of immigrants deepens as institutionalized racism seeps across borders through the exportation of U.S. militarism.

7. THE MILITARIZATION OF BOTH SIDES OF THE BORDER

We are witnessing the northern Mexican and southern Mexican borders being further militarized as the composition of its people adjusts to absorb the asylum seekers expelled from U.S. borders including those who were never allowed to enter. Sassen claims that, "the notion of expulsion takes us beyond the more familiar idea of growing inequality as a way of capturing the pathologies of today's global capitalism" (2014: 1), and, we would add, the further reach of the U.S. to militarize borders. The historical and "real time" push to expel migrants from the U.S. with paramilitary policing tactics reminds us of Sassen's prediction. U.S. expulsion, in our analysis, is evident just outside the U.S. international boundary line including activity within the U.S.–Mexico border region. The practice of expulsion is most evident with Remain in Mexico, metering policies and practices at international bridges, and consequent asylum-seeking protocols prohibiting entry to the U.S.—all used to justify a military presence along nation-state borders.[10]

U.S. historical underpinnings of expansion and empire building ideologies seep into current U.S. influences of militarizing other borders. When migrants arrived at Ciudad Juárez, U.S. army soldiers stationed at Ft. Bliss Army Military Base assisted with the metering practice at the three busy international bridges, by waving people through to the U.S. side if they held up the right form of documentation.[11] "In Ciudad Juárez, the arrival of migrants was 'forced' (removal from the U.S.), and entire communities [were] expelled and displaced towards different regions, both in the U.S. and Mexico due to the presence of armed groups [which include] the army, [and] groups linked to cartels and mercenaries" (Sánchez Díaz and Ravelo Blanca

2019: 111–112). From approximately 2008 to 2010 there was, "an exodus of inhabitants of Ciudad Juárez due to the violence … [due to what] was established by the fight for the city control between cartels and the widespread decomposition that resulted in a large number of homicides and femicides" (Sánchez Díaz and Ravelo Blanca 2019: 108). The violence that predated the arrival of migrants further justified the presence of the Mexican military.

The rhetoric of violence in Ciudad Juárez made the stationing of Mexican military soldiers near the tent encampments a "natural" response, and a defensible one laced with claims of protection for the tent people. Many, however, argued that their presence was to deter or outright stop migrants from attempting to cross into the U.S. as irregular migrants. The proliferation of the Mexican military redefined as border guards at the northern Mexican border spread to the southern Mexican border. According to the Hope Border Institute (2019), the joint agreement known as Remain in Mexico, "paused the tariff threats … [and] emphasized Mexican enforcement" stating:

> Mexico will send 6,000 members of its newly formed National Guard to the Mexico–Guatemala border to prevent further migration to the U.S.; The U.S. will expand the Remain in Mexico program across its entire southern border and will accelerate the adjudication of asylum claims; and Mexico will allow asylum seekers in this program to stay in Mexico while also offering jobs, healthcare, and education according to its principles. (Hope Border Institute 2019)

Aspects of the U.S. Low Intensity Conflict Doctrine (LIC) developed in the 1980s and exported across Latin America is relevant to this discussion. According to Dunn (1996), the LIC is:

> the establishment and maintenance of social control over targeted civilian populations through the implementation of a broad range of sophisticated measures via the coordinated and integrated efforts of police, paramilitary and military forces. One of the doctrine's distinguishing characteristics is that military forces take on police functions, while police forces take on military characteristics. (1996: 4)

The LIC practices were evident everywhere, since the U.S. and Mexican military were deputized as border guards to meter, inspect, and enforce immigration and migration laws at international ports of entry. Some days in Ciudad Juárez and El Paso, the number of policing and military forces seemed to outnumber those of the Mexican *autoasilados* and non-Mexican asylum seekers gathering together in tent settlements, or waiting in shelters or at the international bridges to have their numbers called.

8. TENT CITY ENCLAVES AND THEIR DISPOSABILITY IN PLAIN SIGHT

Over several months in 2019, the landscapes surrounding the international bridges near the Paso del Norte crossing area, the Chamizal International Peace Park near the Bridge of the Américas, and the area bordering the Zaragoza bridge were transformed into Central American and Mexican enclaves. These three bridges are the most traveled crossing points of the five international ports of entry bridging Mexico and the U.S. to each other. Tents dotted pedestrian areas and children, men, and women congregated outside and around their tents. Walking the side streets where the tents were situated felt like one was crossing the threshold of people's homes. It felt as if we were crossing through their living rooms as migrants dusted themselves from a disruptive night's sleep and busily organized their scant belongings inside their tents. Tourist buses would speed by the side street where "tent" people resided, as street vendors set up their stands to sell food to migrant families and passersby. The migrant industry of food posts across the streets from the tents seemed to be the only people pleased with this new settlement.

Tent people, clustered together near their makeshift houses, choking from exhaust fumes as hundreds of cars each day lined the passageways into the U.S. from Ciudad Juárez, came to be known as the "tent cities" of the border. People continued to go along with their daily routines attempting a modicum of normalcy, while the spectacle of the tent settlements formed. We wonder what the young eyes of the three-year-old boys who we once saw sitting cross-legged outside their tents thought, as tourist buses and border crossers zoomed by nearly hitting them. We wonder what the older eyes of their parents felt living in a tent in efforts to keep their children from danger in their hometowns or countries.

Families sat and waited at or near the bridges to have their assigned numbers called. Asylum seekers were given a number to wait to be called to cross the border to meet with an immigration judge. Migrants were fearful of leaving their positions at the bridge, and leaving for a shelter, so they stayed near the bridge for safe keeping. Few migrants were ever able to cross to sit in asylum court proceedings, and even fewer had access to U.S.-based attorneys. Despite the establishment of tent settlements, Mexican shelters swelled with migrants and remained cramped and in need of support to care for so many people (Ortiz Uribe 2019).

The materialization of borderless space through the newly formed enclaves and the reinterpretations of what constitutes community and home in tent settlements reveals the necessity to carve out dignified spaces for those rendered disposable. Forging new relationships and networks of people is representative of the other end of the scale of humanity, the end of the scale that represents relationality through hope and dignity, and a common struggle for rights' assertions across national boundaries and truncated citizenships. "By focusing on the physical rehabilitation of central districts, practices of regeneration have often unrecognized the presence or rights of the communities inhabiting them" (De Carli et al. 2015: 152). One might argue that the tent settlements fostered a unique vibrance to the greater urban landscapes not seen before. Despite their vulnerability and their treatment as symbolic *basurización*, people living in the tent settlements organized themselves and practiced their own brand of agency by creating lists to have their names called during the metering practices at the international bridges, managing their home tents and food scarcity concerns.

Tent people also entered transnational solidarity logics which involved a transgression of the nation-state. A teacher from El Paso established a tent with two sections to provide instruction to 25 children (Net Noticias 2020) in the Chamizal Park. Tent people displayed a resourcefulness and dignity that could only stem organically from within the settlement, as they represented a visual materialization of rebordering spaces that demand urgent responses by border societies and the world order. The most immediate response was reaching across the dry Rio Grande/Rio Bravo riverbed to show our solidarity.

9. DEBORDERING THE MEXICO–U.S. "HYPHEN" THROUGH THE BORDER TUNER ART INSTALLATION

"Cada voz es un puente"[12]

Given our geographic location at the Mexico–U.S. border, a hyper-militarized and volatile geopolitical space, we understand the imminent need to look beyond national, class, and race and ethnic boundaries to come together to form transborder movements of solidarity and forms of communication. Vogt asserts, "Scholars have moved beyond understanding of borders as fixed 'lines in the sand' to reconceptualize the political geographies where borders are 'enacted, materialized and performed'" (2018: 7). We recognize that, at times, we are characterized more so by our differences that manifest in national, social, economic, political and legal boundaries, although our identities as border people bind us together through language, families, culture, and border crossings.

Adding to the complexity of these cultural and border understandings is the displacement and disposability of Mexican *autoasilados*, and Central American migrants and other refugees, through the symbolic basurization of their experiences as migrants, and the establishment of tent cities where they survive their realities as squatters. These experiences speak to a form of structural determinism including, "the idea that our system, by reason of its structure and vocabulary, cannot redress certain types of wrongs ... it is hard to think about something that has no name, and it is hard to name something unless one's interpretative community has begun talking and thinking about it" (Delgado and Stefancic 2012: 27). The unavoidable question then becomes: How can we cross the U.S.–Mexico border, or at least reach what people call "the other side" under such heavy militarized surveillance?

The Border Tuner art installation (Lozano-Hammer 2019) is a recent example that worked as an interlocutor of interpretive community/ies and as an interventionist. The Border Tuner sent light beams across the border between Ciudad Juárez and El Paso. It consisted of three interactive stations on each side of the border wall, which were controlled by "searchlight beams using a small dial wheel. When lights from any two stations [were] directed at each other, microphones and speakers automatically switched-on to allow participants to talk with one another, creating cross-border conversations."[13]

The Border Tuner art installation responded to the question, "What new forms of intimacy and solidarity emerge?" (Vogt, 2018: 7) along la *herida abierta*/the open wound (Anzaldua 1987). During the installation, called activations, people from both sides of the border were invited to engage each other by, literally, listening to each other's heartbeats at one art station, while others radiated light beams across the border pulsating through the sky through the rhythm of their voice and word enunciation. The exchange of feelings and emotions reverberated through the air relaying stories through audio and visual expression that often cannot cross borders. Voices of solidarity traveled across the international border wall, as heartbeat pulses bounced through the border wall, and lights danced across the sky. Messages of solidarity crossed the border wall via airwaves moving in ways that bodies could not. Border Tuner entered a complex discursive and liminal space. Many questioned the cost of the installation in a context of need, yet no one proposed other ways to make possible intimate encounters that are fractured daily by both Mexico and the U.S.

It was an uncensored mechanism of communication between Juarenses, El Pasoans, and others. Every night for two weeks between 6:30pm and 11:00pm people could speak openly and liberally through these sound waves via microphones and mega speakers. People connected with each other, not by seeing each other, but by hearing distinct voices which snuck messages of solidarity and sweet greetings to perfect strangers. This allowed for a kind of displacement of the body to take place, and a debordering to occur. Messages and meaning making transcended the border wall, rendering it useless, as one art installation was temporarily erected at the very place where the largest tent city overtook the Chamizal Federal Park in Ciudad Juárez. The counterpart art installation in El Paso was located across the street from the El Paso Chamizal Park (the international peace parks are in Mexico and the U.S.) and was situated in the grounds of Bowie High School.[14]

The echoing of incantations resisting the border wall, migration, and the human rights atrocities that the U.S. government willed when tent cities formed in Ciudad Juárez were proclaimed through the Border Tuner activations. How were we able to connect our *displaced pláticas* through this resistance medium? The Border Tuner was a new doorway at the U.S.–Mexico border that could not be closed. Air restrictions could not stop messages of solidarity from reaching the other side. Bodies were not crossing, but ideas freely represented the expansions of bodies.

A dialogue took place between two migrant advocates in Ciudad Juárez, Maru and Leticia, and three in the U.S., Cynthia, Cristina, and Zaira. For 30 minutes, we engaged in conversation back and forth in Spanish and English responding to each other across the border, so that a broader audience in Mexico and the U.S. could understand that we would not be limited by languages or borders. Over the course of one week, each evening's activation was distinctly named. Our activation was called "*Las Platicadoras*" and it was described as an "activist and academic collective that works with migrants and refugees in conversation."[15] The following is an excerpt from part of our *displaced pláticas* as *platicadoras* discussing migration:

> *Platicadora* **Zaira in El Paso**, states in Spanish: Remain in Mexico is a program requiring migrants to wait in Mexico as their asylum requests are pending. Asylum Seekers must wait in Mexico for their court hearings in Mexico after being processed by U.S. immigration officials. Migrants can wait for several months while immigration courts scramble to accommodate cases. Since January 2019, close to 70,000 asylum seekers have been returned to various Mexican cities (13,000 are children and 400 infants) …
>
> *Platicadora* **Maru in Ciudad Juárez**, responds in English: Estas cifras nos muestran un patrón que vulnera históricamente a las poblaciones de color. Pero qué hay de los encuentros uno a uno? Que pasa en esos espacios de asilo, de movimiento entre ideas y personas?
>
> *Platicadora* **Cristina in El Paso**, shares a story about an interview with a migrant from the interior of Mexico in Spanish, and
>
> *Platicadora* **Leticia in Ciudad Juárez**, shares a poem about migrants since she operates one of the migrant shelters in that city in Spanish.
>
> *Platicadora* **Cynthia in El Paso**, ends in Spanish with saying that migrants need radical love and radical friendships, and that the migrants at the Parque Chamizal in Ciudad Juárez are not alone.

The rupture of the international boundary line and border wall did not disrupt the *comunitatas* that inspired action and intervention across the dry Rio Grande/Rio Bravo. "Victor Turner calls communitas—the sense of solidarity that people experience through the shared experience of liminality" (Turner 1967, cited in Vogt 2018: 174). Border Tuner was an opportunity to collectively confront and dismantle popular troupes about migrants across forbidden spaces near the U.S. border wall. The Border Tuner activations worked to deborder the international boundary line, and to reborder the relationality across and between migrants and their defenders. The Border Tuner art installation and the *Platicadoras* that spoke in solidarity with migrants worked to undo regime building. If nation-states continue to construct borders, the art installation allows us to deborder and to reimagine the Paso del Norte region without borders or walls. For one night, we were able to reborder an international boundary into a liminal and fluid collective transcendence.

10. THE DISPLACEMENT AND DISPOSAL OF TENT CITIES, DEBORDERING SETTLEMENTS ONE AT A TIME

Throughout the summer of 2019, as temperatures soared, migrant families began to assemble one tent at a time. In the summer, they weathered the incredible heat and dehydration, while the fall proved increasingly difficult as tent settlements swelled, and winter proved intolerable. Spring never came for tent people. Migrants relied on the kindness of strangers, and civil society organizations in Mexico, that coordinated food and clothing efforts for tent settlements, and within Mexican shelters. U.S. organizations worked creatively to get supplies across the border to families. Children were growing ill and fears of a spread of illness and fatigue grew across the settlements. The uncertainty of knowing their fate caused severe anxiety and illness.

In December of 2019, 100 Mexican migrants were removed by Chihuahua state police from the tent cities, after they threatened to separate parents from their children near the Paso del Norte bridge in downtown Ciudad Juárez (Chavez 2020). Near freezing temperatures prompted the eviction. Families were loaded onto shuttles and taken to a government operated shelter, but their whereabouts were not known. Families did not want to leave the tent settlement for fear of losing their place on a list that they initiated to present their asylum claims in the U.S. (Castro 2019). Although there was never a consensus from Juárez officials on exact numbers of migrants living in these settlements at any given time, by December 2019, the number of migrants across the three busiest international bridges was estimated to have dropped to 600 migrants (Castro 2019). As stated earlier, Isacson (2019) claimed roughly 3,000 Mexican migrants had arrived in Juárez in September 2019. As quickly as they had arrived, by early January 2020, the tent cities had vanished, and the migrants were gone. The process of removal was abrupt and justified by inhabitable outdoor weather, although others argued that death threats instigated the demise of tent settlements.[16] They were disposable communities, disposable tents, and disposable bodies. Displaced and disappeared. All migrants' bodies became disposable and forgettable.

The tent city phenomenon was surreal and ephemeral. It is disconcerting how swiftly the settlements vanished and how the visible was rendered invisible and silent. The whereabouts of tent city people is unclear after their eviction and disbandment, and it is unclear if the lists they kept to hold their place in line to seek political asylum was honored, or how, from a distance, they could maintain the network of migrants, communication lines, and order that they organically initiated. Where are the families, the children, and their "at the moment" homes/tents? We return to the paradox again, where the tent people were gone slowly at first, and then almost immediately. In a sea of people and an air of displacement, disposability, and debordering, people vanished into thin air.

11. CONCLUSION: *DISPLACED PLÁTICAS*—LESSONS THAT CHALLENGE DIASPORIC UNDERSTANDINGS

This chapter is an immediate and necessary response to the tent settlements that emerged in Ciudad Juárez. The urgency of seeing the mantling and dismantling of these tent settlements was imperative to bear witness to and to write about, despite our inability to conduct traditional fieldwork. We relied on our ethnographic training to observe what was openly and publicly unfolding in our borderlands' communities, as active witnesses and migrant rights advocates. We developed a method we call *displaced pláticas* that we argue moves relationally between people's temporary settlements and our own historical subjectivities. The tent settlements near international boundaries were spaces of interest, concern, and intimacy for us, as we worked to better understand how migration was unfolding at the Mexican border in ways that had not been seen before.

People living in temporary tents along international bridges at the northern Mexican border with the U.S., challenged popular tenets about migration. We tend to think in paradigms of migrants as people traveling northbound without documents to cross into the U.S., or who move southbound into Mexico as the result of deportation. Tent people created autonomous communities, not only by moving across their home country, but by claiming rights of *autoasilamiento* in Mexico. Although we recognize migration as a historic process, our intention in this chapter is to deepen the understanding of migration as a current and ever changing one. We witnessed the expanding forms of migration taking place, and the real time implications for migrants and local people, as their ways of life shift and take on new meaning.

New forms of diaspora take shape as we begin to comprehend the challenges people confront when moving across multiple contexts of violence. Here, we discuss dispossession as part of the long-term process that is expressed, particularly for tent people, as a displacement from their home communities. Thus, the first challenge we addressed in this chapter was to understand a temporary settlement of mainly Mexican refugees within Mexico, which disrupts ideas around binaries of what is nationality and citizenship, and migrants and foreign status. Central American migrants and other international migrants were joined by an unsuspecting group of *autoasilados* from Mexico, thus, revealing their fermenting internal displacement within Mexico, which helped to shape the complexities around what it means and looks like to flee from violence outside and within one's country. This internal displacement forces us to reconsider how migration is taking shape in the U.S.–Mexican border in ways only heard about in war-torn countries in which citizens are scattered across, yet within their national borders, looking for safe spaces to reimagine home within familiar contexts.

The second challenge we engaged was to frame an interpretation of these tent settlements that captured the tension represented by tent people's desire to be recognized by Mexico as *autoasilados*, and their temporary—or otherwise—living arrangements within their adopted city, which had experienced decades of violence. Their complex realities were magnified by continuously emerging and mercurial U.S. policies like Remain in Mexico, which created a bureaucratic wall by implementing metering practices and increased militarization on both sides of the border. Throughout our chapter, we discussed displacement and basurization (Silva Santisteban 2008), in order to address why people were constantly excluded from asylum protocols to safeguard their rights, and why we argued that migrants were considered by people in power as disposable.

Our decision to use the construct of disposability is one that shows how dehumanization is superimposed on communities which are marginalized, and which results in exile from their home communities for their own protection. This exclusion by their own country has allowed corruption and crime to go unchecked with few to little safety measures in place for *autoasilados* or others seeking refuge. Their hopes for asylum in the U.S. are often thwarted, as their retelling of human rights atrocities are rejected, and migrants are expelled at international bridges without any further thought—thus, our insistence on using symbolic basurization and what scales of humanity conjure.

Although we were not engaging with tent people daily or even weekly, like other border crossers, we observed their settlements grow with each passing week and across several months, and we spent copious amounts of time listening and reading accounts of asylum cases, the development of metering policies, and tent people's concerns and organizational processes, and would lend a hand at shelters or offer other forms of support to migrants. We learned valuable lessons from the people that came and vanished from the public sidewalks and spaces they occupied.

To address these questions and to lend our voices to what was visibly and viscerally occurring in these tent settlements, we participated in the Border Tuner (art installation) that bridged our voices between Juárez and El Paso. We wanted all border people to recognize the human rights injustices occurring under our noses. Border Tuner represented a unique opportunity to reveal the tensions of the parts of our analysis and discussions that could not enter conventional academic mechanisms. By engaging our *displaced pláticas* performatively, we were able, with other migrant advocates, to enter border spaces in unconventional ways to further visibilize migrants in spaces where they were not permitted—the U.S. side of the border.

More research is needed to understand the next steps for people under *autoasilamiento* in border communities. Migration is forever changing as Mexican *autoasilados* have taught us. There is still much to discuss in terms of methodological practices, and how interdisciplinary practices and concepts help us to create more robust approaches that explain the ill-conceived responses to safeguarding people from violence and processes of displacement, disposability, and debordering.

ACKNOWLEDGMENT

We would like to acknowledge the sacrifice and resilience of all the migrants living precariously along the border. We would like to thank the editors of this collection for their meticulous advice, and Zaira Martin for her assistance with this chapter. Thanks also to Leticia Lopez Manzano, Cristina Morales, and Zaira Martin, the other Border Tuner *platicadoras*. To our families, we thank you for your love and patience as we completed this work.

NOTES

1. *Autoasilados* describes Mexican nationals seeking asylum in the U.S., who were internally displaced from their home regions. They sought asylum from within their country as they tried to flee violence, solely to be displaced inside their home country to face other violent experiences.
2. El Paso's population is 680,000 and Ciudad Juárez's population is 1,500,000 (Isacson 2019).

3. The international bridges or entry points between the sister cities of Ciudad Juárez and El Paso consist of five international ports of entry, with two others nearby. One port of entry is east of El Paso in Fabens, Texas/Caseta, Chihuahua, and another is west of El Paso in New Mexico at the Santa Teresa, New Mexico/San Geronimo, Chihuahua crossing. Other entry points dot the international boundary across the 1,952 miles of the international boundary line (Ortiz 2015).
4. A militia known as the United Constitutional Patriots led by 70-year-old Larry Mitchell Hopkins was detaining migrant families at gunpoint near the border in New Mexico; Mitchell Hopkins was arrested for being in possession of several firearms and ammunition in 2019 (Ortiz 2020). On August 3, 2019, a 21-year old from Dallas, Texas killed 22 mostly Mexican and Mexican-Americans and wounded 24 more in a Walmart at El Paso, Texas claiming he wanted to "kill as many Mexicans as he could" (Bogel-Burroughs 2019).
5. Nativists have typically been U.S. born citizens who feel that immigrants do not belong in the U.S. Historically, U.S. nativists included, "eugenicists, xenophobes, scholars, Klan members, labor organizers, and others" who voiced their racism and xenophobia toward immigrant groups including the Chinese, Italians, Polish, Slovanians, and Mexicans (Lytle Hernández 2010: 27). See Mae Ngai's discussion on nativism in her book, *Impossible Subjects: Illegal Aliens and the Making of Modern America* (2004).
6. Ochoa Fierros and Delgado Bernal (2016: 20) address "how *pláticas* can be a strategy to collect data as well as part of a Chicana/Latina feminist methodology." *Pláticas* also represents a "potential space for healing" and "relies on relations of reciprocity, vulnerability, and reflexivity" (Ochoa Fierros and Delgado Bernal 2016: 30).
7. On October 12, 2018, a group of 160 Hondurans decided to travel together to the United States for their safety, and, at one point, the number of migrants grew to thousands when it reached the southern Mexican border (Fry 2019).
8. Seeking political asylum within the U.S. requires meeting five categories. "Asylum is a protection granted to foreign nationals already in the United States or at the border who meet the international law definition of a 'refugee.' The United Nations 1951 Convention and the 1967 Protocol define a refugee as a person who is unable or unwilling to return to his or her home country, and cannot obtain protection in that country, due to past persecution or a well-founded fear of being persecuted in the future 'on account of race, religion, nationality, membership in a particular social group, or political opinion.' Congress incorporated this definition into U.S. immigration law in the Refugee Act of 1980" (https://www.americanimmigrationcouncil.org/research/asylum-united-states).
9. In October 2019, the U.S. Department of Homeland Security launched two programs, the Prompt Asylum Claim Review (PACR) program, and HARP, specific to Mexican citizens to expedite their applications while in Customs and Border Protection custody, although they have little to no access to legal counsel (Isacson 2019).
10. Dunn defines "militarization" as "the use of military rhetoric and ideology, as well as military tactics, strategy, technology, equipment, and forces" (1996: 3).
11. Both authors experienced this process. For several weeks to months in late 2019, army soldiers supervised the metering practice at the midpoint of the international bridge, as young soldiers waved people through the waiting line to cross into the U.S. approving or disapproving border crossers' movements.
12. The Border Tuner Art Installation was curated by León de la Rosa on the Ciudad Juárez side and by Kerry Doyle in El Paso, with programming direction by Edgar Picazo. León made this comment to describe the art installation.
13. See https://www.bordertuner.net/home.
14. This high school is famously known for a student led lawsuit against the El Paso Border Patrol Sector in the early 1990s for racially profiling Latino students. The Latino students won their civil lawsuit against the border patrol (Dunn 2009).
15. See https://www.bordertuner.net/events.
16. Some families claimed that a group of smugglers threatened to burn the settlements if migrants attempted to cross into the U.S. on their own. The Juárez Secretary of Public Safety stated that he was not aware of this claim, but that his office maintained constant vigilance of the tent settlements for the migrants' safety (Martínez Prado 2019).

REFERENCES

Alexander, Michelle. *The New Jim Crow: Mass Incarceration in the Age of Colorblindness*. New York: The New Press, 2012.
American Immigration Council. "Asylum in the United States: Fact Sheet." https://www.americanimmigrationcouncil.org, June 2020.
Anzaldua, Gloria. *Borderlands: La Frontera = the New Mestiza*. San Francisco: Aunt Lute Books, 1987.
Appadurai, Arjun. *Fear of Small Numbers: An Essay on the Geography of Anger*. Durham, NC: Duke University Press, 2006.
Bejarano, Cynthia. "Border Rootedness as Transformative Resistance: Youth Overcoming Violence and Inspection in a US–Mexico Border Region." *Children's Geographies* 8(4): 391–399, 2010.
Bejarano, Cynthia L. and Maria Cristina Morales. "Analyzing Conquest Through a Border Lens: Vulnerable Communities at the Mexico–U. S. and Moroccan–Spanish Border Regions." In *El Río Bravo Mediterráneo: Las Regiones fronterizas en la época de la globalización*, 117–129, Natalia Ribas-Mateos (Ed.). Barcelona: Bellaterra, 2011.
Bello, Chris, Monique Candiff, Tara Ohrtman and Alyssa Epstein. "Violations of Human Rights Occurring in Mexico as a Result of the Remain in Mexico Program. A Report for the Border Institute." Mills Legal Clinic, n.d.
Bogel-Burroughs, Nicholas. "'I'm the Shooter': El Paso Suspect Confessed to Targeting Mexicans, Police Say." *The New York Times*, August 9, 2019. https://www.nytimes.com/2019/08/09/us/el-paso-suspect-confession.html.
Carastathis, Anna. "Identity Categories as Potential Coalitions." *Signs: Journal of Women in Culture & Society* 38(4): 941–965, 2013.
Castillo, Daniel. "Culturas Excrementicias y Postcolonialismo." In *El Debate de la Postcolonialidad en Latinoamérica: Una Postmodernidad Periférica o Cambio de Paradigma en el Pensamiento Latinoamericano*, 235–257, Alfonso del Toro and Fernando del Toro (Eds.). Madrid: Iberoamericana, 1999.
Castro, Salvador. "Exhortan a migrantes a que se refugien en albergues. El Diario de Juárez." https://diario.mx/Juárez/exhortan-a-migrantes-a-que-se-refugien-en-albergues-20191218-1602320.html, December 18, 2019.
Chavez, Julio-Cesar. "Mexican Migrants Removed from Border Camp after Family Separation Threat." https://www.reuters.com/article/us-usa-immigration-mexico-camp/mexican-migrants-removed-from-border-camp-after-family-separation-threat-idUSKBN1Z709R, January 8, 2020.
De Carli, Beatrice, Alexandre Apsan, Benedito Barbosa, Francisco Comarú and Ricardo De Sousa. "Regeneration through the 'Pedagogy of Confrontation': Exploring the Critical Spatial Practices of Social Movements in Inner City São Paulo as Avenues for Urban Renewal." *Dearq Journal of Architecture* (16): 146–161, 2015.
Delgado, Richard and Jean Stefancic. *Critical Race Theory: An Introduction*. Second Edition (Critical America). New York: NYU Press, 2012.
Dunn, Timothy J. *The Militarization of the U.S.–Mexico Border 1978–1992*. Center for Mexican American Studies. Austin: University of Texas at Austin, 1996.
Dunn, Timothy J. *Blockading the Border and Human Rights: The El Paso Operation that Remade Immigration Enforcement*. Austin: University of Texas at Austin, 2009.
Fry, Wendy. "The Massive Caravans that Arrived in Tijuana Last Year Prompted Lasting Policy Changes to U.S. and Mexico Immigration." *San Diego-Union Tribune*. https://www.sandiegouniontribune.com/news/border-baja-california/story/2019-11-17/one-year-later-the-unpredicted-legacy-of-the-migrant-caravan, November 17, 2019.
Galván, T. "Chicana/Latin American Feminist Epistemologies of the Global South (within and outside the North): Decolonizing El conocimiento and creating Global Alliances." *Journal of Latino/Latin American Studies* 6(2): 135–140, 2014.
Giménez, Gilberto. "Materiales para una teoría de las identidades sociales." *Frontera Norte* 9(18): 9–28, 1997.
Hernández Sánchez, Ma. Eugenia. "Institutional Narratives and Migratory Dialogues." ProQuest Dissertations Publishing, 2017.

Hope Border Institute. *Remain in Mexico Updates.* https://www.hopeborder.org/remain-in-mexico-052219, June 7, 2019.

Isacson, Adam. "'I Can't Believe What's Happening—What We're Becoming': A Memo from El Paso and Ciudad Juárez." Washington Office on Latin America, 2019.

Laddaga, Reinaldo. *Estética de la Emergencia: La Formación de Otra cultura de las Artes.* Buenos Aires: Adriana Hidalgo Editora, 2006.

Lozano-Hemmer, Rafael. "Interactive Public Art: Border Tuner: El Paso–Ciudad Juárez." Border Tuner. https://www.border-tuner.net/home, January 29, 2020.

Lytle Hernández, Kelly. *MIGRA! A History of the U.S. Border Patrol.* Berkeley: University of California Press, 2010.

Martínez Prado, Hérika. "Denuncian Migrantes Supuestas Amenazas." *El Diario de Juárez.* https://diario.mx/juarez/denuncian-migrantes-supuestas-amenazas-20191219-1602958.html, December 20, 2019.

Mohanty, Chandra Talpade. *Feminism without Borders: Decolonizing Theory, Practicing Solidarity.* Durham, NC: Duke University Press, 2003.

Monje, Ana María and David Burin. "Dislocando la propiedad. Un análisis sobre usos del espacio en una experiencia colectiva de Rosario, Argentina." *Huellas* 22(2): 35–54, 2008.

Net Noticias. "Instala maestra paseña escuela para ninos migrantes en el Chamizal." https://netnoticias.mx/Juárez/instala-maestra-pasena-escuela-para-ninos-migrantes-en-el-chamizal/, March 5, 2020.

Ngai, Mae. *Impossible Subjects: Illegal Aliens and the Making of Modern America.* Princeton, NJ: Princeton University Press, 2004.

Ochoa Fierros, Cindy and Dolores Delgado Bernal. "Vamos a Plàticar: The Contours of Plàticas as Chicana/Latina Feminist Methodology." *Chicana/Latina Studies Journal* 15(2): 98–121, 2016.

Ortiz, Aimee. "Leader of Right-Wing Border Militia Pleads Guilty to Gun Charge." *The New York Times*, January 3, 2020.

Ortiz, Manuela. *Texas–Mexico International Bridges and Border Crossings Existing and Proposed 2015.* Early, TX: Texas Department of Transportation, 2015.

Ortiz Uribe, Monica. "Trump Administration's 'Remain in Mexico' Program Tangles Legal Process." National Public Radio. https://www.npr.org/2019/05/09/721755716/trump-administrations-remain-in-mexico-program-tangles-legal-process, May 9, 2019.

Razack, Sherene. *Looking White People in the Eye: Gender, Race, and Culture in Courtrooms and Classrooms.* Toronto: University of Toronto Press, 2008.

Rodriguez, Nestor. "Battle for the Border: Notes on Autonomous Migration, Transnational Communities, and the State." *Social Justice* 23(3): 21–37, 1996.

Rosenblum, Marc R. and Isabel Ball. *Trends in Unaccompanied Child and Family Migration from Central America.* Washington, DC: Migration Policy Institute, 2016.

Sánchez Díaz, Sergio G. and Patricia Ravelo Blanco. "Cultura y violencia en Ciudad Juárez. Desplazados y migrantes en medio de la gran violencia (2008–2018)." *El cotidiano*, March–April: 108–117, 2019.

Sassen, Saskia. *Expulsions: Brutality and Complexity in the Global Economy.* Cambridge, MA: Harvard University Press, 2014.

Semple, Kirk and Brent McDonald. "Mexico Breaks Up a Migrant Caravan, Pleasing White House." *The New York Times.* https://www.nytimes.com/2020/01/24/world/americas/migrant-caravan-mexico.html?auth=link-dismiss-google1tap, January 24, 2020.

Silva Santisteban, Rocío. *El Factor Asco: Basurización Simbólica y Discursos Autoritarios en el Perú Contemporáneo.* Lima, Peru: Red para el Desarrollo de las Ciencias Sociales en Perú, 2008.

Turner, Victor. *The Forest of Symbols: Aspects of Ndembu Ritual.* Ithaca, NY: Cornell University Press, 1967.

Vogt, Wendy. *Lives in Transit: Violence and Intimacy on the Migrant Journey.* Oakland: University of California Press, 2018.

Walicki, Nadine. "Los Desplazados Internos en Europa Todavía Marginados." *Revista Migraciones Forzadas* 33: 25–26, 2009.

Wingard, J. *Branded Bodies, Rhetoric, and the Neoliberal Nation-State.* Lanham, MD: Lexington Books, 2013.

4. *Undo/redo* the violent wall: border-crossing practices and multi-territoriality
Marlene Solís

1. INTRODUCTION

This chapter reflects on border-crossing practices and their potential as producers of a social space which functions as a mediation zone for rebordering processes and national identity policies underway, since the beginning of the twenty-first century, that materialized in what we named a violent wall. These processes have affected local populations of the border regions, in particular those who settle in the immediate vicinity of the dividing line between Mexico and the United States.

The point of departure is that we understand the transborder as a network/territory, which is configured by border-crossing practices as a local order characterized by circularity, virtuality, instability and conflict. Throughout the text, both the theoretical basis that supports this idea as well as a description of the most representative border-crossing practices that take place on the border between Mexico and the United States are presented. To think about the transborder as a social space implies considering everyday life as a starting point, and then thinking about a territory with its spatial marks and its own ways of operating autonomously, given the inertia recreated by repetition and in which individuals are able to decipher codes and have their own language. Furthermore, the arrival of Donald Trump as president of the United States in 2017 has marked a turning point in the processes of globalization. Although many of his statements have remained in the discursive terrain, glimpses towards the strengthening of national borders and symbolic borders have been made evident.

At the same time and in a dialectical way, we observe the construction of a transborder territory against these tendencies that follows its own logic, anchored in the local scale of the border coexistence, which can be interpreted under the ideas of Mezzadra and Neilson (2013) that pose precisely the dual character of any border as a place of encounter and avoidance, or as a barrier and contact area. That is, that the border and its processes have ambivalences, which implies figuratively and objectively undoing and redoing the wall. As Pablo Vila (2001: 23) pointed out, the same person could, in a different circumstance or from another perspective, be a border reinforcer or border crosser.

Spencer and Staudt (1998) proposed the idea of the border's dialectic, as an intrinsic attribute of itself, identifying the conjugation of the debordering and rebordering processes in the history of the creation of the border between Mexico and the United States. These processes are presented in multiple dimensions and origin in different scales, may they be global, national, regional or local. The operation of capitalism itself generates forces linked to economic interests that push the opening of the borders. During the last decades two processes prove this dialectic: the intense industrial relocation along the northern border of Mexico, especially after the signing of the North American Free Trade Agreement with the United States and Canada in the 1990s; while – exerting opposing forces – the national security policy in the United States, which intensified after 9/11, had as an effect the drastic decrease of circular migration.

Although a good part of border-crossing practices at a macrosocial level could be understood as a way to legitimize the wall because of the acceptance of the regular entry (leaving behind the illegal crossing), at the microsocial level these systematic crossings of the border by the ports of entry open life-lines against the line of death that enables the violent wall and its technologies.[1] Here it is interesting to ask about the nature of this network/territory in order to understand the border and its reinforcement in this historical moment. Therefore, it is necessary to broaden the discussion about the border as a space for both contact and detachment, analyze the idea of the transborder as a network/territory, and to bring back some concepts of border studies in order to have a theoretical framework for analysis of border-crossing practices, the systems of significance that accompany them and the subjectivities that emerge from this particular way of appropriating a space.

This chapter consists of three sections: the first exposes a theoretical discussion about contemporary multi-territoriality, while, in the second section, different practices and the ways in which they have been studied are analyzed, looking to understand the nature of the transboundary territory and its implications for the processes of rebordering. Finally, a discussion about the role of border-crossing practices in the dialectic of the double function – contact and separation – of the border is presented as a conclusion.

2. THE CROSS-BORDER AS PART OF CONTEMPORARY MULTI-TERRITORIALITY

Generally speaking, globalization is understood as a set of processes that trigger the flows and exchanges between different regions of the planet and that narrow the distances by modifying the space–time relationship between them, and has generated key transformations in national states. Some authors, such as Habermas (2000), propose the idea that we are on the way to a post-national era, given the greater centrality of the capitals and the logic of the markets to define the economic and political direction in the different countries, as well as the importance of the supranational instances in the definition of processes that affect and determine the action of the nation-states.

Until a few years ago, authors such as Noda and Sánchez (2015: 119) had argued that at this particular moment in globalization, democratic governments have a denationalized state whose legal framework and institutions are at the service of global capital, so that the power is decentralized and manifests as a network/power. So the world is not dominated by one, two or even several nation-states, but by various actors at national and global level with particular interests, always searching the privilege at the national level.

In the same direction, Sassen (2006) points out that it is not about the end of states but that there is a dispute over hegemonic power and the nation-state becomes a strategic actor, with new functions. Therefore, the author argues that we are facing denationalization processes, since the state, as guarantor of a nation, has been weakening but not completely eliminated. In her analysis, globalization entails the "disassembly" of the nation-state in three aspects: territory, authority and rights. Although there is a withdrawal of its former functions, the nation-state continues a capitalistic logic that privileges the interests of the owners of capital.

However, we are witnessing new directions from the governments of the United States and Mexico. In the case of the former, there is an interest in strengthening local economies and domestic markets, as well as a series of anti-immigrant policies promoted by President Donald Trump. At the same time, we observe a shift in Mexico with the arrival of President Andrés Manuel López Obrador, who has promoted a new orientation of public policies according to his vision of the role of the State in the redistribution of wealth, thus moving away from neoliberal proposals.

Despite this shift, which probably is going to modify the geopolitical context in the US–Mexico border in the middle and long term, the proposals of Appadurai (1996) are still valid, pointing out that the dynamics of globalization make it necessary to account for the crisis of what is considered national and to identify post-national social forms, such as transnationalism and border-crossing practices.

These transformations within the nation-state disrupt their territoriality. Globalization has been happening as a result of different processes of both deterritorialization and reterritorialization by nation-states (loss of control and at the same time reappropriation of the territory). With regard to geopolitical boundaries, we are witnessing greater tension between the processes of rebordering and debordering (closing and opening of borders). The dialectic of these dynamics is expressed, in turn, in what occurs between the global and the local. While globalization is generating a movement of people, capital, information, merchandise, on the scale of the local, frictions and resistance of different scope and intentionality that stop these flows and allow the reappropriation of the territory are presented. The result of this tension is what Beck (1999), along with other authors such as Jordi Borja and Manuel Castells (1998) and Ronald Robertson (2003), has named as glocalization, thus relating two concomitant and co-dependent processes.

According to Haesbaert (2011), the understanding of space–time compression and in general the dynamics of glocalization have changed the territories from a zone type (zone/territories) to a network type form (network/territories), but this transit takes place without the disappearance of the former, that is, the zone/territory coexists with the network/territory, multiplying the ways of appropriating and giving meaning to a territory. Thus, the production of social space today is distinguished by its multi-territoriality.

From this idea it is interesting to think about the border as a social space generating a multi-territoriality in which the zone/territory is combined with the network/territory. In particular, it seems useful to think of the transborder as a territory that is shaped by the presence of the demarcation of boundaries between national states, but how is the zone/territory different from the network/territory? How do people appropriate this territory? What subjectivities emerge from this experience? How does this help us understand border processes and border-crossing practices facing the violent wall?

Inquiring in the specificity of this territory requires, at first to recover the concept of territory, understanding it as the result of various processes of appropriation of space, both material and symbolic. As Félix (2017) reminds us, the border as a social reality requires not only its material construction, its objectification, but also to be imagined and represented. Likewise, the border is experienced, inhabited and lived in everyday life, referring to the phenomenological dimension of this space. This dimension is fundamental in the proposal of Appadurai (1996) to understand the local, which is more than a matter of spatial scale. The local has a phenomenological quality; it is a relational and contextual category, since it is the referent for the production of subjectivities, sociality and reproducibility.

Unlike a zone/territory, a network/territory implies fluidity, transit and nodes, or anchor points in space. The transborder territory has this quality; as Alonso (2016) and Campos and Hernández (2015) point out, the border-crossing practice implies passing through (by the checkpoints or other point of the border), circular mobility, entering and leaving two contrasting worlds –especially in the case of asymmetric borders – and two different sociocultural formations. Likewise, it is a multi-situated practice, that is, there is a certain discontinuity in the experience of space–time. Therefore, cross-border practices have the quality of developing in and across multiple places.

Defining the transborder as a network-territory leads us to think about its discontinuity and its association with post-national social forms, as well as its unstable and virtual character. The virtual could be understood in two ways: one as a space that some people can access and second – more in line with the idea of limen – for its potential to produce something new, particularly in relation to the identity policies of national states.

According to Jones (2011) there are different forms of resistance to the adscription policies of the nation-states: some are frontal and active, while others weaken, undermine or elude the management capacity of the nation-state borders, generating along the border territories an area of denial of the power of nation-states.[2]

On the other hand, in order to understand the experience of the border, Iglesias (2014) raises the notion of borderism. From this idea, she elaborates a typology of experiences of the border, considering different degrees of exposure to the experience of the border crossing. In this way, the author builds a typology, ranging from those who live in the border region but do not cross it to those who have developed a *modus vivendi* around the customary border crossing. This group of people would be identified by an *habitus* and a cross-border culture; so we are taking for reference Bourdieu's conception of *habitus* as systems of durable and transferable dispositions that can be objectively adapted to their goal without assuming the conscious purpose of certain ends (Bourdieu, 2007: 86).

Returning to the thesis of Appadurai (1996) on the validity of the feeling of belonging to the nation-state, the author points out that this feeling is still present, but it is destabilized by diasporas, communication technologies and queer nationalism. However, patriotism is built not so much by face-to-face contact or by proximity, but through shared imaginary. Following this author, nationalism is reproduced less by "natural" issues – such as language, race, blood – than by cultural aspects; the nation-state in its classical territorial form loses legitimacy, giving rise to transnational forms of belonging, that is, double and even multiple memberships. Therefore, there are more complex and changing forms of identification. This is one of the defining aspects of the transborder territory as a social space for multiple and complex identification.

The transborder is part of the border landscape, the result of the techniques and modes of spatial production of a network-territory. Following the cited author, the relationship between global and local reality requires "the continuous construction, both practical and discursive, of an ethnoscape (necessarily nonlocal) against which local practices and projects are imagined to take place" (Appadurai, 1996: 184). An ethnoscape refers to the fact that the culture of a group of settlers becomes perceptible in the environment, and in the proposal of Appadurai (1996, 2004) it is the result of the action to locate a project of belonging, of distinction, of the tension *them/us*, of symbolic bordering while, as a localized social space, the transborder involves specific social practices, some of which are described in the next section.

3. LOGICS IN BORDER-CROSSING PRACTICES AND SUBJECTIVITIES BEHIND THE VIOLENT WALL

The study of border-crossing practices allows us to better understand the nature of this network/zone/territory, since it is through these practices that a culture is localized and an ethnoscape is built. As Appadurai (1996) points out, "space and time are themselves socialized and localized through complex and deliberate practices of performance, representation and action" (1996: 180), which for the author are cosmological or ritual practices, while expressing a way of understanding and being in the world.

The crossing of people and goods across the border, either regularly or irregularly, implies a series of social practices and these practices are precisely what have been shaping a social space. In the synthesis made by Ariztía (2017) of the theory of social practices, these are defined as ways of doing and/or saying which are present within a space–time, involving competences, meaning and materiality. These three elements are constitutive of social practices; when one of them disappears or changes substantially, they cease to exist. In summary, we can point out that a social practice is germinated from knowledge and skills; it is guided by values, cultural repertoires and teleo-affective aspects; and it makes use of tools, infrastructure and resources.

In different empirical studies on the crossings of people along the checkpoints of the US–Mexico border, some classifications have been made, using various criteria. In a study by Anguiano-Téllez (2005), the searched criteria were the motives behind displacement, the population displaced (children, youth, adults, workers, merchants, civil society organizations, business managers or visitors) and the directionality of the flows;[3] while Odgers and Campos (2012) point out that emotional and utilitarian dimensions make sense of border-crossing practices. They suggest that the motives respond to the idea of crossing as a resource, generating specific scenarios and actors that do appropriate a space. For example, residents from Tijuana working at San Diego county or residents from San Diego county crossing in order to use medical and dental care, or in both directions for visiting their family.

The distinction between the flows according to their direction, that is, if they go from south to north or from north to south, allows us to approach the transborder landscape tessellations. In principle, the data on the crossings allow us to identify that one of the main flows from south to north is the so-called commuters, those who go to work to San Diego every day. According to Orraca-Romano (2019), 52,760 was the number of cross-border workers in 2015, by the checkpoints of Tijuana, Mexicali, San Luis Río Colorado, Nogales, Ciudad Juárez, Ciudad Acuña-Piedras Negras, Nuevo Laredo, Reynosa and Matamoros. Of this number, the majority (41 percent) did cross through Tijuana. In order to approach the sociodemographic profile of this population that experiences the cross-border daily the author emphasizes that a greater proportion are married men with children, who have an older average age than local workers, and a significant percentage declared to have lived five years ago in the United States, although they generally report being born in one of the states adjacent to this country (Orraca-Romano, 2019: 460–61).

Another group that has been studied for its impact on the construction of this territory is that of cross-border students. Rocha-Romero and Orraca-Romano (2018), using 2015 data from the National Institute of Statistics and Geography (INEGI), found that 34,204 people studied in the United States and resided in one of the border cities of Mexico: Tijuana, Mexicali, San Luis Río Colorado, Nogales, Ciudad Juárez, Ciudad Acuña, Piedras Negras, Matamoros,

Nuevo Laredo or Reynosa; Tijuana and Ciudad Juárez represented the main entrance doors. In this count, elementary, secondary, high school, university and postgraduate students were included. Moreover, the group of university students has been studied by Falcón-Orta and Orta-Falcón (2018) in order to show the process of forming a transborder identity among those who cross the border from Tijuana. The authors point to the fact that these students face multiple obstacles while maintaining a transborder lifestyle that relate to the context, discrimination and instability in their worlds of life, among the most important. Also, the authors point out that they manage to form an identity precisely through practices that generate unity and adaptability. In fact, in recent years, transborder student associations of different educational levels have been formed, such as: Latin American Studies Student Organization (LASSO) and the Transfronterizx Alliance Student Organization (TASO). While Morales and Mendoza (2018) describe some of the struggles of the transnational students crossing daily from Ciudad Juárez, Chihuahua, Mexico to El Paso, Texas, United States.

Regarding the north–south flow, a study by Bringas and Verduzco (2008) reveals that 1,282,448 international visitors who crossed the border to some city on the Mexican side arrived in 2004. Of this number, 85 percent were Hispanic; more than half are of Mexican origin. Although these data refer to tourist crossings, they also capture the most regular crossings not necessarily associated with tourism. These data also allow us to account for the importance of the crossing for the population of Mexican or Latin origin in cross-border transit, updating the idea elaborated in previous sections about the superimposed border that has historically generated these crossing social practices in the key of Mexicanness.

Ruiz (1998) analyzed the cross-border topic from the people's crossing experiences from San Diego, United States, to Baja California, Mexico, highlighting the cultural character of this practice that involves physical, emotional and mental aspects and that implies a learning process of multiple forms of interaction and inter-ethnic negotiation, resulting in the construction of a bicultural daily life.

Precisely, in the border city of Tijuana (which is the main referent for this work), tourism has played a very important role in defining the transit of people, especially from north to south, at times being the defining characteristic of the city, as Félix (2011) refers to the construction of the black legend of Tijuana at the time of the prohibition of alcohol in the United States, when the image of Tijuana as a city of vice started to form.

The flows of people for both tourism and labor purposes are defined by the *calculation logic* that drives them, according to Odgers and Campos (2012), since the labor market in the United States and the income derived from this activity place those who participate in it in a privileged position, due to the higher income and greater purchasing power as a result of residing on the Mexican side; while it has been documented that the attraction of tourists to Mexican border cities, is related not only to entertainment, but to the advantages of some services, such as health, dentists and others (more recently to have access to a living place) that are cost prohibitive for those who reside on the US side.

Beyond this instrumental logic, which is sustained by considering the crossing as an opportunity and as a resource, the existence of the border and its border processes have led to the greater density of the social relations, so that in this social fabric the family has become increasingly important to sustain this network/territory, challenging the violent wall. Recently, one of the consequences of the policies of deportation of Mexicans from the United States has been the separation of families. These families have had to rebuild themselves in order to face fragmentation, allowing a new type of transborder family to emerge ever since, as has been documented in some studies (Acosta, 2019 and Ibarra, 2019); a significant number of deported people prefer to live in a border city that allows them some proximity to their family in the United States. This type of family has its antecedents in the transnational families that formed with the diaspora to the United States, as well as in the history of the population of this region (Ojeda, 2005 and 2009). In this sense, the expulsion of Mexicans from the United States has generated a greater density of family visits in both directions; the associated practices would respond according to Odgers and Campos (2012) to a type of *emotional logic*.

Another type of practice of an expressive logic is the one which collective interest drives to continue their ties of belonging, through different rituals and forms of coexistence beyond the borders. These are communities of indigenous people, Christians, artists and other specific populations that frequently live at the border crossing. On the Tijuana–San Diego border, the Binational Front of Indigenous Organizations (FIOB) has a presence on both sides and generates meeting spaces and diverse forms of solidarity that have been deployed with greater intensity by the movement of agricultural workers of the San Quintin Valley in Baja California.

One more reference of crossing practices with an expressive and political sense is the so-called transnational feminism (Solís, 2016). This discourse arises in response to what was initially called global or international feminism, which proposed in a somewhat uncritical manner the internationalization of feminist ideas that emerged from the western hegemonic countries. Transnational feminism as a practice has taken place especially at the borders, as in the case of Ciudad Juárez in northern Mexico, where civil society intervention on both sides of the border has been required to address violence towards women (Aikin, 2011).

From the experience of transnational activism on the US–Mexico border, proposals and organizational forms have emerged that imply a way of understanding otherness, which reinforce the conception of the border as porous, as when organizations come together from diverse realities, problematics and orientations, they have worked on the socialization of shared discourses through dialogue and tolerance.

Beyond activism, other practices that entail the intention of building transnational and transborder communities of different scope and with particular agendas, from those that occur in communities of indigenous people, academics, politicians, professionals and artists, are observed. Thus, along with the daily crossings, there is a certain regular exchange of different scope such as artistic, political and academic events: we could mention El Fandango Fronterizo (The Border Fandango) that is held annually on either side of the wall, or La Ceremonia del Abrazo (The Embrace Ceremony) that has been held for 121 years by the communities of Laredo, Texas and Nuevo Laredo, Tamaulipas.

In this account of border-crossing practices, from the local level, it is necessary also to include the practices generated at other latitudes, and, by that, I am referring to the corridors that are forming the migrant populations, with different migratory projects, some from clandestinity and transgression. In all these experiences there is a recollection of long-standing stories of Mexicans from southern states and Central American people, which during the last decade have also formed a diaspora. Part of the practices of these populations implies circularity and double or triple membership, so that they also contribute to the construction of the transborder territory. Pries (2002) proposes that, in the last decades, a transnational social space has been formed precisely because of the nature of migratory flows, derived from globalization and the advances in information and communication technologies, in such a way that, together with the rise in emigration, processes of remigration and recurring circularity are presented, which has given rise to a new type of migration that he calls: transmigration.

The crossing of borders, regardless of being made with a calculation and/or expressive logic, is experienced and meant differently, similar to what Iglesias (2014) has defined as types of borderism, that is, different ways of giving meaning to the border crossing. These ideal types include: (1) those who reject the border and reinforce their feeling of patriotism – in this case Mexicanness is reinforced; (2) the experience that de-dramatizes and naturalizes the existence of a dividing wall, as Guillermo Arias does with his 2018 documentary *El cerco que nos divide* ("The fence that divides us"); and (3) the most complex, because it recognizes double or multiple memberships and feeds a cosmopolitan ideal that denies the vertical ascription of the nation-state. This would be, then, about different subjectivities that manage their belongings in a strategic way and give rise to processes that involve both ways of undoing and doing the border wall, contributing to an arena of daily dispute over a space, but that, seen in a historical and social plane, contribute to the conformation of this network/territory. Also Martínez (1998) has identified the spectrum of forms of dealing with the adjacency in this border, looking through the cross-border relations, moreover the crossing-border practice. This spectrum goes from the unicultural nationalism to the bicultural binationalism, showing the latter a higher tolerance for ambiguity.

However, in the imaginary of both countries, the border wall has different connotations, as Iglesias (2014) points out; for the United States it represents a defense of the uncivilized, of the wild and the violent. In the imaginary of the inhabitants of the north the wall is rather ignored and few know of it, while from the south, the wall is an offense; it represents the power of the neighboring country north and the disdain for the human rights of thousands of migrant workers.

In geographical terms, regardless of the ways of giving meaning to the border crossing, what is interesting to note is that the transborder in this context implies social practices, which effectively present competences,[4] meaning and materiality, and that shape a particular social space, in which they constitute different subjectivities, and which open different paths to face the typical power relations of national identity policies.

4. CONCLUSIONS

This chapter proposes to understand the idea of the transborder as a network-territory, that is, as a social space that is shaped by practices. These social practices imply knowledge (competences), materiality (space or infrastructure) and meanings (subjectivity). Although there are disparate meanings and instrumental or emotional logics, repetition has allowed the generation of inertia, ways of entering and leaving the border, lifestyles and a particular use of language. In principle, this territory is configured as a zone of denial of the identity policies of the nation-state, although the belongings are managed strategically by the diverse actors, according to their different subjectivities, some of them reproducing the forms of subjection and others resisting them, and according to the different interpretations and ways of facing the power relations that are experienced in the daily crossing of the border between Mexico and the United States.

It is also observed that one way to develop a sense of national belonging is the over-representation and over-valuation of belonging to a minimal and very local territorial unit such as the neighborhood or the family. So, this network/territory forms an ethnoscape whose main feature in this case comes from the experiences of border crossing of Mexicans to the United States that, fundamentally, expresses the disputes of the identity policies of these nation-states. In this dispute there is also a negative charge towards the Mexican sustained by various techniques of devaluation and stigmatization.

Although this chapter has focused on border crossing, we are interested in recovering Vila's criticism (2001 and 2003) of the romantic idea of the border crosser as an ideal type that arises from the contact between two cultural matrices. Therefore, since the introduction we have insisted that the border dialectic (encounter–disagreement, inclusion–exclusion, differentiation–belonging) generates complex dynamics, that are expressed in the multi-territoriality and ambivalence – "Undo and redo the wall" – which is part of the daily tensions of this space.

But from the counting of border-crossing practices elaborated in this chapter, we point out that the transborder network-territory has a density such that the rebordering processes hardly could weaken. Therefore, the material and symbolic violence of the wall, far from guaranteeing the separation of territories, has opened new avenues in the interaction of border populations.

As Jones (2011) has argued, at the local level various forms of denial of the sovereignty of nation-states are gestated, presenting other forms of appropriation and use of territories, giving rise to spaces and specific landscapes of the border. Most importantly, we are talking about a cross-border culture that tends to reproduce by itself despite the brutality of the wall.

NOTES

1. This idea has been raised by Mael Vizcarra (2017). Her phenomenological research on people who cross by car and on foot through the San Ysidro checkpoint in Tijuana–San Diego, shows us the vitality that overflows the traffic through this crossing, noting that, in front of a wall that has involved the death of thousands of people, we can feel the daily effort of thousands of people to cross and find a life on this and the other side of the border, in addition to those who make their lives as street vendors among the cars that circulate through this port of entry to the United States. So lines of life are opposed to the line of death represented by the wall.
2. The notion of the border as interstitial echoes these ideas, since the interstitial is an abyss that opens between one space–time and another, and has a creative potential due to the implicit emptiness that occurs when crossing territories, materially and symbolically (see Stang, 2018).
3. The motivations they identified are: work, study, family and tourist visits, acquire goods and services, receive services, supply business, provide community support, and transit.
4. From the point of view of competences, we can refer to several works that have been carried out to study the knowledge and dynamics of a transborder territory, with a phenomenological perspective: Vizcarra (2017) and Chávez (2016), or a semiotic interpretation the research done by Ramírez (2019).

REFERENCES

Acosta, César M. (2019), *It feels like a normal life but it's not: Familias transfronterizas por deportación en la frontera Tijuana–San Diego*, PhD diss., Mexico: El Colegio de la Frontera Norte.

Aikin, Olga (2011), *Activismo social trasnacional. Un análisis en torno a los feminicidios en Ciudad Juárez*, Mexico City: El Colegio de la Frontera Norte, Instituto Tecnológico y de Estudios Superiores de Occidente, Universidad Autónoma de Ciudad Juárez.

Alonso, Guillermo (2016), 'De los límites simbólicos a las fronteras como artefactos culturales multidimensionales, cambiantes y transhistóricos', in Guillermo Alonso (ed.), *Fronteras simbólico-culturales, étnicas e internacionales: Los efectos en la vida de las gentes y sus sociedades*, Tijuana: El Colegio de la Frontera Norte, pp. 33–71.

Anguiano-Téllez, María Eugenia (2005), 'Vecindad e interacciones fronterizas en la región Tijuana-San Diego', in Tito Carlos Machado de Oliveira (ed.), *Território sem limites: estudos sobre fronteiras*, Campo Grande: Universidade Federal de Mato Grosso do Sul, pp. 279–305.

Appadurai, Arjun (1996), *Modernity at Large: Cultural Dimensions of Globalization*, Minneapolis: University of Minnesota Press.

Appadurai, Arjun (2004), 'The Capacity to Aspire: Culture and the Terms of Recognition', in Vijayendra Rao and Michael Walton (eds), *Culture and Public Action*, Stanford: Stanford University Press, pp. 59–84.

Ariztía, Tomás (2017), 'La teoría de las prácticas sociales: particularidades, posibilidades y límites', *Cinta moebio. Revista de Epistemología de Ciencias Sociales*, **59**, 221–234.

Beck, Ulrich (1999), *What is Globalization?*, Cambridge: Polity Press.

Borja, Jordi and Manuel Castells (1998), *Local y global: La gestión de las ciudades en la era de la información*, Mexico City: Santillana Ediciones Generales.

Bourdieu, Pierre (2007), *El sentido práctico*, Buenos Aires: Editorial Siglo XXI.

Bringas, Nora L. and Basilio Verduzco (2008), 'La construcción de la frontera norte como destino turístico en un contexto de alertas de seguridad', *Región y Sociedad*, **20**(42), 3–36.

Campos, Amelia and Alberto Hernández (2015), 'Vivir en la frontera: una mirada a las prácticas socioculturales en la región Tijuana-San Diego', in Amalia Campos and Alberto Hernández (eds), *Líneas, límites y colindancias: mirada a las fronteras desde América Latina*, Tijuana: El Colegio de la Frontera Norte, Centro de Investigación y Estudios Superiores en Antropología Social, pp. 143–176.

Chávez, Sergio (2016), *Border Lives. Fronterizos, Transnational Migrants, and Commuters in Tijuana*, New York: Oxford University Press.

Falcón-Orta, Vanessa and Alicia Orta-Falcón (2018), 'The Transborder Identity Formation Process: An Exploratory Grounded Theory Study of Transfronterizo College Students from the San Diego–Tijuana Border Region', *Journal of Transborder Studies*, **4**, 1–27.

Félix, Humberto (2011), *Tijuana La Horrible: Entre la Historia y el Mito*, Tijuana: El Colegio de la Frontera Norte.

Félix, Humberto (2017), *De contrabando y mojado. La frontera imaginada (México–Estados Unidos)*, Mexicali: Universidad Autónoma de Baja California.

Habermas, Jurgen (2000), *La constelación posnacional: Ensayos Políticos*, Barcelona: Paidós Ibérica.

Haesbaert, Rogério (2011), *El mito de la desterritorialización: Del 'fin de los territorios' a la Multiterritorialidad*, Mexico City: Siglo XXI.

Ibarra, José Israel (2019), *La integración social de los migrantes deportados y su reconfiguración familiar en la frontera norte de México*, PhD diss., Mexico: El Colegio de la Frontera Norte.

Iglesias, Norma (2014), 'Tijuana provocadora. Transfronteridad y procesos creativos', in José Manuel Valenzuela Arce (ed.), *Transfronteras: Fronteras del mundo y procesos culturales*, Tijuana: El Colegio de la Frontera Norte, pp. 97–127.

Jones, Reece (2011), 'Spaces of Refusal: Rethinking Sovereign Power and Resistance at the Border', *Annals of the Association of American Geographers*, **3**(102), 685–699.

Martínez, Oscar (1998), *Border People, Life and Society in the U.S.–Mexico Borderlands*, Tucson: University of Arizona Press.

Mezzadra, Sandro and Brett Neilson (2013), *Border as Method, or the Multiplication of Labor*, Durham, NC: Duke University Press.

Morales, María Cristina and Juan Mendoza (2018), 'Seeking the American Dream along the United States–Mexico Border', *Practicing Anthropology*, **3**(40), 31–44.

Noda, Eder and Alfredo Sánchez (2015), 'Ciudadanía: un concepto en construcción. Entre el liberalismo y el comunitarismo', *Revista de humanidades y ciencias sociales 'Inclusiones'*, **2**, 111–129.

Odgers, Olga and Amalia E. Campos (2012), 'Crossing the Border: Mobility as a Resource in the Tijuana/San Diego and Tecún Umán/Tapachula Regions', *Estudios Fronterizos*, **13**(26), 9–32.

Ojeda, Norma (2005), 'Familias transfronterizas y familias transnacionales: Algunas Reflexiones', *Migraciones Internacionales*, **2**(3), 167–174.

Ojeda, Norma (2009), 'Reflexiones acerca de las familias transfronterizas y las familias transnacionales entre México y Estados Unidos', *Frontera Norte*, **21**(42), 7–30.

Orraca-Romano, Pedro Paulo (2019), 'Cross-Border Earnings of Mexican Workers Across the US–Mexico Border', *Journal of Borderlands Studies*, **34**(3), 451–469.

Pries, Ludger (2002), 'La migración transnacional y la perforación de los contenedores de Estados-nación', *Estudios Demográficos y Urbanos*, **51**, 571–597.

Ramírez, Daniel (2019), *Semiótica de la vida commuter: Competencias transfronterizas de interacción en la frontera, el muro o la línea entre Tijuana y San Diego*, master's thesis, Mexico: Centro de Investigaciones y Estudios Superiores en Antropología Social.

Robertson, Roland (2003), 'Glocalización: tiempo-espacio y homogeneidad-heterogeneidad', in Juan Carlos Monedero Fernández-Gala (ed.), *Cansancio del Leviatán: problemas políticos de la mundialización*, Madrid: Trotta, pp. 261–284.

Rocha-Romero, David and Pedro Paulo Orraca-Romano (2018), 'Estudiantes de educación superior transfronterizos: Residir en México y estudiar en Estados Unidos', *Frontera Norte*, **30**(59), 103–128.

Ruiz, Olivia (1998), 'Visiting the Mother Country: Border-crossing as Cultural Practice', in Kathleen Staudt and David Spencer (eds), *The U.S.–Mexico Border: Transcending Divisions, Contesting Identities*, Boulder, CO: Lynne Rienner, pp. 105–120.

Sassen, Saskia (2006), *Territory, Authority, Rights: From Medieval to Global Assemblages*, Princeton: Princeton University Press.

Solís, Marlene (ed.) (2016), *Gender Transitions along Borders. The Northern Borderlands of Mexico and Morocco*, Abingdon, New York: Routledge.

Spencer, David and Kathleen Staudt (eds) (1998), *The U.S.-Mexico Border: Transcending Divisions, Contesting Identities*, Boulder, CO: Lynne Rienner.

Stang, Fernanda (2018), 'Pensar desde los intersticios: Algunas reflexiones sobre los estudios de migración y género a partir de un caso de migración LGTBIQ', in María José Magliano (ed.), *Entre márgenes, intersticios e intersecciones: diálogos posibles y desafíos pendientes entre género y migraciones*, Córdoba: Teseo Press, pp. 147–178.

Vila, Pablo (2001), 'Versión estadounidense de la teoría de frontera: una crítica desde la etnografía', *Papeles de Población*, **7**(30), 11–30.

Vila, Pablo (ed.) (2003), *Ethnography at the Border*, Minneapolis: University of Minnesota Press.

Vizcarra, Mael (2017), *Between Lines: Mobility, Temporality, and Performance at a México–U.S. Border Checkpoint*, PhD diss., Emory University.

PART II

ON THE WAY TO THE US

5. The predatory character of today's economies: a focus on borders and migrations
Saskia Sassen

1. INTRODUCTION

My previous work has often focused on the way a financialized global economy has rendered certain types of large-scale violence more or less invisible. One key example in my work is high finance: a complex formation involving admirable forms of knowledge which increasingly functions in fact as an extractive sector. It is a bit like mining in the sense that once you have extracted what is of interest, there is nothing left except destroyed land and broken mountains.

Here I develop a reflection on the predatory character of modern global capitalism and the consequences it has for migration, borders, human security, and human rights more broadly. These are topics I have long researched and given a central place in my previous works. The effort is in good part to make visible, for example, how low-wage jobs are one key element in much of the "admirable" complex digitalized economy.[1] Immigrants are prominent at both ends of such dual labor markets – they are often both the lower paid workers and the advanced technical workers.

1.1 Free Movement and its Many Versions

Existing governmental policies and international agreements have generally deregulated and freed the movement of capital, goods, and information to extract greater profits. This has been the case in low-wage countries especially. At the same time we have increasingly limited and restricted the movement of migrants and refugees, rendering them vulnerable to greater exploitation enabled by neoliberal economic policies, with high finance a key actor also in these domains. One effect has been a massive expelling of older economies and societies. Many modest level households and enterprises have also been displaced and expelled in the Global North given the development of new types of economies.

A major challenge we confront in today's urban economies is the sharp rise of complex types of knowledge that may have started as admirable innovations but increasingly have also enabled predatory operations.[2] These types of knowledge include algorithmic mathematics, some of the more complex forms of law and accounting, high-level logistics, and more. The complexity of these formations tends to camouflage the predatory character of many of them. Further, such formations are systemic in nature: specifically, they are not produced by a straightforward and highly visible seizure of power, such as land grabs, or the invasions of the First and Second World Wars.

In brief, today's emergent predatory formations are often invisible to the average citizen as well as functioning (to variable extents) beyond the reach of ordinary policy responses. This is in good part because they tend to assemble into novel configurations with greater capacities to access what are, still, mostly separate domains. This type of financialized economy is quite different from the traditional economy most people still adhere to.

2. COMPLEX AND ADMIRABLE FORMATS

Among these new types of formations we find high finance. Easily confused with or seen as an extension of banking, today's high finance is radically different from those familiar, long-standing formats.

My particular focus here is on high finance as a capability, both admirable in its complexity and flexibility, and also functioning as one of the more powerful predatory formations of the current period. My effort here is to make visible how even the most sophisticated financial instruments require certain elementary and brutal steps, often resulting in highly degraded socio-economic and environmental outcomes.

One example is that of the sub-prime mortgage developed in the early 2000s: this was a brilliant innovation, quite different from the original 1970s concept of mortgages in that it was centered on an extractive mode. Its aim was not to enable access to housing, but to use the actual physical goods (houses, buildings) to develop asset-backed securities for the financial system itself. The usual way of understanding finance is through a particular set of high-end components, including some of the most advanced uses of digital technologies, the mathematics of physics rather than the more familiar math of standard economics, and other powerful instruments. And it includes some of the best minds in our current period.

Prefiguring today's globalization studies, a major area of research known as "the new international division of labor theory" rose to attention in the 1970s and 1980s. Key elements were the spread of foreign direct investment in developing countries, the shift in manufacturing from North to South, the growth of export processing zones, and the increasing international fragmentation and decentralization of production. The penetration of foreign capital into Third World countries, often in the form of commercial agriculture, disrupted local communities and induced internal migration from rural areas to cities, producing a cheap labor force – disproportionately young women – that could be exploited in the new export processing zones. Thus, since the 1980s these type of studies have been fundamental to explain the asymmetries in the US–Mexico border region, and often beyond, including Central America and other border regions in the world.

I take these observations a crucial step further by linking (a) this expansion of global investment with (b) the pushing out of local communities as (c) a factor leading to the upsurge in international migration. I argue that these two processes, traditionally studied as separate phenomena, or at best as connected at their margins, are in fact mutually constitutive as globalization unfolds. Out of this comes the rise of a transnational space within which the circulation of workers can be regarded as one of several flows, including capital, goods, services, and information.

Soaring income inequality and unemployment, expanding populations of the displaced and imprisoned, accelerating destruction of land and water bodies, these and more have led me to argue that we need added elements besides the familiar poverty and injustice.[3] Today's socio-economic and environmental dislocations cannot be fully understood in these usual terms.

This hard-headed critique updates our understanding of economics for the twenty-first century, exposing a system with devastating consequences even for those who think they are not vulnerable. The current condition includes various types of expulsions – expulsions from professional livelihood, from living space, even from the very biosphere that makes life possible. From finance to mining, the complex types of knowledge and technology we have come to admire are used too often in ways that produce elementary brutalities. These have evolved into predatory formations – assemblages of knowledge, interests, and outcomes that go beyond a firm's or an individual's or a government's project.

Diverse situations in the US–Mexico–Central American region illuminate the systemic logic of these expulsions. The sophisticated knowledge that created today's financial "instruments" is paralleled by the engineering expertise that enables exploitation of the environment, and by the legal expertise that allows the world's have-nations to acquire vast stretches of territory from the have-nots.

In the book *Expulsions* (Sassen 2014) I sought to lay bare the extent to which the sheer complexity of the global economy makes it hard to capture who are the major actors. I traced the lines of responsibility for the displacements, evictions, and eradications it produces. One clear finding I made was that this complexity means, for instance, that the members of Congress have a hard time following the presentations of the financiers and other authorities in charge of regulating complex economic sectors.[4] The legislators give up at some point and basically surrender to the analysis of the experts – that is, the major financiers! This is not the way to handle an inquiry into high finance. Further, under such conditions it becomes equally hard for those who benefit from the system to feel responsible for its depredations.

Migrations, wars, economic crashes, ecological crises, and other phenomena of massive scale have become usual in recent years, especially in certain areas of the world. In this regard, Central America is generally considered one of the most insecure regions in the world. And while they concern us because of their extensiveness and recurrence, we tend to understand them as isolated effects. However, these are only different aspects of the same problem: the "predatory formations" of contemporary capitalism that generate unprecedented levels of inequality.

What is still generally understood in the language of more inequality, more poverty, more imprisonment, more environmental destruction, and so on, is insufficient to mark the proliferation of extreme versions of these well-known conditions.[5] We are seeing the making of a context where many people end up being expelled from the economy and expelled from access to clean water. The key element shaping the expulsions that concern me here is the notion of a "systemic edge" – an edge that exists inside a country, a system, a city. Such systemic edges are proliferating across diverse domains.

Further, I conceive of these systemic edges as the point in sometimes long trajectories when condition "x" becomes invisible, no matter how material it might be, we cannot "see it" conceptually speaking. Let me illustrate briefly with a familiar case: at some point the long-term unemployed fall off the standard categories for measuring unemployment; that is, they become statistically invisible. Another example is our standard measure for economic growth, gross domestic product (GPD) per capita: increasingly the space it measures leaves out significant numbers of people, places, and activities. Thus, it measures a shrunken economic space, and in so doing can come up with some positive growth measure, even as significant numbers of people, small businesses, and places have been expelled from "the" economy. I think of this as a kind of economic "cleansing."

The specific, tightest meaning I develop in the book *Expulsions* is that we entered a new phase of advanced capitalism beginning already, albeit slowly, in the 1980s. What marked this emergent condition was the reinventing of mechanisms for primitive accumulation. In contrast to earlier modes of primitive accumulation, today's is a form of primitive accumulation executed through complex operations and much specialized innovation – ranging from the logistics of outsourcing to the algorithms of finance. And this is a modus operandi that has led to an increase in the concentration of wealth. It has little to do with the preceding period – after the Second World War and up to the 1970s – when the modest middle classes and the working classes gained recognition and saw their wages rise.[6]

3.   ON EXTRACTIVE CAPABILITIES

This is correct as far as it goes, but it is, I argue, an incomplete representation of the domain. We can also link finance with extreme degradation, as has been done, for instance, by corporations that outsource manual work because it lowers production costs. There is a tendency to de-link abusive practices in the actual workplace from the often admirable features of the final product. In the case of the financial scholarship the trend is to emphasize digital capabilities and profits, and to overlook the diverse work functions that are involved. There is rarely, if ever, inclusion of all the kinds of low-paid jobs which directly and indirectly also enable the financial sector. It is simply not considered as part of the general scholarship about finance nor is finance usually linked to degraded manual labor. Finance is also a contrast with many advanced economic sectors where we can make such links easily, notably the degraded and unhealthy moments in the actual production of electronic components.

To incorporate physical degradation into the case of the financial sector requires expanding the understanding of finance. That is to say, I consider "high finance" as a far more expansive domain than is usually done. Seeing finance through the lens of such an expanded domain allows us to get at a far more inclusive assemblage of elements than is usual in studies of finance: it is not only the work of developing complex instruments, it is also the work of its high-end as well as low-wage workers. Further, such an expanded assemblage of elements can include some very simple or familiar components rarely associated with high finance. Constructing such an expanded domain for finance makes visible that even extremely complex and sophisticated financial instruments can actually include some very elementary and brutal steps in the production chain as well as highly degraded socio-economic conditions we never associate with high finance.[7]

In brief, the aim is to capture a more encompassing operational field for finance than is usually deployed. Yes, finance is an assemblage of algorithmic math and advanced technologies. But it needs grist for its mill and often does so by incorporating very modest elements at the other extreme of the knowledge and technical vector. Finance is an abstract domain that depends on massive material capabilities and on rarely recognized workers – from cleaners and miners to truckers. Most major migrations of the last two centuries, and often even earlier, can be shown to start at some point: they have beginnings generated by a mix of conditions. Poverty is not enough of an explanation, or we should be seeing billions of migrants across the world. This suggests that there is a larger context within which migration flows emerge.[8] And it is this larger context that interests me. I will focus on three types of flows, each very different from the other. Yet they share one major factor: a massive loss of habitat generated by either the destructions produced by war or the destructions produced by particular modes of so-called "economic development."

This multi-decade history of destructions of rural economies and expulsions dressed in the clothing of "modernization and development" has reached extreme levels today: vast stretches of land and water bodies are now dead due to mining, plantations, and water extraction by the likes of Nestlé. At least some of today's localized wars and conflicts in Africa arise out of such destruction and loss of habitat; climate change further reduces livable ground. And access to Europe is no longer what it used to be. This mix of conditions – wars, dead land, and expulsions of smallholders from their modest economies in the name of "development" – has produced a vast loss of life options for a growing number of people in more and more communities. We see this in areas as diverse as Africa, Central America, and parts of Asia, notably India and Myanmar.[9]

4. THE EXAMPLE OF UNACCOMPANIED MINORS FROM CENTRAL AMERICA TO THE US

European and US "development" practices over several decades, as well as their shaping influence on international institutions, such as the International Monetary Fund (IMF) and the World Bank, are key factors in the analysis of such context. Generally, IMF debt management policies from the 1980s onwards can be shown to have worsened the situation for the unemployed and poor. Much research on poor countries documents the link between hyper-indebted governments and cuts in social programs. These tend to affect particularly women and children through reduced education and health care.

The above is part of a larger history in the making. In my reading it includes as one key element a *repositioning* of much of Africa and major parts of Latin America and Asia in a new massively restructured global economy. Weakened governments and the destruction of traditional economies have launched a new phase of extraction by powerful states and firms and a new phase of survival economies by the impoverished middle classes and the long-term poor.

At its most extreme this meant the immiseration of growing numbers of local people who ceased being of value as workers and consumers. What mattered was access to natural resources, rather than people as workers and consumers. But it also meant that traditional petty bourgeoisies ceased being of value. Such repositioning and destructions have contributed to the current duality marked by the rise of a new class of highly educated professionals and an impoverishment of rural people who have lost their land and wind up in urban slums.

One brutal way of putting it is to say that the natural resources of much of Africa and good parts of Latin America and Asia have long counted more for extractive sectors than the local people counted as consumers and as workers. The lack of both genuine development and distributed economic growth *is* a mode of growth that benefited elites and foreign investors. It was basically extractive and thereby used a country's people, but did not bring genuine development to their lives. One key legacy of such extractive sectors is a shrunken habitat for more and more of these countries' peoples and their local economies.

With this background in mind, I now turn to the types of migrations that are to variable extents an outcome of such destructive modes of economic "development." But with one sharp difference: the vast extractions and destructions of the past many decades have produced a massive loss of habitat. And this, in turn, has made the expulsions of rural people more immediate and more brutal. These past restructurings have created a whole new extreme struggle for land and resources. And the indigenous populations are often the first victims.

New migrations are often far smaller than ongoing older migrations. But catching them at the beginning offers a window into larger dynamics that catapult people into migrating. Emergent migrations have long been of interest to me: this is the migrant as indicator of a history in the making. In contrast, once a flow is marked by chain migration, it takes far less to explain that flow. My focus is mostly on that larger context within which a new flow takes off. Each of these flows is easily seen as part of older ongoing flows. My focus is on specific factors in each of these new flows that lead me to argue that there is something in play that is not usually recognized. One of these is the sharp increase in 2014 of the migration to the US of unaccompanied minors from Central America, specifically, from Honduras, Salvador, and Guatemala. Central America is one of the key regions where the flight of unaccompanied minors rose sharply a few years ago. "Urban violence" has become the leading explanation among those studying this escape of minors from the cities and the decision to try getting to the US, which means crossing the whole of Mexico.

Yet there is more to be brought into the picture. In my reading, we need to trace this violence back to the destruction of smallholder rural economies. This is one key, overlooked factor at the origins of the disastrous outcomes. Powerful families with vast lands know how to extract wealth from land. They are key actors in pushing out smallholders to develop large-scale commercial plantations, mining, water grabs, and more. Private armies help execute the project of expelling the smallholders, and take care of threatening or even killing human rights activists fighting for the rights of smallholders. Some smallholders have been killed by private armies. Others have escaped to poorer quality lands of little interest to the big land-owners. Many of these expelled families eventually wound up in the cities of Central America. Cities are increasingly the only option for those expelled from their land. But the cities lack jobs and options for displaced rural families. The drug trade is one of the few, easily accessible economies in these cities. It has often been the only one where expelled rural smallholders can get some income in the cities. One outcome is that many of the displaced rural workers have been killed in the drug battles in Central America's cities.

Out of this disastrous mix of conditions comes the desperate hope of getting to the US. While Central America has long been an emigration region, for both political and economic reasons, this flow of unaccompanied children is new. They are driven by extreme fear because of urban violence that has left growing numbers of minors without adult caretakers. They are on their own.

The US Customs and Border Protection data show that a first major flow of about 63,000 unaccompanied minors, most from Central America, crossed the southern US border between October 1, 2013 and July 31, 2014. This is nearly twice the number of child migrants who came during the same period the previous year. The estimate is that by the end of 2014, up to 90,000 unaccompanied children had crossed the border into the US; Prior to 2012, more than 75 percent of unaccompanied children were from Mexico. By 2015, only 28 percent were from Mexico, and the rest from Guatemala, El Salvador and Honduras.[10]

What we do not know is how many of these minors never made it. We only know the numbers for those who arrived in the US, driven by fear. Being forced off their land by private armies marks the beginning of harsh high-risk lives in these cities rendered violent by the drug trade and the absence of reasonable economies.

I examine a case of extreme migration flows that have much to do, even if unrecognized, with our "modernizing" development modes and their massive expulsions of smallholders. One is the flight of unaccompanied minors from Central America to the US that took off in 2014. Important in my analysis is the lack of recognition in law of this third kind of migrant, one evicted from her land to make room for a mine or a plantation. This migrant fits neither of the two established subjects in law: the refugee and the immigrant. This third subject is invisible to the eye of the law as she is a refugee of what is registered as positive: certain modes of "economic development." Nor is there law that recognizes the fact that much "economic development" and wealth is based on land grabs from rural smallholders, destruction of land and water bodies by mining and plantations, and more. Migrants who lose their land or have their water supplies poisoned by nearby mines *are* refugees of such modes of economic development. There should be law that recognizes them as such. But for now the basic interpretation is that those development modes are good for a country. What I seek to present here are the social and economic conditions that render this third subject invisible to existing law. And my hope is that there are legal scholars who might be interested in making this migrant subject visible in law.

5. CONCLUSION

By emphasizing the interplay between the global and the local, we can understand new forms and conditions such as global cities, transnational communities, and commodity chains that are increasingly common. Such interplay offers interpretive and analytic tools to understand the complex ideas of global interdependence in the world's borders and the proliferation of expulsions.

There are other such much admired and respected domains represented by complex forms of knowledge, which can also be shown to function in a far more expansive operational space than is usually mentioned. Thus many an admired product includes spaces of production marked by extreme degradation – elements typically left out of the description of the final product. We need to re-position such domains in ways that allow us to capture the full operational spaces through which they are constituted. The tendency is to go in the opposite direction: separate the most complex knowledge functions from other moments that might contain physical degradation of workers.

We need to recover the full geographies of our leading contemporary economic sectors. This involves examining a range of advanced sectors through this type of framing: that is, an expanded frame that includes a far broader operational field. This becomes an angle for observation that includes the less impressive and less admirable tasks and needs of what we mostly see as highly admirable and innovative systems.

Such an expanded recognition of the full array of workers and tasks enabling production could lead to a broader understanding of how even the most complex sectors of our economies still need a very broad range of workers. This can bring recognition of sectors and workers who are increasingly invisible in our current world where the focus is on outcomes much more so than the tasks and the people involved in producing.

The flows I have described are mostly refugee flows even if not formally recognized by the international system. They are to be distinguished from the almost 300 million regular immigrants in the world today, who are mostly modest middle class and, increasingly, high-level professionals functioning in the global economy. Today's immigrants are not the poorest in their countries of origin. Nor are they generated by the extreme push factors feeding the two flows described here. And these refugees, in turn, are also not usually the poorest in their countries, even if leaving their home countries leaves them without any resources; many have advanced educations and started out with resources.

These new refugees are one component of a larger population of displaced people whose numbers are approaching 80 million. They stand out by their sudden surging numbers and by the extreme conditions in the areas where they originate. Extreme violence and extreme destruction of local economies are two key factors explaining this surge. Climate change is likely to have extreme effects in some of these regions due to what we might describe as development malpractice – with its disastrous consequences for local economies and societies in the Global South. It all amounts to a massive loss of habitat, and migration will be one mode of survival.

NOTES

1. See, for example, Albrow et al. (2008); Amin (1970); and Bonilla et al. (1998).
2. See, for example, Braverman (1974); Buechler (2014); Desmond (2016).
3. See, for example, Nashashibi (2007); Ribas-Mateos (2015).
4. See, for example, Sassen (2013, 2018). See also Buechler (2014).
5. See the classic Braverman (1974). See also Sassen (2018).
6. See, for instance, Gutman (2016). See also Gill (2015); Knorr Cetina and Preda (2012); and Parnreiter (2015).
7. See also this type of experimenting, for instance, in Rose et al. (2014). See also, on a very different vector Sassen (2015); Sklair (2017).
8. See, for instance, Swiaczny and Hillmann (2017); US Customs and Border Protection (2016).
9. See Sassen (2016).
10. See Swiaczny and Hillmann (2017); US Customs and Border Protection (2016).

BIBLIOGRAPHY

Albrow, Martin, Helmut Anheier, Marlies Glasius, and Mary Kaldor. 2008. *Global Civil Society 2007/8: Communicative Power and Democracy*. Thousand Oaks, CA: Sage.
Amin, Samir. 1970. *L'Accumulation a l'échellemondiale*. Paris: Anthropos.
Bonilla, Frank, Edwin Melendez, Rebecca Morales, and María de los Angeles Torres. 1998. *Borderless Borders*. Philadelphia, PA: Temple University Press.
Braverman, Harry. 1974. *Labor and Monopoly Capital: The Degradation of Work in the Twentieth Century*. New York: Monthly Review Press.
Buechler, Simone Judith. 2014. *Labor in a Globalizing City: Economic Restructuring in São Paulo, Brazil*. Bern, Switzerland: Springer.
Desmond, Matthew. 2016. *Evicted: Property and Profit in the American City*. New York: Crown.
Gill, Stephen, ed. 2015. *Critical Perspectives on the Crisis of Global Governance: Reimagining the Future*. London: Palgrave Macmillan.
Gutman, Margarita. 2016. "The Fight for the Future." In *The Futures We Want: Global Sociology and the Struggle for a Better World*. Selected Writings from the WebForum, edited by Markus S. Schulz. Germany and USA: Initiative for Transnational Futures, International Sociological Association, 228–229.
Kaldor, Mary, and Saskia Sassen. 2020. *Cities at War*. New York: Columbia University Press.

Knorr Cetina, Karin, and Alex Preda, eds. 2012. *The Oxford Handbook of the Sociology of Finance*. Oxford, UK: Oxford University Press.

Nashashibi, Rami. 2007. "Ghetto Cosmopolitanism: Making Theory at the Margins." In *Deciphering the Global: Its Scales, Spaces and Subjects*, edited by Saskia Sassen. New York: Routledge, 243–264.

Parnreiter, Christof. 2015. "Las Ciudades Latinoamericanas en la Economía Mundial: La Geografía de Centralidad Económica y sus Transformaciones Recientes." *Economía UNAM* 12(35): 3–22.

Portes, Alejandro. 2016. "International Migration and National Development: From Orthodox Equilibrium to Transnationalism." *Sociology of Development* (2): 73–92.

Ribas-Mateos, Natalia. 2015. *Border Shifts: New Mobilities in Europe and Beyond*. New York: Palgrave Macmillan.

Robinson, William I. 2014. *Global Capitalism and the Crisis of Humanity*. New York: Cambridge University Press.

Rose, Gillian, Monica Degen, and Clare Melhuish. 2014. "Networks, Interfaces, and Computer-Generated Images: Learning from Digital Visualizations of Urban Redevelopment Projects." *Environment and Planning D: Society and Space* 32(3): 386–403.

Sassen, Saskia. 2013. "Global Finance and Its Institutional Spaces." In *The Oxford Handbook of the Sociology of Finance*, edited by K. Knorr Cetina and A. Preda. Oxford, UK: Oxford University Press, 13–32.

Sassen, Saskia. 2014. *Expulsions: Brutality and Complexity in the Global Economy*. Cambridge, MA: Harvard University Press.

Sassen, Saskia. 2015. "Digitization and Work: Potentials and Challenges in Low-Wage Labor Markets." Position Paper, New York, Open Society Foundations.

Sassen, Saskia. 2016. "A Massive Loss of Habitat: New Drivers for Migration." *Sociology of Development* 2(2): 204–233.

Sassen, Saskia. 2018. *Cities in a World Economy*. 5th ed. Thousand Oaks, CA: Sage.

Sklair, Leslie. 2017. *The Icon Project: Architecture, Cities and Capitalist Globalization*. New York: Oxford University Press.

Swiaczny, Frank, and Felicitas Hillmann. 2017. "Migration und Flucht im Globalen Süden" ("Migration and Flight in the Global South"). *Geographische Rundschau* 3: 46–50.

US Customs and Border Protection. 2016. *Southwest Family Unit Subject and Unaccompanied Alien Children Apprehensions Fiscal Year 2016*. Washington, DC: US Department of Homeland Security.

6. New security: threat landscape and the emerging market for force

Blanca Camps-Febrer and John Andrew Carter, Jr.

1. INTRODUCTION

There is a long history of private endeavors in policing and military affairs (Spitzer and Scull 1977; Spitzer 1993; Abrahamsen and Leander 2016). The East India Company achieved its highest global influence in 1778, amassing more than 67,000 mercenaries that imposed the company's law and order throughout the vast Asian territories (Bryant 2008). So-called "company towns" popped up around the United States in the aftermath of its civil war due to the commercial efforts involved in the restoration of public and private infrastructure. Profiting from the vulnerability and lack of formal protections amid the uncertain security landscape, private militias and vigilantes were hired to protect labor forces and industrial facilities. The London Metropolitan Police was established in 1829, designed in the likeness of a model put forth by the Thames River Police, initially funded by maritime merchants to protect their commercial fleets, cargo and sailors to insure and defend their transactions (Spitzer 1993). In 1933, a law was passed in French colonial Morocco promoting and formalizing the use of private police contractors by French settlers to protect their land and private property against expropriation or seizure by bandits or rebellious natives (Aït-Taleb 2014).

The central position of the nation-state in the West during the twentieth century seems to have clouded the historical memory of a stuttering monopoly of violence by the state. Indeed, some authors argue that the monopoly of violence was not established by the modern state, not even in the West, but rather through an advanced phase of capitalism where the state acquired growing responsibilities and roles amid an expanse of private property (Spitzer 1993; Weiss 2007). In other terms, the "bureaucratic–democratic" state, as Mann acknowledges, gained in infrastructural power[1] as military and political powers merged through "formally monopoliz[ing] the means of military violence" (Mann 1993, 44). These configurations and their subsequent utility comprise the foundations of the modern security paradigm, granting further responsibility and notions of jurisdictional control to the state, its security forces, and its network of contractors over threats within its territory.

At the international level, the political understanding of the world has been short sightedly rooted in the supremacy of the state, especially in terms of security. From the First World War until the end of the Cold War, the discipline of International Relations (IR) has supported this state-centric view. Most scholars within their centers of intellectual production (with close financial and political ties to state actors and institutions) were naturally concerned with pressing issues of interstate war and diplomacy, positioning the state as the central and sole actor with authority to utilize and deploy the use of force against perceived threats to its populace or its assets.

However, after the onset of the US war in Afghanistan (2001–) and Iraq (2003–), the rise of third-party, private sector involvement by security contractors has produced an emerging

111

market with increasingly specialized product and service offerings, probably unlike that of any other period in history. Private Security Contractors (PSCs)[2] and "commercial security" forces (Chisholm 2016) have also increasingly penetrated civil spaces, dispatched to secure private spheres within the boundaries of maintaining law and order in "peaceful" contexts. This is commonly realized through public procurement calls in which a project seeks a private contractor to provide services or assist in state-sponsored projects, such as a call for private guards to supplement or assist public forces in the securitization of public infrastructure, such as in the management of prison facilities as well as borders and points of entry.

Security has traditionally been a primary function of the social contract between citizens and allocated within the central authority of the state. But with an evolving threat landscape, how does the provision of increasingly privatized security differ from that of older historical periods? What does the increased utility of PSCs mean for the philosophical and moral foundations of the modern nation-state? And, more importantly, what impact does its internationalized private security activity have on the ordinary lives of people around the world?

To approach these questions, traditional international relations scholars seem preoccupied in their attempt to adjust their assumptions of identity politics into state-centric analyses. Decolonized proposals, which decenter IR through multidisciplinary paradigms, seem to provide better tools for understanding.[3] Outside mainstream IR, cross-sectoral approaches by anthropologists, sociologists, historians, criminologists, and even activists – already veterans in certain issues – are barely surfacing as principal and legitimate IR research agendas on security.[4]

The chapter that follows deals with the apparent paradox of the current economic landscape of neoliberal globalism and a consequent outsourcing and privatization of security amid the reinforcement of nation-states and of social control. This, as the authors will show, amounts to an issue of accountability and proper governance, pointing to a wave of militarization of critical infrastructure regarding capacities to provide essential security services.

First, the chapter investigates the evolving landscape of global threats that international institutions and nation-states identify as primary in the construction of current security affairs. In the authors' understanding, these threats are intersubjectively produced through political and institutional discourse and practice; and are also embedded in a particularly economic and political order.

Second, the authors will identify the relationship of these threats with their current proposed solutions, specifically through the specialized market of private security provision within the security governance paradigm.

Third, the chapter attempts to point in the direction of further research into the consequences that this imperfect security governance has for the current political and economic order and, ultimately, for the moral and philosophical foundations of human life.

2. THREAT LANDSCAPE, SOCIAL PERCEPTIONS, AND THE TRINITY OF INSECURITY

Do threats define desired security apparatuses, or is a specific model of security rather constraining to the kind of threats societies deem important? How do societies/communities collectively acknowledge or perceive certain threats and exclude others? In the field of IR, constructivists and critical scholars have long engaged with the ideational structure of the world and its actors (Tickner 1988, 1997; Wendt 1992, 1999; Katzenstein 1996; Finnemore and Sikkink 1998; Acharya 2004). Scholars have busied themselves with understanding the methods by which states or state actors perceive and operate in IR, providing explanations for the timing, context, and communication of threats to a state security agenda.

There is a clear relation between asking why "500 British nuclear weapons are less threatening to the United States than five North Korean nuclear weapons" (Wendt 1995, 73); and from an anthropological perspective, arguing that around the globe, "the relationship between fear and danger is starkly disproportionate" (Comaroff and Comaroff 2016, 6). For instance, traditionally in South Africa, white populations perceived risk over their own life as much higher than those of poor black populations in cities such as Cape Town, despite the fact that in 2013 the homicide ratio was actually 0 to 262 (Comaroff and Comaroff 2016, 42).

Even in the context of armed conflict, war is a social experience. "Violent experiences and traumatic events do not shape social action by themselves but require specific cultural coding in order to do so" (Malesevic and Olsson 2018, 725). This cultural coding comes in the form of narratives, understood as discourses and social practices, whereas some are globally and others are locally produced.

However, national security continues to persist among decision-makers as the main framework for identifying threats and implementing protective (and often extra-judicial) measures against them. Threats occasionally become the authorship of non-state groups such as terrorist organizations, or narco- and human-trafficking cartels, which constitute some of the main concerns of and threats to contemporary borders. In addition, threats can come in non-human form, such as that of the increasing escalation of the climate crisis and global warming (although understood as a consequence of human behavior). However, the apparent object of security has not changed: that which has to be protected from threats at the local, regional, and international level continues to be the same – a certain state order, as expressed through sovereignty and the social contract under which citizens live.

As the nature of threats change, the actors that define and promote certain risks and threat assessments remain the same. From their positions, security scholarship is promoted by elite think tanks, academia and policy-makers, who base(d) their ideas of national security on specific outlooks of the world[5] and the means by which they intend to protect it.

In 1998 Buzan, Wæver and de Wilde proposed a constructivist framework for analyzing security in their now-classic work *Security: A New Framework for Analysis*, which came to be known as the theory of securitization. Their analysis examines how the narrative is framed and which actors it comes from. They understood that threats are based on an intersubjective and performative nature. It is the collective narrative that determines how these perceived threats will be inserted in a political agenda and by which instruments they will be addressed, even if through extra-constitutional or extra-judicial means.

Instrumental or functionalist analyses of securitization speech bring the risk of selectively falling into decontextualized meta-narratives (Wilkinson 2007, 2011). Critical theory helps us navigate the contextual nature of these narratives. In this sense, the "securitizing actors" could be instrumentalizing the narrative of a particular threat, and, as such, their agency would be paramount. Alternatively, their position in the political and economic structure could be the explanatory factor in the formulation of the threats. In any case, the agency–structure debate remains open, and, as such, a functionalist approach would ignore the complexity of the issue. Instead, the focus is placed on the constitutive nature of discursive and ordinary practices as contextualized practices of security.

2.1 The Trinity of Threats

A common and underlying global discourse has become salient in the narrative of global threats. It is inscribed in the everyday practices of border security regimes (Côté-Boucher, Infantino, and Salter 2014) and evident in the militarization of police and policization of the military (Kraska 2007; Resteigne and Manigart 2019). This global discourse is articulated through three axes that Berda calls the "Trinity of Threats" (Berda 2013).

Migrations and human mobility are as old as human nature. Current mobilities, however, are explained within the context of a specific political and economic order. Migration is currently transposed under the narrative that it presents a direct threat to national, cultural, and religious identities and associated values; but, also, as a threat to prosperity and wealth. In this context, migration is a security as well as a civilizational threat that transcends social and economic structures within the state's jurisdiction (Persaud 2004). Thus, borders become increasingly militarized through the strengthening of vetting processes and are equipped with modern technologies to better facilitate their fortification to address these perceived threats to the wellbeing of the state (Akkerman 2016; Ruiz Benedicto and Brunet 2018). This, in turn, renders mobility as a scarce resource due to heightened restrictions or enhanced screening, that is arguably reserved for and favorable to the privileged (Shamir 2005).

The tensions that arise from human rights regimes and sovereign territoriality are especially acute when confronting discursive narratives with border practices. Nevertheless, the narratives of threat are not an *ad hoc* construction, but rather emerge "entangled in broader narratives on mobility, security, sovereignty, and the regime boundaries" (Weinblum 2017, 115). Having said that, migrants do not rid their suspicions when they cross the border, but rather, carry them – allowing these suspicions to linger and ferment throughout their social and personal life on the other side. Where enhanced border patrol could produce sentiments of safety and wellbeing as being in place to protect "those on the inside," it could simultaneously have the opposite effect, producing feelings of insecurity or vulnerability due to the visibility and necessity of armed security personnel and apparatuses.

Following migrations, the second grand threat is entangled in the first narrative of "suspected mobilities." Terrorism,[6] and, specifically, jihadist, or radical terrorism emerged as global enemy number one after the Cold War. In 2006, Buzan asked himself if terrorism would be able to become the explanatory force behind world politics after the fall of the Berlin Wall (Buzan 2006). Even though he rejected the idea, terrorism had justified open-ended global war and continues to reinforce authoritarian measures under the banner of the war on terror, providing the necessary justification for an invasion of privacy and the limitation of freedoms for the sake of protection and security (Bigo 2005, 2008). The terrorist threat, moreover, has been the driving force for enhanced measures of surveillance and, thus, has permitted the extended use of biopolitics by and within an "included" citizen group, permitting further control and exclusion of those deemed suspicious to its wellbeing.

Third, as not all migrants can be regarded as potential terrorists, they can still be regarded as prospective criminals or "crimmigrants" (Aas 2011). This is embedded in the third perceived threat identified by states: crime. Law and order are a pornographic spectacle – produced "for the specific purpose of being seen ... to fight crime and assorted urban disorders [that] must be methodically orchestrated, exaggerated, dramatized, even *ritualized*" (Wacquant 2009, xii). Law in the colony mean(t)(s) violence, according to the court, is a weapon of the colonial mission. Beyond the colony, law transforms into a weapon that can be deployed against the weak, against minorities and against workers due to its complexities and its presumed financial burden. Petty crime and international criminal organizations – as well as irregular migrant networks – are united in a logic of security that legitimizes the use of force:

> Preventing cross-border crime (i.e. terrorism, human trafficking, drug smuggling and illicit arms traffic) has been, at least on the discursive level of policy formation, the main driving force and justification for systems such as the Schengen Information System and Eurosur. (Aas 2011)

The conflation of this "Trinity of Threats" (Berda 2013),[7] reinforces the importance of racial structures of the current political–economic system, as the only potential authors of these threats, or at least those that are explicitly identified, are the racialized[8] bodies and the excluded, those who represent the exploited and the subjugated. Migrants and racialized people are thus regularly treated as a threat, conflated with increased perceptions of risks of terrorist or criminal behavior, not as a consequence of global political and economic decisions, nor as a historical behavior of all species – and are subjected to necropolitical technologies (Mbembe 2003).

2.2   What is New about These Threats?

The way the modern threat landscape is narrated is considered to have blurred the internal–external divide. Threats can as easily come from inside the borders as they can from outside. Thus, security seems to merit a two-sided or transnational approach that cannot differentiate internal from external measures (Eriksson and Rhinard 2009; Bigo 2005). The terrorist inside is not treated as a criminal but rather as an enemy combatant from the outside that has infiltrated the inside, and therefore, their punishment by extra-judicial measures or even death by sentence of the state[9] is justified. Consequently, the logics of war become pervasive on and off the battlefield (Kraska 2007; Grassiani 2017). Moreover, citizens that help irregular migrants are also criminalized, as the territorial spaces of sovereignty must be preserved not only at the border, but through social control and surveillance.[10]

In this sense, what is new about the innovative security technologies that are deployed as preventative tools against these threats? Militarized and violent experiences have been ordinary occurrences for colonial and racialized bodies for centuries (Rigouste 2007; Gržinić and Tatlić 2014; Howell and Richter-Montpetit 2019). Rather, the novelty resides in its spatial locations, its pervasiveness, and its uncontested nature within liberal states (Eriksson and Rhinard 2009). Following Shamir's rationale on mobility regimes in globalization, the security practices that these narratives claim cannot be explained as exceptions, but rather as mechanisms that ensure a specific type of globalization. Security and risk-management practices are highly specialized, and therefore globalized and exported, while most people become enclosed and immobilized within their secured spaces.

Second, the depoliticization of those threats becomes much more novel to understanding of current meta-narratives of threat identification. The political goals of terror attacks are hardly discussed (Baker-Beall 2009) or dismissed as irrational and savage (Mamdani 2004). According to securitization theory, issues of social relevance could be treated as a non-political, as political, or as security issues. Security issues ensure prominence and urgency in the agenda, and the exceptional and executive measures to tackle them are justified and are often permitted without question due to the extreme perceptions, potential externalities and time sensitivity regarding their risk. The excessive securitization of certain issues endangers proper debates and discussions of questions of significant social importance. At the state level, this means a lack of parliamentary debate, expedited measures and the militarization of policies, as is the case in the management of migrations (Huysmans 2006). At the global level, for instance within the UN, this could mean that an issue can be treated by the Security Council instead of the General Assembly, whereas its debate is restricted to fewer voices and to an underrepresentation of related concerns (Oels 2012).

3. SECURITY GOVERNANCE: TECHNICAL MANAGEMENT OF THREATS

Depoliticization opens the door to technical solutions. In line with the narrative of the managerial account of the neoliberal world (Ong 2006), the concept of security governance entails a technical and market-based idea of politics and public procedures. It is as such that "depoliticized" threats and the narrative entanglement of crime, migration and terrorism further reinforce the "conceptual blueprint for the organization of global risk-management strategies" (Shamir 2005, 197) within "a new (postmodern) era of pluralized security arrangements" (White 2010, 10).

This trend of business-like management of public affairs can be traced alongside the expansion of neoliberalism in the 1970s. It transfers the processes and mechanisms of corporate governance to public governance, where the state is recast with "the introduction of market standards as a guideline and a measure for bureaucratic efficiency" (McLean and McMillan 2009). Whereas the state sets the regulative and governance parameters in which the private sector operates, the state evolves and adapts according to private sector innovation in approaches to bureaucratic and administrative processes. However, a key difference is that the survival of the private sector is contingent on the degree to which it is innovative, agile, and effectively governed.

This security governance paradigm works to affect the state and its reliance on privatization and outsourcing for allegedly cost-effective purposes. Private businesses are confronted with *efficient and objective* solutions to threats. Companies, much like states, include private security and risk-management models in order to be competitive and efficient, but differ in the sense that they have enhanced capacity or are more specialized as compared to the in-house capabilities of the state.

As Buzatu and Buckland (2015) point out, there is both an increase in outsourcing state security in all domains – from intelligence operations to prison facilities – and an overall increase in the number and type of clients seeking security services – from international to humanitarian organizations, while the primary clients of private security contractors are still state (or publicly funded) agencies,[11] but also transnational corporations investing in conflict-ridden or occupied zones, such as post-2003 Iraq (Raphael 2016). These two phenomena, the increased outsourcing of state functions and increasing number of clients, constitute a continuum between border security and gated communities (Shamir 2005), between the managerial narrative of security at the state level and the pervasive nature of security technologies in private spaces. They all feed from and are fueled by the logic of "security fetishism" (Neocleous 2007), which is based on an economic model where those with more resources are able to obtain higher levels of security.

Paired with the transformation and expansion of threat identification at the national and international level, outside the scope of state governments, the outsourcing of military and security tasks has consequently led to the increased employment of private sector specialists to supply conventional military and security efforts on behalf of a wide variety of actors, permeating the state monopoly on the use of force, challenging the role of the state as the sole security actor and directly influencing security policy. This is exemplified by the gradual increase in the outsourcing of security efforts, establishment of public–private sector partnerships and the augmentation of defense contracts allocated to third-party, specialized private firms. The estimated value of the global private military and security industry in 2016 is as high as US$200 billion (Transparency International 2016).

Different challenges arise from the privatization of the security sector. Among them, the very nature of a for-profit organization entails that profit is based on the actual existence of threats, and vice versa, whereas successful eradication of a threat is unprofitable – and has the possibility to threaten a business's or consultancy's survival in a given market. Companies need their clients to perceive the permanent existence of a threat that can nevertheless be managed but not completely neutralized. This means that companies, much like private investigators in nineteenth-century England (Joh 2006), have no incentive to entirely rid the threat. Instead, they are incentivized to control or harness a threat but not eliminate it due to the market dynamics of the contractual relationship with their client. Arguably, this can be both seen as an industry conscious strategy or as an unintended consequence of raising subjective awareness of risks (White 2010).

Second, the private and profit-driven model of PSCs makes it an asymmetric provision that is thus centered not on the potential risks, but on the capital capacities of those seeking protection. This fact is predicated on a focus on cost-effectiveness as an incentive to cut expenditures, and, thus, may signify a reduced quality of services or labor conditions of those involved to maximize profit (Trevithick 2015). This is still an under-researched issue, but some authors are starting to investigate the gendered and racialized hierarchies of the security industry logic (Chisholm 2016) –from elite businessmen to ex-guerrilla soldiers from Central Asia or Latin America that have become the cannon fodders on the frontlines of conflicts around the world (Chisholm 2014). The expendable nature of contractors is reinforced by their legal standing outside international and human rights law and they are subsequently bound by different rules of engagement.

Third, the utility of the private sector is considered an incentive for executive branches of government due to the opportunity it provides to circumvent parliamentary oversight while utilizing public sector finances, significantly lowering the political costs of accountability regarding securitization activities or decision-making. Short-term leasing or the purchase of a service is regarded as more cost-efficient than maintaining internal capabilities, thus propelling the rate at which security services are privatized and bolstering the market for private sector security specialists (Singer 2009). The ability for political leaders or public officials to hire contractors for military and security operations also enables them to terminate those contracts (for example, when facing public backlash or growing discontent, especially in election years), which provides them with considerable power to reduce their accountability.

Finally, internationalized private sector activity prompts a thorough debate on governance apparatuses and oversight mechanisms applicable to firms operating around the globe. Regulation and governance, in this context, are the government-led mechanisms pertaining to the industry that address issues such as transparency and accountability, its personnel, resources and the nature of subcontracting, or its utility of third-party affiliates (Schreier and Caparini 2005). The absence of consistent and uniform approaches to the legal parameters in which the sector is governed enables firms to circumvent states and regions with unfavorable regulatory regimes. On many occasions, private firms are accountable only to their contracting entity and there are few mechanisms of protection in the wake of malpractice or malcontent.

3.1 Mapping and Embodying Private Security Provision

The traditional IR narrative contends that the modern state is formed based on its ability to monopolize and consolidate the legitimate use of force over perceived security threats. It is through this central means of coercion that the modern state can offer protection to its citizens from internal and external threats, prompting a social contract that eliminates the alleged lawlessness that existed before the state's legitimacy,[12] evokes a considerable responsibility of the state and right to its citizens.

Considering the economic obligations of the state, the picture that emerges is rather different. On one hand, the state has never legitimately monopolized force due to the ability of non-state actors to engage in violence. The varying degree to which states provide security renders its provision as asymmetrical or uneven when comparing two unique states. For many people around the world, however, life within their state "seems merely nasty, brutish and shortsighted" (Comaroff and Comaroff 2016, 30) or the contrary. Historically, misconduct by police forces, gender-based violence, repression of social dissidence, and other non-legitimate and non-monopolistic violent behaviors have existed in parallel with the construction of the Leviathan. Indeed, the history of policing and crime are intrinsic, as criminal behavior cannot exist outside the rule of law and without the framework of administrative justice (Comaroff and Comaroff 2007).

On the other hand, the forms and uses of coercion and force in their private/public shapes have been inextricably linked to capital. Spitzer and Scull tried to explain the evolution of policing with the increased dependence on the international political economy. They argued that the necessities of capital in the different phases of capitalism explained a progressive centralization of coercion and the socialization of the cost of security forces (Spitzer and Scull 1977). Nevertheless, the triangular relation between state–security–capital is a matter of contention between Marxist and liberal positions. The ways in which the emergence of a multimillion-dollar industry of private security affects the nature of the state is thus primordial. Weiss compares the role of PSCs in the US invasion and occupation of Iraq as assisting the new capitalist expansion and accumulation by dispossession with the new frontiers of the westbound expansion of cowboys in nineteenth-century North America (Weiss 2007).

The narratives of threat convey a specific sense of where security provision must be in that same logic. In the European Union and through the European Schengen area, borders and biometrical control are expanded with public funds and technology patented by private companies. As media and politicians celebrated the 30 years since the fall of the Berlin Wall in 2019, more than 600 miles of border walls have been built in and around the European Union and Europe in the time since its collapse. Physical borders through walls and technological fences are built by private companies such as Dragados or Ferrovial; securitized with radars, sensors and drones from Thales or Leonardo; maritime patrols are equipped with Indra technologies (Akkerman 2016, 2019), etc. Technological companies help develop the "protection and control" the EU has outlined in detecting threats – and these technologies are not only deployed at the borders. Their biometrical control is embedded further into the "security governance" within the EU through the "virtual walls" of digital infrastructure (Ruiz Benedicto and Brunet 2018).

It might seem paradoxical that new technologies of biometrical control are first deployed or trialed outside the most-economically advanced (and sometimes the producer) countries. As Breckenridge shows, the Global South is most commonly where these technologies are first installed and operated (Breckenridge 2014). This phenomenon is supported by international institutions and their initiatives, such as that of the World Bank's Identification for Development (Id4D)program:

> The goal of the ID4D is for all people to be able to access services and exercise their rights, enabled by digital identification. This will be achieved by supporting countries to build inclusive and trusted identification systems, including civil registration, using multi-sectoral approaches and appropriately leveraging innovative digital and other solutions. (World Bank 2020)

At the humanistic level, the use of force must be regarded as a continuum where Foucauldian power is deployed and technologically enhanced through surveillance, granting managerial control of life in the name of "security and modernity." Ultimately, the use of force understood as direct physical violence is only possible as the last step in the policies of inclusion and exclusion of life and death.

4. THE DESIDERATUM OF SECURITY: EXCLUSIONS AND INCLUSIONS

One might be tempted to think that the privatization of the mechanisms in which states use force, while still in small proportion to relative military capacity, has become a scholarly issue because of its quantitative growth. We can also point, as aforementioned and described above, at its relatively recent emergence as an academic area of study in the West. However, the most challenging feature within the phenomenon is the power of this "new security" to shake the philosophical and political foundations of the modern state and the perceived and supported realist paradigm in which the legitimacy of the state is founded.

Are states bound to reform and restructure their security governance in a globalized world where security is increasingly supplemented by private actors? Has the central function of the state as a security provider ceased to exist? As classic critiques of neoliberalism have already predicted (Polanyi 2001), it seems quite clear that the state still plays a fundamental role in sustaining and regulating the myth of free-markets. In the case of PSCs, states are and will continue to be primary clients. As some identify states as both competitors and sources of revenue for the private military and security industry (White 2010), they are also providing the regulatory and normative framework for a market-oriented "security governance" and for a certain consistency required in an "(in)security narrative." It is this commodification of security that makes it an interesting site for capital investment and accumulation.

The focus on privatization of security within neoliberalism has tended to convey the idea of a weakening of the state. The new security landscape rather presents a "re-articulation of public–private and global–local relations" (Abrahamsen and Williams 2009, 3). It is not a hollowing-out of the state, but, as Neocleous argues, "the ideology of (in)security is central to the political logic of capital, as well as to the logic of the state" (2007, 341). By the 2020s, a sense of newly reinforced nationalism and leadership around the world seem to deny allegations of weakening states. Conversely, it might be the weakening that is at stake, not of the state as a powerful structure and resource, but of its moral democratic rationale.

The use of force by private actors is sanctioned and framed by a narrative where states are central. States become a source of funds as well as a source of legitimacy for a specific deployment of force, for specific necropolitics that control and ultimately manage the life and death of humans and non-humans. This growing market for force culminates as a specialized and innovative private security industry and is thus grounded on the exclusion/inclusion of different social groups – some embody the threat, and force is used against them and as a performative ritual. Others reproduce the ideology of insecurity through biopolitical technologies of surveillance and control.

NOTES

1. Michael Mann, in his classic book *The Sources of Social Power* develops a theory of the modern state by looking at the state's power through two dimensions: the infrastructural power and the despotic power. Infrastructural power is "institutional capacity of a central state, to penetrate its territories and logistically implement decisions" (Mann 1993: 59).
2. Henceforth we will use the term PSCs, although a distinction could be argued between Private Security Contractors and Private Military Contractors. Others use the all-encompassing term of Private Military and Security Companies. *The Montreux Document* of 2008, a soft and non-binding regulatory attempt, defines private military and security companies (PMSCs) as "private business entities that provide military and/or security services, irrespective of how they describe themselves. Military and security services include, in particular, armed guarding and protection of persons and objects, such as convoys, buildings and other places; maintenance and operation of weapons systems; prisoner detention; and advice to or training of local forces and security personnel" (*The Montreux Document* 2008: 9). Since the distinction between military and security is not clear-cut and it can even sometimes help obscure situations of the use of force by the former, we adopt here the more generic acronym of PSC.
3. Among others, these approaches help us problematize timelines, decenter geographies, and recast subjects and actors of international politics.
4. See, for example, issues such as the continuum between war and gender-based violence; the colonial legacy of social control, etc. An indispensable read is the compilation of approaches on private security studies edited by Rita Abrahamsen and Anna Leander (2016).
5. Feminists point at the patriarchal structure of academia and politics as the main reason why war is a national threat and gender-based violence inside and outside wartime is not. Postcolonial and structuralist scholars are perceived to have identified the racist world system through the lens of privileged intellectuals and policy-makers.
6. "Terrorism" is also a concept of semiotic contention, as there is no agreed definition of what terrorism is (see Ramsay 2015).
7. Other threats can be identified at the global level. The climate crisis, for instance, is increasingly salient in media and political discourses. The amount of funds and instruments deployed to tackle the issue provides an interesting research agenda as compared to the three threats identified in this chapter. News seems to populate our forecast, and yet, so far, they only contribute to enhancing the perception of a certain risk. Since the subject of the threat is not directly explicit regarding its authorship, opinions diverge, and the threat can be redirected to other actors – such as migrant or displaced populations. The dangers of securitizing the climate crisis have also been addressed in published work by some academics (Detraz and Betsill 2009; Detraz 2011; Oels 2012).
8. The term "racialized" refers to the process in which certain people are categorized into a closed compartment of identity, with their bodies and identities processed accordingly.

9. As was the case of Osama bin Laden's assassination in Abbottabad, Pakistan in 2011; Abu Bakr al-Baghdadi in Idlib, Syria in 2019; and Qassem Soleimani in Baghdad, Iraq in 2020.
10. Activists in Morocco denounced the role of bus companies and their employees in controlling IDs in addition to the situation of racialized people in the country, especially of those traveling towards cities near state borders. According to journalistic accounts, bus drivers and conductors were pressured by authorities and the companies' management to control passengers. See Zine (2019).
11. In a 2012 Freedom of Information Act request, the British government acknowledged that "The Foreign and Commonwealth Office (FCO) had centrally awarded contracts to PSCs in conflict zones to a value of approximately" £454.5 million between 2002–2012. The company G4S was awarded "global contracts totaling some £36+ million per annum" (https://assets.publishing.service.gov.uk/government/uploads/system/uploads/attachment_data/file/35502/0669-12.pdf).
12. This view is rooted in the work of absolutist Jean Boudin's sixteenth-century work, *Les Six Livres de la République* as well as Thomas Hobbes' publication, *Leviathan*, published in the seventeenth century. It was later expanded upon in Max Weber's 1919 essay, *Politics as a Vocation*, which introduces the notion that the modern concept of state legitimacy exists through the consent of its constituents, generated through social contracts, among other means, and is intrinsically linked with the principle of territoriality (Weber 1919). Alternatively, neoliberals attempting to justify the privatization of security provision claim that the idea of coercion as a core function of the state does not mean that other private actors cannot provide it, so long as the state retains its oversight powers and responsibility in regulating it.

REFERENCES

Aas, Katja Franko. 2011. "'Crimmigrant' Bodies and Bona Fide Travelers: Surveillance, Citizenship and Global Governance." Edited by Kevin D. Haggerty, Dean Wilson, and Gavin J. D. Smith. *Theoretical Criminology* 15 (3): 331–46. https://doi.org/10.1177/1362480610396643.
Abrahamsen, Rita, and Anna Leander, eds. 2016. *Routledge Handbook of Private Security Studies*. London; New York: Routledge, Taylor & Francis Group.
Abrahamsen, Rita, and Michael C. Williams. 2009. "Security Beyond the State: Global Security Assemblages in International Politics." *International Political Sociology* 3 (1): 1–17. https://doi.org/10.1111/j.1749-5687.2008.00060.x.
Acharya, Amitav. 2004. "How Ideas Spread: Whose Norms Matter? Norm Localization and Institutional Change in Asian Regionalism." *International Organization* 58 (2). https://doi.org/10.1017/S0020818304582024.
Aït-Taleb, Ahmed. 2014. *Le secteur public de securité: Architecture, action et éthique: essai sur l'institution sécuritaire au Maroc*. Paris: L'Harmattan.
Akkerman, Mark. 2016. "Border Wars: The Arms Dealesr Profiting from Europe's Refugee Tragedy." Transnational Institute and Stop Wapenhandel.
Akkerman, Mark. 2019. "The Business of Building Walls." Transnational Institute, Centre Delàs, Stop Wappenhandel.
Baker-Beall, Christopher. 2009. "The Discursive Construction of EU Counter-Terrorism Policy: Writing the 'Migrant Other', Securitisation and Control." *Journal of Contemporary European Research* 5 (2): 188–206.
Berda, Yael. 2013. "Managing Dangerous Populations: Colonial Legacies of Security and Surveillance." *Sociological Forum* 28 (3): 627–30. https://doi.org/10.1111/socf.12042.
Bigo, Didier. 2005. "La mondialisation de l'(in)sécurité? Réflexions sur le champ des professionnels de la gestion des inquiétudes et analytique de la transnationalisation des processus d'(in)sécurisation." *Cultures & conflits* 58 (June): 53–101. https://doi.org/10.4000/conflits.1813.
Bigo, Didier. 2008. "Globalized (in)Security: The Field and the Ban-Opticon." In *Terror, Insecurity and Liberty*, edited by Anastassia Tsoukala and Didier Bigo. Vol. 20083125. London: Routledge. https://doi.org/10.4324/9780203926765.ch2.
Breckenridge, Keith. 2014. *Biometric State: The Global Politics of Identification and Surveillance in South Africa, 1850 to the Present*. New York: Cambridge University Press.

Bryant, Gerald. 2008. "Officers of the East India Company's Army in the Days of Clive and Hastings." *The Journal of Imperial and Commonwealth History*, July. https://doi.org/10.1080/03086537808582508.
Buzan, Barry. 2006. "Will the 'Global War on Terrorism' Be the New Cold War?" *International Affairs (Royal Institute of International Affairs 1944–)* 82 (6): 1101–18.
Buzan, Barry, Ole Wæver, and Jaap de Wilde. 1998. *Security: A New Framework for Analysis*. Boulder, CO: Lynne Rienner Publishers.
Buzatu, Anne-Marie, and Benjamin S. Buckland. 2015. "Private Military & Security Companies: Future Challenges in Security Governance." DCAF Horizon 2015 Working Paper no. 3: 93, Geneva Centre for the Democratic Control of Armed Forces.
Chisholm, Amanda. 2014. "The Silenced and Indispensible: Gurkhas in Private Military Security Companies." *International Feminist Journal of Politics* 16 (1): 26–47. https://doi.org/10.1080/14616742.2013.781441.
Chisholm, Amanda. 2016. "Postcoloniality and Race in Global Private Security Markets." In *Routledge Handbook of Private Security Studies*, edited by Rita Abrahamsen and Anna Leander, 177–86. London; New York: Routledge, Taylor & Francis Group.
Comaroff, Jean, and John L. Comaroff. 2007. "Law and Disorder in the Postcolony." *Social Anthropology* 15 (2): 133–52. https://doi.org/10.1111/j.0964-0282.2007.00010.x.
Comaroff, Jean, and John L. Comaroff. 2016. *The Truth about Crime: Sovereignty, Knowledge, Social Order*. Chicago; London: The University of Chicago Press.
Côté-Boucher, Karine, Federica Infantino, and Mark B. Salter. 2014. "Border Security as Practice: An Agenda for Research," edited by Karine Côté-Boucher, Federica Infantino, and Mark B. Salter. *Security Dialogue* 45 (3): 195–208. https://doi.org/10.1177/0967010614533243.
Detraz, Nicole. 2011. "Threats or Vulnerabilities? Assessing the Link between Climate Change and Security." *Global Environmental Politics* 11 (3): 104–20. https://doi.org/10.1162/GLEP_a_00071.
Detraz, Nicole, and Michele M. Betsill. 2009. "Climate Change and Environmental Security: For Whom the Discourse Shifts." *International Studies Perspectives* 10 (3): 303–20. https://doi.org/10.1111/j.1528-3585.2009.00378.x.
Eriksson, Johan, and Mark Rhinard. 2009. "The Internal–External Security Nexus: Notes on an Emerging Research Agenda," edited by Johan Eriksson and Mark Rhinard. *Cooperation and Conflict* 44 (3): 243–67. https://doi.org/10.1177/0010836709106215.
Finnemore, Martha, and Kathryn Sikkink. 1998. "International Norm Dynamics and Political Change." *International Organization* 52 (2): 887–917.
Grassiani, Erella. 2017. "Commercialised Occupation Skills: Israeli Security Experience as an International Brand." In *Security/Mobility: Politics of Movement*, edited by Matthias Leese and Stef Wittendorp, 57–73. Manchester: Manchester University Press.
Gržinić, Marina, and Šefik Tatlić. 2014. *Necropolitics, Racialization, and Global Capitalism: Historicization of Biopolitics and Forensics of Politics, Art, and Life*. Lanham, MD: Lexington Books.
Howell, Alison, and Melanie Richter-Montpetit. 2019. "Racism in Foucauldian Security Studies: Biopolitics, Liberal War, and the Whitewashing of Colonial and Racial Violence." *International Political Sociology* 13 (1): 2–19. https://doi.org/10.1093/ips/oly031.
Huysmans, Jef. 2006. *The Politics of Insecurity: Fear, Migration, and Asylum in the EU*. The New International Relations. London; New York: Routledge.
Joh, Elizabeth E. 2006. "The Forgotten Threat: Private Policing and the State." *Indiana Journal of Global Legal Studies* 13 (2): 357–89.
Katzenstein, Peter J. 1996. *The Culture of National Security: Norms and Identity in World Politics*. New York: Columbia University Press.
Kraska, P. B. 2007. "Militarization and Policing – Its Relevance to 21st Century Police." *Policing* 1 (4): 501–13. https://doi.org/10.1093/police/pam065.
Malesevic, Sinisa, and Christian Olsson. 2017. "Chapter 40: War." In *The Sage Handbook of Political Sociology, 2v*, edited by William Outhwaite and Stephen Turner, 1st edition. Thousand Oaks, CA: Sage Publications.
Mamdani, Mahmood. 2004. *Good Muslim, Bad Muslim: America, the Cold War, and the Roots of Terror*, 1st edition. New York: Pantheon Books.
Mann, Michael. 1993. *The Sources of Social Power: The Rise of Classes and Nation-States, 1760–1914*. Vol. 2. Cambridge [Cambridgeshire]; New York: Cambridge University Press.

Mbembe, Achille. 2003. "Necropolitics." *Public Culture* 15 (1): 11–40.
McLean, Ian, and Alistair McMillan. 2009. "Governance." In *The Concise Oxford Dictionary of Politics*. Oxford: Oxford University Press. https://www-oxfordreference-com.ezp-prod1.hul.harvard.edu/view/10.1093/acref/9780199207800.001.0001/acref-9780199207800-e-1539.
Neocleous, Mark. 2007. "Security, Commodity, Fetishism." *Critique* 35 (3): 339–55. https://doi.org/10.1080/03017600701676738.
Oels, Angela. 2012. "From 'Securitization' of Climate Change to 'Climatization' of the Security Field: Comparing Three Theoretical Perspectives." In *Climate Change, Human Security and Violent Conflict*, edited by Jürgen Scheffran, Michael Brzoska, Hans Günter Brauch, Peter Michael Link, and Janpeter Schilling, 8: 185–205. Berlin, Heidelberg: Springer Berlin Heidelberg. https://doi.org/10.1007/978-3-642-28626-1_9.
Olsson, C., and S. Malesevic. 2018. Chapter 40, "War." In *The Sage Handbook of Political Sociology, 2v*, edited by W. Outhwaite and S. Turner (1st edn, pp. 716–33). SAGE Inc.
Ong, Aihwa. 2006. *Neoliberalism as Exception: Mutations in Citizenship and Sovereignty*. Durham, NC: Duke University Press.
Persaud, Randolph B. 2004. "Situating Race in International Relations: The Dialectics of Civilizational Security in American Immigration." In *Power, Postcolonialism and International Relations Reading Race, Gender and Class*, edited by Chowdhry Geeta and Sheila Nair, 56–81. Abingdon, UK: Taylor & Francis.
Polanyi, Karl. 2001. *The Great Transformation: The Political and Economic Origins of Our Time*. 2nd Beacon Paperback ed. Boston, MA: Beacon Press.
Ramsay, Gilbert. 2015. "Why Terrorism Can, but Should Not Be Defined." *Critical Studies on Terrorism* 9153 (July): 1–18. https://doi.org/10.1080/17539153.2014.988452.
Raphael, Sam. 2016. *Mercenaries Unleashed, 2016.Pdf*. London: War on Want. https://waronwant.org/sites/default/files/Mercenaries%20Unleashed%2C%202016.pdf.
Resteigne, Delphine, and Philippe Manigart. 2019. "Boots on the Streets: A 'Policization' of the Armed Forces as the New Normal?" *Journal of Military Studies* 8 (Special Issue): 16–27.
Rigouste, Mathieu. 2007. "L'ennemi intérieur, de la guerre coloniale au contrôle sécuritaire." *Cultures & conflits* 67 (November): 157–74. https://doi.org/10.4000/conflits.3128.
Ruiz Benedicto, Ainhoa, and Pere Brunet. 2018. *Building Walls: Fear and Securitization in the European Union*. 35. Centre Delàs Report. Barcelona: Centre Delàs d'Estudis per la Pau i el Desarmament; TNI; Stop Wapenhandel. http://www.centredelas.org/images/INFORMES_i_altres_PDF/informe35_BuildingWalls_ENG.pdf.
Schreier, Fred, and Marina Caparini. 2005. "Privatising Security: Law, Practice and Governance of Private Military and Security Companies." Geneva Center for Democratic Control of Armed Forces. http://www.isn.ethz.ch/DigitalLibrary/Publications/Detail/?lang=en&id=14077.
Shamir, Ronen. 2005. "Without Borders? Notes on Globalization as a Mobility Regime." *Sociological Theory* 23 (2): 197–217. https://doi.org/10.1111/j.0735-2751.2005.00250.x.
Singer, P. W. 2009. "Outsourcing War: Understanding the Private Military Industry." January 28. https://www.foreignaffairs.com/articles/2005-03-01/outsourcing-war.
Spitzer, Steven. 1993. "The Political Economy of Policing." In *Crime And Capitalism: Readings in Marxist Crimonology*, edited by David Greenberg, 568–94. Philadelphia: Temple University Press. http://qut.eblib.com.au/patron/FullRecord.aspx?p=547424.
Spitzer, Steven, and Andrew T. Scull. 1977. "Privatization and Capitalist Development: The Case of the Private Police." *Social Problems* 25 (1): 18–29.
The Montreux Document. 2008. Montreux: International Committee of the Red Cross; FDFA.
Tickner, J. Ann. 1988. "Hans Morgenthau's Principles of Political Realism: A Feminist Reformulation." *Millennium: Journal of International Studies* 17 (3): 429–40.
Tickner, J. Ann. 1997. "You Just Don't Understand: Troubled Engagements Between Feminists and IR Theorists." *International Studies Quarterly* 41 (4): 611–32. https://doi.org/10.1111/1468-2478.00060.
Transparency International. 2016. "Private Military and Security Companies: A Call for Better Regulation by Transparency International." Press release. TransparencyInternational. https://www.transparency.org/news/pressrelease/private_military_and_security_companies_a_call_for_better_regulation.

Trevithick, Joseph. 2015. "A Colombian Merc Firm Was the Pentagon's Shadiest Afghanistan Contractor." *Medium*. March 9. https://medium.com/war-is-boring/a-colombian-merc-firm-was-the-pentagon-s-shadiest-afghanistan-contractor-38be49b01da8.

Wacquant, Loïc. 2009. *Punishing the Poor: The Neoliberal Government of Social Insecurity*. Durham, NC; London: Duke University Press.

Weber, Max. 1919. *Politics As a Vocation*. Philadelphia: Fortress Press, 1965.

Weinblum, Sharon. 2017. "The Management of African Asylum Seekers and the Imaginary of the Border in Israel." In *Security/Mobility: Politics of Movement*, edited by Matthias Leese and Stef Wittendorp, 114–31. New Approaches to Conflict Analysis. Manchester: Manchester University Press.

Weiss, Robert P. 2007. "From Cowboy Detectives to Soldiers of Fortune: Private Security Contracting and Its Contradictions on the New Frontiers of Capitalist Expansion." *Social Justice; San Francisco* 34 (3/4): 1–19.

Wendt, Alexander. 1992. "Anarchy Is What States Make of It: The Social Construction of Power Politics." *International Organization* 46 (2): 391–425.

Wendt, Alexander. 1995. "Constructing International Politics." *International Security* 20 (1): 71–81.

Wendt, Alexander. 1999. *Social Theory of International Politics*. Cambridge Studies in International Relations 67. Cambridge, UK; New York: Cambridge University Press.

White, Adam. 2010. *The Politics of Private Security*. Crime Prevention and Security Management. Houndmills, Basingstoke: Palgrave Macmillan.

Wilkinson, Claire. 2007. "The Copenhagen School on Tour in Kyrgyzstan: Is Securitization Theory Useable Outside Europe?" *Security Dialogue* 38 (1): 5–25. https://doi.org/10.1177/0967010607075964.

Wilkinson, Claire. 2011. "The Limits of Spoken Words: From Meta-Narratives to Experiences of Security." In *Securitization Theory: How Security Problems Emerge and Dissolve*, edited by Thierry Balzacq, 95–115. PRIO New Security Studies. Milton Park, Abingdon, Oxon; New York: Routledge.

World Bank. 2020. "Overview: The ID4D Initiative." https://id4d.worldbank.org/about-us.

Zine, Ghita. 2019. "Maroc: Titre de séjour obligatoire pour acheter un ticket d'autocar pour les Subsahariens", *Yabiladi*, October, 29. https://www.yabiladi.com/articles/details/85011/maroc-titre-sejour-obligatoire-pour.html.

7. An anti-Latin@ policing machine: enforcing the U.S.–Mexico border along the Great Lakes and the 49th Parallel

Geoff Boyce and Todd Miller

1. INTRODUCTION

In popular and social media in the United States, the country's border with Canada is frequently characterized as quiet, tame and bucolic – in marked contrast to how the U.S. border with Mexico is treated as a source of anxiety and fear. Nevertheless, over the past two decades the U.S./Canada border has been the focus of a remarkable and unprecedented build-up of Homeland Security-related infrastructures, technology and personnel. The authors have collectively spent more than a decade investigating this Homeland Security build-up, often conducting our research in tandem. Drawing on original interviews with government officials, activists and residents from a diversity of communities across the United States' northern frontier, as well as internal government records obtained via the U.S. Freedom of Information Act, this chapter sheds light on the everyday patterns of policing that have resulted.

As we discuss below, rather than concentrating their efforts on persons entering the United States without authorization from Canada, U.S. Border Patrol agents along the northern border mostly apply their extraordinary legal authority to surveil, arrest and detain U.S. citizens and long-term U.S. residents. When the targets of these enforcement activities actually prove to be noncitizens, the vast majority are found to have first entered the United States not from Canada, but from Mexico. In this way, we argue that Homeland Security activity along the U.S./Canada border is best understood as an operational extension of the militarization of the U.S./Mexico border, and of the racial logics that animate this endeavor. To summarize, our work suggests that, whether operating along the country's southern or its northern land border, U.S. Border Patrol agents in practice operate essentially (although not exclusively) as an anti-Latin@[1] policing and paramilitary institution, coordinating with local, state and other federal law enforcement partners to focus disproportionate scrutiny and state violence on persons and communities of Latin American origin and descent.

The results for these communities are often devastating. Consider, for example, the small rural town of Sodus, New York. The second-largest apple-producing region in the country, during harvesting season some 8,000 people show up to work, crowding into the rudimentary housing that proliferates along the edges of the area's abundant orchards. In 2004, Customs and Border Protection (CBP) opened a new Border Patrol station in Rochester, just down the road from Sodus. CBP said that this station would address potential problems that could emerge from a ferry service that was to travel to Rochester from Toronto across Lake Ontario. When the ferry service was suspended in 2006, CBP did not close their new station. Instead, the Border Patrol increased the number of agents in its Rochester Station from seven to 27, and Homeland Security personnel began to target small businesses like Mi Ranchito, a typical

Mexican *abarrotes* (a small neighborhood shop that sells tortillas, tostadas, salsas and all kinds of Mexican brands). Previously, Mi Ranchito had bustled with business. Many of the people working on the farms and orchards originally came from Mexico, and since opening in 1992 the store had come to serve as a hub of social activity. But after green-striped vehicles started to stake out Mi Ranchito – sometimes two at a time, ordering arriving customers to show their papers – business dried up; and Primitivo Vásquez, who owned the store, feared that he might have to close his shop. Elsewhere in Sodus, cases have been documented of Border Patrol agents pursuing people into grocery stores and pharmacies, such as Market Place, Dollar General, and CVS. Border Patrol has arrested people in front of, and on the very steps of, the local Catholic parish during Spanish-language mass, resulting first in a dramatic decline in attendance, and ultimately the closure of the parish. Meanwhile, New York state troopers have been photographed operating joint checkpoints with Border Patrol, ensnaring drivers traveling to or from mobile home parks, or attempting to access Sodus's only laundromat where working people, mostly noncitizens, can wash their clothes on their day off.

Because of enforcement activities like those described above, John "Lory" Ghertner, of Migrant Support Services of Wayne County, New York, calculated in 2013 that more people had been deported from Sodus than were deported following the infamous 2008 Immigration and Customs Enforcement (ICE) raid in Postville, Iowa. The Postville raid – one of the largest in U.S. history – resulted in the arrest of nearly 400 undocumented foreign nationals, mostly from Guatemala, at a kosher slaughterhouse and meatpacking plant. The difference in Sodus, Ghertner told us, is that "it just hasn't happened at the same time." Reflecting on the impacts on his neighbors, Ghertner offered that "this is just like 1955 Tennessee racism. You may've survived the Southwest. You may've survived the border, the Border Patrol, the checkpoints. But unless you were born here, you are not going to survive Sodus, New York."

2. A GENEALOGY OF THE ENFORCEMENT BUILD-UP ALONG THE U.S./CANADA BORDER

An enforcement focus on the Canadian border is in some ways as old as the Border Patrol itself. Initially founded in the 1920s to enforce the racist "Asiatic Barred Zone" and the national origins quota system, the U.S. Border Patrol quickly expanded its operations to include enforcing Prohibition. During its first decade of operation, a majority of agents were sent to the northern border, while the agency counted just two main offices – one in El Paso, the other in Detroit (Hernández, 2010). The modern era of U.S./Canada boundary enforcement, however, can be traced to the terrorist attacks of September 11, 2001. Before 9/11 more than half the border crossings between the United States and Canada were left unguarded at night. But as scholars like Andreas (2005), Nicol (2006), Gilbert (2007), and Salter and Piché (2011) have observed, the terrorist attacks triggered an immediate reorientation of the national security paradigm in North America, away from a Cold War-era outward-looking framework of continental "perimeter security" and toward a much more granular focus on civilian movement across the two countries' shared border. After 9/11, U.S. officials began to associate the possibility of unauthorized cross-border movement with the spectre of terrorism, thereby imagining this as posing an existential threat to the nation's security. As one former high-level CBP official who worked in Detroit described in a May 2013 interview:

before [September 11] the northern border was never perceived to be a threat. For narcotics, for anything else. But suddenly we have a terrorist trying to enter in Washington state. And we have another one trying to enter through Buffalo. Now suddenly there's a northern border situation where perhaps we have people coming out of Canada that are a threat to us ... So the concept that the northern border is not a threat has now just gone away, I mean the idea is now we have to secure all our borders, not just the southern border but the northern border as well.

The 2001 Patriot Act tripled the number of Border Patrol and frontline customs agents deployed along the U.S./Canada border, and provided an additional $50 million for technology and equipment. In 2002 the U.S. customs service and Border Patrol were then reorganized, along with the paramilitary Office of Air and Marine, into U.S. Customs and Border Protection, part of the newly created Department of Homeland Security (DHS). In 2004, additional legislation mandated that 20% of all new Border Patrol hires be stationed along the northern border. In 2006 Congress again doubled the size of the Border Patrol, resulting in an active national workforce of around 21,000 agents.

These changes produced an unprecedented concentration of resources and personnel mandated to undertake Homeland Security-related police operations across the interior of the continent. In 2001 only 340 Border Patrol agents were deployed along the entire U.S./Canada border. That number jumped to more than 1,000 by 2005. As of 2018, some 2,306 agents were operating in the northern border arena buttressed by a steady expansion of new state-of-the-art stations like the one in Pembina, North Dakota (at a cost of $13 million) and International Falls, Minnesota ($6.8 million), among other places. CBP has also invested in expansive surveillance platforms and technologies, which include Predator B drones, sometimes in the air for 20 hours at a stretch, flying from Grand Forks, North Dakota, to Spokane, Washington; as well as the SBInet surveillance system deployed along the shores of the St. Clair River in southeastern Michigan (part of a larger $3.7 billion contract to the Boeing corporation that also included an experimental deployment along the U.S./Mexico border in Arizona's Altar Valley).

Meanwhile, congressional actors like Candice Miller, the powerful former chairwoman of the House Subcommittee on Border and Maritime Security (who from 2003 to 2016 represented Macomb County, a suburban area of Detroit with a high concentration of defense and security industry), used her authority to hammer at the DHS's lack of "operational control" along the northern border, and to demand that ever-greater security resources be deployed. Again, much of this initiative was justified based on the spectre of terrorism. As Karen Czernel, one of Miller's staffers, insisted in July 2013 to a group of activists protesting the security build-up "the northern border *is* vulnerable. We have known cases of terrorists trying to come in from Canada. When we talk to officials from Homeland Security they tell us that the northern border is wide open!" (quoted in Boyce 2014).

But although arguments like Czernel's suggest a set of security concerns associated with the international border itself, the actual arena in which U.S. Border Patrol personnel operate is expansive. The Immigration and Nationality Act grants U.S. Border Patrol agents jursidiction within a "reasonable distance" from *all* U.S. land and sea borders (including the country's east, west and gulf coasts). Since 1953 the U.S. Department of Justice has held that this "reasonable distance" extends as far as 100 miles inland.[2] As a result, the American Civil Liberties Union (ACLU) points out that some two thirds of the U.S. population lives in an area defined under the law as Border Patrol jurisdiction (ACLU, 2020). Along the northern border, this jurisdiction includes the cities of Seattle, Detroit, Cleveland, Buffalo and Rochester, and the entire states of Maine, Massachusetts and New Hampshire. And although the shores of Lake Michigan fall entirely within U.S. territory, the government has used the lake's connection to international waterways to designate it as a "functionally equivalent border," extending the Border Patrol's jurisdiction across the entire state of Michigan, as well as into the cities of Chicago, Green Bay and Milwaukee.

Meanwhile, a series of court decisions including *United States v. Brignano-Ponce* (1975), *United States v. Martinez-Fuerte* (1976) and *United States v. Preciado-Robles* (1992) grant the Border Patrol extraordinary authorities to surveil, question and detain any individual they suspect of being unlawfully present in the United States. This includes the ability to initiate investigatory stops on streets, sidewalks and transit stations for anybody who an agent is able to articulate a "reasonable suspicion" might be in the country unlawfully (the "reasonable suspicion" threshold is a much lower legal threshold than "probable cause," the standard to which most other civilian law enforcement is held).[3] It further includes the ability to use "Mexican appearance" as one criteria (so long as it is not the only one) for establishing "reasonable suspicion." Within 25 miles of a land or sea border, agents have the ability to enter private property (land but not buildings) without a search warrant. Finally, the Border Patrol maintains the authority to board trains and buses and to operate traffic checkpoints at which all occupants of a vehicle must answer questions about their citizenship, and may be required to show ID (agents can also take additional action, such as searching a vehicle and enforcing laws against illegal drugs and other contraband). In 2008, when he was traveling 125 miles south of the U.S./Canada border in upstate New York, Senator Patrick Leahy of Vermont was detained at one such checkpoint and ordered to exit his vehicle. When he inquired "What authority are you acting under?" Leahy reports that the agent simply pointed to his gun and stated: "That's all the authority I need" (Ortega, 2014). Although stories like Leahy's are alarming by revealing how cavalier agents can be in their exercise of extraordinary legal authority, the larger patterns that obtain across the agency's everyday policing activities have mostly remained opaque to journalists, scholars and the public.

3. AN ANALYSIS OF INTERNAL RECORDS IN THE BORDER PATROL'S BUFFALO AND DETROIT SECTORS

In May 2015 a Freedom of Information Act (FOIA)[4] request was filed by the Michigan Immigrant Rights Center, the ACLU of Michigan, and Drs. Geoff Boyce and Elizabeth Oglesby of the University of Arizona, in order to obtain internal records from the U.S. Border Patrol related to policies, practices and intergovernmental agreements in the agency's Detroit Sector (a jurisdictional area that encompasses all of the state of Michigan, parts of Illinois, Indiana and much of northeast Ohio). Daily apprehension logs were also requested for the agency's Tucson and Buffalo Sectors, to provide a basis for comparison between patterns of arrest along both the country's southwest and northern land borders.

Initially, the Border Patrol failed to respond to the above FOIA request. It then dragged its feet on the release of most data – requiring the applicants to go to court. Following successful litigation and a negotiated settlement, in October 2018 the DHS began releasing the data in batches, which eventually came to include daily apprehension logs from Fiscal Year 2012 through June 30 of Fiscal Year 2019, and a random sample of 738 Detroit Sector I-213 "records of deportable/inadmissible alien" – documents that provide a narrative description of the circumstances of and official justification for any arrest that resulted in some kind of immigration-related action (this sample of 738 I-213s captures about 10% of all Detroit Sector immigration arrests during the period January 1, 2012–July 31, 2017).

The portrait that this data paints is damning. Between October 2011 and June 2019 the Border Patrol's records reveal a total of 13,239 arrests in the agency's Detroit Sector and 6,855 in the Buffalo Sector (an area encompassing upstate New York and areas of Pennsylvania proximate to Lake Erie), for a total of 20,094 arrests (as the N for our data). Among these arrests, a total of 11,498 (57%) were initiated by the Border Patrol itself, through enforcement tactics that range from roving patrol stops, to document checks on trains, buses, and transit stations, to targeted enforcement involving arrests at peoples' homes or workplaces, based on some pre-existing intelligence. As will be explained below, only a very small proportion of these arrests involved persons who recently entered the United States from Canada.

The data show that the Border Patrol generally uses extremely minor, highly questionable, and almost non-existent evidence to stop people. When a person is first detained by Border Patrol directly, the legal threshold an agent must meet is that they be capable of articulating specific facts that lead that agent to a "reasonable suspicion" that the person may be a noncitizen who is unlawfully present in the United States. Agents frequently refer to more than one issue as a basis for suspicion. Twenty percent of the time, this includes a person's "Hispanic" appearance, or the person being overheard speaking in the Spanish language, or speaking English with difficulty. In 52.2% of cases it was a person's perceived reaction to having seen Border Patrol that serves as a basis for suspicion; while in close to half of cases (48.9%) it is simply a person's or vehicle's appearance that is recorded as "suspicious," with little or no additional commentary (although in some cases this commentary was redacted). Twenty-one Detroit Sector arrests documented in the sample of I-213 records were the result of a "citizen complaint" requesting that the Border Patrol initiate an immigration investigation on a particular individual.

Meanwhile, 8,596 persons (43%) arrested by the Border Patrol in the agency's Detroit and Buffalo Sectors were first detained by a third-party law enforcement agency. An overwhelming majority (90.6%) of these "other agency" arrests in the Detroit Sector were a result of a vehicle accident, a disabled vehicle or a traffic stop. But I-213 records also reveal incidents whereby local police summoned Border Patrol following a routine wellness check; or because the individuals was a victim or witness to a crime; or after an individual or a member of their family dialed 911 for emergency assistance. This is to point out that those Border Patrol arrests initiated by another agency were overwhelmingly tied to routine service calls and low-level traffic enforcement efforts having nothing to do with the border itself; while many lacked any allegation of any legal offense.

There are various justifications recorded to explain why another police agency contacted Border Patrol for assistance, and detained an individual or multiple individuals until an agent could arrive to conduct an immigration investigation. Here, too, more than one justification is recorded: 26.3% of the time, this included "translation assistance," or because a person was found to be speaking Spanish (in at least one of these cases a Border Patrol agent pointedly notes upon arrival that the individual in question "was in fact able to communicate in the English language without difficulty"); 46% of the time Border Patrol was contacted for "identification assistance," even though many times the detained individual was in possession of a valid foreign-issued identification document, such as a passport. In more than 20% of such "identification assistance" cases this applied *only* to a passenger or pedestrian – persons who are not required by law to carry or produce any such ID. For about 40% of "other agency" arrests no justification is recorded whatsoever for having contacted the Border Patrol.

Just as revealing as the mechanism of arrest are demographic records about who is being apprehended. Only a tiny portion are recent border crossers, 2.5% of total arrests (n = 622) are recorded as occurring "at entry" or "within 72 hours" of entry to the United States, while 9,112 individuals (45%) are recorded as having been in the United States for longer than one year (the field "Time in US" is left blank in an additional 4,906 of apprehension records – or 19.8% – of the time). Analysis of Detroit Sector I-213 records reveals that among those who have been in the country longer than one year and who are arrested in Michigan, 81.5% are long-term residents of that state; while in Ohio 57.4% are long-term Ohio residents (there is a lower proportion of in-state residents from Ohio because of the number of arrests that take place along Ohio's interstate highway system, revealing how the Border Patrol uses the proximity of these routes of transit to the Canadian border as an excuse to undertake frequent pretextual traffic stops).

An overwhelming proportion of persons arrested in the Detroit and Buffalo Sectors are Latin@, and entered the United States from Mexico, not from Canada. Although neither the race nor ethnicity of those detained is explicitly tracked by Border Patrol, 85.6% of noncitizens arrested in the Detroit Sector are recorded as being of Latin American origin – this despite Latin@ persons comprising only 4.9% of the population of Michigan and 3.9% in Ohio (United States Census Bureau, 2020). Even if we look at the foreign-born population, still Latin@ persons comprise only 16.8% and 17.2% of foreign-born persons in each state, respectively (United States Census Bureau, 2020). Similarly, a full 86.1% of persons arrested are recorded as having first entered the United States at the U.S./Mexico border, while an additional 9.2% arrived through an airport or seaport. According to I-213 records, only 4.6% of Border Patrol arrests in the Detroit Sector involved persons who first entered the United States across the Canadian border, whether this entry was lawful or not. Meanwhile, as reported in a 2011 report published by Families for Freedom and the New York Civil Liberties Union, Border Patrol agents track a field of data titled "complexion" for all persons they arrest (New York Civil Liberties Union and Families for Freedom, 2011). The agency's daily apprehension logs for the Detroit Sector reveal fully 95.6% of noncitizens arrested having a complexion recorded as "Black," "Dark Brown," "Dark," "Light Brown," "Medium Brown," or "Medium." Only 4.2% of those arrested have a complexion recorded as "Fair" or "Light," while one person was recorded as having a complexion using the racist category "Yellow."

But it is important to point out that it is not only immigrants or noncitizens who are arrested by the Border Patrol – one third of those apprehended in the Detroit Sector and one fifth in the Buffalo Sector are recorded as being United States citizens. Some of these arrests involve persons who are detained because either their identity or citizenship are initially questioned, but upon investigation and confirmation they are subsequently released. Others are individuals who are first stopped by Border Patrol to conduct an immigration investigation, and are then identified as having an outstanding warrant issued by some other local or state law enforcement agency. In addition, among those 14,106 noncitizens recorded in Buffalo and Detroit Sector daily apprehension logs, fully 2,121 persons – or 15% – are eventually found to be non-deportable, meaning they have some lawful status in the United States and they are not suspected of any criminal offense that would allow that status to be revoked. Thus, close to 40% of those arrested in the Detroit and Buffalo Sectors combined were either U.S. citizens or persons otherwise lawfully present in the country. These figures likely represent just a tip of the iceberg of overall field detentions, given that a random sample of roving patrol vehicle stops found that as many as 25 persons are stopped and investigated by Border Patrol for every one person who is actually taken into custody (meaning a 4% "hit rate"), and who would therefore appear in the agency's daily apprehension logs. And there is every reason to believe that these investigative stops follow the same patterns of ethnicity, complexion and nationality documented above (for more, see Barrick, 2015; Boyce, 2018).

4. THE IMPLICATIONS FOR IMPACTED COMMUNITIES

Given the formal justifications recorded by the Border Patrol for either initiating an immigration investigation, or for responding to a civilian complaint or third-party law enforcement agency, and given the agency's overwhelmingly disproportionate apprehension of persons of Latin American origin and ethnicity, it is fair to conclude that along the U.S./Canada border the agency operates as a police institution that principally and specifically targets Latin@ persons and communities (and communities of color more broadly). Indeed, despite the myriad security rationales cited to justify the build-up of enforcement resources and personnel along the U.S./Canada border, in practice agents rarely apprehend persons who are entering the United States from Canada, or who recently entered the country without authorization. Instead, agents use their authority proximate to the Canadian border as a convenient pretext to focus disproportionate police scrutiny and state violence on one subset of U.S. citizens and long-term residents, based principally and often explicitly on their perceived ethnicity, national origin and/or use of language.

What's more, a 2013 report *Uncovering USBP: Bonus Programs for United States Border Patrol Agents and the Arrest of Lawfully Present Individuals*, revealed that agents in New York State were actually, for a time, given material incentives to increase the number of people they sweep up (Families for Freedom, 2013). These incentives included Home Depot gift certificates, cash bonuses and vacation time. Drawing on internal records obtained via FOIA, the authors track how this policy led to thousands of spurious arrests of U.S. citizens and others lawfully present in the United States, who wound up being arrested because they were not carrying a form of ID that an agent chose to find satisfying (the report also finds that "agents are not genuinely interested in what documents the law might require noncitizens to carry. Instead, USBP's demand for 'papers' is universal, resulting in an enforcement culture that maximizes arrest rates" [Families for Freedom, 2013, v]). The disproportionate concentration of scrutiny and arrests on Latin@ residents and communities of color generates considerable vulnerability and harm to people's everyday security and wellbeing. We have already discussed some of these impacts on rural agricultural areas like Sodus, New York. But to appreciate the scale and scope of this harm, let us now turn to the City of Detroit.

Once celebrated as "the arsenal of democracy," Detroit has suffered one of the steepest population declines of any major U.S. city – from a height of two million residents in the 1950s (when Detroit was the fourth-largest city in the United States) to a little over 670,000 residents today. However, since the 1990s, the Latin American (and mostly Mexican) immigrant population has grown considerably, reaching more than 52,000 residents (United States Census Bureau, 2020). As Elena Herrada, director of the Detroit-based Centro Obrero, told us, "People started coming to Detroit after NAFTA," referring to the North American Free Trade Agreement and its impact on Mexican states like Jalisco and Michoacan, the geographic origin of much of the recent migration to the city. But Herrada, whose claim to national fame was evoking the ire of Glenn Beck when she compared ICE to the Klu Klux Klan, is herself testament to the long-standing presence of the Mexican community in Detroit. Like so many families in the city, hers arrived early in the twentieth century to work in the city's automobile factories. During the Great Depression, some 15,000 Mexican Americans from Detroit were forcibly repatriated to Mexico, part of a nationwide pattern that impacted U.S. citizens and noncitizens alike. But through it all, a robust Mexican-American and Latin@ community persisted in the southwestern corner of the city, sandwiched between the Detroit River and the Henry Ford-created suburb of Dearborn.

The recent post-NAFTA influx of immigrants has driven something of an economic renaissance in southwest Detroit. If you drive along Vernor Highway, the neighborhood's main thoroughfare, you will observe streets full of taquerías, tortillerías and lavanderías (laundromats). Windows are filled with red-green-and-white Mexican flags. There are businesses where you can send money south. Clark Park, a well-maintained public area in the center of the neighborhood, fills on evenings and weekends with children, families, activity, people – sitting, walking, chatting and recreating. But southwest Detroit is also a neighborhood under siege.

Everybody has a story. There was the guy from Mexico arrested on his way to work at 4:00am at a bus stop. There were the two other Mexican men fishing on the banks of the Detroit River whom Border Patrol agents approached and arrested as they were casting their lines into its greenish-blue water. CBP and Border Patrol loiter outside the stately Ste. Anne de Detroit Catholic Church, and, like in Sodus, they have even made arrests during Spanish-language mass. These encounters are often brutal. Mexican-American activist and lawyer Jonathan Contreras described to us how on one cold November night a Border Patrol agent pulled a taser on him when he refused to get out of his truck:

> he [the agent] comes around and he starts asking me questions again, "what's your status? Are you a US citizen? What's your citizenship?" and I said "I'm a US citizen." And [then] I said "no, you know what? I'm not going to answer any questions, I don't need to answer anything. I want to talk to my lawyer." He said "Oh. You want to talk to your lawyer?" I'm like "Yeah." And he's like, "okay, that's fine, I'll be back." They go back to the car. And then ... one of the officers came up on my side and says "get out of the car." And I said "Why? What did I do wrong?" "Get out of the car now." I'm like "I haven't done anything wrong, why should I get out of the car?" And then that's when he pulls out his little taser gun, and then I see the – the laser pointing, and going right through the glass of my window and pointing at my chest. And then that's when I, I got scared, I got scared and am like "okay, I'll get out ..."

Contreras' only offense was attempting – and apparently failing – to assert his constitutional rights.

Lidia Reyes, the former Executive Director of the now-defunct Latino Family Services, offered another story about how as she arrived at work on a cold April morning, she saw a Border Patrol agent questioning one of the center's volunteers, a man named Clemente. They were on the sidewalk in front of the gray two-story building, which used to offer various services to the Latin@ community, including a food pantry, youth tutoring and English language classes. When Reyes asked what the agents were doing, another one boxed her in with his green-striped Dodge Charger – what Reyes viewed as a blatant act of intimidation. The agent arrested Clemente, and Homeland Security later deported him. This was only one, Reyes said, of a long list of incidents that both she and her husband had undergone. Once, she described, a half-dozen Border Patrol agents on bikes surrounded Latino Family Services during a women's forum (when "I had about 50 moms here"). Reyes went outside and asked them to leave. "Up until this," Reyes described, "I took the side of the law. I figured that their rationale for doing this was A, B or C. But now since I've been director of Latino Family Services [since 2010], the stuff that they do is just horrible."

Stories like those above illustrate how Homeland Security policing practices disseminate everyday insecurity among those individuals and communities impacted along the U.S./Canada border. This includes fear of leaving one's home and circulating in public, out of worry for a loved one who might be arrested and permanently removed from the family; or fear that one might oneself be stopped, harassed and asked to show one's papers – or worse. These fears also extend to local police. For example, the Detroit Police Department is responsible for the third greatest proportion (following the Michigan State Police and the Macomb County Sheriff's Office) of the thousands of arrests initiated by a third-party law enforcement agency within the Detroit Sector. With the understanding that undocumented people are less likely to contact the police, a spate of crimes in southwest Detroit has targeted street vendors selling tacos, *paletas*, and other items, as well as individuals carrying large sums of cash to be sent to loved ones abroad.

5. CONCLUSION

Over the past 20 years, the United States has undertaken an unprecedented build-up of its enforcement capacity along the country's border with Canada. Officially, this enforcement build-up is justified with reference to the spectre of terrorism and the kinds of security concerns that proliferated in the aftermath of the terror attacks of September 11, 2001. However, we have shown here that Border Patrol agents stationed along the northern border spend very little of their energy and resources focusing on their formal mission of "preventing terrorists and terrorists weapons, including weapons of mass destruction, from entering the United States" (U.S. Customs and Border Protection, 2020). Indeed, agents rarely intercept individuals engaged in any kind of unauthorized activity that crosses the U.S./Canada border; while there is no documented evidence of a "terrorist" attempting to sneak into the country from Canada between official ports of entry (the Border Patrol's official area of operations) in order to attack the United States (in the handful of known cases involving individuals who did attempt to enter the United States from Canada and who were later prosecuted for terrorism-related crimes, these individuals lawfully presented themselves for inspection at an official Port of Entry). Instead, Border Patrol agents stationed along the U.S./Canada border mostly – and often explicitly – target persons and communities because these individuals are perceived to be of Latin American origin, or are observed speaking Spanish. Many of these individuals prove to be U.S. citizens or to have a lawful visa status; and even when the United States undertakes an immigration action against a noncitizen, the overwhelming majority of these noncitizens are found to have first entered the United States from Mexico and most are long-term residents of the country. It is for this reason that we argue that U.S./Canada border enforcement operates principally as an extension of policing and militarization along the U.S./Mexico border, and of the racial logics that animate this project.

Reflecting on the analysis above, there are several issues that deserve to be considered further. The first is that it may prove profitable to decouple our thinking about the border and border enforcement from the issue of migration. Indeed, in the case of the U.S./Canada border, the two issues can often be shown to have little to do with one another – as even when noncitizens appear in the Border Patrol's apprehension records, they are generally found to be established residents with a long-standing commitment to communities in the United States. But the same can be observed in other areas of the country where the Border Patrol operates, including the southwest border. Although along the U.S./Mexico border agents arrest many more individuals who are actively seeking to enter the United States, here too apprehension records reveal the arrest of hundreds of U.S. citizens and thousands of individuals who are long-term U.S. residents, through the very same kinds of practices observed above – transit checks, roving patrol stops, highway checkpoints and third-party law enforcement custody-transfer.

This raises a final issue we think merits urgent attention. As we have shown extensively in our reporting and scholarship (e.g. Miller, 2014; Boyce, 2018) the Border Patrol increasingly operates as a *de facto* national police force. Setting aside how such a development violates fundamental principles of federalism, the agency's consistent and disproportionate application of extraordinary authority to target the nation's largest minority group, Latin@ individuals and communities, appears to replicate some of the most egregious abuses associated with "stop and frisk"-style policing. In the case of stop and frisk, the federal courts have recently stepped in, ruling these practices unconstitutional due to their racially discriminatory application (see *Floyd, et al. v. City of New York, et al.* [2013]). Yet with the U.S. Border Patrol we have a federal agency implementing a similar logic of policing nationwide, and doing so with very few available mechanisms for accountability or even for obtaining basic information about the agency's routine activities. Indeed, it took considerable time, effort and alliance with volunteer lawyers to obtain the data discussed in this chapter, and the DHS dragged its feet and fought this data release every step of the way. Meanwhile, in February 2020 Mark A. Morgan, the acting commissioner of CBP, designated CBP to be a "security agency," allowing the agency to claim additional loopholes to exempt itself from the FOIA (Klippenstein, 2020a). This is a worrisome development that further highlights the need for a radical overhaul of the principles and priorities guiding the U.S. government's current approach to border enforcement and to border communities, both north and south.

6. CODA, APRIL 2020

As we were completing this chapter, once again a national and international crisis began to be exploited in the United States to justify expanded border policing, this time in the name of combating the Covid-19 pandemic. On April 10, 2020 *The Nation* magazine revealed that CBP had sent an internal memo seeking an emergency diversion of $145 million and 916 military personnel to support surveillance and enforcement operations along the Canadian border, along with 540 additional military personnel to supplement the 5,000 already deployed to the U.S./Mexico border, arguing that "CBP does not have the resources required to maintain public health standards and national security requirements to enforce immigration laws without additional DoD [Department of Defense] support" (Klippenstein, 2020b). Meanwhile U.S. Attorney General William Barr has publicly stated a belief that Covid-19 can be leveraged to push through additional border restrictions – suggesting during an interview with Laura Ingram on Fox News that "As horrible as this is and as tragic as it is, there are a couple of good things that can flow from this experience," and continuing that "as much as people talk about global warming … the real threat to human beings is microbes and being able to control disease, and that starts with controlling your border" (Boboltz, 2020). These developments were unfolding despite the demonstrable fact that the country's current vulnerability to the pandemic was the outcome of the fragility of its privatized approach to medical care and health-related infrastructure, and of the Trump administration's failure to prepare for the virus long after it became clear that community spread in the United States was inevitable (to the contrary, as was widely reported, the Trump administration had spent years systematically undermining the country's pandemic monitoring and response capacity, while well into this current pandemic it continued advocating budget cuts to the federal Centers for Disease Control). Meanwhile, rates of infection in both Canada and Mexico were so far much lower than those in the United States. The discrepancy considered in this chapter between the formal justification for the expansion of Homeland Security policing after 9/11, and the actual practices this expansion facilitated, should provide a cautionary lesson for this period, as any effort to resolve a complex social problem (such as a public health crisis) through the militarization of nation-state borders is liable to amplify community vulnerability while doing nothing to address the long-term public disinvestment and socio-economic inequality that the virus has exposed.

NOTES

1. Although we recognize the problems with the label "Latin," which erases the indigenous and African contributions to the multiplicity of peoples who share a geographic, linguistic and cultural heritage derived from Latin America, we follow the general U.S. practice of using this as an umbrella term. We are furthermore persuaded here by Hernández's (2018) argument in favor of the affix "@" over the increasingly common use of "x" as a way to disrupt the gender binaries that permeate the Spanish language. After all, observes Hernández, rather than gesturing toward singularity or negation, the affix "@" designates "the existence of a multiplicity within a unity," and "just as importantly, the @ predates the Latin script. The latter is older than Spanish colonialism proper, for it first appeared as an Arabic marking in al-Andalus signifying a unit of weight, a part of a whole … In other words, if one wants to honor and make visible the processes of dehumanization that rendered entire peoples less than whole human beings, then @ is precisely a pre-Spanish symbol that demarcates both a form of collectivity and a part of a whole, and thus one suited to convey all that has been raised as reasons to abandon the *a/o* affixes" (Hernández, 2018, 34).
2. The Border Patrol's 100-mile jurisdiction refers to 100 linear miles (e.g. "as the crow flies") from a sea cost, lake shore or land border. Frequently the agency's checkpoints are much farther away by highway from any designated border crossing.
3. "Reasonable suspicion" requires that a law enforcement agent or officer be able to articulate facts "based upon a totality of circumstances" that would lead a "normal" or "reasonable" person to suspect that a criminal or legal violation *may* have occurred, and that a specific individual person *may* have been involved. "Probable cause" requires much stronger evidence that establishes the probability that a crime or legal violation *has in fact* been committed, and that furthermore directly connects responsibility for this legal or criminal violation to a specific individual person. In the United States the distinction between these legal categories is partially derived from *Terry v. Ohio*, a 1968 U.S. Supreme Court ruling that among other things continues to provide a legal foundation for practices of "stop and frisk" policing.
4. The Freedom of Information Act is a public transparency law in the United States dating to the 1960s that allows scholars, journalists and other members of the public the right to petition and access a majority of internal government records, with only a handful of exceptions intended to protect personal privacy, national security and foreign policy interests, trade secrets, and ongoing police investigations.

REFERENCES

ACLU. 2020. The Constitution in the 100-Mile Border Zone. https://www.aclu.org/other/constitution-100-mile-border-zone.

Andreas, P. 2005. The Mexicanization of the US–Canada border: Asymmetric interdependence in a changing security context. *International Journal* 60(2), pp. 449–462.

Barrick, L. 2015. "Possible criminal activity afoot": The politics of race and boundary-making in the United States Pacific Northwest borderland. *ACME: An International E-Journal for Critical Geographies* 14(3). https://acme-journal.org/index.php/acme/article/view/1064.

Boboltz, S. 2020. Bill Barr says Coronavirus crisis should lead to stricter border control. *Huffington Post*, 9 April. https://www.huffpost.com/entry/bill-barr-coronavirus-crisis-stricter-borders_n_5e8f2651c5b6b371812cfdd4.

Boyce, G. 2014. Border (In)Security and the "Unknown Unknown." Public Political Ecology Laboratory, May 14. http://ppel.arizona.edu/?p=587.

Boyce, G.A. 2018. Appearing "out of place": Automobility and the everyday policing of threat and suspicion on the US/Canada frontier. *Political Geography* 64, pp. 1–12.

Families for Freedom. 2013. *Uncovering USBP: Bonus Programs for United States Border Patrol Agents and the Arrest of Lawfully Present Individuals*. New York: Families for Freedom.

Gilbert, E. 2007. Leaky borders and solid citizens: Governing security, prosperity and quality of life in a North American partnership. *Antipode* 39(1), pp. 77–98.

Hernández, K.L. 2010. *Migra!: A History of the US Border Patrol*. Berkeley: University of California Press.

Hernández, R.D. 2018. *Coloniality of the U-S/Mexico Border: Power, Violence, and the Decolonial Imperative*. Tucson: University of Arizona Press.

Klippenstein, K. 2020a. Exclusive: Customs and Border Protection gains an extra layer of secrecy. *The Nation*, 4 February. https://www.thenation.com/article/politics/cbp-security-agency/.

Klippenstein, K. 2020b. Exclusive: Inside Trump's failed plan to surveil the Canadian border. *The Nation*, 10 April. https://www.thenation.com/article/politics/canada-border-covid-security/.

Miller, T. 2014. *Border Patrol Nation: Dispatches from the Front Lines of Homeland Security*. San Francisco: City Lights Publishers.

New York Civil Liberties Union and Families for Freedom. 2011. Justice derailed: What raids on trains and buses reveal about Border Patrol's interior enforcement practices. http://www.nyclu.org/files/publications/NYCLU_justicederailedweb_0.pdf.

Nicol, H. 2006. The Canada–US border after September 11th: The politics of risk constructed. *Journal of Borderland Studies* 21(1), pp. 47–68.

Ortega, B. 2014. Interior border guard checks spark ACLU complaint. *USA Today*, 16 January. https://www.usatoday.com/story/news/nation/2014/01/16/aclu-border-patrol-complaint/4518711/.

Salter, M.B. and Piché, G., 2011. The securitization of the US–Canada border in American political discourse. *Canadian Journal of Political Science/Revue canadienne de science politique* 44(4), pp. 929–951.

United States Census Bureau. 2020. QuickFacts. https://factfinder.census.gov/faces/tableservices/jsf/pages/productview.xhtml?pid=ACS_17_5YR_S0501&prodType=table.

U.S. Customs and Border Protection. 2020. What is the Border Patrol and what is its mission? https://www.cbp.gov/faqs/what-border-patrol-and-what-its-mission.

8. The invisible dimension of institutional violence and the political construction of impunity: necropopulism and the averted medicolegal gaze

Bilgesu Sümer

> Are you ready to wear your burial robes? Are you ready to follow the footsteps of our ancestors?
> Turkish president Recep Tayyip Erdoğan during the 946th anniversary celebrations for the Battle of Malazgirt, 26 August 2017

> Last night was a great night for the United States and for the world. A brutal killer, one who has caused so much hardship and death, has violently been eliminated. He will never again harm another innocent man, woman, or child. He died like a dog. He died like a coward. The world is now a much safer place.
> US president Donald Trump referring to ISIS Leader Abu Bakr al-Baghdadi, 27 October 2019

1. INTRODUCTION

In this chapter, I conceptualize necropopulism and the averted medicolegal gaze as two political processes that should be recognized as immanent problems in world politics for causing violence accompanied by the global rise of populism. My goal is to broaden the debate on what United Nations (UN) bodies point to as the systematic character of impunity (Orentlicher 2005) using Turkey, Mexico and the USA as illustrative examples. I argue that necropopulism and the averted medicolegal gaze can help explain the institutional configurations that play central roles in the construction of impunity that is a central feature of power that enables populist leaders to hold on to power despite the overwhelming evidence indicating abuse of power.

A set of compelling evidence can be found in how dead bodies recovered from borders are not properly investigated. This is an example of the averted medicolegal gaze,[1] which is possible when there is a lack of defendants for the victims. Lack of institutional gaze enables authorities to absolve themselves of guilt, along the lines of allegations of misconduct. Political discourse is shaped to absolve administrative responsibility to investigate the causes of death thoroughly. Populist leaders take this state capability further to construct a necropopulist[2] discourse that normalizes the violence that killed these faceless victims.

Necropopulism and the averted gaze, as the proposed concepts, are meant to make visible the invisible violence that populist leaders cause. Due to the averted medicolegal gaze, legal institutions actively erase the political status and personal identity of those who perish on the borders. They do not directly act to devalue human life. They simply neglect humans when they can get away with it. Governments set the expenses for dealing with the death of migrants to a minimum and no one can be hold accountable for this policy under the current world order. Necropopulist discourses can add to this picture to justify further dismantling of a state's responsibility to protecting human rights of non-nationals. On the ground, state institutions look away from crime scenes instead of resolving them; they avert their medicolegal gaze away from crime scenes and frame them as tragedies.

In the following, I begin by conceptualizing necropopulism and the averted medicolegal gaze, grounded in literatures conducting interdisciplinary studies of political violence. I argue that these concepts can explain the power behind the global rise of populism, as it causes political violence and prevents protection of human rights. After, I delve into the history of politicization of the dead in order to demonstrate how international medicolegal norms emerged to challenge necropopulist political agendas. In the penultimate section, I advance an analysis of various discourses of dehumanization from the contemporary period, as a way to complete the picture depicted in this chapter.

2. NECROPOPULISM

My conceptualization of necropopulism is meant to add to the current debate on populism. Populism is a type of political discourse that presupposes an organic distinction between elites and ordinary people (Müller 2016). Populist politicians claim to represent ordinary people and defend them from elite indifference. The populism debate returned in the 2010s, after the global economic recession caused by the 2008 financial crisis. The 2010s have seen the rise of populist leaders, some of whom are new while others have been present for some time.[3] Müller (2016) frames a common thread of populist political discourse as blaming an imagined form of "established elites" for the prevailing problems while positioning themselves against pluralism. Necropopulism fits Müller's framing as a discursive field where populist leaders position themselves against cultural groups designated as the "others" of their imagined "national" community (Anderson 2006).

While my definition fits Müller's framing, it also extends the debate because necropopulism is a particular deployment of populism. Its content concerns itself with the subject of death, which can be approached through examining its relation to statecraft (Auchter 2014) and legitimization (Jackson 2006) of sovereign right to kill (Mbembe 2003). My understanding adds that modern states are entrusted in building and maintaining infrastructure for dealing with dead bodies. Similarly, nation states construct an infrastructure of care for the politically significant dead bodies. Necropopulist discourse builds on this infrastructure of the imagined national past where there are specific cultural understandings related to dead heroes and slain enemies; it is a form of politicizing the dead (Pérez 2012) through speech acts. Populist leaders can use necropopulist discursive formation for proposing new cultural understandings of political order and legitimacy for national aspirations. Through this discourse, populist leaders are utilizing the symbolic meaning of death for constructing political message.

As political scientist Aucthter (2014) elaborates, everyday practices of modern states dwell on making the subject of death meaningful. Similarly, cultural anthropologist Verdery's examination (1999) focusing on political lives of dead bodies shows that cultural politics of modern nationalism performs a mode of ancestry worship. Everyday construction of state activities symbolizes this worship in many ways. In the epigraph above, Turkish president Erdoğan's speech commemorating the Battle of Malazgirt is mentioned, in which I understand a ritual of ancestor worship shaped by necropopulism. It is dwelling on symbols of martyrdom and conquest. This sort of cultural performance normalizes the exercise of sovereign right to kill.

Mbembe (2003) rightfully points out that modern states killing their own citizens corresponds to the legacies of colonialism and histories of European conquest. Erdoğan frequently speaks of past conquests and performs rituals around these ideas, as his government conducts military operations within the country and across its borders. Necropopulist discourses play a significant role in devaluing those who do not belong to the nation, or those who died as enemies of the nation. The other epigraph serves as an example, as it demonstrates how the 45th President of the USA Donald Trump refers to the death of ISIS leader al-Baghdadi.

In order to deal with the real problem of dead bodies, modern states build and maintain certain infrastructures shaped by prevailing cultural norms. Preventing proper burial to certain dead bodies can become a mode of abusing state power shaped by the cultural understanding of undignified treatment, as evidence of necropolitics in Turkey clearly demonstrates (Bargu 2016). My argument is that, when state sponsored, necropopulism discourses gain power to inflict invisible violence in all forms: symbolic (Whitehead 2004), cultural (Galtung 1990) and structural (Farmer 2004). Of structural violence Bourgois writes that "despite its invisibility, structural violence is shaped by identifiable institutions, relationships, force fields, and ideologies, such as the unequal market-based terms of trade between industrialized and non-industrialized nations, carceral systems, discriminatory laws, gender inequity, and racism. It manifests visibly in health disparities resulting in distinct morbidity burdens, mortality rates, and occupational injury levels across class, ethnicity, and citizenship status" (2009, 18–20).

3. THE AVERTED MEDICOLEGAL GAZE

> All 212 were undocumented immigrants who died in Texas trying to evade Border Patrol checkpoints by walking across the rugged terrain. Most died from dehydration, heatstroke or hypothermia.
> Manny Fernandez, "A Path to America, Marked by More and More Bodies",
> 4 May 2017

Necropopulism works as the discursive representation of border as a site of legitimate and expected violence, which authoritarian governments utilize for two reasons. First, the death of migrants promotes the idea of protected borders that the popular base desire. Second, the symbolic meaning of death at the border sends a deterrent message to the potential migrants, implying a similar fate waits for them. Despite the fact that people keep dying, no one can be held accountable. I propose an understanding of the averted medicolegal gaze to explain the institutional mechanisms behind this phenomenon that prevents the protection of human rights. Impunity becomes systematic when dead bodies recovered from borders are not properly investigated by courts and other juridical bodies. Instead of conducting proper forensic investigations following international medicolegal principles, the authorities avert their gaze away from the dead bodies as a site of criminal conduct. In this fashion, human rights violations occur due to the lack of access to medicolegal gaze, where there is not a fair and sound investigation of state sponsored crimes by trustworthy authorities capable of enforcing legal decisions.

The averted medicolegal gaze constitutes a form of invisible violence, reminding how direct violence is not the only mode of state sponsored killing. Migrants dying while crossing dangerous geographies also reflects back how state sponsored violence occurs. Economic disparities and restrictions placed on workers create global structures that force displacement while punishing mobility. The effects of the global system later get normalized. The following excerpt from a July 16, 2015 report published by oppositional media outlet *Democracy Now* perfectly hints at the discourse that gets used in normalizing the state bodies neglecting to uphold international medicolegal principles:

> Texas says there is "no evidence" of wrongdoing after mass graves filled with bodies of immigrants were found miles inland from the U.S.–Mexico border. The bodies were gathered from the desert surrounding a checkpoint in Falfurrias, Texas, in Brooks County. An investigation was launched after the mass graves were exposed last November in a documentary by The Weather Channel in partnership with Telemundo and The Investigative Fund. The report also found many of the migrants died after crossing into the United States and waiting hours for Border Patrol to respond to their 911 calls.

Together with the epigraph above, this statement reveals multiple levels of institutional neglect. First, the constructed evidence absolves all guilty parties, which implicitly includes the authorities. In other words, the function of medicolegal gaze is used to grant impunity to state authorities. For instance, the identification of the victims is not considered a duty of the government. Second, the statement cites a report evidencing state neglect. US authorities let migrants die by ignoring their calls for help. I want to add the epigraph above to this picture as it hints at how the border architecture corners illegally crossing migrants to their own deaths.

Necropopulist argument establishes itself a rationality by arguing that it is virtually impossible for US officials to conduct thorough investigations. The US authorities do not have any information that can help with identification because they are not US nationals. They also do not have any information about their nationality either. They do not have any incentive to properly identify these victims since there are no US citizens claiming them either. Thus, there is no wrongdoing in their indecent burial, and it is normalized. The truth of the matter is that US authorities are focused on eliminating these corpses from existence; asking them to deal with this problem runs contrary to their governance logics.

The averted medicolegal gaze absolves the governments from being accountable to upholding human rights and erases the political status and personal identity of the dead persons. However, there is always resistance pushing back against the prevalent policy. Texas authorities are pushed to make such a statement because there are media and civil society organizations placing pressure on them by exposing mass graves in the desert. But this will not change the institutional mechanism alone. It is supported by a very potent cultural understanding grounded in the history of White supremacy. Necropopulism functions through supremacist undertones that frame death of migrants as legitimate and expected.

4. THE EMERGENCE OF INTERNATIONAL MEDICOLEGAL PRINCIPLES

Surveying the history of the politicization of the dead allows for a sound understanding of the emergence of the international medicolegal principles. By politicization of the dead I refer to the use of dead bodies for sending political messages (Pérez 2012) – where the victors of violent conflict display their slain enemies as a way of sending political messages. The mode of display changes depending on cultural and historical context. Human rights conventions are a major factor that shapes the mode of display. Although they prohibit the undignified and immoral treatment of persons and dead bodies (Fujii 2013), politicization of the dead still occurs adding an element of horror to the performative side of international politics (Debrix 2016; Cavarero 2009).

We can think about symbolic and material uses of dead bodies and humans as distinct but related activities, in order to grasp a difference that human rights make. Human rights norms prohibit the material use of dead bodies. This prohibition largely shapes contemporary state behavior where symbolic and indirect interventions are preferred. For example, the Skull Tower of Nis is an example of politicization of the dead occurring before human rights conventions start to take place. The construction of the Skull Tower occurs in the context of the Serbian Revolution (1804–1835) against the Ottoman Empire. The main material used in the construction of the Skull Tower was the skulls of Serbian revolutionaries who were captured dead. During the onset of the revolution, the Serbian rebels and the Ottoman forces found themselves fighting a bloody war. The Ottoman forces were led by Hurshid Pasha and by 1809 his forces had lost more than 15,000 soldiers. In a final standoff, the Serbian rebel army had close to 2,000 remaining fighters and they were cornered. The rebels blew up their armory and died in the process. Afterwards, Hurshid Pasha ordered the construction of a tower with the skulls of more than nine hundred dead Serbian insurgents in Nis, which stands on the road to Istanbul from Belgrade.

The tower stayed in its place until 1861 when Midhat Pasha became the governor of Nis. Known as one of the most prominent figures of Ottoman liberalism, he ordered the dismantling of the Skull Tower. This policy change signals a shift towards biopolitical governance that seeks to establish a positive relationship between the Ottoman state and its ethnically diverse population. These reforms did not prevent the loss of these territories. In 1878, the structure was rebuilt when Serbian territories were liberated from Ottoman rule. Some of the dismantled pieces were reassembled and the site was put under a chapel structure. As such, the Skull Tower continues to serve as an important heritage site for Serbian national identity. It is a political site laden with cultural potential for necropopulism to flourish, as well as a collective memory reflecting the horrors of the past that can be a reminder to resist necropopulism.

US governments in the past century also engaged in politicization of the dead as a means of disseminating messages about their power as the new global hegemon. A well-known example is the circulation of images showing the dead body of Ernesto Guevara, the Argentinian revolutionary who was killed in Bolivia in 1967. US policy, however, changed over time. Four decades after Guevara's death, when US security agents killed Osama Bin Laden, the images of Bin Laden's corpse were not circulated, and the body was disposed in a secret location. This change can be interpreted as a reflection that US government believes any display of horrific images would provoke unnecessary reaction, serving as a rallying call. I also think that the decision to deny marked burial for Bin Laden reflects the belief that a burial site could help set up a cult of martyrdom.

Comparably, the US government treats the burial sites of its own dead agents with utmost reverence. The graves of dead US military service personnel and veterans are adorned with US flags and this practice is maintained by local state institutions. This reverence has political foundations that have shaped cultural understandings and funerary practices in the US. For example, open casket funerals owe their popularity to necropopulist agendas from the nineteenth century. In this epoch, the US military was waging a war of extermination against Native Americans and facing deadly resistance. The dead soldiers had to be buried in their communities of birth, which were far away from combat zones. As archaeologist Pearson

(1999) underlines, their corpses were intentionally mummified in ways that made them look as lively as possible in order to conceal the horrors of war from the American public.

Although the practice of using dead bodies and human parts for sending political messages continues to the present day (Gregory 2016), it is nonetheless prohibited in international law and criminalized under modern rule of law regimes. This advancement is due to collective work of transnational advocacy networks (Keck and Sikkink 1999). The human rights conventions increased moral value placed on the human body starting with the formation of the UN in 1945. However, disabling politicization of the dead as a technique of power became possible after the democratization of forensic sciences. This shift also paved way to the emergence of international medicolegal norms. A major turning point in history was the assassination of the US president John F. Kennedy in 1963. US government officials became more interested in application of scientific methods for solving crimes and this paved a way in the proliferation of forensic expertise.

Dr. Clyde Snow was a US forensic anthropologist who was politically very influential. In 1973, he prepared a scientific report about Kennedy's assassination and presented it to the US senate. Together with forensic pathologist Dr. Robert Krischner, Dr. Snow spent a significant amount of time in Argentina in the 1980s. Both worked on exposing the crimes of the Argentinian junta that led to its end and helped to train local experts (Keck and Sikkink 1998). Together, they were present at the drafting of the 1991 Minnesota Protocol (Manual on the Effective Prevention and Investigation of Extra-Legal, Arbitrary and Summary Executions). This protocol set the stage for constructing international medicolegal principles.[4] These principles are detailed in international documents, but they are non-binding treaties. Although signatory states are advised to adapt these manuals and the principles behind them, they are not legally bound. Implementation of international medicolegal principles requires a shift in practices of sovereignty, which is a major challenge for protection of human rights.

The Minnesota Protocol details how to use scientific procedures while investigating human rights violations. Its content reflects the experiences of Dr. Snow and Dr. Krischner, who were among the authors of the protocol. In a way, they worked with legal experts and human rights advocates to devise a manual that can universally translate science to law. They often traveled to train other scientists and medical experts, if not conduct investigations themselves (Rosenblatt 2015). After the protocol was ratified by the UN in 1991, Dr. Snow traveled to Guatemala and helped set up the Guatemalan Forensic Anthropology Association. The association has worked ever since to investigate mass graves and clandestine burials and identify victims (Sanford 2003). With the emergence of international medicolegal norms, science and expert knowledge became a tool for proving state sponsored crimes and a method for disabling the abuse of political power. However, state sponsored violence has continued and the problem of dealing with dead bodies has remained as a core issue.

5. CONTEMPORARY DISCOURSES OF DEHUMANIZATION

Examining contemporary necropopulist discourses shows that they dehumanize groups impacted by endemic and systemic outcomes of structural inequalities (Rylko-Bauer, Whiteford, and Farmer 2009; Singer and Hodge 2010). In a way, it is victim blaming. In their framing of violent symptoms as pathologies, populist leaders often refer to borders, migration and violence in pragmatic and untruthful ways. They deploy various discourses of dehumanization that imagine the border that naturally kills the enemies of the nation. In certain instances, these enemies are potential migrants who are blamed for domestic problems and violence. Generally, the targets can be groups under the "others" of the nation, those who do not belong to and are positioned against the nation as it is imagined by a populist leader.

For example, during the summer of 2016, a group within the Turkish military attempted to overthrow Erdoğan's regime. While they failed, the government consolidated its authoritarian hold on political power in the aftermath of the violent clashes. The three major political parties in the parliament conducted a joint public meeting to celebrate "democracy" and condemn military interventions. The pro-Kurdish political party was excluded from these events named "Democracy and Martyrs' Patrols." Erdoğan spoke about the logic of exclusion by invoking a hypothetical situation where they could not have explained their attendance to "the martyrs of democracy." In this phrasing, Erdoğan referred to the victims who died during the coup while defending his regime and excluded the victims who died while attempting the coup. This is a symbolic assault against the memory of those who died based on their political beliefs. The assault occurs in the context of their beliefs having caused the violent killing of those who defended Erdoğan. Erdoğan glorifies his supporters using the cultural understanding of "martyrdom" together with democracy, implying those killed opposing him were excommunicated from religion for their illegitimate dissidence. Altogether, this is cultural violence that Erdoğan generates from a layered context of structural inequalities.

In this framing, governance of life as a problem of sovereignty disappears from the political agenda. The other loss is constructing better ways of governance. Institutional neglect couples with dehumanization, which invites collective resistance. Since the problem is political at the core, in many instances resistance transforms into social movement organizations, collective action and protest, and even armed insurgency (Tarrow 2011; Alvarez, Dagnino, and Escobar 1998; Irvin 1999; Juris and Khasnabish 2013; Wood 2003). For example, Black Lives Matters in the USA is an example of a social movement organization that pushes back against the demonization of Black victims of police violence in the USA. The movement is a discursive other for Trump who denigrates professional athletes performing their approval of the movement in public spheres.

Trump has many groups that he frames as others: Mexicans, Muslims, women, minors, disabled persons and LGBTI+ (lesbian, gay, bisexual, and transgender+) identities. Looking at this set of identities, it is important to recognize how the mode of othering reflects intersectionality of power and domination. For instance, while Trump demonizes Mexicans as criminals, there is also a major debate in Mexican politics about the problem of crime and cartel violence. It is well recognized that the country is going through an epidemic of violence and the main perpetrators are men. Feminicide is increasingly becoming a subject of protest in Mexico. Rightfully so, since the problem has been a major subject of political debate for the past decades (Fregoso and Bejarano 2010).

The way in which Trump utilizes the Immigration and Customs Enforcement (ICE) agency also offers a window to see necropopulism at work in justifying the violence deployed by its agents. Since 2017, the agency has been under the spotlight due to the multiple reports of death. Some of the victims were minors and transgender people and almost exclusively all of them were Central American. In addition, the agency has set up detention centers that are notorious for the way in which inmates are treated. They have been called out for being concentration camps, because the critical perspective in public see this administrative move as a display of state power.

Trump deploys the institutional infrastructure targeting populations who cannot legally hold him accountable. Given the structural conditions of impunity, he displays his power as a leader by causing unnecessary harm to migrant communities. In this picture, the negative treatment of inmates leading to their deaths creates a display of power for White supremacist spectators to enjoy. Thus, the cause of death is neglect, which is not a direct form of violence but a structural one. State power stages a publicly sanctioned spectacle of killing people of color, where state agents remain unpunished, as they would not have been a century ago when public lynching was common in the USA.

Mexican policy is heavily criticized for being in line with US interests. Mexican authorities treat Central Americans just like US authorities treat all border crossers. Most notably, both governments use physical geography as a political tool (De León 2015). The US–Mexican border is a vast desert that is extremely hard to trek, just like Mexico's southern border with Guatemala, which is divided by mountains, jungles, rivers and ravines. Throughout its southern states, migrants crossing Mexico have to go through checkpoints established by the notorious "La Migra," the Mexican federal agency that enforces customs and immigration law. Added to the state repression, transnational criminal networks prey on migrants crossing Mexico. Mexican authorities passively support these activities by not enforcing the law, failing to investigate these organizations and looking away from the violent outcome. Since their corpses do not belong to the nation in which they perished, neither government feels it should be a priority for their legal teams to identify the countless dead bodies surfacing from the risk ridden migration patterns.

Given the evidence, I read the political border as a metaphorical wall constructed with human remains and dead material. It is constructed as a powerful metaphor meant to spread terror and deter further crossings. The metaphor confirms that the imagination of border is a site of legitimate and expected violence. For the popular base of the populist, the death of migrants imply that borders are protected. For the discursive others, the metaphor implies a similar fate waits for them. The way in which the victims are not recognized as human beings can be sensed by the lack of mention in the political speeches. The victims are faceless persons whose lives and afterlives do not matter. In this sense, the border is an open-air site of totalitarian power that punishes migrants to the point of oblivion.

6. CONCLUSIONS

Since populism is increasingly getting hold of state institutions, I think it becomes important to pay attention to how state power is deployed in the making and remaking of border, migration and violence. The current wave of governments seems to disregard the need for maintaining the international political system that is constructed upon the will to uphold human rights. Nonetheless, there is a global civil society that is able to intervene in critical cases, but not every case that needs attention.

Scientists and experts are still working transnationally and mobilizing towards offering resolutions. For example, the work of Eyal Weizman (2012) amplified through the project Forensic Architecture is now a global actor. As a team of researchers and experts, they prepare reports for court purposes. Their architectural approach is easily available to the public because they use 3D graphic illustrations to depict crime scenes. The use of architecture in this manner has amplified the voices of many human rights advocacy groups over recent years. This work adds to the existing networks of forensic experts and medical doctors. There are teams of experts in Argentina, Peru, Chile, Brazil, Mexico and Spain, and they travel internationally to work in other geographical contexts. There are many forensic experts elsewhere who continue to take an oppositional stance against their governments, even when they are not allowed to practice legally. These are important for retaining hope for a better future. However, at the end of the day, increasing our capacity to identify human remains should not be the long-term plan; it should be dismantling the structures that kill them.

NOTES

1. I draw from cultural anthropologist Scheper-Hughes (1992) in formulating my understanding of averted medicolegal gaze. She uses Foucault's concept of gaze in her ethnography of everyday violence in Brazil, not to demonstrate how power is used to discipline but to give evidence for how institutional neglect takes place. She demonstrates that medical gaze is absent or averted from certain bodies where discriminatory behaviors fit prevailing forms of racism, sexism and classism. Medical doctors do not want to treat poor and mostly Black Brazilians. There is a genocide of infants that goes unaddressed because the "gaze" of biopolitical power is averted from the population.
2. Cultural studies scholar Bratich (2019) also uses "necropopulism" in a public talk, which he defines as modes of populist expressions that are meant to keep the dead body alive through performances and embodiments. Bratich's main example is how Trump revives Nixon through speech and gestures. Based on cultural anthropologist Taussig's (1997) work, Bratich frames this form of politics as a mode of spirit possession, which invokes the past and embodies the "necrotic" through the living. For Bratich the issue is getting at the fascist aesthetics that inundate white supremacist political expressions. My goal is different in the sense that I want to get at how the institutional configurations of state are manipulated and reconfigured through necropopulist discourses. Following political scientist Auchter's (2014) methodological intervention to the study of statecraft, I examine how populist discourses register death as an ontological problem in defining what nation is and who belongs to the nation. In this sense, the social and political value of national political borders get to be expressed through the body of the living and the dead ancestors, which must be protected from those who are not part of the nation, i.e. the others.
3. This debate is concerned with major shifts in world politics and it is triggered by the election of Donald Trump as the president of the USA in 2016. Another example is the 2019 election of Boris Johnson as the leader of the Conservative Party in the UK, which elevated him to the office of prime minister.
4. The Minnesota Protocol was the first document to detail the international medicolegal principles. New additions were made as new challenges arose and new methods/procedures became available to experts. There have been two key updates to the original set of documents. In 2004, the UN ratified the Istanbul Protocol, which became the basis of holding governments accountable for torture and other misconduct. In 2016, the original Minnesota Protocol was revised based on experiences from other parts of the world. The original protocol was heavily modeled on the transitional justice framework of Argentina. The updated protocol incorporated insights from other geographies (for example, Peru, Bosnia, Sierra Leone, Cyprus) where forensic experts became involved in digging up the dead after mass atrocities in the light of international medicolegal principles.

REFERENCES

Alvarez, Sonia E., Evelyn Dagnino, and Arturo Escobar, eds. 1998. *Cultures of Politics/Politics of Cultures: Re-Visioning Latin American Social Movements*. Boulder, CO: Westview Press.
Anderson, Benedict R. O'G. 2006. *Imagined Communities: Reflections on the Origin and Spread of Nationalism*. London; New York: Verso.

Auchter, Jessica. 2014. *The Politics of Haunting and Memory in International Relations*. Hoboken: Taylor and Francis.
Bargu, Banu. 2016. "Another Necropolitics." *Theory & Event* 19 (1): 1–11.
Bourgois, Philippe. 2009. "Recognizing Invisible Violence: A Thirty-Year Ethnographic Retrospective." In *Global Health in Times of Violence*, edited by Barbara Rylko-Bauer, Linda M. Whiteford, and Paul Farmer, 17–40. Santa Fe: School for Advanced Research Press.
Bratich, Jack. 2019. "The Aesthetics of Decline: Necro-Populism, Downsurgency, and Wars of Restoration." Presented at the WHAP! Lecture Series, California, April 12. https://art.calarts.edu/events/jack-bratich-the-aesthetics-of-decline-necro-populism-downsurgency-and-wars-of-restoration.
Cavarero, Adriana. 2009. *Horrorism: Naming Contemporary Violence*. New Directions in Critical Theory. New York: Columbia University Press.
De León, Jason. 2015. *The Land of Open Graves: Living and Dying on the Migrant Trail*. California Series in Public Anthropology 36. Oakland, CA: University of California Press.
Debrix, Francois. 2016. *Global Powers of Horror: Security, Politics, and the Body in Pieces*. London; New York: Routledge.
Democracy Now. 2015. "Mass Graves of Immigrants Found in Texas, But State Says No Laws Were Broken." July 16, 2015. http://www.democracynow.org/2015/7/16/mass_graves_of_immigrants_found_in.
Farmer, Paul. 2004. "An Anthropology of Structural Violence." *Current Anthropology* 45 (3): 305–25.
Fernandez, Manny. 2017. "A Path to America, Marked by More and More Bodies." *The New York Times*, May 4, U.S. section. https://www.nytimes.com/interactive/2017/05/04/us/texas-border-migrants-dead-bodies.html.
Fregoso, Rosa Linda, and Cynthia L. Bejarano. 2010. *Terrorizing Women: Feminicide in the Américas*. Durham, NC: Duke University Press.
Fujii, Lee Ann. 2013. "The Puzzle of Extra-Lethal Violence." *Perspectives on Politics* 11 (2): 410–26.
Galtung, Johan. 1990. "Cultural Violence." *Journal of Peace Research* 27 (3): 291–305.
Gregory, Thomas. 2016. "Dismembering the Dead: Violence, Vulnerability and the Body in War." *European Journal of International Relations* 22 (4): 944–65.
Irvin, Cynthia L. 1999. *Militant Nationalism between Movement and Party in Ireland and the Basque Country*. Minneapolis, MN: University of Minnesota Press.
Jackson, Patrick Thaddeus. 2006. *Civilizing the Enemy: German Reconstruction and the Invention of the West*. Ann Arbor: University of Michigan Press.
Juris, Jeffrey S., and Alex Khasnabish, eds. 2013. *Insurgent Encounters: Transnational Activism, Ethnography, and the Political*. Durham, NC; London: Duke University Press Books.
Keck, Margaret E., and Kathryn Sikkink. 1998. *Activists Beyond Borders: Advocacy Networks in International Politics*. 1st edition. Ithaca, NY: Cornell University Press.
Keck, Margaret E., and Kathryn Sikkink. 1999. "Transnational Advocacy Networks in International and Regional Politics." *International Social Science Journal* 51 (159): 89–101.
Mbembe, Achille. 2003. "Necropolitics." Translated by Libby Meintjes. *Public Culture* 15 (1): 11–40.
Müller, Jan-Werner. 2016. *What Is Populism?* Philadelphia: University of Pennsylvania Press.
Orentlicher, Diane. 2005. "Set of Principles to Combat Impunity – Updated Set of Principles for the Protection and Promotion of Human Rights through Action to Combat Impunity." E/CN.4/2005/102/Add.1.
Pearson, Michael Parker. 1999. *The Archaeology of Death and Burial*. College Station: Texas A & M University Press.
Pérez, Ventura R. 2012. "The Politicization of the Dead: Violence as Performance, Politics as Usual." In *The Bioarchaeology of Violence*, edited by Debra L. Martin, Ryan P. Harrod, and Ventura R. Pérez, 13–29. Gainesville: University Press of Florida.
Rosenblatt, Adam. 2015. *Digging for the Disappeared: Forensic Science after Atrocity*. Palo Alto, CA: Stanford University Press.
Rylko-Bauer, Barbara, Linda M. Whiteford, and Paul Farmer, eds. 2009. *Global Health in Times of Violence*. Santa Fe: School for Advanced Research Press.
Sanford, Victoria. 2003. *Buried Secrets: Truth and Human Rights in Guatemala*. New York: Palgrave Macmillan US.

Scheper-Hughes, Nancy. 1992. *Death without Weeping: The Violence of Everyday Life in Brazil*. Berkeley: University of California Press.
Singer, Merrill, and G. Derrick Hodge, eds. 2010. *The War Machine and Global Health*. Lanham, MD: AltaMira Press.
Tarrow, Sidney G. 2011. *Power in Movement: Social Movements and Contentious Politics*. 3rd edition. Cambridge; New York: Cambridge University Press.
Taussig, Michael T. 1997. *The Magic of the State*. New York: Routledge.
Verdery, Katherine. 1999. *The Political Lives of Dead Bodies: Reburial and Postsocialist Change*. The Harriman Lectures. New York: Columbia University Press.
Weizman, Eyal. 2012. *Hollow Land: Israel's Architecture of Occupation*. 1st edition. London; New York: Verso.
Whitehead, Neil L., ed. 2004. *Violence*. Santa Fe: School of Advanced Research.
Wood, Elisabeth Jean. 2003. *Insurgent Collective Action and Civil War in El Salvador*. New York: Cambridge University Press.

9. 'Migrant trash' or humanitarian responsibility? Central American government state responses to deported nationals

Isabel Rosales Sandoval

1. INTRODUCTION

Long before Central American migrants reach the US–Mexico border, they travel for weeks or months through some of the most impoverished regions of Mexico, some riding on the roofs of freight trains. It is a difficult journey even for those who make it to the US, because they sometimes face deportation. Each week a steady stream of migrants is arrested and deported from the US to El Salvador, Guatemala and Honduras, the Northern Triangle of Central America. In the last decade there has been an increase in the number of Central American migrant deportations; after the Mexicans, Northern Triangle emigrants are the most numerous. In this chapter I examine how migrant-sending states are institutionalizing reception policies for deported migrants. These policies vary from country to country and can include the creation of institutions, programmes or statistical databases, or short-term actions such as providing snacks, phone calls and currency exchange to deported citizens. I ask which factors make some sending states reluctant to implement reception policies and argue that since deported migrants represent neither a political nor an economic gain, governments give limited attention to reception policies. Hence the title of this chapter and its reference to whether deported migrants are 'migrant trash'[1] or rather part of the humanitarian responsibility of migrant-sending states.

I draw on material collected from the *Dirección de Atención al Migrante* in El Salvador, the *Bienvenido a Casa* programme in Guatemala and the *Centro de Atención para el Migrante Retornado* in Honduras, programmes designed to receive deported migrants. Despite sharing similar contexts, Central American governments respond differently towards their emigrants. I end the chapter with a typology of state actions regarding deportation programmes. While El Salvador's government has taken the initiative to provide services and protection to its migrants arrested abroad and receive the deported, Honduras has delegated these functions to non-governmental organizations (NGOs). Guatemala, on the other hand, has allied with intergovernmental organizations (IGOs), and its consulate services provided abroad are not as proficient as those of El Salvador.

2. NORTHERN TRIANGLE OF CENTRAL AMERICA: THE CONTEXT

Emigration from the Northern Triangle of Central America (hereinafter, NTCA) to the US through Mexico is largely a result of the political conflicts that took place in the region during the 1970s and 1980s. The wars in El Salvador and Guatemala and the various levels of

Table 9.1   NTCA population by country and estimated emigrant population in the US in 2019

Country	Total population (millions)	Emigrant population in the US (%)
El Salvador	6.5	25
Guatemala	16.3	7
Honduras	9.2	9
Total NTCA	32	11

Source: Prepared by the author based on total population data from El Salvador (DIGESTYC 2017), Guatemala (Instituto Nacional de Estadística Guatemala 2019) and Honduras (Instituto Nacional de Estadísticas Honduras 2019). Estimated percentage of NTCA emigrant population in the US from the International Organization for Migration (IOM 2019a).

repression culminated in the displacement of approximately 1.5 to 2 million people to Mexico and the US (Torres-Rivas and Jiménez 1985). Even though Honduras did not suffer the high costs of internal military conflict, the country received more than 30,000 refugees fleeing the conflict in El Salvador. There have been four types of migration from El Salvador, Guatemala and Honduras, the NTCA: internal, regional, transit and, after the mid-1990s, international migration driven by economic rather than political factors (Andrade-Eekhoff and Silva-Avalos 2003).

Since the 2000s, the number of international emigrants from the NTCA to the US has increased from 1.8 to more than 3.6 million in 2019 (IOM 2019b). Despite the peace accords signed in the 1990s and US pressure to impose strict migration controls in the region, undocumented migration from the NTCA continued. As can be seen in Table 9.1, in 2019, 11 percent of the NTCA's total population was living in the US and for countries like El Salvador, 25 percent of its population lives abroad.

After reaching record high levels in 2014, the flow of NTCA emigrants arriving at the US–Mexico border declined sharply in 2015.[2] Numerous factors contributed to the decline. First, the US intensified its enforcement efforts at the US–Mexico border, targeting more resources to investigate and prosecute migrant smugglers and working with the NTCA governments on a public information campaign to discourage outflows (Alonzo 2015). Additionally, the three NTCA countries announced a large-scale development strategy in 2014 known as the Alliance for Prosperity Plan (Rosenblum and Ball 2016). Mexico implemented a major enforcement effort, the Southern Border Programme, to secure its borders with Guatemala and Belize and block emigrant flows. Shortly afterwards, in 2015 the consulates of the NTCA and Mexico signed a joint declaration to create a consular coordination group in McAllen, Texas to promote collaborative actions on matters of protection and consular assistance, called TRICAMEX. Thus, while the drop in the number of migrants from the region in 2015 led some to believe that the regional migration 'crisis' had been resolved, recent data are a reminder that humanitarian and migration pressures in the Northern Triangle remain a major concern. As Table 9.2 illustrates, in 2018 migrants from the NTCA outnumbered those from Mexico.

Despite the hardening of immigration policies in North America, NTCA emigrant flows have been steady. If increased regional enforcement explains falling emigrant arrivals in 2015, what accounts for the resurgence of flows beginning in 2016? Powerful push factors in the region and pull factors in the US appear to be overwhelming the regional enforcement efforts.

In general, the underlying drivers of migration from Central America remain in place and have intensified. The region suffered a crisis in the agricultural sector and was hit by severe disasters such as Hurricane Mitch in 1998 and Hurricane Stan in 2005. In a survey asking

Table 9.2   *US apprehensions of Central American and Mexican migrants (2011–2018)*

Country	2011	2012	2013	2014	2015	2016	2017	2018
El Salvador	27 652	38 976	51 226	79 321	51 200	78 983	59 687	42 132
Guatemala	41 708	57 486	73 208	97 151	66 982	84 649	81 909	135 354
Honduras	31 189	50 771	64 157	106 928	42 433	61 222	60 169	91 141
Total NTCA	100 549	147 233	188 591	283 400	160 615	224 854	201 765	268 627
Mexico	517 472	468 766	424 978	350 177	267 885	265 74	220 138	252 267

Source: Prepared by the author using data from Homeland Security (2018).

recent NTCA migrants residing in the US about their motivations for leaving, the main reason was economic. Almost 90 percent of Guatemalan migrants report economic reasons as the main motivation behind leaving their country of origin. Among the economic reasons reported are unemployment (43 percent), lack of sufficient work to cover needs (22 percent) and low wages (15 percent) (Abuelafia, Del Carmen, and Ruiz-Arranz 2019). Economic growth in the NTCA countries is below their peers in Latin America, with the three countries having some of the highest poverty rates in Latin America and the Caribbean. In 2017, 53 percent of Hondurans, 49 percent of Guatemalans and 29 percent of Salvadorans lived on less than US$5.50 per day (International Monetary Fund 2019).

The region also has high levels of postwar violence. For several years, El Salvador, Guatemala and Honduras have accounted for the highest murder rates in the world, with deaths frequently connected to drug trafficking and organized crime (UNODC 2019). In El Salvador, a truce between rival gangs led to a reduction in homicides in 2012–13. However, violence intensified when the truce fell apart in 2014, and the country's homicide rate climbed in 2015 to the highest monthly total since the country's civil war (which ended in 1992); there was one murder every hour in El Salvador that year (Lakhani 2015; Watts 2015).

According to a UNODC report, in 2016 El Salvador and Honduras were the countries with highest homicide rates in the world,[3] with 62.1 and 41.7 homicides for every 100,000 inhabitants respectively (UNODC 2019). These numbers, along with the homicide rates in Guatemala, give a total of 25.9 homicides per 100,000 people and confirm that Central America is one of the most insecure regions in the world (UNODC 2019; Dalby and Carranza 2019). It is possible to find medium-sized cities with homicide rates far above the national average (e.g. San Pedro Sula, Honduras) and cities of over 1 million inhabitants with above-average homicide rates, e.g. Tegucigalpa (Honduras) with 91 homicides per 100,0000 people and Guatemala City with 65 homicides per 100,0000 people (UNODC 2019).

The pull factors driving migration flows from the NTCA migrants vary. After three decades of migration from the region, about one in five Salvadorans and one in 15 Guatemalans and Hondurans already live in the US, making the US an obvious destination for most families fleeing the region (Rosenblum and Ball 2016). In 2014, the US responded to the surge of unaccompanied children and family units by increasing its reception and adjudication resources to begin hearings within three weeks of their arrival. However, chronic funding shortfalls for immigration courts meant that more than half of the cases opened in 2014 were still pending in 2015. Smugglers have used these slow processing times to lie to families, telling them that they will be granted immediate permission to reside in the US (Gianopoulos 2015).

On 12 October 2018 a group of about 160 Hondurans set forth from the town of San Pedro Sula, which has been often referred to as the 'murder capital of the world', in hopes of presenting themselves for asylum in Mexico or the US. By 15 October, the Associated Press estimated that around 1,600 Hondurans had gathered at the border with Guatemala (Pradilla 2019). On 15 January 2020 another caravan leaving from Honduras started its journey to the US. The NTCA caravans forced the governments of the NTCA, Mexico and the US to come up with yet another regional enforcement plan, the Comprehensive Development Plan (Plan de Desarrollo Integral) presented in December 2018. The plan's aim is to address the growing migratory flows from the Northern Triangle to the US, based on a human security and rights perspective (Comisión Económica para América Latina y el Caribe 2019). Despite all regional enforcement plans, it is clear that economic and security conditions in Central America continue to push people to leave their homes.

3. MIGRATION POLICY AIMED AT INTEGRATING THE EMIGRANT COMMUNITY: SENDING STATES PROTECTING EMIGRANTS' RIGHTS

Sending states are emigration states that can influence ties with their citizens even beyond the reach of their territorial coercive powers. They do this through mechanisms that go beyond their borders and operate on a transnational scale within policies (Gamlen 2019; Østergaard-Nielsen 2016). The three Central American sending states examined in this chapter have gone from having no policy to playing a major role in migration policy. Together with political, social, religious and international institutions, sending states are creating and reinforcing transnational ties.

In the region, three main actors have asked the governments to pay more attention to policies that respond to the needs of emigrants and their families to improve, among other things, deportation services. The main actors making claims in the civil society sector are: academics and migrant organizations abroad, NGOs, the Church and human rights organizations and IGOs such as the UN and the International Organization for Migration. Some policies are being debated on the political agenda, while bills are in their first or second reading in congress. Some claims go directly to the executive branch, but many are channelled through political parties to reach the legislature.

In the NTCA, it is impossible to speak of a single migration public policy with clear macro-orientations and common, long-term institutional goals. On the contrary, the policies are outside the normative idea of public policy. In the countries under study, public policies are fragmented between different institutions, which largely act in an isolated, uncoordinated and inconsistent way. This happens when public policies are the outcome of a reaction, which means that their actions are oriented to mitigate short-term needs. However, fragmentation is one of the main characteristics of migration policies in El Salvador, Guatemala and Honduras. The states have somehow organized themselves to lead the policy-making process, and different actors have struggled to put the topic on the political agenda.

Based on the existing categories discussed by many scholars (among them Gamlen 2015; Østergaard-Nielsen 2016; Levitt and de la Dehesa 2003) for the particular case of Central America, I have divided these policies into four categories:

(a) recognizing the emigrant community;
(b) cultivating loyalty among the emigrant community;

(c) extending emigrants' rights; and
(d) extracting resources from emigrants.

These categories are an important part of the state policy mechanisms that I have addressed in my own research. Table 9.3 shows the country result based on documents collected during various fieldwork trips to the three countries between 2012 and 2017.

In sum, differences regarding migration policies are the product of the mechanisms used by each sending state. But, why are these policies different? I argue that these differences are strongly related, on the one hand, to the relationship between the state and non-state actors and, on the other, to a specific policy theme. This can be seen in the combination of actors involved in each policy. Those actors either facilitate or impede certain policies in the pursuit of particular interests, which sometimes ignore collective interests in order to be put on the political agenda.

Clearly, the three sending states have taken different paths when it comes to protecting the emigrant community abroad. The next section presents an analysis of the different strategies that states use to 'protect' their emigrant community when, in reality, most Central American governments are merely providing services.

Table 9.3 State policy mechanisms to engage with the emigrant community

	Emigrant community building		**Emigrant community integration**	
Countries	**Recognizing the emigrant community**	**Cultivating loyalty among the emigrant community**	**Extending rights**	**Extracting resources**
	Expansion of consular unit services, improving statistics, creating institutions, extensive bilateral agreements.	Symbolic days, celebrating national holidays, announcing responsibility for the migrant.	Dual nationality, right to vote abroad, legislative representation, support of hometown organizations, providing health and education services. Reception of deported citizens, aiding missing migrants' families, assisting arrested migrants, labour rights protection.	Investment services, matching fund programmes, offering financial products, facilitating sending remittances, promoting temporary workers' programmes.
El S	X	X	X	X
GT	X	X	X	X
HON		X	X	X

Source: Based on Gamlen's categories of Diaspora Policy Mechanisms (2008) and collected data.

4. THE RECEPTION OF CENTRAL AMERICAN DEPORTED MIGRANTS

This work builds upon three detailed case studies that trace the sources of emigrant policies in Central America. I collected data from academic and civil society publications, government reports, pieces of legislation and legislative and executive decrees. I conducted 74 in-depth interviews with former and current high-ranking public officials in El Salvador, Guatemala,

Honduras and Mexico (as a migrant-transit country) in 2012, 2015 and 2017, and visited the *Dirección de Atención al Migrante* in El Salvador, the *Bienvenido a Casa* programme in Guatemala and the *Centro de Atención para el Migrante Retornado* in Honduras. Lastly, I coded the information with a qualitative analysis software and then created a database with over 300 official reports, laws and bills from the three countries.

State services for deportees start abroad when emigrants are arrested and consist mainly of consulate activities, starting with a visit from the Guatemalan, Honduran or Salvadoran consul general in a US prison upon detention of one of its citizens. Through a series of mechanisms and inter-institutional coordination, the consul verifies the identity of the detained migrant. Then, consuls provide documentation called 'consular cards', although only in the case of El Salvador is there a systematized database containing the deportee's information. Consulates are part of Ministries of Foreign Affairs and are located where a considerable number of a country's citizens are living abroad. The services offered by the mobile consulates include the issuance of a consular identification card. As of 2019 in the US, El Salvador had 18 consulates, Guatemala 17 and Honduras 10, numbers that demonstrate a quite extensive network of consulates in the US for such small countries (Ministerio de Relaciones Exteriores de El Salvador 2019; Ministerio de Relaciones Exteriores de Guatemala 2020; Secretaría de Relaciones Exteriores y Cooperación Internacional de Honduras 2017).

In 2019 in Guatemala, approximately three to five flights arrived weekly from the US with 300 deported Guatemalans (Gutiérrez and Manzanedo 2019). According to the 2011 Report on Actions and Achievements in Consular and Migration Matters: 'The Ministry of Foreign Affairs provides daily assistance to all Guatemalans that are returned from the United States. The Ministry welcomes the deported citizens by providing a snack, free national and international calls, as well as currency exchange in a bank if they are bringing dollars that they want to exchange to quetzales, the Guatemalan currency' (Ministerio de Relaciones Exteriores de Guatemala 2011). The Human Rights Ombudsman visits the air force facilities several times a month to interview deported migrants. During this process, a survey is filled in with data from each respondent taken in confidence to profile and identify trends such as age, gender, place of origin and whether the migrant was abused or suffered at the hands of organized crime or authorities in Mexico or the US. When there is a human rights violation, Migrant Advocacy opens a file with all the information and sends it to the Ministry of Foreign Affairs. This Ministry is responsible for filing a report against Mexico or the US, although there is no known resolution for any of the reports filed against abuses committed by these countries' authorities (Reynosa 2012).

In El Salvador, the General Directorate of Migration (DGM) is in charge of receiving deported migrants. When the Welcome Home Programme started, it was administered by Catholic Relief Services, a US agency. After that, the programme was handed over to a local NGO, the National Development Foundation (FUNDE). However, since 2008, El Salvador's General Directorate of Migration has been in charge of the programme. In Honduras, the Centre for Returned Migrants (CAMR), a NGO founded in Tegucigalpa in 1999 on the initiative of the Pastoral Care of Migrants and with the involvement of volunteers (Scalabrinian missionaries), is the institution in charge of receiving deported migrants. Through its Directorate General of Immigration, the Honduran government has delegated its functions to civil society (the National Forum for Migration in Honduras (FONAMIH), Family Network of Missing Migrants), among many other actors, primarily the Scalabrinian nuns. It is notable that Tegucigalpa's former mayor, Ricardo Álvarez, called the director of CAMR, Sister Valdette

Table 9.4 Programmes and actors involved in the reception of Central American deported migrants

Policy category	El Salvador	Guatemala	Honduras	Actors involved
Protection and extension of emigrant rights	Reception of migrants (a)	Welcome Home Programme (b)	Returned Migrant Care Programme (c)	– (a) State – (b) State/Civil Society International Organizations (IOs) – (c) IO/State
	People tracking system (a)	–	People tracking system (b)	– (a) State – (b) Civil Society
	Consular interview and consular card	Consular interview and consular card	Consular interview and consular card	State
	Monitoring of formal complaints	–	–	State

Source: Prepared by the author based on fieldwork collected data.

Table 9.5 US deportations of Central American and Mexican migrants (2011–2018)

Country	2011	2012	2013	2014	2015	2016	2017	2018
El Salvador	17 945	18 910	21 130	26 671	21 900	20 264	18 452	14 877
Guatemala	30 871	38 885	47 013	54 406	33 379	33 887	33 060	49 149
Honduras	22 675	31 724	36 636	40 877	20 298	22 016	22 168	28 452
Total NTCA	**71 491**	**89 519**	**104 779**	**121 954**	**75 577**	**76 167**	**73 680**	**92 478**
Mexico	287 502	300 589	307 120	265 615	234 296	238 074	192 334	217 919

Source: Prepared by the author using data from Homeland Security (2018).

Willeman 'the mother of migrants'. Although this is symbolic, it shows how the government promotes civil society to be responsible for deported citizens (Table 9.4).

The aim of these programmes is to provide protection to emigrants detained abroad and later deported to their countries of origin. However, it ends up being merely a service provision in the case of Honduras and Guatemala, where states delegate their functions to civil society or to IOs.

Beginning in the mid-1990s, a hardening of US immigration policies elevated the power of the federal government to arrest and deport undocumented migrants. This led to increased deportation, now strategically referred to as 'removals' (Hagan, Eschbach, and Rodriguez 2008). During fiscal year 2012, the US Immigration and Customs Enforcement's (ICE's) Office of Enforcement and Removal Operations deported the largest number of undocumented migrants (409,849) from the US in the agency's modern history. Guatemala was the destination of the highest number of air repatriations to any country in the world (Wainer 2012). However, after reaching record levels in 2014, the number of NTCA deported emigrants declined, but remained steady (Rosenblum and Ball 2016). Behind the numbers, deportees consist of a diverse group of migrants, spanning settled migrants who have lived and worked for years in the US and new arrivals apprehended during a first attempted unauthorized entry.

The numbers in Table 9.5 must be multiplied at least by two to estimate how many more Central Americans have been deported by land from Mexico. The sociopolitical ramifications of current mass deportations remain very much underexamined and insufficiently explored in the region. In addition to the problems faced by individual migrants, US deportation policy undermines long-standing family reunification principles and has direct social, economic and psychological costs for deportees and their families in the US and in the country of origin.

The three countries have arranged a place at the airport with plastic chairs to receive deported migrants, away from the place where commercial flights land. In Guatemala, for instance, deported Guatemalan migrants come back to a country of origin lacking an effective state programme for reception and integration. Deportees are not received at the airport, but at the air force base, not because the military are handling them, but apparently to keep them out of sight of the other passengers. When the authorities are done interviewing them, they exit through a door that takes them directly out to a busy street far from the exit area for other international travellers and from public view.

In my three visits to the three facilities for deported migrants in El Salvador, Guatemala and Honduras, I interviewed members of civil society either running the facilities, as in Honduras, or verifying the respect for the human rights of that population, as in Guatemala, along with public officials from the General Directorate of Migration who run the programme in El Salvador.

In El Salvador, the *Ley Especial para la Protección y Desarrollo de la Persona Migrante Salvadoreña y su Familia*, a law to protect migrants and their families, incorporates a few initiatives identified with the reintegration of deported emigrants into the nation, for example, the *Proyecto de Cooperación Productiva y Cooperación Técnica*, a cooperation project (Asamblea Legislativa de la República de El Salvador 2011). As soon as migrants arrive, they are provided with a snack (a traditional Salvadoran stuffed tortilla and coffee), allowed to make a phone call and given some money for their bus ride back home. There is an official work database in the facilities that deported migrants must fill out to encourage the incorporation of the deported emigrants into the economy, according to the capacities and skills they learned abroad. The General Directorate of Migration and Immigration also offers services for deported emigrants (Olán 2015). The Directorate for Attention to Migrants is made up of the Return Reception Centre, where land returns from Mexico and air returns from the US are received daily, located in Colonia Quiñonez, San Salvador.

The commitment of the Salvadoran state has made it possible to implement an exemplary model at the regional level for the reception of returned Salvadoran people, based on an effort to articulate and coordinate various government institutions and on the support of NGOs, foundations and IOs in order to provide comprehensive and immediate care for their needs when they return to the country, but always led by the state. Priority is given to caring for people in vulnerable conditions, with strict adherence and respect for human rights (Dirección General de Migración y Extranjería de El Salvador 2020). In this line, the *Programa de Reinserción Sociolaboral*, promoted by the *Instituto Salvadoreño del Migrante* (INSAMI), with the support of the Ministry of Labour, Vice-Ministry for Salvadorans Abroad and the Executive Secretary of CONMIGRANTES, is an initiative that has carried out activities to provide counselling to deported emigrants from the US regarding financial matters. INSAMI created the *Red Nacional de Emprendedores Retornados de El Salvador* (RENACERES), a network to provide seed funding to deported Salvadorans (Ríos 2018).

In Guatemala, deported migrants arrive at the air force base on daily flights, seven days a week, and sometimes on two flights a day. As soon as the planes touch ground, the deportees are escorted to the deportation reception facility, each carrying a black plastic bag containing their belongings. Once inside the building, the deportees are assigned a plastic chair, where sandwiches and coffee are distributed. They are welcomed by Foreign Ministry posters saying

'You are finally in your own country and with your own people – Welcome to Guatemala'. On the day I was there, a representative from the DGM made a motivational speech and told the deported migrants 'Welcome home! No worries, surely there is chicken broth waiting for you at home' (ignoring the fact that these people probably left their country because there is not much to eat in their houses). Despite this welcome, the deportees are subject to state authority, enacted, for example, by not allowing them to go to the toilet or make phone calls. Some hours later, deported migrants go through the first ordinary migration control procedure, followed by a second check by the national police (for felonies committed in Guatemala). In addition to the modest meal, the services offered consist of an international phone call, paid for by the International Organization for Migration (IOM), while the Ministry of Foreign Relations (MINEX) gives deported migrants access to a local call. IOM also pays for half the transportation costs of the migrants who will travel outside the capital, but pays them directly to the transport company. Those arriving on afternoon planes and whose home communities are located far from Guatemala City are dropped off at the *Casa del Migrante*, the migrant shelter operated by the Catholic Church, but very few sleep there (Reynosa 2012). Ironically, the only existing reception programme – The Guatemalan Repatriates Project – is funded by USAID (US Agency for International Development) and operated by the IOM. Since the project was launched in June 2011, it has provided basic communication and health services, transportation and shelter to about 23,000 returnees. Apart from a few basic and immediate services, there is no long-term reintegration plan for deportees.

In Honduras, the Centre for Returned Migrants (CAMR), *Casa Alianza*, the Network of Migrant Committees and Families (RED COMIFAH) and other individual member organizations of the FONAMIH provide vital social infrastructure and humanitarian assistance to migrants and deportees, as well as more accurate data about the Honduran migration situation than can be obtained from official statistics. Much work is done on a voluntary basis. Over the years, these NGOs have had success with improving public policies in some areas (e.g. in the area of unaccompanied minors) and with compensating for a lack of public policies in other areas (e.g. providing migrant shelters and receiving deportees).

While religious NGOs express some concern about migration-related family breakdown, they also view migration in part as a consequence of high levels of intrafamily violence. Only representatives from the private sector reproduce some form of migrant marginalizing discourse when they refer to contingents of deported women as prostitutes and potential carriers of AIDS. State actors generally seem too embarrassed to ascribe blame to anyone.

'Welcome to Honduras, a country of five stars, and you are one of the seven million stars that inhabit this beautiful country' is the encouraging message Sister Valdette Willeman gives to arriving deportees when she steps up to greet them from the chartered 'removal flights' arriving on a daily basis. She runs the Centre for Returned Migrants at the international airport of Tegucigalpa. The majority have spent three months awaiting their deportation in US prisons. Only when they have been released from the plastic flexi handcuffs used during the journey is Sister Valdette allowed to enter the plane. She is escorted by two Honduran migration police officers. The deportees are then walked to the CAMR building, where a migration check-in is done by the authorities and an interview is conducted by CAMR staff. Inside the reception hall, Sister Valdette mentions that their aim is to treat all deported migrants with dignity, and they are offered medical and psychological assistance, one phone call, a lunch that includes a tortilla, a drink and money to pay for the bus ride to their final destination (Willeman 2012).

Outside the CAMR building, family members struggle with taxi drivers and mobile phone vendors to be the first to greet the exiting deportees.

For all three countries, state engagement stops the moment the deportees leave the reception area. Outside the gate, money exchangers, 'coyotes' (illegal migration border smugglers) and loan companies line up with family members to 'welcome' deported citizens.

5. FACTORS THAT MAKE SOME SENDING STATES RELUCTANT TO IMPLEMENT RECEPTION POLICIES

5.1 Size and Potential Impact of an Emigrant Community

As indicated in the previous section, El Salvador is the only country out of the three that takes complete responsibility for its deported nationals. One possible factor to explain the lack of interest or commitment in the Honduran and Guatemalan governments could be the importance of the size and potential impact of an emigrant community in the country of origin.

The Honduran government and local migrant organizations quote a figure of 1.2 million Hondurans abroad. This figure is also reported by the World Bank (World Bank 2015), although these are only estimates, because it is difficult to determine an exact number when studying undocumented emigrants. Local media use the astonishing breakdown made by the National Forum for Migration, which calculates that 185,000 Hondurans leave their country each year (15,000 per month, 3,500 per week, 21 per hour) (FONAMIH 2006). The majority migrate to the US. The figures also suggest a rapid transformation from Honduras being primarily a country of reception during the 1970s and 1980s (receiving more than 100,000 war refugees from Nicaragua, El Salvador and Guatemala) to becoming a country of mass emigration, with the vast majority migrating within the last 15 years (Endo et al. 2010). As in the case of other Central American migrations, the Honduran experience was once connected to earlier periods of conflict that never resulted in the migration of more than a few thousand people at a time. Current mass migration patterns are linked to structural adjustment packages and massive state corruption during the 1990s, state failure to reconstruct the country after the devastating effects of Hurricane Mitch and the subsequent increase in unemployment, poverty, inequality and insecurity (Meza 2011).

In comparison to Guatemalans and Salvadorans, Honduran migrants have less experience because they started to migrate later, and appear to have fewer networks and weaker links to earlier and more well-established groups in the US. The substantial numbers of Hondurans who have fallen victim to human trafficking, accidents that result in amputation, like falling off a train, abuse, abduction and even murder on their journey northwards, suggest that travelling migrants have to rely more on smugglers and other criminal migration actors than on well-established transnational social networks (Kaye 2010; Sørensen 2013b).

Until the 1970s, migration in the region was generally characterized by internal or regional movements of a transborder, binational and temporary character aimed at sustaining local livelihoods (Morales et al. 2011). However, the armed conflicts in El Salvador and Guatemala changed this pattern, first by causing massive forced displacements due to political violence during the second half of the 1970s and throughout the 1980s (Torres-Rivas and Jiménez 1985). Most affected people became displaced internally, while others found refuge in neighbouring countries, and fewer went to the US, Canada or Europe. When peace accords were finally reached, one significant outcome was a massive return of Central American refugees (Castillo 1994). Others continued their transnational community formation by either staying in the countries of refuge or moving further on, paving the way for later social network-based labour movements (Castillo 1994).

While migration is an enduring aspect of Central American livelihood strategies, the volume and dynamics have changed tremendously during recent decades. Armed conflict, political instability, human rights violations and natural disasters drove Central Americans to migrate in the 1980s and early 1990s, while continuing socioeconomic problems and widespread violence are the main factors behind the present movements (Sørensen 2013a). However, migration has not affected the different Central American countries in the same way and to the same extent. The armed conflicts of El Salvador, Guatemala and Nicaragua have produced larger migration flows from those countries than from more stable countries such as Costa Rica and Panama, and within each country the conflictive zones have generated more migrants (Morales 2007). When new conflicts occur – like the 2009 overthrow of Honduran President Manuel Zelaya – migration flows are instantly affected (Sørensen 2013b).

The distinction between earlier refugee movements (motivated by fear) and post-conflict migrations (economically motivated) is difficult to uphold in Central America. More recent migrants no longer qualify for refugee status according to country of reception, although they often share several experiences with earlier pioneer refugees, in particular regarding exposure to regime instability and increasing levels of insecurity and extensive violence (Sørensen 2013a).

5.2   The Delegation of Functions to Private Actors

Another possible factor to explain the reluctance of the Honduran and Guatemalan governments to invest in more adequate reception policies for its deported citizens is that there are other actors involved, especially private ones, that profit from the deportation regime. Moreover, as undocumented migration has become a business for them, governments do not pay much attention to deported nationals, knowing that cooperation agencies will give them more money to 'deal with' deportations (Rosales Sandoval 2013). The Honduran and Guatemalan governments have outsourced several humanitarian services to NGOs, primarily because of a lack of state capacity. For example, in 2001 the reception of deportees was delegated to the Catholic Church, first to Caritas and then subcontracted to the Scalabrinian sisters.

Hondurans have become the second largest migrant group apprehended and deported by US authorities. According to Homeland Security (2018) statistics, the number of apprehended migrants has risen from around 31,189 in 2011 to 91,141 in 2018. Those deported by air are most likely transported by the New Mexico-based CSI Aviation Services Inc., which, due to US privatization of its detention and deportation operations, makes huge profits on the removal business (Gammeltoft-Hansen 2009). The company has become the largest provider of US deportation flights to Central America, with million dollar contracts awarded by ICE within the US Department of Homeland Security (Kaye 2017).

Nathalie Peutz and Nicholas de Genova have recently called attention to the normative and administrative role of deportation in global migration regulation. Deportability – the protracted possibility of being deported – profoundly weighs on individual lives. Deportation is rendering greater numbers and more diverse categories of migrants subject to arrest, detention and deportation (Genova and Peutz 2010). In terms of practice, deportation entails the sociological production of deportable populations that are not limited to bilateral transactions between receiving and sending states, but rather must be comprehended as an increasingly unified, effective global response to a world that is being actively remade by transnational human mobility.

5.3 Remittance Dependence

Apart from the fact that emigration and deportations are a business for many private and public actors, governments do not do enough to provide deported migrants with a job, health, education or reintegration opportunities once they are back in their home country. This suggests that governments are applying a 'policy of no policy' by letting migrants re-emigrate so that they continue to send economic remittances. Table 9.6 details what remittances represent for these countries.

The high number of deportations in relation to migration attempts leaves the impression that Honduran migration is repetitive. According to FONAMIH activists, 90 percent of the deportees will attempt to migrate again as quickly as possible. From the perspective of the remittance-dependent states, this may mean that rather than being invested in local development, substantial sums are used on repeated migration attempts. Consequently, expectations for a developmental impact from incoming remittances might be far too high. Apart from such purely economic considerations, the high deportation number in Honduras calls for a calculation of the enduring human costs of the current deportation regime for deportees, their families and the communities from which they migrate and to which they are deported. However, this does not reflect the situation in El Salvador, which is the second most remittance-dependent country of the three according to the data in Table 9.6, because the government also takes the most responsibility for assisting deportees of the three countries. For that reason, it is important to take into account the longer history of migration and the greater organization of migrants.

In sum, it is clear that deportation effectively subverts the myth of success through migration. By being physically constrained, forcibly relocated, dumped back into Honduras in chains and with no luggage, movement once again becomes restricted due to the double stigma attached to the deportee body: 'polluted' by prison sentences (even if the felony was nothing but a lack of proper documentation) and 'polluted' by the myth of deportees bringing social ills, such as the female deportees suspected of prostitution. The deportee, in other words, becomes the victim of disgrace, shame and speculation, while simultaneously transforming from a remittance provider into an economic burden (Sørensen 2013b). Yet, not all deportees conform to such victim identities, as some are fully aware of the global and national structures

Table 9.6   *Emigrant remittance inflows ($ million) from 2000 to 2019 and as a share of GDP*

Country	2000	2005	2010	2015	2019	Remittances as a share of GDP in 2019 (%)
El Salvador	1765	3029	3472	4275	5609	20.8
Guatemala	596	3067	4232	6573	10 696	13.0
Honduras	484	1805	2618	3666	5283	21.4
Total NTCA	**2844**	**7900**	**10 322**	**14 514**	**21 588**	–

Note: All numbers are in current (nominal) US $. GDP: gross domestic product.
Source: Prepared by the author using data from World Bank (2019).

to blame. Others use deportation as an occasion for a US government-sponsored 'free' home visit.

Several NGOs acknowledge their business function. Even if their main concern is the creation of migration policies that aim to protect the emigrant community, their actual activities are focused on deportation reception and anti-trafficking campaigns, simply because these are the issues for which they can obtain international funding. At the same time, secular and faith-based NGOs compete for the same meagre national and international resources available for information campaigns, migrant shelters and deportee reception. Particularly after the caravan phenomenon, NGOs are in a stiff competition for funding related to migration, due to the recent drain on international funding in Central America.

To the deported migrant, deportation represents a disaster. To the state from which they originally migrated, the deportee represents a burden. Stripped of his or her economic capacity, the 'migrant hero' of the remittance-dependent nation instantly becomes 'deportee trash' (Sørensen 2010). The disposability of deportees is apparent during their reception in the three countries studied here, as they are kept invisible to the dominant social order.

6. CONCLUSION

The aim of this chapter has been to determine which factors make some sending states reluctant to implement reception policies. I argue that, since deported migrants represent neither a political nor an economic gain, governments give limited attention to those policies. The differences among migrant-sending states became clear during the course of my study and, as a result, I propose a typology of sending states in Central America regarding deported migrants: (a) states that lead the action; (b) states that outsource to private actors; and (c) states that use a mixed system, involving international cooperation with groups such as USAID.

In contrast to Guatemala and Honduras, El Salvador is the sending state that is most active in receiving and providing some resources to welcome its deported citizens. Honduras is the sending state that outsources its functions completely to the Church to receive and protect migrants who have been deported. Guatemala is in the middle, since, although the government receives the deported citizens, migrants face many risks as soon as they leave the air force facilities, and most embark upon their journey back to the US. Ironically, a programme sponsored by USAID is outside waiting for them, offering assistance to pay for the bus or a phone call.

The Salvadoran government has a long history of working with the emigrant community on projects like roads and schools, but they have not been as engaged in projects that generate income and jobs. Government authorities in El Salvador in 2012 stated that they wanted to provide potential migrants with alternatives to migration. Even if change has been slow, at least a statement has been made. In contrast, the governments of Guatemala and Honduras are even less involved in working with migrants and their families. 'There is no administrative capacity', said a Guatemalan Catholic Church leader.

USAID, IOM and some Northern Triangle governments are providing immediate assistance to deportees. There is a visible outsourcing tendency, mainly from Guatemala and Honduras, to delegate protective functions for deported citizens to IOs or the Church, while these organizations only provide basic services. Even if the main concern of many of the NGOs and IOs that are taking over the states' role is to protect citizens, their actual activities are focused on providing services for the reception of emigrants, simply because these are the activities for which international funding is available.

The lack of interest or commitment on the part of the Honduran and Guatemalan governments could be explained by the importance of the size and potential impact of each country's emigrant community. This variable indicates how much a government is willing to give and do for its emigrant community, depending on how big the community is. It is also related to the size of the community, how organized it is abroad and the value of the economic remittances sent. In the case of the deported nationals, it is clear that they will not be sending money if they are in their home country. As a result, it makes sense that governments would be reluctant to provide opportunities at home when re-migration is more beneficial for the countries' economies.

Deportations have legal, economic, embodied and spatial consequences and, in addition to studying the deportees' experience, researchers need to look at the state agencies charged with apprehension and deportation, the private corporation or corporate mercenaries that benefit from these practices, the transnational organizations or local networks that assist arriving deportees and activist groups whose political work opposes deportation. This chapter has shown how and why migrant-sending states differ in their policy actions towards deported migrants and which factors make some countries reluctant to implement those actions.

NOTES

1. The term 'migrant trash' is inspired by Sørensen's article: 'The rise and fall of the "migrant superhero" and the new "deportee trash": Contemporary strain on mobile livelihoods in the Central American region', in which she discusses how the image of migrants changes when they are no longer in the US sending money home and how they go from being perceived as superheroes to 'deportee trash', no longer useful to their home countries (Sørensen 2010).
2. Measured by total apprehensions at the southern border of the US.
3. Excluding subregions of Africa that might show higher rates, but for which complete data are not available (UNODC 2019).

REFERENCES

Abuelafia, Emmanuel, Giselle Del Carmen, and Marta Ruiz-Arranz. 2019. *Tras Los Pasos Del Migrante: Perspectivas y Experiencias de La Migración de El Salvador, Guatemala y Honduras En Estados Unidos*". New York: Inter-American Development Bank. https://publications.iadb.org/publications/spanish/document/Tras_los_pasos_del_migrante_Perspectivas_y_experiencias_de_la_migraci%C3%B3n_de_El_Salvador_Guatemala_y_Honduras_en_Estados_Unidos.pdf.
Alonzo, Areli. 2015. "Campaña '¡Quédate!' Para Evitar Migración de Menores, Se Oirá En Idiomas Mayas." February 17, 2015. https://www.deguate.com/artman/publish/migrantes_actualidad/campania-quedate-para-evitar-migracion-de-menores-se-oira-en-idiomas-mayas.shtml.
Andrade-Eekhoff, Katharine, and Claudia Marina Silva-Avalos. 2003. *Globalización de La Periferia: Los Desafíos de La Migración Transnacional Para El Desarrollo Local En América Central*. San Salvador, El Salvador: FLACSO Programa El Salvador.
Asamblea Legislativa de la República de El Salvador. 2011. *Ley Especial Para La Protección y Desarrollo de La Persona Migrante Salvadoreña y Su Familia*.
Castillo, Manuel Ángel. 1994. "A Preliminary Analysis of Emigration Determinants in Mexico, Central America, Northern South America and the Caribbean." *International Organization for Migration (IOM)*, Quarterly Review, XXXII (2): 269–306.

Comisión Económica para América Latina y el Caribe. 2019. *Hacia Un Nuevo Estilo de Desarrollo: Plan de Desarrollo Integral El Salvador–Guatemala–Honduras–México. Diagnóstico, Áreas de Oportunidad y Recomendaciones de La CEPAL*. LC/MEX/TS.2019/6. Ciudad de México: Naciones Unidas. https://www.gob.mx/cms/uploads/attachment/file/462720/34.Hacia_un_nuevo_estilo_de_desarrollo___Plan_de_Desarrollo_Integral_El.pdf.
Dalby, Chris, and Camilo Carranza. 2019. "Balance de InSight Crime Sobre Los Homicidios En 2018." January 22, 2019. https://es.insightcrime.org/noticias/analisis/balance-de-insight-crime-sobre-los-homicidios-en-2018/.
DIGESTYC. 2017. *Encuesta de Hogares de Propósitos Múltiples*. El Salvador: Ministerio de Economía.
Dirección General de Migración y Extranjería de El Salvador. 2020. "Retorno a Casa." http://www.migracion.gob.sv.
Endo, Isaku, Sarah Hirsch, Jan Rogge, and Kamil Borowik. 2010. *The U.S.–Honduras Remittance Corridor: Acting on Opportunities to Increase Financial Inclusion and Foster Development of a Transnational Economy*. World Bank Working Paper, no. 177. Washington, DC: World Bank.
FONAMIH. 2006. *Ejes de Un Proceso Migratorio*. Tegucigalpa, Honduras: Publigráficas S. de R.L.
Gamlen, Alan. 2008. "The Emigration State and the Modern Geopolitical Imagination." *Political Geography* 27 (8): 840–56.
Gamlen, Alan. 2015. "The Rise of Diaspora Institutions." In *Diasporas Reimagined: Spaces, Practices and Belonging*, edited by Nando Sigona, Alan Gamlen, Giulia Liberatore, and Hélène Neveu Kringelbach, 166–71. Oxford: Oxford Diasporas Programme.
Gamlen, Alan. 2019. *Human Geopolitics: States, Emigrants, and the Rise of Diaspora Institutions*. Oxford: Oxford University Press.
Gammeltoft-Hansen, Thomas. 2009. *Access to Asylum: International Refugee Law and the Offshoring and Outsourcing of Migration Control*. Aarhus: Institute of Law, Aarhus University.
Genova, Nicholas de, and Nathalie Peutz, eds. 2010. *The Deportation Regime: Sovereignty, Space, and the Freedom of Movement*. Durham, NC: Duke University Press Books.
Gianopoulos, Kimberly. 2015. "Unaccompanied Alien Children. Improved Evaluation Efforts Could Enhance Agency Programs to Reduce Migration from Central America." United States Government Accountability Office. https://www.gao.gov/assets/680/673414.pdf.
Gutiérrez, Blanca, and Cristina Manzanedo. 2019. "Los invisibles de las políticas migratorias: los deportados." *El País*, July 12, 3500 Millones section. https://elpais.com/elpais/2019/07/10/3500_millones/1562794341_175507.html.
Hagan, Jacqueline, Karl Eschbach, and Nestor Rodriguez. 2008. "U.S. Deportation Policy, Family Separation, and Circular Migration." *The International Migration Review* 42 (1): 64–88.
Homeland Security. 2018. *Yearbook of Immigration Statistics*. https://www.dhs.gov/immigration-statistics/yearbook.
Instituto Nacional de Estadística Guatemala. 2019. *Principales Resultados Censo 2018*. Guatemala: Gobierno de la República de Guatemala.
Instituto Nacional de Estadísticas Honduras. 2019. "Población Total 2019." https://www.ine.gob.hn/V3/.
International Monetary Fund. 2019. *World Economic Outlook: Global Manufacturing Downturn, Rising Trade Barriers*. Washington, DC: IMF.
IOM. 2019a. "Global Migration Data Portal." http://migrationdataportal.org/es/data.
IOM. 2019b. "Migration Data Portal: The Bigger Picture." Migration Data Portal. http://migrationdataportal.org/themes/diasporas.
Kaye, Jeffrey. 2010. *Moving Millions. How Coyote Capitalism Fuels Global Immigration*. Hoboken, NJ; Canada: John Wiley & Sons.
Kaye, Jeffrey. 2017. "For Immigration Crackdown Proponent, Deportations Mean Business." *HuffPost*. December 6. https://www.huffpost.com/entry/for-immigration-crackdown_b_594426.
Lakhani, Nina. 2015. "Violence Escalates in El Salvador as End to Gang Truce Proves Deadly." *The Guardian*, April 6, World News section. https://www.theguardian.com/world/2015/apr/06/el-salvador-violence-end-to-gang-truce-proves-deadly.
Levitt, Peggy, and Rafael de la Dehesa. 2003. "Transnational Migration and the Redefinition of the State: Variations and Explanations." *Ethnic and Racial Studies* 26 (4): 587–611.
Meza, Víctor, ed. 2011. *Honduras: Retos y Desafíos de La Reconstrucción Democrática*. Tegucigalpa, Honduras: Centro de Documentación de Honduras CEDOH.

Ministerio de Relaciones Exteriores de El Salvador. 2019. "Directorio de Embajadas y Consulados de El Salvador." http://embajadasyconsulados.rree.gob.sv/index.php?option=com_content&view=featured&Itemid=323.
Ministerio de Relaciones Exteriores de Guatemala. 2011. "Acciones y Logros En Materia Consular y Migratoria." Departamento de Reproducciones MRE.
Ministerio de Relaciones Exteriores de Guatemala. 2020. "Directorio de Embajadas y Consulados de Guatemala." https://www.minex.gob.gt/Directorio.aspx?ID_TIPO=6.
Morales, Abelardo. 2007. *La Diáspora de La Posguerra. Regionalismo de Los Migrantes y Dinámicas Territoriales En América Central*. San José, Costa Rica: FLACSO Costa Rica.
Morales, Abelardo, Susan Kandel, Xenia Ortiz, Oscar Díaz, and Guillermo Acuña. 2011. *Trabajadores Migrantes y Megaproyectos En América Central*. San Salvador, El Salvador: PNUD/ UCA.
Olán, Eunice. 2015. Statistics Director, General Directorate of Migration. Interview.
Østergaard-Nielsen, Eva. 2016. "Sending Country Policies." In *Integration Processes and Policies in Europe*, edited by Blanca Garcés-Mascareñas and Rinus Penninx, 147–65. Cham: Springer International Publishing. https://doi.org/10.1007/978-3-319-21674-4_9.
Pradilla, Alberto. 2019. *Caravana: Cómo el éxodo centroamericano salió de la clandestinidad*. Debate. Mexico: Penguin Random House. https://www.casadellibro.com/ebook-caravana-ebook/9786073180528/9640006.
Reynosa, Flora. 2012. Defensoría del Migrante, Procuraduría de Derechos Humanos, Guatemala. Interview.
Ríos, César. 2018. Executive Director of Instituto Salvadoreño del Migrante (INSAMI) and of Asociación Salvadoreña de Educación Financiera (ASEFIN). Interview.
Rosales Sandoval, Isabel. 2013. "Public Officials and the Migration Industry in Guatemala: Greasing the Wheels of a Corrupt Machine." In *The Migration Industry and the Commercialization of International Migration*, edited by Thomas Gammeltoft-Hansen and Ninna Nyberg Sørensen. Global Institutions. London, New York: Routledge.
Rosenblum, Marc, and Isabel Ball. 2016. "Trends in Unaccompanied Child and Family Migration from Central America." Migration Policy Institute. https://www.migrationpolicy.org/research/trends-unaccompanied-child-and-family-migration-central-america.
Secretaría de Relaciones Exteriores y Cooperación Internacional de Honduras. 2017. "Observatorio consular y migratorio de Honduras, CONMIGHO." https://www.conmigho.hn/.
Sørensen, Ninna Nyberg. 2010. "The Rise and Fall of the 'Migrant Superhero' and the New 'Deportee Trash': Contemporary Strain on Mobile Livelihoods in the Central American Region." *Border-Lines* 5: 90–120.
Sørensen, Ninna Nyberg. 2013a. "Central American Migration, Remittances and Transnational Development." In *Handbook of Central American Governance*, edited by Diego Sanchez-Ancochea and Salvador Martí i Puig, 45–58. London: Routledge.
Sørensen, Ninna Nyberg. 2013b. "Jumping the Remains of the Migration Train Honduran Migration and Criminal Co-Optation of the Migration Industry." In *The Migration Industry and the Commercialization of International Migration*, edited by Thomas Gammeltoft-Hansen and Ninna Nyberg Sørensen. Global Institutions. London/New York: Routledge.
Torres-Rivas, Edelberto, and Dina Jiménez. 1985. "Informe Sobre El Estado de Las Migraciones En Centroamérica." *Anuario de Estudios Centroamericanos, University of Costa Rica*, 1985: 25–66.
UNODC. 2019. "Global Study on Homicide 2019." Booklet 2. Vienna, Austria. https://www.unodc.org/documents/data-and-analysis/gsh/Booklet2.pdf.
Wainer, Andrew. 2012. "Exchanging People for Money: Remittances and Repatriation in Central America." 18. Briefing Paper. Bread for the World Institute. https://www.bread.org/sites/default/files/downloads/briefing-paper-18.pdf.
Watts, Jonathan. 2015. "One Murder Every Hour: How El Salvador Became the Homicide Capital of the World." *The Guardian*, August 22, World News section. http://www.theguardian.com/world/2015/aug/22/el-salvador-worlds-most-homicidal-place.
Willeman, Valdette. 2012. Scalabrinian missionary director of Centre for Returned Migrants (CAMR). Interview.

World Bank. 2015. "Migration and Remittances Data. Bilateral Remittances Matrices." http://www.worldbank.org/en/topic/migrationremittancesdiasporaissues/brief/migration-remittances-data.

World Bank. 2019. "Migration and Remittances Data." World Bank. https://www.worldbank.org/en/topic/migrationremittancesdiasporaissues/brief/migration-remittances-data.

10. Biopolitical governmentality at Chile's northern border (Arica–Tacna)

Luis Iturra Valenzuela

1. INTRODUCTION

Chile's Norte Grande borders have been historically known for the migratory circularity between the inhabitants of the surrounding countries. Nevertheless, the current migratory flow has attracted the attention of social scientists, as well as politicians (Tapia, 2017, 2018), especially the latter, whose opinion is split in favor of or against the migratory process.

At the border control facilities of Arica–Tacna and Colchane–Pisiga, the commercial networks of complementarity that involve profits for the Chilean side are not disrupted (Dilla, 2015, 2016), yet simultaneously discourses and security mechanisms emerge at the border hampering other crossings (García Pinzón, 2015). An example of this is the *Plan Frontera Norte* that was established in 2012 to tackle drug trafficking and included immigration as one of the flows to be controlled (Aranda and Ovando, 2017), which was updated in 2018 under the name of *Plan Frontera Segura*. Both plans were launched under the governments of Sebastián Piñera.

This selection rationale of the commercial and migratory flows, between the desirable and the undesirable, is framed within the Foucaultian terms of a neoliberal governmentality and more precisely as an operation of biopolitics where there is a desired and a non-desired migratory population (Foucault, 2007; Tijoux and Díaz, 2014; Bolaños, 2017). Here it becomes evident that the Tacna–Arica urban complex operates as a space of integration but that it necessarily generates an asymmetry which allows the exploitation of the Peruvian migrant who inserts him-/herself to work in the agricultural lands of Arica (Dilla and Álvarez, 2018); or that President Piñera is stressing bilateral trade relations and promoting aid to countries undergoing humanitarian crises, but at the same time denies the entry of impoverished Venezuelans in order to protect the border (Emol, 2019c) at a time where hundreds of Venezuelans are gathered outside the Chacalluta border post looking for refuge. Therefore, it is interesting to report and investigate the various discourses and "dispositifs" of biopolitical governmentality that have been reproduced at the Arica–Tacna border. Chile's northern border is a dynamic cross-border space in terms of trade and human flows, but where selection dispositifs operate over the non-desired migrant population, which constitutes another body, an alien one, and bearer of the poverty collective imagination.

2. THE CONCEPTS OF GOVERNMENTALITY AND BIOPOLITICS

In simple words, governmentality is the rationalization of the art of governing and its practice turns into politics. Conversely, biopolitics turns out to be an extension of economic rationality and biopower, that is, an expression of the modern state (Fassin, 2010). From these definitions we can further deepen these concepts in order to better grasp certain phenomena, using these as a toolbox, otherwise we risk the fetishization of the social. We must go along the different paths the concept has taken since its introduction by Foucault and its subsequent authors who took up these two concepts, of which Agamben and Negri stand out.

Foucault points out that biopower was the power of the king to decide whether to end someone's life or not. It was a power that belonged to a sovereign's law, which decided upon death. Later on, a turn would be made, it was no longer death that mattered but life itself or more so the way of life. Biopolitics, unlike the dispositif of sovereignty, aims to make people live or to let them die (Castro, 2007). It pretends to understand and to control the way of life of a community, therefore it is interested in the computation of these and to be able to administer by configuring a society of security that subsumes the disciplined society which was interested in the conduction of individuals (Foucault, 2006). Biopolitics is exercised on a group, on a social body, a population.

The emergence of biopolitics did not imply the extinction of the dispositifs of sovereignty or discipline; these are latent in today's societies. Another point that should be clarified is that for the French philosopher the concept is neutral despite the fact that its maximum expression was manifested in the society of Nazi Germany. However, Agamben is one of the authors where the concept has negative overtones, while other authors considered biopolitics as a battlefield, visualizing ways of resistance (Negri, 2006). The positivity of the concept of biopolitics is found in the way of life that the population itself promotes by resisting the capitalist government, which we will name affirmative biopolitics (Avila, 2009).

Governmentality implies an understanding of how a population reproduces itself, what is the rationale of government and what are those practices. Neoliberal governmentality interested in migration is the one which, while accounting for it as a normal result of globalization, also points out that it is essential to be counteracted by selection. This way of governing migration makes a segmentation between regulated market-based openness and the restriction of undesired migration, encompassing agents, practices, technology and a migrant's moral discourse (Estupiñán Serrano, 2014).

In the Chilean case, this type of rationality was introduced by an influential economists group known as the *Chicago Boys* during the dictatorship of Augusto Pinochet and deepened into democracy under the administrations of the *Concertación de Partidos por la Democracia* (1990–2010), Sebastián Piñera (2010–2014), *Nueva Mayoría* (2014–2018) and currently with the re-election of Piñera, which have intensified this way of governing life.

3. ANALYZING THE DISCOURSES

Analyzing the discourses involves analyzing a type of social action (Santander, 2011). We assume the fact that society is asymmetric and therefore every social relationship entails such a distinction between groups that have more or less power than others. A way of production and reproduction of power is the discourse (Van Dijk, 2005, 2010). Moreover, groups that have power over others also control the context in which they operate in favor of the interests of the ruling group (Van Dijk, 1999). However, the question of the dominated also raises discourses disputing the meanings (Valle, 2019). Long-term field research started in 2014 and also included a few months' stay in the mountain border. The main methods were discourse listening, informed conversation as well as border photography.

There are contexts in which the discourse of domination/dominated is reproduced, where a single member is able to crystallize in his/her discourse the discourse and belief systems of the group to which he/she belongs. Therefore, the discourse has a fundamental role in the process of construction and reproduction of knowledge (Foucault, 2004), where the shared knowledge of a group, viewed as an epistemic community, allows the reproduction of it into an ideological discourse (Londoño, 2015: 330). For this reason it is interesting to research the discourse that both governors and other institutions deliver since they provide the ideological coherence of the beliefs of each group.

4. A BRIEF HISTORY OF THE CHILEAN NORTHERN BORDER

Chile's northern border was incorporated late into the national territory after the War of the Pacific, also known as the Saltpeter War. This war was fought between Peru, Bolivia and Chile from 1879 to 1883. After the war, which Chile won, the Bolivian saltpeter territories of Antofagasta and the Peruvian territories of Tarapacá were annexed, leaving the regions of Tacna and Arica at the crossroads, which were partitioned by the Treaty of Peace and Friendship of Lima on July 28, 1929 (González, 2008).

It is necessary to understand these historical events of the current border between Peru and Chile, as well as the borders between Bolivia and Chile, because, despite the years, they remain latent, displacing the warlike conflict with diplomatic ones. The subsequent integration of these regions, won by force, gave way to processes of cultural assimilation in order to assert sovereignty over them: the so-called "chilenization," which went from the occupation of the former countries' political and administrative structures to the exercise of symbolic violence in the educational system, or even physical violence against the Peruvian population by means of paramilitary groups called *Ligas Patrioticas* (patriotic leagues), culminating with the expulsion of Peruvians from the Tarapacá province in the years 1910 and 1918. This process was not homogeneous, but started out from spots of saltpeter capital and population concentration, the coast and the pampas, and spread to the Andean foothills and finally to the Highlands.

During the nitrate expansion cycle, the urbanization of the city of Iquique was central in the process of "chilenizing" the Tarapacan territory, becoming the "main urban geosymbol of the border area at the country's north" (González, 2009a: 24), while the Pampa based its importance on the saltpeter industry. It was these dynamics during the nitrate cycle that allowed the opening of the borders to supply the nitrate industry with commercial traffic and cross-border migration.

After the saltpeter boom and subsequent nitrate crisis, the strategic interest of the Chilean State in the pampas and the coast, a legacy of the nitrate industry began to shift to the problem of the precarious presence of state agencies in the Andean border region (Castro, 2014).

Despite this, the dynamic that prevailed was the free flow of goods and merchandise from the annexation until these days, mainly due to a liberal economic rationality promoted by the nitrate entrepreneurs and updated from the government's premises.

During the military dictatorship (1973–1990), an Immigration Act was established which would be in force until the present year 2019 and whose philosophy is the National Security Doctrine, embracing the idea of the other as an enemy (Stang, 2016). At the same time, a policy was to be implemented to materialize its defense in the border areas, where "obeying a defensive strategy, the country planted anti-personnel and anti-tank mines in the border areas during that period" (Aranda and Salinas, 2016: 64).

In 2013, a 21-year-old Colombian citizen tried to cross the border ignoring the existing minefields. The young man would lose one of his legs when an anti-personnel mine exploded and "after the accident, the victim of the explosive approached the Chacalluta border complex asking for help" (on October 3, 2013). By 2017, 157 people were dead or mutilated under the same circumstances, most of them in unmarked areas (Rojas, 2017).

Following the 2010 report of the United Nations International Narcotics Control Board, which revealed the increase in coca crops in Bolivia and Peru, the Board laid the groundwork for the creation and launch of *Plan Frontera Norte* in 2012, during the first government of Sebastián Piñera, in order to combat organized crime and drug trafficking in the far north of the country. However, this Plan also aimed to control migration by criminalizing migrants (Iturra, 2018). On the other hand of this conflict, the geographical proximity and, furthermore, the dynamics of both commercial and human flows make the cities of Tacna and Arica cross-border regions which in turn comprise a multidimensional, multiscale and hierarchical space (Dilla, 2018) due to the way in which the border is crossed, the reason to cross and the population crossing it. However, a system of differentiated flows that Heyman places in a triangle where at each angle or point they intersect: the reified frontier, globalization (flows and connections) and the underprivileged population (Heyman, 2011).

4.1 Regions in which History Often Overlaps and Cultures Hybridize

This is how Haroldo Dilla (2018: 225) describes the city of Arica:

> a place that fascinates and disconcerts. The view of the city is dominated by a natural landmark, the Morro, whose upper plateau features a museum designed to commemorate a decisive – and particularly bloody – battle of the War of the Pacific, which took place there in 1880. It is probably the darkest museum in the whole country, where death is vividly remembered, and where the good hand of the dictator Augusto Pinochet is still alluded to. At the foot of the Morro lies what is called the Peruvian Arica, that is, the oldest area in town, where along with architectural pieces of various types and styles, a Peruvian consular office stands crowned by what could be one of the largest flags that adorn the city: a red-and-white banner that is impossible not to see from any angle downtown.

The commercial dynamic itself manifests in the way in which transport is carried out by Chilean companies that supply Asian goods to the Tacna Free Zone. However, the most significant thing is the movement of people whereby:

> the Chacalluta border post can be considered as one of the most transited by people in the continent. In 2017 (according to Customs statistics, 2017), 3,297,847 people entered Chilean territory via this border crossing point and 3,229,959 people left through it, that is, more than six and a half million crossings per year. (Dilla, 2018: 229)

In fact, the regional migration authorities of both countries allow Peruvian and Chilean citizens to enter with identity documents or passports through authorized crossings (Santa Rosa–Chacalluta) as tourists (with a maximum time of 90 days), something that enables the circulatory movement of people.

4.2 A Dynamic of Complementarity that has its Asymmetries

The migration of Ariqueños to Tacna is mainly due to medical tourism, since Tacna has two hospitals and 72 health centers, while Arica has one hospital and 21 health centers, and this has combined with the economic benefits for the Ariqueños of being in Peru (Contreras, Tapia and Liberona, 2017).

As for the Tacneño who crosses, he/she does so for work purposes, mostly in informal jobs such as seasonal agricultural and construction work. That configures biocapital, an economic social body that establishes itself in the most precarious labor sources where "the worker's 'freedom' to dispose of his vital force and to sell it in the market takes with it, in a simultaneous but hidden way, to put at the disposal of other the capital, which is his very own existence" (Osorio, 2006).

> The flow that has relation with the Peruvians is very settled in the area of the terminal, and in the area of the Azapa Valley from the 30th kilometer upwards that is the sector of the Rapids, where it is another flow, that under the same context, look for employment, they come down from the valley between 5 and 6am to be able to establish themselves in a place which is the place called *Pan de Azucar*, so that an employer will pick them up, both men and women alike ... they work as a construction worker or seasonal agricultural laborer, and the women as housekeepers or waitresses. The residence thing is since they are only seasonal workers, they can only earn a sum between 10,000 and 12,000 CLP, nothing more than that. (Social worker living in Arica, Servicio Jesuita a Migrante, as cited in Contreras, Tapia and Liberona, 2017: 134–137).

This issue is not questioned by the central government, as it is a productive and mainly economic social body validated by integration mechanisms based on 90-day travel mobility and this has not been interrupted either by diplomatic conflicts following the return of the democracies of both countries, running on separate lines the political and the economic aspects of the bilateral relationship.

But the migrant is also categorized by his or her origin, phenotypic features, demographic background and countries of origin. The causes of Venezuelan migration, as in general the Latin American migrations of the twenty-first century, are due to political and economic reasons. In this case, social instability during the presidency of Nicolás Maduro (García Arias and Restrepo Pineda, 2019) causes migration to Chile, both as a country of transit and settlement, driven by an image of stability that has been projected internationally (Stefoni, Leiva and Bonh, 2017).

In this way, we can explain the differentiation and decisions that governments like Piñera's administration have promoted. During his second term, the Chilean president decided to dismiss the UN migration pact as an encouragement to illegal migration. He delivered a public statement and then posted it on his social networks:

> "Chile has a policy that seeks an orderly, safe and regulated migration open to those who come looking for a better life, respecting our laws and integrating them into our society. But it is not open for those who come to harm us as criminals or drug dealers," he declared, adding, "Chile respects and protects the human rights of all, including those of migrants. However, the UN Migration Pact contradicts some of these principles, encourages illegal migration, restricts our sovereignty and can be detrimental to our compatriots. That is why we decided not to endorse it." (Sebastián Piñera through his Twitter account, as quoted by CNN Chile, 2018)

Just a few months earlier, Piñera himself had announced the *Visa de Responsabilidad Democrática* ("democratic responsibility visa") for Venezuelan migrants given the crisis in their country but did not have any effect on the Haitian migration as such. This was a selective discourse of the migrant, pointing at an ideal migrant. This was felt by the public itself:

> "Chile was used to welcome immigrants who came from Europe, to do business. Afterwards, more people from Latin America and the Caribbean arrived. There is a Haitian migratory flow and it is black. The issue of color has been a global issue for a long time, and there is a lot of racism involved," says Wadner Maigman to the BBC (in Molina, 2018), "it operates as a demand for a different corporality that allows – once again – the construction of a white Chilean self and, therefore, different and separated from that which constitutes it and from that which must be excluded or separated. The difference marks the other body as a way of dehumanizing, dispossessing feelings and sometimes animalizing." (Tijoux, 2014: 3)

Tijoux points out that the Chilean state has been historically racist, given its policies of inviting European migrants to "improve the race" at the end of the nineteenth century and the denial of blacks and Indians as identifying components of the Chilean being. In addition, the current Immigration Act was passed under a dictatorship whose policy is the national security doctrine, meant to deal with an enemy. Within this framework, the indigenous and black migrant bodies on the border constitute the other, the excluded for control dispositifs and police agents.

This form of exclusion and denial would be consolidated with the so-called humanitarian aid that the government would provide in October 2018:

> "The priority is not to send the person back to his country. It is a method of deportation. It's not a matter of goodwill," stated Line François on behalf of the Sociocultural Organization of the Haitians in Chile (OSCHEC). (CNN Chile, 2018)

It is interesting how that humanitarian discourse disguises the expulsion strategy, since the plan commits Haitian immigrants to two points: (1) not to return to Chile in nine years; and (2) the plan involves the entire family group.

But the discourse towards Venezuelan immigrants and the democratic responsibility visa begins to take a turn in mid-2019 when hundreds of poor Venezuelan families flock to the border trying to enter Chile. On June 19, the newspaper *El Mostrador* headlined "Jesuits denounce the critical situation of Venezuelans stranded at the border: 'It's not Cúcuta, it's Chacalluta.'" That story made evident the problem that was occurring on the Arica–Tacna border:

> A complex situation is taking place in the Chacalluta area in the far north of the country, where foreign citizens, mainly Venezuelans, are stranded without being able to enter Chilean territory.
>
> Organizations working with migrants warned of the critical conditions faced by foreign citizens. "It's not Cúcuta, it's Chacalluta," warned the director of the Jesuit Migrant Service, José Tomás Vicuña, who compared the situation in our country with the situation on the Colombian–Venezuelan border.
>
> According to Vicuña, there are about 200 people, most of them Venezuelan, although other versions report 300 or 500 cases. "These people have children, many of them under the age of five, who have been sleeping at the border for three or four nights. Some of them are in poor health and have been mistreated by police officers." Vicuña told El Mostrador. (Emol, 2019a)

Despite the accusations of the Jesuits, the representative of the government, Mijail Bonito, stated that "there is no humanitarian issue, nor are there any queues. At this moment there should be no more than 50 people. Border crossing officials are resolving all cases individually" (Emol, 2019b).

This is a turn in the discourse regarding the same group of people, the Venezuelan community, and yet why, if the democratic crisis in Venezuela still exists, is this shift taking place? Why had Piñera given his support to Juan Guaido, who represented Maduro's opposition and ensured that Venezuelan migrants were welcomed? Because it was no longer the businessmen and doctors who had originally migrated, but now poor migrants who arrived at the Chacalluta border post.

Eight days later, during the G20 Leaders' Summit, the President would announce "we do not want those people who cause us harm to enter our country and that is why we are taking special precautions to better protect our borders and especially the northern borders of our country" (Emol, 2019c).

But in contrast to that power exercised at the border, those who promoted the crossing also were mobilized, mainly from the Department of Migration of the Catholic Institute of Migrations (Incami) and the National Institute of Human Rights (INDH). The director of the INDH pointed out that:

> "We are especially concerned about children and women, who according to testimonies have been insulted and mistreated," said the director of the entity, Consuelo Contreras, who warned that the issue "can lead to the emergence of human trafficking networks … they are worrisome given the high vulnerability in which people are, many have been unable to enter. They are being sent to Tacna to do a series of procedures that make it difficult for them to be admitted. Approximately 90% of the people who are here have relatives in Chile, who have their documentation in order and who are waiting for their arrival." (Fernández, 2019)

This raises the tension between the security of the individual as a migrant and the security of the State in terms of territorial sovereignty. The latter is responding by regulating the border zone, normalizing certain spaces in the political and social order of a State, the Nomos (Schmitt, 2005).

When the President says "we have the doors open for those who have been observing our laws, without deceiving our authorities, in order to integrate themselves into our country and work in an honest way" (Emol, 2019c), he is referring to the observance of the Immigration Act dating from the beginning of the dictatorship and whose origin is rooted in the doctrine of national security.

That grand idea of national order and exclusion are securitizing constructs. The discursive construction of context or subject referring to threats constitutes an elaboration of the groups of power. It also occurs in the instrumentalization of the concept of human security, where the priority is to restrict the concept and reproduce the status quo. Human security discourses and policies can be widened or restricted. The first focuses on the protection of human rights and the second is limited to specific fields such as the fight against drug trafficking, social and ethnic conflicts, or migration, among others (Pérez de Armiño, 2013). Both terms are used on the border, but the central government favors limited human security.

South–south migration towards Chile is motivated by the imaginary of the "oasis in Latin America" due to macroeconomic growth, but it hides the social disparities and inequity existing in the country (Casen, 2017).

The Piñera administrations were noted for their development of policies that reinforced border security, such as the *Plan Frontera Norte* and *Plan Frontera Segura*, strengthening border controls in response to the various flows regarded as negative, in which they also included migrants. In these texts, an exhaustive analysis was made of the government's discourse during the second administration, focusing on the issue of Venezuelan migration. The following points can be inferred from the abovementioned case:

- The Arica–Tacna border reveals itself as a biopolitical space or biopolitical fighting field. A space that from the neoliberal governmentality is expressed as a space of control over the bodies of populations occasionally non-desired or instrumentalized as a "war horse" by the speeches of politicians.
- In the book *Estados amurallados, soberanía en declive*, Wendy Brown remarks: "Today the picture of foreign danger is therefore literally overdetermined and includes economic, political, security-related and cultural effects caused by globalization. These dissimilar elements merge into one by the construction of 'the alien' as a multi-headed dragon" (2015: 169–170). It is therefore very interesting to see how this can be easily extended to this triple border.

5. CONCLUSIONS: THE MEANING OF BIOPOLITICS IN CHILE'S NORTHERN BORDER

The management of non-desired population would also be expressed as heterophobia, namely, a fear of everything that is different from the cultural group to which one belongs, and, from this, feelings of racism and aporophobia would arise; fear or rejection of the poor (Cortina, 2017). This would be the cause of the reproduction of discourses and practices that justify discrimination against immigrants: this appears to be the case among migrant groups of Haitians and poor Venezuelans who congregated on the outskirts of the Chacalluta border crossing.

The fact that one group of Venezuelans was accepted over another, mainly linked by their economic conditions of origin, reinforces the idea that the Chilean policy (at the very border) is not only xenophobic but also a repulsive policy towards the poor.

5.1 Towards an Affirmative Biopolitics

But the border also brings an affirmative biopolicy. Returning to Heyman (2011) when he mentions unequal classifications and treatments on the border, we add to that statement that the border is also a field of biopolitical disputes. The contrasting discourses between the central government and non-governmental bodies in the case of Venezuelan migration are proof of this. Thus, the Arica–Tacna border is established not only as a space of biopolitics, but more as a battleground between governments and forms of resistance. The Venezuelan migrants crowded the border, living in precarious conditions, but betting on the dream of a new life in a country that was denying them entry. Also the procedures in favor of entry are part of this affirmative biopolitics from institutions like INCAMI and INDH.

The reaction of organizations from the local level attempt to unravel the problem by advocating on behalf of the immigrants is the opposition to political decisions taken from the central government (Silva and Padilla, 2019). In the abovementioned case, these organizations raise the voice of the immigrant, but also configure another form of governmentality over them. The importance of these institutions lies in the fact the immigrant is at the center as a subject and not as an object, appealing to an expanded rather than restricted human security.

It is worth mentioning that this chapter was written in the midst of a social upheaval in Chile, where the political–economic model inherited from the dictatorship has been put in question. Today I write in the midst of burning streets, among people fighting for their rights against the oppressive state apparatus. The population has taken the streets as a battlefield for an affirmative biopolicy against the neoliberal government, demanding equity and dignity for the worker, the scientist, the student, the elderly, the native peoples and the immigrant. "To establish a new way of living."

BIBLIOGRAPHY

Aranda, Gilberto, y Cristian Ovando. "Nociones de seguridad en el plan frontera norte: una expresión de teichopolítica." *Revista Relaciones Internacionales, Estrategia y Seguridad* 13, n° 1 (2017): 67–92.

Aranda, Gilberto, y S. Salinas. *El laberinto de la globalización: fronteras duras y suaves en la historia y el presente*. Santiago: RIL Editores, 2016.

Avila, Gina P. H. "Biopolítica afirmativa de los movimiento sociales: el caso del movimiento sin tierra y piqueteros." *Criterios* 2, n° 1 (2009): 155–183.

Bolaños, Bernardo. *Biopolítica y migración. El eslabón perdido de la globalización*. México: UAM-Cuajimalpa, 2017.

Brown, Wendy. *Estados amurallados, soberanía en declive*. Barcelona: Herder Editorial, 2015.

Casen, Encuesta. *"Observatorio Social." Previsión social: sintesis de resultados*. Santiago de Chile: Ministerio de Desarrollo Social y Familia, 2017.

Castro, Estevan. "Biopolítica y gubernamentalidad." *Revista Temas & matices* 11, n° 6 (2007): 8–18.

Castro, Luis. "Tráfico mercantil andino, comerciantes indígenas y fiscalización estatal (Tarapacá, norte de Chile 1880–1938)." *Revista de Indias* 74, n° 261 (2014): 561–590.

CNN Chile. "Piñera justifica rechazo a Pacto Migratorio de la ONU: 'Incentiva la migración irregular'." 10 de diciembre de 2018. https://www.cnnchile.com/pais/pinera-justifica-rechazo-a-pacto-migratorio-de-la-onu-incentiva-la-migracion-irregular_20181210/ (último acceso: agosto de 03 de 2019).

Contreras, Yasna, Marcela Tapia, y Nanette Liberona. "Movilidades y prácticas socioespaciales fronterizas entre Arica y Tacna. Del sentido de frontera a la transfrontericidad entre ciudades." *Diálogo Andino*, n° 54 (2017): 127–141.

Cortina, Adela. *Aporofobia, el rechazo al pobre: un desafío para la democracia*. Barcelona, España: Paidós, 2017.

Dilla, Haroldo. "Los complejos urbanos transfronterizos en América Latina." *Estudios Fronterizo* 16, n° 31 (2015): 15–38.

Dilla, Haroldo. "Chile y sus fronteras: notas para una agenda de investigación." *Revista Polis* 15, n° 44 (2016): 309–327.

Dilla, Haroldo. "Arica entre tres fronteras." *Estudios Atacameño*, n° 57 (2018): 221–238.

Dilla, Haroldo, y Camila Álvarez. "Arica/Tacna: Los circuitos económicos de un complejo urbano transfronterizo." *Diálogo Andino*, n° 57 (2018): 99–109.

Emol. "Jesuitas denuncian crítica situación de venezolanos varados en la frontera: 'No es Cúcuta, es Chacalluta'." *El Mostrador*, 20 de junio de 2019a.

Emol. "'No hay ningún tema humanitario': asesor del Gobierno le baja el perfil a situación de venezolanos en Chacalluta." *El Mostrador*, 20 de junio de 2019b.

Emol. "Piñera sobre migrantes en Chacalluta: 'Estamos tomando medidas para proteger nuestras fronteras'." *El Mostrador*, 28 de junio de 2019c.

Estupiñán Serrano, Mary Luz. "Gestión internacional de las migraciones como una racionalidad política." *Migraciones internacionales* 7, n° 3 (2014): 249–259.

Fassin, Didier. "Otra política de la vida es posible: crítica antropológica del biopoder." En *Michel Foucault: neoliberalismo y biopolítica*, de Vanessa Lemm, 21–49. Santiago de Chile: Ediciones Universidad Diego Portales, 2010.

Fernández, F. "INDH asegura que venezolanos varados en Chacalluta deben ingresar al país y no descarta acciones legales." *Emol*, 26 de junio de 2019.

Foucault, Michel. *El orden del discurso*. Buenos Aires: Tusquets, 2004.

Foucault, Michel. *Seguridad, Territorio, Población. Cursos en el Collège de France (1977–1978)*. México: Fondo de Cultura Económica, 2006.

Foucault, Michel. *Nacimiento de la biopolítica: Curso en el College de France*. México DF.: Fondo de Cultura Económica, 2007.

Gallardo, Karla. *24horas*. 03 de octubre de 2013. https://www.24horas.cl/nacional/colombiano-herido-al-estallar-mina-antipersonal-en-arica-871512 (último acceso: 10 de agosto de 2019).

García Arias, Manuel Felipe, y Jair Restrepo Pineda. "Aproximación al proceso migratorio venezolano en el siglo XXI." *Hallazgos* 16, nº 32 (2019): 63–82.

García Pinzón, Viviana. "Territorios fronterizos: Agenda de seguridad y narcotráfico en Chile: El Plan Frontera Norte." *Estudios Internacionales* 47, nº 181 (2015): 69–93.

González, Sergio. *La llave y el candado. El conflicto entre Perú y Chile por Tacna y Arica (1883–1929)*. Santiago: Ediciones Lom, 2008.

González, Sergio. "El Norte Grande de Chile: la definición histórica de sus límites, zonas y líneas de fronteras y la importancia de las ciudades como geosímbolos fronterizos." *Revista de Historia Social y de las Mentalidades* 7, nº 13 (2009a): 9–42.

González, Sergio. "La presencia boliviana en la sociedad del salitre y la nueva definición de la frontera: auge y caída de una dinámica transfronteriza (Tarapacá 1880–1930)." *Chungará (Arica)* 41, nº 1 (2009b): 71–81.

Heyman, Josiah. "Cuatro temas en los estudios de la frontera contemporánea." En *El Río Bravo Mediterráneo: Las regiones fronterizas en la época de la globalización*, de Natalia Ribas-Mateos (ed), 81–98. Edicions Bellaterra, 2011.

Iturra, Luis. "El cuerpo otro y los otros espacios. El discurso soberano en los agentes estatales de seguridad sobre la inmigración." En *El a fán de cruzar la frontera. Enfoques transdisciplinarios sobre migraciones y movilidad en Sudamérica y Chile*, de Marcela Tapia y Nanette Liberona, 365–383. Santiago: RIL Editores, 2018.

Londoño, Oscar. "Discurso y conocimiento: Una mirada a los Estudios Críticos Epistémicos del Discurso Entrevista a Teun A. van Dijk." *Literatura y Lingüística*, nº 32 (2015): 325–338.

Molina, Paula. "Por qué Chile facilita la llegada de inmigrantes de Venezuela y pone dificultades a los de Haití." *BBC*, 11 de abril de 2018.

Negri, Antonio. *Movimientos en el Imperio: pasajes y paisajes*. Vol. 142. Madrid: Grupo Planeta (GBS), 2006.

Núñez, Andrés, Rafael Sanchez, y Federico Arenas. *Fronteras en movimiento e imaginarios geográficos. La cordillera de Los Andes como espacialidad sociocultural*. Santiago: Geolibros-RIL Editores, 2013.

Osorio, Jaime. "Biopoder y biocapital: El trabajador como moderno homo sacer." *Argumentos (México, D.F.)* 19, nº 52 (2006): 77–98.

Pérez de Armiño, Karlos. *¿Más allá de la Seguridad Humana? Desafíos y aportes de los estudios críticos de seguridad*. Cursos de Derecho Internacional y Relaciones Internacionales de Victoria-Gasteiz 2011, Madrid: Editorial TECNOS, 2013.

Rojas, Jorge. *Cosecha explosiva: civiles mutilados por siembra de minas antipersonales*. 13 de marzo de 2017.

Romero, María Cristina. "Piñera y situación migratoria en Chacalluta: 'Estamos tomando medidas especiales para proteger mejor nuestras fronteras'." *Emol*, 28 de junio de 2019.

Santander, Pedro. "Por qué y cómo hacer análisis de discurso." *Cinta de moebio* 41 (2011): 207–224.

Schmitt, Carl. *El Nomos de la tierra. En el Derecho de Gentes del jus publicum europaeum*. Argentina: Struhart y Cía., 2005.

Silva, Aída, y Vianney Padilla. "Instituciones en crisis y acción colectiva frente a las migraciones globales. El caso de la llegada de haitianos a Tijuana, B.C." *Desafíos*, 2019: 2016–2017.

Stang, María Fernanda. "De la Doctrina de la Seguridad Nacional a la gobernabilidad migratoria: la idea de seguridad en la normativa migratoria chilena, 1975–2014." *Polis (Santiago)* 15, n° 44 (2016): 83–107.

Stefoni, Carolina, Sandra Leiva, y Macarena Bonh. "Migración internacional y precariedad laboral. El caso de la industria de la construcción en Chile." *REMHU-Revista Interdisciplinar da Mobilidade Humana* 25, n° 49 (2017): 95–112.

Tapia, Marcela. "Las fronteras, la movilidad y lo transfronterizo: Reflexiones para un debate." *Estudios fronterizos* (18) 37 (2017): 61–80.

Tapia, Marcela. "Prácticas sociales fronterizas entre Chile y Bolivia, movilidad, circulación y migración. Siglos XX Y XXI." *Leggere Historia* 12, n° 1 (2018): 66–86.

Tapia, Marcela, y Cristian Ovando. "Los Andes Tarapaqueños, nuevas espacialidades y movilidad fronteriza: ¿barrera geográfica o espacio para la integración?" En *Fronteras en movimiento e imaginarios geográficos*, de A. Núñez, R. Sánchez, y F. Arena, 243–274. Santiago: RIL Editores, 2013.

Tapia, Marcela, Nanette Liberona, y Yasnna Contreras. "El surgimiento de un territorio circulatorio en la frontera chileno-peruana: estudio de las prácticas socio-espaciales fronterizas." *Revista de geografía Norte Grande*, n° 66 (2017): 117–141.

Tijoux, María. "El otro inmigrante 'negro' y el nosotros chileno. Un lazo cotidiano pleno de significaciones." *Boletín Onteaiken* 17 (2014): 1–15.

Tijoux, María, y Letelier Díaz. "Inmigrantes, los 'nuevos bárbaros' en la gramática biopolítica de los estados contemporáneos." *Rivista Internazionale di Filosofia Contemporanea* 2, n° 1 (2014).

Valle, G. "'Los dominados y el arte de la resistencia'. Una reseña de James C. Scott." *Revista Chakiñan de Ciencias Sociales y Humanidades* 7 (2019): 94–103.

Van Dijk, Teun. "El análisis crítico del discurso." *Anthropos*, n° 128 (1999): 23–36.

Van Dijk, Teun. "Ideología y análisis del discurso." *Utopìa y Praxis Latinoamericana* 10, n° 29 (2005): 9–36.

Van Dijk, Teun. "Discurso, conocimiento, poder y política. Hacia un análisis crítico epistémico del discurso." *Revista De Investigación Lingüística*, 13 (2010): 167–215.

PART III

CHALLENGING MEDITERRANEAN BORDERS

11. Major changes in "migrations and borders" after the "revolution" of globalized liberalism
Salvatore Palidda

1. CONNECTING "MIGRATION PARADIGMS" AND BORDERS

The history of migration is marked by periods of racism and violent rejection and also by periods of peaceful integration and assimilation in immigration countries. In fact, capitalist development of the nineteenth and twentieth centuries was nourished by both domestic and international migration. However, since the beginning of 1990, migration has become the spectre that haunts wealthy countries as if it were a very dangerous threat. The so-called immigration threat has even become a permanent war against migration, with a continuous proliferation of military and police means and forces, as well as a range of sophisticated technological devices and the expenditure of huge economic resources. It has been framed as one of the most serious threats of the twenty-first century. This represents a paradigm shift in the understanding and treatment of immigration and borders, which in turn has led to more desperation, tragedies, and deaths among migrants.[1]

We can begin to understand this shift in the paradigm of migration and borders by noting that the literature on migration and borders has undergone enormous development over the past 20 years. Many authors have described different aspects of actual dramatic situations of migration regarding human and humanitarian dignity. However, much of this has been partially constructed as a reiteration of previous works, and the narratives frequently follow a pattern of dominant discourse based on a nineteenth-century "science of migration studies," lacking a deconstruction or questioning of this discourse and its purpose.[2]

My main argument in this chapter is that this change in the paradigm of migration and borders, so often unrecognized in scholarly work, is due to two serious shortcomings. First, there has been too little attention devoted to the understanding of the consequences of the economic neoliberal global "revolution," which began in the 1970s in the Global North (though an important exception is the work of Sassen, 1999, 2008, 2014). The second shortcoming is the perception among dominant-country elites of the so-called uncontrolled growth of world population (especially in poorer nations of the Global South). More recently this has been linked with escalating climate change, which together are seen by elites as likely to generate very "dangerous invasions" of poor migrants to rich countries (Miller, 2017). This is the fearful "spectre" that preoccupies dominant-country elites and is the principal reason for the transition from a more tolerant biopolitics of migrations favourable to the migrant integration into the receiving society to a more coercive thanatopolitics of death and exclusion (well-established concepts that refer to Foucault's work). This is basically the radical shift in the meaning of migration policies: from *let live* to *let die*. Therefore, migration and borders shift and the migrants become "wasted lives" (Bauman, 2003) or get trapped as "excess humanity".

In order to fully understand such a paradigm shift, I focus in detail on what has actually changed in the paradigm of migration and borders, in the context developed after decades of development of globalized economic neoliberalism. I argue that migration and borders, conceived as *total political facts* (I seize here a classic concept that reinterprets Mauss[3]), have previously always been governed in response to the paradigm of *biopolitics*. Accordingly, policies have aimed to integrate immigrants – apart from periodic rejection, racialization, and attempts to remove "bad immigrants". This concept of integration involved turning them into docile labour as well as good citizens who pay their taxes, and who are also prepared to die in the wars of the new country of their integration/assimilation. The cases of the United States and France are good illustrations of such classic immigrant integration practices. Migration has always been essential for the economic development of these countries, which have thus become economic, political and military powers in the world. And it is thanks to the continuous arrival of migratory flows that the United States and other countries have had great economic growth since 1990 and have overcome the crisis of 2008. In fact, the population of the United States went from 250 million in 1990 to 320 million in 2017, including 11 million undocumented immigrants subject to hyper-exploitation. Thus, migration has played a key utilitarian role as this migration paradigm has been functional to the development of industrial society governed by the sovereign national state.

The origins of the change of this classic migration paradigm emerged in the 1970s and onward with the acceleration of the global economic neoliberal revolution. It started by a dismantling process of much of the industrial apparatus in the most developed countries in the Global North, which has been relocated to the Global South low-wage, less regulated countries (and eventually including tertiary activities such as the opening and expansion of call centres). Therefore, the wealthy countries have experienced a lesser need for migrant labour to integrate/assimilate into stable manufacturing, but rather instead they have displayed a need only for precarious labour in the semi-shadow and shadow economies, due to the outsourcing of all sorts of economic activities. Such an epochal transformation was made possible by the technological revolution in communications, transport, and production and also by the financial revolution (which also further impoverishes the Global South). Furthermore, the technological revolution also triggered changes in the military-police affairs.

The so-called Revolution in Military (and police) Affairs (RMA) is another key change that has contributed to the shift in the paradigm of migration and borders during the contemporary period. It is characterized by new technologies and resources of surveillance and coercion in which police and military increasingly overlap and collaborate, in "security efforts" against international migrants, among other types of population. This process consequently generates tension in power relations, creating a greater asymmetry of domination in relation to subordinated people (including migrants). On one side of the extreme, one can locate the wealthy with an ever-greater concentration of resources, ever-more narrowly shared, on the other side, the expanding ranks of the vulnerable and disadvantaged, with expanding poverty on a global scale. Such a polarized scenario reinforces an increasing asymmetry of power. Such power permits the dominant-country elites to impose bad working conditions, lower incomes and poor conditions of life on the growing impoverished and highly exploited working class, particularly those from poorer developing nations. At the extremes, these practices are found in shadow economies and neo-slavery activities. The RMA is a coercive tool reinforcing this social order of drastic inequality.

Another factor explaining this global transformation is the intensification of neo-colonial practices through the over-exploitation of resources and land devastation in the Global South. Similar to the way in which Sassen discusses (in Chapter 5 of this volume), this process involves the depredation and expulsion phenomenon of global capitalism, which is in turn linked to the aggravation of the global ecological–political crisis. Consequently, such process involves new mass migrations, in which people flee from devastated territories where not even a blade of grass grows nor fish swims in the rivers. Increasingly, migration is the outgrowth of ecological and political disasters provoked on a global scale by the dominant-country elites and their multinational corporations and financial institutions. These consequences of global neoliberal economic revolution generate the new humanitarian disasters and threats to human security described by Gros (2008).

The next factor underlying the shift in the paradigm of migration and borders relates to demography and the lack of social justice associated with population changes. The view of dominant-country elites is that the so-called uncontrolled world population growth, especially in poorer nations, in conjunction with climate change will generate more and more "invasions" of immigrants into rich countries. On the contrary, it is the unequal distribution of wealth and of access to technological innovations and scientific discoveries – in addition to the devastation of the environment by extractive multinational corporations – which prevents 7 (eventually 10) billion humans from living decently on earth.

The last factor relates to security translated into the intensification of military and police devices. Immigration from the Global South is today perceived as a threat to the Global North. Therefore, migration is a central object of attention for security services, military and police, which frame migrants as enemies (a fact known in the past only for the political migrations). In this framework some military, geo-engineers and experts in new technologies also speculate about "climate wars", which obviously would target emigration countries (Miller, 2017). Fortunately, these hypotheses seem for now not feasible or at risk of boomerang/blowback for rich countries. The current Covid-19 pandemic risks being an even greater scourge for poor countries, that is, countries of emigration.

Before moving on to a further elaboration of my theoretical interpretation of the paradigm shift in migrations and borders, I first turn to the contemporary consequences of the Covid-19 pandemic for migrants and border zones, for it is both intrinsically important and also serves to highlight in dramatic fashion key features of the paradigm shift.

2. THE VIOLENCE OF BORDERS AND THE VIOLENCE POST-GLOBAL PANDEMIC

Pandemics are also part of the understanding of the migration paradigm and borders. Among the first measures adopted by nearly all governments in the Covid-19 crisis was the closure of borders (or large-scale restriction of migration), and the abandonment of any duty to help refugees, which has resulted in the tragic aggravation of the situation of migrants located near borders, exemplified especially on the Turkish–Greek border zone. During global capitalism, pandemics circulate internationally with ease and flourish not only in large metropolises but also spread to sparsely populated regions. I should also add that prior to Covid-19 we have experienced many other epidemics in recent years, such as Ebola, SARS, avian and swine influenza, which appear to have left China or Southeast Asia. China has also suffered greatly from swine fever. Thus, the global mapping in the origin of pandemics is exactly at the centre of capitalist production for the world. Nevertheless, there are many more places where the environmental risks of mutation and spread are high. The "black death", or plague, started in

Mongolia, the "Spanish flu" of 1918 extended across national borders from France, HIV/AIDS is thought to have originated in Africa as have the West Nile and Ebola viruses, while dengue seems to flourish in Latin America. There are different origins of pandemics, but we can see the economic and demographic impact of viruses spread across borders, facilitated by increasing globalization over the years. In the case of Covid-19, many refer to it as a "vengeance" of the violent, global, deregulated neoliberal extractivist system.

In all countries, one of the first consequences of the pandemic was to aggravate the working and living conditions of the weakest and least protected people: irregular workers, homeless people, precarious workers, imprisoned people, migrant women who are the carers of the vulnerable population (as domestic workers and carers), and, in general, people with uncertain and low incomes. It is, for example, emblematic that the majority of Covid-19 deaths in the United States (more than 70 percent in some states) are among African Americans as well as Hispanics (and in New York the death rates of Hispanics and Blacks were double those of Whites and Asian Americans[4]). Is this a racist pandemic or yet another demonstration of class discrimination, which is accentuated by public health destroyed by neoliberalism? Among these same categories in Europe we see there are obviously many regular and irregular immigrants who continue to work in particular in the so-called essential labour force of the economy, such as the collection of fruit and vegetables in the countryside, cleaning work, the care of the elderly, children, teenagers and the sick, often with families of workers who are not confined to their home or with elderly people alone. Among many paradoxes, the case of Austria should be noted, the country that is most hermetically closed; the urgent need for agricultural labour to harvest asparagus and potatoes has forced the government to authorize charter flights to transport workers from Romania or other Eastern European countries. Even in hard hit Italy the emergence of the need for labour in the countryside has prompted the union of farmers to put pressure on the government to authorize the arrival of at least 300,000 immigrants (but according to the unions there is the possibility of regularizing the 500,000 undocumented immigrants).

In contrast, during April 2020 Italy used the pandemic as an excuse to close its ports to ships that rescued migrants at sea.[5] The situation of immigrants locked up in deportation centres is as high risk as that of the inmates of normal prisons. Even worse, however, is the situation of migrants stranded at the borders, for example at the border between Turkey and Greece, as well as the situation of migrants stranded on the Greek islands (see later). These are often people who are weakened, at risk of respiratory diseases, pneumonia and bronchitis, and therefore particularly vulnerable to the Covid-19. These are people who are often forced to live in crowded and unhealthy spaces and are not given any help or medical material for prevention (personal protective equipment –PPE – facemasks, etc.). In the same period, President Erdoğan of Turkey ordered the deportation of migrants from the Greek border, which does not bode well for this population.[6] At the Ventimiglia border (Italy), France continues to expel migrants to Italy despite the blockade of European borders justified for the pandemic situation; meanwhile the people expelled are left with health risks under conditions of serious risk of contagion.[7]

The conditions of the refugee camps where thousands of people are crammed into Greece are now hell. But nobody talks about refugees or migrants anymore and in particular about children. For example, nobody talks about the many Mexicans who flee the United States to return to Mexico (testimony of Mexican emigrants), nor the Central American refugees stranded in precarious situations on the Mexican side of the border waiting for their asylum applications to be addressed. Furthermore, the media has no space to make the fate of migrants known. Only a few non-governmental organizations (NGOs) continue to be present near the borders. The Ocean Viking ship of Medici Senza Frontiere (Doctors Without Borders) and SOS Méditerranée managed to bring 274 migrants to Sicily. But immediately the fascist–racist leader Matteo Salvini asked for them to be expelled.[8] The authorities had decided to quarantine all of them together with the crew, although there is no proof that either the migrants or the NGO workers were affected by the virus.

The situation is dramatic in the refugee camps in Greece. The first case of Covid-19 in Lesbos Island Refugee Camp was confirmed in March 2020. But the Athens authorities had not provided any concrete help, not even for unaccompanied minors. According to the International Rescue Committee (IRC), Human Rights Watch and the Danish Refugee Council many children are not properly registered and protected and pandemic prevention procedures are lacking. The fires in the camps are frequent. A child died in the flames that flared up in one of the containers where the refugees are housed in the Moria refugee camp. According to Stephan Oberreit, head of the mission of Doctors Without Borders in Greece: "This fire comes only two months after the fire in the Kara Tepe camp, and only five months after the fire in the Moria camp in September 2019." And recently, some NGOs have had to reduce their presence or abandon the area due to the violence against humanitarian workers. According to UNHCR (United Nations High Commissioner for Refugees) spokesman Andrej Mahecic "there are more than 36,000 asylum seekers who stay in reception centres in five islands, originally designed for 5,400 people."[9] As regarding the situation of migrants, the NGO Doctors Without Borders fears that the Covid-19 epidemic will result in a new unjustified public anxiety towards those who have been saved at sea and serve as an "excuse to prevent Ocean Viking from resuming its control work in the central Mediterranean."[10]

The quasi-total closure of borders by all states only accentuates the ban on migrants. Therefore, once again, the notion of thanatopolitics is crucial to understand this situation – i.e. to let these people die without rights, seen and conceived as "humanity in excess" (a concept that has been mainly used in the field of the holocaust studies, in humanitarian crisis and in the studies of refugee camps).

Thus, the cynical and brutal logic of the frontiers of globalized economic neoliberalism becomes, with all these detailed examples, even more concrete in migration humanitarian tragedy as a key illustration of what happens at global borders.

A dramatic chapter in the consequences of the pandemic on migration is the one that emerges from the autumn of 2020 in immigration countries, where the immigrants have been blocked and without work and without income. The International Organization of Migration (IOM) has estimated 2.750 million (July 2020) of the migrants remained "stranded", that is, blocked against their will, in the countries of immigration, mostly the Gulf countries. In fact, in the Emirates, immigrants are often also deprived of their passport and in any case are unable to find a flight to return to their country of origin. They are therefore forced to live in conditions of indigence and without any help (see their dramatic situation in the Reportage broadcast by l'ARTE "Emirats: la fin de l'Eldorado?": https://www.youtube.com/watch?v=6L4X9tOOKrA). Furthermore, this scourge of the pandemic has caused a worsening of the living conditions of tens of millions of families supported by the remittances of their emigrant relatives. Remittances from emigrants have been an element of stability and economic development for the countries of origin, and a strong support for the families who have remained at home.

3. THE ORIGIN OF THE CHANGES

The drastic pandemic circumstances and draconian migration policies find their roots in earlier changes in globalization. The technological revolution has been accelerated since the early 1970s. Such changes have also impacted other economic, social, cultural and political changes – e.g. in communications, financial activities, transports, the production system, controls, etc. Everything has changed in that sense, first of all in the most developed countries and in the projections of all sorts of activities on a local and global scale. Information technology and robotics have allowed the dismantling of large and medium-sized industries in rich countries in the Global North and their relocation to the Global South. A consequence of this trend is that more developed countries have had less and less need for stable and assimilated immigrants to work in industry according to the traditional paradigm of biopolitics, but only instead increasingly use immigrants for slavish, inferior, precarious jobs.

The closing of traditional labour migration was the "halt" of migration adopted by the OECD (Organisation for Economic Co-operation and Development) and wealthy countries in 1974, after the 1973 oil crisis. However, in the context of Southern Europe, mass emigration continued in the 1970s and 1980s especially after the end of the Salazar regime in Portugal and that of Franco in Spain. Migration also accelerated following the economic and political dictatorships in various countries of Latin America, Africa, and Asia. We can also add the phenomenon of boat people from Southeast Asia after the end of the Vietnam War and the consequences of the Pol Pot regime in Cambodia. After the Cold War period, there was also the subsequent mass migration from the Eastern European countries, that is, after the collapse of the USSR in 1991. Subsequently, stopping migration (or at least pushing it far underground to heighten the vulnerability and exploitation of migrants) became a principal goal of rich countries. Since the late 1980s, tens of thousands of migrants have died during migration attempts to reach wealthy countries (especially at the borders of the United States and Mediterranean Europe). Although such reality received much media attention, it is important to remember that the majority of migrations take place between the countries of the Global South, and, among those, between the poor and the rich countries (such as the Emirates, Saudi Arabia where the immigrants are in extreme cases of slavery and lost lives).

The financial revolution – which has been studied by many authors such as Sassen (see her two chapters in this volume) – has facilitated the rise of stock market speculation and tax havens. Nation-states have lost control of these financial manipulations (in part due to the neoliberal imperative of deregulation), and thus financial transnationalization has increased. This process has also allowed the global rise of the powerful financial troika (i.e. World Bank, World Trade Organization, and International Monetary Fund (IMF)), fully displayed in the dominant structure of transnational politics. In addition, the European troika (i.e. European Commission, European Central Bank, and IMF) as well as the power of the private multinational banks of the wealthy dominant countries (United States, China and Japan) all play a key role in the global neoliberal economic configuration. Therefore, the impact of the powerful global financial system has caused even more impoverishment of the less developed countries, particularly an increasingly unequal distribution of wealth and income as well as an increase in poverty (apart from China, where poverty has been greatly reduced).

In conjunction with the global neoliberal economic domination, the so-called RMA allows the military conversion of the police forces and the police conversion of the military. The RMA began in the 1980s, developed by the US think tanks in the pursuit of stopping the decline of the United States' economic and political hegemony. A military–police apparatus was established to restore direct US domination, and is less and less shared with other NATO countries. At the same time, such countries do allow the development of new technologies that facilitate destructive actions (see for example, the use of drones since the first Gulf War) and subjugation via financial speculation (see "financial coups", Perkins, 2005). Under such conditions, the United States claims to have the international "right to protect", namely to be able to intervene with "surgical strikes" in any country in the world where its "vital interests" are supposedly threatened (see Dal Lago and Palidda, 2010; Bigo and Guild, 2005). Since then, control has been further developed, with all new military and police technologies increasingly used against the so-called migration threat, via satellite espionage, video surveillance, drones, and not only with traditional devices such as patrol boats or border police units, but also even military force at times. In addition, privatized "migrant hunters", or private militia men or fascist gangs, often enter with the approval of military and police to participate in this war against migration.

During the same approximate period since the 1970s, the development of neo-colonialism, or, more precisely, globalized neoliberal economic neo-colonialism, and the increased exploitation of natural and human resources has significantly increased. This activity has become increasingly unrestrained and provokes more and more disasters, putting at risk the survival of the vulnerable populations of the Global South. The mindset driving this phenomenon is illustrated in the notorious comments in 1991 by Lawrence Summers, then head of the economic department of the World Bank (later the US Secretary of Treasury), who wrote in a private note leaked to the press:

> Subpopulated African countries are largely poorly polluted. ... We must encourage significant migration from polluting industries to less developed countries ... the economic logic requires that the masses of toxic waste be thrown where wages are low is unquestionable. (Extracts published by *The Economist* (2 August 1992) and *The Financial Times* (2 October 1992) under the title "Saving the planet of economists")[11]

He adds, again in 1991:

> The risk of an apocalypse due to global warming or any other cause is non-existent. The idea that we should impose limits on growth due to natural limits is a profound mistake; also, the idea whose social cost would be surprising if the choice of development were applied.[12]

Since then, "desperate migrations" have increased exponentially. Consequently, it is not a question of future "climate migrations", but of migrations that subsume all the disasters provoked by the impact of dominant-country multinational corporations in the Global South (see Palidda, 2016 and Palidda, 2018).

4. ON THE CONTEXT OF HARD BORDERS

Continuing with the core issue of this handbook we can relate the changes in the paradigm of migration to the construction of hard borders, as has been mentioned in the introduction to this book. According to Heyman and Ribas-Mateos (2019), three key kinds of relationship are involved in such a border regional context: (i) Militarized barriers (combined natural and human made) that prevent the entry of peasant-workers and working classes from the Global South. This includes both uninspected entry of unauthorized workers and asylum-seeker attempts. But mixed with official rejection is humanitarianism of various kinds, both state management of migrant bodies to avoid bad political publicity, as well as resistant humanitarianism from below by activists and organizations. (ii) A permeable membrane (a system of entry inspections) that allows a range of other people to enter the space of relative wealth, including elites, tourists and shoppers, non-immigrant temporary labourers, some family members, etc., as well as massive flows of commercial goods. These are crucial to global alliances of economic, political, and intellectual elites. (iii) However, not all labour crosses the border; indeed, most does not. Border enforcement reinforces a global division of labour, which often places low-wage production sites in the Global South, and prosperous consumption sites mostly in the North (Heyman and Ribas-Mateos, 2019).

Searching for an answer, Heyman and Ribas-Mateos advocate for the need to give attention not only to the geopolitical analysis of borders, which mainly focuses on the political relationship of (unauthorized) migrants and asylum seekers to the state (e.g. militarized border enforcement and humanitarianism), but also to other dimensions. Specifically, they present a framework that identifies a few key themes that remain particularly salient but underexplored in border studies; they highlight the multiple relationships involved in the global neoliberal economic changes and their intersections with bordering processes worldwide. Thus, the rich and dominant countries tend increasingly to entrench their borders in the face of supposed "new threats", among which – for the first time in history – migration is also considered as such (previously only used for relatively few political militant migrants). Also considered new border threats are international terrorism as well as mafias and drug cartels, which are often conflated with migration.

5. DEFENCE AND SECURITY AS A CENTRAL EXPLANATION

The paradigm shift towards viewing migration as a security threat is the "spectre" of the twenty-first century, which causes anguish among elites of the world (those who build new bunkers, equip themselves with sophisticated and powerful military–police defence devices or hope to escape into space). This view foresees greater migration due to the alleged overlap between climate change and unchecked population growth in the developing world. Their great fear is that this would lead to increasingly gigantic and desperate migrations that would threaten rich countries (Miller, 2017). Obviously, the elite do not consider "realistic" the possibility that thanks to new technologies and scientific discoveries it would be possible to feed even over 10 billion people and, above all, to eliminate extractivism and the abuse of toxic and devastating minerals on the planet, and therefore the causes of desperate migrations today (see oil, coal, gas, uranium, etc.). This could be done on condition of abolishing profits that must increase year by year while poverty and, in general, the extreme disparity in the distribution of wealth also increases. From 2000 to the present day, the degradation of the ecosystem has worsened and many territories have become unhabitable due to the devastation caused largely for and by multinational corporations. This is the first cause of desperate migrations that precisely subsume all the disasters on the planet (Palidda, 2016 and 2018) – i.e. environmental insecurity as an element of human security. It is no coincidence that, in response to this twenty-first-century "spectre", some military, geo-engineers and experts in new technologies claim to imagine "climate wars" capable of causing earthquakes, tsunamis and other biblical catastrophes no longer with atomic bombs but with the sun's rays intercepted and diverted, capable of eliminating a few billion human beings (see *negationism, scepticism* ...[13]).

The militarization of borders as well as the outsourcing and subcontracting of control to third countries or militias (as in Libya or Somalia and in part other countries such as the Congo), becomes more and more important together with the construction of new walls and sophisticated border control devices. In this respect we have to acknowledge that there has never been such an increase in the investment in the construction of new walls and in the militarization of borders with sophisticated devices and forces. Within this process, ironically, NGOs and all the so-called reception services are in fact functional to a management of migration that produces "excess humanity" or "disposable" labour.

The only effective alternative to this scenario could be the effective stopping of the devastation by multinational corporations in the countries of emigration, and, in migrant-receiving countries, the regularization of all *sin papeles* (without papers, unauthorized) migrants, allowing their peaceful and regular integration. It could also be said that the countries of emigration do not need help, but above all they need to no longer be devastated and massacred in every sense, especially economically and environmentally.

This new context explains the total closure of European borders and Trump's choice of a wall – as well as temporary worker migration for over-exploitation. This total closure corresponds with the shift from the *biopolitics* of migration towards *thanatopolitics* instead, that is to let migrants die – whereas before, despite the moments of racism and refusal, there was a tendency to include and forge migrants into new citizens who pay taxes, provide docile economic labour as well as soldiers that go to war. This is the main element that characterizes the paradigm shift in migration and borders, but also with respect to all the constitutive aspects of the political organization in contemporary society on a national and world scale. So, we are facing here a *total political fact* that obviously derives from the increasingly intense and uncontrollable intertwining of the dynamics of other economic, social, cultural and political phenomena.

6. CONCLUSION

The change in the paradigm of migration and borders cannot be understood if two main fundamental aspects are not fully taken into account: the consequences of neoliberalism and the intensification of neo-colonial practices. Therefore, the consequences of the triumph of global economic neoliberalism as well as the great increase in the world population and the ecological instability commonly understood as climate change confirm two key axes in the comprehension of the paradigm. These two aspects have radically transformed the economic, social, cultural and political structure of the world at local and global level, to the point that it can be said that, since the 1980s, we have entered a new era. The previous era was marked by capitalist development more or less framed by the nation-states with a large use of internal and international migration. All economic, military and political powers, led by the United States, have developed their societies thanks to these migrations, by integrating them, assimilating them, or adapting them to be docile workers and also good citizens. This was the model established during the time of biopolitics: accomplishing the integration and full assimilation of the majority of immigrants and acting towards the rejection of the "bad immigrant", i.e. those unable or unwilling to became docile workers and good citizens (see Preciado, 2020).

Today, however, economic development has much less need for stable workers than back in the 1970s, but rather "flexible labour" is prioritized in the global neoliberal economic model. Thus, it requires "disposable" labour, even to be enslaved or hyper-exploited both at the very heart of the big cities of the rich world and in the countryside. The abundant availability of immigrant labour together with the erosion of workers' protections offers employers the possibility of lowering them, sometimes enslaving them, making them "disposable" labour or disposable migrants (as shown in various chapters of this volume). This possibility becomes even greater due to the continuous influx of migrants fleeing devastated lands that have become uninhabitable. In this line of argument, today's migrations subsume all the disasters caused by capitalist development, past colonialism and global economic neoliberalism over the past 30 years. The unravelling of the more traditional incorporation of migrants into society is dramatically illustrated in the precarious survival of migrants in rich countries (including the Emirates and Saudi Arabia).

To sum up, the tendency to choose such a contemporary option – to let migrants die (thanatopolitics) – has been adopted by all wealthy countries, including those that claim to be democratic and respectful of human rights, and particularly in their treatment of migrants during the acute Covid-19 crisis. As a consequence, we can refer somehow to witnessing a massacre. This is not only perceived as a crucial part impacted by the population in devastated territories – devastated not only by wars directly or indirectly fuelled by the great powers as well as by Islamist terrorism – but also of migrants left to die en route and at borders. Migrants are in fact designated as a fearsome threat in the eyes of the elites, whose main concerns are the increase in population and ecological imbalances, primarily because they are responsible for the inability to govern this situation. The only sustainable solution would be the equitable distribution of wealth, the abolition of profits, the abolition of all the devastating activities that cause health and environmental disasters and the majority of deaths due to diseases due to toxic contamination and work conditions and of unsustainable life – i.e. a dramatic increase in human security.

However, even if the situation tends to worsen in the short and medium term, migration will inexorably continue and, in spite of obstacles, migrants will be successful in at least partially integrating into the arrival/receiving countries. The resistance of migrants, as well as other subordinated people, to oppression is a matter of survival and an expression of the never-dormant aspiration for economic, social, cultural, and political emancipation.

NOTES

1. An introduction to such a border shift can also be seen in the European context in relation to external or internal borders (see Ribas-Mateos, 2015).
2. The deconstruction of such a dominant discourse in migration studies makes reference to the works of Foucault, whereas the critique of the "science of migration" was proposed by Abdelmalek Sayad (2004).
3. The much quoted anthropologist Marcel Mauss (grandson of Durkheim) revises his grandfather Durkheim's concept of social fact, proposing the idea of a "total social fact," which would include all aspects of a particular phenomenon. I think that today it is fundamental to revisit such a concept, considering this "fact" as a total political fact because all aspects involved contain a strong political significance.
4. See https://www.nytimes.com/2020/04/08/nyregion/coronavirus-race-deaths.html.

5. Among other sources see: https://www.repubblica.it/cronaca/2020/04/10/news/migranti_porti_chiusi_per_il_coronavirus_casarini_il_covid_non_puo_essere_il_motivo_-253694321/?ref=RHPPLF-BH-I253495487-C8-P8-S2.4-T1.
6. See https://www.dailymail.co.uk/news/article-8092315/Germany-child-migrants-trapped-Greek-islands-prioritise-sick-girls-14.html.
7. See https://www.ilfattoquotidiano.it/2020/03/21/coronavirus-la-francia-continua-a-respingere-i-migranti-a-ventimiglia-ma-con-lemergenza-vengono-abbandonati-senza-precauzioni/5744702/; and https://www.notiziegeopolitiche.net/grecia-coronavirus-migranti-e-profughi-dimenticati-nei-campi-di-lesbo-e-moria/.
8. See https://www.notiziegeopolitiche.net/grecia-coronavirus-migranti-e-profughi-dimenticati-nei-campi-di-lesbo-e-moria/.
9. See https://www.notiziegeopolitiche.net/grecia-coronavirus-migranti-e-profughi-dimenticati-nei-campi-di-lesbo-e-moria/.
10. See https://www.fanpage.it/politica/coronavirus-perche-chiudere-le-frontiere-ai-migranti-come-chiede-salvini-non-ha-alcun-senso/.
11. "Furor on Memo At World Bank," February 7, 1992, *The New York Times* 2017, https://www.nytimes.com/1992/02/07/business/furor-on-memo-at-world-bank.html; Office Memorandum from Lawrence M. Summers, Subject: GEP, the World Bank/IMFMIGA, 12 Dec 1991. This was an internal memo at the World Bank, not intended for the public – reportedly sarcastic, rather than sincere, according to its authors – that highlighted the economic logic of dumping waste in less-developed countries. See https://en.wikipedia.org/wiki/Lawrence_Summers.
12. L. Summers, at the annual meeting of the World Bank and the IMF in Bangkok in 1991, interview with Kirsten Garrett, "Background Briefing," Australian Broadcasting Company. See https://fr.wikipedia.org/wiki/Lawrence_Summers: and also the Cadtm Committee for the abolition of illicit debt LIEGE – BELGIUM: www.cadtm.org and https://www.les-crises.fr /. https://www.cadtm.org/English.
13. See the reference in: http://effimera.org/negazionismo-scetticismo-o-resistenze-dove-va-lecologia-politica-di-turi-palidda/.

BIBLIOGRAPHY

Aradau, Claudia and Tazzioli, Martina (2020) "Biopolitics multiple: Migration, extraction, subtraction", *Millennium*, 48(2), pp. 198–220. http://research.gold.ac.uk/27738/1/Biopolitics%20multiple%20Accepted%20manuscript.pdf.

Bauman, Sigmund (2003) *Wasted Lives: Modernity and Its Outcasts*, Cambridge: Polity.

Bigo, Didier and Guild, Elspeth (2005) "Policing at a distance: Schengen visa policies", in *Controlling Frontiers: Free Movement into and within Europe*, edited by Elspeth Guild and Didier Bigo, London: Routledge, pp. 233–63.

Cuttitta, Paolo (2017) "Delocalization, humanitarianism, and human rights: The Mediterranean border between exclusion and inclusion". https://onlinelibrary.wiley.com/doi/full/10.1111/anti.12337.

Dal Lago, Alessandro and Palidda, Salvatore (eds.) (2010) *Conflict, Security and the Reshaping of Society: The Civilisation of War*, London: Routledge. http://www.oapen.org/search?identifier=391032.

Foucault, Michel (2007) *Security, Territory, Population: Lectures at the Collège de France, 1977–1978*, London–New York: Basingstoke: Palgrave Macmillan.

Foucault, Michel (2008) *The Birth of Biopolitics: Lectures at the Collège de France, 1978–1979*, London–New York: Basingstoke: Palgrave Macmillan.

Gros, Frédéric (2008) "Désastre humanitaire et sécurité humaine.Le troisième âge de la sécurité". https://esprit.presse.fr/article/gros-frederic/desastre-humanitaire-et-securite-humaine-le-troisieme-age-de-la-securite-14470.

Guild, Elspeth and Bigo, Didier (eds) (2005). *Controlling Frontiers: Free Movement into and within Europe*, London: Routledge.

Heyman, Josiah and Ribas-Mateos, Natalia (2019) "Borders of wealth and poverty: Ideas stimulated by comparing the Mediterranean and U.S.–Mexico borders", *Archivio antropologico mediterraneo*, 21 (2). https://doi.org/10.4000/aam.2019.

Martini, Francesca and Palidda, Salvatore (2018) "Continuità e mutamenti delle migrazioni nel confine tral'Italia e la Francia", *Altreitalie*, 56, pp. 117–129. https://www.altreitalie.it/pubblicazioni/rivista/n-56/acquista-versione-digitale/continuita-e-mutamenti-delle-migrazioni-nel-confine-tra-litalia-e-la-francia.kl.

Miller, Todd (2017) *Storming the Gate: Climate Change, Migration, and Homeland Security*, San Francisco: City Lights.

Palidda, Salvatore (ed.) (2011) *Racial Criminalisation of Migrants in the Twenty-first Century*, London: Ashgate/Routledge, https://www.routledge.com/products/9781409407492.

Palidda, Salvatore (ed.) (2016) *Governance of Security and Ignored Insecurities in Contemporary Europe*, London: Routledge. https://www.academia.edu/35552034/Extract_of_Governance_of_Security_and_Ignored_Insecurities.pdf.

Palidda, Salvatore (2018) *La guerre aux migrations ou la subsomption de tous les désastres de la derive néo-libériste- le fait politique total du XXI siècle*. https://www.academia.edu/37936402/La_guerre_aux_migrations_ou_la_subsomption_de_tous_les_d%C3%A9sastres_de_la_d%C3%A9rive_n%C3%A9o-lib%C3%A9riste-_le_fait_politique_total_du_XXI_si%C3%A8cle.

Palidda, Salvatore (2019) "Negazionismo, scetticismo o resistenze: dove va l'ecologia politica?". http://effimera.org/negazionismo-scetticismo-o-resistenze-dove-va-lecologia-politica-di-turi-palidda/.

Perkins, John (2005) *Confessions of an Economic Hit Man*, London: Ebury Press.

Preciado, Paul B. (2020) "Les leçons du virus", *Mediapart*, April 11. https://www.mediapart.fr/journal/culture-idees/110420/les-lecons-du-virus.

Ribas-Mateos, Natalia (2015) *Border Shifts. New Mobilities in Europe and Beyond*, Basingstoke: Palgrave.

Sassen, Saskia (1999) *Globalization and Its Discontents: Essays on the New Mobility of People and Money*, New York: New Press.

Sassen, Saskia (2008) *Territory, Authority, Rights: From Medieval to Global Assemblages*, Princeton: Princeton University Press.

Sassen, Saskia (2014) *Expulsions: Brutality and Complexity in the Global Economy*, Cambridge, MA: Harvard University Press.

Sayad, Abdelmalek (2004) *The Suffering of the Immigrant*, Cambridge: Polity Press.

Squire, Vicki (2016) "Governing migration through death in Europe and the US: Identification, burial and the crisis of modern humanism", *European Journal of International Relations*, September 16. https://journals.sagepub.com/doi/full/10.1177/1354066116668662.

12. Documenting and denouncing violence at eastern European borders: the socio-legal relevance of refugee voices through the production of audio-visual material
Chiara Denaro

1. INTRODUCTION

Since 2011, a time characterized by an increase in migratory pressure at the borders of the European Union (EU) related to political and socioeconomic changes in the Middle East and North Africa (MENA) region, the Mediterranean space has become, once again, the crossroads for several migration paths, within which the forced component of migration has emerged as the dominant one (Ribas-Mateos, 2016). The insufficiency of resettlement policies and the absence of humanitarian corridors to Europe have forced people to challenge the European border regime, and a growing number of scholars have analysed the so-called transformation of refugees into 'illegal migrants' (Black, 2003; Schuster, 2011; Castles, 2014; Scheel & Squire, 2014), who are, as such, obliged to trust in smuggling networks in order to cross the borders of the EU.

In the reconfiguration of the Mediterranean space that occurred after 2011, affecting both migration routes and flow compositions, the eastern Mediterranean corridor has become increasingly important. The number of arrivals reached its peak in 2015 and then started to decrease in parallel with a more effective system of land and sea interceptions, followed by pushbacks to Turkey after the signing of the EU–Turkey statement of March 2016, primarily aimed at managing migration flows. Nevertheless, in 2019 there were 43,683 sea arrivals and 11,665 land arrivals in Greece (UNHCR, 2019a)[1] and the situation on the Greek islands – where most seaborne refugees are accommodated – is still quite critical. According to data provided by the Greek Ministry of Interior, on 30 August 2019, 24,673 persons were being held on the Greek islands (Lesbos, Chios, Samos, Leros and more) where there was an official reception capacity for 8,863.

Violence is a structural component of contemporary border regimes, in particular at the Greek–Turkish border. It is transversal to sea and land border crossings, in which people risk, and often lose, their lives; to border management operations, which are strongly characterized by the use of force; and to the reception policies put in place within the framework of the so-called hotspot approach, which plans to systematically hold people on the islands for several months in extremely poor reception conditions. The EU borders, built to 'protect' and delimit an area of supposed 'freedom, security and justice', are configured as sites of struggle between opposite tendencies (Mezzadra & Neilson, 2013): the people's will to move and the institutional will to contain them in determined spaces. Nevertheless, several scholars have been able to go beyond this rigid opposition by focusing on borders as 'grey zones' and tackling the in-between structures, the superposition of filters and the ambivalence of such a scenario (Knudsen & Frederiksen, 2015). However, as Balibar (2001) has observed:

> the traditional institution of borders which ... can be defined in the modern era as a 'sovereign' or non-democratic condition of democracy itself, mainly works as an instrument of security control, social segregation and unequal access to the means of existence and sometimes as an institutional distribution of survival and death: it becomes a cornerstone of institutional violence. (2001: 16)

Inside and outside the borders are human beings entitled to specific universal rights and increasingly aware of this entitlement. Although established as one of the EU's priorities, the protection of these fundamental rights, including the right to asylum, clashes with some prescriptions imposed by the configuration of each border regime. As many non-governmental organization (NGO) reports have demonstrated, the relationship between borders and violence in some cases is so deep that it generates the perception of borders as a violent entity (Jones, 2016). Notwithstanding, violence at the borders is still a 'missing discourse' (Fine, 1988), both in official and public documents and humanitarian and security rhetoric (Walters, 2010; Campesi, 2014; Tazzioli, 2015).

Beginning in 2013, *prise de parole* initiatives organized by Syrian refugees (what Hirschman defined as 'voice', 1970, 1978) multiplied transversally according to the geographies of the migration routes. The production and diffusion of audio-visual material on social networks and so-called 'new media' have been at the core of these processes of 'voice through exit' and they have often shown a different reality from that of the official media (Denaro, 2016a, 2020b). The places of sharing and diffusion of this material were often virtual communities (such as WhatsApp and Facebook groups of refugees and activists) on social media, and it is reasonable to hypothesize that digital technologies and digital connectivity played a key role in the phenomena. It is possible to identify different kinds of 'voices': voices aimed at documenting a particular reality, at denouncing rights violations, at requesting help. In these voices, the violence experienced at the borders ceases to be a missing discourse by contributing to building counternarratives about European border management policies.

In some cases, the production of audio-visual material by persons on the move, documenting both violence at the borders and undignified detention and reception, has played a key role in strategic litigation cases by providing evidence for various kinds of appeals before judicial authorities. In this regard, this chapter sheds light on the possible legal significance of audio-visual testimonies, as they provide a more evidence-based picture of alleged human rights violations.

The analysis of these processes is guided by a series of research questions aimed at exploring the cultural, social and legal relevance of the processes. How do the practices of documenting border violence help to make it emerge as an explicit discourse? Is it possible to identify elements of agency, empowerment and resistance in persons on the move in these practices? How do these practices contribute to refugees' claims for rights, both within processes of advocacy and strategic litigation cases? Finally, what is the role of social media and new technologies in facilitating these processes of *prise de parole*/self-representation and the production of evidence for legal purposes?

The main hypothesis of this chapter is that the production of audio-visual material takes shape as a result of the combination of a wide gamut of social, cultural and relational factors and that it is not merely ascribable to access to social media and Web 2.0 (O'Reilly, 2005) or to the possession of new technologies. Accordingly, the chapter analyses how the violence experienced at the borders emerges through images, as both individual and collective testimonies, focusing on the processes of sharing the audio-visual material with other collectives and spreading it around the world. Coherent with Couldry's reflection concerning the need to 'rethink voice' (2009), refugees' narratives through images are considered in terms of dialogue, with a wide range of listeners: other refugees, volunteers, activists, journalists, NGO members and even the authorities. In particular, the role of media has not only been qualified as a vehicular form of action, but as a fundamental hypothesis of change in political action. Additionally, the chapter explores the role of digital technologies and social media in documenting border violence as communication infrastructures, which may increase the sociocultural and legal relevance of those processes.

Starting with a brief reflection on the configuration of the Greek border and migration management regime – characterized by violence at different levels – the chapter explores the concept of border violence in general and how counternarratives provided by persons on the move, NGOs, activists and human rights experts may cause it to emerge as an explicit discourse by going beyond the mainstream narratives that often hide violence behind a technical use of language to present some operations.

The chapter then brings empirical evidence from a number of key cases of visual narratives – namely pictures and videos – aimed at documenting border violence to explore the multiple contexts surrounding the production of audio-visual material, as well as the different purposes behind these processes. In this context, it reflects on the voices of refugees as an interactive process, which involves particular listeners and takes place through the use of social media. The selected cases were collected during an ethnographic research study, combined with visual sociology conducted between 2013 and 2019 in some of the key sites at the eastern European borders, in particular between Turkey and Greece.

Finally, the chapter analyses the sociocultural and legal relevance of audio-visual testimonies of violence. From a sociocultural perspective, the conclusions shed light on the mechanisms of self-determination and empowerment that make the violence experienced emerge through images as an individual and collective testimony that needs to be shared with other collectives and disseminated around the world, and as a trauma that must be faced and highlighted as an explicit discourse. The processes explored lead to the conclusion that the production of audio-visual material may be significant from a legal perspective as well, especially in the framework of strategic litigation processes, where it may help to strengthen the evidence-based nature of the cases.

2. THE CONFIGURATION OF THE GREEK–TURKISH BORDER: SEA AND LAND CROSSINGS, VIOLENT PUSHBACKS AND THE HOTSPOT APPROACH

Although it has been an important migration corridor since the 1990s and even earlier, the eastern European migration route took on increasing significance after 2011, becoming the most travelled during the so-called migration crisis. In 2015, more than 861,630 people reached the EU via this route (UNHCR, 2019a). Although the number of border crossings decreased after the signing and implementation of the EU–Turkey deal[2] in March 2016, they continued to be significant: 177,234 in 2016, 36,319 in 2017, 50,508 in 2018 and 55,348 in 2019 (UNHCR, 2019a).

Table 12.1   Possible border interceptions and returns to Turkey

Agency/year	UNHCR – arrivals	Frontex – border crossing attempts	Possible interceptions – returns to Turkey
2015	861,630	885,000	23,370
2016	177,234	182,227	4,993
2017	36,319	42,319	6,000
2018	50,508	56,561	6,053

Source: Author's creation using UNHCR/Frontex statistics.

The primary nationalities (83.7%) of persons crossing the Greek–Turkish borders in 2019 reflect the world's top ten refugee producing countries: Afghanistan (38.2%), Syrian Arab Republic (25.3%), Democratic Republic of the Congo (7.8%), Iraq (6.8%) and the State of Palestine (5.6%) (UNHCR, 2018, 2019a). Therefore, as previously noted by McMahon and Sigona (2016, 2018), 'the so-called "migration crisis" can be more accurately described as a crisis of refugee protection'. This trend is confirmed by statistical data from the Greek Asylum Service (7 June 2013–30 October 2019), according to which asylum applications by year were 48,554 in 2019, 66,966 in 2018, 58,638 in 2017 and 51,053 in 2016.[3]

A comparison of UNHCR data for sea and land arrivals and Frontex (2019) statistics gives an account of the possible number of interceptions made by joint border patrol operations, also in cooperation with the Turkish authorities[4] (see Table 12.1).

Despite the prevalence of the forced component in mixed migration flows, the interceptions at EU land and sea borders done as part of the joint Frontex border surveillance operations are reported to be quite systematic, and several scholars, NGOs and institutions have questioned their compliance with the non-refoulement principle and with international human rights standards and obligations (Human Rights Watch, 2011; Mountz & Loyd, 2014; Aas & Gundhus, 2015; Pallister-Wilkins, 2015; Fink, 2016, and others). In particular, the illegitimate use of violence by interforce police authorities during interceptions at land and sea borders has been widely reported by the local and international media and often documented in audio-visual material produced by refugees.

A recently reported case of violent pushback in the Aegean dates back to 14 November 2019 when 27 migrants (including 17 Syrian and 10 Somali nationals) spoke of having been attacked by the Greek Coast Guard when they were only 20 metres from Chios, and forced to return to Turkish waters. 'They [the Greek Coastguard] had no light on their boat', the Syrian refugee told the newspaper *Daily Sabah*, 'and then they turned on their lights about 200 meters away from our boat. They started firing into the air but we kept moving. They fired on us when we approached the island. It lasted for about 20 minutes and I counted about 100 rounds fired on us' (Daily Sabah, 2019). In this case, pictures of the damaged boat were published in the newspaper as evidence of the attack.

According to the Aegean Boat Report,[5] similar pushbacks at sea from Greek to Turkish waters were quite frequent, and visual evidence of several episodes has been collected and shared by the association on Facebook in order to document this practice, with the most recent cases being those of 10 and 21 July and 8 August 2019, when pushback operations were reportedly performed near the islands of Farmakonisi and Agathonisi.

For those who manage to successfully cross the Aegean Sea, a further possible scenario of human rights violation is the Greek reception system for asylum seekers and refugees, of which the detention and reception facilities set up on the Aegean islands as part of the hotspot approach represent a key component (European Commission, 2015, Migreurope, 2016). In November 2019, the situation on the islands was extremely critical: approximately 30,000 people were trapped in facilities with an intended capacity for only 6,178 people (Greek General Secretariat for Information and Communication, 2019) in extremely dangerous and unsuitable conditions, all within the framework of the geographical restriction imposed by the EU–Turkey Statement (Greek Refugee Council (GCR), 2019, UNHCR, 2019b). In particular, the GCR (2019) expressed deep concern for 'the limited, up to non-existent provision of medical and psychosocial services', with significant consequences for the identification of persons belonging to vulnerable groups,[6] and for 'the absence of new reception places in the mainland and the significant delays in the examination process of international protection applications all over the country' (GCR, 2019).

In recent years, the inadequacy of Greek policies concerning border and migration management has been denounced by numerous institutional and non-governmental stakeholders at both national and international level. Several cases have been brought before the European Court for Human Rights for alleged fundamental rights violations which were founded on a number of cases. Particularly significant was the decision 'M.S.S. v. Belgium and Greece (application no. 30696/09)',[7] where the European Court of Human Rights (ECtHR) found a violation of the European Convention on Human Rights (ECHR) Art. 3 (prohibiting inhuman or degrading treatment or punishment) by Greece, both because of the applicant's detention conditions and because of his living conditions in Greece, in addition to Art. 13 (right to an effective remedy), because of the deficiencies in the asylum procedure followed in the applicant's case. Another decision, 'Sharifi and Others v. Italy and Greece (application no. 16643/09)',[8] found a violation of Art. 13 and Art. 3 on the part of Greece due to the lack of access to asylum procedures and the risk of deportation to Afghanistan, where the plaintiffs were likely to be subjected to ill-treatment. The most recent significant decision was passed down by the ECtHR on 13 June 2019 concerning case No. 14165/16 'SH.D. and others v Greece, Croatia, Hungary, Northern Macedonia, Serbia and Slovenia',[9] where the Court found violations of Art. 3 with regard to five unaccompanied Afghan minors and Art. 5 (right to liberty and security) with regard to three of them due to unlawful detention in police stations justified by so-called 'protective custody' and undignified reception conditions at Idomeni Camp.

Although no alleged violation of Art. 3 was found in the subsequent 'Kaak and Others v. Greece' case despite the very critical living conditions in the hotspots of Vial and Souda (Chios), the SH.D. case opened the path to the recognition of human rights violations beyond the detention system in relation to inadequate reception and living conditions for unaccompanied minor asylum seekers. Nevertheless, the unlawful detention of unaccompanied minors remains a key issue – especially in light of the policy of 'protective custody' – and is being increasingly addressed using ECHR appeals under Rule 39 (on urgent measures). On 18 March 2019, the ECtHR approved interim measures in favour of two unaccompanied girls who were detained in the pre-removal centre of Tavros, telling the Greek government to transfer them immediately to a dedicated shelter and to ensure reception conditions in accordance with ECHR Art. 3.[10] A similar decision was issued on 4 November 2019, when the ECHR instructed the Greek government to transfer two unaccompanied boys detained in police stations – in breach of Art. 3 – to suitable shelters.[11]

Unfortunately, the recent bill on International Protection, published by the Greek government on 15 October 2019, does not seem to be designed to improve the current situation. In particular, the GCR has expressed its deep concern about the proposed reform, stressing that it significantly undermines the fundamental rights of asylum seekers and refugees in violation of, inter alia, the EU, International and Greek Law as well as the principle of non-refoulement.[12]

3. BORDER VIOLENCE AS A MISSING DISCOURSE

'Violence matters. It wrecks and shortens lives, causes pain and suffering, and is often part of rapid social change' (Walby, 2013: 95). Violence is as an emerging core issue in sociology but – ontologically and disciplinarily – it has generally been classified into two major forms: (a) interpersonal violence, mainly qualified as deviance and at the core of criminology studies; and (b) inter-state war, or warfare by the state, mainly explored by international relations and political science theorists, with a few sociological exceptions (Giddens, 1985; Mann, 1986 and others). Against the common theoretical background of the monopolization of legitimized violence by the state (Weber, 1968; Tilly, 1990), the shift in governance from state brutality to discipline and securitization has been thoroughly explored by several scholars (amongst them Foucault, 1991, 1997), who focused their attention on new and more sophisticated forms of power. The hypothesis of the decline of violence with modernity produced a sort of marginalization of violence in contemporary debates, and a consequent 'uncovering of new forms of violence' (Walby, 2013). Border violence can be understood as a new form of violence, characterized by the deployment of military forces by a state against unarmed civilians, whose supposed 'crime' is that of attempting to cross a border. According to Balibar (2001):

> the traditional institution of borders which ... can be defined in the modern era as a 'sovereign' or non-democratic condition of democracy itself, mainly work as an instrument of security control, social segregation and unequal access to the means of existence and sometimes as an institutional distribution of survival and death: it becomes a cornerstone of institutional violence. (2001: 16)

Most victims of border violence – especially those who lose their lives – have very limited access to public mourning (Butler, 2004), and remain invisible. Borders are violent entities (Jones, 2016) and sites of struggle (Mezzadra & Neilson, 2013), where a sad match between death and life is played daily against a background of the progressive detachment of legality and justice (Denaro, 2020a).

In the words of journalist Lee May, 'Violence against undocumented immigrants has always been there, but very little has been done about it because illegal immigrants have been terrified to file complaints against abusing officers' (May, 1987, cited in Trevino, 1998). Not all the violence at the borders is visible as affecting migrants' bodies, and several subtle but systematic forms of violence characterize the contemporary global border regime (Jones, 2016). Scholar Reece Jones – who brings evidence from the US–Mexico border region – has defined the violence narrated by refugees – often through images and videos – as 'the overt violence of border guards and border security infrastructure' and 'the use of force or power – threatened or actual – that increases the chances of injury, death or deprivation'. Less visible forms of violence may be related to the construction of walls or the deployment of border patrol agents on a border to prevent easy crossings, pushing migrants towards possibly lethal routes. In particular, border violence seems able to exceed the operations carried out at the borders as such, by encroaching upon detention and reception regimes as well as undignified living conditions in which persons on the move are often forced to exist. As seen earlier, the ECtHR has repeatedly found violations of Art. 3 in recent years with regard to the Greek reception system for asylum seekers and refugees, providing the grounds to extend the definition of violence beyond borders.

Despite being quite transversal to migration flow management policies, the concept of border violence is little defined and sometimes deliberately obscure and vague. In particular, in most official legal and policy documents concerning borders, violence remains a missing discourse (Fine, 1988). European Council Regulation 2007/2004, which established the Frontex Agency (2004),[13] is a good example of how a particular use of language may expose the violent operations entailed in border control through the use of non-violent words. Border control activities use quite violent verbs, such as 'obstruct' or 'impede' free mobility, or 'stop', 'arrest', 'capture' and 'detain'. Although these actions imply physical contact and coercion, here they are presented as 'management' and 'surveillance' (actions that do not imply contact between people) while, in the same spirit, violent words such as 'pushback' and 'expulsion' are replaced by non-violent ones, such as 'return' (see Chapter 1, Art. 1; Chapter 2, Art. 2 and 9).

The same lack of explicit references to violence characterizes European Regulation 1052/2013, establishing the European Border Surveillance System (Eurosur),[14] and European Regulation 1624/2016 on the European Border and Coastguard.[15] The only exception is represented by the term 'forced return', but the reference made to mandatory compliance with fundamental rights, international law, refugee law and child protection law does not really make it possible to perceive the violence behind this kind of operation. The new Regulation of the European Parliament and Council on the European Border and Coast Guard (COM/2018/631)[16] seems to introduce a more explicit reference to violence, through Art. 83, which addresses the 'tasks and powers of the members of the teams' and includes the use of weapons and ammunition (paragraph 5) in accordance with Member State legislation (paragraph 6). In addition, a dedicated annex V on 'Rules on the use of force, including the supply, training, control and use of service firearm weapons and non-lethal equipment applicable to the Agency's statutory staff when acting as team members during their deployment from the European Border and Coast Guard standing corps' should be introduced.

In recent years, Frontex's discourse on human rights has strengthened significantly, particularly through the concept of compliance with fundamental human rights (Art. 87), the introduction of a complaint mechanism (Art. 88) and of a specific professional figure tasked with safeguarding the respect for human rights obligations (Fundamental Rights Officer, Art. 89). While, on the one hand, Frontex seems to have appropriated the language of fundamental rights as a standard item of its self-presentation (Aas & Gundhus, 2015), on the other, the concept of violence has been replaced by that of 'force' which – as underlined by Hannah Arendt in her sage *On Violence* (1970) – does not include the component of the 'intentionality' of the behaviour, representing more a sort of 'natural power'.

Against the structured attempt to obscure the violent nature of border management policy behind a technical and aseptic language, there has been a proliferation of stakeholders engaged in the production of counternarratives on border management, in which violence emerges as a cornerstone that provides a different picture of what have been defined as 'border games' or 'border spectacle' (Andreas, 2012; De Genova, 2013). These include refugees – and more generally, persons on the move – who are the only first-hand providers of evidence and who often bear visible traces of the very meaning of border management on their bodies. Their pictures, videos, narratives, testimonies, accounts and lawsuits allow NGOs, international organizations and human rights officers to provide counternarratives and to challenge the dominant technical discourse on border management.

4. DOCUMENTING EXPLICIT BORDER VIOLENCE: CONTEXTS, TOOLS AND STRATEGIES IN VISUAL NARRATIVES BY PERSONS ON THE MOVE

The production of audio-visual material by refugees during their journeys and its dissemination through social media is an emergent phenomenon that is quite absent from the academic debate and little addressed by the mass media (Grandjean et al., 2014; Denaro, 2016a). At the same time, while increased attention has been paid to the impact of new digital technologies on the lives of migrants who live in Europe, the use of technology by persons on the move has little been explored (Leurs & Ponzanesi, 2014, 2018; Witteborn, 2015). As Witteborn (2015) observes, 'virtual practice enables ways of knowing and relating for forced migrants that challenge concepts of border through information sharing, transnational grouping and political learning' (2015: 350). Nevertheless, in the frame of the new 'network society', where the possession and use of digital technologies that make it possible to produce and rapidly share audio-visual material is increasingly transversal with respect to social classes and sociopolitical contexts (Castells, 2004), new technologies play a key role in the lives of refugees forced to cross borders illegally.

It is possible to identify a number of contexts in which these 'visual narratives' take shape: geographic contexts, namely migration routes, and sociopolitical contexts, namely border and migration regimes. Before further exploring these contexts, some features of forced mobility to and through Europe need to be explored. First, the will of the refugees to reach Europe comes up against well-known difficulties in entering the Schengen Area legally. This involves travelling on 'irregular' routes, which continuously evolve in order to overcome new barricades and obstacles (Castles, 2014; Fargues & Bonfanti, 2014; Scheel & Squire, 2014; Ribas-Mateos, 2015; Denaro, 2016c). Second, between 2013 and 2016, Syrian refugees who reached southern Europe, mainly Italy and Greece, by crossing the Mediterranean Sea, did not want to stop in these first arrival countries, and put in place several strategies of resistance against the circulation restrictions imposed by the Dublin Regulation in order to pursue their travels (Denaro, 2016b). Finally, during their struggles to reach central and northern Europe, migrants were able to interact with local and transnational solidarity movements engaged in critical sea-watching phenomena (Denaro, 2015), the provision of primary goods and the facilitation of transit through Europe.

In the context of these reflections it is possible to define some specific circumstances in which refugees have started to express their voices through images and videos, such as very dangerous phases of their journeys (e.g. sea crossings), happy 'turning points' (e.g. successful border crossings, transfers to new places), demonstrations, protests, hunger strikes – especially those held in order to continue journeys – inadequate reception and living conditions, cases of illegitimate detention and physical violence or human rights violations. Looking at these circumstances, it is possible to identify at least three main aims pursued through the production of audio-visual narratives: documentation, denouncement and requests for assistance at sea and on land (Denaro, 2016a). Even the main contents and messages of the pictures and videos vary widely, coherent with the nature of the 'listeners' and the aim of the communication. Launching an SOS at sea or sending out help requests on land is often done using voice messages via WhatsApp, Viber or Imo, supported by pictures and videos. They often concern cases of real or symbolic violence, deeply connected with the operation of the borders.

This chapter argues that the intrinsic violent nature of borders, as sites of legalized violations of fundamental rights, emerges and becomes visible through refugees' voices, ceasing to be a missing discourse (Fine, 1988). Moreover, it hypothesizes that the self-narratives of refugees, disseminated across social media, could challenge some traditional classifications and representations concerning migrations, migrants and borders. Finally, this production can be interpreted as an attempt to correct the narrative, one of the main goals of the revolutionaries committee in Syria after 2011 (Yassin-Kassab & Al-Shami, 2016).

5. DOCUMENTING, DENOUNCING, REQUESTING HELP: VOICES FROM THE BORDERS CONCERNING VIOLENCE

Audio-visual material constitutes a particular language that is able to contemporaneously transmit implicit or explicit messages to a large group of listeners. In particular through social media, refugees express their own voices and share them in real time with geographically distant people. However, these voices require an interpretation, like any other form of communication. The potential of photographs to give voice to the members of marginalized communities has been analysed by different studies that look at, for example, the capacity to promote processes of empowerment. Notwithstanding, as Chalfen et al. (2010) suggest, the production of visual narratives is not self-evident. In other words, the mere fact of producing and disseminating images does not coincide per se with having a voice, and it is not intrinsically or automatically a tool of empowerment (2010: 201), agency or resistance (Pauwels, 2015).

That said, in order to interpret the voices of refugees that emerge through pictures and videos, it is necessary to frame them in the specific circumstances in which they were produced, in terms of both events, or moments, and the interactions and relationships in which they took shape. In the following paragraphs, I discuss four cases of refugees' voices related to violence that were narrated through pictures and videos and spread through social media. The first case concerns a pushback in the Aegean Sea, carried out by the Turkish authorities (Figure 12.1); the second case is related to a shipwreck in the Aegean observed by unknown authorities (presumably Turkish coastguards) (Figures 12.2 and 12.3); the third case focuses on the use of audio-visual material by the Border Violence Monitoring Network;[17] and the fourth concerns the use of audio-visual material for strategic litigation purposes by the Still I Rise association.

5.1 A Pushback in the Aegean Sea

One case of violence at the EU borders denounced via new technologies and social media concerns the pushback at sea of 35 Syrian refugees that occurred during the night of 24–25 October 2014. The refugees were sailing to the Greek island of Chios when, after an engine failure, they were rescued by a Russian merchant vessel (presumably Danapris 5). According to refugee witnesses, the captain of the ship called the Greek authorities, because the rescue had taken place in Greek waters, but disembarkation in Greece was not authorized and the ship went in the opposite direction, towards Izmir. When the refugees learned they had been pushed back to Turkey, they decided to launch an SOS to the Italian human rights activist Nawal Soufi,[18] supported by a picture (Figure 12.1).

She forwarded the case to the Watch The Med Alarm Phone project, which also got in touch with the refugees on the boat. Both alerted the Greek coastguard, but it did not intervene,

Figure 12.1   Pushback toward Izmir, followed by Nawal Soufi SOS and Watch The Med Alarm Phone

declaring that the rescue did not happen in its territorial waters. This kind of pushback from Greece to Turkey was nothing new and, although in open violation of the non-refoulement principle (Art. 33 of the Geneva Convention) and the right to not be exposed to the risk of inhuman and degrading treatment (Art. 3) and collective expulsions (Art. 4 of Protocol 4), it constitutes a common praxis in Frontex's work along the Greek–Turkish borders (Amnesty International, 2013, 2016; Archer, 2014; Goodwin-Gill, 2011; Pro Asyl, 2013).

In the picture that the refugees sent to the activists, they depict themselves in a group, including women and children, arranged as in a family portrait. Their looks are direct and serious. Their eyes are full of the determination of people who are still struggling, refusing to disembark in an unsafe country, combined with the sadness of people who have risked their lives in vain and who will be forced to do so again. There is also a plea for help and intervention from the activists to stop the pushback. The dignity that emerges from each look, which show no fear of repercussions, contrasts with the official, dominant representation of refugees as victims whose identity is never recognized, except as statistics on migration flows.

5.2   A Shipwreck in the Aegean

Amongst the visual narratives produced to request rescue and help are pictures related to shipwrecks. The photographs in Figures 12.2 and 12.3 concern a shipwreck that occurred on 19 September 2015 on one of the seaborne routes from Turkey to Greece. Reportedly, the people on board launched several SOS calls to both institutional (e.g. coastguards) and

Figure 12.2   Interception of a boat in distress

Figure 12.3   Shipwreck

non-institutional actors (e.g. activists), and in the second case they supported the request for assistance with photographs. The man who took the picture was transferred onto a coastguard boat (presumably the Turkish coastguard) to 'help in the rescue operations', but in the end the authorities did not intervene promptly, and the people were rescued – and brought back to Turkey – at the very last moment.

These pictures were received by Nawal Soufi via WhatsApp and shared on Facebook with the primary aim of condemning the failure to rescue.

> When you receive a picture that depicts a person in a river or at sea, you understand that ok, stop, you can't do any reasoning. You have to intervene. This is not only useful in order to document, after days, months and years, something that is really happening. This is useful to call for immediate intervention. (Interview with Nawal Soufi, human rights activist, 20 May 2015)

5.3 Violent Pushbacks at the Greek Land Border

Starting in 2015, volunteers operating along the so-called Balkan route began to gather witnesses to the violence experienced by persons on the move. Some of these documented experiences have been put into an Internet database in order to report the violence at the borders, with the particular focus on pushback operations. One particularly important project is the Border Violence Monitoring Network,[19] which started operating at the border between Serbia and Hungary and then extended to all the Balkan route countries (Bosnia-Herzegovina, Montenegro, Macedonia, Greece). The database updated by the Border Violence Monitoring Network includes monthly reports with detailed information on single events of violence against persons on the move. From a methodological perspective, the information is collected – and reports compiled – by volunteers on the ground, either working independently or with NGOs.[20] The reports are often supported by pictures taken by persons on the move as testimonies to the violence suffered.

With regard to Greece, in 2019 the network mainly received reports from Info Mobile Team[21] and the Philoxenia association concerning seven cases of border violence and pushbacks at the Greek–Macedonian (5 cases) and Greek–Turkish borders (2 cases). The different reports are supported by photographs taken by migrants, which provide evidence of reported injuries. On 22 July, one person was pushed back from Macedonia (Gevgelija) to Greece:

> According to the respondent, the two policemen arrived in a police car and arrested him. He was ordered to walk from the point of apprehension until the police station in the injured condition for 15 minutes.
> The respondent tried to explain to the police that he could not walk in this injured condition. Instead of listening to his plea, the policemen started pressing his wounds to force him to walk.[22]

A few months later, on 26 September 2019, another violent pushback of two young men occurred near the Gevgelija train station, and they were reported to have been beaten with batons, hands and other tools, threatened with guns and attacked by dogs (pictures of the injuries are included in the report).[23]

5.4 The Living Conditions of Unaccompanied Minors at the Vathy Hotspot: The Use of Audio-visual Material to Claim Rights through Strategic Litigation

As highlighted in several reports by NGOs and the media (Doctors Without Borders, 2019; Smith, 2019), despite having a capacity of 648, the Vathy hotspot on Samos Island holds around 6,000 refugees. Unaccompanied minors are amongst the most vulnerable population and are lodged in very poor living conditions. According to a report by the Italian–Greek NGO Still I Rise, based on daily testimonies of child abuse collected in the field for over two years, the NGO, in collaboration with Help Refugees UK, filed a criminal case on 12 June 2019 with the Prosecutor's Office of Samos, in Greece, against the management of the reception and identification centre of the island, to condemn the human rights violations perpetrated against unaccompanied children living in the camp. The same complaint was filed with the Rome prosecutor's office on 19 June 2019 (Act 11587).[24]

At the core of the complaint were 'abuses and living conditions of unaccompanied minors in the Hotspot', with particular reference to: (i) the initial reception and identification of unaccompanied minors; (ii) the limited access to clothes and hygiene products, as well as to hygiene services; (iii) very poor living conditions and inadequateness of the allocation provided to unaccompanied minors in the hotspot (promiscuity with adults, no dedicated space); (iv) limited access to medical assistance; (v) limited quantity and quality of food; (vi) police violence against minors; (vii) violation of the right to family unity; and (viii) consequences of living conditions on the mental health of minors.

The report shared by Still I Rise concerning the complaint includes a reference to violence and to the use of audio-visual material to document it:

> The children report multiple and regular instances of violence against them, also documented with videos and pictures – they write. One reports that he was kicked by an officer during the queue for food and was wounded in the hand. Another was arrested on 28/10/2018 for trying to break up a fight. After handcuffing him, police officers threw him to the ground and repeatedly kicked him, breaking his arm. He claims all his medical records were then destroyed by the authorities. Another incident occurred on 20/07/2018: three unaccompanied Syrian minors were attacked and injured by a policeman while they waited to enter the camp and were subsequently illegally detained for 24 hours.

6. THE SOCIOCULTURAL AND LEGAL RELEVANCE OF 'VOICES (CONCERNING VIOLENCE) THROUGH EXIT'

Inspired by Hirschman's conceptualization of 'exit and voice' and its re-working in migration and diaspora studies, I have chosen to focus on refugee 'voices through exit' (Denaro, 2016a, 2020b) when referring to the narratives of refugees that emerged along their exit pathways from Syria and migration to Europe. While defining the concept and exploring 'voice through exit', I have always borne in mind the sociocultural background of the speakers. In this respect I also focused on the Arab revolutions, especially in Syria, which were a fertile ground for the diffusion of the habit of documenting everyday life to denounce violations and to provide counternarratives to the dominant ones. This is exactly what refugees do as well, by documenting their travels, denouncing violations and providing new narratives concerning themselves, their migration paths and contemporary border regimes (Denaro, 2020b). In doing so, refugees help to challenge the stereotype that qualifies them as 'speechless emissaries' (Malkki, 1996) by demonstrating awareness of their rights and their ability to present autonomous claims.

As Nick Couldry (2009) suggests in the essay 'Rethinking the politics of voice', the mechanisms of voice have to be recognized as bidirectional communications that develop through dialogical processes. Each voice acquires meaning when a listener receives it. Moreover, according to the author, the act of listening is like a duty, which corresponds to the right to provide an autonomous account of one's own story, which must exist for each human being. In his reading, listening is an act of the recognition of humanity.

In the case of refugees' voices during exit, it was possible to observe the presence of a wide and variegated plethora of listeners: institutional and non-institutional actors, individuals and collectives, political and apolitical subjects. Amongst them were certain innovative listeners, or interlocutors, especially from the world of associations, volunteerism or activism, which traditionally revolve around migration phenomena. The focus on interlocutors for refugees was critical, because very often the messages that emerged from the *prise de parole* processes, through words and pictures, were the result of an interaction. Indeed, it arose from some interviews that the content of the audio-visual material was at times co-produced and came about through specific requests from interlocutors, as it could be useful for advocacy in the future.

> It is often a process of co-production of messages. Some people are very conscious of their rights, and it is not a coincidence if they [refugees who voice by producing and sharing audio-visual material through social media] are Afghans – because many of them have already been in England and have an idea about rights in the EU – or Syrians, maybe from higher social classes. People who come directly from Pakistan have no idea about 'his capacity to say or to do'. He has to discuss this with you. So, this is a co-production. They want to say something, but they have also to discover what their rights are here. (Interview with Y.A., Italian teacher and activist, 15 May 2015)

As in the case of refugees, sea and land borders and migration routes all constitute the setting where unusual forms of activism and volunteering take place. They offer at least two new forms of support provided to people on the move. The first case concerns the reception of SOS calls from sea, the (not only linguistic) mediation between refugees on board and southern European coastguards and political pressure in the case of delayed or non-assistance. These actions – which I previously conceptualized as 'critical sea-watching phenomena' (Denaro, 2015) – are mainly ways of 'listening to the voice of those at sea and amplifying their political demands' (Schwarz & Stierl, 2019). This is exactly the mission of the Watch The Med Alarm Phone project, an activist hotline that migrants in distress at sea can call 24 hours a day.[25] The amplification of voices of persons on the move – and those who risk their lives at sea – is mainly carried out through social media work, reporting activities and advocacy. A second interactive scenario, where refugees' voices are heard and amplified, is that of the provision of humanitarian aid to refugees on the move by individuals, associations and the refugees themselves. This may consist of providing instructions to facilitate travel, rides or essential supplies such as food, water and clothing.

Concerning voices of, or rather, dialogues about so-called seaborne refugees, there are several pages especially dedicated to sea crossings: pictures that people post about journeys, information concerning specific boat departures, SOS calls, people in distress, shipwrecks, missing people and the like.[26] Volunteers or activists manage other kinds of pages, which in some cases are the expression of quite large networks – such as that of Alarm Phone, which involves more than 200 activists in different countries – and in other cases are managed by individuals, who perform solidarity tasks. Interesting examples of the latter category are Nawal Soufi,[27] Alaa Hasan[28] and Helena Maleno,[29] who for several years have received SOS calls from the sea and assistance requests from borders, detention centres and other sites of violations around Europe and beyond.

Social media play a crucial role in the interactions between refugees and activists, both concerning the possibility to request help or launch an SOS by sharing one's own GPS position via

WhatsApp or Viber, and in terms of solidarity movement organization. Self-geolocalization is one of the most innovative functions introduced by new technologies, and it has completely revolutionized the way people deal with forced and voluntary mobilities. Especially on migration paths that involve one or more clandestine phases, the obligation of invisibility precludes any possibility of satisfying the human need to position oneself in the world. Indeed, the severing of the relationship between the individual and their external environment is exactly one of the most oppressive and violent aspects of clandestine migration.

The self-geolocalization of seaborne migrants and sharing GPS positions also facilitate new and more sophisticated forms of advocacy, denunciation and strategic litigation by activists and researchers. One key example is represented by the Forensic Oceanography project,[30] which reconstructs events in which human rights violations have taken place by providing analysis and reports based on the employment of a wide range of digital mapping and modelling technologies.[31] 'In combining these technologies to elucidate the chain of events of this particular case, Forensic Oceanography also suggest new ways in which these emergent technologies could be applied to the field of international law and human rights advocacy' (Heller, Pezzani & Situ Studio, 2012; Forensic Oceanography, 2019). One great example of the potential of these new forms of documenting and denouncing human rights violations is the 'Nivin case', in which the Global Legal Action Network (GLAN) lodged an appeal with the UN Human Rights Committee to challenge the practice of so-called 'privatized pushbacks' – consisting of the engagement of commercial ships by EU coastal states to return migrants to non-safe countries (e.g. Libya), in which their lives are at risk, using merchant ships as a proxy.[32]

The sociocultural relevance of interaction processes between speakers and listeners, which visibilizes and amplifies the voices of refugees and persons on the move, is therefore quite high. It contributes to building counternarratives on migration and border management policies and including a perspective that is generally excluded: that of persons experiencing violence on their bodies. In particular, there is an attempt to 'correct the narrative' (Yassin-Kassab & Al-Shami, 2016) by reaffirming the illegitimate nature of violence against unarmed people which, according to the international human rights legal framework, should respect their right to life (Art. 2 ECHR) and protect them from undergoing inhuman and degrading treatment (Art. 3 ECHR) and from the possibility of being returned to countries where these rights may be at risk, in accordance with the non-refoulement principle (Art. 4, ECHR and Geneva Convention). The respect for human rights is at the very core of the political claims made by persons on the move through their voices, making their relevance not only sociocultural but also legal.

From a legal perspective, collecting and presenting audio-visual testimonies may have a disruptive impact on judicial proceedings, but the requirement that these products have to be considered credible evidence has still been little explored. As stressed by Della Ratta (2018) in her analysis of the production of audio-visual materials during the Syrian revolution, 'having too many pictures is like to have none of them', as the overproduction of audio-visual material may significantly affect its credibility. Once more, the effectiveness of evidence of violence experienced by persons on the move to support rights claims at the judicial level very much depends on the interaction between speakers and listeners, who can work together to ensure their legal worth.

There is no doubt that the potential audience of these refugee voices exceeds those who have been previously defined as 'listeners' – namely volunteers, activists, journalists and human rights defenders. A wider public could be reached both directly by refugees – through

Facebook and other social media – and indirectly – through the work of journalists and traditional media, but also through the narration of the ongoing legal struggle of human rights defenders. Refugee voices can play a key role in countering, and correcting, the anti-immigrant, xenophobic narratives of right-wing politicians, and thus influence European culture and society.

7. CONCLUDING REFLECTIONS

By bringing empirical references from an ethnography of forced mobilities along the eastern Mediterranean corridor – in particular between Turkey and Greece – this chapter reflects on the sociocultural and legal impact of the production of audio-visual materials by persons on the move, aimed at documenting and denouncing violence experienced at the borders. Digital technologies and social media have an impact on forced migrations. Refugees' voices through exit (Denaro, 2016a, 2020b), which emerge from producing and sharing audio-visual narratives through social media, are at the core of the analysis here. They have been interpreted in light of some contextual elements and, following Couldry's suggestion, they have been hypothesized as the result of complex interactions between speakers and listeners. Relationships between refugees and activists are often entirely mediated by social media and digital technologies, which constitute the infrastructure that allows the dialogue between them to take shape, overcoming spatial–temporal distances.

Against a background in which border violence is a missing discourse, and characterized by a mainstream narrative built upon the technical management of borders and migration flows (presented as being fully respectful of human rights standards and obligations), refugees' voices and testimonies help to change the cultural perception of border regimes as neutral entities and to 'correct the narrative' by making the violence explicit. This correction process – in which violence is clearly shown through audio-visual recordings and emerges as a cornerstone of border management policies – takes shape through the dialogue between speakers and listeners, where activists work as amplifiers of refugee voices (Schwarz & Stierl, 2019). Refugee voices documenting and denouncing violence at the borders also have a social relevance: they are able to challenge the view of refugees as passive victims of smugglers and make them emerge as agents, as people who are able to speak, to denounce violations and to claim rights, including the right to life, to be protected from inhuman and degrading treatments and to choose where to live (Denaro, 2016a).

Finally, after transforming border violence from a missing discourse to a dominant, intrinsic feature of contemporary border regimes, refugees' counternarratives and audio-visual testimonies can play a key role in strengthening claims for human rights and denouncing violations experienced at the borders. Audio-visual testimonies can have a truly significant legal relevance, serving as part of the evidence collected to provide grounds for appeal before judicial authorities. They can document troubling living conditions, injuries suffered and other inhuman and degrading treatments, as well as pushbacks. Of course, at the core of these voices are human rights related claims, and a crucial role remains to be played by the refugees' listeners, who – through a constant dialogue with persons on the move – can contribute to the systematization of the evidence collected, report on border violence to a broader audience and amplify messages, all in order to make refugee voices heard.

NOTES

1. The UNHCR provides disaggregated data by type of border crossing (sea or land) and year.
2. The EU–Turkey deal was signed on 18 March 2016 and was mainly aimed at stopping the flow of irregular migration via Turkey to Europe. According to the EU–Turkey statement, all new irregular migrants and asylum seekers arriving from Turkey to the Greek islands and whose application for asylum has been declared inadmissible must be returned to Turkey. A more comprehensive explanation is provided at http://www.europarl.europa.eu/legislative-train/theme-towards-a-new-policy-on-migration/file-eu-turkey-statement-action-plan (accessed on 2 February 2020).
3. Data are available at http://asylo.gov.gr/en/wp-content/uploads/2019/10/Greek_Asylum_Service_data_September_2019_en.pdf (accessed on 2 February 2020).
4. The section on the eastern Mediterranean route reports: 885,000 attempted border-crossings in 2015, 182,227 in 2016, 42,319 in 2017, 56,561 in 2018.
5. See Aegean Boat Report, https://www.facebook.com/pg/AegeanBoatReport/videos/?ref=page_internal (accessed on 2 February 2020).
6. According to Greek legislation – Law No. 4375 of 2016 on the organization and operation of the Asylum Service, the Appeals Authority, the Reception and Identification Service, the establishment of the General Secretariat for Reception, the transposition into Greek legislation of the provisions of Directive 2013/32/EC, Gazette 51/A/3-4-2016 – only vulnerable persons are entitled to be transferred to the mainland and thus overcome the so-called 'geographical restriction' (ECRE & ELENA, 2019; Christides & Stefatou, 2017).
7. Judgement available at https://hudoc.echr.coe.int/eng#{"fulltext":["M.S.S.%20belgium"],"documentcollectionid2":["GRANDCHAMBER","CHAMBER"],"itemid":["001-103050"]} (accessed on 2 February 2020).
8. Judgement available at https://hudoc.echr.coe.int/eng#{"languageisocode":["FRE"],"appno":["16643/09"],"documentcollectionid2":["CHAMBER"],"itemid":["001-147287"]} (accessed on 2 February 2020).
9. Judgement available at https://hudoc.echr.coe.int/eng#{"itemid":["001-193610"]} (accessed on 2 February 2020).
10. See https://www.gcr.gr/en/news/press-releases-announcements/item/1069-the-european-court-of-human-rights-grants-interim-measures-in-favour-of-two-detained-unaccompanied-girls (accessed on 2 February 2020).
11. See https://rsaegean.org/en/european-court-of-human-rights-asks-greece-to-transfer-two-unaccompanied-boys-detained-in-police-station-to-suitable-shelter/ (accessed on 2 February 2020).
12. See https://www.gcr.gr/media/k2/attachments/GCR_on_bill_about_International_Protection_en.pdf (accessed on 2 February 2020).
13. Regulation available at https://eur-lex.europa.eu/legal-content/EN/TXT/?uri=CELEX%3A32004R2007 (accessed on 2 February 2020).
14. Regulation available at https://eur-lex.europa.eu/legal-content/IT/TXT/?uri=CELEX%3A32013R1052 (accessed on 2 February 2020).
15. Regulation available at https://eur-lex.europa.eu/legal-content/EN/TXT/?uri=CELEX%3A32016R1624 (accessed on 2 February 2020).
16. Proposal available at https://eur-lex.europa.eu/legal-content/EN/TXT/?uri=celex:52018PC0631 (accessed on 2 February 2020).
17. Website at https://www.borderviolence.eu/about (accessed on 2 February 2020).
18. Further information on Nawal Soufi and her activities is available at https://en.wikipedia.org/wiki/Nawal_Soufi (accessed on 2 February 2020).
19. More information is available at https://www.borderviolence.eu/about/ (accessed on 2 February 2020).
20. Some of the NGOs involved in the project include No Name Kitchen, Rigardu, [Re:]ports Sarajevo, Aid Brigade, Balkan Info Van, Escuela con Alma, BASIS, BelgrAid and Fresh Response.
21. See the Info Mobile Team website at https://www.mobileinfoteam.org/pushbacks and last report (November, 2019) *Illegal Pushbacks in Evros: evidence of human rights abuses at the Greece–Turkey border* available at https://static1.squarespace.com/static/597473fe9de4bb2cc35c376a/

t/5dcd1da2fefabc596320f228/1573723568483/Illegal+Evros+pushbacks+Report_Mobile+Info+Team_final.pdf (accessed on 2 February 2020).
22. See report, 'They treated me like a dog', available at https://www.borderviolence.eu/violence-reports/july-22-2019-0930-gevgelija-north-macedonia/ (accessed on 2 February 2020).
23. See report, 'I said just leave me to die here, whatever, I don't care anymore', available at https://www.borderviolence.eu/violence-reports/september-26-2019-0000-nearby-gevgelija-train-station/ (accessed on 2 February 2020).
24. According to the information shared by Still I Rise, the recipients of the criminal complaint are the director of the Samos Reception and Identification Centre, the General Secretary for Reception and Identification, Greek Ministry of Migration and any other responsible person.
25. Active since 2014, Watch The Med Alarm Phone is a project that manages a self-organized hotline for refugees in distress in the Mediterranean Sea. Its main objective is to offer boat people in distress an additional option to draw attention to their SOS. The Alarm Phone documents the situation, informs the coastguards, and, when necessary, mobilizes additional rescue support in real time. This way, they are able, at least to a certain extent, to put pressure on the responsible rescue entities to avert pushbacks and other forms of human rights violations against refugees and migrants at sea. Official website available at https://alarmphone.org/en/ (accessed on 2 February 2020).
26. The analysis intentionally does not take into account the issue of smugglers who use social media to propose journeys.
27. Facebook page available at https://www.facebook.com/Nananoborder (accessed on 2 February 2020).
28. Facebook page available at https://www.facebook.com/ali.surveyor.7 (accessed on 2 February 2020).
29. Facebook page available at https://www.facebook.com/helena.malenogarzon (accessed on 2 February 2020).
30. Forensic Oceanography is part of the European Research Council project Forensic Architecture and the Centre for Research Architecture, Goldsmiths, University of London. More information is available at http://www.forensic-architecture.org (accessed 12 February 2020).
31. These include the use of Synthetic Aperture Radar (SAR) imagery, geospatial mapping and drift modelling.
32. The case refers to 'a group of 93 migrants fleeing Libya in November 2018', which was forcefully returned to the war-torn country after they were 'rescued' by a merchant ship flying the Panama flag heading towards Libya, the *Nivin*. The reconstruction of the case was also possible thanks to the migrant's self-geolocalization process and the GPS position shared with Watch The Med Alarm Phone, in the form of a help request.

REFERENCES

Aas, K. F. and Gundhus, H. O. (2015), 'Policing humanitarian borderlands: Frontex, human rights and the precariousness of life', *British Journal of Criminology*, 55(1), 1–18.
Amnesty International (2013), 'Frontier Europe: Human rights abuses on Greece's border with Turkey', accessed 2 February 2020 at: https://www.amnestyusa.org/wp-content/uploads/2017/04/greece_embargoed_until_7am_tomorrow.pdf.
Amnesty International (2016), 'Greece: Evidence points to illegal forced returns of Syrian refugees to Turkey', accessed 2 February 2020 at: https://www.amnesty.org/en/latest/news/2016/10/greece-evidence-points-to-illegal-forced-returns-of-syrian-refugees-to-turkey/.
Andreas, P. (2012), *Border games: Policing the US–Mexico divide*. Ithaca, NY: Cornell University Press.
Archer, C. (2014), 'The EU's failure to protect: Violations of the non-refoulement principle in the EU Asylum System', accessed 2 February 2020 at: http://europe.unc.edu/wpcontent/uploads/2014/02/TheEU.pdf.
Arendt, H. (1970), *On violence*. Boston, MA: Houghton Mifflin Harcourt.
Balibar, E. (2001), 'Outlines of a topography of cruelty: Citizenship and civility in the era of global violence', *Constellations*, 8(1), 15–29.

Black, R. (2003), 'Breaking the convention: Researching the "illegal" migration of refugees to Europe', *Antipode*, **35**(1), 34–54.

Butler, J. (2004), *Precarious life: The powers of violence and mourning*. London & New York: Verso.

Campesi, G. (2014), *Frontex, the Euro–Mediterranean border and the paradoxes of humanitarian rhetoric*. Rochester, NY: Social Science Research Network.

Castells, M. (2004), *The network society: A cross-cultural perspective*. Cheltenham, UK and Northampton, MA, USA: Edward Elgar Publishing.

Castles, S. (2014), 'International migration at a crossroads', *Citizenship Studies*, **18**(2), 190–207.

Chalfen, R., Sherman, L., and Rich, M. (2010), 'VIA's visual voices: The awareness of a dedicated audience for voices in patient video narratives', *Visual Studies*, **25**(3), 201–209.

Christides, G. and Stefatou, O. (2017), 'The Greek island camp where only the sick or pregnant can leave', *The Guardian*, 4 November, accessed 2 February 2020 at: https://www.theguardian.com/world/2017/nov/04/the-greek-island-camp-where-only-the-sick-or-pregnant-can-leave.

Couldry, N. (2009), 'Rethinking the politics of voice: Commentary', *Continuum*, **23**(4), 579–582.

Daily Sabah (2019), 'Migrants claim Greek Coast Guard fired on them', *Daily Sabah*, 14 November, accessed 2 February 2020 at: https://www.dailysabah.com/europe/2019/11/14/migrants-claim-greek-coast-guard-fired-on-them.

De Genova, N. (2013), 'Spectacles of migrant "illegality": The scene of exclusion, the obscene of inclusion', *Ethnic and Racial Studies*, **36**(7), 1180–1198.

Della Ratta, D. (2018), *Shooting a revolution: Visual media and warfare in Syria*. London: Pluto Press.

Denaro, C. (2015), 'The Mediterranean Sea as transnational space and (struggle) field. Reflections on the critical "sea-watching" phenomenon as a new form of citizenship', *Feministische Geo-Rund Mail. Informationenrund um feministische Geographie*, **64**, 15–20.

Denaro, C. (2016a), '"We have the right to choose where to live". Agency e produzione di materiale audio-visuale nei percorsi di fuga dalla Siria', *Mondi Migranti*, **2**(1), 123–145.

Denaro, C. (2016b), 'Agency, resistance and (forced) mobilities. The case of Syrian refugees in transit through Italy', *REMHU: Revista Interdisciplinar da Mobilidade Humana*, **24**(47), 77–96.

Denaro, C. (2016c), 'The reconfiguration of Mediterranean migration routes after the war in Syria: Narratives of the "Egyptian route" to Italy (and beyond)', in N. Ribas-Mateos (ed.) *Migration, mobilities and the Arab Spring: Spaces of refugee flight in the Eastern Mediterranean*. Cheltenham, UK and Northampton, MA, USA: Edward Elgar Publishing, pp. 71–104.

Denaro, C. (2020a), 'Legalità e giustizia nelle pratiche di gestione dei flussimigratori verso l'Europa. Riflessioni a partire dall'utilizzo "legittimo" della violenza', *Convegno "Legalità e Giustizia"*, Rivista Studi sulla Questione Criminale, Università di Roma 3, Facoltà di Giurisprudenza, Rome 23–24 January 2020.

Denaro, C. (2020b), 'Voice through exit: Syrian refugees at the borders of Europe and the Struggle to Choose where to Live', in S. Pasquetti and R. Sanyal (eds.) *Global conversation on refuge*. Manchester: Manchester University Press.

Doctors Without Borders (2019), 'Greek and EU authorities deliberately neglecting people trapped on island', accessed 2 February 2020 at: https://www.msf.org/deliberate-neglect-greek-and-eu-authorities-towards-those-trapped-islands.

ECRE (European Council on Refugees and Exiles) and ELENA (European Legal Network on Asylum) (2019), 'The living conditions for migrants and refugees on the Eastern Aegean islands. Information note', accessed 2 February 2020 at: https://www.asylumlawdatabase.eu/sites/default/files/aldfiles/ELENA%20Information%20Note%20-%20The%20living%20conditions%20for%20migrants%20and%20refugees%20on%20the%20Eastern%20Aegean%20islands.pdf.

European Commission (2015), 'The hotspot approach to managing exceptional migratory flows', accessed 2 February 2020 at: https://ec.europa.eu/home-affairs/sites/homeaffairs/files/what-we-do/policies/european-agenda-migration/background-information/docs/2_hotspots_en.pdf().

Fargues, P. and Bonfanti, S. (2014), 'When the best option is a leaky boat: Why migrants risk their lives crossing the Mediterranean and what Europe is doing about it', Migration Policy Centre, Policy Brief 2014/05.

Fine, M. (1988), 'Sexuality, schooling, and adolescent females: The missing discourse of desire', *Harvard Educational Review*, **58**(1), 29–54.

Fink, M. (2016), 'A "blind spot" in the framework of international responsibility? Third-party responsibility for human rights violations: the case of Frontex', in T. Gammeltoft-Hansen and J. Vested-Hanses (eds.) *Human rights and the dark side of globalisation*. Abingdon, UK: Routledge, pp. 286–307.

Forensic Oceanography (2019), 'The Nivin Case: Migrants' resistance to Italy's strategy of privatized push-back', Forensic Architecture Project, Goldsmiths, University of London, accessed 12 February 2020 at: https://content.forensic-architecture.org/wp-content/uploads/2019/12/2019-12-18-FO-Nivin-Report.pdf.

Foucault, M. (1991), 'Governmentality', in G. Burchell, C. Gordon and P. Miller (eds.) *The Foucault effect: Studies in governmentality*. Chicago: Chicago University Press, pp. 87–105.

Foucault, M. (1997), *Discipline and punish: The birth of the prison*. London: Penguin.

Frontex (2019), 'Migratory routes', accessed 2 February 2020 at: https://frontex.europa.eu/along-eu-borders/migratory-routes/eastern-mediterranean-route/.

GCR (2019), 'Press briefing of 12 organisations, The Aegean Islands again in the "red": When is this vicious cycle going to stop?', 18 September 2019, accessed on 2 February 2020 at: https://www.gcr.gr/el/news/press-releases- announcements/item/1257-ta-nisia-tou-aigaiou-kai-pali-sto-kokkino-os-pote-aftos-o-faylos-kyklos.

Giddens, A. (1985), *The nation-state and violence*. Berkeley and Los Angeles: University of California Press.

Goodwin-Gill, G. S. (2011), 'The right to seek asylum: Interception at sea and the principle of non-refoulement', *International Journal of Refugee Law*, 23(3), 443–457.

Grandjean, G., Khalili, M., Roupell, A., and Topham, L. (2014), 'Death at sea: Syrian migrants film their perilous voyage to Europe', *The Guardian*, accessed 23 January 2020 at: http://www.theguardian.com/world/video/2014/oct/20/death-sea-syrianmigrants - film-europe-video.

Greek General Secretariat for Information and Communication (2019), 'National situational picture regarding the islands at Eastern Aegean Sea (07/10/2019)', accessed on 2 February 2020 at: https://infocrisis.gov.gr/6338/national-situational-picture-regarding-the-islands-at-eastern-aegean-sea-07-10-2019/?lang=en.

Heller, T., Pezzani, L. and Situ Studio (2012), 'Report on the "Left-To-Die Boat"', Forensic Architecture Project, Goldsmiths, University of London.

Hirschman, A. O. (1970), *Exit, voice and loyalty. Responses to decline in firms, organizations, and states*. Vol. 25. Cambridge, MA: Harvard University Press.

Hirschman, A. O. (1978), 'Exit, voice, and the state', *World Politics*, 31(1), 90–107.

Human Rights Watch (2011), 'The EU's dirty hands: Frontex involvement in ill-treatment of migrant detainees in Greece', accessed 3 February 2020 at: https://www.hrw.org/report/2011/09/21/eus-dirty-hands/frontex-involvement-ill-treatment-migrant-detainees-greece.

Jones, R. (2016), *Violent borders: Refugees and the right to move*. London and New York: Verso Books.

Knudsen, I. H. and Frederiksen, M. D. (ed.) (2015), *Ethnographies of grey zones in Eastern Europe: Relations, borders and invisibilities*. London: Anthem Press.

Leurs, K. and Ponzanesi, S. (2014), 'On digital crossings in Europe', *Crossings: Journal of Migration & Culture*, 5(1), 3–22.

Leurs, K. and Ponzanesi, S. (2018), 'Connected migrants: Encapsulation and cosmopolitanization', *Popular Communication*, 16(1), 4–20.

Malkki, L. H. (1996), 'Speechless emissaries: Refugees, humanitarianism, and dehistoricization', *Cultural Anthropology*, 11 (3), 377–404.

Mann, M. (1986), *The sources of social power*. Cambridge: Cambridge University Press.

May, L. (1987), 'Violence by border agents against aliens grows, coalition charges', *Los Angeles Times*, 21 November.

McMahon, S. and Sigona, N. (2016), 'Boat migration across the Central Mediterranean: Drivers, experiences and responses', MEDMIG Research Brief, 3.

McMahon, S. and Sigona, N. (2018), 'Navigating the Central Mediterranean in a time of "crisis": Disentangling migration governance and migrant journeys', *Sociology*, 52(3), 497–514.

Mezzadra, S. and Neilson, B. (2013), *Border as method, or, the multiplication of labor*. Durham, NC: Duke University Press.

Migreurope (2016), 'Hotspot at the heart of the archipelago of camps', accessed on 2 February 2020 at: http://www.migreurop.org/IMG/pdf/note_4_en.pdf.

Mountz, A. and Loyd, J. M. (2014), 'Constructing the Mediterranean region: Obscuring violence in the bordering of Europe's migration "crises"', *ACME: An International E-Journal for Critical Geographies*, **13**(2), 173–195.

O'Reilly, T. (2005), 'What is web 2.0. Design patterns and business models for the next generation of software', accessed on 2 February 2020 at: http://facweb.cti.depaul.edu/jnowotarski/se425/What%20Is%20Web%202%20point%200.pdf.

Pallister-Wilkins, P. (2015), 'The humanitarian politics of European border policing: Frontex and border police in Evros', *International Political Sociology*, **9**(1), 53–69.

Pauwels, L. (2015), *Reframing visual social science: Towards a more visual sociology and anthropology*. Cambridge: Cambridge University Press.

Pro Asyl (2013), 'Pushed back', accessed on 2 February 2020 at: http://www.proasyl.de/en/press/press/news/pro_asyl_releases_new_report_pushed_back/.

Ribas-Mateos, N. (2015), 'The Mediterranean Rio Grande/Rio Bravo: Envisioning global borders', Focus on International Migration II, Universitat Autònoma de Barcelona, CER-Migracions-Servei de Publicacions, Bellaterra Catalunya/España.

Ribas-Mateos, N. (ed.) (2016), *Migration, mobilities and the Arab Spring: Spaces of refugee flight in the Eastern Mediterranean*. Cheltenham, UK and Northampton, MA, USA: Edward Elgar Publishing.

Scheel, S. and Squire, V. (2014), 'Forced migrants as illegal migrants', in E. Fiddian-Qasmiyeh, G. Loescher, K. Long and N. Sigona (eds.) *The Oxford handbook of refugee and forced migration studies*. Oxford: Oxford University Press, pp. 188–199.

Schuster, L. (2011), 'Turning refugees into "illegal migrants": Afghan asylum seekers in Europe', *Ethnic and Racial Studies*, **34**(8), 1392–1407.

Schwarz, N. V. and Stierl, M. (2019), 'Amplifying migrant voices and struggles at sea as a radical practice', *South Atlantic Quarterly*, **118**(3), 661–669.

Smith, H. (2019), 'Aid workers warn of catastrophe in Greek refugee camps', *The Guardian*, 17 September 2019, accessed on 2 February 2020 at: https://www.theguardian.com/world/2019/sep/17/aid-workers-warn-of-catastrophe-in-greek-refugee-camps.

Tazzioli, M. (2015), 'The desultory politics of mobility and the humanitarian–military border in the Mediterranean. Mare Nostrum beyond the sea', *REMHU: Revista Interdisciplinar da Mobilidade Humana*, **23**(44), 61–82.

Tilly, C. (1990), *Coercion, capital and European states*. Oxford: Blackwell.

Trevino, J. A. (1998), 'Border violence against illegal immigrants and the need to change the Border Patrol's current complaint review process', *Houston Journal of International Law*, **21**, 85.

UNHCR (2018), 'Global trends', accessed on 2 February 2020 at: https://www.unhcr.org/5d08d7ee7.pdf.

UNHCR (2019a), 'Operational portal. Mediterranean situation: Greece', accessed on 2 February 2020 at: https://data2.unhcr.org/en/situations/mediterranean/location/5179.

UNHCR (2019b), 'Greece must act to end dangerous overcrowding in island reception centres, EU support crucial', 1 October 2019, accessed on 2 February 2020 at: https://www.unhcr.org/gr/13070-i_ellada_prepei_na_drasei_amesa.html.

Walby, S. (2013), 'Violence and society: Introduction to an emerging field of sociology', *Current Sociology*, **61**(2), 95–111.

Walters, W. (2010), 'Foucault and frontiers: Notes on the birth of the humanitarian border', in U. Bröckling, S. Krasmann and T. Lemke (eds.) *Governmentality*. Abingdon, UK: Routledge, pp. 146–172.

Weber, M. (1968). *Economy and Society*, ed. G. Roth and C. Wittich. New York: Bedminster Press.

Witteborn, S. (2015), 'Becoming (im) perceptible: Forced migrants and virtual practice', *Journal of Refugee Studies*, **28**(3), 350–367.

Yassin-Kassab, R. and Al-Shami, L. (2016), *Burning country: Syrians in revolution and war*. London: Pluto Press.

13. Transnational humanitarianism: blurring the boundaries of the Mediterranean in Libya
Natalia Ribas-Mateos

1. INTRODUCTION

The general background to this study is an examination of the detention conditions of migrants trapped in Libya. It is set within a complex framework that considers the proliferation of spaces pertaining to the situation of migrants who cannot leave Libya, and the proliferation of borders and actors involved in this topic. The study is based on action research (human rights development) with a gender perspective that gives the reader a complex understanding of leaving extreme violence in the broader context of humanitarian policies along the southern central Mediterranean route.

The chapter draws on a literature review, desk analysis and in-depth qualitative interviews carried out between October and November 2018 in Tunisia and Sicily (Italy), especially Tunis, Medenine, Ben Gardane and Palermo. Given the security situation in Libya, it was difficult for the researcher to conduct fieldwork in the country as initially planned. In addition to interviews, the work includes a review of relevant reports, statements and other documents issued by United Nations (UN) bodies, in particular the International Organization for Migration (IOM), the United Nations High Commission for Refugees (UNHCR), the UN Support Mission in Libya (UNSMIL), the Office of the UN High Commissioner for Human Rights (OHCHR) and the UN Special Rapporteur on the human rights of migrants; European Union (EU) bodies, including the European Commission, the European Council and the European Parliament; the Italian government; international and local non-governmental organizations (NGOs); as well as declarations from informal intergovernmental meetings and information from online media sources, social media platforms and a variety of YouTube videos (mainly from NGOs and the so-called hegemonic and independent media).

This study shows that more empirical than theoretical knowledge regarding the topic of violence along the Libyan route has been produced, and it comes from NGOs and practitioners more than social science scholars. The original focus of this chapter planned to combine empirical knowledge with key theoretical questions regarding violence and transnational humanitarian policies. I carried out 32 semi-structured qualitative interviews, 25 of which were face-to-face (in some cases more than once with the same respondent), and seven were remote (using the WhatsApp phone service). The snowball sampling technique provided a greater degree of flexibility to accommodate sudden openings and locate hidden individuals. Targets included: UN staff, members of international organizations, academics (to a lesser extent), media actors, NGOs and migrants in various contexts. Fieldwork was conducted in Tunis and Sicily from October to November 2018. Different data collection methods were employed: (1) a document review prior to in-country data collection to identify and summarize existing data along the Libyan, Tunisian and central Mediterranean route and in Italy; and (2) interviews with international humanitarian responders, service providers, cultural mediators, human rights experts and government officials (some key informants had previously worked or were currently working in Libya or on search and rescue boats in the Mediterranean).

The initial question underlying the research concerned the nature of migrant detention in Libya. Detention has been a matter of grave concern, a primary source of human rights abuse. According to the UN, detainees are forced to live in severely overcrowded facilities with little food, water or medical care and are subject to physical abuse, forced labour, slavery and torture. The IOM has also reported on the emergence of 'slave markets' along migrant routes where migrants are 'being sold and bought by Libyans, with the support of Ghanaians and Nigerians who work for them' (IOM 2017; Global Detention Project 2018: 7). Women and children are not recognized as requiring special attention and thus remain particularly vulnerable to abuse and ill-treatment, including rape and human trafficking, which can involve extreme violence, as indicated by international organizations, and leaves an open debate regarding the dilemma of care and violence.

Bearing in mind this complex situation involving widespread violence, what kind of recommendations can be made for the different transnational actors? In addition to extreme violence, many other phenomena lead to reflections on how to understand suffering, distant suffering[1] (viewed from a distance and as an outsider), when considering the responses from the different actors to the humanitarian crisis within a social policy context, as well as the question of humanitarian accountability and NGO advocacy in cases of extreme violence.

2. STATE OF THE ART, OR SOME CONTEXTUAL THINKING

Issues such as the securitization of borders, humanitarian intervention in border areas and the analysis of the conditions of violence exercised on people in transit (using a careful gender perspective regarding such mobilities) reveal a changing, urgent reality that needs to be studied in detail by academics, border activists and policy-makers. In general, the gap between the protection that migrants formally enjoy under international law – and even national laws – and the actual experiences of individuals reveals a severe absence of human rights. In this glaring contradiction, many of the main issues related to global borders also emerge: securitization, the search for re-routing, irregular migration, racism, complex gender issues, the autonomous migration of minors, human trafficking, globally networked surveillance and so forth. At these Mediterranean border sites, the challenges of humanitarian aid are also on display, as are the varying reactions of civil society in border regions. In brief, within this humanitarian challenge lies the importance of the politics of compassion as the moral–political manifestation of humanitarianism present among the different social actors at a particular global border.

One clear example of this contradiction of policies in the Mediterranean is explored in the theoretical–empirical work by Poguisch (2018) on the central Mediterranean route. She focuses her analysis of these policies on the period after 2013 and the Mare Nostrum Operation, where 'saving lives was put on the European Agenda', and later on the treaties between Italy and Libya, which tried to synthesize the humanitarian rhetoric into migration management, where the humanitarian is inserted into governmental policies. However, she points out the ambiguity of such humanizing policies expressed in multiple ways – for example, within the existing contradictions between border control and humanitarian rescue that prevent many migrants from reaching Europe.

First, works like the one by Poguisch (2018) reveal what 'the vulnerability of human rights' means today by shedding light on the experiences of vulnerable populations in border regions. These peoples are impacted by the restructuration of industries and its effect on the labour market, gender and class inequality, extreme violence, as well as forms of resistance against human rights abuses that particularly occur in border areas. Such a context is ripe for a discussion of the issues of solidarity, transnational humanitarianism and border activism as a global action in these specific sites and as key ways of analysing the humanitarian and contemporary violence against migrants in Libya and beyond.

Second, a theme that often appears in border literature concerns the 'fabrication of corpses'. This can be clearly associated with 'the manufacture of corpses' that Hannah Arendt identified as a characteristic of a totalitarian regime, wherein the limits of human experience can be analysed (Arendt 2006). She was referring to the fabrication of corpses or the factories of destruction related to the totalitarianism of the Holocaust. I refer to specific zones as zones of oblivion, where rights are annihilated and forgotten and, as Rancière (2003) adds, where not even humanitarianism is enough. Many independent journalists and activists are working on these same issues along the central Mediterranean route, and in some interviews they discuss how parallels can be made, even using the concept of 'genocide' (for example, in comments made by two interviewees to independent journalists working in Libya).

In fact, borders attract a variety of activists both from outside and within the border regions. Activists range from people broadly supportive of state enforcement, such as those who play-act enforcement at borders (for instance, militia groups), to pro-immigrant activists who provide humanitarian aid and advocate for migrants and asylum-seekers. In the last decade, much important work on activism in the Mediterranean has been made public, especially since 2015, and particularly regarding displacement and camps, research on the forms of mobility and violence in border areas and the politics of compassion. Within this wide variety of work, this study highlights the contradictions inherent in border security and humanitarian policies as well as the politics of compassion, critically moving beyond the classic paradigms of victimhood, which mostly address women and children. This is not completely new. Many authors have considered this humanitarian work during their different fieldwork projects. One classic example in the Middle East concerns the humanitarian pictures that politically position the concepts of 'refugee' and 'camp' as moral indictments of the states and agencies that influence refugees' lives (see the case of the Bekaa Valley in Lebanon, Ribas-Mateos forthcoming). In the past and still today, the case of the Palestinian camps has been paradigmatic in this context, where the idea of not settling into new countries has been seen as a form of agency, with the refugees focused instead on their return and economic survival. They were usually seen as revolutionaries rather than recipients of international aid or subjects of humanitarian crises (Marron 2016). However, from the perspective of the NGOs in the Mediterranean today, there is a new form of humanitarianism that is both rational and emotional, containing a fraternal spirit and a concern for the situation of other human beings, by expressing compassion and solidarity. This has arisen along with the new displacement of millions of additional individuals in a brief time, stemming from multiple conflicts. All of this highlights how humanitarianism is a response that is embedded in politics, as seen in the moral need to save lives,[2] which has become the motto of any NGO working on sea rescue in the Mediterranean in recent years.

Third, and drawing on Sjoberg (1999) and his analytic framework of 'bureaucratic capitalism', the chapter provides sensitizing concepts that are general enough to be applied to the diverse detention migration regimes observed. From the standpoint of Sjoberg's 'bureaucratic capitalism', I highlight human agency, the state–corporate nexus and rationalization processes. I add that bureaucratic power structures (whether state-directed security forces or corporations contracting with the state) in a surrounding social environment like the Mediterranean, are the key means by which the human rights of vulnerable groups, especially non-citizens, are undermined. Further, human agency rooted in people's ability to engage in critical reflection as well as counter-system tendencies also emerge to challenge these human rights abuses, although this is in an asymmetrical, if also dialectical, relationship with the powerful organizations. This idea fits the Libyan case very well, as when examining the transnational humanitarian work done with migrants in the face of hostile, externalizing EU policies and a range of abusive social actors in Libya.

Fourth, the Mediterranean setting as the context for this chapter is constructed by a scenario that takes into account socioeconomic changes in southern European countries, mobility changes impacted by the Arab Spring, post-revolution situations, shipwreck events in the Mediterranean, EU emergency policies, the proliferation of pushbacks and so forth. They have all pushed an externalization of the borders towards the South, towards sub-Saharan Africa, especially from 2011 to 2015 and from 2015 to date, in step with the crisis of border externalization and a new phase of turbulence at the maritime frontier. Policies have been event driven. For instance, in the aftermath of a major shipwreck involving a migrant boat on the central Mediterranean route (April 2015, 700 migrant deaths), the Council of the EU launched 'Operation Sophia', which was mandated to undertake systematic efforts to identify, capture and dispose of vessels as well as enable assets used or suspected of being used by migrant smugglers or traffickers as part of a broader EU effort to block South–North migration. Its justification was to disrupt the business model of human smuggling and trafficking networks in the southern central Mediterranean and prevent the further loss of life at sea.

One key example of these complex compassion policies is the case of reimposed border externalization in Libya and the closing off of the central Mediterranean route by driving rescue NGOs out of the area, expanding Libyan Coast Guard interceptions under EU coordination and refoulement/migrant return southward. These EU policies, which are mainly implemented via Italy to stem migration across the central Mediterranean, deploy a strategy of delegitimizing and criminalizing migrant rescue operations by NGOs.

In the case of the migrants trapped in Libya, the methodology for the interviews involves a focus on the human rights approach to violations and the defence of human rights and a gender perspective. I have particularly focused on the conditions of gender vulnerability and extreme violence. The general context was the articulation of the following triangle: spaces of violence, politics of border compassion and mobilities.

3. WHAT ARE WE OBSERVING?

Nearly half a million people have crossed the Mediterranean in the last three years; over 10,000 have died in the attempt. A further half a million, maybe more, are currently stranded in Libya as of 2017. Over the past decade, tens of thousands have been exposed to arbitrary detention, torture and other ill-treatment, including sexual violence, extortion and forced labour in Directorate for Combatting Illegal Migration (DCIM) detention centres. (Amnesty International 2017).

Armed groups across Libya, including those affiliated with the state, hold thousands of men, women and children in prolonged arbitrary and unlawful detention, and subject them to torture and other human rights violations and abuses. Victims have little or no recourse to judicial remedy or reparations, while members of armed groups enjoy total impunity (United Nations Human Rights Office of the High Commissioner in cooperation with the United Nations Support Mission in Libya 2018).[3]

In this Libyan scenario, which is always changing, a culture of impunity prevails within a legal vacuum (where transitional justice groups are trying to work). Some of the stories of violence I heard from women in Medenine (Tunisia) reminded me of the phenomenon of 'rape trees', the bushes and trees from which rapists hang their victims' garments as a type of trophy, which have become a symbol of crossing the Mexico–United States border deserts. Violence comes in many forms, but the migrants' voices heard in interviews in Medenine and Sicily have been particularly explicit about it. On the other hand, some actors indirectly imply that the worse the suffering, the more effective the migration policies, where violence would be the outcome of an acute involution of social policies.

3.1 On the Complexity of the Proliferation of Spaces, Borders and the Proliferation of Actors in the Time of Globalization

I first consider the different spaces, taking into account the entire scope of the research. They range from being very space focused in terms of physical space (sea/land/border/detention) to other conceptions/adjectivations of space, particularly related to the concept of safe space, which is articulated in different ways during the interviews, meaning safe country (in the case of migrants and refugees, this means pushbacks). Finally, interviewees also referred to the idea of safe places, meaning a place apart for the victim when dealing with gender-based violence and a safe place in general as a place where one can enjoy protection rights.

The denegation of neutrality and safe space has become a constant in contemporary wars. The most exaggerated form is genocide (French independent journalist interview). This is when safe space is abolished. For example, the IOM recommends creating protected places ('safe houses'), spaces that should already be identified at the time that migrants disembark in Libya, so that they can be separated from traffickers and immediately activate specific assistance services. From the advocacy recommendations for the situation of migrants trapped in Libya, 'places of safety' are found in the IOM's 2004 Rescue Guidelines, which indicate that a place of safety is a place where the survivor's life is no longer threatened, where basic human needs (such as food, shelter and medicine) can be met, and from which transportation arrangements can be made for the survivor's next or final destinations. Furthermore, such spaces comprise multiple locations which act simultaneously and involve numerous agencies and feedback loops. As different bases and forms of violence are convertible into many different types, they are exerted in different spatial layers and articulated in the larger space of Mediterranean territories.

Second, when I reflect on borders and the transformation of borders in this context, taking into account the importance of the view of the *Carrefour de la Mediterraneé* (Crossroads of the Mediterranean). Other reflections recall the way that borders are understood in the broader context of the Mediterranean as an export of a model of border securitization, which is multi-scalar, for example, considering the intervention in Libya and the use of remote management by international entities.

Third, when I reflect on the proliferation of actors at play, I refer to all types of actors from international organizations, different types of NGOs, national governments, journalists and the like. Such a proliferation makes the analysis of violence very complex. Additionally, the complexity is even more aggravated considering how many topics are very often managed in a cluster dynamic (for example, between international agencies and NGOs).

Apart from extreme violence, many other concepts lead to considerations of the understanding of suffering, such as distant suffering when examining the responses to the humanitarian crisis, as well as the question of humanitarian accountability and NGO advocacy in cases of extreme violence (which uses and concerns the reconstruction of human testimony). This complexity is revealed in every finding in consistent and repeated patterns of extreme violence and in the exploration of testimony and evidence in the digital age.

3.2 On the Complexity of the Situation in Libya

The complex political situation is rooted in a scenario of three different governments and many types of militias. In Libya, there are very few truly national actors. Most figures are local players, some of whom are relevant at the national level while representing the interests of their region, or, in most cases, their city. Particularly outside the largest cities, many important actors also have tribal allegiances. Several types of actors scramble for power in today's Libya: armed groups, city-states – particularly in western and southern Libya – and tribes, which are especially important in eastern and southern Libya.

4. TRANSNATIONAL HUMANITARIANISM WITH MIGRANTS TRAPPED IN LIBYA

This empirical research reviews transnational solidarity as a relationship within the forms taken by the transnational dynamics that mark contemporary economic and political globalization in the Mediterranean region. The first focus is on transnational humanitarianism in contemporary economic and political globalization. Studying transnational humanitarianism in this case requires an analysis of the politics of immigration within the global differences between wealth and poverty, as well between race and gender inequalities. To study the humanitarian as a reality that unfolds across multiple scales, I use the details of the micro-approach – for example, fragments of violence inserted in the case – as an entry point from which I will unpack the larger dynamic of the humanitarian. This approach seeks to make connections between close-up cases – even ethnographic cases – and extreme far shots of understanding. This transnational approach is backed up by a particular space, a topological approach that shows a myriad set of different cases and transnational dynamics, cases that use heterogeneous materials – from interviews, reports, academic references, YouTube images and ethnographic notes – to piece together concrete positions to understand transnational humanitarianism within global politics. I try to comprehend these processes across a transnational perspective of the Mediterranean.

Studies of humanitarianism really started in the late 1980s, when humanitarianism began to assume a particular moral and political project in the formation of transnational NGOs. It follows both the evolving relationship of anthropologists to humanitarianism – initially as allies, then as critics, alternately embracing and challenging their conjoined humanist legacy – and the growing field of the anthropology of humanitarianism (Ticktin 2014). Such studies have also been common in the area of development and migration, but they are always difficult to define, especially when ethics comes into play. In the Libyan case, I focus on the practices of humanitarianism and on the way these practices have been regarded from the spaces of humanitarian intervention, especially in the case of the camps (as indicated by Agier 2014), the view of actors polarized between victims/survivors and agents of humanitarian intervention, and the arena of mobilities and borders in the Mediterranean, in particular, in the case of the fieldwork done on migrants trapped in Libya.

Since the beginning of the fieldwork in October/November 2018, the disproportionate violence meted out to the increasing number of migrants detained in Libya has become particularly aggravated due to the war in the country (the advance of commander Khalifa Haftar taking Tripoli), which has caused not only a large number of fatalities, as the migrants were also an open target in the war, but also produced disappearances and displacement. Therefore, 'migrants trapped in Libya' became 'migrants trapped in war'. This state of the humanitarian catastrophe can be viewed in terms of the disputed politics between the interests of the EU (blocking migration to the North) and the Libyan authorities – in particular the Libyan Coast Guard – defending the right to sovereignty by taking action in their own territory (see interviews conducted in Sicily). This reveals the contradictions of migration governance between the restrictive conception of the EU (through a particular mix of securitization, humanitarianism and rescue) openly clashing with the concept of the national sovereignty of the Libyans. Here, the humanitarian crisis takes on the wreckage of a broader critical situation related to the political, military and financial crisis in post-revolution Libya.

At the international level, after the open criticism of detention conditions expressed by many transnational actors and in interviews conducted with NGOs, the UNHCR has become more broadly visible in its role as global spokesperson for the Mediterranean in Africa. In August 2019, for instance, the organization tried to obtain the release of the refugees held in various detention centres, especially in the north of the country.

One of the primary cases of such humanitarian suffering has been reflected in the neoliberal sexualized gender violence against women at border crossings (in the terms used by Tellez et al. 2018), as noted in my fieldwork in southern Tunisia. In this case, dehumanization and commodification was seen in the evidence of mass sexual violence against detainees and crossers, especially in the case of women from Nigeria (particularly from Edo State) and the Gambia. For them, the structural vulnerability is a result of the fact that most of them travel alone. Another key case of such suffering has been seen at sea, in a humanitarian void in which renewed humanitarian action was seen in civic mobilization in reaction to the tragedy in the Mediterranean (concerning multiple vessels; from Cap Anamur in 2004 to Sea-Watch in 2019), as reflected in the interviews conducted with NGOs in Sicily.

5. INTERPRETING THE INTERVIEWS

The fieldwork on migrants trapped in detention discovered an entangled framework, considering the proliferation of spaces (which all play a role along the Mediterranean route), the situation of migrants trapped in Libya and the proliferation on the borders (from Italy to the South, from Libya to the East, from Tunisia to the West) and the variety of actors. The idea of being trapped in different contradictions was expressed in the 32 interviews conducted in Tunisia (Tunis and Medenine) and in Italy (Sicily) with UN staff, members of international organizations, academics, media actors, NGOs and migrants. The concept of being trapped in Libya or Tunisia was expressed in most interviews, for example, with witnesses aware of the contradictions involved in the migration project, which entailed, on the one hand, 'the beautiful side of the project of what it was before Libya, or today's Italy or Germany' and the reality that 'migrants could go to Europe and say, of course, I want to go there, but in the end it was a trap'.

These types of contradictions are expressed in the form of contradictory policies of compassion. Most actors identified a contradiction in EU policies that manifests itself in a multi-layered way, and all the NGOs interviewed were very critical about such policies. For example, a representative from a local NGO in Palermo said with respect to human smuggling: 'Europe is not doing anything to control the regional mafia that controls the central Mediterranean route. Europe is only putting a band-aid on the central Mediterranean, meaning Libya. But Europe is not going into the origin of the networks that makes people slaves and victims'.

5.1 The Interplay of Actors

There is a multifaceted interplay of actors in these policies. Many examples of this can be found, as indicated by one of the members of the UN Office for Project Services. The NGOs working in Libya in detention centres are from the IOM and UNHCR (for resettlements and assisted voluntary return) and at disembarkation points along the west coast, in collaboration with the international medical corps. The interplay of actors was seen in the multi-connections with UN offices who work in clusters (for example, involving institutional and non-institutional actors in humanitarian assistance). Agencies like the IOM are active at many levels and work in many different collaborations on humanitarian action, as the IOM interviewee in Tunis expressed: 'In 2012/2013 we also tried a combination of assistance, direct assistance like humanitarian assistance [...] The UN evacuated their personnel again, basically to Tunis.'

Regarding this interplay of actors in the politics of compassion, a clear distinction can be made between the assistance that is provided, for example if it is an NGO working on advocacy or assistance or if they focus on some target groups (such as women and children). In the border area of Ben Gardane (Tunisia), this multifaceted interaction of actors was witnessed as far back as 2011–12 in the Choucha refugee camp (17 km from Ben Gardane). One interviewee speaks of a camp of 80,000 people, a mix of different nationalities and actors: Islamic Relief, Adra, Qatar Charity, UNHCR, Tunisian Army and so forth (local NGO worker in Ben Gardane).

As for international agencies, humanitarian assistance is also linked to many sectoral objectives; we see this in an interview with IOM Libya:

> IOM Libya (from the Tunis offices) deals with the following areas: displacement tracking matrix, community stabilization, humanitarian repatriation and reintegration, life-saving humanitarian assistance, capacity building, saving lives at sea, protection of vulnerable migrants. The IOM Mission in Libya seeks to provide tailored assistance to vulnerable (a) migrants, (b) IDPs [internally displaced people] and (c) host communities through the following programmes: life-saving humanitarian assistance (urgent needs rescued at sea) [...]. Regarding saving lives at sea: working together with the Libyan Coast Guard, port authorities and the DCIM, the Italian Coast Guard.

In this interplay of actors, the media plays a central role, working closely with organizations like rescue NGOs:

In 'suffering at a distance', the use of video is very widespread. We acknowledge horror and then we amplify it, but there is no action. We have an unlimited number of images but politics remain, without action on real refoulement. For example, on the vessel Lady Sham, which was directly returned to Misrata. [...] This lack of action is a paradox. It is the representation of the inhumane in today's media [...] the video with direct shipwreck recording is the spectacle of the inhumane [...] And we are trapped in this historical contradiction: the vision of live genocide without action. (Independent researcher in a sea rescue NGO)

Other voices echo these thoughts. 'We always board with a journalist, as I told you with the case of Josepha and Open Arms [the logistic sector in a sea rescue NGO]. [...] In Josepha's case, some volunteers painted her nails in order to distract her. However, this is what has been criticized about Open Arms' (which also, incidentally, leads to the question of 'fake news', debunker David Puente and the false reconstruction of events on social media).

In this type of activism, people from civil society, who do not correspond to the traditional militant profile, are also engaged in the Mediterranean: 'On all rescue vessels we see the novelty of a new volunteer sector from civil society, as in 2004 with Cap Anamur' (an international NGO based in Palermo).

In addition to numerous UN offices, governments and semi-institutional actors like advocacy and operational NGOs, the migrants themselves also play a role. In their stories of migration trajectories, they provide rich details concerning their role in the migration project:

They take our telephones from us, they would beat you up if they find a cellphone. They take away take our telephones, our bras, socks, they want to get rid of weight. It is a crazy system. My *kockser* [intermediary] had 15 passengers, a list with real names [...] They never care about your interests, they only ensure their own benefits, that is all. The family directly pays the *mudir* [the boss], the boss buys the boat, he offers you a simple meal and water. (Migrant minors in Barcellona, Sicily)

It is because of this violence that we decided to go to Tunisia. The police took my little girl from me. We went on a non-official border route. (Migrant at Ibn Khaldoun migrant centre, Medenine)

My ex-husband followed me to Libya. I went to Tripoli and someone employed me as a domestic worker [...] He had power. Anytime he wanted to sleep with me he tried, if I did not want to, he would say he would take me to prison [...] I feel protected here (migration centre in Tunisia). (Woman at Ibn Khaldoun migrant centre, Medenine)

5.2   A Demand for Safety

The research done here has emphasized the idea of a safe place, safe country, safe harbour. Safe means staying at a distance from violence, for example gender violence, a safe country, and a demand for safe routes and non-refoulement. It also applies to a safe harbour for disembarkation, as seen in interviews with the representatives of NGOs who work saving lives at sea:

In 2015 they started NGOs like MOASS, MSF, Sea-Watch, they wanted to fill a void from the different institutions and from Italy. We started with a very small vessel, we wanted to call the centre in Rome so they could rescue the people and take them to a safe harbour. At that time the NGOs were using a discourse totally aligned with the Italian Guard Coast. After the Malta declaration and the alliance between Italy and the Libyan Guard Coast there was a shift; it meant the total departure of the European institutions. [...]

Safe ways, legal ways. People have to be evacuated from Libya. [...] We have the discourse of criminalization–security, it is a paradox. One case in point is the ship Nave Diciotti in Catania, financed by Italy. The role of the NGOs here is to put a dressing on the wound, but one must figure out how to not produce the wound. A person who has been through all that, what kind of rights do they have? There is a double standard of human rights, there are two levels of application of human rights, this acknowledges a different country for us. When the witnesses say: 'In Libya they break us up. It is a psychic phenomenon.' (European NGO, rescue ship)

Second, the concept of the border is another important axis of research, from specific locations in Tunisia bordering Libya and what it means to have this transborder life:

We are 45 km away from Zwara. This is the main municipality, but it has political problems with the surrounding villages; some are revolutionaries, others anti-revolutionaries. Remember that in Libya there are three big main powers, but to that you have to add that each village has its own power and its circles of complexity. In truth, this Libyan reality has not affected us so much, as each one in the family has their own security system. (NGO in Ben Gardane)

5.3 Conditions of Violence

Narratives of a system of violence are a feature of all migrant testimonies:

The *kockser* can be an intermediary, also called *aboga*. This is the person who speaks Arabic, this concerns migrants who were already in Libya in the time of Gaddafi [...] He is the one who calls the families to receive the payment. (Minor in Barcellona, Sicily)

The reality of migrants exposed to arbitrary detention, torture and other ill-treatment, including sexual violence, extortion and forced labour in DCIM detention centres is also a central theme in the interviews and especially criticized by NGOs:

The difference between being arrested by the government and being arrested by the Asma boys (street gangs) is that the government takes the migrant to official detention centres, whereas the Asma boys take them to 'connecting houses'. For them, it is always a prison. They ask the families to have a negotiator with an extortion. (Minor in Barcellona, Sicily)

Women and children are not recognized as requiring special attention and, thus, are particularly vulnerable to abuse and ill-treatment, including rape and human trafficking. The vulnerability attributed to women and children as victims of extreme violence by international organizations is under-addressed, leaving an open debate regarding the dilemmas of care and violence:

Since 2015, I understood through interviews with disembarked people in Augusta and Pozallo that it was a matter of mass violence, of systematic violence [...] In the last years I have reflected on this context around the genocide against the 'migrant people', according to the lawyer Luigi Ferrajoli. [...] The testimonies reflect the existence of systematic torture and the idea of the elimination of the Other. The media does not have a long perspective of time, they use the terminology of the 'castaway', 'case', 'accident', like there was a fatality. They are all elements of a mediatized narration, as if there was a fatality. (Independent journalist in Italy)

Rape on this central route is a constant feature [...] Men symbolize money and they take their money, if there is no money, they hit them, whereas the woman always has rape involved in the negotiation, and they pass the woman around them. This route is not made for women. But, what can they do? If you want food, I have to use you. In Agadez we saw it, they took all the women who were with us in rotation. The *kockser* also does the same thing even. If he is black, they use the same system. (Migrant minor in Barcellona, Sicily)

Rape is committed by the guards, it cannot be by their own partners. Many men do not say it, because they want to turn the page and not to have to explain it. In my sample, 436 out of a total of 790 women acknowledge having suffered sexual violence [...] The data from SMS did not take into consideration the factor of homosexuality, it is very difficult to do the screening. It is a problem from the start, because men do not declare their own homosexuality [...] I know the case of two sisters in Libya raped by nine different men. The older one tries to resist, the younger does not. They try to persuade the younger one, and how did everything end? In the end they shot the older one. This is a very grave trauma for the younger woman here in Italy. (Doctor in Palermo)

6. CONCLUSION

Detention is a matter of grave concern and is the focus of the question of human rights abuse in this chapter. In this case, the work combines empirical qualitative knowledge with key theoretical questions mainly regarding violence and transnational humanitarianism. Most actors refer to a scenario of 'human rights crisis', while institutions speak of humanitarian responses in the form of a strategy of prevention, protection, responsibility and caring.

Most interviewees focused on the existing contradictions and possible solutions and recommendations in the final part of their interviews. Regarding contradictions, there is a regular use of double speech, for example, the fact that the IOM deals with Libya even though it has not signed the Geneva Convention or the contradiction between repatriation and evacuation (to Niger) used by different international organizations. Migration governance here finds a humanitarian void expressed in many different ways, like the action that NGOs take along the central Mediterranean route. Furthermore, such migration governance is often represented on one side as an issue of national sovereignty, which uses the discourse of national security, and on the international side as an issue of international cooperation, which currently includes refugee regimes, labour migration and counter-trafficking initiatives.

Human rights concerns are put as a priority for most actors on the political scene. Such rights are seen as the main content of the humanitarian instrument, but defending them is also perceived as a tool for social development and a cooperation instrument. Serious human rights concerns about the situation of migrants trapped in Libya have been expressed by all actors and all the interviewees met in the different fieldwork encounters. Solutions are expressed as the demand for safe routes, recommendations concerning non-refoulement and sea and rescue legislation, for example UNCLOS, the 1982 United Nations Convention on the Law of the Sea.

While most interviewees see their own solutions to the humanitarian crisis not only in demands for safe routes, but also evacuation from Libya, applying coherent policies and the like, they are also looking for legal measures. Examples include the Maastricht Principles on the extraterritorial obligations of states in the area of economic, social and cultural rights and legal forms of ending the impunity of institutions regarding human rights violations and abuse. NGOs go further, looking to international human rights law, which prohibits violations related to the right to life, arbitrary detention, torture and enforced disappearance. Other solutions use a multi-level approach that is international, regional and national. In the case of Italy, some NGOs mention the efforts made by the Corte de Milano to address issues of genocide against migrants.

The research has also shown disparate political narratives between actors and within actors (for example Italian Deputy Prime Minister Matteo Salvini and other people from his government saying that Libya is a safe place). The research also found evidence of different views of humanitarianism and the difficulty of handling distinct views of the humanitarian (from Tunis, managing Libya; from Italy, managing Libya), forms of contemporary violence and new humanitarian actions (the rhetoric on humanitarian assistance and repatriation, the clash between humanitarianism and securitization policies, the activist slogan of 'save lives, protect and try to compile testimonies').

In addition to extreme violence, many other ideas were discussed by NGOs in order to understand the concept of suffering provoked by contemporary violence. Most interviewees who considered such issues focused on the question of humanitarian accountability and NGO advocacy in cases of extreme violence.[4]

Many interviewees see their solutions in a discourse based on trying to stop violence in mobility.[5] Recommendations that refer to the problems of the 'new wars' and the denegation of a safe space were repeated by most actors when referring to gender and violence. They mention one of the most recent known international cases: the elimination of the secure spaces, such as in the cases of genocide in Rwanda. Concerning gender difference, they also emphasize the problematic lack of protection for female detainees from sexual- and gender-based violence and sexual exploitation, as well as ensuring that children are separated from adults to whom they are not related. Advocacy NGOs cite an urgent need for safe spaces for migrants and refugees, alternative detention and better access to monitoring (life-saving assistance and monitoring for places of detention).

The last focus is the situation of violence against women along the central Mediterranean route, which in many ways is reminiscent of the situation in the Sonoran Desert, the site of disconcerting scenes of women's undergarments hanging on the branches of a tree, signifying a 'rape tree', which have come to represent the sexual and physical domination of women by marking them with the remnants of sexual violence. This amplifies the way that large numbers of migrants, especially women, continue to be dehumanized and commodified in the region. According to Tellez et al. (2018), this also happens in the Mediterranean, and the level of aggression is palpable. Yet there is neither recourse nor support for the migrant woman who has been deemed rapeable, disposable and unworthy of recognition along the borderlands, deprived of human rights because her humanity has been denied.

This kind of common metaphor indicates the need for specific recommendations regarding peace-making from a woman's perspective concerning women against violence, which can also be transferred to the Libyan case study. For example, the Security Council adopted resolution S/RES/1325 on women and peace, reaffirming the role of women in conflict resolution and peace-building. Resolution 1325 discusses measures to protect women and girls from gender-based violence, particularly rape and other forms of sexual abuse, in situations of armed conflict. In border settings, these women are largely missing from the #MeToo women's movement. The cases seen in this study particularly reveal how sex-based violence refers to any act that is perpetrated against a person's will and is based on gender norms and unequal power relationships. Testimonies are, then, fundamental as a form of agency for the near future. These women's voices must be heard, as Save the Children notes in several reports concerning the vulnerability of migrants coming from Libya: 'Listen to the voices of migrant and refugee children and adolescents and youth in how they exercise agency and show resilience during their journeys.'

NOTES

1. In its study of this phenomenon, this chapter draws, in part, on the work of Luc Boltanski (*grammaire de la pitié* or 'distant suffering', 1993) and his *'pragmatique'* framework, which is the inductive approach of observing actors in order to discern the principles of their actions and contradictions.
2. See the 'right to life at borders' by Helena Maleno, an activist calling for rescue ('*Salvamento Marítimo*' in Spain and Morocco) at the Strait of Gibraltar for the last ten years (Maleno 2020). She fights for the right to live at the border crossing as a part of human rights that is not fully recognized by the 'colonial nation-state'.
3. Published by the OHCHR in cooperation with the UNSMIL, this summarizes the main human rights concerns in the context of detention in Libya since the signing of the Libyan Political Agreement (LPA) on 17 December 2015. The findings in this report are based on first-hand accounts and other information gathered by OHCHR/UNSMIL from a broad range of sources inside Libya, visits to prisons and other detention facilities, a review of legal and medical documents and an analysis of photographic and audio-visual evidence.
4. See, for example, these fragments from some interviews:
   We did not start as an advocacy NGO. This is different. Now it is a very political theme, we are an operative NGO. Amnesty International is different, they were born as an advocacy NGO, as a lobby, this is different. We started as Sea Rescue. But afterwards they criminalized us and we have to react. We do not make any political propositions, you do not do this at sea, you don't do politics at sea. We are there to cure the symptoms [...] We save lives and we make complaints based on testimonies, but this has been later, it is different from our initial objective. (European NGO, rescue ship)
   The IMO [International Maritime Organization] in London cannot recognize a Libyan SAR because it means recognizing that Libya is a safe harbour. (Human rights activist)
   They now apply the concept of criminal collective guilt, which used to be a fascist concept, instead of the individual concept of democracy. (Human rights activist)
5. See, for example, the following fragment from an interview:
   At the beginning, people only talked about the network of Nigerian women and their vulnerability on the trip, but then there were more and more ships every day, there were much younger and more women on the ships. There are two anti-exploitation projects, one in western Sicily (the Maddalena project) and the other in eastern Sicily (the Penelope Project). The objective was that women could be in a protected house in a dual sense: to free themselves from their debt and to solve the voodoo ritual [...] But what has happened after all this time? The cases, the testimonies are now bounded by generalized vulnerability due to externalization policies. In contrast to 2005, they are all victims of intentional violence, torture and dehumanizing treatments. Before, when you would analyse the case you could see how they depended on concrete variables (for examples, kidnappings by the Asma boys), this is all a slaughter. Now they are very young girls, it is much worse. It is no longer like the Nigerian women ten years ago holding a plane ticket and a visa. There is a health implication, they all reveal cases of torture, not only physical torture, but torture as an erosion of the very identity of the person [...] There are now Gambian mediators, but they do not have specific training in trauma. (Violence therapist in Sicily)

BIBLIOGRAPHY

Agamben, G. (2005). *Lo que queda de Auschwitz: El archivo y el testigo*. Homo sacer III. Valencia: Pre-textos.
Agier, M. (ed.) (2014). *Un Monde de camps*. Paris: La Découverte.
Altai Consulting (2017). *Leaving Libya: Rapid Assessment of Municipalities of Departures of Migrants in Libya*, June. Tunis: Altai Consulting.
Amnesty International (2017). "Libya's dark web of collusion: Abuses against Europe-bound refugees and migrants" (Index: MDE 19/7561/2017).
Arendt, H. (2006). "Nosotros, los refugiados", in M.L. Knott (ed.), *Tiempos Presentes*. Barcelona: Editorial Gedisa.
Boltanski, L. (1993). *La souffrance à distance*. Paris: Métailié.
Boltanski, L. (1999). *Distant Suffering: Morality, Media and Politics*. Cambridge: Cambridge University Press.

Copelon, R. (2000). "Crímenes de género como crímenes de guerra: Integrando los crímenes contra las mujeres en el derecho penal internacional". *McGill Law Journal*, 46: 2017–2040.

Denaro, C. (2016). "The reconfiguration of Mediterranean migration routes after the war in Syria: Narratives on the Egyptian route to Italy and beyond", in N. Ribas-Mateos (ed.), *Spaces of Refugee Flight: Migration and Mobilities after the Arab Spring in the Eastern Mediterranean*. Cheltenham, UK and Northampton, MA, USA: Edward Elgar Publishing (71–104).

EEAS (2017). "Strategic review on EUBAM Libya, EUNAVFOR MED Op Sophia & EU Liaison and Planning Cell". Brussels, 15 May.

European Commission (2017). "339 Action plan on measures to support Italy, reduce pressure along the Central Mediterranean route and increase solidarity". Brussels, 4 July.

European Commission (2019). *Migration Compact. European Commission – Fact Sheet*. Brussels: European Commission.

Fassin, D. (2007). "Humanitarianism as a Politics of Life". *Public Culture*, 19(3): 499–520.

Fassin, D. (2008). "The humanitarian politics of testimony: Subjectification through Trauma in the Israeli–Palestinian Conflict". *Cultural Anthropology*, 23: 531–558.

Fassin, D. (2013). *Humanitarian Reason: A Moral History of the Present*. Berkeley: University of California Press.

Fassin, D. and Rechtman, R. (2009). *The Empire of Trauma: An Inquiry into the Condition of Victimhood*. Princeton, NJ: Princeton University Press.

Forensic Oceanography (2018). "MARE CLAUSUM Italy and the EU's undeclared operation to stem migration across the Mediterranean: A report by Forensic Oceanography (Charles Heller and Lorenzo Pezzani), affiliated to the Forensic Architecture agency", Goldsmiths, University of London, May 2018. http://www.forensic-architecture.org/wp-content/uploads/2018/05/2018-05-07-FO-Mare-Clausum-full-EN.pdf (accessed 29 January 2019).

Global Detention Project (2018). "Immigration detention in Libya: 'A human rights crisis'", 30 August.

IOM (2017). "IOM learns of 'slave market' conditions endangering migrants in North Africa". 4 November.

IOM (2019). *Displacement Tracking Matrix (DTM): Libya's Migrant Report*. Geneva: International Organization for Migration.

Lagarde, D. (2016). "Mapping the encampment of the world and its consequences on refugees' itineraries". Paper presented at the Refugees on the Move Conference, CER-Migrations, Barcelona, 21–22 April.

Loschi, C., Raineri, L. and Strazzari, F. (2018). "The implementation of EU crisis response in Libya: Bridging theory and practice". Deliverable 6.02, January. Working Paper. EUNPACK. A conflict sensitive unpacking of the EU Comprehensive Approach to Conflict and Crisis mechanism.

Maleno, H. (2020). *Mujer de Frontera*. Barcelona: Editorial Península.

Malkki, L. (2015). *The Need to Help: The Domestic Arts of International Humanitarianism*. Durham, NC and London: Duke University Press.

Marron, R. (2016). "Introduction. On the humanitarian cause. Humanitarian rackets and their moral hazards. The case of the Palestinian refugee camps in Lebanon", in *Humanitarian Rackets and their Moral Hazards. The Case of the Palestinian Refugee Camps in Lebanon*. Abingdon and New York: Routledge (1–29).

Médecins Sans Frontières (MSF) (2017). "MSF warns EU about inhumane approach to migration as leaders meet to discuss cooperation with Libya," 3 February. https://prezly.msf.org.uk/msf-warns-eu-about-inhumane-approach-to-migration-management-as-leaders-meet-today-to-discuss-cooperation-with-libya#

Musarò, P. (2015). "The banality of goodness: Humanitarianism between the ethics of showing and the ethics of seeing". *Humanity: An International Journal of Human Rights, Humanitarianism, and Development*, 6(2): 317–335.

OHCHR (2016). *Investigation by the Office of the United Nations High Commissioner for Human Rights on Libya: Detailed Findings*. Annual report of the UN High Commissioner for Human Rights and reports of the Office of the High Commissioner and the Secretary-General, February. Geneva: OHCHR.

OHCHR (2017a). *Report of the United Nations High Commissioner for Human Rights on the Situation of Human Rights in Libya, Including on the Effectiveness of Technical Assistance and Capacity Building*

Measures Received by the Government of Libya. Annual report of the UN High Commissioner for Human Rights and reports of the Office of the High Commissioner and the Secretary-General, January. Geneva: OHCHR.

OHCHR (2017b). "EU 'trying to move border to Libya' using policy that breaches rights – UN experts". Geneva, August.

OHCHR (2017c). "UN human rights chief: Suffering of migrants in Libya outrage to conscience of humanity". Geneva, November.

Poguisch, T. (2018). "I confini Fantasma dell'Europa", in *Decolonizzare le migrazioni. Razzismo, confini, marginalità. A cura di Bellinvia*. Milano: Mimesis/Cartografie Sociale (41–60).

Rancière, J. (2003). *El maestro ignorante. Cinco lecciones sobre la emancipación intelectual*. Barcelona: Laertes.

Ribas-Mateos, N. (2015). *Border Shifts. New Mobilities from Europe and Beyond. Series: Frontiers of Globalization*. Basingstoke: Palgrave Macmillan.

Ribas-Mateos, N. (ed.) (2016). *Migration, Mobilities and the Arab Spring*. Cheltenham, UK and Northampton, MA, USA: Edward Elgar Publishing.

Ribas-Mateos, N. (2019). "Migrants trapped in Libya: Is detention and human rights' abuse the 'solution'?" Seminar. Department of Social and Policy Sciences. University of Bath. March.

Ribas-Mateos, N. (forthcoming). "The proliferation of the desert in the Mediterranean: The Lebanese case".

Sen, A.K. (1995). *Las mujeres desaparecidas*. Nueva Economía del Bienestar. Escritos seleccionados, Valencia: Ediciones de la Universidad de Valencia.

Sheller, M. and Urry, J. (2006). "The new mobilities paradigm". *Environment and Planning A*, 38(2): 207–226.

Sjoberg, G. (1999). "Some observations on bureaucratic capitalism: Knowledge about what and why?", in J. Abu-Lughod (ed.), *Sociology for the Twenty-First Century: Continuities and Cutting Edges*. Chicago: University of Chicago Press (43–64).

Tellez, M. Simmons, W.P. and del Hierro, M. (2018). "Border crossings and sexual conquest in the age of neoliberalism in the Sonoran Desert". *International Feminist Journal of Politics*, 20: 524–541.

Ticktin, M. (2011a). "How biology travels: A humanitarian trip". *Body and Society*, 17(2–3): 139–158.

Ticktin, M. (2011b). "The gendered human of humanitarianism: Medicalizing and politicizing sexual violence". *Gender and History*, 23(2): 250–265.

Ticktin, M. (2012). *Casualties of Care: Immigration and the Politics of Humanitarianism in France*. Berkeley, CA: University of California Press.

Ticktin, M. (2014). "Humanitarianism as planetary politics", in S. Perera and S. Razack (eds.), *At the Limits of Justice: Women of Colour on Terror*. Toronto: University of Toronto Press (406–420).

Toaldo, M. (2015a). "Migrations through and from Libya: A Mediterranean challenge". IAI Working Paper 15, Istituto Affari Internazionali, Rome, May.

Toaldo, M. (2015b). "Libya's migrant-smuggling highway: Lessons for Europe". Policy Memo, European Council on Foreign Relations, Rome, November.

Uehling, G.L. (2008), "The international smuggling of children: Coyotes, snakeheads and the politics of compassion". *Anthropological Quarterly*, 81(4): 833–872.

UNICEF (2017). *A Deadly Journey for Children: The Central Mediterranean Migration Route*. New York: UNICEF.

United Nations Human Rights Office of the High Commissioner in cooperation with the United Nations Support Mission in Libya (2018). *Abuse behind Bars: Arbitrary and Unlawful Detention in Libya*. Geneva, New York: Office of the United Nations High Commissioner for Human Rights in cooperation with the United Nations Support Mission in Libya.

UNSMIL and OHCHR. (2016). "Detained and dehumanized. Report on human rights abuses against migrants in Libya". Geneva, December 2016.

Walters, W. (2010). "Foucault and frontiers. Notes on the birth of the humanitarian border", in U. Bröckling, S. Krasmann and T. Lemke (eds.), *Governmentality: Current Issues and Future Challenges*. Abingdon: Routledge (138–164).

14. Migration policies at the Spanish border in Southern Europe: between 'welfare chauvinism', hate discourse and policies of compassion[1]

Belén Fernández-Suárez

1. INTRODUCTION

A spectre is haunting Europe – the spectre of migration. In the mass media, any reference to migration is synonymous with crisis: the 'Mediterranean migration crisis' or 'refugee crisis'. The ever-present reference to crisis in discourses related to the mobility of people coincides with several factors: Europe's emerging economic recession, austerity policies, the consolidation of right-wing populist projects and the political crisis of the European Union (EU) project (Sirriyeh, 2018). Between 2015 and 2017, roughly 1.6 million migrants crossed the Mediterranean to reach Europe. An estimated 110,000 were rescued at sea and some 15,000 drowned (Cusumano, 2018). These deaths have clearly created a state of emergency in international asylum law and the very concept of human rights. The lack of empathy, compassion and care in our societies is becoming a serious concern. The philosopher Martha Nussbaum (2014: 142–3) defines compassion as a 'basic social emotion' that serves as a link between the collective and individual dimension to emphasize feelings of solidarity and suffering towards others. But to understand this process we must go back in time and analyse the main social transformations that have affected immigrants in recent times.

Over the course of the first two decades of the twenty-first century, liberal states have undergone a transformation, shifting from promoting policies that expand social and civil rights to restricting access and allocation. This dominant strain of restrictive liberalism is willing to defend the values which they consider to be essential to a 'Western' society through the coercive use of the power of the state (Joppke, 2007; Goodman, 2010; De Giorgi, 2010; Wonders, 2017; Casella Colombeau, 2019). The restrictive turn goes beyond the paradox of accepting unwanted migration in the immigration policies of Western countries, that is, governments promoting discourses of rejecting irregular immigration while, at the same time, allowing for the entry and residence of immigrants in an irregular situation (Cornelius, Martin and Hollifield, 1994). This reaction may be linked to the rapid change caused by the rising diversity in their societies and the growing social inequality that began to occur in the early 1980s and continues today. The rise of multiculturalism in the 1980s and 1990s occurred in parallel with the rise of neoliberalism, which caused part of the citizenry to associate diversity with a neoliberal process to increase competition in a global market. It is in this context of conservative criticism, the fall of multiculturalism and the rise of neoliberalism, that the term 'welfare chauvinism' should be framed. This is defined as the opinion that immigrants are less entitled to welfare benefits than natives (Van der Wall, De Koster and Van Oorschot, 2013; Kymlicka, 2015).

Currently, within the paradigm of late neoliberalism, the way in which states regulate belonging and citizenship is deeply influenced by austerity, scarcity and racist presumptions, leading to the emergence of what has been called a hostile environment for immigrants, namely, a condition of fear and uncertainty that increasingly penetrates different aspects of everyday life (Bowling and Westenra, 2018; De Giorgi, 2010; Brandariz-García and Fernández-Bessa, 2017). Bowling and Westenra (2018) point out that, in the early 1970s, the criminalization of immigrants was launched to control, punish, stop and expel those unwanted migrants, with the goal of having control prevailing over the objective of justice, and making this criminalization system work requires a link between national and global systems. For De Giorgi (2010), this process of criminalization also arose in the mid-1970s in Europe at a time of economic deregulation through globalization that was accompanied by a border emergency and the criminalization of migration. This author highlights that the hyper-criminalization of this collective contributed to the reproduction of a vulnerable labour force whose insecurity made it suitable for the segmented labour markets of post-Fordist economies. Finally, Brandariz-García and Fernández-Bessa (2017) foreground how the economic crisis in 2008 caused a managerial turn in migration control policies in Spain by taking advantage of the decline in inflows. This change consisted of improving the management of immigration control to make it more efficient and introducing administrative changes to increase the effectiveness of these policies.

This chapter examines how the European migration policies of the twenty-first century have led to the tightening of migration control and internal control policies through more stringent requirements for the integration of immigrants. These tougher measures have been influenced by a greater rejection of immigration, an increase in views that favour restricting the social welfare rights of immigrants, and, lastly, by a surge in right-wing populist attitudes against immigration. This process is related to neoliberalism and its austerity policies, which serve to combat growing inequality and rapid social change.

This chapter is divided into four sections. The first looks at internal and external migration control policies and the shift towards more restrictive measures. The second section presents an analysis of radical right-wing populist party discourse regarding immigration and the rise in hate speech linked to 'welfare chauvinism'. The third section discusses the shift in the dominant discourse: from compassion to the implementation of exclusion practices directed at immigrants in Europe which jeopardize the principle of solidarity and human rights. Finally, I draw a few brief conclusions on the connection between the different issues discussed in the chapter.

2. MIGRATION POLICIES IN EUROPE AND THE SHIFT TOWARDS THE APPLICATION OF MORE RESTRICTIVE MEASURES IN INTERNAL AND EXTERNAL BORDER CONTROL

At the 1999 Tampere European Council, the member states agreed that the EU would develop Community policies on immigration and asylum. This common Community policy was to provide for the use of a global approach to cooperation with the countries of origin and transit, the development of a common European asylum system, the assurance of fair treatment of third country nationals residing in the EU and the efficient management of migration flows (Ferrero-Turrión and Pinyol-Jiménez, 2016). The progress in Community policy depended on the member states, which expressed their opposition to transferring state powers to the collective government of the EU.

The link between immigration and security in the EU has grown stronger since 2000. Readmission agreements and cooperation in fighting irregular migration have been developed more specifically than other instruments, such as visa facilitation or the promotion of legal migration channels. These strategies, aimed at improving safety and strengthening policies to control irregular immigration, are linked to a view of immigration as unlawful. Immigrants are perceived as posing competition in the job market or as potential seekers of benefits from the welfare state (Pinyol-Jiménez, 2012).

Moreover, although states try to push migration control away from their territorial boundaries, the rights of personhood continue to be resolutely territorialized in practice (FitzGerald, 2019). Border externalization refers to a 'series of processes of territorial and administrative expansion of a given state's migration and border policy to third countries' (Casas-Cortes, Cobarrubias and Pickles, 2016: 231). The externalization of migration control shifts understandings of how states monopolize the legitimate means of movement (Torpey, 2018). The most powerful states externalize migration control to neighbouring countries that offer these contention management services. By removing control policy from their borders, the states manage to evade their own internal controls based on criteria of justice and citizenship rights (Guiraudon and Lahav, 2000). This externalization attempts to extend the border to restrict the access of immigrants to the rights granted by the liberal states (FitzGerald, 2019).

In Europe, dynamics are at play that point to a shift towards restrictiveness – a 'restrictive turn' or punitive turn – in migration policies (De Hass, Natter and Vezzoli, 2016) which is marked by increased migration control, the 'criminalization' of the immigrant population and the creation of obstacles that hinder their prospects for an improved standard of living through restrictions on social rights. This drastic change is responsible for the policy enforced by nation-states – and aggregate organizations – and is based on neoliberal economic principles. This change, of course, has also led to the strengthening of the EU's internal borders, challenging the notion of free movement within the Schengen area. Moreover, this situation has triggered a crisis in the Schengen agreement, which states that external borders should be reinforced to guarantee free movement within Europe (Joppke, 2007; Goodman, 2010; De Giorgi, 2010; Wonders, 2017; Casella Colombeau, 2019).

The states create a regime of migration management based on a lengthy probationary period called 'apprenticeship in illegality'. This institutional production is the result of the formal legalization of certain types of movement, or the exclusionary dimension of citizenship, but it also copies a racialized sociopolitical condition that causes immigrants to live in fear of being expelled from the territory (De Genova, 2004; Moffette, 2014). The process criminalizes the immigrant, by associating immigration with crime. This concept involves the enforcement of laws that increase the deportability of migrants who commit a crime, leading to policies that result in the illegality of the immigrant and the criminalization of undocumented migrants because they committed a crime by crossing the border (Stumpf, 2006; Gonzales, 2012; Wonders, 2017). Irregular immigration is a phenomenon which started to appear with the emergence of the so-called Fortress Europe strategy, associated with the closure of external EU borders and highly restrictive immigration legislation. In the case of the United States, Gonzales (2012) uses the language of 'anti-migrant hegemony' to name a type of ideological leadership that naturalizes the adoption of authoritarian solutions to the immigration crisis.

This criminalization has generated an attitude of intolerance towards activists who defend the rights of immigrants. The repression against these activists and their solidarity with the immigrants goes hand in hand with the new developments in border control (López-Sala and Barbero, 2019). The criminalization of dissent leads to the repression of protest and erodes democracy. The repression of solidarity and activism defending the rights of irregular immigrants has been called the punitive turn. For example, this is the case with the Catalan non-governmental organization (NGO) Proactiva Open Arms, which was threatened with fines by the Spanish authorities for rescuing refugees stranded in the Mediterranean. What is at play is an involution of human rights. It is not only a matter of strengthening immigration control policy, but of negativizing the manifestations of solidarity, and, by extension, the compassion policy itself that has third-sector entities as one of the main executing arms.

In Europe, and in the case of Spain as well, there has been a paradigm shift towards a restrictive or punitive turn (Goodman, 2010; De Giorgi, 2010; Wonders, 2017) in the migration policies developed since the beginning of the economic crisis in 2008. This shift boils down to an increase in border control measures, particularly a reluctance to resettle refugees, and the reinforcement of internal borders, resulting in restrictions on the social rights of immigrants. Examples in Spain include the exclusion of undocumented immigrants from health care coverage under Royal Decree-Law 16/2012 (Martínez et al., 2015; Peralta-Gallego, Gené-Badia and Gallo, 2018) and the introduction of criteria for civic integration in the Alien Act itself under the Law Reform of 2011, which establishes the principle of 'integration effort' from the perspective of individual logic and imposes a basis for conditionality to administer residence and work permits (Baldi and Goodman, 2015). Far more serious in the humanitarian sense have been the processes to exclude the rights of immigrants in Italy, such as the anti-immigrant measures used by former Deputy Prime Minister Matteo Salvini and implemented by some mayors from the Northern League party, who found innovative ways as of 2010 to restrict access to basic rights like medical care, restrict the right to residency through mayors' orders and to implement regulations that modified national requirements in an exclusionary way (Gargiulo, 2017).

This restrictive trend in Spain also includes social and political resistance, especially at the municipal level. The economic crisis in Spain produced enormous social and political unrest. Citizens organized themselves critically to create protest movements such as the 15-M anti-austerity movement in 2011. This cycle of political resistance reached its maximum expression when far-left citizen candidates supported by social movements, including immigrant support organizations, came to power in large cities like Madrid and Barcelona. The municipal 'governments of change' in these two cities tried to act as a counterbalance to neoliberal policies and the restrictive turn in migration in state and regional measures.

In summer 2015, coinciding with the most acute period of the so-called refugee crisis in the Mediterranean, municipalities declared their welcoming orientation, and created a network of cities to support the arrival of refugees that the state government rejected. This municipal solidarity towards the refugees led by Madrid and Barcelona was a reaction against the restrictive politics towards these refugees implemented by the Spanish government (García Agustín and Bak Jørgensen, 2019). The governments of the municipal candidates in those two cities fought the restrictive turn on immigration by expanding citizenship rights and trying to lessen the unjustified police control of immigrants. First, they broadened citizenship and granted rights to excluded social sectors, i.e. immigrants in vulnerable situations and under irregular administrative status, aiming to guarantee access to social services. The second area of action addressed the social emergency resulting from the extension of policing and the crimmigration control system based on identification, detention and deportation (Fernández-Suárez and Espiñeira-González, 2019). This reaction and the political measures are similar to those adopted by sanctuary cities around the world. Even though restrictions on the foreign population have advanced, there are also frequent signs of resistance and solidarity on the part of social movements and some of the political parties of the alternative left.

3. THE RISE IN RIGHT-WING POPULIST PARTIES IN EUROPE AND HATE SPEECH LINKED TO SOCIAL WELFARE

What is happening in Europe that has led to this growing fear of 'others'? There has been a proliferation of political forces in the Western world that advocate fighting immigration: the Freedom Party (FPÖ) in Austria, the National Rally (RN) in France, Alternative for Germany in Germany, the United Kingdom Independence Party (UKIP) in the UK, the Dutch Party for Freedom (PVV) in Holland, Vox in Spain and the like. An increasing number of governments with authoritarian leanings in Western countries have also appeared, such as Donald Trump of the Republican Party in the United States, Jair Bolsonaro of Alliance for Brazil in Brazil, Viktor Orbán of the Fidesz-Civic Union in Hungary and Mateusz Morawiecki of the Law and Justice Party (PIS) in Poland.

The common denominator between these European populist radical forces is the defence of their national identity, culture and language, the preservation of their cultural values and ways of life, and the defence of economic territorial rights based on autarkic policies. When these concepts are applied to the presence of the immigrant population, it means that these individuals must assimilate and renounce their own culture (Hepburn, 2009; Mellón and Hernández-Carr, 2016). These forces can be distinguished from fascist or right-wing parties because they identify with democracy – although they do criticize some of its aspects – as opposed to the far right, which is openly anti-democratic and opposes the principle of the sovereignty of the people (Mudde, 2007). The key issue is that these discourses sometimes trickle down into the messages of centrist and leftist forces, which means that they spread on a social level and seek hegemony through the 'contagion effect' (Jupp, 2003). This growth has caused the cultural polarization of European societies between the followers of the values of tolerance and diversity and the authoritarians of the new right (Koster et al., 2014). The central importance of the migration issue in the emergence and development of populist conservative proposals at the political level makes it increasingly necessary to search for answers in the field of the sociology of migrations.

Anti-immigration and alt-right parties and their supporters have used hate speech against foreigners, especially certain ethnic minorities. This discourse has three characteristics: (a) it is directed against a specific or easily identifiable individual or, more usually, a group of individuals based on aspects of their identity; (b) it stigmatizes the target group by implicitly or explicitly attributing to it qualities widely considered undesirable; and (c) due to its alleged negative qualities, the target group is seen as an unwelcome presence and a legitimate object of hostility (Parekh, 2012). This alt-right discourse is plural due to its diverse composition and central arguments. However, what defines this narrative is the idea that 'non-privileged' whites are victims of unfair governmental policies, such as affirmative action, sanctuary for illegal migrants and the cultural cleansing of so-called white history (Phillips and Yi,

2018). The national-populists have polarized opposition between 'us' and 'them' in two dimensions: the Trumpian opposition between 'the people' and 'the elite' and the opposition between insiders and outsiders. The outside also includes institutions that are seen as threatening a way of life or security, such as globalization, the EU, radical Islam and so forth. According to Brubaker (2017), different types of populism include civilizational, defined by its identitarian 'Christianism', a secularist posture, a philosemitic stance and an ostensibly liberal defence of gender equality, gay rights and freedom of speech, as found in northern and western Europe (one example of this type of populism is the PVV in Holland). This populism contrasts with that of Trump, who rejects liberal values, embraces religious freedom and objection on religious grounds, reinforces America-firstism, positions himself against gender equality and sexual diversity, and, finally, is clearly favourable to white hegemony with an anti-immigration discourse.

The explanations for this social phenomenon, with its long-standing tradition in sociology, are many and complex in nature. Liberal democrats are questioned, particularly in regard to the two pillars considered to be fundamental: their own capacity to exercise sovereignty as a nation-state in their domestic policy and the social perception of the crisis of liberal societies as institutions that are unable to guarantee fundamental rights or to promote the extension of new rights to the citizens (Freeman, 2003; Joppke, 2007; Triadafilopoulos, 2011; Loch, 2014). In response to the challenges wrought by globalization and neoliberal policies, governments have increased immigration enforcement to demonstrate state sovereignty and placate aggrieved citizens (Anderson, 2013). This line of questioning has led to a more restrictive kind of liberalism that is prepared to defend the values considered essential to a society through the coercive use of state power as a reaction to the change brought about by the rise in the diversity of their societies, among other issues (Triadafilopoulos, 2011).

The moral foundation of the welfare state has been described as 'a common obligation to care for one's fellow citizens and, in particular, people with fewer resources or in vulnerable life-phases' (Bergmark, Thorslund and Lindberg, 2000: 241). However, at the present time, anti-foreigner sentiment is on the rise in Western countries, which can be seen in the increasing reluctance to expand social rights to include this group, a phenomenon termed by some academics as welfare chauvinism. This concept can be defined as the fear harboured by less privileged social groups towards the immigrant population, whom they perceive as their competitors vying for limited welfare resources. Therefore, this fear transforms into a demand for the separation of social groups into levels that would limit the foreign-born population's access to the welfare state to make it easier for the native population to have access to this right (Faist, 2009; Wimmer, 1997; Kymlicka, 2015).

The transition from class solidarity to national solidarity in the social democratic forces of Europe, where they have taken on a role generally played by nationalist parties, involves the idea that the welfare state is an expression of solidarity based on a shared sense of belonging (Kymlicka, 2015). Some of the circumstances that may give rise to the harshest version of neoliberal nationalism – entailing exclusion without solidarity – which has been adopted as a measure by Western populist parties (Kriesi, 2015) include: restrictive liberalism (the idea that redistribution should be only for nationals); civic integration policies, which argue that 'others' should behave like nationals as much as possible to ensure peaceful coexistence; and a toughening of the criteria to determine who is part of the community, that is to say, cutting off access to this coexistence through more dehumanizing migration control policies. Burgoon and Rooduijn (2020) have shown that attitudes towards immigration in Europe affect support for welfare redistribution and moderate growth of the economy in countries with a strong presence of immigrants produces more anti-solidarity attitudes.

Spain appeared to be a cultural exception within a European context characterized by a populist wave and the rise of anti-immigrant parties and actors (Alonso and Rovira Kaltwasser, 2014; Dennison and Mendes, 2019; Turnbull-Dugarte, 2019). Populist radical right parties were almost non-existent in the country, even during the economic crisis that irrupted in 2008. The 2018 regional elections in Andalusia, however, brought an end to this situation when the far-right political party Vox gained representation in the Andalusian parliament. This was later repeated in the general elections of 2019. Vox is a political party characterized by authoritarian conservatism, Spanish nationalism and its defence of political positions contrary to what they call 'gender ideology', same-sex marriage and immigration (Turnbull-Dugarte, 2019; Franquesa, 2019).

The analysis of this case shows how the consensus around immigrant integration and gender equality policies is broken, and how Vox's discourse provokes a social reaction that attempts to demonize the migrant community (as well as its environment: NGOs and specialized public workers) and the feminist movement, as well as the experts aimed at implementing these measures. The nativist discourse, based on a discriminatory and deeply conservative national sentiment, rejects the whole 'new left' ideology that emerged in the late 1960s in light of multiple demands from different social sectors. The attempt to break the consensus of immigrant integration policies and gender equality policies in Andalusia and Madrid has encountered strong political and social opposition with different degrees of rejection, but Vox has somehow managed to dichotomize a negative discourse that makes its voice be perceived as an alternative to that social consensus.

Finally, it can be concluded that Vox's discourse has similar characteristics to other European forces such as RN in France and Northern League in Italy, but it also incorporates elements typical of Spanish conservatism, such as its ties to Francoist sectors and the rejection of political decentralization, exemplified by its position against the political representation of nationalist (peripheral) parties. The presence of Vox is a brake on diversity and equality, and, what is more worrying, its antagonistic position results in a more amplified discourse. Due to its recent emergence, it is still difficult to ascertain whether its presence will produce a drift to the right in the other political parties concerning migrants' and women's rights, but it is still a plausible hypothesis that deserves further analysis.

4. ARE SOLIDARITY AND COMPASSION IN A STATE OF CRISIS IN EUROPEAN SOCIETIES?

The tension between discourses and practices of compassion and repression has always existed in migration policies, especially in the case of asylum and refuge. For example, it is possible to be compassionate towards refugees who cross the border and allege unacceptable persecution in the destination society, such as political persecution in socialist regimes like Venezuela, persecution for reasons of sexual orientation or gender violence and the like. On the other hand, immigrants who are not granted refugee status are deported to a buffer zone outside the state border, where their lives may be in danger because their human rights are violated. This is done by the states which, even knowing the risks to their lives, assign a different value to the various reasons for granting refuge.

However, even this tension should be linked to the moral principles that define the socially accepted norms and obligations as to how a society should function. These principles, which are constantly changing, are also connected with biopolitics, a concept related to the political practices behind the management of human lives that are responsible for deciding what undesirable people are most likely to suffer. In this case, expendable persons may be poor, illegal immigrants, ethnic minorities, women and so forth (Fassin, 2005). Fear aligns bodies with a particular sense of belonging and exclusion. Feminist theorist Sara Ahmed (2004) highlights the fact that after the events of 9/11, the American response was to protect the free movement of economic capital, while arresting bodies suspected due to their Arab or Asian racial profile. Community solidarity becomes based on the perceived insecurity of shared risk.

Borders produce divisions and exclusions, but they are also catalysts for relations of solidarity between migrants and citizens, or bordering solidarities. However, the literature on solidarity focuses primarily on how migrants and citizens come together to support migrant rights (Rygiel, 2011; Franko, Woude and Barker, 2019). The implicit assumption is that the solidarity is between relatively privileged citizens and marginalized migrants. The Italian philosopher Giorgio Agamben speaks of the refugee as a subject of human rights, rights that are suspended by the primacy of the rights of the citizen associated with belonging to the nation-state (Agamben, 1998).

However, the emergence of neoliberalism as a paradigm does not seem to have left any room for twentieth-century redistribution and solidarity. Society is in the process of a transformation to a period of sinister post-humanism, which according to Rosi Braidotti (2017: 15) is characterized by an increase in migrations:

> as a result of dispossession, expulsions and terror [...] the refugee camps and other zones of detention are multiplying, as are our militarized borders and humanitarian interventions. Whole sections of humanity are downgraded to the status of infra-humans, extra-territorial, like the refugees, trying to cross the solid sea that is the Mediterranean, by now turning into a liquid grave. They are the alien others, not meant to be here to stay.

As applied to Europe-bound immigration, necropolitics – understood as the replacement of the liberal paradigm by a neoliberal one – can be linked to the unrecorded deaths of immigrants who lose their lives while attempting to cross the borders into Europe or the United States, mainly by sea (Mezzadra and Neilson, 2017; Domingo, 2018a; Rosas, 2019). Indeed, the very violation of the right to seek asylum and of the Geneva Convention of 1951 constitutes an unprecedented crisis of values in the EU (Ferrero-Turrión and Pinyol-Jiménez, 2016). This reality is similar at the US–Mexico border, which has become a zone of sacrifice. This border and American immigration policy are conceived as a necro-subjection, in other words, garnering asylum or other relief from deportation increasingly demands accounts of deep victimization on behalf of individuals and collectivities, playing to a deeply ingrained paternalism found in racial liberalism (Rosas, 2019).

The fall of the liberal paradigm gives way to nomadism as an exercise in survival which, when applied to refugees who want to enter Europe, makes them 'zombies' who must be confined in militarized camps. Another example of this concept of necropolitics is the militarization of the camps receiving refugees bound for Europe or militarized barriers that prevent the entry of immigrants and refugees at the US–Mexican and Mediterranean borders (Heyman and Ribas-Mateos, 2019). These camps have replaced humanitarian and third-sector organizations, leading to the subsequent criminalization of these agencies (Domingo, 2018a). Refugees and unwanted immigrants are conceptualized by states as a surplus population. They are seen as a marginal population whose distinguishing feature is stigmatization and alienation. They are dispossessed of humanity and therefore of human rights (Domingo, 2018b). One example of this process of the militarization of refugee camps can be seen in the 2019 British television series *Years and Years* (HBO, 2019, dir. Russell T. Davies), a show set in a post-Brexit time that features the emergence of a neoliberal populism with restricted freedoms and that transfers fear to a dystopian future that is present.

The processes described above are linked to the crisis of empathy and compassion in the political class and part of society towards the 'others' (Sirriyeh, 2018). This process consists of increasing stereotypes and prejudices to maximize the distance between the perceived differences. Ultimately, it increases the empathy gap between the 'others', perceived as substantially more different than they really are, and even imagines the danger of maintaining contact with these unwanted subjects. As I noted at the beginning of the chapter, Martha Nussbaum (2014) defines compassion as 'the basic social emotion', and relates this emotion to a path towards justice. Nussbaum's perspective is contrary to the viewpoint of compassionate conservatism, the American doctrine that argues that conservatism and compassion are complementary and produce an increase in social welfare. This philosophy defends the traditional family, welfare state reforms to promote individual responsibility and increased spending on security and the police, since, according to this doctrine, these measures would help improve the situation of those most in need. This approach was applied in the 1990s in the United States during the presidency of George W. Bush.

The rise in deportations, persecutions and deaths during refugee and immigrant entry processes has given rise to the creation of social movements, collective demonstrations and a growing number of municipalities that are opposed to these dehumanizing European and state migration policies (Patler, 2017; Karakayali, 2017; Sirriyeh, 2019). In this sense, emotions play an important role in motivating people who are committed to helping refugees (Doidge and Sandri, 2019). Additionally, in the United States there is a reaction that can be called 'compassionate migration', which consists of a counter-hegemonic response to the institutions and systems that criminalize unauthorized immigration, including compassionate assistance from those who aid migrants (Bender and Arrocha, 2017).[2]

In some cases, these social movements have been criminalized, resulting in the repression of acts of solidarity with undocumented immigrants or refugees (Cuttita, 2018; López-Sala and Barbero, 2019). A good example of this type of process is the criminalization of the activists of Open Arms, a non-governmental, non-profit organization whose main mission is to protect people who try to reach Europe fleeing from war, persecution or poverty by being present at sea in the area. Open Arms emerged from a company providing rescue services and first aid at sea with extensive experience on the Spanish coasts. Like other similar organizations such as Sea-Watch, Open Arms rejects the idea that people should die when trying to cross a border (Cuttitta, 2018). The fact that these organizations have been banned from leaving ports and fined for rescuing immigrants at sea, with their activists threatened with prison sentences, is a clear indication that the principles of solidarity, empathy and compassion, like human rights, are experiencing a severe crisis in Europe.

Since the 2001 attacks in the United States, there has been a restrictive turn towards migration on a global level. Beyond border control and the reduction of access rights to the welfare state, internal controls for the foreign population have increased. In this context, civic integration programmes were also incorporated in a hostile context towards multiculturalism as a liberal commitment to diversity. These programmes are decentralized from the state to municipalities across Europe and are a representative case of multilevel governance. They have a strong assimilationist emphasis, by demanding that greater effort be made for foreign people, specifically in the acquisition of linguistic and civic skills (Caponio, 2010; Gebhardt, 2016).

5. CONCLUSION

The rise of individualism in the neoliberal era and the emergence of xenophobic political parties in Europe have led to the disruption of well-established de facto agreements such as the Universal Declaration of Human Rights. One example of this rupture in the political consensus and the questioning of human rights can be seen in Spain in the discourse of the populist far-right Vox party, which questions laws and policies to protect women survivors of gender violence and also defends the expulsion of unaccompanied foreign minors, bypassing international and national laws for the protection of minors.

The violation of the right to asylum and refuge has brought about the so-called refugee crisis, which has gone far beyond that action to become a crisis of democracy itself as a political system. On the social level, rejection and the lack of compassion, which are characteristic of a society increasingly dominated by the fear of 'others' and especially of social inequality, complete this bloodless image of the great European civilization. However, given this turn, an organized part of civil society and some local administrations have tried to respond to this loss of humanity through two mechanisms: denunciation and actions – such as, for example, the maritime rescue of refugees in the Mediterranean itself – and through political organization to denounce, create solidarity networks and expand rights at the local level, as in the case of sanctuary cities in many countries. These initiatives have elicited a strong political response in the form of the repression of 'no-borders' activism achieved by criminalizing it and the demonization of policies to expand rights for migrants in sanctuary cities by conservative forces.

Before this refugee crisis started, voices had been crying out in alarm to warn of the restrictive turn towards immigration accompanied by the criminalization of foreigners in European societies. This reactive turn entailed the promotion of welfare chauvinism, which denied social rights to foreigners and made social conditions for immigrants in irregular administrative situations more difficult. This was coupled with an emphasis on the need for integration to be an individual effort made by the foreign population and a reduction in multicultural and intercultural policies, all of which were demonized.

We are currently entering a new phase of exclusion characterized by necropolitics and based on the consideration that certain lives are not worth saving or that they do not have the same rights as the native population. The externalization of borders, the criminalization of the solidarity of third-sector organizations dedicated to saving lives in the Mediterranean, and the questioning of subsidies to the third sector working to promote the social inclusion of migrants are part of this new restrictive stage, in which irregular immigrants go from being unwanted to becoming a dispensable population for whom social rights can be cut. A chilling image of this institutional state violence are the thousands of people abandoned and left to die by the nation-states.

Solidarity and compassion seem to have been abandoned in the logic of the state, reduced to agencies that function on a human scale. These include the municipalities that make up the global solidarity network, some third-sector organizations that specialize in maritime rescue services and, lastly, some people who are aware of the situation and demonstrate their solidarity proactively by demanding compliance with human rights. Once again, the empathy crisis can be found more at the forefront of political power – populist right-wing states and parties – than at the foundation of civil society and the organizations closest to the citizens.

NOTES

1. I would like to thank the Faber Foundation in Olot (Girona) for their welcome at their Diversity Policies research residence in 2019, which provided me with the environment and time to write this chapter.
2. A more extensive definition can be found in Bender and Arrocha (2017: 11): 'Compassionate migration is a concept and praxis that describes how individuals, collectives, organizations, and governments express humanity towards victims of conditions that oblige them to leave behind their homes, countries, families, friends, and livelihoods in search of refuge or a better life for themselves and their families. As a praxis it requires a deep empathy towards others as well as an understanding of the reasons for their often forced migration. Practices of compassionate migration tend to be carried out at the margins of the established legal and policy frames, for many of these existing frames are based on control, punishment, rejection, and repression. Compassionate migration has at its conceptual core a deep sense of humanity which through concrete actions strives to extend and ensure fundamental human rights, including the right of movement for all individuals, regardless of their nationality or immigration status.'

REFERENCES

Agamben, Giorgio (1998), *Homo sacer: Sovereign power and bare life*, Palo Alto, CA: Stanford University Press.
Ahmed, Sara (2004), *The cultural politics of emotion*, Edinburgh, UK: Edinburgh University Press.
Alonso, Sonia and Cristóbal Rovira Kaltwasser (2014), 'Spain: No country for the populist radical right?', *South European Society and Politics*, 20 (1), 21–45, doi: http://dx.doi.org/10.1080/13608746.2014.985448.
Anderson, Bridget (2013), *Us and them? The dangerous politics of immigration controls*, Oxford: Oxford University Press.
Baldi, Gregory and Sara W. Goodman (2015), 'Migrants into members: Social rights, civic requirements, and citizenship in western Europe', *West European Politics*, 38 (6), 1152–1173.
Bender, Steven W. and William F. Arrocha (2017), *Compassionate migration and regional policy in the Americas*, London, UK: Palgrave Macmillan.
Bergmark, Åke; M. Thoslund and E. Lindberg (2000), 'Beyond benevolence – solidarity and welfare state transition in Sweden', *International Journal of Social Welfare*, 9, 238–249.
Bowling, Ben and Sophie Westenra (2018), 'A really hostile environment: Adiaphorization, global policing and the crimmigration control system', *Theoretical Criminology*, doi: https://doi.org/10.1177/1362480618774034.
Braidotti, Rosi (2017), 'Posthuman, all too human: The memoirs and aspirations of a posthumanist', Tanner Lectures, Yale University.
Brandariz-García, José and C. Fernández-Bessa (2017), 'The managerial turn: The transformation of Spanish migration control policies since the onset of the economic crisis', *The Howard Journal of Crime and Justice*, 56 (2), 198–219, doi: http://dx.doi.org/10.1111/hojo.12201.
Brubaker, Rogers (2017), 'Between nationalism and civilizationism: The European populist moment in comparative perspective', *Ethnic and Racial Studies*, 40 (8), 1191–1226, doi: https://doi.org/10.1080/01419870.2017.1294700.

Burgoon, Brian and Matthijs Rooduijn (2020), '"Immigrationization" of welfare politics? Anti-immigration and welfare attitudes in context', *West European Politics*, doi: https://doi.org/10.1080/01402382.2019.1702297.

Caponio, Tiziana (2010), 'Conclusion: Making sense of local migration policy arenas', in Tiziana Caponio and Maren Borkert (eds.), *The local dimension of migration policymaking*, Amsterdam: Amsterdam University Press, pp. 161–195.

Casas-Cortes, Maribel; S. Cobarrubias and J. Pickles (2016), '"Good neighbours make good fences": Seahorse operations, border externalization and extra-territoriality', *European Urban and Regional Studies*, **23** (3), 231–251.

Casella Colombeau, Sara (2019), 'Crisis of Schengen? The effect of two "migrant crises" (2011 and 2015) on the free movement of people at an internal Schengen border', *Journal of Ethnic and Migration Studies*, doi: https://doi.org/10.1080/1369183X.2019.1596787.

Cornelius, Wayne; Philip Martin and James Hollifield (1994), *Controlling immigration: A global perspective*, Stanford, CA: Stanford University Press.

Cusumano, Eugenio (2018), 'The non-governmental provision of search and rescue in the Mediterranean and the abdication of state responsibility', *Cambridge Review of International Affairs*, **31** (1), 53–75.

Cuttitta, Paolo (2018), 'Repoliticization through search and rescue? Humanitarian NGOs and migration management in the Central Mediterranean', *Geopolitics*, **23** (3), 632–660.

De Genova, Nicholas (2004), 'The legal production of Mexican/Migrant "Illegality"', *Latino Studies*, **2**, 160–185.

De Giorgi, Alessandro (2010), 'Immigration control, post-Fordism, and less eligibility: A materialist critique of the criminalization of immigration across Europe', *Punishment & Society*, **12** (2), 147–167.

De Hass, Hein; K. Natter and S. Vezzoli (2016), 'Growing restrictiveness or changing selection? The nature and evolution of migration policies', *International Migration Review*, doi: https://doi.org/10.1111/imre.12288.

Dennison, James and Mariana Mendes (2019), 'When do populist radical right parties succeed? Salience, stigma, and the case of the end of Iberian "exceptionalism"', *Salience, Stigma, and the Case of the End of Iberian 'Exceptionalism:'* (April), Robert Schuman Centre for Advanced Studies Research Paper No. RSCAS 26 (2019).

Doidge, Mark and E. Sandri (2019), '"Friends that last a lifetime": The importance of emotions amongst volunteers working with refugees in Calais', *The British Journal of Sociology*, **70** (2), 463–480.

Domingo, Andreu (2018a), 'Postveritat i demografía a la "Crisi dels refugiats". El plec thanatopolític a la Unió Europea', *Treballs de la Societat Catalana de Geografia*, **85**, 9–30.

Domingo, Andreu (2018b), 'Analyzing zombie dystopia as neoliberal scenario: An exercise in emancipatory catastrophism', *Frontiers in Sociology*, **3** (20), doi: https://doi.org/10.3389/fsoc.2018.00020.

Faist, Thomas (2009), 'Diversity – a new mode of incorporation?', *Ethnic and Racial Studies*, **31** (1), 171–190, https://doi.org/10.1080/01419870802483650.

Fassin, Didier (2005), 'Compassion and repression: The moral economy of immigration policies in France', *Cultural Anthropology*, **20** (3), 362–387.

Ferrero-Turrión, Ruth and Gemma Pinyol-Jiménez (2016), 'La mal llamada "crisis de refugiados en Europa: crisis, impactos y retos para la política de inmigración y asilo de la Unión Europea', *Documentación Social*, **180**, 49–69.

Fernández-Suárez, Belén and Keina Espiñeira-González (2019), 'Can local policies undermine internal borders? Conditional and exclusionary welfare affecting undocumented migrants in Madrid and Barcelona', paper presented at the Workshop 'Governing the poor – Migration and Poverty', University of Neuchâtel, Switzerland, 11 December, 2019.

FitzGerald, David Scott (2019), 'Remote control of migration: Theorizing territoriality, shared coercion, and deterrence', *Journal of Ethnic and Migration Studies*, https://doi.org/10.1080/1369183X.2020.1680115.

Franko, Katja; M.V.D. Woude and V. Barker (2019), 'Beacons of tolerance dimmed? Migration, criminalization, and inhospitality in welfare states', in Synnøve Bendixsen and Trygve Wyller (eds.), *Contested hospitalities in a time of migration: Religious and secular counterspaces in the Nordic region*, Milton Park, UK: Routledge, pp. 55–75.

Franquesa, Jaume (2019), 'The vanishing exception: Republican and reactionary specters of populism in rural Spain', *The Journal of Peasant Studies*, **46** (3), 537–560, doi: https://doi.org/10.1080/03066150.2019.1578751.
Freeman, Gary P. (2003), 'Incorporating immigrants in liberal democracies', CMD Working Papers, Center for Migration and Development, Princeton University, Princeton.
García Agustín, Ó. and M. Bak Jørgensen (2019), 'Solidarity cities and cosmopolitanism from below: Barcelona as a refugee city', *Social Inclusion*, **7** (2), 198–207, doi: http://dx.doi.org/10.17645/si.v7i2.2063.
Gargiulo, Enrico (2017), 'The limits of local citizenship: Administrative borders within the Italian municipalities', *Citizenship Studies*, **21** (3), 327–343, https://doi.org/10.1080/13621025.2016.1277982.
Gebhardt, Dirk (2016), 'When the state takes over: Civic integration programmes and the role of cities in immigrant integration', *Journal of Ethnic and Migration Studies*, **42** (5), 742–758, https://doi.org/10.1080/1369183X.2015.1111132.
Gonzales, Alfonso (2012), *Reform without justice: Latino migrant politics and the homeland security state*, New York: Oxford University Press.
Goodman, Sara Wallace (2010), 'Integration requirements for integration's sake? Identifying, categorising and comparing civic integration policies', *Journal of Ethnic and Migration Studies*, **36** (5), 553–772.
Guiraudon, Virginie and Gallya Lahav (2000), 'A reappraisal of the state sovereignty debate: The case of migration control', *Comparative Political Studies*, **33** (2), 163–195, https://doi.org/10.1177/0010414000033002001.
Hepburn, Eve (2009), 'Regionalist party mobilisation on immigration', *West European Politics*, **32** (3), 514–535, https://doi.org/10.1080/01402380902779071.
Heyman, Josiah and Natalia Ribas-Mateos (2019), 'Borders of wealth and poverty: Ideas stimulated by comparing the Mediterranean and U.S.–Mexico borders', *Archivio antropologico mediterraneo* [Online], **21** (2), doi: https://doi.org/10.4000/aam.2019.
Joppke, Christian (2007), 'Beyond national models: Civic integration policies for immigrants in western Europe', *West European Politics*, **30** (1), 1–22, https://doi.org/10.1080/01402380601019613.
Jupp, James (2003), 'Immigration, asylum and extremist politics: Europe and Australia', *National Europe Centre Paper* **70**. Paper presented at The Challenges of Immigration and Integration in the European Union and Australia Conference, University of Sydney, Australia, 18–20 February.
Karakayali, Serhat (2017), 'Feeling the scope of solidarity: The role of emotions for volunteers supporting refugees in Germany', *Social Inclusion*, **5** (3), 7–16.
Koster, Willem De; P. Achterberg, J.V.D. Wall, S.V. Bohemen and R. Kemmers (2014), 'Progressiveness and the New Right: The electoral relevance of culturally progressive values in the Netherlands', *West European Politics*, **37** (3), 584–604.
Kriesi, Hanspeter (2015), 'Enlightened understanding, Empowerment and leadership – three ways to enhance multiculturalism: Comment on Will Kymlicka´s article: "Solidarity in Diverse Societies"', *Comparative Migration Studies*, **3** (17), 3–18, https://doig.org/10.1186/s40878-015-0019-2.
Kymlicka, Will (2015), 'Solidarity in diverse societies: Beyond neoliberal multiculturalism and welfare chauvinism', *Comparative Migration Studies*, **3** (17), https://doi.org/10.1186/s40878-015-0017-4.
Loch, Dietmar (2014), 'Integration as a sociological concept and national model for immigrants: Scope and limits', *Identities: Global Studies in Culture and Power*, **21** (6), 623–632, https://doi.org/10.1080/1070289X.2014.908776.
López-Sala, Ana and I. Barbero (2019), 'Solidarity under siege: The crimmigration of activism(s) and protest against border control in Spain', *European Journal of Criminology*, https://doi.org/10.1177/1477370819882908.
Martínez, Omar; E. Wu, T. Sandfort, B. Dodge, A. Carballo-Dieguez, R. Pinto, S.D. Rhodes, E. Moya and S. Chavez-Baray (2015), 'Evaluating the impact of immigration policies on health status among undocumented immigrants: A systematic review', *Journal of Immigrant and Minority Health*, **17** (3), 947–970.
Mellón, Joan Antón and A. Hernández-Carr (2016), 'El crecimiento electoral de la derecha radical populista en Europa: parámetros ideológicos y motivaciones sociales', *Política y Sociedad*, **53** (1), 17–28, http://dx.doi.org/10.5209/rev_POSO.2016.v53.n1.48456.
Mezzadra, Sandro and B. Neilson (2017), *La frontera como método*, Madrid: Traficantes de Sueños.

Moffette, David (2014), 'Governing immigration through probation: The displacement of borderwork and the assessment of desirability in Spain', *Security Dialogue*, **45** (3), 262–278.
Mudde, Cas (2007), *Populist radical right parties in Europe*, Cambridge: Cambridge University Press.
Nussbaum, M.C. (2014), *Emociones políticas. ¿Por qué el amor es importante para la justicia?*, Barcelona: Paidós.
Parekh, Bhikhu (2012), 'Is there a case for banning hate speech?', in Michael Herz and Peter Molnar (eds), *The content and context of hate speech: Rethinking regulation and responses*, New York: Cambridge University Press, pp. 37–56.
Patler, Caitlin (2017), '"Citizens but for papers": Undocumented youth organizations, anti-deportation campaigns, and the reframing of citizenship', *Social Problems*, **65**, 96–115.
Peralta-Gallego, Leia; J. Gené-Badia and P. Gallo (2018), 'Effects of undocumented immigrants' exclusion from health care coverage in Spain', *Health Policy*, **122** (11), 1155–1160.
Phillips, Joe and Joseph Yi (2018), 'Charlottesville paradox: The "liberalizing" alt-right, "authoritarian" left, and politics of dialogue', *Society*, **55** (3), 221–228, doi: https://doi.org/10.1007/s12115-018-0243-0.
Pinyol-Jiménez, Gemma (2012), 'The migration–security nexus in short: Instruments and actions in the European Union', *Amsterdam Law Forum*, **4** (1), 36–57.
Rosas, Gilberto (2019), 'Necro-subjection: On borders, asylum, and making dead to let live', *Theory & Event*, **22** (2), 303–324.
Rygiel, Kim (2011), 'Bordering solidarities: Migrant activism and the politics of movement and camps at Calais', *Citizenship Studies*, **15** (1), 1–19, https://doi.org/10.1080/13621025.2011.534911.
Sirriyeh, Ala (2018), *The politics of compassion. Immigration and asylum policy*, Bristol, UK and Chicago, USA: Bristol University Press.
Sirriyeh, Ala (2019), '"Felons are also our family": Citizenship and solidarity in the undocumented youth movement in the United States', *Journal of Ethnic and Migration Studies*, **45** (1), 133–150.
Stumpf, Juliet (2006), 'The crimmigration crisis: Immigrants, crime and sovereign power', *American University Law Review*, **56** (2): 367–419.
Torpey, John C. (2018), *The invention of the passport: Surveillance, citizenship and the state*, Cambridge: Cambridge University Press.
Triadafilopoulos, Triadafilos (2011), 'Illiberal means to liberal ends? Understanding recent immigrant integration policies in Europe', *Journal of Ethnic and Migration Studies*, **37** (6), 861–880.
Turnbull-Dugarte, Stuart J. (2019), 'Explaining the end of Spanish exceptionalism and electoral support for Vox', *Research & Politics*, doi: https://doi.org/10.1177/2053168019851680.
Van der Wall, Jeroen; Willem De Koster and Wim Van Oorschot (2013), 'Three worlds of welfare chauvinism? How welfare regimes affect support for distributing welfare to immigrants in Europe', *Journal of Comparative Policy Analysis: Research and Practice*, **15** (2), 164–181.
Wimmer, Andreas (1997), 'Explaining xenophobia and racism: A critical review of current research approaches', *Ethnic and Racial Studies*, **20** (1), 17–41, https://doi.org/10.1080/01419870.1997.9993946.
Wonders, Nancy A. (2017), 'Sitting on the fence – Spain's delicate balance: Bordering, multiscalar challenges, and crimmigration', *European Journal of Criminology*, **14** (1), 7–26.

15. The wall and the tunnels: crossings and separation at the border between Egypt, Israel and the Gaza Strip[1]

Lorenzo Navone

1. INTRODUCTION

The 11-kilometre border between the Gaza Strip and Egypt is the northernmost segment of the Israeli–Egyptian border. The border follows a more or less straight line, about 200 kilometres long, drawn in the arid space between the Sinai Peninsula, the Negev Desert, the Mediterranean Sea and the Gulf of Aqaba. Still scarcely studied by social scientists (Anteby-Yemini 2008; Hanafi and Sanmartin 1996), this partially fortified line in the desert is criss-crossed by electrified and barbed wire, constantly monitored by a camera system, and patrolled by the Israeli army on one side and by the Egyptian police on the other. It can be legally crossed at three crossings: Rafah, Nitzana/Al-Auja and Taba. The Rafah Border Crossing, the only transit point between Egypt and the Gaza Strip, should be under the joint control of Egypt and the Palestinian National Authority (PNA). However, since 2007 the Hamas political movement has controlled the Palestinian side.[2]

In order to better understand this border, it is necessary to look back at the past and outline a brief genealogy of the processes that have contributed to defining the current configuration in the area. Since the British "Sinai and Palestine campaign" (1915–1918) during the First World War, the Sinai Peninsula has been the theatre of multiple tensions, conflicts, and wars that have deeply shaped the physiognomy of its territory and social space. The borderline separating Israel, Egypt and the Gaza Strip has emerged as a mobile frontier, "both as instrument and goal, a means and an end" (Lefebvre 1991: 411) of the main conflicts that have affected the region during the twentieth century: the first Arab–Israeli War (1948), the Suez Crisis (1956), the Six Days War (1967), the War of Attrition (1969), and the Yom Kippur or Ramadan War (1973).

The events that have shaped the border space of North Sinai as a battlefield for almost a century must be examined within the broader context of the Arab–Israeli and Israeli–Palestinian conflicts. The Arab–Israeli conflict dominated the political and military scene in the Middle East from 1948 until the Camp David agreements of 1978; the Israeli–Palestinian conflict began between the 1980s and 1990s and has been marked by gradual "Palestinization",[3] which consists in turning the Palestinian conflict, a regional issue (involving the countries bordering Israel), into a local one, affecting the heart of the territory corresponding to the former Mandatory Palestine, namely Israel and the OPT (Occupied Palestinian Territories). The OPT are made up of the West Bank, a portion of land between the Jordan River and the Green Line, and the Gaza Strip.

Over the course of such tensions – which have encompassed the entire spectrum of possible forms of conflict in modern times – the territorial matrix has had, and still has, a decisive relevance. More precisely, these tensions inevitably converge primarily *on the borders*. In the case of Israel and the OPT, over the years we have witnessed a twofold phenomenon, divergent but complementary, of multiplication of borders: on the one hand, a phenomenon of deterritorialization and dematerialization of borders, which can be observed within "Israel proper" in the processes of fragmentation and partitioning of citizenship in ethnic terms (Smooha 1997; Yiftachel 1997); on the other, a movement of rematerialization and re-territorialization of the borders, lending them a renewed territorial intensity, giving way to the production of a complex and integrated system of confinement and segregation devices targeting the Palestinians living in the OPT (from the separation wall to the bypass roads to the refugee camps), accompanied by a legal arsenal in support of this regime (Ben-Naftali et al. 2018).

Today, the OPT are a discontinuous and fragmented territory, made up of a group of "islands", roughly corresponding to the main urban centres, separated by an "archipelago" of Israeli colonies and outposts connected by a network of roads and surrounded by a large "sea" under exclusive Israeli military control, which is off-limits to the Palestinians (Petti 2019). This separation regime was legally established by the Taba Agreements, or Oslo-II Accord (1995), which led to the partition of the West Bank into three control areas:

- Area A: 18 percent of the West Bank, under civil control of the Palestinian Authority (PA), which is responsible for security. This area includes the main Palestinian urban settlements.
- Area B: 21 percent of the West Bank, including about 450 villages and smaller towns. The PA is responsible for general administration, but the security is under Israeli control.
- Area C: 60 percent of the territory, under complete Israeli military control. It includes colonies, outposts, bypass roads, all strategic areas and security infrastructure. Approximately 300,000 Palestinians and 400,000 Israeli settlers live in this area.

The Gaza Strip is not part of this segmentation and officially it is entirely contained in Area A. Likewise, following the 1979 peace agreements, Sinai was fragmented into three gradually demilitarized zones (Zones A, B and C, from the Suez Canal to the East), which are monitored by the Multinational Force and Observers (MFO). Despite the formal process of demilitarization of the region, the presence of the Egyptian Army and its military operations are steadily increasing, thanks to *ad hoc* amendments to the agreements, justified by the threat of Islamic terrorism.

The process of multiplication of borders, well visible in the Israel/Palestine conflict, shows that the very concept of border is basically inseparable from the ideas of *frontier* and *frontline*, and therefore of war itself: the frontier, a shifting device by definition, constitutes a "virtual military environment that gravitates around the political border" (Dal Lago 2006: 8). On the one hand, the war turns the frontier into the initial front of the conflict and redefines the political borders of the territory of the defeated enemy; on the other hand, the frontier always embodies potential war, because it incorporates relations of force and power that are ready to emerge, as it is clear from the very etymology of the term: the Latin word "frons, frontis" (Moatti 2010). As Scheper-Hughes and Bourgois recall, war is only a polarity within "the continuum of violence": from the state of war, violence is prolonged in peacetime in various daily practices, to include "all expressions of radical social exclusion, dehumanization, depersonalization, pseudo speciation, and reification which normalize atrocious behaviour and violence" (Scheper-Hughes and Bourgois 2004: 21). In other words, war, as an act of extreme violence aimed at imposing one's will on the adversary (Von Clausewitz 1989 [1832]) and producing death (Bouthoul 1970), is the plastic representation of the extreme violence of borders; and if borders represent the place of "necropolitics" *par excellence*, the processes of multiplication and overlapping of borders in the OPT make the latter a paradigmatic and exemplary place of "necropower" in the making (Mbembe 2003: 27–28).

In the first part of this contribution, I present the field of my research, a disputed and conflict-laden territory, over-determined by the presence of the border and a network of tunnels aimed at smuggling goods into the Gaza Strip. In the second part, I describe the social fragmentation affecting the Palestinian community in Egypt, a phenomenon in which border shifts throughout history have played a decisive role. In the third part, the border is analysed as the centre of gravity around which a complex system of legal, informal and illegal economies is built. Finally, in the conclusions, I examine the particular triangulation of the North Sinai border in the light of the general process of multiplication and "three-dimensionalization" of contemporary borders, where tunnels represent its material, tangible and ethnographically observable phenomenon.

2. A BORDER THAT DOES NOT WORK

Between 2009 and 2011 I spent several months in the city of Al Arish, on the north-eastern coast of Sinai, about 40 kilometres from the border with the Gaza Strip. Since Israel completed its withdrawal from the peninsula (25 April 1982), the border has divided the town of Rafah into two sectors: one half is in Egypt, the other half is in the OPT. Under the 11-kilometre wall shaping this border a network of tunnels has been expanding for several years. The tunnels were illegally dug and aimed at the smuggling of all kinds of goods and commodities and at the passage of people.

This chapter is the ethnographic account of my experience on the field, in the Northern Sinai borderland, and it is based on direct observation of border life, informal conversations with the people living in the area (Bedouins, Palestinians, Egyptians and international activists) and a dozen interviews conducted over the course of multiple fieldwork stays in the border area between 2009 and 2011.[4] The main focus of my research was the functioning of the border, understood as a total social fact affecting all spheres of social life. In order to understand how the border shapes the frame of daily relationships and interactions, some questions immediately emerged: who can cross it? Who governs its functioning? What knowledge, practices, conflicts and resistance does the presence of the border generate and reflect? In particular, this contribution focuses on the political economy of the border, namely the complex intertwining of economic activities generated by the presence of the border itself – whether they are considered legal, informal or criminal by local social actors.

During my stays in Egypt, when I asked for clarification about the functioning of the Rafah Border Crossing, the answer I got was often a laconic "It doesn't work!", followed by laughter. In fact, the Rafah crossing has been almost sealed for several years now: following the Israeli disengagement from Gaza (2004/2005) the PNA gradually took control of its part of the terminal. Following the electoral victory of Hamas (January 2006) and the failure of negotiations to form a government of national unity, a bloody civil war broke out (2007), the civil mission of the EU observers (EU Border Assistance Mission Rafah) withdrew from the terminal, Israel imposed a state of siege and Egypt materially "closed the door".

During my fieldwork in Egypt, the border was largely perceived as non-functioning: this perception was not only due to the "normality" of its closure, but also to the arbitrariness of the mechanism by which it was governed: a border is activated and actually works as a device of government of life at the very moment of its crossing, by filtering and selecting people and goods. Otherwise, it isn't a border.

Between 2007 and 2011, border openings were discontinuous and erratic, on average three or four days each month. Only individuals holding a Palestinian passport and certain categories of people defined as VIPs (international investors, non-governmental organization (NGO) staff, healthcare staff, members of international organizations, diplomats) were entitled to cross the border. The opening days were defined by the Egyptian authorities, which communicated the dates to the national media about a week in advance; then, the Palestinian Embassy and the Hamas government submitted a list with the names of several hundred people intending to pass through to the Egyptian authorities. Through the information services (*mukhabarat*), the Egyptian government decided the opening dates and allowed (or denied) the transit. The principle serving as the basis for this decision remained unknown, but waiting lists were extremely long and even in case of acceptance the actual date of transit remained unpredictable (UN OCHA – OPT 2009). I witnessed the daily life of the people waiting for the opening of the border and the moment of the race to the terminal in the hope of crossing: I was able to observe, follow the human events and talk to some individuals, out of the thousands of people who went to the Rafah Terminal. Most of them waited, often in vain, to cross the border to enter Gaza; others waited there for someone to leave the Gaza Strip. When the crossing was closed, I was based in Al Arish, where I focused on daily life in this border town and on the interactions produced by the presence of the border.

Both in the cases of waiting and in the case of crossing, the frontier constitutes the *frame* articulating multiple practices and narratives. In accordance with current practice, the names of my interviewees have been changed.

3. PALESTINIAN PRESENCE

The human presence in this region is heterogeneous: besides an almost sedentary Bedouin population, there is a local Arab component[5] (non-Bedouin), as well as government officials, settlers and Egyptian workers from the *Wadi Nil* (Nile Valley). In addition, several people are staying in the region "temporarily": a small number of foreign workers or tourists (mostly from other Arab countries, but also Chinese) and many Palestinians.

Egypt is the only country bordering Israel not to have locked up Palestinians expelled after the 1948 and 1967 wars in refugee camps (El-Abed 2009). Palestinians permanently residing in Egypt are estimated at several tens of thousands, but there is no such thing as a single, unified Palestinian community: over 70 years of Palestinian diaspora have produced a wide spectrum of different situations. Behind the category of the Palestinians in Egypt lies an extremely fragmented reality. For analytical convenience, the different coexisting Palestinian communities can be identified by cross-checking socio-economic capital with time of arrival in Egypt. This gives us a range of situations covering almost all possible labels of *humanity in excess*, defined as "a human condition that exceeds every idea of exclusion, and is instead 'included', according to a radically differential logic tantamount to apartheid, as confinable and deportable" (Rahola 2010: 192). Since 1948, Palestinians in Egypt have faced multiple forms of "differential inclusion" (Mezzadra and Neilson 2012: 67). Thus, the social fragmentation of the Palestinian diaspora in Egypt can be summarized through the following empirical categories:

- "Egyptians of Palestinian origin": namely, the descendants of those Palestinians who have obtained full nationality, due to their professional position and economic status.
- "Palestinians in Egypt": those with a temporary visa for health, work or study reasons.
- "Palestinians of Egypt": those Palestinians who only have the right of residence, but not full citizenship, despite having being born in Egypt.[6]
- "Illegal Palestinians": namely, those Palestinians permanently living in Egypt without an entry visa as well as those who were born in Egypt to undocumented parents, living therefore without any residency or property right (El-Abed 2009).
- "Exiled Palestinians": several thousands of former members of the Fatah security forces who fled Gaza following the 2007 civil war.

The last of these mainly used to live in Al Arish, in a tourist district near the sea, called the *Corniche*, and did not have any specific legal status. They arrived with temporary visas after the Hamas takeover of the Gaza Strip and they were tolerated by the authorities, although constantly under surveillance: they were not allowed to work or leave Al Arish to go to Cairo, not even to Rafah, without the permission of the *mukhabarat*. They still received their salary from Ramallah and spent their time in Sinai either waiting to go back to Gaza, where many of them had left their families, or dreaming of moving to Europe as refugees.

One effect of the selective permeability of the border is the production of narratives that reinforce the idea of separation and contribute to the construction of new barriers, both between different "ethnic" communities and within each community, as highlighted by Pablo Vila (2000) in the El Paso/Ciudad Juárez borderland, between Mexico and the USA. In the case of the infra-Palestinian barriers, economic, political and temporal factors play a role. Omar was about 40 years old at the time of our meeting and was in Al Arish following what he called the Hamas coup (*inqilab*, overthrowing). In his account, the social relations between members of different communities emerges as a relevant topic: the *Arishi* (the people from Al Arish) and their cuisine cannot be trusted, unlike the Bedouins, who, although they have made money (*flus*) thanks to trafficking with Gaza, are respectable, because they have a history and traditions (*adat wa-taqalid*) and have smuggled weapons into Palestine during the last conflicts. Otherwise, with regard to the Palestinians of Al Arish, the relations were initially tense, since the Hamas propaganda had created a climate of distrust towards Fatah exiles, but subsequently improved.

Abu Mohammed was about 30 years old and had been in Al Arish for about two years when I met him. After the murder of two of his brothers, also members of Fatah, he fled Gaza and was later joined by his wife and son, who was born in Khan Yunis during his absence. While Abu Mohammed was chatting in a courtyard with other exiles, I noticed his two-year-old playing with other children, apparently local. A few minutes later, during the conversation, I heard someone say: "Here so many say they are Palestinians. But those are not ours [*min aind-na*], they are Egyptians." In fact, as they will explain to us later, these children were all of Palestinian origin, which was clearly not enough to be considered as "real" Palestinians: being born in Palestine and having migrated at a different time are perceived as further barriers to full cultural and national recognition, even if the inhabitants of the Gaza Strip and Northern Sinai share long stretches of their recent history in addition to the language, and the material distance that separates the two cities – Khan Yunis and Al Arish – amounts to around 50 kilometres.

In other circumstances, the intergenerational transmission of displacement, through memories and narratives, can contribute to the production of new borders. Naji was about 30 years old and worked at the Palestinian Cultural Centre, a structure housed in the complex of the Palestinian Embassy in Cairo. Naji was a Palestinian refugee born in Damascus. Following his university studies in Syria, he travelled to several Arab countries before settling in Cairo, where we met. Naji, who spoke fluent English and had never been to the OPTs before, offered his point of view about the difference between exiles and refugees. First, he reminded me that many prominent figures of Palestinian culture and politics studied or lived in Cairo, such as Edward Said and Yasser Arafat. Afterwards, he nevertheless distanced himself from the community of exiles then present in Al Arish (although they too, like almost everyone in Gaza, were probably refugees[7]):

Naji: They are just security officers, they have no political culture. They are militants of a faction, like those of Hamas.

The mistrust and the differences that exist between exiles, refugees and, in general, Palestinians abroad, can lead to some considerations: the fragmentation of the Palestinian society of the diaspora is an effect of the continuous processes of reconfiguration of the social and material borders that have crossed Palestine from 1948 to the present day. The different legal statuses of members of the Palestinian diaspora generate different perceptions of the right to return. The latter can be envisioned in mythical–geographical terms, as a *nostos* for a homeland where some have never set foot, or in a more practical sense, in terms of family reunification opportunities. The right to return is less often seen as a means to achieve coexistence in the future or to organize politically (Hanafi 2006). In short, while nostalgia is a recurring trope, this feeling is directed to the land more than to the people.

4. BORDER ECONOMIES

Border areas are by definition spaces of interaction, transit and economic exchange. The opportunity represented by the presence of an interstate border can generate a quick economic development, but it can also be the cause of an abrupt decline, due to the variable material conditions in which these cross-border activities flourish: border permeability, presence or absence of infrastructures, market demand. The peripheral location of physical borders, far from centralized state authority, may encourage the development of activities that are often considered as illegal or informal. However, the stark distinction between legal and illegal activities does not prove useful in this case. In border areas, the boundary between these concepts is blurred and fluctuating: legal and illegal practices seem to blend into each other and intertwine.

For over 20 years Northern Sinai (*Shamal Sina'*) has been the target of an integrated development plan that is part of a wider process of economic liberalization: the open-door policy (*infitah*, literally "opening") launched by President Sadat in 1974. The goal of the development plan is to complete a set of industrial, urban, infrastructural, agricultural and tourism modernization projects by 2022 with the aim of repopulating the region by offering new employment opportunities that encourage the voluntary displacement of several million people from the overpopulated areas of *Wadi Nil* in North Sinai. Although the "reconquest" of the region is also considered a strategic goal for national security, only a part of the plan has been completed. The region remains among the poorest in Egypt: it is still poorly industrialized and there is no QIZ (Qualified Industrial Zone) in this area. The main economic resource of the region seems to reside in the tertiary sector. The beaches of Al Arish are one of the main destinations of low-cost Egyptian internal tourism, but they also welcome some tourists from the Gulf countries, especially Saudi Arabia. However, despite major development plans and the opportunity offered by tourism, the economy seems to gravitate mainly around the existence of the border.

When the opening of the Rafah Crossing Point was announced, several hundreds of Palestinians from all over the world headed towards the Rafah Terminal. They spent at least a few days there, with the aim of entering Gaza or waiting for someone on the other side of the border to get out of the Gaza Strip (Navone 2016). Achieving the border crossing, in both directions, was not guaranteed: most Palestinians were either rejected or just arrived too late at the terminal, once it was already closed. In such cases, they had to wait until the next opening, at least one month, having to face the expenses that an unforeseen and prolonged stay can generate. While the presence of people in transit in Al Arish or Rafah can be an additional source of income for the tourism industry (carriers, hoteliers, property owners, traders, and so on), the presence of people on hold mainly feeds other markets and spaces for exchange. In the square in front of the border crossing there was a small building with toilets, a small prayer room, and most importantly a cafeteria, selling water, soft and hot drinks, food, and Egyptian SIM cards, which cost twice as much as in Al Arish.

The border area and the presence of thousands of people waiting represented a huge opportunity to earn money, especially for Bedouins, who marketed themselves as the only keepers of a practical border knowledge. According to the United Nations, the two largest military offensives in recent years, "Cast Lead" (December 2008–January 2009) and "Pillar of Defense" (October 2012),[8] caused the destruction or serious damage to more than 6,000 homes. The blockade that endures since 2006 and the embargo on the import of building materials through Israel are still decisive obstacles to the reconstruction or rehabilitation of these homes.[9] In the villages between Rafah and Al Arish, cement bags and all kinds of home appliances (such as ovens, televisions, refrigerators, gas cookers, and so on) were on sale, mostly delivered to the terminal through an informal paid service provided by the Bedouins. Moreover, the Palestinians waiting to enter the Gaza Strip were often carrying so much luggage that they needed porters, usually young Bedouins, who were the only people allowed to enter the terminal. In addition, it is worth mentioning that while in Egypt the official currency is the Egyptian Pound, and in Palestine it is the Israeli Shekel, for many operations it is convenient to use American dollars or euros, which is why at the border Bedouins operate as currency changers at more or less arbitrary rates. Informal Bedouin taxi drivers shuttled non-stop between the border crossing and Al Arish, where the bus station to Cairo is located. Lastly, along the 40-kilometre road leading to the crossing point, several Bedouin families sold local agricultural products as well as water, soft drinks, sandwiches, eggs, and so on.

The effect of the restrictions resulting from the economic blockade imposed by Israel and Egypt and the consequences of the material isolation of Gaza were amplified by the most recent wars, which produced a catastrophic humanitarian, health and environmental impact on the Strip. Gaza has become absolutely dependent on outside resources. The underground economy of the tunnels therefore regulates the balance between the inhabitants' need for survival and the opportunity of rapid enrichment for those who operate in the smuggling sector.

The direct connection between economic embargo, border strengthening measures and clandestine economic activities is quite common: criminal and smuggling networks are a constant in conflicts and a typical post-conflict legacy (Andreas 2004), but examining a concrete case from the micro-analytical perspective of ethnography, mostly in an area as little known as Northern Sinai, can yield unforeseen insights.

Firas, a Palestinian from Khan Yunis, was a member of the Fatah community in exile in Al Arish and a friend of an informal entrepreneur, a Bedouin who ran a tunnel. While sitting in Firas's living room, I witnessed a Skype video call between him and his wife, who had remained in the OPT, not even 50 kilometres away. Firas's wife confirmed that the refrigerator he had "sent" had just arrived, that it actually seemed to work well. She also said that she needed a new stove since the old one was broken. Following their conversation, Firas explained to me that about ten days before our meeting, during the opening of the crossing, he was able to send a new fridge to his wife as she had requested, through an acquaintance who was returning to Gaza. However, on the supposed date for the crossing, the authorities suddenly decided that appliances were not allowed on that day: the unexpected decision required a change of route. In addition to the $100 cost of the refrigerator, Firas had to add around $200 for "travel expenses" (*agr tariq*) in order for the appliance to finally arrive to its destination. This circumstance lead Firas to claim that "when they did not have the tunnels, the Bedouins were starving. Now they are rich thanks to the Palestinians."

What are the tunnels and how do they work? Starting from some easy-to-find information and from the testimonies I collected, during the period of my fieldwork there was an unspecified number of underground tunnels between the Gaza Strip and Egypt, a few hundred certainly, which connected the two sides of the city of Rafah and were used mainly for the smuggling of merchandise and goods. While on the Palestinian side the tunnels, being relatively easy to access, have long been the subject of journalistic investigations, on the Egyptian side they are very difficult to access for external observers. The first tunnels that were dug during the 1990s were aimed at smuggling rare Israeli products from Israel to Egypt via Gaza, and at the same time functioned as means to maintain cross-border family relations between Palestinians separated by the border fences in Rafah. The tunnels increasingly attracted the attention of the Egyptian Government, which in 1995 ordered the demolition of some houses along the border in order to prevent smuggling. Between 2000 and 2004, the IDF discovered and destroyed a hundred tunnels under the border with Egypt. In May 2004, the Israeli army then launched Operation Rainbow, which consisted in demolishing entire districts in the south-western part of the Palestinian side of Rafah, with the aim of extending the buffer zone along the border, the so-called "Philadelphi route" (HRW 2004).

The isolation imposed on the Gaza Strip marked a crucial turning point for the economy of the tunnels: between 2007 and 2014 the number of tunnels had increased significantly. They were more and more sophisticated and deeper, and offered employment to many people. The tunnels allowed the inhabitants of the Gaza Strip to get most of the goods they needed. The blockade imposed on Gaza was not limited to building materials; it also pertained to gasoline and diesel for private use, which was essential for electric generators. Scarcity feeds the black market, resulting in inflated prices and in a general increase of the cost of living for the inhabitants of the Strip. In addition, tunnels have a terrible human cost: due to structural collapse, bombardment, explosion or suffocation, hundreds of people have died in them. The information that I was able to collect directly regarding the tunnels is limited, essentially because the local authorities altogether banned foreigners from the centre of the border town of Rafah, surrounded by a complex system for monitoring and filtering movements of people. While I was only partially able to access the world of tunnel owners or operators, I was more successful with the customers, who provided useful information about the functioning of the underground economy.

First of all, it is not easy to precisely quantify the exact number of tunnels in operation during my stay in Egypt, since this complex network is composed of actual tunnels and access tunnels, often hidden in civil homes. A new access point can then lead to several existing tunnels through connecting tunnels. The construction of a tunnel always begins on the Palestinian side, mostly in a basement or in a private apartment, more rarely outdoors, and it ends on the Egyptian side always in apartments or in private terrains of Bedouins with whom an agreement has previously been established. The construction of a tunnel requires engineering expertise and a substantial initial capital investment: in addition to the cost of the workforce employed in the excavation, the manufacturer is required to pay Hamas a "licence", which can cost several thousand dollars. While Hamas does not participate directly in the construction of the tunnels, they remain under its direct or indirect control, according to a few simple rules: the tunnels allow the passage of all kinds of goods and merchandise that are necessary for the population's survival, except for drugs, which are prohibited; the passage of weapons, ammunition and people must be authorized directly by Hamas. As a matter of fact, bans contribute to exacerbating the market logic and the power relations that it entails: in other words, they lead to an increase in the prices and tariffs of those goods and services that suddenly become scarce or whose traffic involves a greater risk for the smuggler (Parizot 2008). As it happens with goods prohibited by Israel such as diesel, petrol and cement, the same can apply to drugs, which are banned by Hamas: in both cases, all these products cross the border through the tunnels. Several of my interviewees confirmed the massive circulation in Gaza of painkiller drugs such as Tramal, an opiate sold over the counter in Egyptian pharmacies (UNODC 2017).[10]

There are differences and similarities between the functioning of the tunnels and the Rafah crossing. First of all, although they saw them as an imposition, my interviewees perceived the rules established by Hamas as clear and explicit, while the opening of the Rafah crossing was perceived as random and its regulation was subject to the total arbitrariness of the Egyptian authorities (and of their Israeli counterparts). Second, unlike the border crossing, the tunnels used to operate non-stop: waiting times were due to their limited number and to the large quantity of goods that passed through them every day. Finally, both the tunnels and the official border crossing can be considered as "selective borders" and as generators of social exclusion. The tunnels guarantee the crossing of the border to a certain number of goods and people. While on the one hand they allow for the enrichment of a few and the survival of a large part of the population of Gaza, on the other hand even successful passage through the tunnels may often push their users towards a condition marked by further exclusion and subalternity.

In this sense, the story of Nada is meaningful: originally from Gaza City and a graduate in foreign literature, she spoke good English and had been in Cairo for a couple of months when we met, in a cafe in the district of Zamalek. Nada had made the decision to leave the Strip, where she lived with her parents, following the deterioration of the general living conditions after Operation Cast Lead. She came into contact with the owner of a Rafah tunnel and after an initial refusal was offered the possibility of crossing the border for a fee of about 800 dollars, which, moreover, as claimed by Nada, was more or less the same amount that Hamas asked her to cross "legally" in Rafah. Having reached an agreement for about half of the amount requested, Nada had to wait for the go-ahead from the smuggler. After a few days she received the call: the entrance to the tunnel was in a private apartment, it was about a dozen metres deep and provided access to an unlit, small tunnel, mainly used for the traffic of small goods, about 200 metres long and requiring crawling. Nada reached the Egyptian side of Rafah, in the courtyard of a Bedouin, in whose house she spent the rest of the night, before she was taken to Al Arish. She went through the checkpoints without any hassle, and in the morning she arrived in the town, where Canadian volunteers she had met in Gaza expected her. A passport loaned by one of them allowed her to easily pass all the checkpoints along the road and the customs on the Suez Canal, until Cairo. As Nada had entered Egypt illegally, with no entry visa, she had no official existence. She lived in precarious economic conditions and had a vague plan to secure a visa in some way and, subsequently, to contract a marriage with a Western citizen, in order to eventually obtain a new nationality and a new passport, one that would be more useful than the Palestinian one.

This story, like the other testimonies I have collected, represents an important contribution to our understanding of the functioning of the tunnels: there are tunnels for small goods, such as suitcases, and tunnels for larger goods, such as household appliances or people. In the second case they are called "VIP tunnels", as they are spacious enough to be able to walk almost upright. Goods were smuggled mainly towards Gaza, and in some cases towards Egypt: some exiles would have their relatives in the Gaza Strip send them products such as tea, coffee, honey, spices, sometimes even sweeteners for diabetics.

The social actors running the tunnel economy (owners, middlemen, businessmen) have grown richer in last few years (Pelham 2012). However, it is important to note that most often had both an initial capital to invest and an already successful business to order, distribute and sell products, like any other supply chain. In Egypt, it was generally believed that the police tolerated the tunnels, or even participated in their management: in fact, it is almost unthinkable that goods for more than a million inhabitants could be smuggled across the border, in such a small city surrounded by police checkpoints and subject to almost daily police roundups.

Adel was a young Bedouin I met near Rafah: although he was unemployed, he always seemed to have a certain amount of money and owned a luxury car. According to Adel, a large part of Rafah's economic activity was linked to the tunnel industry, a sector that involved different types of social actors, including security forces:

Lorenzo: Is this about *bakshish*[11]?

Adel: No, they're in the business.

Several interviewees agreed that the tunnel business in some way included all the actors involved on the border, including the Egyptian police. This perception, of course, cannot be confirmed empirically, but it is not surprising. The fact that the Egyptian police occasionally collapsed some tunnels indicates that they were probably used also to trade goods not tolerated either by Egypt or Israel, such as weapons, explosives or ammunition.

Aiming to crush the tunnel economy, in 2014, the Egyptian government began carrying out an extensive demolition campaign in the city of Rafah,[12] in order to create a buffer zone similar to the Philadelphi route on the Palestinian side. Then, the Egyptian authorities, in partial agreement with the PNA, proceeded to flood over 1,500 tunnels discovered along the border (HRW 2015) with sea water or sewage, causing an environmental disaster as well as serious damage to both the underground and the official economy of the Gaza Strip.

The border between Egypt, Israel and the Gaza Strip 249

The growing tensions in Northern Sinai and the emergence of armed groups affiliated with ISIS (Ansar Beit al-Maqdis – Wilayat Sina') and Al-Qaeda (AQSP (Al-Qaeda in the Sinai Peninsula)) made direct access to the field increasingly risky. The Egyptian Army's extensive and yet ongoing military operation, called "Sinai 2018", has further contributed to the isolation of Northern Sinai and makes it even more difficult for independent researchers, journalists and observers to gain access to the area. As a result, recent information on the tunnel economy is scarce and comes mostly from military sources: although their number is certainly smaller than in the previous decade, in 2019 the demolition of the tunnels is still ongoing, which is an indirect proof of the existence, the extent and the resilience of the tunnel economy.

The economic activities taking place at the border between Egypt and the Gaza Strip do not seem to fully adhere to a "classic" definition of a criminal economy.[13] In this disputed and fragmented territory, the tunnels are not a parasitic threat to state order and to the "legitimate" capitalist economy. Indeed, this phenomenon can be understood as a process of entrepreneurial integration in the frame of the market economy, in which, whether it is legal, informal or criminal, the border is an unquestionable resource, an opportunity and the theatre of all operations.

5. CONCLUSIONS

Illegal activities are often considered residual with regard to legitimate activities because they are perceived as peripheral, in different ways: they often take place on the geographical margins of the state (the borders), are located on the margins of economic activity (smuggling) and mainly involve social actors considered "deviant". Probably, the very use of the term "informal" contributes to this marginalization: it is often used to identify and describe illegitimate activities, whereas, as suggested by Janet Roitman (2005: 20), it would be more consistent to define them as "unregulated", because they cannot be interpreted as belonging to a sphere that is completely distinct from the official economy, or maybe "clandestinely regulated", since there is a certain degree of self-regulation in such activities.

In order to better understand the functioning of the border between Egypt and the Gaza Strip it is necessary to integrate different levels of analysis. First, we must consider the idea of "the partial unbundling of traditional territorial national borders and the formation of new bordering capabilities" (Sassen 2005: 524): the multiscalar dimension of contemporary borders goes beyond the infrastate/interstate framing. The increasing complexity of borders lies in their disarticulation and re-articulation of space–time: the multiplication of border spaces and their temporal extension create differential and gradual forms of exclusion and inclusion. Second, the social production of material and metaphorical borders can result in the emergence of new identities and new diversities, as pointed out by American border studies, although focusing mostly on the US–Mexican border (Vila 2003).

The tunnels thus represented a component of the general process of multiplication and three- dimensionalization of borders in Israel and Palestine (and elsewhere). The horizontal dimension of the border (the actual crossing) is multiplied by its vertical dimension: this does not consist only in the multiplication of the border actors, but above all in the phenomenon of space–time extension of the border, whose multidimensionality defies traditional cartography. Between walls and tunnels, surveillance technologies, territorial waters and air space under exclusive Israeli control, the very border surrounding the Gaza Strip appears to be a complex, irregular and paradoxical three-dimensional volume, rather than a line; notwithstanding, vertical and temporal discontinuities are obliterated by common cartographic representations (Weizman 2002).

The "wall" and the "tunnels" may be both considered here as metaphors of the process of border crossing/reinforcing and as more situated border devices. In the specific context of the divided city of Rafah, where I conducted my ethnographic fieldwork, the tunnels worked as an underground counterpart of the "overground" border(s). Overall, by keeping the situation in an effective and precarious state of balance, the tunnels actively participated in the state of confinement and seclusion of Palestinians inside and outside Gaza. In other words, the tunnels existed because of the border, and produced further segregation, exploitation, filtering, differential temporalities, social power relations and class segmentation. Arguably, the power of death of the border itself worked along with the power that is exercised over life by other border devices (tunnels, border knowledge). Therefore, keeping a population alive or condemning the same population to death (or survival) are two sides of the same coin (Foucault 1998).

Arguably, the tunnels serve a purpose for all involved: on the one hand, they still feed part of the local Egyptian and Gaza economy; on the other hand, they guarantee to Israel and Egypt a minimum flow of non-tolerated goods (weapons, explosives, prisoners, etc.) to Gaza. At the same time, the tunnels maintain the precarious balance at the border by allowing smugglers to perform their activities, within the framework of an established endogenous control, as long as they do not cross the "red line".

Besides the unstable and precarious balance between these main actors, Israel's and Egypt's depiction of the tunnels as smuggling routes became a strong argument to justify draconian security measures (closure of crossings, isolation, embargo) and further brutality (home demolitions, precision bombings, targeted killings, large-scale military operations, and so on). In the meantime, Hamas continues to exploit the tunnel economy and to play a legitimate role in the popular Gaza border protests that erupted in 2018 against the Israeli blockade of the Gaza Strip (Mills et al. 2019).

In this scenario, several actors, discourses, representations and strategies appear to benefit from the tunnels' existence. Tunnels work as filtering and selecting devices, which legitimate policies and practices of border reinforcement. They are the hidden, or the less visible, side of a three-dimensional frontier operating as a tool for segregation. In other words, the tunnel system is a crucial cog in the complex border mechanism, enabling both border crossing and border reinforcing.

NOTES

1. This chapter received support from the Maison Interuniversitaire des Sciences de l'Homme d'Alsace (MISHA) and the Excellence Initiative of the University of Strasbourg.
2. Already addressed in the Israeli–Egyptian Peace Treaty of 1979, the crossing of the Rafah border was further regulated by the Taba Agreements (Oslo II, September 1995). In particular, provisions are to be found in Annex I, Article 6 (Security Arrangements in the Gaza Strip), paragraph 6 (The Egyptian Border) and Article 8 (Passages). Since 15 November 2005, under the Agreed Principles for Rafah Crossing, the Rafah border has been jointly administered by Egypt and the Palestinian Authority, with a supervisory role for the European Union (EU) and Israel.
3. This turning point is especially marked by the first Intifada (1987–1993). See Sela (2012).
4. The fieldwork was part of my PhD programme in Sociology, University of Genoa (Italy).

5. Part of this component of the local population is the result of demographic movements within the Ottoman Empire. Some descend from the Bosnian and Albanian soldiers who lived in the outpost of Al Arish during the "Khedivate of Egypt" (1867–1914) (ICG 2007: 11).
6. Most of them have a blue, passport-like document, written in Arabic and French, issued since the early 1960s and called the "Travel Document for Palestinian Refugees". This travel document has five subcategories: according to the date of arrival in the Arab country, such categories also define the holder's rights and obligations (such as the right to travel abroad, the legal duration and the renewability terms).
7. Seventy-three percent of the population of the Gaza Strip is made up of registered refugees (1.4 out of a 1.9 million total). Source: United Nations Relief and Works Agency (UNRWA), https://www.unrwa.org/where-we-work/gaza-strip (accessed 3 November 2020).
8. These are two large-scale military operations conducted by the Israel Defense Forces (IDF) in order to stop the launch of hand-made rockets from the Gaza Strip to Israel by Hamas and other factions. Cast Lead, in particular, caused the deaths of 1,417 Gazans, most of them civilians (including 313 children). According to the UN Human Rights Council "Goldstone Commission", the operation proved disproportionate since it turned into a collective punishment for the whole population living in the Palestinian enclave (1.85 million inhabitants). For a critical analysis on the Cast Lead operation, see Shlaim (2019).
9. UN OCHA – OPT, *The Humanitarian Monitor*, May 2009.
10. See also Cunningham (2009).
11. The Arabic term "bakshish" generally indicates tipping, but it can also be used to refer to corruption practices, such as bribes. In this case, the word corresponds to the Spanish "mordida" (literally "bite"), as it "alludes to police officers and other public officials being seen as dogs, on the lookout for an innocent citizen to 'have a bite of'" (Baez-Camargo 2018: 171).
12. The demolitions are clearly visible from the satellite imagery published on easy-to-access tools, such as Google Maps.
13. In Michel Peraldi's words (2007: 111), a criminal economy includes those activities "aimed at the production, circulation and marketing of products that are morally or legally prohibited, activities whose organisation and execution incorporate a degree of physical violence actually or potentially present in the very organisation of the production cycle, and activities carried out by individuals, marginal or deviant groups, in conditions of total or relative clandestinity".

REFERENCES

Andreas, Peter (2004), 'Criminalized Legacies of War. The Clandestine Political Economy of the Western Balkans', *Problems of Post-Communism*, 51 (3), 3–9.
Anteby-Yemini, Lisa (2008), 'Migrations africaines et nouveaux enjeux de la frontière israélo-égyptienne', *Cultures & Conflits*, 72, 77–99.
Baez-Camargo, Claudia (2018), 'Mordida (Mexico)', in Ledeneva, Alena (ed.), *The Global Encyclopedia of Informality (Volume 1)*, London: UCL Press.
Ben-Naftali, Orna, Michael Sfard, and Hedi Viterbo (2018), *The ABC of the OPT: A Legal Lexicon of the Israeli Control over the Occupied Palestinian Territory*, Cambridge: Cambridge University Press.
Bouthoul, Gaston (1970), *L'infanticide différé*, Paris: Hachette.
Cunningham, Eric (2009), 'Drug Addiction on the Rise in Besieged Gaza', *The Electronic Intifada*, 30. Online: https://electronicintifada.net/content/drug-addiction-rise-besieged-gaza/8323 (accessed 3 November 2020).
Dal Lago, Alessandro (2006), 'Fronti e frontiere. Note sulla militarizzazione della contiguità', in *fronti/frontiere*, Conflitti globali, 2, Shake: Milano, 7–15.
El-Abed, Oroub (2009), *Unprotected: Palestinians in Egypt since 1948*, Washington-Ottawa: Institute for Palestine Studies-International Development Research Centre.
Foucault, Michel (1998), *The History of Sexuality: 1: The Will to Knowledge*, London: Penguin Books.
Hanafi, Sari (2006), 'Return Migration and the Burden of Borders', *Cairo Papers in Social Science*, 29, (1), 51–66.

Hanafi, Sari and Olivier Sanmartin (1996), 'Histoires de frontières: les palestiniens du nord-sinaï', *Maghreb-Machrek*, 151.
HRW (Human Rights Watch) (2004), *Razing Rafah: Mass Home Demolitions in the Gaza Strip*, New York: Human Rights Watch.
HRW (Human Rights Watch) (2015), *'Look for Another Homeland': Forced Evictions in Egypt's Rafah*, New York: Human Rights Watch.
ICG (International Crisis Group) (2007), *Egypt's Sinai Question*, Middle East/North Africa Report, 61, Brussels: ICG.
Lefebvre, Henri (1991), *The Production of Space*, Malden: Blackwell Publishing.
Mbembe, Achille (2003), 'Necropolitics', *Public Culture*, 15 (1), 11–40.
Mezzadra, Sandro and Brett Neilson (2012), 'Between Inclusion and Exclusion: On the Topology of Global Space and Borders', *Theory, Culture & Society*, 29 (4/5), 58–75.
Mills, David, Mads Gilbert, and Bram Wispelwey (2019), 'Gaza's Great March of Return: Humanitarian Emergency and the Silence of International Health Professionals', *BMJ Global Health*, 4, e001673.
Moatti, Claudia (2010), 'La terre de personne', *Médium*, 24–25 (3), 51–69.
Navone, Lorenzo (2016), 'The Field before the Battle: Palestinian Mobilities and the Gaza–Israel–Egypt Triangular Border before (and after) the 2011 Egyptian Uprising', in Natalia Ribas Mateos (ed.), *Migration, Mobilities and the Arab Spring. Spaces of Refugee Flight in the Eastern Mediterranean*, Cheltenham, UK and Northampton, MA, USA: Edward Elgar Publishing, 127–141.
Parizot, Cedric (2008), 'Tightening Closure, Securing Disorder: Israeli Closure Policies and Informal Border Economy During the Second Intifada (2000/2006)', *Refugee Watch*, 31, 54–64.
Pelham, Nicolas (2012), 'Gaza's Tunnel Phenomenon: The Unintended Dynamics of Israel's Siege', *Journal of Palestine Studies*, XLI (4), 6–31.
Peraldi, Michel (2007), 'Economies criminelles et mondes d'affaires à Tanger', *Cultures & Conflits*, 68, 111–125.
Petti, Alessandro (2019), "Archipelagos and Enclaves: On the Border between Jordan and Palestine–Israel", in A. Pieris (ed.), *Architecture on the Borderline*, London: Routledge, 77–99.
Rahola, Federico (2010), 'The Space of Camps. Towards a Genealogy of Places of Internment in the Present', in Alessandro Dal Lago and Salvatore Palidda (eds), *Conflict, Security and the Reshaping of Society: The Civilization of War*, London and New York: Routledge, 185–199.
Roitman, Janet (2005), *Fiscal Disobedience. An Anthropology of Economic Regulation in Central Africa*, Princeton: Princeton University Press.
Sassen, Saskia (2005), 'When National Territory is Home to the Global: Old Borders to Novel Borderings', *New Political Economy*, 10 (4), 523–541.
Scheper-Hughes, Nancy and Philippe Bourgois (eds.) (2004), *Violence in War and Peace: An Anthology*, Hoboken, NJ: Blackwell.
Sela, Avraham (2012), 'The First Intifada: How the Arab–Israeli Conflict Was Transformed', *Haaretz*, December 13. Online: https://www.haaretz.com/.premium-first-intifada-a-watershed-moment-1.5272288 (accessed 3 November 2020).
Shlaim, Avi (2019), 'Ten Years after the First War on Gaza, Israel Still Plans Endless Brute Force', *The Guardian*, 7 January.
Smooha, Sammy (1997), 'Ethnic Democracy: Israel as an Archetype', *Israel Studies*, 2 (2), 198–241.
UN OCHA – OPT (United Nations Office for the Coordination of Humanitarian Affairs – Occupied Palestinian Territories) (2009), *Locked in: The Humanitarian Impact of Two Years of Blockade of the Gaza Strip*, Jerusalem: UN OCHA OPT.
UNODC (United Nations Office on Drugs and Crime) (2017), *Estimating the Extent of Illicit Drug Use in Palestine*, Vienna: UNODC.
Vila, Pablo (2000), *Crossing Borders, Reinforcing Borders. Social Categories, Metaphors and Narrative Identities on the US–Mexico Frontier*, Austin: University of Texas Press.
Vila, Pablo (ed.) (2003), *Ethnography at the Border*, Minneapolis: University of Minnesota Press.
Von Clausewitz, Carl (1989 [1832]), *On War*, Princeton, NJ: Princeton University Press.
Weizman, Eyal (2002), *The Politics of Verticality*, Open Democracy, Online: http://www.opendemocracy.net/ecology-politicsverticality/article_801.jsp (accessed 3 November 2020).
Yiftachel, Oren (1997), 'Israeli Society and Jewish–Palestinian Reconciliation: "Ethnocracy" and its Territorial Contradictions', *The Middle East Journal*, 51 (4), 505–519.

16. Spanish–Algerian border relations: tensions between bilateral policies and population mobilities

María-Jesús Cabezón-Fernández, Juan-David Sempere-Souvannavong and Arslan Mazouni

1. INTRODUCTION

The circularity of migrants has been analysed as a key aspect of the complexity of global migrations. Since the 1990s, the post-Fordist model has encouraged us to consider different approaches to understand European international migrations. During that decade, authors such as Alain Tarrius indicated the relevance of that model and the emergence of circularity trends amongst Algerians and Moroccans in southern Europe. In this Mediterranean region, Ribas-Mateos has previously referred to the idea of the 'Mediterranean Caravanseray', which suggests the idea of diverse and intensified circulation (Ribas-Mateos, 2005: 1). Since 2011, a time characterized by an increase in migratory pressure at the borders of the European Union (EU) related to political and socioeconomic changes in the Middle East and North Africa (MENA) region, the Mediterranean space has become, once again, the crossroads for several migration paths, within which the forced component of migration has emerged as the dominant one.

In contrast to the ongoing attention reserved for a variety of classic perspectives on integration (which may be termed as adaptation or acculturation, and refer to the idea of settlement), and the predominance of unilocal, unilinear, unidirectional migration, the existence of various, multidirectional human mobilities (of varying durations and in different directions, even opposing ones, hence the idea of circularity), tends to be overlooked. Furthermore, it must also be remembered that people build their lives around references to the assortment of social worlds in which they spend considerable amounts of their time, and that the actions of individuals and groups, in this case immersed in migratory movements, contribute to the modification of the contexts in which they move.

This work considers the overall universe of the Algerian and Spanish populations in relation to the migration context, where family strategies cover an extended geographical space intertwined by strong family ties. At the same time, such flows can be studied under the longue durée of Mediterranean migration history (see the chronology in the next section). It is in this context that we review the case of Algerians and Spaniards in the Mediterranean, a case that provides an interesting picture of circular itineraries related to transborder practices between neighbouring countries and the political responses.

Most of the complexities around the circular nature of migration have been inspired by Tarrius' work (1995, 2000) on Mediterranean mobility. He is able to elucidate how migrant identities are not reaffirmed as characteristically stable but through populations marked by their movements; they operate through a combination of territory and movements. Tarrius (2000) introduces the term 'circular territories' to refer to certain population groups that are hallmarked by movements, coming and going, the type of entry and exit between worlds designed as different (2000: 8). Studies like the one developed by Tarrius make it possible to ask critical questions about the study of the social structure of migration on the basis of time–space geographies beyond the limits of the national space. Notwithstanding, those circularities cannot only be expressed by the actual physical mobility of the people themselves, but can also be related to the circuits of information which bind transnational communities, flows of information with the help of today's technologies and peoples' social lives between border cities and the migrants' dispersal around the globe. Therefore, the concept of territorial circularities will be emphasized to give relevance to the different groups in the population for whom movement is an essential characteristic, both coming and going and entering and leaving worlds represented as separate from one another. These mobilities will be located at case-study level when considering such categories in borderland settings, and how people express and consider them when managing their survival strategies. One case in point is Marseille, both a border and harbour city, and its '*Marché aux Puces*' entrepreneurs. There, rather than corresponding to the dynamics of ethnic business, family and community networks are widened to extra-kin relations (such as those formed by the peer group), combining transborder mobility, flexibility and relational competencies. Goods come from all over the world, and they combine the business circuits of southern Europe with the Algerian and Moroccan markets (Tarrius, 2000: 16). Tarrius refers here to an *économie de bazar*, the bazaar being the place where the different stages of the economic market can be found, the place of equilibrium between the logic of the economic rationalization of exchange and the logic of the different social orders.[1]

However, circular dynamics and migration flows must coexist with the administrative procedures that national states design to regulate such population trends. The flows between Spain and Algeria combine an amalgam of phenomena, for instance those analysed by the authors mentioned above. In this particular scenario, the visa procedure among countries began to be applied in the early 1990s, after Spain became a member of the European Economic Community in 1986. Since then, the visa policy has constituted a boundary that the political class is unwilling to take down, while citizens from both sides of the Mediterranean demand better living conditions through the amelioration of the visa procedure in order to continue these traditional flows, which constitute a particular transnational scenario in the Mediterranean arena.

This chapter sheds light on the tensions and distensions in Spanish–Algerian relations regarding the control of migrations and mobilities taking place in the transnational arena. In doing so, we include data from several research studies performed by the authors from the 1990s to the present, focusing on the migratory dynamics of Algerians and Spaniards and the public discourses of the Spanish political class regarding Spanish–Algerian bilateral relations. This takes the migration and mobility dynamics the authors have worked on into consideration from a qualitative perspective, using in-depth interviews from several fieldwork expeditions in Spain and Algeria between 1990 and 2016. Additionally, regarding the analysis of public discourse, a longitudinal study was conducted between 1985 and 2014 by analysing Spanish parliamentary bills and data from the Foreign Policy Database (BDPEX in Spanish).[2]

2. ESTABLISHING A CHRONOLOGY

The European Mediterranean region has interconnected neighbouring countries that have exchanged flows of goods, commodities and individuals for centuries. It offers an 'interesting laboratory' (Withol de Wenden, 2000) in which to study migration flows and responses from different social agents (politicians, the media) of the countries involved interacting in a multiplicity of processes. Migration in the Mediterranean region means an interweaving of different dynamics, from '*commerce à la valise*' – suitcase traders – (Tarrius, 1995), a circular migration perspective between France, Spain and Algeria, and the migration of refugees from Africa and the Middle East to Italy, Greece, or Portugal, to the labour mobilities from Spain to Algeria to cope with the constraints of the economic crisis after the financial crash of 2008 (Cabezón-Fernández, 2018) and the lifestyle migrations of EU citizens to Morocco, Algeria or Tunisia to retire in the sun (Le Bigot, 2016), with a lesser impact on local society than the mobilities of northern Europe to the Spanish Costa del Sol.

In these dynamics of people moving back and forth in this transnational social field (Pries, 2001; Levitt & Glick Schiller, 2004; Faist, 2010), borders have their own particularities depending on supranational migration policies (multilateral Euro-Mediterranean policies, which are less obvious in the cases of Morocco and Tunisia), national migration policies and binational migration policies. The last of these are articulated between countries that share borders and/or particular historical relationships, such as the physical borders shared by Spain and Morocco in Africa or the symbolic border between Spain and Algeria. This is due not only to historical cultural exchanges but also to the visa requirements for citizens who pretend to cross the border in either direction.

Southern European countries like Italy and Spain became the 'doors to Africa' with regard to the migratory policies of the EU after the 1985 signing of the Schengen Agreement, which promoted the free movement of individuals with an EU passport in the Schengen Area. Nevertheless, the migration flows between North Africa and southern European countries became a security issue on the EU international agenda, leading to the creation of so-called 'fortress Europe' (Morokvasic, 1991; Gil Araujo, 2003; Sassen, 2013) by increasing control and restricting flows from Africa to EU member states. Furthermore, a securitization approach in multilateral and bilateral relations in the Euro-Mediterranean region intensified after the 9/11 terrorist attacks in the United States, when international relations became aware of the issue of extremist terrorism, and the need to manage it occupied international public discourse, particularly in those countries that receive flows from the African continent and the Middle East, as well as the countries of North Africa most heavily impacted by the terrorist attacks.[3]

At a micro level, for those individuals who envision a long-term migration project or for those who choose to live transnationally in two or more nation-states, physically crossing a border is a key moment, usually preceded by a number of long administrative procedures to obtain a visa. In the case of Morocco and Spain there is no need for a visa, while a visa requirement was introduced in 1990 for Algeria and Spain.[4] At present, Algeria is a strategic country for the Spanish economy, particularly since 1974, when Spain signed the first agreement to import Algerian gas. Since then, diplomatic exchanges have been increasingly intense in order to achieve a cooperation compromise regardless of the national issues at play during different periods (for example the transition process in Spain from a dictatorship to a democratic nation in 1975 or the Algerian Civil War of 1990[5]). Furthermore, the distance between the two national coastlines is only 308 kilometres, which has fostered population flows, particularly between the northwest region of Algeria (Oran, Tlemcen) and southeast Spain (Alicante, Murcia, Almeria, Mallorca).

Managing migrations has been a steady concern, related to other matters such as trade and business relations and creating a secure space in the Mediterranean, with migration being linked to irregular migrations and the need to increase security to control possible terrorist movements. That securitization trend affects not only migration, but also mobility dynamics in the form of short-term strategies that are controlled by visa procedures. In the last two decades, there has been a disconnect between the political discourse and bilateral relations agenda between Spain and Algeria and the discourse of the population's demands (Soler i Lecha & Vianello, 2012; Cabezón-Fernández, 2017) about the need to ameliorate the visa procedure.

2.1 From 1962 to 1986: Initial Relations and Tensions Characterized by Domestic Situations

Algerian independence from France in 1962 marked the beginning of a period of almost 30 years without war in either Algeria or Spain. Although policies diverged and there were conflicts between the two governments, they did not affect the peace at the border during these decades.

After independence, the myth that Algeria had conquered imperialism took root. It expelled the 'colonists' and was once again an Arab-Muslim country with few foreigners in it. However, the reality was somewhat different. In addition to the hundreds of thousands of French people who still lived in the country, Algeria between the 1960s and 1980s was one of the great leaders of third-worldism, which made it an important destination for political migrants. In addition to exchanges with communist countries, some Westerners moved to Algeria to work on behalf of the country and the ideals represented by its revolution (Simon, 2009). Algeria also lent its support to Marxist liberation movements, particularly African ones, that were fighting against authoritarian regimes, as well as to other movements in the West, like the Movement for the Self-determination and Independence of the Canarian Archipelago (MPAIAC) and Euskadi Ta Askatasuna (ETA) in the Basque Country.[6] Several ETA militants, in particular, lived in Algeria during this period, with Algiers hosting the first negotiations between ETA and the Spanish government between 1986 and 1989 (Bustos, 2006).

For its part, Spain followed a divergent political trend, completing its integration into the European system and the West after the beginning of democracy in 1977. The country was also the site of Algerian political movements. During the presidencies of Chadli Bendjedid (1979–92) and, especially, Houari Boumédiène (1965–78), Algeria was a single-party dictatorship, and many Algerian activists took refuge in Spain. Ahmed Ben Bella, the first president of Algeria (1962–65) and founder of the underground Movement for Democracy in Algeria (MDA) party, was taken in by Spain in 1979. On 8 October 1988, the newspaper *Información de Alicante* ran a frontpage story entitled 'The MDA in Alicante claims to be leading the revolt in Algiers' (Gil, 1988).[7] After the article appeared, the Algerian authorities suspended the Alicante–Oran maritime connection between 11 October 1988 and 18 February 1989. In short, the population exchange motivated by political reasons was not large, but was continuous between the countries during this period.

In the same line, there was little economic migration between the 1960s and 1980s. One of the reasons for this, according to the World Bank, is that between 1960 and 1985, the per capita Gross National Product (GNP) in current dollars in Spain was between two and four times greater than that of Algeria. While this difference may be significant, it is far below the disparity found between 1991 and 2009, when the Spanish GNP was between eight and ten times greater than the Algerian GNP. At this time, Spaniards were no longer travelling to North Africa in search of employment, while the Algerians who lived abroad were concentrated exclusively in France, the primary destination since 1950. The French census reports from 1982 and 1990 indicate 805,116 and 614,207 Algerians living in the country, respectively, while only 1,183 Algerians appear in the 1991 Spanish census. Spain was still a long way from being a country of immigration and had few Algerian residents. However, some incipient movement in both directions detected at the time connected to transport, tourism and commerce began to expand as the 1980s progressed.

2.2 From 1986 to 2001: The Beginning of Spanish Migration Policies and Algerian Exceptionality

Spanish migration policies began to develop in the late 1980s in response to demands from the EU (at that time the EEC), which had scarcely begun to draw up measures to manage migration. The first EEC policies were established in 1970 as European Political Cooperation (later the Common Foreign and Security Policy or CFSP), the result of the Luxembourg/Davignon Report (Barbé, 1994), a document that laid the foundations for European migration policy to come after the signing of the Schengen Agreement in 1985. That same year, Spain's foreign policy began to take shape and the country passed its first Immigration Law in 1985 as a prerequisite for joining the EEC. Until that point, Spain had almost no legislation to control migration flows, since immigration was not perceived as a threat. Khader (2010) notes that, in 1985, there were 85,000 immigrants living in Spain, a number that rose to 211,100 in 1991 (not including data on foreigners living on irregular administrative situation), a year when 1,626,580 Spaniards were living abroad, in other words 'four and a half times the total number of foreign residents in Spain, i.e., 360,655' (Khader, 2010: 460). However, after the 1986 first regularization programme,[8] migration trends began to change, although this shift would not be considered critical by the political elite until the mid-1990s (Izquierdo, 1996). The legislation on immigration from the period indicates as much: (1) the management of admissions (the Immigration Law or Organic Law 7/1985), visa facilitation (upon approval of the implementation of a visa regime for non-EU countries after Spain joined the Schengen Agreement in 1991) and the quota system put into effect in 1993 to determine the social and labour profile of immigrants and the number of persons allowed; (2) control policies (border control, such as the construction of a fence in Melilla in 1998 and the creation of the Sea Civil Guard in 1993, holding facilities, management of repatriation and the various 'crossing the Strait' operations to coordinate vacationers travelling from Europe to Africa); and (3) integration policies (the 1991 and 1996 regularizations).

The Algerian dynamics reflect the political and economic situation in the country. The oil crisis, the lack of diversification in the economy and problems inherited from the colonial period exacerbated by the policies of the first post-independence governments led to a series of riots in 1988 after the price of basic commodities rose. With foreign collaboration limited to a few areas like oil and the government stuck in the discourse of independence without any real improvements for its citizens, Islamism began to rise. After the riots, the government of President Chadli Bendjedid passed the Law on Parties, took economic measures and held local and legislative elections (Volpi, 2003). However, this process of opening was interrupted by the military in January 1992, which effectively took control of the government when the Islamic Salvation Front won the first round of the parliamentary elections, sparking a civil war and the so-called 'dark decade', which finally came to an end in 2001. During this convulsive period, Algerian migration policies developed 'inside out', with the aim of protecting and managing the large Algerian community living in France and other countries. For the Algerian government, the value of this community was twofold: the importance of their vote and the income from remittances amidst deficits and international isolation.

In addition to these domestic contexts, the geographic proximity between the countries and the existing routes at that time, particularly the Alicante–Oran ferry line, which facilitates mobility and traffic between Spain and Algeria, as well as Algeria and France via Spain, continued to foster different kinds of dynamics, even though the flows were not that intense due to the contexts discussed above. This traffic increases during the summertime above all, when many Algerians living in France return to their country for vacation, passing through Spain instead of going directly from France. However, the intensity of the transit is not comparable to the port of Marseille. Driving from France to Alicante to take the ferry to Oran can be both faster and cheaper than going from France to Oran by boat, making it a particularly attractive option for families. As traffic has increased since the 1980s, Alicante has become the site of a flourishing bazaar-based economy. Beginning in the 1970s, Algerians would come to Spain to procure a wide variety of products that were not easy to obtain in a country with a planned economy like Algeria's. In the area around the port infrastructure in Alicante, an entire system of trade and an economy based on bazaars developed to sell products to Algerians for later export to Algeria by ferry (Sempere-Souvannavong, 2000; Sandoval-Hernández, 2018[9]).

To better picture the immigration situation in Spain, we looked at the survey conducted with irregular foreigners in 1996 by the Spanish Centre for Sociological Research (CIS in Spanish). From this data, 12 per cent of the surveyed population had emigrated before 1981, with the largest number of immigrants arriving between 1986 and 1990 (41.5 per cent). Of 1,981 people, 33.7 per cent had been born in Morocco, followed by 7.5 per cent in America, 7.3 per cent in Peru and 6 per cent in Algeria. Of the Algerians, 69.2 per cent had arrived as tourists and 74.2 per cent had already gone through an earlier regularization process as the holder of a work and/or residence permit. An analysis of foreigners in the 1996 Municipal Registry finds 4,614 Algerians in absolute terms. As in the survey, these numbers are much lower than the Moroccan population at the time (88,087).

Nevertheless, mobilities were the primary dynamic, meaning that the data for the Algerian population was insufficient to explain the bigger picture, including short-term dynamics. In this line of reasoning, the data on the visas issued by Spanish consulates in the Maghreb between 1996 and 1999 show that Algeria received the second highest number of visas, behind Morocco (Cabezón-Fernández, 2017). In a worldwide comparison, in 1996 Algeria ranked third with 24,571 visas issued, behind Morocco with 68,812 and 62,437 for Russia, where conditions governing travel abroad had been loosened (Marcu, 2007: 33). An analysis of the long- and short-term visas issued from 1996 to 2019 by the Spanish consulates in Algeria (Figure 16.1) shows both dynamics.[10] Whereas long-term visas remain almost constant over the whole period, the short-term visas issued indicate the importance of the dynamics associated with mobilities compared to migration dynamics associated with settlement processes. For instance, in 1999, 21,455 short-term visas were issued, while there were 455 long-term visas. Additionally, regarding the period between 1996 and 2000, the particular contexts are also reflected in this data, with a decrease in the number of visas in 1997 and an increase in

Spanish–Algerian border relations 259

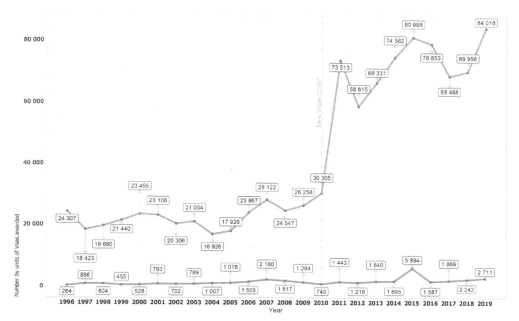

Source: Observatorio Permanente de la Immigración.

Figure 16.1   Evolution of visas awarded by Spanish consulates in Algeria (1996–2019)

1999, in sum, the hardest years of the Algerian Civil War and its end in 2000. Furthermore, the data from the Municipal Registry mentioned above shows that there were 4,614 Algerians with an official residence registered in Spain and 24,307 short-term visas issued the same year.

Despite the quite intense mobility shown by the visas, the Spanish public discourse focused on the phenomena related to the Algerian political migration due to the Civil War without paying particular attention to mobilities. For example, bills proposed by the Spanish parliament during the first two terms that coincide with this period, 1986–89 and 1989–93,[11] reveal that during the first term, the government's interest continued to centre around energy and negotiations with ETA (Cabezón-Fernández, 2017). It was only later that Islamism and the Algerian Civil War garnered interest, giving the agenda a more political and security-based cast. Questions related to the migration and mobility of Algerians were not a cause for concern in Spanish policy-making bodies at the time. It was only during the 1996–2000 parliamentary term that Spanish political attention began to focus on migration. Topics including granting visas to Algerians, surveillance of the Alicante–Oran ferry, the status of Algerian refugees and irregular immigrants in Melilla,[12] requests for asylum and how to manage the expulsion of Algerians all became the object of political attention in Spain. At this time, additionally, several bills addressed the 'political destabilization process in Algeria' and mentioned a 'possible mass exodus of Algerians to Spain'.

In brief, the beginning of the visa procedures between Spain and Algeria led to an awareness of the need to manage one type of migrations, but not all the phenomena taking place on the Spanish–Algerian scene. From a security perspective, the main concerns of the Spanish political class were related to maintaining trade relations, despite the political context in Algeria, a concern shared by Algeria at a time when their international connections were limited due to the war. Managing migrations for political reasons was the first step in the bilateral management of shared migrations and mobilities.

2.3 2001–2008: Terrorism and an Increasing Security Discourse in the Face of Rising Migration

Spanish–Algerian relations deepened in the early twenty-first century due, above all, to an improvement in the economic and political situation in Algeria. The end of the Algerian Civil War and the subsequent Civil Concord led to a period of stability, accompanied by economic improvements and the country's recovery of its international presence after the political blockade that characterized the years of conflict. However, in an international context distinguished by Islamic terrorism, bilateral relations became increasingly securitized. This included the management of migration, which continued to be a secondary theme within the shared agenda.

The attacks on the World Trade Center in the United States marked a turning point that influenced the security question in relations between the West and the Arab world. Strengthened by its experience during the Civil War, Algeria asserted itself as a standard-bearer in the fight against terrorism as a way of recovering its international position. In fact, in June 2001, a few months before 9/11, the Algerian Mohamed Bensakhria, the leader of a commando unit with ties to Al-Qaeda, was arrested in Alicante as part of an international operation. This congruity with Algeria represented an opportunity for Spain, which wished to offset the problems between the government of Prime Minister José María Aznar and Morocco. In July 2000, Aznar made the first official visit of a European leader to Algeria since the end of the Civil War (Thieux, 2007). This outreach was consolidated in 2002 with the signing of the Treaty of Friendship, Good Neighbourliness and Cooperation between Spain and Algeria and, indirectly, with the crisis between Spain and Morocco over Perejil Island. The combination of the conflict with Morocco, collaboration on security issues and gas imports led Spain to consider Algeria a top-tier partner, and high-level meetings between the two countries began to be held in 2003.

The terrorist bombings of 11 March 2004 in Madrid reaffirmed Spain's political line with respect to the Maghreb. During this period, Spain developed border control policies that aligned even more with European trends, while at the same time dealing with the question of how to manage the immigration of several hundred thousand people a year during the first decade of the century. With migration at the centre of the political agenda, migration policies began to multiply, especially after 2006 (Pinyol Jiménez, 2007), when 31,678 Africans arrived in the Canary Islands during the 'Cayuco Crisis', so called for the wooden boats they used. During these years, irregular emigration from Algeria to Spain was revealed when the number of *Harragas*,[13] young Algerians trying to cross the Mediterranean in makeshift boats, increased. This situation had a substantial impact on Algerian and Maghrebi civil society as hundreds of young people left to cross the sea and dozens disappeared.

As a consequence of this rise in illegal entries and the transformation of the Spanish southern border into the EU border, the Spanish government decided to harden its southern border and accelerate the installation of the Integrated System of External Vigilance (SIVE), a network of high-technology stations (radars, cameras, long-range acoustic sensors) that made it possible to detect illegal maritime entries. The installation of the SIVE system along the entire southern maritime border of Spain – from the Canary Islands to the Balearic Islands, passing across the Peninsula and Ceuta and Melilla – was completed in 2012.

Moreover, since the early 2000s and particularly the 'Cayuco Crisis', Spain and the EU have promoted the externalization of the EU's borders, by which countries of origin and, especially, countries of transit for Africans headed to Europe control migration themselves. This process, which continues to be reinforced and extended, consists of supporting training for the border police in these countries, signing conventions to readmit migrants and convincing these countries to pass laws that penalize the illegal entry, transit and exit of people. Since Morocco passed the first of these laws in 2003 – Law 02-03 on the entry and stay of foreign nationals and irregular immigration and emigration – all African countries north of the Sahel, including Algeria, have signed on to the policy to control migration towards Europe. Thus, the border between Spain and Algeria, in other words between Spain and Africa, was transformed during the 2000s into a key piece in the external border of the Schengen space. As a consequence of both this process of externalizing the Spanish and European borders and an increase in emigration in the Sahel countries, Algeria, like Morocco and Tunisia, has witnessed an unexpected increase in foreign immigration. Since the first decade of the century, hundreds of thousands of Africans have been living and working in the Maghreb. In Algeria, these people have recently been joined by refugees from Arab countries at war like Libya, Syria and Iraq.

Immigration appears in some specific pieces of legislation, two of which are related to the Civil War as a source of Algerian emigration. The Spanish 2000–2004 parliament, for instance, proposed a bill to improve the situation for 700 Algerian immigrants living in Melilla (Bill 25), some of whom were fleeing the war. Spanish political concern was also directed at the consequences of the war for Spanish citizens living in Algeria; Bills 26 to 29 requested registries from the consular offices in Oran and Algiers and the number of deceased (Cabezón-Fernández, 2017). The Algerian community in Spain has also figured on the bilateral agenda in the form of bills calling for the registries of requests for Spanish nationality in the municipalities of Burgos and Murcia in addition to requests for family reunification. The discourse on immigration in these bills corresponds to international and national trends linking irregular immigration and terrorism, as seen in Bill 65, which contains language about the number of interns from Morocco and Algeria possibly fomenting extremist behaviour.

With an eye towards increasing border security, bills have requested information about the progress made in collaboration with the Algerian National Gendarmerie regarding the Judicial Police and immigration since 6 May, 2005 (Bill 56) and the signing of an extradition agreement between the People's Democratic Republic of Algeria and the Kingdom of Spain (Bill 55) that was negotiated after an Algerian terrorist commando unit was detained in Almeria. These bills all dovetail with general Spanish trends in immigration management, focusing on admission and fledgling integration efforts while trying to understand an immigration situation that is just starting to make itself known, all at a time when Algeria was beginning to be confronted by the illegal emigration associated with the *Harragas* and working with the destinations where its international community had settled.

During this period, the administration of visas is only reflected with regard to the Sahrawi question, with Bills 30 to 34 requesting information about the number of Sahrawi refugees in Tindouf and visa administration for this group and the signature of a protocol on the circulation of persons, a topic that emerged at the end of 2020 due to the political crisis amongst the Moroccan and the Polisario Front. Spanish visa policy aligns with Schengen policy, prioritizing security and control of immigration (Macías-Aymar et al., 2012: 55) to the detriment of mobility. Finally, with a view to participating in the market development plans, the Spanish business sector made a comparative study of visa administration processes in India, Algeria and Colombia (Ibid: 61), and although the investigation went no further, it is one of the few actions that reveals an interest in mobility towards Algeria related to economics.

2.4 2008–2019: Ever-increasing Mobility, Despite Border Securitization

The evolution of migration and mobility dynamics in this period highlights the diversification of phenomena linked to domestic contexts. First, an international trend has influenced the securitization of migration control, in particular the irregular flows linked first to international terrorism and then to the increase in the number of asylum seekers in Europe due to instability in Afghanistan, Syria and other countries experiencing violent conflicts. Second, at national level, Spain was affected by the international economic downturn due to the financial crash that began in 2008. Third, a time of bonanza in the Algerian economy led to the emergence of a middle class and the diversification of the national economy. In brief, the population dynamics correspond in some way to these two phenomena: the diversification of the Algerian dynamics vis-à-vis Spain and the renewed dynamics of Spaniards towards Algeria. Both share a commonality: criticisms of the visa procedure, a public demand from Algerian migrants since the 1990s, has now become a demand shared by Spaniards who have begun to live transnationally between the two countries.

2.4.1 The Algerian lifestyle migration and the renewal of 'trade in a suitcase'

During the 2000s, the bazaar-based commerce discussed above transformed when the Algerian economy opened up and a number of significant changes took place in the country. Thanks to the rising price of hydrocarbons, the per capita GNP in Algeria multiplied by 2.4 between 1997 and 2007 and by 3.6 from 1997 to 2014. Despite the non-convertible nature of the Algerian dinar and the requirement to obtain a visa to enter Spain, Algerian society continues to import products from the country, especially Alicante. However, consumption trends have changed. While basic consumer products purchased in the bazaars were exported to Algeria in the 1980s, in 2010, luxury products began to be purchased in franchises, department stores and shopping centres in Alicante and the surrounding area. These exports are done through a network of people and services that has been reproduced over decades. Each time that a ferry arrives from Algeria, dozens of merchants and carriers disembark in the morning, buy products while they are in Alicante, and embark again in the afternoon to return to Algeria on the same vessel. The products transported are legal and their export is tolerated, but the import process is irregular.

In addition to this commercial mobility, Algerian tourism in Spain has increased at an astonishing rate since the 2000s thanks to rising Algerian purchasing power. The coast of the province of Alicante and, most notably, the city of Benidorm are highly valued tourist destinations for thousands of Algerians who spend their family vacations in hotels or rented apartments. They particularly appreciate the infrastructure, security and peacefulness, as well as the welcoming treatment they receive from the local population, in comparison with their perception regarding their welcome in France. Another growing trend in Algerian tourism is the consumption of cultural and health services, such as ophthalmology and aesthetics in private consultancies oriented to the elite.

These renewed circular mobilities indicate how Algerians choose Spain as a regular tourism destination as well as for medical treatments. Like the British on the Costa del Sol and the

Germans in Majorca, some Algerians have decided to acquire a second residence in Spain to reduce costs and facilitate the organization of their daily life when living in the country. This is possible because a type of middle class emerged in Algeria right when prices in the real estate sector were falling in Spain and, as a consequence, a significant number of Algerians purchased low- or mid-range housing in the Alicante region. This consumption trend also corresponds to a fear of the instability that is always latent in Algeria, as reflected by the 2011 Arab Spring uprisings and the 2019 demonstrations that convinced President Bouteflika not to run for a fifth term. According to the Spanish yearbook of the Association of Property Registrars of Spain, in 2013 Algerians ranked ninth among foreign property buyers in the country, the third largest non-EU group after the Russians and Norwegians and the highest ranking non-European group (Fabra Garcés, 2013). As a result, Algerians come to Spain on a regular basis, and those who have bought homes in the country have been particularly insistent over the years in asking the Spanish Embassy in Algeria to establish visa facilities and guarantees.

2.4.2 Contemporary Spanish expatriates: transnational dynamics

Spaniards have largely forgotten their shared migration past with Algeria. The flows of Spaniards in the nineteenth century and at the end of the Spanish Civil War represent the last period when Algeria was an important country of destination for Spaniards. It is only in the current decade that the population flows from Spain to Algeria have become reactivated due to trade. During the 1990s, companies in sectors like energy and fishing became interested in the country's resources, despite the civil conflict. Later, in the 2000s, the rising Algerian GNP and massive state investments in housing and infrastructure attracted large companies from those sectors. Finally, beginning in 2008, when the financial crisis erupted in Spain, many Spanish small and medium-sized enterprises (SMEs), particularly in the construction sector, tried to find business solutions in Algeria. They participated in a large number of construction projects, including a potable water project overseen since 2008 by a subsidiary of the company Aguas de Barcelona; the building of the Oran Convention Centre between 2008 and 2011 by the OHL Group, and, most notably, the construction of the first tram line in Oran by Isolux Corsán (2008–12), a milestone in the city's transportation image. Although these projects were directed by large companies, numerous SMEs were subcontracted and these undertakings were accompanied by the constant movement of Spanish workers between Algeria and Spain, which reached its zenith between 2010 and 2015. Since then, a decline in currency reserves in Algeria due to falling gas prices has limited the country's ability to hire foreign companies for construction work and, consequently, lessened the movement of Spanish workers in the direction of Algeria.

One indicator of the increase of the exchange of population flows between countries is the data published by Aeropuertos Españoles y Navegación Aérea, the Spanish National Airlines Service (AENA, 2020), on the number of passengers on flights from Spain to Algeria and vice versa. Figure 16.2 shows the increase in the number of passengers (regardless of nationality) in 2001 and 2002, coinciding with the end of the Algerian Civil War. The numbers then decrease slightly until 2007, when they increase to 200,000 passengers, largely concentrated between three Spanish airports: Alicante, Barcelona and Madrid. After 2012, regular commercial flights between the two countries were operated by Air Algerie and Iberia, the two national airline companies. Around 2011, some low-cost airlines such as Vueling started to operate regular commercial flights from Alicante and Barcelona to Oran and Algiers. This trend has

264 *Handbook on human security, borders and migration*

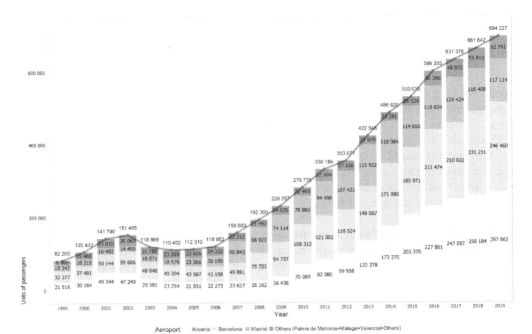

Source: Aena 2020.

Figure 16.2   *Evolution of passenger flows between Spanish and Algerian airports (1999–2019)*

continued, with more than 600,000 passengers being served since 2016, and was not even affected by the financial crisis in Spain.

As more Spaniards become transnational migrants – or contemporary Spanish expatriates – they have been forced to face the issue of the visa procedure. For third-country-national expatriates, their company usually takes care of the paperwork. However, the businesspeople and entrepreneurs working in freelance activities, such as, for instance, architecture, need to navigate the visa procedure themselves. The qualitative data gathered between 2012 and 2016 indicates that a key issue when living transnationally is the visa procedure. In some cases, businesspeople lost professional opportunities due to delays in the procedure that caused them to miss deadlines to apply for public contracts in the infrastructure or construction sector. Spanish demands regarding delays in acquiring visas now coincide with the demands of the Algerians discussed in Soler i Lecha and Vianello (2012) criticizing the constant change in the requirements for periodic business trips from Algeria to Spain (2012: 207) and the difficulties for Algerian students and professors wanting to participate in transnational research projects, due to the denial of their visa (2012: 205). These difficulties are solved, in some cases, by Spaniards' changing their itineraries to spend more time in Algeria (Cabezón-Fernández, 2018), where they create better social networks and gain access to, for example, construction projects that are unavailable to them when they reside only in Spain. Nevertheless, the visa procedure remains unchanged.

3. CONCLUSION

Algeria and Spain are two neighbouring countries that share a maritime border over which people, ideas and merchandise have moved for centuries. There has been no war between the two countries since the nineteenth century, but the various internal conflicts in each of the individual countries has had an impact on the other in the form of refugees, as at the end of the Spanish Civil War and the Algerian War of Independence. This Euro-Mediterranean border does not represent an example of a 'violent border', but a border that has evolved due to several tensions at different levels: the political tensions related to the management of secure relations for domestic and shared economies; and the tensions caused by visa procedures in the daily lives of Algerians and Spaniards who seek to work or spend time in the other country.

As this chapter has shown, circular dynamics are not new in the Mediterranean or between Spain and Algeria. As Tarrius and Peraldi have observed, circularity has evolved from being a dynamic performed only by the low or mid-to-lower classes to involve the middle class. While trade has served as a motivation, other new catalysts have produced circular dynamics of different types that can be included under the theoretical umbrella of lifestyle migration. Tourism, leisure activities and health treatments are a new interest for the Algerian middle class seeking these services beyond its borders. One particularly new trend appearing in European lifestyle migration literature (Benson & O'Reilly, 2009; Gustafson, 2008; Huete et al., 2013) concerns individuals from countries in the north looking for locations in the south for retirement, leisure or other kinds of services. The main destinations studied were Italy, Spain and Portugal, but other researchers have recently analysed the logic of north–south trends, flows from Europe (Bredeloup & Gois, 2016) to countries like Morocco (Escher & Petermann, 2013), Tunisia (Faranda, 2015) and Algeria. Spaniards became involved in these circular dynamics for labour reasons, a result of the financial crisis that began in 2008 and intensified after 2012, years when Spain recorded the highest amounts of social exclusion, unemployment and the destruction of small businesses. These contemporary Spanish expatriates (Cabezón-Fernández, 2018), some of whom were wealthier migrants (Meier, 2014) (like the Algerian middle class in this case), looked for job opportunities in response to the precarization of their lives at a time of instability and risk (Beck & Grande, 2010). The data analysed in this chapter demonstrates how the population flows between the two countries have increased considerably since the 2000s, largely thanks to the growth of airlines making regular daily flights between them. However, the political discourse has paid less attention to these phenomena. Nonetheless, this study has clearly shown that the transnational dynamics between the two countries are more intense than ever, with the nature of the motivations behind the circular dynamics and the individuals involved having diversified.

From the historical analysis made in this chapter, it is clear that bilateral relations between the two countries led to a hardening of migration control policies (in particular regarding irregular migration) in order to sustain economic relations, the basis of the shared agenda between Spain and Algeria. The imposition of a visa and the establishment of a detection system for irregular entries into Spain reveal how the border has gone from being a boundary between two countries with a similar degree of development to what increasingly appears to be a wall against migration between what is perceived as rich, ageing Europe and poor, young Africa. Soler i Lecha and Vianello (2012) have stated that visa procedures usually establish an asymmetrical relationship between countries, leading to a clear disadvantage for the population coming from the south. Nevertheless, this case study has shown that the visa procedure causes difficulties for both Algerians and Spaniards. In response to the constraints resulting from the financial crisis of 2008, individuals from Spain have been involved in making demands for better conditions regarding the visa procedure, as the Algerians have been doing for decades. The visa procedure, then, represents a shared issue for both Algerians and Spaniards moving within the logic of mobilities instead of migrations. For the first time in these shared relations, Algerian and Spanish civil societies are making the same demand to the political class: to ameliorate visa procedures and, thus, promote better conditions in the current mobility dynamics in the transnational Mediterranean arena created by flows of various individuals. Although there is an Algerian immigration of workers and family members in Spain, the bulk of the movements between the two countries is related to leisure, business and commercial mobility. Since the late 1990s, this mobility has diversified and grown dramatically, irrespective of the periods of crisis that have occurred in the two countries. In other words, migration is on the agenda, while mobility is still an issue ripe for control (because it takes place between 'fortress Europe' and Africa), but not for in-depth management.

NOTES

1. Beginning in the 2000s, ethnographies on Mediterranean cross-border trade began to be produced. Early works by Tarrius, followed by Peraldi (2001), led to a proliferation of such ethnographies within the framework of '*globalisation par le bas*' or grassroots globalization.
2. Database available: https://bdpexonline.org/acerca.php.
3. For some articles on terrorist attacks, for instance in Casablanca, 2003, see *El País*, 13 May 2003, retrieved from: https://elpais.com/diario/2003/05/18/internacional/1053208801_850215.html; and Madrid, 2004, see *El País*, 11 April 2004, retrieved from: https://elpais.com/elpais/2004/03/11/actualidad/1078996617_850215.html.
4. With the introduction of the visa for the three North African countries, Spain (which, with Denmark, stood alone among the EU members in not requiring visas for the three Maghrebi states of Morocco, Algeria and Tunisia), moved closer to the Schengen Group (see Ignacio Cembrero in *El País*, retrieved from: https://elpais.com/diario/1990/12/10/espana/660783616_850215.html.
5. See Volpi (2003).
6. Between 1958 and 2018, ETA was a Basque nationalist organization that resorted to violence to fight for the independence of the Basque Country.
7. Once one of the historical figures of the Algerian Revolution and an activist opponent of the regime, Mohamed Khider was a refugee in Madrid who was killed in 1967.
8. According to Aguilera Izquierdo, this legal procedure paved the way for the legalization of foreign workers in Spain without the corresponding administrative authorizations: 'The first procedure known as "regularization" or "normalization", consists of granting the legally required administrative authorizations to foreigners who meet the requirements of the rule that approves the corresponding regularization process at any point.'
9. The author analyses the commerce of second-hand clothes in the Mediterranean, especially between Spain and Morocco. The two main points are Muro and Cocentaine, two locations in Valencia, near Alicante. They are not very far from the Alicante harbour. Here, the '*balas*' (packs) are organized to reach not only Ceuta and Melilla and Oran, but also other points in Africa, and are divided by their quality. Some are sent as far away as Paraguay.
10. Although the methodology to categorize the long-term visas changed, we refined the data in order to create Figure 16.1.
11. According to the Spanish Senate's dictionary of parliamentary terms, a bill is an 'act whereby parliamentary proceedings are initiated which can be legislative in nature or might pertain to authorization, supervision and political impetus or the election of other bodies'. Tracking these bills reveals the issues of concern for Spanish policy-making bodies at any given time.

12. Since the closure of the land borders in August 1994, the region of Maghnia in Algeria, like that of Oujda in Morocco, has been linked by roadways essential for the maintenance of family ties, as well as for smuggling. The populations in the border areas largely live off the illicit trade of 'food' smuggling via organized networks, mules or the trunks/boots of cars. Working in *'trabendo'* (a contraction of the Spanish *'contrabando'*) is tantamount to conducting informal trading activities which, prima facie, are beyond the control of the state. This black or parallel market is closely linked to the question of borders, passage and transgression.
13. *Harraga* is an Arabic word used to refer to the candidates for emigration (adults and minors) who try to illegally cross the Mediterranean.

REFERENCES

Aguilera Izquierdo, Raquel, "El acceso de los inmigrantes irregulares al mercado de trabajo: Los procesos de regularización extraordinaria y el arraigo social y laboral". *Revista del Ministerio de Trabajo e Inmigración*, 63, (2006): 175–196.

Barbé, Esther, "Entre Europa y América Latina: la diplomacia española frente al conflicto de las Malvinas". *Estudios Internacionales*, 106, (1994): 222–251.

Beck, Ulrich & Grande, Edgar, "Varieties of second modernity: The cosmopolitan turn in social and political theory and research". *The British Journal of Sociology*, 61(3), (2010): 409–443.

Benson, Michael & O'Reilly, Karen, "Migration and the search for a better way of life: A critical exploration of lifestyle migration". *The Sociological Review*, 57(4), (2009): 608–625.

Bredeloup, Sylvie & Gois, P., "De l'Europe vers les Sud: Nouvelles itinérances ou migrations á rebours?". *Autrepart*, 1(77), (2016): 3–15.

Bustos García de Castro, Rafael, "Las relaciones España–Argelia, una mirada desde España". *Anuario internacional CIDOB*, 1, (2006): 499–506.

Cabezón-Fernández, María-Jesús, "Las migraciones en la agenda hispano-argelina. De la realidad social a la invisibilidad bilateral". *Revista de Estudios Internacionales Mediterráneos*, 22, (2017): 77–108.

Cabezón-Fernández, María-Jesús, "North to south. The Spaniards' mobility strategies in Algeria in times of crisis. Postcolonial continuities from contemporary expatriates' bubbles". Thesis, Alicante, University of Alicante, 2018.

Escher, Anton & Petermann, Sandra, "Marrakesh Medina: Neocolonial paradise of lifestyle migrants?". In M. Janoschka & H. Haas (eds.) *Contested spatialities, lifestyle migration and residential tourism*. Abingdon, UK: Routledge, 2013, 45–62.

Fabra Garcés, Luis A., *"Estadística Registral Inmobiliaria". Anuario 2013*, Madrid: Colegio de Registradores de la Propiedad, Bienes Muebles y Mercantiles de España, 2013.

Faist, Thomas, "Towards transnational studies: World theories, transnationalisation and changing institutions". *Journal of Ethnic and Migration Studies*, 36(10), (2010): 1665–1687.

Faranda, Laura, "La vita è altrove? L'autunno mediterraneo dei pensionati italiani in Tunisia, tra conflitti e crisi". *Etno Antropologia*, 3(1), (2015): 97–112.

Gil, Juan R., "El MDA asegura que organizó en Alicante la revuelta de Argel", *Diario Información de Alicante* (8 October 1988): 1–3.

Gil Araujo, Sandra, "Las migraciones en las políticas de la Fortaleza. Sobre las múltiples fronteras de la Europa comunitaria". In S. Gil Araujo & M. Dahiri (eds.) *Movimientos migratorios en el Mediterráneo occidental.¿Un fenómeno o un problema?*, 2003: 31–58.

Gustafson, Per, "Transnationalism in retirement migration: The case of North European retirees in Spain". *Ethnic and Racial Studies*, 31(3), (2008): 451–475.

Huete, Raquel, Mantecón, Alejandro & Estévez, Jesús, "Challenges in lifestyle migration research: Reflections and findings about the Spanish crisis". *Mobilities*, 8(3), (2013): 331–348.

Izquierdo, Antonio, *La inmigración inesperada. Análisis de la población extranjera en España (1990–1994)*, Madrid: Editorial Trotta, 1996.

Khader, Bichara, *El mundo árabe explicado a Europa: historia, imaginario, cultura, política, economía, geopolítica*, Barcelona: Icaria, 2010.

Le Bigot, Brenda, "Les migrations hivernales des Européens vers le Maroc: circulations et constructions des espaces de vie". *Autrepart*, (1), (2016): 51–68.
Levitt, Peggy & Glick Schiller, Nina, "Conceptualizing simultaneity: A transnational social field perspective on society". *International Migration Review*, 38(3), (2004): 1002–1039.
Macías-Aymar, Íñigo, De Pedro, Nicolás & Pérez, Francisco A., "La dimensión económica de la política de visados de España". In E. Sánchez-Montijano, J. Vaquer i Fanés & E.Viilup (eds.) *La política de visados para el siglo XXI: más allá de la cola del visado*, Barcelona: CIDOB, 2012: 55–78.
Marcu, Silvia, "España y la geopolítica de la inmigración en los albores del siglo XXI", *Cuadernos Geográficos*, 40, (2007): 31–51.
Meier, Lars, *Migrant professionals in the city: Local encounters, identities and inequalities*, Abingdon, UK: Routledge, 2014.
Morokvasic, Mirjana, "Fortress Europe and migrant women". *Feminist Review*, 39(1), (1991): 69–84.
Peraldi, Michael (ed.), *Cabas et containers. Activités marchandes informelles et réseaux migrants transfrontaliers*, Paris: Maisonneuve et Larose, 2001.
Pinyol Jiménez, Gemma, "España en la construcción del escenario euroafricano de migraciones" *Revista CIDOB d'afers internacionals*, 79–80, (2007): 87–105.
Pries, Ludger, "The disruption of social and geographic space: Mexican–US migration and the emergence of transnational social spaces". *International Sociology*, 16(1), (2001): 55–74.
Ribas-Mateos, Natalia, *The Mediterranean in the age of globalization: Migration, welfare, and borders*, Piscataway, NJ: Transaction Publishers, 2005.
Sandoval-Hernández, Efrén, Rosenfeld, M. & Peraldi, M, "La fripe du Nord au Sud. Production globale, commerce transfrontalier et marchés informels de vêtements usagés", Paris: Editions PETRA, 2019.
Sassen, Saskia, *Inmigrantes y ciudadanos: De las migraciones masivas a la Europa Fortaleza*, Spain: Siglo XXI España, 2013.
Sempere-Souvannavong, Juan-David, "El tránsito de argelinos por el puerto de Alicante". *Investigaciones geográficas*, 24, (2000): 111–130.
Simon, Catherine, *Algérie, les années pieds-rouges. Des rêves de l'indépendance au désenchantement (1962–1969)*, Paris: La Découverte, 2009.
Soler i Lecha, Eduard & Vianello, Alvise, "La inalcanzable tercera 'M': visados y movilidad de personas en las relaciones euromediterráneas". In Sánchez-Montijano et al. (eds.), *La política de visados para el Siglo XXI. Más allá de la cola del visado*. Barcelona: CIDOB, 2012.
Tarrius, Alain, *Arabes de France dans l'économie mondiale souterraine* (Monde en cours), La Tour d'Aigues: Éditions de l'Aube, 1995.
Tarrius, Alain, *Les nouveaux cosmopolitismes. Mobilités, identités, territoires*, La Tour d'Aigues: Éditions de l'Aube, 2000.
Thieux, Laurence, "Las relaciones hispano-argelinas desde el final de los años ochenta: el laborioso camino hacia un verdadero partenariado estratégico", *Anales de Historia Contemporánea*, 23, (2007): 241–258.
Volpi, Frédéric, *Islam and democracy. The failure of dialogue in Algeria*, London: Pluto Press, 2003.
Withol de Wenden, Catherine, *¿Hay que abrir las fronteras?*, Barcelona: Bellaterra, 2000.

17. Neighbour or stranger? Bordering practices in a small Catalan town

Martin Lundsteen

1. INTRODUCTION

European politics is at a turning point. Faced with increasing migration, extremism, transnational crimes, and a variety of other ostensible external security threats, most European countries have recently taken new and alternative steps to police and secure internal borders. Contrary to agreed-upon doctrines of globalisation and free mobility in the European Union (EU), member states have reinserted physical border controls, invested heavily in surveillance technologies, and furthered legalisation to surveil and minimise the means and mobility of many non-citizens, unintentionally affecting many citizens alike (Yuval-Davis, Wemyss and Cassidy, 2017). These socio-political and -legal practices conform a crucial pattern which might indeed have far-reaching consequences for the social cohesion of the increasingly diverse societies of the EU (Hage, 2000) to the point where we might even be faced with a new social question (Lundsteen, 2020c).

Until recently, several thought-provoking studies have been conducted in the fields of sociology and criminology, thoroughly highlighting the problematic legal and political elements of this transition. In fact, this chapter builds on the ideas of this path-breaking research, often designated interchangeably as *crimmigration* (Stumpf, 2006). In this tradition the criminological concepts reflect how contemporary criminal law and criminal justice are increasingly being used to police the boundaries of legal or illegal practices in society, and how jurisprudence in a growingly globalised world is used to demarcate the line between wanted citizens and unwanted non-citizens forcefully, and to reinforce racialised, classed, and gendered hierarchies around citizenship and belonging. Criminal law and justice are, thus, replacing border checks as a primary present-day technology of inclusion/exclusion (Carbado and Harris, 2011; Provine and Doty, 2011; Armenta, 2017).

While social control of populations deemed dangerous or contaminating is nothing new – sociology, urbanism and criminology indeed emerged from this preoccupation (Wolf, 1982; Lundsteen, 2015) – we are certainly seeing new path-breaking trends in the social policies and jurisprudence of the advanced liberal societies of the EU in the last decades. Hence, recent investigations have devoted attention to the counter-terrorist legislation and its adverse effects on Muslims (Kundnani, 2014), on the deportation regime and its social consequences (De Genova and Peutz, 2010; Kalir, 2019), and on the functioning and political consequences of the cross-national anti-drug enforcement and transnational organised drug trade and smuggling between Africa and Europe (Vigh and Sausdal, 2018). Similarly, although border and migration scholars have emphasised the 'downgrading' (Walters, 2002), 'loosening' (Guittet, 2017) or 'dissolution' (Rozakou, 2017) of internal intra-state EU borders in an area of free movement, ubiquitous boundaries – and bordering practices have arisen in parallel with the reinstating of borders and border regimes (Walters, 2002; Kallius, Monterescu and Rajaram, 2016).

What this recent work on borders shows us is how there is no single, unitarian organising logic at work; instead, the border constitutes a site of constant encounter, tension, and contestation. One should, therefore, rather speak about *bordering practices*, recognising the ongoing process involving social relations that are historically constituted and often politically contested (Mezzadra and Neilson, 2013; Dijstelbloem and Walters, 2019). Consistent with this viewpoint, a rich body of scholarship has developed to explain how these practices have transformed nation-states, economies, subjectivities, and citizenship (see Dauvergne, 2008; Pickering and Weber, 2006; Weber, 2015).

These *bordering practices* are measures taken by state institutions to attain social order and gain legitimacy by demarcating categories of people to incorporate some and exclude others (Guentner et al., 2016), a subtle policing of the internal boundaries of the citizenry which has quite often been ignored (Anderson, 2013; Anderson and Hughes, 2015). In fact, we see a rise in community policies targeting uncivil behaviour, especially informal economic practices, implemented with the explicit aim of making certain neighbourhoods 'more secure' (Lundsteen and Fernández González, 2020). However, only little attention has been paid to the unintended social and political effects on society in general, and more specifically, on what Ghassan Hage – paraphrasing Bourdieu (1990) – has called the 'field of belonging' (Hage, 2000). This chapter aims to engage with this bourgeoning line of research by bridging several theoretical traditions of critical scholarship that scrutinise the political use of notions of civility and the negotiation of what is considered appropriate behaviour or out-of-place in the urban space; this way drawing attention to what I call, paraphrasing Fassin (2008), a 'moral economy of belonging'.

2. THE CASE: A SMALL TOWN IN CATALONIA

To this end, the small town of Salt, located in the northern part of Catalonia, is optimal. On the one hand, the aspiration of Catalan independence (Guibernau, 2013; Lluch, 2014) promises a new state that will be a step towards a fairer and more just world, while, on the other hand, being a response to various local and non-local demands for social rights and sovereignty. As an occurrence which happens in a specific historic context, the impact of the political, economic and institutional crisis in the local–global contexts, with its spatial expression or *spatial fix* (Harvey, 1982), makes it relevant to look at the different idioms or *dispositifs* with which people try to give meaning to these changing times.

For instance, although officially the Catalan nation strives to be intercultural (Conversi and Jeram, 2017), the question remains how this is actually lived out and perceived on the local scale of the cities and neighbourhoods. While several authors have been interested in the conceptualisation of 'convivència' (Erickson, 2011), a concept which has no clear translation into English, but which is often used to refer to a situation that goes beyond mere 'coexistence', meaning an attitude of 'live and let live' (Lundsteen, 2020b), indeed, quite often it is conceptualised in positive terms as 'the practices of everyday living together that everyone should strive for' (Heil, 2014: 456) – others also point to the social stratification inherent to these romantic depictions of everyday life in Catalonia (Clua i Fainé, 2011). Elsewhere I have analysed the relationship between cultural conflicts and the production of space through the opposition to the building of a mosque in another small town (Lundsteen, 2020a). Here I propose a more grounded description and analysis of the workings of this *convivència* in practice. Because, in order to fully comprehend the workings of bordering in practice, one must indeed rely on an inter- and intra-groupal study at local level *situated* within the specific politic and economic context of study, and its multiple scales:

> If we are to understand what happens in villages within complex systems [...] we need not only a better understanding of political economy, of the processes of economic funding of power capabilities, but also one of political ecology, of the system of relationships between groups possessed of differential access to resources, power, and symbols. (Cole and Wolf, 1974: 286)

3. EVERYDAY BORDERING PRACTICES IN SALT (GIRONA)

For several years (from 2011 to 2014 and from 2016 to 2019) I have been conducting research in Salt, a small town right next to Girona. Salt constitutes a spatial expression of the existing social and ethnic inequalities in the region. It has around 30,000 inhabitants, many of whom are working-class, a large number of unemployed (24.56% of the active population in 2012), and the general level of income per habitant is the second lowest in all of Catalonia (Spanish Statistical Office, 2012). Of these inhabitants around 40% have a nationality other than Spanish. The majority settled in the town at the beginning of the 2000s, arriving often from Morocco, Senegal, Gambia or Honduras. At the same time some of the old inhabitants moved out, leaving behind them broken neighbourhoods in terms of social ties and the material condition of the houses; a social production of space which further divided an already segregated town, and left areas socially unattended and degrading (see Lundsteen, 2015, 2019).

During the period of 2011–2014 I carried out extensive fieldwork living in three different locations of the town, focusing observations mainly on the social interactions and the way people were living together in the central neighbourhood where the majority of the social problems were taking place. My research is comprised of an initial qualitative and open-ended period of data collection, which I later complemented with informal conversations and more formal interviews.

Through my study I was able to see how, in contrast to the static descriptions often portrayed in the media, the inhabitants would negotiate boundaries of the social groups through their daily encounters and relations. Some people seem to know each other, others recognise someone as 'one of them', while the distance from others seems greater, but through the daily interaction the border and boundaries are continuously (re)drawn and crossed. The following is an observation from my field notes:

> Today in Mari Carmen's bar I met an elder lady called Josefa, she was 89 years old and Mari Carmen's mother-in-law. Both of them were originally from Andalusia. When I entered the bar with Mostafa they were talking together, while a Moroccan-looking guy was reading the newspaper at one of the tables. Mostafa said 'Hi' to the ladies, and greeted the guy shaking his hand and then putting it to the heart. We then sat down with the guy at the table and ordered a coffee, when suddenly the 'grandmother' started to talk to us. She said that today she wasn't feeling quite alright and that she had a hard time getting out today, which is why she hadn't gone dancing. And then adds that she is old. Mostafa tells her that she's not old, the ones who are really old they're permanently in their beds. She says she doesn't want to be like that. She then continues saying that her neighbours really take care of her, they worry about her. 'They're *moros*, but they're good people'. Mostafa laughs while he

replies 'oh, in spite of being *moros*, eh!?' Afterwards, Josefa tells us how the last time they had been to Morocco they had brought her tons of gifts, and that they really treat her very well. They've grown quite attached to each other. But the whole time she refers to them as 'moors'. Later on she tells us that the other day she had to knock on the door of her neighbours and scold them. Apparently they were celebrating a birth and they were dancing and making a lot of noise, 'boom, boom, boom, just like the black people do it'. (24 September 2011, first diary: 35–37)

First thing to be noticed in this case is how the categories are used in an apparently much more descriptive way, as a simple stating of the facts, with no clear negative undertone nor pejorative implication. Indeed, as symbolic interactionism explains, the attribution to one group or another depends to a certain degree on the person who enounces, and more concretely, on the symbolic, cultural and economic capital at their disposal (i.e. the intertwined power relations), in order to be considered socially effective or valid. This is an agentic approach which must be paired with a view on the more structural aspects, in a more Althusserian approach perhaps: what are the symbolic representations offered via the media, culture and the state in general. Pierre Bourdieu was able to articulate this tension quite successfully, via his notions of the *field* and *habitus*. While the field is the socially constructed possibilities of action and enunciation in their interplay and tensions, observable via the sociological and discursive analysis, the habitus is the sum of possibilities that a specific individual has within these structuring structures (Bourdieu, 1977). Let us have a look at another example.

During fieldwork I took part in Catalan language classes. Although one of the main reasons for doing this was to meet potential new informants, during the lessons I was able to observe the negotiation of belonging and bordering practices regarding the abovementioned socio-cultural logics. During the classes we as students would be encouraged to present 'culture' in a static way and, more specifically, as bound to the territory where we 'come from'. We students would then talk about 'what we do there' [i.e. the country where we are from] while the teacher would then explain 'what we [Catalans] do here'. This way cultural borders would clearly be established, assigning a territory to each culture and defining what is 'normal' in each national context, and what would be considered 'native' or 'appropriate'.

In fact, given the insights from research in social sciences that point out how culture is a never-finished and relational product of local–global processes, we might as well have considered the habits the students practise as new and hybrid 'here'; after all, they are living in Salt and in Catalonia at the moment, not in Morocco or India. However, in the classes each would be considered, and to a certain degree each was presented as representing their origin, in this way strengthening the hegemonic ideas and cultural logics regarding what is considered normal and an adequate cultural expression in the town, Catalonia or Spain. There is no doubt that the predominance of a celebratory multicultural pedagogy in Catalan language classes – a result of what Sahlins called the 'Culture of cultures' (1993: 19) – has certainly had an influence on the prevalence of this classroom dynamic. But why indeed did the students not contest and therefore reproduce the categories that would exclude them from any claim of belonging, and establish these boundaries between themselves? To explain this, one would have to bear in mind the field in which the interactions took place, as well as the social agents at play in this.

The ideas of the Lebanese–Australian anthropologist Ghassan Hage are of great use here. Following his theoretical–analytical proposal (2000), one may indeed understand the classroom as a field constituted by cultural and symbolic capital which situates the social agents in social positions and unequal power relations. In the national field, those with more capital are in the position of having more legitimacy to decide what belongs and what does not in terms of cultural practices and therefore have 'the power to position others in it' (Hage, 2000: 55). Hence, the teacher is the dominant one, followed closely by those who have Spanish nationality and comply with the expected ethno-racial characteristics; they are the ones who define the socio-cultural dynamics and eventually how they can be presented and in what order. This conceptualisation of the logics at play reveals a close and fundamental relation between bordering practices, belonging and space.

Although truly ethno-cultural identification is a mundane yet complex phenomena – indeed multidirectional in that it can be appropriated and put into force by anyone – the fact is that the process is not void of unequal power relations. While any normative identification implied in the communication taking place in an apparently egalitarian public sphere has been widely criticised (see for instance Fraser, 1990 and Calhoun, 2010), the critique could as easily be transferred to any kind of racialised communication: racism is indeed exercised from a powerful position, otherwise we simply would not be talking about racism (Miles and Brown, 2003). Therefore, when analysing the use of labels, discourses or, in this case, bordering practices, one must always bear in mind the locus of enunciation as well as the immediate and more global context surrounding the speech-act.

So, both during language classes and in the street I was able to see how migrants with a whiter skin colour and middle-class (high cultural capital, but often working in precarious conditions) positioned themselves differently from other migrants, often either from Africa, or American migrants of darker skin colour. Veronica is particularly representative in this regard. Originally from Portugal, although she had lived for several years in both Switzerland and Venezuela, she had a bachelor's degree in biochemistry and had been living in the more recently created neighbourhood *la Massana* for the last three years. During our conversations she would regret having only a little interaction with her fellow neighbours. In fact, according to her, the neighbourhood was exempt of any social life. At that time, she was unemployed, but would attend language classes, amongst others the introductory course to Catalan where we had met. When talking about the central neighbourhood, where she had been working doing interviews for a social survey, she would refer to migration and would instantly make a distinction between her and them, often using the African migrants as point of reference. Somewhat similar to this, Conchita, an Argentinian woman who was also studying Catalan and was living in the borderland between Salt and Girona, states:

> I've had a hard time familiarizing myself with the fact that there are Blacks and *moros* here ... and I'm a migrant, eh ... but in Argentina if you see a Black guy he'd often be a football player ... and a *moro* is very unusual [to see], you'd see them on the telly dancing belly-dance ... but the girls dressed like nuns you'd see them in the nun's school ... so, obviously, it's a bit of a shock ... moreover, the perception that we have ... of the women who are dressed that way ... that they're ... sometimes when I see one of them in the street passing me by, and you can only see their eyes, I think to myself 'what has that women done, to be obliged to walk the street dressed like that?' [laughing] ... I think of it and laugh because then I think 'how can I think this way, if she dresses like this it must be because she wants to' ... I don't know honestly, that's what I understand now ... what's more, in the building where I live there's a lot of people, it's multi-ethnic ok, I get along much better with the ones from here maybe because we're much more alike. (Conchita, 53 years old, resident in the area surrounding the Catalunya square)

While observing other common neighbourhood spaces such as the staircases, I was able to observe similar dynamics of negotiating belonging. Hence, in the three different places where I stayed during fieldwork, at one point or another I would be able to witness a group of Spanish women gathered at the bottom of the stairs, in the entrance of the building, discussing news and stories while indiscreetly also checking and controlling who entered the building, who lived where and with whom:

> Throughout the day I have encountered two Spanish women in the entrance to the building. Each time I opened the door for them, and they were both equally surprised that I was living in the building, they weren't familiarized with me yet. One of them even asked me how and where I lived. When I told her that I was living in the mezzanine she responded 'but, with the Brown[1] ones?'(24 May 2012, fourth diary: 110)

This kind of social control of the community relates to the abovementioned field of belonging: these practices of filtering influence the feelings of belonging that the neighbours experience and establish borders between those who are in and those who are out, those who belong and those who do not; they indeed constitute practices of everyday bordering in the local communities (Yuval-Davis, Wemyss and Cassidy, 2017).

A friend of mine experienced another example of bordering practices. Some months after a Senegalese friend, Demba, had moved in with him, he told me he was having problems with his landlord. It turns out that when he had called the landlord to get them to fix the water heater, his wife had blurted 'oh, but you're the one who rents out a room to some Black guys?' Moreover, he told me, since Demba had moved in some of the neighbours had stopped greeting him. A fact I had myself been able to confirm, experiencing strange looks when I visited Demba or went out with him. One might argue that this is an example of an everyday bordering practice of a local space of the town located in an area in dispute, at the margins of both the stigmatised central neighbourhood and the middle-class old neighbourhood. And indeed it is. However, if we observe some other examples from much more stigmatised and therefore non-conflictual areas in that sense, we can observe more clearly how this also relates to socio-cultural dynamics that go beyond the mere local space.

4. 'AT HOME': BORDERING PRACTICES IN URBAN SPACE

> Familiarity is essential for a sense of community, but the latter also requires a sense of shared symbolic forms and the existence of support networks of friends and relatives. (Hage, 2000: 40)

Influenced by Ghassan Hage (2000) I will here take my point of departure as the idea of a 'field of national belonging'. An idea which stresses that while certain cultural differences might be tolerated in one country or territory, some cultural practices considered originary or native tend to dominate over others. Hage argues that the 'natives' (i.e. people from the hegemonic socio-cultural group) employ what he calls 'nationalist practices' via a spatial/territorial discursive projection. This conceptualisation explains very well how concepts such as 'home' and 'nation' are closely linked and why they have such a symbolic power: They are all based on some kind of territoriality, one which the ethnography is full of. In fact, the following quotation from an interview with Pilar, a 58-year-old women who lives in the area of the Catalunya square, is a good example of this:

> What I can't stand ... is that they don't know how to live with us ... that is, I'm not supposed to adapt to them, I'm sorry but ... I'm at home you know ... Carolina [a Peruvian woman living in the town for almost 30 years] explained it very well the other day ... It's as if I was at home and somebody from

outside came and dictated some norms that I'd have to follow, right? That is, if somebody comes from outside the normal thing would be to follow the existing rules and norms of living together in that country ... one can't just come here and try to change everything ... I'm against that.

So we see how the idea of 'home' – in socio-cultural terms and implying a territorial identification – serves to justify some cultural practices over others. Some practices are presented to belong more to one territory than to another, a move which, at the same time, justifies a more privileged position of some people over others, and the right to discursively manage others, including any symbolical and material inclusion and exclusion:

> The discourse of 'home' is one of the most pervasive and well-known elements of nationalist practices. Strangely enough, however, it has become part of an anti-racist common sense to consider 'go home' statements as mere 'racism'. Yet, surely, the expressed wish to send undesirable others to their 'home' is as clear a nationalist desire as can be, even if it involves a racial categorisation of those one wishes to see 'go home'. In the desire to send the other 'home', subjects express implicitly their own desire to be at home. [...] Furthermore, because 'home' refers more to a structure of feelings than a physical, house-like construct, it is fragmentary images, rather than explicit formulations, of what the homely nation ought to be like that we obtain by listening to people's comments. Together, however, these fragments show the national home to be structured like many other images of homely life, around the key themes of familiarity, security and community. (Hage, 2000: 39–40)

Although a minority, we can indeed find alternative viewpoints that resort to class or neighbour as socially relevant categories and discourses when talking about the groups in town. Amongst these, probably the most interesting and surprising category is that of neighbour. It renders residency and implication in the neighbourhood or the town more relevant than ethno-cultural aspects, gender or citizenship. This way apparently it allows for an equal inclusion of people with other nationalities and minorities in general, and creates an egalitarian sense of belonging. However, I argue, there is a catch, and possibly a risk, with this reading of the social reality. One might ignore the actually existing structural inequalities, thus projecting an illusion of equality which might finally help reproducing or rather naturalising these self-same inequalities, thereby blaming the victim individually.

In fact, in some of these local settings in Catalonia, where social conflicts – often dubbed as cultural conflicts – take place, recent attempts to bridge solidarity across an increasing plurality of identity markers, often perceived as something negative to social cohesion, have taken place. Hence can be seen a proliferation of the use of the category of 'neighbours' as an alternative marker, a categorisation which is being promoted especially by activists and non-governmental organisations (NGOs), with the aim of creating an alternative and local community of belonging.

The slogan that 'we are all neighbours', as a social worker expressed it in a documentary on TV3 (Corporació Catalana de Mitjans Audiovisuals, 2010), visualises an idealised horizon in which everybody who lives in the neighbourhood or town fits. Nonetheless, this apparently neutral idea is constituted by unequal relations of power and specific cultural logics, just like the notion of public space is (Fraser, 1990). Some residents are able to manage the cultural codes, symbols, and so on, better than others. The entrance and belonging to an imagined community is always negotiable and negotiated, boundaries and borders are (re)created and crossed, and the same thing goes for the social category of 'neighbour', just like we can see in the following extract:

I entered a bar which I'd categorized as 'Spanish' due to its regulars and ordered a small beer which I'd drink in the bar. Many people were outside the bar or in the doorway [observing a police raid]. After a few sips I would join them outside. I wouldn't take a minute before some of them would ask me if I was a journalist (a young guy of around my own age and an older one). When I refuted such a claim they said 'that, or secret police'. I told them that 'I'm from the neighbourhood' and laughed at the secret police claim, the younger guy said that they were just kidding, and told the others to 'leave Bojan [a Catalan football player of Croatian descent] alone'. Meanwhile the other insisted in me being a journalist, and said 'you're from the neighbourhood? But I've never seen you here, you're not from the neighbourhood', talking to the others and drawing attention to my [foreign] presence. (14 October 2011, first diary: 52–53)

Although the symbolic community of neighbours at first seems like an open and inclusive category, which does not depend on nationality or ethnicity or the like, in practice it is wedded to implicit ideas regarding who belongs, what neighbourhood and neighbourliness are, and what living together means, which all transcend the initially civic and inclusive notion.

Following Edensor's work on the a-symbolic aspects of nationhood (2004, 2006), one might conclude that unremarkable material aspects such as house styles, leisure facilities, urban design in general, and subtler aspects such as 'soundscapes' and 'smellscapes', 'contribute making the nation a visible, tangible presence in people's routine experience of space' (Antonsich, 2015: 302). In fact, it was the famous Spanish writer Goytisolo who often referred to this when talking about his sensory experiences with the plurality of cultures, cuisines and people in places such as Paris, New York or Berlin (Goytisolo, 1985). Hence, we can deduce that, in relation to a specific space such as that of the territory of the nation-state but also that of a neighbourhood, some forms of being and belonging, smells and sounds (language) might be rendered more natural and 'at home' than others, and similarly that some subjects might be perceived as more 'indigenous' in racial and ethnic terms than others, and some cultural expressions more genuine than others. This is a phenomenon that Hage (2000) has named a homely imaginary, i.e. 'an idealised image of what this national spatial background ought to be like' (Hage, 2000: 39).

In practice this would explain why some residents might want to resort to a uniquely and privileged position, regarding belonging in moral, cultural and ethnic terms, such as we have seen above, and to a lesser extent to an abstract urban belonging to the neighbourhood or the town, which might cause them to lose their relative privilege. The neighbourhood is indeed 'a politically charged category that gives symbolic meaning to the social space: it can promote forms of exclusionary belonging reproducing class inequalities [...] or challenge them' (Palomera, 2013: 11). Therefore, we would have to study the relation between the social space and the symbolic communities arising from this, and how these communities are composed: what national and/or ethno-cultural ideas about belonging and what it means to be a neighbour are implicit, and what contending visions of the neighbourhood are present, and so on. The obvious deduction from this is that conflicts might arise around contending conceptualisations of how to live in-space and with-each-other, and who the shared space belongs to.

In the following section we will take a closer look at how this homely imaginary plays out in the ethnography. We see how, oftentimes, people who feel and are perceived as native refer to the insolent and contingent appropriations of space by those perceived as foreigners (in their eyes) as 'invasions' and 'occupations'. These discourses often take the shape of moral judgements regarding the belonging or not of certain values and social practices. To this end, they resort to a greater legitimacy based on their moral–cultural–ethnic belonging, and to a lesser degree on citizenship status. They define and decide which practices are acceptable and which are not, this way projecting the latent logics of the nation-state upon the scale of the neighbourhood, all in all, the product of a nationalist–culturalist reading of the social world and space, which is hegemonic in the social field, according to which a Muslim is considered less of a national or 'from here' in Salt, despite being born in the country or even in the town. The same thing goes for a Black guy (due to his skin colour) or the Arab language. So, instead of creating a symbolic community of neighbours, certain symbols such as the veil or phenotypes are considered the contours of incommensurable cultural borders.

5. THERE GOES THE NEIGHBOURHOOD: THE OUTSIDERS AS MORAL–CULTURAL TRANSGRESSORS AND THE SYMBOLIC COMMUNITIES IN THEIR HISTORICAL FORMATION

If we adopt the widely accepted idea that there is a dialectical relation between space and social relations (Lefebvre, 1991), a process which, following Low (1996, 2000), can helpfully distinguish between 'the social production of space', which includes all the factors – social, economic, ideological and technological – which pretend to construct the material setting physically, and 'the social construction of space', which refers to the spatial transformation of space – through the social interactions, conversations, memories, sentiments, imaginations, and uses – into scenes and actions that convey symbolic meaning (Low, 2000: 112). From this point of view, the neighbourhood should not merely be understood as a geographical physical space, but also both a social process and collective project; a practical and sensorial experience and common sense, emerging from the everyday experiences of living together (including any more or less conflictual situations); an experience which translates into a kind of collective conscience, a *structure of feelings* (Williams, 1977).

Oftentimes when I spoke to inhabitants in Salt who had been living in the town for decades, I would hear stories about how nice things were before and how well everything had worked. Especially relevant was the tour around the central neighbourhood that I would take with a social worker. In one of the buildings in the Esteve Vila Street we met an elder man of around 70 years old – a Catalan-speaking, retired worker. He assessed the changes in the building, and with it the town at large, in the following manner. First of all, he said that 'the migrants' had eroded the social space of all the 'native folks', following which he explained that he had been living in the building for the last 15 years, and that beforehand it had been a 'working-class haven', according to him, united and in good condition: 'the door would always be closed, the intercom always worked, the glass would never be broken'. But the most interesting part is when he explained how they lived together as a community:

> Right here a man called Joan lived ... Asunción lived on the second floor, Fina on the third floor ... On the first floor a widow lived together with her two sons, on the third floor everybody was from here, on the fourth floor everybody was from here ... The community expenses were paid for ... And one would only hear two languages spoken in the staircase, Spanish and Catalan, and everybody understood each other ... Now nobody does.

Although indeed he hints at a sense of abandonment, which the broken windows literature would applaud – despite much more well-founded critiques of it (Harcourt, 2001) – in his memory of the neighbourhood we can detect a certain sense of *being in* and *belonging to* a community, which has been lost with the arrival of new inhabitants with other nationalities and cultures. Very similar to the traditional sense of community about which Durkheim, Weber and Tönnies so famously have written – at least, according to more contemporary readings of them (Putnam, 2000, 2007) – this conceptualisation of community implies cultural homogeneity (fictitious as it may be). This is a view of the community and the erosion of it which coincided with that of many other older Spanish residents with whom I spoke during fieldwork. And while these memories might exactly be a product of recent changes, many of the people recognised some cultural commonality in their shared histories of migration, often from a rural setting in Andalusia, as the former mayor recounts:

> The central district where the majority of the migrants arriving in the 60s and 70s had settled ... Where the majority were homeowners ... Well the neighbours more or less knew each other, if they weren't from the same town, often it was from a town close to, in Andalusia, or wherever that was ... And so Maria, Puri and Paquita they knew each other and they lived together more or less peacefully and in harmony. (Iolanda Pineda, former mayor of Salt (Catalan Socialist Party – PSC))

And let's not forget, apart from sharing similar histories of migration, they also shared residential and convivial spaces (of social reproduction and leisure), and that a lot of them even worked together in the same factories (such as Coma-Cros, Maret or Gassol). They were traditional working-class, an identity which was also based on experiences of spatial injustice, in opposition to the middle-class Catalan-speaking populations of the Old Neighbourhood (Barri Vell).

Therefore, I believe it is fair to say that the local community at least shared some set of moral values or 'structures of feelings' as Williams (1977) would have it, emerging from the everyday experiences – of both conflict and peace – in the social space that the neighbourhood or its territorial subdivisions offered, a *habitus* of place or neighbourhood conscience, similar to the working-class conscience in the sense that Thompson (1968) conferred on it. The Catalunya square is exemplary in this regard.

Through several accounts of the old-timers of the area, many of them with more than 30 years of residence, and others who have moved out, I have been able to recount how certain feelings of belonging and community developed in the neighbourhood from neighbourhood struggles aimed at improving the infrastructures and urban settings of the area. Indeed a certain memory of the place has been produced, which is often in stark contrast to the younger generations.[2] However, these feelings, never completely institutionalised nor clearly defined, coexist alongside a romantic vision of cultural homogeneity, as we have seen. A memory of a united neighbourhood, a unified and unifying identity which opposes those coming from outside be they young or older, the outsiders, which in the narratives of the older and younger middle-class residents in other neighbourhoods, are often perceived and portrayed as moral–cultural transgressors, responsible for the erosion of the neighbourhood community or simply the social conflicts taking place in the town (Lundsteen, 2020b). The fact is that these experiences of social conflict or cooperation might as well serve as grounds for a common identity, so why is that not the case?

Hage (2000) invites us to analyse these disputes and conflicts in terms of what he refers to as 'categories of spatial management', as he explains:

> Most humans perceive ants as a different species, and certainly as an inferior species. Yet, just on the basis of this belief, they do not perceive them as 'undesirable' or as 'too many'. They do so only

when these ants are seen to have invaded spaces where humans find their presence harmful such as in their houses or on their plates. And it is only in such situations that practices of violence are directed against them. Consequently, categories such as 'too many', while embodying some form of 'racist' belief, are primarily categories of spatial management. (2000: 37–38)

When justifying this *spatial management* oftentimes those in a position to carry it out refer to extreme cases of transgression of civic norms, as we can see from the following conversation:

Federic: Well one of the typical problems in the communities is that they keep them to themselves, they forget about the shared spaces of the community ... They think they can do whatever they want ... Some smoke joints ... This is my home ... And it's not, it's a community space, you have to behave, like anybody else ... They are often sitting in the staircase, everybody smoking ... And that's the problem

Toñi: Well you see that's what such a culture from other countries brings with it ... There are no rules ... But well, now they're here, and here we've got another reality ... Although you might not understand that ... But they also have to understand, that in the receiving country, you have to comply with the rules that apply ... What one cannot tolerate in any case is those kind of situations that Federic mentions or other kinds of situations we have experienced where people have peed or defecated in the staircases ... Well, thing are changing ... But in the beginning that's what we found ... And these kinds of situations created a neighbourhood which wasn't well functioning you know ... In fact, everybody would isolate and defend their own little territory in their home and wouldn't want to know nor share anything with anybody else.

(Toñi, 50 years old, neighbour in the central district (Barri Centre) and former president of the neighbourhood community; Federic, 65 years old, neighbour in the central district)

So, from what we have seen here it becomes clear that there is indeed a set of hegemonic socio-cultural practices which derive from the historic experiences of the dominant ethnic group. This would indeed explain why some find themselves in the (valid) position of saying, 'we've been invaded by them', positioning and signalling the 'outsiders' from the insiders, drawing boundaries and setting borders, this way justifying and naturalising their superior position. At the same time, through the example we see just how *public*, public space is (i.e. in the sense of it being an egalitarian and shared space): everybody can apparently access and make use of it, but when outsiders do it, they are apparently breaking a moral code and doing it in a way that the established residents see as invasion or occupation; opposed to their 'normal ways'. They therefore reclaim a privative use of space, theirs, resorting to discourses of national–cultural belonging, in which they have more right to the space than others, via the use of civic notions (culturally based as they are) of what activities are correct and which are not. Often this right and the inherent power inequalities is not questioned by local politicians or civil servants, either because they share the vision of the 'native' inhabitants in their exclusive right to manage the space, or because they want to cater for them due to political interests. Either way, a comprehensive analysis of the actual workings of these bordering practices is much needed.

6. CONCLUSIONS

The main aim of this chapter has been to put forward arguments supporting the idea that we as social scientists dealing with migration as a social phenomenon will have to pay attention to the urban transformations and differing communities in their interplay in our analysis by, for instance, focusing on emerging bordering practices.

Especially in these times of large-scale socio-economic transformations, there is an intensification of mobility and an awareness around this, as well as an increasing effort to control and police certain migrations and bodies. Faced with these tasks, often unequally distributed territorially, many states, regional administrations and cities find it an urgent task to create affinities and communities that cohere the social fabric. But rather often these Others are portrayed as somebody who has just arrived instead of somebody who will stay and create a future. A central argument of this chapter is that critical research on both the solidarities and bordering practices is much needed.

In this way the chapter relates to the emerging literature on 'homing' in migration studies (see Boccagni and Brighenti, 2017), looking at how a sense of community is created at a local level, be that through the creation of bottom-up identities or by locating larger-scale movements. At the same time, it engages with a new strand of research which has been building up, mainly within geography and sociology (Antonsich, Mavroudi and Mihelj, 2016), and which questions the dichotomy and the rather optimistic portrayal of 'the urban' and simplistic accounts of the nation(al) (the conjunction of the nation and the national). Drawing on ethnographic data this strand of research shows 'more nuanced, complex or even positive and hopeful conceptualisations of the nation' (Antonsich, 2015; Rossetto, 2015: 170).

The final argument of the chapter is rather simple. Any kind of community-building, be it a nation, an urban formation or social class, will have to review and deal with the underlying and inherent social inequalities first *and* in the making. Contemporary attempts at creating bonds between neighbours in multicultural or super-diverse areas run into problems because of this neglect. The mere reliance that some of these actions have on 'public space' as an adequate arena for meaningful and egalitarian intercultural communication or dialogue is simply too naïve. While Fraser (1990) pointed to many of the problems with this belief in her critique of the public *sphere*, other authors have shed similar critiques regarding public *space* (Staeheli and Thompson, 1997; Di Masso and Dixon, 2015).

However, one important question remains: if any kind of group-creation entails establishing boundaries, maybe the problem is much more structural than we think. Maybe we *do* need to rethink the social categories we use to navigate in social science and in society politically (Anderson, 2019); they frame our conceptualisation of the world and our understanding of it, the way we understand the social tensions, and therefore also the way we deal with them, and more importantly our futures. At the same time, maybe boundaries and the borders are not so problematic *in themselves*; in the end they are something we share with each other, our nexus. The real problem is rather the structural inequalities that make exploitation possible and division natural, and sometimes even exclusion a desirable option for some (because they fear losing the little privilege they have).

I therefore think we should focus on building up a radical urban politics of belonging from below. Although this will have to be located in a specific space and time, it will have to attend to and struggle against all forms of social inequality in order to foster the building up of egalitarian communities, in plural, while at the same time creating the social conditions necessary for a socially just production of the space for and controlled by these people. 'For only in a disalienated city produced by citizens in their everyday life can we as creative human beings hope to find our true identity amidst real difference' (Goonewardena and Kipfer, 2005). Only this way would we be able to talk about the right to the city for every*body*.

NOTES

1. Brown is often used as a more politically correct way, as opposed to Black, of referring to people who are dark-skinned.
2. In another place it would be interesting to reflect upon this generational cleavage. In fact, a large majority of the younger generations, no matter their ethnic background, do not share this vision. Most certainly many of the older people will proudly refer to this experience in the neighbourhood and having taken part in its making as yet another reason why their voice should be heard.

REFERENCES

Anderson, B. (2013), *Us and Them? The Dangerous Politics of Immigration Control*. Oxford: Oxford University Press.
Anderson, B. (2019), 'New directions in migration studies: Towards methodological de-nationalism', *Comparative Migration Studies*, 36(7), 1–13. doi: 10.1186/s40878-019-0140-8.
Anderson, B. and V. Hughes (eds.) (2015), *Citizenship and its Others*. London: Palgrave Macmillan UK.
Antonsich, M. (2015), 'Nation and nationalism', in Agnew, J. et al. (eds.), *The Wiley Blackwell Companion to Political Geography*. London: Wiley-Blackwell, pp. 297–310.
Antonsich, M., E. Mavroudi and S. Mihelj (2016), 'Building inclusive nations in the age of migration', *Identities*, 24(2), 156–176. doi: 10.1080/1070289X.2016.1148607.
Armenta, A. (2017), 'Racializing crimmigration: Structural racism, colorblindness and the institutional production of immigrant criminality', *Sociology of Race and Ethnicity*, 3(1), 82–95. doi: 10.1177/2332649216648714.
Boccagni, P. and A. M. Brighenti (2017), 'Immigrants and home in the making: Thresholds of domesticity, commonality and publicness', *Journal of Housing and the Built Environment*, 32(1), 1–11. doi: 10.1007/s10901-015-9487-9.
Bourdieu, P. (1977), *Outline of a Theory of Practice*. Cambridge: Cambridge University Press.
Bourdieu, P. (1990), *Logic of Practice*. Stanford, CA: Stanford University Press.
Calhoun, C. (2010), 'The public sphere in the field of power', *Social Science History*, 34(3), 301–335. doi:10.1017/S0145553200011287.
Carbado, D. W. and C. I. Harris (2011), 'Undocumented criminal procedure', *UCLA Law Review*, 58, 1543–1616.
Clua i Fainé, M. (2011), 'Catalan, immigrants and charnegos: "Race", "cultura" and "mixture" in Catalan Nationalist Rhetoric', *Revista de Antropología Social*, 1, 55–75.
Cole, J. W. and E. R. Wolf (1974), *The Hidden Frontier: Ecology and Ethnicity in an Alpine Valley, Studies in Social Discontinuity*. New York etc.: Academic Press.
Conversi, D. and S. Jeram (2017), 'Despite the crisis: The resilience of intercultural nationalism in Catalonia', *International Migration*, 55(2), 53–67. doi: 10.1111/imig.12323.
Corporació Catalana de Mitjans Audiovisuals (2010), *Salt: assaig de convivència*, TV3 [documentary].
Dauvergne, C. (2008), *Making People Illegal: What Globalization Means for Migration and Law*. Cambridge: Cambridge University Press.
De Genova, N. and N. Peutz (eds.) (2010), *The Deportation Regime: Sovereignty, Space, and the Freedom of Movement*. Durham, NC: Duke University Press.
Dijstelbloem, H. and W. Walters (2019), 'Atmospheric border politics: The morphology of migration and solidarity practices in Europe', *Geopolitics*, 1–24. doi: 10.1080/14650045.2019.1577826.
Di Masso, A. and J. Dixon (2015), 'More than words: Place, discourse and the struggle over public space in Barcelona', *Qualitative Research in Psychology*, 12(1), 45–60.doi: 10.1080/14780887.2014.958387.
Edensor, T. (2004), 'Automobility and national identity', *Theory, Culture and Society*, 21(4–5), 101–120. doi:10.1177/0263276404046063.
Edensor, T. (2006), 'Reconsidering national temporalities', *European Journal of Social Theory* 9(4), 525–545. doi:10.1177/1368431006071996.
Erickson, B. (2011), 'Utopian virtues: Muslim neighbors, ritual sociality, and the politics of convivència', *American Ethnologist*, 38(1), 114–131. doi: 10.1111/j.1548-1425.2010.01296.x.

Fassin, D. (2008), 'Moral economies revisited', *Annales. Histoire, Sciences Sociales*, 64(6), 1237–1266. doi:10.3917/anna.646.1237.

Fraser, N. (1990), 'Rethinking the public sphere: A contribution to the critique of actually existing democracy', *Social Text*, 25/26, 56–80. doi: 10.2307/466240.

Goonewardena, K. and S. Kipfer (2005), 'Spaces of difference: Reflections from Toronto on multiculturalism, bourgeois urbanism and the possibility of radical urban politics', *International Journal of Urban and Regional Research*, 29(3), 670–678. doi: 10.1111/j.1468-2427.2005.00611.x.

Goytisolo, J. (1985), *Contracorrientes*. Barcelona: Editorial Montesinos.

Guentner, S., S. Lukes, R. Stanton, B. A. Vollmer and J. Wilding (2016), 'Bordering practices in the UK welfare system', *Critical Social Policy*, 36(3), 391–411. doi: 10.1177/0261018315622609.

Guibernau, M. (2013), 'Secessionism in Catalonia: After democracy', *Ethnopolitics*, 12(4), 368–393. doi: 10.1080/17449057.2013.843245.

Guittet, E.-P. (2017), 'Unpacking the new mobilities paradigm: Lessons for critical security studies?', in Leese, M. and Wittendorp, S. (eds.), *Security/Mobility: Politics of Movement*. Manchester: Manchester University Press, pp. 209–216. doi: 10.1162/glep.2001.1.1.158.

Hage, G. (2000), *White Nation: Fantasies of White Supremacy in a Multicultural Society*. New York: Routledge.

Harcourt, B. H. (2001), *Illusion of Order: The False Promise of Broken Windows Policing*. Cambridge, MA: Harvard University Press.

Harvey, D. (1982), *The Limits to Capital*. Oxford: Basil Blackwell.

Heil, T. (2014), 'Are neighbours alike? Practices of conviviality in Catalonia and Casamance', *European Journal of Cultural Studies*, 17(4), 452–470. doi: 10.1177/1367549413510420.

Kalir, B. (2019), 'Departheid', *Conflict and Society*, 5(1), 19–40. doi: 10.3167/arcs.2019.050102.

Kallius, A., D. Monterescu and P. K. Rajaram (2016), 'Immobilizing mobility: Border ethnography, illiberal democracy, and the politics of the "refugee crisis" in Hungary', *American Ethnologist*, 43(1), 25–37. doi: 10.1111/amet.12260.

Kundnani, A. (2014), *The Muslims Are Coming! Islamophobia, Extremism, and the Domestic War on Terror*. London: Verso.

Lefebvre, H. (1991), *The Production of Space*. Cornwall: Wiley-Blackwell.

Lluch, J. (2014), *Visions of Sovereignty. Nationalism and Accommodation in Multinational Democracies*. Philadelphia: University of Pennsylvania Press.

Low, S. M. (1996), 'Spatializing culture: The social construction and social production of public space in Costa Rica', *American Ethnologist*, 23(4), 861–879.

Low, S. M. (2000), *On the Plaza: The Politics of Public Space and Culture*. Austin: University of Texas Press.

Lundsteen, M. (2015), *Conflicts and Convivencia: An Ethnography of the Social Effects of 'The Crisis' in a Small Catalan Town*. Barcelona: Department of Social Anthropology, University of Barcelona. Available at: http://www.tdx.cat/bitstream/handle/10803/363197/LUNDSTEEN_PHD_THESIS.pdf?sequence=1.

Lundsteen, M. (2019), 'Challenging narratives of "native flight" in a small town. Reflections on moral economies and space', *GRITIM-UPF Working Paper Series*, 40, 1–27. Available at: https://repositori.upf.edu/handle/10230/41977.

Lundsteen, M. (2020a), 'Conflicts in and around space: Reflections on "mosque conflicts" through the case of Premià de Mar', *Journal of Muslims in Europe*, 9(1), 1–21. doi: 10.1163/22117954-12341410.

Lundsteen, M. (2020b), 'An iron fist in a velvet glove: Towards a new governance of the migrant other in Catalonia?', *Dialectical Anthropology*, 44(1), 1–17. doi: 10.1007/s10624-019-09579-w.

Lundsteen, M. (2020c), *Conflicts and Convivencia: A Critical Ethnography of Migration and Urban Transformation in a Small Catalan Town*. Challenging Migration Studies Series, London: Rowman & Littlefield International.

Lundsteen, M. and M. Fernández González (2020), 'Zero-tolerance in Catalonia: Policing the other in public space', *Critical Criminology*, pp. 1–16. doi: 10.1007/s10612-020-09533-1.

Mezzadra, S. and B. Neilson (2013), *Border as Method, or, the Multiplication of Labor*. Durham, NC: Duke University Press.

Miles, R. and M. Brown (2003), *Racism*. 2nd ed. London and New York: Routledge.

Palomera, J. (2013), *Reciprocity and Conflict: The Urban Poor in a Bubble-and-Bust Economy*, PhD Dissertation, Department of Social Anthropology, University of Barcelona.
Pickering, S. and L. Weber (2006), *Borders, Mobility and Technologies of Control*. The Netherlands: Springer.
Provine, D. M. and R. L. Doty (2011), 'The criminalization of immigrants as a racial project', *Journal of Contemporary Criminal Justice*, 27(3), 261–277. doi: 10.1177/1043986211412559.
Putnam, R. D. (2000), *Bowling Alone: The Collapse and Revival of American Community*. New York: Simon & Schuster.
Putnam, R. D. (2007), 'E pluribus unum: Diversity and community in the twenty-first century. The 2006 Johan Skytte Prize Lecture', *Scandinavian Political Studies*, 30, 137–174.
Rossetto, T. (2015), 'Performing the nation between us: Urban photographic sets with young migrants', *Fennia*, 193(2), 165–184. doi: 10.11143/45271.
Rozakou, K. (2017), 'Nonrecording the "European refugee crisis" in Greece', *Focaal*, 77, 36–49.
Sahlins, M. (1993), 'Goodbye to tristes tropes: Ethnography in the context of modern world history', *The Journal of Modern History*, 65(1), 1–25.
Spanish Statistical Office (2012), Website. Available at: https://ine.es/.
Staeheli, L. A. and A. Thompson (1997), 'Citizenship, community, and struggles for public space', *Professional Geographer*, 49(1), 28–38.
Stumpf, J. (2006), 'The crimmigration crisis: Immigrants, crime, and sovereign power', *American University Law Review*, 56(2), 367–420.
Thompson, E. P. (1968), *The Making of the English Working Class*. Harmondsworth, Middlesex: Penguin.
Vigh, H. and D. Sausdal (2018), 'The anthropology of crime', in Wydra, H. and Thomassen, B. (eds.), *Handbook of Political Anthropology*. Cheltenham, UK and Northampton, MA, USA: Edward Elgar Publishers, pp. 441–461.
Walters, W. (2002), 'Mapping Schengenland: Denaturalizing the border', *Environment and Planning D: Society and Space*, 20(5), 561–580. doi: 10.1068/d274t.
Weber, L. (2015), *Rethinking Border Control for a Globalising World: A Preferred Future*. New York: Routledge.
Williams, R. (1977), *Marxism and Literature*, Oxford: Oxford University Press.
Wolf, E. (1982), *Europe and the People without History*. Berkeley: University of California Press.
Yuval-Davis, N., G. Wemyss and K. Cassidy (2017), 'Everyday bordering, Belonging and the reorientation of British immigration legislation', *Sociology*, 52(2), 1–17. doi: 10.1177/0038038517702599.

PART IV

REGIONS, PARTITIONS AND EDGES

18. Border regions, migrations and the proliferation of violent expulsions
Saskia Sassen

1. BORDERS, MIGRATION AND CAPITALISM

We have given a lot of attention to borders and how they matter in the configuration of capitalism. We have seen how surveillance of the nation-state is also very visible in border regions but we do not see it completely. Borders are a very powerful category and bordering capabilities seem central to them. Borders are able to show us the making of histories, in this current area in a global geography of exploitation. The weakening of national borders is important but what happens with all the rebordering process too. In this chapter I will try to expose my analytic tactics in order to de-stabilize the concept of the border in the context of depredatory practices based on expulsions and extractive logics (see for example here Chapter 20 on the Amazones in this volume) in different regions of the Global South.

Borders are also able to display new actors in the making of globalization. For example, when a foreign country or big powerful private actors buy lands in Zambia and in Congo in order to establish their own plantation, of course affecting flora, fauna, villagers, rural districts, manufacturing ... Borders are sites of uneven capitalist development and inequalities. There are scenarios of global inequalities, especially experiencing severe expulsions.

Therefore, one angle into the question of national territory, at a time of global and digital capabilities, is the border. It is one of the critical national institutions that those capabilities can unsettle and even neutralize. Borders, in turn, bring up the national state as the key historic actor shaped partly by the struggle about and institutionalizing of territorial borders. The globalization of a broad range of processes is producing ruptures in the mosaic of border regimes underlying the international system of exclusive territorial demarcations. There is much disagreement about the effect of these global and digital capabilities on state territorial jurisdictions, with some seeing much and others little real change. But both sides of the debate tend to share one assumption, often implicit: the territorial exclusivity of the nation-state which makes of the border a line that divides the national and the global into two mutually exclusive domains. And yet, the changes under way are shifting the meaning of borders, even when the actual geographic lines that demarcate territories have not been altered. Perhaps more importantly, these changes are contributing to the formation of new types of borders. Such changed meanings and new types of borders make legible the fact that bordering takes place in far more sites than geographic borderlines and their linked institutions, such as consulates and airport immigration controls. And they make legible the extent of state capture in the historiography and geography covering the geopolitics of the last two centuries, an issue that has received considerable attention in the last few years. State sovereignty is usually conceived of as a monopoly of authority over a particular territory. Today, it is becoming evident that national territories may remain demarcated along the same old geographic borderlines, but that novel types of borderings resulting from globalization are increasingly present inside national territory. Sovereignty remains as a systemic property, yet its institutional insertion and its capacity to legitimate and absorb all legitimating power have become unstable.

The second analytic tactic is to look at what happens in migrations with this new bordering. Most major migrations of the last two centuries, and often even earlier, can be shown to start at some point: they have beginnings generated by a mix of conditions. Poverty is not enough of an explanation, or we should be seeing billions of migrants across the world. This suggests that there is a larger context within which migration flows emerge. And it is this larger context that interests me: a massive loss of habitat generated by either the destructions produced by war or the destructions produced by particular modes of so-called "economic development" (Sassen 2016a).

New migrations have long been of interest to me in that they help us understand why a given flow starts.[1] Hence they can tell us something about a larger context that generates such a beginning. This means that the migrant becomes an indicator of a change in the area where s/he comes from. This contrasts with a later stage in a flow – when it becomes chain migration – which takes far less to explain than the start of a new flow. The beginning of a migration flow is a specific phase. Once chain migration sets in it is typically the family that authorizes one or another member to migrate for the good of the household. Until quite recently chain migration has been the dominant mode in the West since the 1950s as many of those migrations were by then in the second or third generation. It is these routinized migrations that have received most of the attention from immigration experts in the West. In all these diverse situations, survival has become a major challenge for local residents, even for the relatively small proportion able to get a job in the plantations and mines.

Migrating to the cities is one major option. New migrations co-exist with older migrations. The rapid changes at point of origin also explain why most migrations are to cities. And they explain new types of migration, from rural areas to the Global North (notably from several sub-Saharan countries to Europe). In effect, expulsions are being rebranded as migrations, a phenomenon that will not cease anytime soon, given the ongoing search for land for crops, mining and water by governments and firms from a growing number of countries. The generic term "migration" tends to obscure the fact that our firms and government agencies, and those of our allies, may have contributed to expulsions.

Each of these three very diverse types of flow points to a larger context marked mostly by extreme conditions. Factoring in how those conditions came about allows us to see at least some of the larger dynamics generating migration as an option – for a better life or for bare survival. Each of these three flows emerges from situations larger than the internal decisions of households, and larger than the ups and downs of national or local economies. The extreme and sharply delineated conditions from which they arise operate at diverse levels – ranging from individual needs to macro-level dynamics. And they do so with variable degrees of visibility.

Extreme violence is one key factor explaining these migrations. But it is not the only one. I add a second key factor: 30 years of international development policies have left much land dead (because of mining, land grabs, plantation agriculture) and have expelled whole communities from their habitats. Moving to the slums of large cities, or, for those who can afford it, migration, has increasingly become the last option. This multidecade history of destructions and expulsions has reached extreme levels made visible in vast stretches of land and water bodies that are now dead. At least some of the localized wars and conflicts arise from these destructions, in a sort of fight for habitat. And climate change further reduces livable ground.

On the basis of these destructions and on the characteristics of the three emergent migration flows, I argue that this mix of conditions – wars, dead land, expulsions – has produced a vast loss of habitat for a growing number of people. These, then, are not the migrants in search of a better life who hope to send money and perhaps return to the family left behind. These are people in search of bare life, with no home to return to. This chapter will focus on different regions of the world but it will particularly illustrate one case: the expulsion of Rohingya from Myanmar – reaching 800,000 in three months in late 2017; this amounts to a whole new phase in their long-time persecution as Muslims in a majority Buddhist country.

2. THE CONTEXT OF EXPULSIONS IN THE GLOBAL SOUTH

Many of today's negative features in Global South countries (e.g., the sharp growth of poverty and of expulsions of smallholders from their land) originated partly in the development strategies launched by major international institutions and global firms in the 1980s and the 1990s. Mining and plantation agriculture are among the notable examples of a mode of development that is basically extractive, and leaves behind dead land and poisoned water. Further, by insisting on opening up these countries to imports, much of the international system has wound up enabling large multinational consumer enterprises to enter markets where once local producers and shops were the key.

The outcome has been a significant destruction of local enterprises and local manufacturing. Opening up these fragile economies to global firms ready to supply all needs gradually reduced them to consumption economies. The extractive sector, largely under the control of foreign firms, has grown in importance and has become an enabler, not of countrywide development but of the emergence of rich local elites.

A major factor in the late 1970s and early 1980s, rarely mentioned nowadays, was the push by the so-called "transnational banks" to sell debt to less developed countries (Sassen 1988). Two clarifications are necessary here. One is that the rise of OPEC (Oil Producing Export Countries) in the 1970s brought with it a vast concentration of money in the oil-producing countries. Instead of "storing" this money in their countries, the major Arab oil producers decided to work with Western banks to grow that money.

That was a time when the multiple financial instruments available today to multiply the value of cash did not yet exist. Selling debt for an interest rate was the way of gaining a quick profit. African countries, especially, were pressured or persuaded to buy such loans – which meant taking on debt. And eventually many if not most of these governments wound up paying a very high price for those seemingly cheap loans: elites got rich but the economic development of these countries ceased being of interest to their governments and elites.[2]

For much of the 1980s and onwards indebted poor countries were asked to pay a share of their export earnings toward debt service that was much higher than that asked in other instances of country indebtedness; this share stood at about 20 percent. For instance, in 1953, the Allies canceled 80 percent of Germany's war debt and insisted on only 3 to 5 percent of export earnings for debt service. And they asked only 8 percent from Central European countries in the 1990s. But the debt service burdens on today's poor countries have wound up being extreme, as I discuss below. It does suggest that the aim regarding Germany and, later, Central Europe, was reincorporation into the capitalist world economy of the time.

The fact is that well over 30 years of international "development" policies in sending countries have left much land dead due to mining, land grabs, plantation agriculture, and more. The most extreme case is Africa. The result was and continues to be the expulsion of whole communities from their rural habitats. But it all gets registered as gross domestic product (GDP) per capita growth, even though these types of "development" exhaust the land and poison water bodies. Smallholders know how to keep the land alive, but their production was rarely considered in measures of GDP per capita growth. As they were pushed out of their land across several decades, moving to the slums of large cities increasingly became, and continues to be, the last option for the expelled. And, for those who could afford it, leaving their country, with Europe a common destination. This, then, is not the migrant in search of a better life who hopes to send money to the family left behind. This is people in search of bare life.

Thus, I discuss here some of the key international development policies deployed as of the 1980s.[3] The central focus in that section is on Africa and on the key role of the key international development organizations, notably the International Monetary Fund (IMF) and the World Bank; European and United States economic interests have also played a key role in shaping policy. My aim here is not a full review of the good and the bad development programs. It is rather a tracing of how a rapidly growing share of the less developed areas of the world wound up with massive corporate mines and plantations leaving behind destroyed habitats. Directly, and indirectly via their corporations, rich Western states have often been major players in these destructions of habitats far away from their own lands. We can now add China to the list of such major players.[4]

In contrast, the aim vis-à-vis the Global South countries in the 1980s and 1990s was more akin to a disciplining rather than enabling regime, starting with forced acceptance of loans and restructuring programs from the international system. These were measures that helped large extractive firms (such as mining and plantations), and consumer multinationals enter these economies on very profitable terms. After 20 years of this regime, it became clear that it did not deliver on the basic components for healthy development. The discipline of debt service payments was given strong priority over infrastructure, hospitals, schools, and other people-oriented development goals. The primacy of this extractive logic became a mechanism for systemic transformation that went well beyond debt service payment. It included the devastation of large sectors of traditional economies, including small-scale manufacturing, the destruction of a good part of the national bourgeoisie and petty bourgeoisie, the sharp impoverishment of the population, and, in many cases, the impoverishment and thereby corruptibility of the state.

By the 2000s, the rapid growth in the debt of mostly poor countries led global regulatory institutions to implement the so-called structural adjustment programs (SAPs). Key to this project were, and are, the IMF and the World Bank, and, eventually, the World Trade Organization. These have shaped the evolution of much of the Global South over the past two decades. Debt servicing was the instrument for this disciplining: it weakened the governments of those countries by forcing them to use growing shares of national revenue for interest payments on their debts rather than for economic development (Sassen 2008a: Ch. 5). Further, it made them susceptible to signing unfavorable deals with global firms in extractive industries rather than furthering mass manufacturing and local commerce by national firms. These arrangements did little to promote local capacities for developing manufacturing and commerce, two sectors that could have generated a modest but effective middle class.

Debt and debt servicing problems have long been a systemic feature of the developing world.[5] But what concerns me here are the particular features of IMF-negotiated debt rather than the fact of debt per se. A further concern is how the gradual destruction of traditional economies prepared the ground, literally, for some of the new needs or aims of advanced capitalism. Examples are the acquisitions by national and foreign enterprises of vast stretches of land – for agriculture, for accessing underground water tables, for mining, and more (Sassen 2014: Chs. 2 and 4). The third concern is the survival struggles of the poor and of the impoverished middle classes.

While each one of these three components is familiar and has been present before, my argument is that they are now part of a new organizing logic that changes their valence and their interactive effects. Even as we see the rise of a robust well to do middle class in the last decade or two, there are also growing numbers of poor households and impoverished villages.

From the 1980s to the early 1990s, governments' debt *service* payments to the international system had increased to $1.6 trillion, more than the actual debt. From 1982 to 1998, indebted countries paid four times their original debts, and at the same time their debt stocks went up by four times. For instance, for every $1 African countries received as aid in 1998, they paid $1.40 in debt service. Africa's debt to Gross National Product ratios were especially high in the late 1990s: 123 percent, compared with 42 percent in Latin America and 28 percent in Asia.[6]

Thus Global South countries had to use a significant share of their total revenues to service these debts (Amen and Gills 2010; Bello 2004; IMF 2015c). The IMF, the World Bank, and sister institutions established the criteria and processed these debts, thereby functioning as a global disciplining regime rather than an enabler of local development.

The Heavily Indebted Poor Country (HIPC) initiative, set up in 1996 by the World Bank and by the IMF, amounted to a recognition that the earlier restructuring programs did not work. The aim became to assist countries with debts equivalent to more than one and a half times their annual export earnings. By July 1, 2009, 26 countries had completed the HIPC process, and 9 had "passed the decision point".[7]

As of 2006, the poorest 49 countries (i.e., "low-income countries" with less than $935 per capita annual income) had debts of $375 billion. If to these 49 we add the "developing countries," together these 144 countries had a debt surpassing $2.9 trillion, and had already paid $573 billion just for debt servicing (Jubilee Debt Campaign 2013a, 2013b).

But HIPC soon showed its shortcomings. The Multilateral Debt Relief Initiative (MDRI) went into full force in July 2006. It was intended to address many of the critiques of the HIPC initiative. MDRI promised cancellation of debts to the World Bank (incurred before 2003), to the IMF (incurred before 2004), and to the African Development Fund (incurred before 2004) for the countries that completed the HIPC initiative. According to one estimate, the major cancellation schemes (including HIPC and MDRI initiatives and the Paris Club) have written off $88 billion so far (Jubilee Debt Campaign 2013a, 2013b).

From a social development angle, the IMF and World Bank restructuring programs have been highly problematic. The debt burden that built up in the 1980s and the 1990s had negative effects on state spending composition. Zambia, Ghana, and Uganda were three countries that global regulators such as the World Bank and the IMF saw as cooperative, responsible, and successful at implementing SAPs. These three countries illustrate some of the issues even for countries held in high esteem by global regulators.

Thus, at the height of these programs in the early to mid-1990s, Zambia's government paid $1.3 billion in debt but only $37 million for primary education; Ghana's social expenses, at

$75 million, represented 20 percent of its debt service; and Uganda paid $9 per capita on its debt and only $1 for health care. In 1994 alone, these three countries remitted $2.7 billion to bankers in the North. This may have been great for the lenders, but not for a majority of the poor in those countries. Nor was this great for their governments. And this became clear when the new programs (HIPC and MDRI) became an option: all three countries joined them and they accepted the Poverty Reduction Strategy Paper requirements, and it worked for them.[8]

Generally, IMF debt management policies from the 1980s onwards can be shown to have worsened the situation for the unemployed and poor (United Nations Development Programme (UNDP) 2005, 2008). Much research on poor countries documents the link between hyper-indebted governments and cuts in social programs. These tend to affect particularly women and children through reduced education and health care (for data overviews, see UNDP 2005, 2008, 2015; World Bank 2005, 2006, 2015a, 2015b).

The above is part of a larger history in the making. In my reading it includes as one key element a *repositioning* of much of Africa and major parts of Latin America and Asia in a new massively restructured global economy. Weakened governments and the destruction of traditional economies have launched a new phase of extraction by powerful states and firms and a new phase of survival economies by the impoverished middle classes and the long-term poor (for a more detailed analysis, see Sassen 2008a, 2008b, 2014).

In brief, after several decades of these "development initiatives", centered on debt and extractive sectors, most IMF program countries had been left with larger government debts, devastated local economies and enterprises, and poorer populations. It also enabled the proliferation of predatory elites of all sorts, some in the domain of politics and some in the economy.

At its most extreme this meant the immiseration of growing numbers of local people who ceased being of value as workers and as consumers even as national elites emerged and got rich. What mattered was access to natural resources, rather than people as workers and consumers. But it also meant that traditional petty bourgeoisies ceased being of value. Such repositioning and destructions have contributed to the current duality marked by the rise of a new class of highly educated professionals and an impoverishment of rural people who have lost their land and wind up in urban slums.

The migrations to Europe in the 1970s and 1980s in good part were a response to this absence of options for the more modest households and the failure of the international system to enable genuine development and stop the massive land grabs and mining operations of mostly foreign firms. Those same conditions have now become extreme, and generated massive conflicts of all sorts. The rise of a prosperous middle class is not enough to counteract the disastrous effects of ill-conceived policies by the IMF, the World Bank, and other international institutions. Nor have the new rich African elites helped much.

One brutal way of putting it is to say that the natural resources of much of Africa and good parts of Latin America and Asia have long counted more for extractive sectors than the local people counted as consumers and as workers. The lack of both genuine development and distributed economic growth *is* a mode of growth that benefited elites and foreign investors. It was basically extractive and thereby used a country's people, but did not bring genuine development to their lives. One key legacy of such extractive sectors is a shrunken habitat for more and more of these countries' peoples and their local economies.

More recently we are seeing the rise of a strong, highly educated middle class in several African, Latin American and Asian countries keen on productive modes of development. This is a good turn of events, even if so much extraction has already destroyed much land and water bodies in some of those countries. The hope is that these new generations will care about genuine development that can bring economic openings to larger sectors of their populations.

With this background in mind, I now turn to the types of migrations that are to variable extents an outcome of such destructive modes of economic "development." But with one sharp difference: the vast extractions and destructions of the past many decades have produced a massive loss of habitat. And this, in turn, has made the expulsions of rural people more immediate and more brutal. These past restructurings have created a whole new extreme struggle for land and resources. And the indigenous populations are often the first victims. Important in my analysis is the lack of recognition in law of this third kind of migrant, one evicted from her land to make room for a mine or a plantation. This migrant fits neither of the two established subjects in law: the refugee and the immigrant. This third subject is invisible to the eye of the law as she is a refugee of what is registered as positive: certain modes of "economic development". Nor is there law that recognizes the fact that much "economic development" and wealth is based on land grabs from rural smallholders, destruction of land and water bodies by mining and plantations, and more. Migrants who lose their land or have their water supplies poisoned by nearby mines *are* refugees of such modes of economic development. There should be law that recognizes them as such. But for now the basic interpretation is that those development modes are good for a country.

European and US "development" practices over several decades, as well as their shaping influence on international institutions, such as the IMF and the World Bank, are key factors in the analysis of Africa. This is the most complex of the migration in border regions. But it is also the one that makes visible how even well-intentioned development practices can destroy habitats and thereby engender "development" refugees. The political and economic actors enabling these expulsions should be made accountable. And "development" refugees should be recognized as such.

This multidecade history of destructions of rural economies and expulsions dressed in the clothing of "modernization and development" has reached extreme levels today: vast stretches of land and water bodies are now dead due to mining, plantations, and water extraction by the likes of Nestlé (as I have also mentioned in Chapter 5). At least some of today's localized wars and conflicts in Africa arise out of such destruction and loss of habitat; climate change further reduces livable ground. And access to Europe is no longer what it used to be. This mix of conditions – wars, dead land, and expulsions of smallholders from their modest economies in the name of 'development' – has produced a vast loss of life options for a growing number of people in more and more communities. We see this in areas as diverse as Africa, Central America, and parts of Asia, notably Myanmar.

3. SOUTHEAST ASIA'S REFUGE SEEKERS AS AN EXAMPLE OF THE GLOBAL SOUTH

3.1 Southeast Asia's Refuge Seekers: The Andaman Sea

We are witnessing the shaping of a new extreme phase in Southeast Asia, a region that has long seen slavery and the smuggling of desperate refugees. The massive post-Vietnam War refugee flows have mostly sorted themselves out – in good and bad ways. This new emergent crisis arises out of a different mix of conditions; it is not a continuation of the earlier crisis. Two very recent facts signal alarming developments. One concerns several small Muslim communities escaping evictions from their land and persecution for being Muslim. Most visible is the case of the Rohingya. While some of the Rohingya have escaped from Myanmar using Bangladeshi passports, they are an old Muslim minority that has been part of Myanmar for centuries. Unlike the Rohingya, the Bangladeshis living in Myanmar have economic reasons for being there, and it is the search for employment that brings them to Myanmar, even if they may also be persecuted for being Muslims. Here I focus mostly on the Rohingya, the population living in Myanmar; they are not recognized as citizens. There is scattered evidence of active persecution of the Rohingya. The US Department of State finds that least 500,000 have been evacuated to neighboring countries

The country's opening and its enabling of foreign investors coincides with a somewhat sudden vicious persecution of the Rohingya by particular groups of Buddhist monks. That it is these particular Buddhist monks who have led this assault and, further, rewritten some parts of the doctrine so as to justify the expulsion of the Rohingyas from their land, and even the killing of Muslims, does point to larger vested economic interests that are likely to go well beyond these monks. Could this signal a deeper unsettlement? That Buddhists should become brutal persecutors of a small, peaceful Muslim minority may be only one of several other indicators pointing to a struggle for land. Could this violence signal something about the loss of habitat? There is considerable evidence in various areas of Southeast Asia about significant evictions of small farmers from their land to make way for mining, plantations, and office buildings. Foreign firms have been among the major investors since Myanmar opened its economy to foreign investment. Indeed, freed opposition leader Aung San Suu Kyi has lost considerable support among the rural population precisely because she has not contested these land grabs (at least publicly) or openly supported the local movements against land grabs. One key first public reckoning came through press reports in the summer of that about an estimated people in dozens of overloaded vessels had been floating aimlessly for up to two months in the vast Andaman Sea. This sea is bordered on the east by Myanmar and Thailand and on the south by Malaysia and Indonesia. These, and perhaps other, regional governments were aware of this surge in fleeing people but had made it clear they were going to push them back to sea if they dared to land. It was the press that sounded the alert about some of these ships, where people were piled up over each other with no water or food left. When the facts went public, Indonesia, mostly, took in about half of that estimated population, forced by the global uproar as the horrifying details went viral. The struggle to get countries to accept them was not easy. Their rescue added even more information about the horrific conditions. And that rescue still left an estimated 4,000 people floating in that vast ocean in precarious vessels. These are but one component of a larger desperate search for bare life on the part of a rapidly growing number of men, women, and children. Even as those ships were brought to land, other ships crammed with Rohingya and Bangladeshis were found off Malaysia's coast and turned away, and thousands of migrants were still believed to be stranded at sea (Tribune Wire Reports 2015). Under pressure from international bodies, Southeast Asian nations agreed at a meeting in Bangkok to set up an antitrafficking task force and to intensify search-and-rescue efforts to help vulnerable "boat people" stranded in the region's seas. How far it will all go is not clear. Nor is it clear how long it will all last, including the willingness of governments to take in desperate people. These governments have already turned back overloaded boats that are ready to sink. The current reversal of position is, to some extent, a willingness enforced by the glare of the media. And the flows are not about to end anytime soon. This alarming development concerns the enslavement of poor Thai men from the isolated mountain areas. It has long been known that the huge Thai and Malaysian fishing industries use Thai workers; it has also been known that they have often been de facto slaves. And rumors have circulated about slave camps and mass graves. But the findings of up to a hundred mass graves on the border zone between Thailand and Malaysia went beyond much that had been suspected or rumored. These extreme conditions are indicative of a larger and disturbing dynamic. There is considerable evidence confirming that the Malay military control that region: it is one of their operational spaces.

3.2 The Expulsion of the Rohingya

It is the example of a whole new phase of forced evictions: the expulsion of 800,000 Rohingya from their land by Myanmar's military – all in a short period of a few months in late 2017. These two migrations are not necessarily representative of the larger world of migrations. Rather, they serve as indicators of how bad it *can* get. Local wars and violence against mostly rural people and communities are major factors often mentioned in academic research and in the media. But they are not the only ones. A key, but mostly unrecognized explanation of these flows has to do with current development modes – by private corporations, international institutions, and quite a few governments – that are seen as positive economic growth. The Rohingya, a Muslim minority, have long lived in Rakhine state. This is one of the poorest and most isolated provinces of Myanmar, on the western side of the country, facing Bangalore across a narrow water body. They also have long been persecuted by Myanmar's military.

This persecution took on a more extreme than usual violence in 2012, when the country passed new laws that opened up its vast resources to foreign investors from a growing number of countries. Over a hundred thousand Rohingya were expelled from their villages in a fairly central part of Rakhine state. The villages were burnt down, and the Rohingya placed in camps, with the promise of a return to their villages. They are still in the camps today, their former villages evidently put to better economic uses given their proximity to Sitse, Rakhine state's main city.

Myanmar has several other minoritized peoples who have also suffered losses of their land and resources at the hand of the army. Even minoritized Buddhists have suffered land grabs. Behind these grabs of lands long used and occupied by diverse minoritized peoples lie major investors, both national and foreign. These are interested in natural resources – timber, mining, water.

But the extreme events of late 2017 mark a whole new phase in the scale of evictions of the Rohingya: an estimated 100,000 shot or burnt to death in their homes, 700,000 escaping to Bangalore in a few months, over 350 villages burnt down to the ground. Local peoples, the military, and a vast international world of concerned people and institutions invoked religious persecution as the only explanation.

Clearly religion was and is a central factor. But I find it difficult to accept that religion was the only explanation. I knew too much about the massive development projects the military were enabling and authorizing which brought them great wealth: a third of the vast Myanmar forest lost to the timber industry, a river rerouted so it brought its water to China, while leaving local rural communities without water, vast mining developments that were displacing local peoples, including minoritized Buddhists.

At this point I want to emphasize one specific aspect which led me to a whole other understanding of a critical, but overlooked element in this short brutal history. I can accept the explanation centered on religious persecution – in this case anti-Muslim persecution; this was and remains a major factor. But the risk of such a strong and effective explanation is that it can easily obscure other factors in play. Yes, there are extreme Buddhists who have proclaimed that killing Rohingya is a necessary act. And, yes, the Rohingya evidently never mixed easily with the other inhabitants, and in the current period this persecution has become extreme.

But when the military burn 350 villages, most of them in one month – September 2017 – then there is more in play.

I had already researched the massive land grabs and development projects (see Sassen 2017) that the military were enabling across the country. My question then became, what is happening in Rakhine state, that long forgotten and marginal part of Myanmar? What do the Myanmar military want to do there? By early 2017 I had information about a huge development taking place further south from the area where the 350 villages were burnt. I found it by researching China's Road and Belt project. The shadow effect of such a large development would sharply raise the price and the value of the land occupied by the Rohingya further north. Most of the responses from the international media was, no, it is all about religion.

4. CONCLUSIONS: EXTREME MIGRATIONS OR THE PROLIFERATION OF VIOLENT EXPULSION

Among the many migrations that mark today's world, my focus here is on the rise of a new type of migrant in the border regions of the Global South, one evicted from her small farm (or shop in the urban periphery) by what we commonly refer to as 'economic development' – plantations, mining, water grabs, and other large projects. This is a migrant subject for whom we lack a designation. The core feature marking this new migrant subject is that she is the victim, directly or indirectly, of a mode of "economic development" centered on extractions – of land, metals, water, and more. These are, thus, refugees who have been expelled from their land by modes of development that are measured as positive economic growth.

The presented case study brings to the fore an additional feature: extreme violence. When this is in play it has the power to obscure other factors that may actually feed the violence. Among such factors are land and water scarcity, and vast new development projects such as mines and plantations. As indicated earlier, these are de facto refugees who have been expelled from their land by what is measured as positive economic development.

Thus when they appear at our borders they are not recognized as refugees who have lost their livelihood because their countries' standard economic measures show growth in advanced economic sectors. And we lack a category that recognizes that millions of smallholders and modest middle classes every year are expelled from their land directly by major firms and major development projects. These refugees of "economic development" are invisible to the eye of the law.

Recognizing that migrations tend to happen inside systems helps explain why poverty as such is not enough to explain migration, and why the estimated total of under 300 million migrants in the world is relatively small, given the almost 3 billion poor in the world. Communities that have long been poor may not have emigrations. Or, if they do, it can be shown that they start at some point – even when a household or a community has long been poor. Most major migrations of the last two centuries, and often even earlier, can be shown to have beginnings, they are not simply there from the start. It also explains why we do not have far more migrations – especially in earlier periods when it was easier to enter another country.

Central to my analysis in this text is a concern about specific mis-representations in the general discussion about each of these two flows. This is evident in the exclusive emphasis on religion in the case of the Rohingya, such factors are in play, but there are also deeper causes behind them that need to be recognized. It is especially important because these deeper causes are obscured by overwhelming, though unwarranted, certainty regarding the standard explanations – in both the general debate and in more specific research. While specific factors are indeed in play, wars do not fall from the sky ready-made. They are made, and so is violence. And often it is the logics behind the wars and violence that we must understand: war and violence can be outcomes of a deeper condition.

NOTES

1. My work on migration has long focused on that larger context within which a new flow takes off (e.g., 1988, 1990, 1996, 1999, 2016a). At the heart of my work on the subject is that migrations happen *inside* systems, but these systems are not countries: they are the larger operational space within which the powerful countries of an epoch pursue their aims. Examples are the British Empire, the Pax Americana, and such.
2. For a full analysis of how this extraordinarily destructive modus operandi came about, see Sassen 1988. See also Sassen 2016b.
3. See also, for some of the early pioneering work, notably Frank 1969; Quijano 2000; Robinson 2008.
4. I develop these issues in great detail elsewhere. See Sassen 1988, 2014, 2016a, 2018.
5. The research literature on this subject is vast. For understanding on how the international community addressed the matter, which is just one approach, see, e.g., IMF 2015a, 2015b, 2015c. For a critical analysis, see the multiple reports produced by the Jubilee Debt Campaign (e.g., 2013a, 2013b). Elsewhere I argue (Sassen 2014: Ch. 1) that today's "austerity programs" for the Global North are a kind of equivalent of these older restructuring programs in the Global South.
6. There were also some reasonably good outcomes. Thus by 2003, debt service as a share of exports (not overall government revenue) ranged from extremely high levels for Zambia (29.6 percent) and Mauritania (27.7 percent) to significantly lowered levels (compared to the 1990s) for Uganda (down from 19.8 percent in 1995 to 7.1 percent in 2003) and Mozambique (down from 34.5 percent in 1995 to 6.9 percent in 2003).
7. To be eligible, countries have to have been compliant with the IMF for at least three years. The HIPC process begins with a "decision point" document. This sets out eligibility requirements. Among these is the development of a Poverty Reduction Strategy Paper (PRSP) that replaces the earlier Structural Adjustment Programs (SAPs). PRSPs describe "the macroeconomic, structural, and social policies and programs" that a country is required to pursue in order to be eligible for debt relief (IMF 2015a, 2015b, 2015c).
8. Thus Zambia's debt service in 1997 was 18.3 percent of income on exports but 1.3 percent by 2007 (IAEG 2009). For Ghana these figures were 27.1 percent and 3.1 percent respectively, and for Uganda 19.7 percent and 1.2 percent (IAEG 2009).

BIBLIOGRAPHY

Ackerman, Spencer, Tom Dart, Daniel Hernandez, and David Smith. 2016. "Immigration Activists Condemn US Deportation Asylum Seekers." *Guardian*, January 4. Retrieved January 10, 2016 (http://

www.theguardian.com/us-news/2016/jan/04/immigration-activists-condemn-deportationsasylum-central-america).

Albert, Eleanor. 2015. "The Rohingya Migrant Crisis." CFR Backgrounder, Council on Foreign Relations. Retrieved January 10, 2016 (http://www.cfr.org/burmamyanmar/rohingya-migrantcrisis/p36651).

Alhamad, Karam, Vera Mironova, and Sam Whitt. 2015. "In Two Charts, This Is What Refugees Say about Why They're Leaving Syria Now." *Washington Post*, September 28. Retrieved January 11, 2016 (https://www.washingtonpost.com/news/monkey-cage/wp/2015/09/28/in-two-charts-thisis-what-refugees-say-about-why-they-are-leaving-syria-now/).

Alund, Aleksandra, Branka Likic-Brboric, and Carl-Ulrik Schierup. 2015. "Migration, Precarization and the Democratic Deficit in Global Governance." *International Migration* 53(3): 50–63.

Ambrogi, Thomas E. 1999. "Goal for 2000: Unchaining Slaves of National Debt." *National Catholic Reporter*, March 26, 3–5.

Amen, Mark, and Barry Gills, eds. 2010. "Globalization and Crisis." Special issue, *Globalizations* 7(1–2).

Amin, Ash. 2012. *Land of Strangers*. Cambridge: Polity Press.

Anseeuw, Ward, Liz Alden Wily, Lorenzo Cotula, and Michael Taylor. 2012. *Land Rights and the Rush for Land: Findings of the Global Commercial Pressures on Land Research Project*. Rome: International Land Coalition.

AP. 2015a. "Deportations in Mexico up 79% in First Four Months of 2015." *Guardian*, June 11. Retrieved May 12, 2016 (http://www.theguardian.com/world/2015/jun/11/deportations-mexicocentral-america).

AP. 2015b. "Despite Border Crackdown in Ethiopia, Migrants Still Risk Lives to Leave." Guardian, August 25. Retrieved January 11, 2016 (http://www.theguardian.com/global-development/2015/aug/25/despite-border-crackdown-ethiopia-migrants-risk-lives).

Archibold, Randal C. 2014. "On Southern Border, Mexico Faces Crisis of Its Own." *New York Times*, July 19. Retrieved May 12, 2016 (http://www.nytimes.com/2014/07/20/world/americas/on-southernborder-mexico-faces-crisis-of-its-own.html?_r=3).

Arrighi, Giovanni. 1994. *The Long Twentieth Century: Money, Power, and the Origins of Our Times*. New York: Verso.

Barney, Keith, Margarita Benavides, Michael DeVito, Dominic Elson, Marina France, Alain Karsenty, Augusta Molnar, Phil Shearman, Carlos Soria, and Petro Tipula. 2011. *Large Acquisition of Rights on Forest Lands for Tropical Timber Concessions and Commercial Wood Plantations*. Rome: International Land Coalition.

Bello, Walden. 2004. *Deglobalization: Ideas for a New World Economy*. London: Zed Books.

Beneria, Lourdes, and Shelley Feldman, eds. 1992. *Unequal Burden: Economic Crises, Persistent Poverty, and Women's Work*. Boulder, CO: Westview Press.

Borras, Saturnino M., Jr., Ruth Hall, Ian Scoones, Ben White, and Wendy Wolford. 2011. "Towards a Better Understanding of Global Land Grabbing: An Editorial Introduction." *Journal of Peasant Studies* 38(2): 209–16.

Borwick, Summer, Mark Brough, Robert D. Schweitzer, Jane Shakespeare-Finch, and Lyn Vromans. 2013. "Well-being of Refugees from Burma: A Salutogenic Perspective." *International Migration* 51(5): 92–105.

Bradshaw, York W., Claudia Buchmann Sershen, Laura Gash, and Rita Noonan. 1993. "Borrowing against the Future: Children and Third World Indebtedness." *Social Forces* 71(3): 629–56.

Cockburn, Patrick. 2015. "Refugee Crisis: Where Are All These People Coming from and Why?" *Independent*, September 7. Retrieved January 11, 2016 (http://www.independent.co.uk/news/world/refugee-crisis-where-are-all-these-people-coming-from-and-why-10490425.html).

Colchester, Marcus. 2011. *Palm Oil and Indigenous Peoples in South East Asia*. Rome: International Land Coalition.

Cotula, Lorenzo. 2011. *The Outlook on Farmland Acquisitions*. Rome: International Land Coalition.

De Schutter, Olivier. 2011. "How Not to Think of Land Grabbing: Three Critiques of Large-Scale Investments in Farmland." *Journal of Peasant Studies* 38(2): 249–79.

Foo, Wen, and Simon Scarr. 2015. "Asia's Migrant Crisis." Reuters Graphics. Retrieved January 10, 2016 (http://graphics.thomsonreuters.com/15/rohingya/index.html).

Frank, Andre Gunder. 1969. *Sociology of Development and Underdevelopment of Sociology*. Stockholm: Zenit.
Frank, Andre Gunder. 1998. *Re-Orient: Global Economy in the Asian Age*. Berkeley: University of California Press.
Friis, Cecilie, and Anette Reenberg. 2010. *Land Grab in Africa: Emerging Land System Drivers in a Teleconnected World*. GLP Report No. 1. Copenhagen: Global Land Project International Project Office.
Gecker, Jocelyn. 2015. "Asia's Migrant Crisis: Who's Going to Friday's Summit, and Where Do They Stand?" *Globe and Mail*, May 28. Retrieved January 13, 2016 (http://www.theglobeandmail.com/news/world/asias-migrant-crisis-whos-going-to-fridays-summit-and-where-do-they-stand/article24659168/).
Gorra, Vanessa, and Roel R. Ravanera. 2011. *Commercial Pressures on Land in Asia: An Overview*. Rome: International Land Coalition.
Hall, Ruth. 2011. "Land Grabbing in Africa and the New Politics of Food." Future Agricultures, Policy Brief 41, June. Retrieved April 13, 2016 (http://www.future-agricultures.org/publications/researchand-analysis/1427-land-grabbing-in-africa-and-the-new-politics-of-food/file).
Hampshire, James. 2015. "Europe's Migration Crisis." *Political Insight* 6(3): 8–11.
Harvey, David. 2003. *The New Imperialism*. Oxford: Oxford University Press.
International Monetary Fund (IMF). 2015a. "Factsheet: Poverty Reducing Strategy in IMF-supported Programs." International Monetary Fund, Washington, DC.
International Monetary Fund (IMF). 2015b. "Financial Soundness Indicators (FSIs)." International Monetary Fund, Washington, DC.
International Monetary Fund (IMF). 2015c. "Vulnerabilities, Legacies, and Policy Challenges: Risks Rotating to Emerging Markets. Global Financial Stability Report." International Monetary Fund, Washington, DC.
Jubilee Debt Campaign. 2013a. "Life and Debt: Global Studies of Debt and Resistance." Retrieved November 13, 2020 (https://jubileedebt.org.uk/wp-content/uploads/2013/10/Life-and-debt_Final-version_10.13.pdf).
Jubilee Debt Campaign. 2013b. "Vulture Finds Cause Chaos over Argentina." Retrieved November 13, 2020 (https://jubileedebt.org.uk/news/vulture-funds-cause-chaos-argentine-debt).
Kanupriya, Kapoor, and Amy Sawitta Lefevre. 2015. "SE Asia Vows to Rescue 'Boat People'; Myanmar Seizes Migrant Vessel." Reuters, May 29. Retrieved January 11, 2016 (http://www.reuters.com/article/us-asia-migrants-us-idUSKBN0OE05T20150529).
Kingsley, Patrick. 2015a. "It's Not at War, but Up to 3% of Its People Have Fled. What Is Going On in Eritrea?" *Guardian*, July 22. Retrieved January 11, 2016 (http://www.theguardian.com/world/2015/jul/22/eritrea-migrants-child-soldier-fled-what-is-going).
Kingsley, Patrick. 2015b. "Refugee Crisis: Apart from Syrians, Who Is Traveling to Europe?" *Guardian*, September 10. Retrieved January 11, 2016 (http://www.theguardian.com/world/ 2015/sep/10/refuge-crisis-apart-from-syrians-who-else-is-travelling-to-europe).
Koslowski, Rey, and David Kyle. 2001. *Global Human Smuggling: Comparative Perspectives*. Baltimore: Johns Hopkins University Press.
Land Matrix. 2015. *Land Matrix Newsletter*. November. Retrieved January 13, 2016 (http://www.landmatrix.org/media/filer_public/95/1c/951c640e-3cda-4a0b-821c-3c5142b901b7/7365_up_ispa_land_matrix_newsletter_261115.pdf).
Land Matrix. 2016a. "Dynamics Overview." Land Matrix. Retrieved January 13, 2016 (continuously updated) (http://www.landmatrix.org/en/get-the-idea/dynamics-overview/).
Land Matrix. 2016b. "Land Matrix: The Online Public Database on Land Deals." Land Matrix. Retrieved January 13, 2016 (http://www.landmatrix.org/en/).
Lucas, Linda E., ed. 2005. *Unpacking Globalization: Markets, Gender, and Work*. Kampala: Makerere University Press.
Mala, William. 2011."Chinese Trade and Investment and the Forests of the Congo Basin: Synthesis of Scoping Studies in Cameroon, Democratic Republic of Congo and Gabon." Working paper, Center for International Forestry Research, Bogor, Indonesia. Retrieved April 13, 2016 (http:// www.cifor.org/publications/pdf_files/WPapers/WP67Putzel.pdf).
Maldonado-Torres, Nelson. 2007. "On the Coloniality of Being." *Cultural Studies* 21(2): 240–70.

Marx, Karl. 1992. *Capital*. Vol. 1. London: Penguin Classics.
Mignolo, Walter. 2007. "Delinking: The Rhetoric of Modernity, the Logic of Coloniality, and the Grammar of De-coloniality." *Cultural Studies* 21(2): 449–514.
Quijano, Anibal. 2000. "Coloniality of Power, Euro centrism and Latin America." *Nepantla: Views from the South* 1(3): 533–80.
Rahman, Aminur. 1999. "Micro-credit Initiatives for Equitable and Sustainable Development: Who Pays?" *World Development* 27(10): 67–82.
Robinson, William I. 2004. *A Theory of Global Capitalism: Production, Class, and State in a Transnational World*. Baltimore: Johns Hopkins University Press.
Robinson, William I. 2008. *Latin America and Global Capitalism: A Globalization Perspective*. Baltimore: Johns Hopkins University Press.
Sassen, Saskia. 1988. *The Mobility of Labor and Capital*. Cambridge: Cambridge University Press.
Sassen, Saskia. 1990. *The Global City: New York, London, and Tokyo*. Princeton, NJ: Princeton University Press.
Sassen, Saskia. 1996. *Losing Control? Sovereignty in the Age of Globalization*. New York: Columbia University Press.
Sassen, Saskia. 1999. *Guests and Aliens*. New York: New Press.
Sassen, Saskia. 2008a. *Territory, Authority, Rights: From Medieval to Global Assemblages*. 2nd, rev. ed. Princeton, NJ: Princeton University Press.
Sassen, Saskia. 2008b. "Two Stops in Today's New Global Geographies: Shaping Novel Labor Supplies and Employment Regimes." *American Behavioral Scientist* 52(3): 457–96.
Sassen, Saskia. 2013a. "Global Finance and Its Institutional Spaces," pp. 13–32 in *The Oxford Handbook of the Sociology of Finance*, edited by K. Knorr-Cetina and A. Preda. Oxford: Oxford University Press.
Sassen, Saskia. 2013b. "When Territory Deborders Territoriality." *Territory, Politics, Governance* 1(1): 21–45.
Sassen, Saskia. 2014. *Expulsions: Brutality and Complexity in the Global Economy*. Cambridge, MA: Belknap Press of Harvard University Press.
Sassen, Saskia. 2016a. "A Massive Loss of Habitat: New Drivers for Migration." *Sociology of Development* 2(2): 204–33.
Sassen, Saskia. 2016b. "Economic Cleansing: Failure Dressed in Fine Clothes." *Social Research* 83(3): 673–87.
Sassen, Saskia. 2017. "Is Rohingya Persecution Caused by Business Interests rather than Religion?" *The Guardian*, January 4. Retrieved November 18, 2020 (https://www.theguardian.com/global-development-professionals-network/2017/jan/04/is-rohingya-persecution-caused-by-business-interests-rather-than-religion).
Sassen, Saskia. 2018. "Embedded Borderings: Making New Geographies of Centrality." *Territory, Politics, Governance* 6(1): 5–15.
Sassen-Koob, Saskia. 1982. "Recomposition and Peripheralization at the Core." *Contemporary Marxism* 5: 88–100.
Toussaint, Eric. 1999. "Poor Countries Pay More under Debt Reduction Scheme?" TWN (Third World Network), July. Retrieved May 12, 2016 (http://www.twn.my/title/1921-cn.htm).
Tribune Wire Reports. 2015. "Another Boat Found at Sea as Rohingya Refugee Crisis Deepens." *Chicago Tribune*, May 13. Retrieved January 13, 2016 (http://www.chicagotribune.com/news/nation-world/ct-rohingya-refugees-20150513-story.html).
UNDP. 2005. *A Time for Bold Ambition: Together We Can Cut Poverty in Half*. Annual Report. New York: UNDP.
UNDP. 2008. *Human Development Report, 2007–2008*. Annual Report. New York: UNDP.
UNDP. 2014. *Human Development Report 2014*. Annual Report. New York: UNDP.
UNDP. 2015. *Human Development Report 2015*. Annual Report. New York: UNDP.
UN High Commissioner for Refugees (UNHCR). 2015a. "Facts and Figures about Refugees." Retrieved January 11, 2016 (http://www.unhcr.ie/about-unhcr/facts-and-figures-about-refugees).
UNHCR. 2015b. "2015 UNHCR Country Operations Profile—Pakistan." Retrieved January 11, 2016 (http://www.unhcr.org/pages/49e487016.html).

UNHCR. 2015c. "2015 UNHCR Subregional Operations Profile—East and Horn of Africa." Retrieved January 11, 2016 (http://www.unhcr.org/pages/ 49e4838e6.html).
UNHCR. 2015d. *World at War. UNHCR Global Trends 2014.* Retrieved January 9, 2016 (http://www.unhcr.org/556725e69.html).
UN Inter-agency and Expert Group on MDG Indicators (IAEG). 2009. *The Millennium Development Goals Report.* New York: United Nations. Retrieved April 13, 2016 (http://www.un.org/millenniumgoals/pdf/MDG_Report_2009_ENG.pdf).
Vanderklippe, Nathan. 2015. "In Transit to Nowhere: Rohingya Move from One Bleak Horizon to Another." *Globe and Mail*, May 28. Retrieved January 13, 2016 (http://www.theglobeandmail.com/news/world/in-transit-to-nowhere-rohingya-move-from-one-bleak-horizon-to-another/article24624679/).
VanderPijl, Kees, ed. 2015. *Handbook of the International Political Economy of Production.* Cheltenham, UK and Northampton, MA, USA: Edward Elgar Publishing.
Von Braun, Joachim, and Ruth Meinzen-Dick. 2009. *"Land Grabbing" by Foreign Investors in Developing Countries: Risks and Opportunities.* Washington, DC: International Food Policy Research Institute.
Wiener Bravo, Elisa. 2011. *The Concentration of Land Ownership in Latin America: An Approach to Current Problems.* Rome: International Land Coalition.
World Bank. 2005. "Increasing Aid and Its Effectiveness," pp. 151–188 in *Global Monitoring Report: Millennium Development Goals: From Consensus to Momentum.* Washington, DC: World Bank.
World Bank. 2006. *Global Economic Prospects: Economic Implications of Remittances and Migration.* Washington, DC: World Bank.
World Bank. 2015a. *Global Economic Prospects: The Global Economy in Transition.* Washington, DC: World Bank.
World Bank. 2015b. *Global Monitoring Report: Development Goals in an Era of Demographic Change.* Washington, DC: World Bank.
World Bank. 2015c. "Intentional Homicides (per 100,000 People)." World Bank Database. Retrieved January 10, 2016 (http://data.worldbank.org/indicator/VC.IHR.PSRC.P5?order=wbapi_data_value_2013+wbapi_data_value+wbapi_data_value-last&sort=desc).
World Bank. 2015d. "Latin America and Caribbean." Poverty and Equity. Retrieved January 10, 2016 (http://povertydata.worldbank.org/poverty/region/LAC).
Yearwood, Edilma L. 2014. "Let Us Respect the Children: The Plight of Unaccompanied Youth." *Journal of Child and Adolescent Psychiatric Nursing* 27(4): 205–6.

19. Borders and violence in Burundi: regional responses, global responsibilities
Niamh Gaynor

1. INTRODUCTION

Situated within the volatile Great Lakes region of Africa, Burundi has suffered decades of violence, displacement and re-displacement, most notably following the third-term bid in 2015 by the country's president, Pierre Nkurunziza. The unrest preceding and following these elections has cost more than 1,000 lives and, in a country of just 10 million, an estimated 400,000–500,000 have been displaced and re-displaced over the last four years (UNHCR, 2019a). Clearly, efforts at peacebuilding and conflict transformation have failed. Examining the reasons for this, in this chapter I argue that the global aid community bears some responsibility for this failure through both its failed peacebuilding model and its implicit sanctioning of ongoing political intimidation and violence. Given this global complicity in fomenting and sustaining the current crisis, I argue for an attendant globalised politics of responsibility in responding to it. This includes lifting the glass ceiling on migration, thereby affording Burundians the opportunity and agency to seek employment elsewhere and assist their home communities directly.

The chapter proceeds as follows. In the next section I set out the background to the ongoing violence and displacement in the country. Exploring the reasons for this, I move beyond simplistic ethnic explanations and highlight the fundamentally political nature of the unrest whereby, with implicit if not explicit Western collusion, the country's wealth has been and continues to be siphoned off by a political elite which is determined to remain in power at any cost. I then go on to examine regional policies and responses to the ensuing crisis. I highlight the detrimental effects of the lack of international support for regional initiatives which have left displaced households in limbo, living in deplorable conditions, with few opportunities for employment, and under threat of forced repatriation. Arguing for a global politics of responsibility in this regard, in the final section I develop this concept and flesh out what such a politics would entail.

2. VIOLENCE AND DISPLACEMENT IN BURUNDI – SOME BACKGROUND

Burundi is a small landlocked country in Central Africa. With a per capita Gross National Income (GNI) of just $702 and a Human Development Index ranking of 185 (out of 189 countries), it ranks as one of the poorest countries in the world (UNDP, 2018). It is also one of the most unequal, with a Gini coefficient of 33.3 per cent (UNDP, 2018). As the second most densely populated country in Africa, land stresses are significant and local conflicts over land are exacerbated by displaced people returning to find other families on their land (Kirchhof,

2009). Food insecurity is almost double the average in sub-Saharan Africa (SSA). According to the World Bank, some 1.8 million people are food insecure, with over half the children (six in ten) suffering from stunting in 2017.[1]

2.1 Ongoing Violence and Displacement

Since attaining independence from Belgium in 1962, Burundi has been plagued by internal conflict and violence as different political actors mobilise for power and control over the country's resources. This has resulted in successive waves of displacement and re-displacement over the decades. In 1993, the country descended into a brutal civil war. Hundreds of thousands of Burundians were displaced, fleeing internally, to neighbouring countries and further afield. A peace agreement was signed in Arusha, Tanzania in 2000 but the war still dragged on as two rebel groups continued to fight. Elections were held in 2005 leading to a new power-sharing executive with ethnic quotas. It was not until 2009, however, that the war finally came to an end when members of the rebel groups were integrated into the army (Reyntjens, 2005). While there was hope and stability for a short time, with the 2000 peace negotiations internationally hailed as a "success",[2] the 2010 elections were marred by intimidation and violence by all contesting parties and unrest continued thereafter, with ongoing reports of political intimidation, repression and extra-judicial political assassinations (Gaynor, 2014a).

This violence escalated with the ruling party's announcement, on April 25, 2015, that the sitting president, Pierre Nkurunziza, would run for a third term in the forthcoming elections scheduled for June 26, 2015, even though the constitution limits presidential tenure to two terms of office. Opposition parties and their adherents took to the streets. Security forces responded with force and the country once again descended into violent chaos (Wilén, 2016). When Nkurunziza won the disputed election,[3] violence once again escalated. There were numerous grenade attacks, including on civilian targets and police forces, with the violence reaching a peak on December 11 with attacks on army barracks. The government crackdown that followed reportedly left 34 people dead in the streets of the capital, Bujumbura, in addition to those killed in the attacks (Jacobsen and Engell, 2018). Although 2016 saw a reduction in general violence toward civilians, repression, intimidation and political assassinations increased. More than 300,000 people were displaced and remained outside the country. During 2017, 60,000 more people fled, bringing the total refugee population to over 400,000. Many of those fleeing were doing so for a second or third time, having been repatriated over ten years previously (Purdeková, 2016).

Although the Burundian government now insists that the instability is over, ordinary Burundians do not seem to agree and internal and external displacement continues (UNHCR, 2019a). Human Rights Watch (2019: 102), cataloguing a long list of human rights abuses, characterises the humanitarian situation as "dire", while a recent report by the United Nations (UN's) Commission of Enquiry on Burundi (UNHCR, 2019b) notes that "Serious human rights violations, including crimes against humanity, have continued to take place since May 2018", with the main perpetrators being the ruling party's youth wing. In the run up to the elections in May 2020, there were reports that members of a newly formed opposition party had been arrested, beaten, disappeared and killed by the authorities and their affiliated youth militia.[4] Meanwhile, as regional and international support for refugees dwindles, the UN Refugee agency claims that hundreds of new refugees are still fleeing from the country each month.[5]

2.2 The Failure of Peacebuilding and the Global Community

It is clear, therefore, that violence and unrest continues, and that there has been a profound failure in addressing the root causes of conflict despite the internationally acclaimed Peace and Reconciliation Agreement of 2000. There are two principal reasons for this failure. The first is an overly reductionist approach to the peacebuilding process which, according to evidence, over-emphasised the ethnic dimensions of the violence over its political nature. While ethnic tensions have certainly been one of the key drivers of violence in the past (see Reyntjens, 2005; Daley, 2006; Lemarchand, 2007; Curtis, 2013), these are just one dimension of a much more complex political and social picture where inequality, political power and violence intersect, and where ethnic tensions can be, and have been, mobilised by a small group of powerful political elites to maintain their position of status and privilege (Ndikumana, 2005; Daley, 2006). Peter Uvin (2010: 170) describes it well.

> In Burundi ... high inequality was produced and maintained by the control of a small elite on the levers of the state (foremost the army). Corruption and rent-seeking, unequal access to education and privileged control over aid funds were the main pathways through which these elites managed to reproduce their advantages.

Indeed, the Arusha Peace and Reconciliation Agreement begins by stating that the civil war was "fundamentally political, with extremely important ethnic dimensions; it stems from a struggle by the political class to accede to and/or remain in power".[6] Yet, the agreement that followed focused largely on the ethnic dimension, and a culture of impunity for political elites from past and ongoing atrocities was allowed to develop (Lemarchand, 2007; Wilén, 2016). Wilén (2016: 70), pointing to the blind eye turned by global actors to the state's growing authoritarian tendencies, argues that "international actors have adopted a comfortable 'laissez-faire' approach in the case of Burundi, characterized by a 'good enough' peace. Relative stability has been exchanged for autocratic tendencies and an increasingly limited political space." This mirrors the attitude of global actors in neighbouring Rwanda where the state has grown increasingly authoritarian and repressive also (see Reyntjens, 2004; Beswick, 2010; Gaynor, 2016). As in the case of neighbouring Rwanda, the global community's need for a success story dominated international narratives and strategy around the Burundian process from 2000 forward. As Campbell (cited in Grauvogel, 2016: 8) notes: "in the wake of the 'unexpected success of Arusha', the international community, and especially Western donors, ignored the negative patterns that became visible from 2006 onwards".

The second reason for the failure in peacebuilding has been the international community's prioritisation of short-term relative stability over more long-term conflict transformation in its programming and support. A number of specific shortcomings can be identified. First, security sector reform, which has constituted a cornerstone of international peacebuilding since 2000, failed to prevent a renewed politicisation of the armed forces. In particular, and as seen elsewhere (see Kilroy, 2015), the "R" of the DDR (disarmament, demobilisation, reintegration) process was never fully funded or implemented. The result is that, as Grauvogel (2016: 10) argues, "it is now easy for the government to remobilise the former rebels to carry out violent attacks on the opposition", which, as we have seen, is precisely what is happening today. Second, in relation to governance and democracy, the focus has been largely on high-level politics while ignoring local societal concerns. Both Curtis (2013) and Gaynor (2014b) have demonstrated the exclusionary nature of new governance arrangements, despite their inclusionary rhetoric. Citizens remain marginalised from local political fora and have little or no voice in the governance of their affairs. Third, the concerns of returning refugees post-war and pre-2015 were never met. While both the international community and the Burundian government have hailed the repatriation of large numbers, Purdeková's research among displaced and re-displaced Burundians both highlights the cyclicality of this displacement and the fundamentally political motivations underpinning it. As she notes (2016: 3), one of the principal reasons for their displacement and determination not to return is the profound sense of distrust in the state and its institutions – "The picture that emerges is one of citizenship defined by broken political promises, unclear state motives, the lack of vertical accountability and resulting in feelings of distrust and deception". And, finally, again as in the case of neighbouring Rwanda (see Hayman, 2011; Gaynor, 2016), the global community's need for a successful peacebuilding example dominated international narratives and strategy around the Burundian process from 2000 forward.

Thus, international and regional peacebuilding efforts, in prioritising stability over more long-term peace, failed to address the root causes of violence. This contributed to the development of a highly fragile post-war climate, one which stood ready to explode at any moment. As we will now see, when that moment came, international actors proved equally ineffective in rising to the resultant challenges, most notably in relation to support for the displaced, both regionally and internationally.

3. REGIONAL POLICIES AND RESPONSES

As we have seen, ongoing political tensions and violence coupled with rising food insecurity has resulted in a deterioration of the humanitarian situation within Burundi and waves of displacement and re-displacement continue. Yet, according to the UNHCR, the Burundian refugee crisis was the least funded internationally in 2018.[7] In 2019 a shortfall of 78 per cent in the required funding was reported.[8] As this section demonstrates, this international failure to adequately respond to the political and humanitarian crisis is both irresponsible and unjust. As a political stalemate continues between regional governments and international agencies over who is responsible and who should take action, displaced households are left in limbo, living in deplorable conditions, with few opportunities for employment, and under a threat of forced repatriation.

3.1 Migration Figures – Where Are the Displaced Going?

International migration figures for Burundi tell an interesting story. Numbers of migrants to non-African countries have traditionally been and remain extremely low in comparison to regional migration figures. The principal recipient countries internationally are Canada (which received 635 migrants in 2016), the United States (which received 415 migrants in 2016), Belgium (which received 333 migrants in 2016), France (which received 127 migrants in 2016), Australia (which received 120 migrants in 2016) and Sweden (which received 94 migrants in 2016).[9] While the reasons for such low figures are of course complex, the restrictive migration policies in non-African countries coupled with the expense and danger of travel are undoubtedly key factors.

Regionally, migration figures from Burundi are much higher. Of the 400,000 plus Burundians who have fled the country since 2015, over half of these have fled to Tanzania, while Rwanda, the Democratic Republic of the Congo (DRC) and Uganda have hosted 72,612, 45,447 and 42,334 respectively (UNHCR, 2019a). While these countries, most notably Tanzania, have traditionally been very generous in opening their borders to Burundians (see also below), the acute shortfall in international support coupled with domestic challenges means that borders are now closing and options to cross regional borders are becoming more and more difficult. According to the UNHCR, refugees are no longer being granted refugee status on a *prima facie* basis in Tanzania, Uganda and DRC (UNHCR, 2019a).

Internally within Burundi, many other people have been displaced, with people fleeing from urban to remote rural areas in the hills. Although it is hard to determine exactly how many people are internally displaced, the most recent figures (May 2019) from the International Organization for Migration (IOM) estimate that there are 124,578 internally displaced people (IDP) within the country.[10]

3.2 Living Conditions of the Displaced

Whether internally displaced or settled in refugee camps across the border, living conditions for displaced individuals and households are reported to be extremely poor. According to the IOM, 57 per cent of internally displaced households have access to just one meal a day; 37 per cent have no access to clean drinking water; and 94 per cent have no access to services following incidents of gender-based violence. In certain provinces, over 90 per cent of IDP cannot afford health care; over 90 per cent have no access to a latrine; and over 50 per cent of children from IDP household do not attend school.[11]

Conditions in refugee camps across the border are also reported to be poor, with widespread overcrowding and cholera reported. According to Lukunka (2011), while in the refugee camps, displaced people are subject to attacks from roaming bandits. Incidents of violence against women are extremely high. Moreover, refugees in camps in Tanzania are not allowed to leave the camps in search of food or work and are forced to remain completely reliant on the limited services offered by camp authorities and international agencies such as the UNHCR.[12] The UNHCR (2019a) reports that 54 per cent of Burundian refugees are children. These face specific challenges, including family separation, early marriage, teenage pregnancy, child neglect, child labour, domestic violence, sexual and gender-based violence, and psycho-social distress.

3.3 Border and Refugee Policy in Tanzania

As the above figures illustrate, Tanzania has long been extremely generous in opening its borders and providing refuge to Burundian displaced people. The 1972 genocide against the Hutu population produced one of Africa's most prolonged refugee situations as an estimated 275,000 fled. Although a number returned thereafter, 220,000 opted to stay. Under Tanzania's then "Open Door" policy, these were allocated 5 hectares of land per family in three designated settlements in western Tanzania. By 1985, they were largely self-sufficient (Milner, 2014). More arrived later and were hosted in refugee camps in north-west Tanzania.

In 2007, the Tanzanian and Burundian governments in partnership with the UNHCR adopted an innovative strategy which offered a choice between repatriation and naturalisation to the 220,000 refugees living in three settlements in western Tanzania. The TANCOSS, as it was known (Tanzania Comprehensive Solutions Strategy), was an unprecedented intervention designed to offer stability and security to the long-term displaced families and it attracted much international attention and support (Milner, 2014). Only 20 per cent of the 1972 Burundian refugees in Tanzania elected to go home. Many returned to find their land occupied after their long absence, with these secondary occupants having accrued certain legal rights. Land tenure conflicts are thus common among internally displaced and externally repatriated people in Burundi (Thomson, 2009). The vast majority of the displaced expressed a desire to remain in Tanzania where they were promised citizenship and relocation to new plots of land.

While this strategy received widespread international acclaim, it was not without its shortcomings. Most notably, it fell victim to domestic opposition in relation to local integration and was never fully implemented (Milner, 2014). Plans for resettlement were abandoned and the newly naturalised migrants were permitted to remain in the areas of the settlements in which they had lived for the past four decades. As a result, it remains unclear when and how a transition to local governance will take place and what rights to the land the newly naturalised migrants in these settlements have (Kuch, 2018). As Kuch describes it, it is like being "left in limbo". As one migrant notes, "people here don't have ownership, you can be taken off your land at any time… It's like a marriage with no certificate".[13]

The Tanzanian government has since pulled back further in its accommodation of migrants. In 2012, refugees were forcibly repatriated from a camp in Mtabila by, first, having all services removed, then enduring a prohibition on all income-generating activities and finally, being forced to return to Burundi.[14] In 2017, the Tanzanian president suspended the granting of citizenship to Burundian refugees.[15] And in January 2018, the Tanzanian government halted the naturalisation of another group of more recently arrived Burundian refugees. It has since pulled out of the UN's Comprehensive Refugee Response Framework due to shortfalls in international funding.[16] Little of the $103 million earmarked for relocation and integration of naturalised refugees in the 2011–15 United Nations Development Assistant Plan has materialised, and a stalemate has developed between humanitarian organisations and the government with each accusing the other of broken promises. Residents of the settlements have been forced to live in uncertainty as they wait for citizenship documents and investment in infrastructure like access to clean water. Their situation worsened considerably with the announcement of forced repatriation after October 1, 2019.[17] While both the Tanzanian and Burundian government claim that conditions in Burundi have now stabilised, refugees fear otherwise. As one anonymous refugee, speaking to the BBC has noted, "It's very unfortunate. What have the international community or Tanzania done to stop Nkurunziza's government from persecuting people? There are killings, abductions and dead bodies found later. They are pushing us back to be killed."

While "unfortunate" is certainly an understatement, the refugee's comment neatly encapsulates the international community's egregious abdication of responsibility in the face of ongoing violence and insecurity. As the promised resources and supports for displaced individuals and families have failed to materialise, with shortfalls of 78 per cent reported for 2018, it has largely been left to regional neighbours to deal with the crisis. Yet, as we have seen in the preceding section, the international community bears a degree of responsibility for this crisis. It therefore should bear some of the responsibility for its resolution. This necessarily involves moving beyond the failed initiatives of the past which sought to contain rather than transform the underlying conditions of insecurity. It involves moving beyond piecemeal and uncertain funding supports in the region to a more globalised politics of responsibility. In the following section I develop this concept and flesh out in more detail what this might entail.

4. FROM COMPASSION TO CULPABILITY: THE CASE FOR A GLOBALISED POLITICS OF RESPONSIBILITY

Promoting charity, assistance and support, the international humanitarian system is underpinned by ideals of compassion, sympathy and empathy for others. Confronted with distressing images of suffering and hardship, we are exhorted to dig deep and demonstrate compassion and charity. This is reflected, *inter alia*, in the identities and titles of a number of leading international non-governmental organisations (NGOs) such as Care International, Concern International, Caritas (meaning "charity" in Greek and "love for all" in Latin), and Trócaire (meaning "mercy" in Irish). Yet, such framing negates the globalised nature of many humanitarian crises – both past and present – thereby negating the shared culpability of the Global North in fomenting, sustaining and, in some instances, exacerbating these crises. The causes of specific crises are often underdeveloped or, where they are, these are identified as being internal to Southern countries themselves, as opposed to being linked to broader structural constraints, or indeed, the failures or shortcomings of the global community and its interventions. The South is the problem, not the North. Moreover, the agency of Southern actors (state and civil society) in addressing these obstacles is largely negated as Southern actors are generally represented as constituting their principal architects. It therefore falls to Northern actors and institutions – i.e. the global aid community – to intervene and assist, thus laying the foundation and rationale for the global aid industry. The language of the aid community is replete with such ideology. To take an example, in a commentary on a World Bank's recent poverty report, Nirav Patel of the Brookings Institute notes "the remarkable progress *the world has achieved* toward ending extreme poverty" (Patel, 2018: 20 – emphasis added), yet goes on to speak of "sub-Saharan Africa's much slower fight against poverty". Successes are attributed to the global community, while any failures are the Global South's alone. This Northern saviour complex is not just damaging and demeaning to Southern actors and communities, it also masks the shortcomings and errors of Northern actors and institutions, negating their complicity in the production and reproduction of global inequality and unrest. In this section I outline four ways in which this complicity and culpability for the ongoing violence and unrest has played out in Burundi and its neighbouring region. I go on to make the case for a concomitant globalised politics of responsibility in addressing, in a sustainable and transformative way, both the fallout from and the roots of this violence.

First, colonial legacies continue to play a key role in contemporary politics within the region. Specifically, the ethnic tensions which have been identified as constituting one dimension of past and ongoing unrest are rooted in the "divide and rule" tactics of former European colonising powers (Young, 1988). In addition, the neo-patrimonial spoils politics which underpinned both the president's third-term bid in 2015 and the opposition's reaction to this are also a direct legacy of the colonial administration's system of indirect rule in the region (Young, 1988). Burundi's violent, extractive "big man's politics" was not born yesterday or in the recent past. Rather, it is the inevitable outcome of decades of violent, extractive colonial administration where the objective was neither equality or development, but suppression and exploitation (Ndikumana, 2005).

Second, although it is now 60 years since the colonial occupiers officially left the region, global extraction and exploitation continues apace. According to one account (Honest Accounts, 2017: 7), although African countries receive around $19 billion in aid each year, over three times that much ($68 billion) is taken out in capital flight, mainly by multinational companies (MNCs) deliberately misreporting the value of their imports or exports to reduce tax (Honest Accounts, 2017: 2). Moreover, MNCs legally extract $32 billion each year, while illegal logging, trade in wildlife, and fishing account for $17 billion, $10 billion, and $1.7 billion respectively (Honest Accounts, 2017: 2). While specific figures for particular countries are difficult to source, one study estimates that illicit outflows from Burundi amounted to $92 million in 2015 (GFI, 2019: 31), while its resource rich neighbour, the DRC, lost a total of $15.5 billion in illicit capital flight from 1980 through to 2006 (GFI, 2008).

Third, although often celebrated in the Global North for its achievements in reducing poverty in poorer countries, the empirical evidence on international aid's effectiveness in this regard is far more mixed, both in terms of quantities of aid dispensed and in terms of its effectiveness. Overall, volumes of aid to the Global South are falling. They fell by 3 per cent in 2018, with humanitarian aid falling by 8 per cent.[18] Aid flows to Burundi have followed a similar trend with the country's aid receipts amounting to just 12 per cent of its per capita GNI ($290) in 2017. In contrast, neighbouring Rwanda, which has a per capita GNI of $720, received aid amounting to 14 per cent of its GNI that same year, while Malawi, a country somewhat on a par with Burundi in terms of poverty (its per capita income was $320 in 2017) received aid amounting to 25 per cent of its GNI that same year.[19] According to the UNHCR, the Burundian refugee crisis was the least funded internationally in 2018. In 2019, there was a shortfall of 78 per cent in the required funding, with just $64 million of the $293 million required secured (UNHCR, 2019b). More broadly, as we have already seen, aid that has been dispensed has proven less than effective, as the global community has prioritised of short-term relative stability over more long-term conflict transformation in its programming and support. Although peace negotiations, held in Arusha, Tanzania, were widely declared a "success",[20] ongoing reports of political intimidation in the years that followed, and the overt insecurity and violence that has characterised the last four years (Human Rights Watch, 2019; UNHCR, 2019b) indicate a profound failure in aid efforts from 2000 forward.

And, fourth, although Burundi ranks as one of the poorest countries in the world with its refugees receiving one of the lowest levels of support globally, Burundian migrants are also largely denied access to employment opportunities in the Global North. During the last four years, of the 400,000 people who have fled the country, over half have been welcomed in the neighbouring country of Tanzania, while Rwanda, the DRC and Uganda have hosted 72,612, 45,447 and 42,334 respectively (UNHCR, 2019a). International migration figures are significantly lower, registering in the hundreds per annum in contrast to regional figures. This is in stark contrast to broader trends more globally. The World Bank reports that the worldwide number of international migrants has been increasing steadily from a level of 18 million in 2010 to 270 million in 2019 (2019: 9). Included in these figures are asylum seekers and refugees. By mid-2018, the global stock of refugees recorded by the UNHCR reached 20.2 million (World Bank, 2019: 9). These migrants and refugees are estimated to have sent a combined $698 billion back home in 2019 (World Bank, 2019: 9). This is over three times the volume of aid flows. As aid flows dwindle and stagnate, remittances are rising at a rapid rate in those countries that choose to welcome them.

While certainly not a panacea for poverty reduction and distributional justice, migrant remittances can and are assisting individuals and communities in real, tangible ways. They therefore represent another – potentially very significant – dimension of a global politics of responsibility. Remittances already play an important role in development within many Southern countries, amounting to over 25 per cent of some country's annual Gross Domestic Product (GDP) (for example, Haiti, Nepal, Tonga and Tajikistan) (World Bank, 2019: 3). As well as assisting families and communities to purchase necessities such as food, clothing and housing, these direct flows can also help in the development of livelihoods and businesses. Yet remittances to some of the world's poorest countries, notably those in SSA, remain at a much lower level. At the high end, remittances to some SSA countries[21] amount to between 7 and 15 per cent GDP (World Bank, 2019: 23), yet some of the continent's poorest countries such as Burundi receive less than 1 per cent GDP,[22] as the vast majority of Burundian migrants and refugees are forced to remain in neighbouring countries where employment opportunities are limited.

The reason for this is the failure of countries in the Global North to embrace their global responsibilities. Despite European proclamations of a migration "crisis" in the face of different conflicts worldwide, countries in the Global South have historically hosted and continue to host by far the largest share of refugees. This was around 85 per cent of the global total in 2018 (UNHCR, 2018). Meanwhile, the approval rate for asylum applications in the European Union (EU) has been falling – from 46 per cent in 2017 to 37 per cent in 2018. With a total stock of over 870,000 pending asylum applications at the end of 2018 and also considering detected undocumented economic migrants, the World Bank (2019: 11) estimates the number of migrants refused entry into EU countries in 2018 at over 6 million. The growing anti-immigration sentiment in many European countries is clearly having an influence. Although, in December 2018, the UN General Assembly voted to formally adopt a Global Compact for Safe, Orderly, and Regular Migration as a step toward managing migration in a more humane and orderly manner, the withdrawal of several countries (mostly from within the EU) from this is indicative of heightened political sensitivities toward immigration.[23] A glass ceiling exists and, as political sensitivities toward immigration heighten, the ceiling is turning to concrete. Such trends are indicative of an abrogation of culpability and responsibility on the part of the global community and undermine efforts toward building a global politics of responsibility.

There is, therefore, a fundamental hypocrisy at the heart of the global system. While the global community bears a significant degree of responsibility for this current crisis in Burundi and its neighbouring region, it is reluctant to share responsibility for its resolution. This is most starkly apparent in its lack of support for refugees in the region, leaving it to much poorer and crisis-ridden countries to bear the burden, and in its hardening stance on migration and the important remittance opportunities that this can offer. Global actors need to take responsibility for their role in the current, ongoing crisis. This responsibility needs to be matched with concrete support – both for people and communities displaced within the region, and for those making the difficult and challenging journey to the Global North to earn money and assist their families and communities directly through remittances. While the instrumental reasons for such a politics of responsibility are clear – greater support should lead to greater stability in the region, in turn leading to less displacement and lower levels of hazardous, informal migration – the moral and political reasons override these. The Global North has been and continues to be part of the problem. It therefore behoves it to be part of a just and sustainable solution.

5. CONCLUSION: REGIONAL RESPONSES YET GLOBAL RESPONSIBILITIES

The limitations and, at times, abject failure of the international aid model is exemplified by the case of Burundi where a combination of flawed programming and international inertia has left over 400,000 Burundians without homes, livelihoods, or any secure prospects for the future. International institutions and actors need to acknowledge that they have played a role in developing and sustaining the current crisis. They also need to accept that they have a responsibility to be part of a just and sustainable solution. This means going beyond erratic, though often well-meaning, displays of generosity and willingness to assist people once they stay at home, or in a neighbouring country, and embracing a global politics of responsibility which actively facilitates migrants and refugees taking the difficult and sometimes necessary choice to leave and assist their countries themselves. A glass ceiling exists and, as political sensitivities toward immigration heighten, the ceiling is turning to concrete. Yet, as the case of Burundi illustrates, given our culpability in sometimes heightening situations of insecurity and poverty, Northern countries have a responsibility to move beyond well-meaning, yet limited, inadequate and sometimes damaging aid interventions to more equitable and economically sustainable pathways to global peace and justice.

NOTES

1. See https://www.worldbank.org/en/country/burundi/overview (accessed September 20, 2019).
2. See Susan Campbell, 'What Burundi's crisis says about UN's capacity to build peace', *Washington Post*, May 18, 2015, https://www.washingtonpost.com/news/monkey-cage/wp/2015/05/18/what-burundis-crisis-says-about-un-capacity-to-build-peace/ (accessed October 7, 2019).
3. Following pressure from the opposition and the international community, the elections were postponed until July 21. Sitting President Nkurunziza won with 69 per cent of the votes.
4. 'Burundi "at risk of fresh atrocities ahead of vote"', Samba Cyuzuzo, BBC Great Lakes, September 5, 2019, https://www.bbc.com/news/topics/ce1qrvlel07t/burundi (accessed September 9, 2019); 'Fears of new atrocities rise in Burundi as Nkurunziza ratchets up his repression', Sam Mednick, Friday, September 6, 2019, https://www.worldpoliticsreview.com/articles/28168/fears-of-new-atrocities-rise-in-burundi-as-nkurunziza-ratchets-up-his-repression (accessed September 9, 2019). See also Human Rights Watch (2019).
5. 'Tanzania to forcibly repatriate Burundi refugees', Bernard Bankukira, BBC Great Lakes, August 28, 2019, https://www.bbc.com/news/topics/ce1qrvlel07t/burundi (accessed September 9, 2019).
6. Article 4 of the Arusha Peace and Reconciliation Agreement, http://www.ucd.ie/ibis/filestore/Arusha%20%28Burundi%29%20.pdf (accessed October 13, 2019).
7. See https://www.unhcr.org/en-ie/burundi-situation.html, (accessed September 12, 2019).
8. Just US$64 million of the US$293 million required has been secured, https://data2.unhcr.org/en/situations/burundi#_ga=2.219327001.1867504319.1567861407-479138521.1563287126 (accessed September 12, 2019).
9. Source: OECD International Migration Database – adapted from https://stats.oecd.org/Index.aspx?DataSetCode=MIG (accessed October 12 2019).
10. See https://www.iom.int/countries/burundi (accessed October 12, 2019).
11. See https://www.iom.int/countries/burundi (accessed October 12, 2019).
12. Lukunka (2011); see also 'Things you should know about refugees in Tanzania', https://www.nrc.no/perspectives/2019/6-things-you-should-know-about-refugees-in-tanzania/ (accessed September 16, 2019); and 'Appalling conditions for Burundi and Congolese refugees in Tanzania', https://www.dw.com/en/appalling-conditions-for-burundi-and-congolese-refugees-in-tanzania/a-44295204, (accessed September 16, 2019).

13. Amelia Kuch, 'Lessons from Tanzania's historic bid to turn refugees to citizens', https://www.newsdeeply.com/refugees/community/2018/02/22/lessons-from-tanzanias-historic-bid-to-turn-refugees-to-citizens (accessed September 12, 2019).
14. Thijs Van Laer (2018), '"There is pressure on us": Burundian refugees in Tanzania pushed to return', https://africanarguments.org/2018/08/21/pressure-burundi-refugees-tanzania-pushed-return/ (accessed September 1, 2019).
15. Thijs Van Laer (2018), '"There is pressure on us": Burundian refugees in Tanzania pushed to return', https://africanarguments.org/2018/08/21/pressure-burundi-refugees-tanzania-pushed-return/ (accessed September 1, 2019).
16. Amelia Kuch, 'Lessons from Tanzania's historic bid to turn refugees to citizens', https://www.newsdeeply.com/refugees/community/2018/02/22/lessons-from-tanzanias-historic-bid-to-turn-refugees-to-citizens (accessed September 12, 2019).
17. 'Tanzania to forcibly repatriate Burundi refugees', Bernard Bankukira, BBC Great Lakes, August 28, 2019, https://www.bbc.com/news/topics/ce1qrvlel07t/burundi (accessed September 9, 2019).
18. OECD International Migration Database, https://stats.oecd.org/Index.aspx?DataSetCode=MIG (accessed September 15, 2019).
19. All figures are drawn from the OECD's interpretative statistical database, https://www.oecd.org/dac/stats/aid-at-a-glance.htm#recipients (accessed September 19, 2019).
20. Susan Campbell, 'What Burundi's crisis says about UN's capacity to build peace', *Washington Post*, May 18, 2015, https://www.washingtonpost.com/news/monkey-cage/wp/2015/05/18/what-burundis-crisis-says-about-un-capacity-to-build-peace/ (accessed 7 October 2019).
21. The top five are The Gambia (15.3 per cent GDP); Liberia (at 12 per cent); Senegal (9.1 per cent); Ghana (7.3 per cent) and Nigeria (6.1 per cent).
22. Calculated by the author from the World Bank's database of development indicators, https://data.worldbank.org/indicator/BX.TRF.PWKR.DT.GD.ZS?locations=BI (accessed October 12, 2019).
23. See Alan Desmond, 'Who's afraid of the UN Global Compact for Migration?', December 11, 2018, https://www.rte.ie/brainstorm/2018/1210/1016278-whos-afraid-of-the-un-global-compact-for-migration/ (accessed September 28, 2019).

REFERENCES

Beswick, Danielle (2010) 'Managing Dissent in a Post-genocide Environment: The Challenge of Political Space in Rwanda', *Development and Change*, **41**(2), 225–251.
Curtis, Devon (2013) 'The International Peacebuilding Paradox: Power Sharing and Post-Conflict Governance in Burundi', *African Affairs*, **112**(446), 72–91.
Daley, Patricia (2006) 'Ethnicity and Political Violence in Africa: The Challenge to the Burundi State', *Political Geography*, **25**(6), 657–679.
Gaynor, Niamh (2014a) 'Bringing the Citizen Back In: Supporting Decentralisation in Fragile States – A View from Burundi', *Development Policy Review*, **32**(2), 203–218.
Gaynor, Niamh (2014b) 'The Tyranny of Participation Revisited: International Support to Local Governance in Burundi', *Community Development Journal*, **49**(2), 295–310.
Gaynor, Niamh (2016) 'Beneath the Veneer: Decentralisation and Postconflict Reconstruction in Rwanda', *Third World Thematics: A TWQ Journal*, **1**(6), 779–798.
GFI (Global Financial Integrity) (2008) 'Capital Flight from the Democratic Republic of the Congo', https://secureservercdn.net/45.40.149.159/34n.8bd.myftpupload.com/wp-content/uploads/2014/05/capital-flight-from-the-drc.pdf?time=1580853010, accessed February 5, 2020.
GFI (Global Financial Integrity) (2019) 'Illicit Financial Flows to and from 148 Developing Countries: 2006–2015', https://secureservercdn.net/45.40.149.159/34n.8bd.myftpupload.com/wp-content/uploads/2019/01/IFF-Report-2019_11.18.19.pdf?time=1580853010, accessed February 5, 2020.
Grauvogel, Julia (2016) 'Burundi after the 2015 Elections: A Conference Report', *Africa Spectrum*, **51**(2), 3–14.

Hayman, Rachel (2011) 'Funding Fraud? Donors and Democracy in Rwanda', in Scott Straus and Lars Waldorf (eds), *Remaking Rwanda: Statebuilding and Human Rights after Mass Violence*, Madison, WI: University of Wisconsin Press, 118–131.

Honest Accounts (2017) *Honest Accounts: How the World Profits from Africa's Wealth*, https://www.globaljustice.org.uk/sites/default/files/files/resources/honest_accounts_2017_web_final_updated.pdf, accessed October 5, 2019.

Human Rights Watch (2019) 'Burundi: Events of 2018', in *World Report 2019*, 101–106, https://www.hrw.org/sites/default/files/world_report_download/hrw_world_report_2019.pdf, accessed September 12, 2019.

Jacobsen, Katja Lindskov and Troels Gauslå Engell (2018) 'Conflict Prevention as Pragmatic Response to a Twofold Crisis: Liberal Interventionism and Burundi', *International Affairs*, **94**(2), 363–380.

Kilroy, Walt (2015) *Reintegration of Ex-combatants after Conflict: Participatory Approaches in Sierra Leone and Liberia*, Basingstoke: Palgrave Macmillan.

Kirchhof, Andreas (2009) 'Burundi: Seven Years of Refugee Return', *Forced Migration Review*, **33**(1), 36–37.

Kuch, Amelia (2018) 'Land and Exile: Revisiting the Case of Burundian Refugees in Tanzania', *Critical African Studies*, **10**(1), 108–125.

Lemarchand, René (2007) 'Consociationalism and Power Sharing in Africa: Rwanda, Burundi, and the Democratic Republic of the Congo', *African Affairs*, **106**(422), 1–20.

Lukunka, Barbra (2011) 'New Big Men: Refugee Emasculation as a Human Security Issue', *International Migration*, **50**(5), 130–139.

Milner, James (2014) 'Can Global Refugee Policy Leverage Durable Solutions? Lessons from Tanzania's Naturalisation of Burundian Refugees', *Journal of Refugee Studies*, **27**(4), 553–573.

Ndikumana, Leonce (2005) 'Distributional Conflict: The State and Peace Building in Burundi', *The Round Table*, **94**(381), 413–427.

Patel, N. (2018) 'Figure of the Week: Understanding Poverty in Africa', 21 November, *Brookings*, https://www.brookings.edu/blog/africa-in-focus/2018/11/21/figure-of-the-week-understanding-poverty-in-africa/, accessed October 2, 2019.

Purdeková, Andrea (2016) '"Barahunga Amahoro – They are Fleeing Peace": The Politics of Displacement and Entrenchment in Post-War Burundi', *Journal of Refugee Studies*, **80**(1), 1–26.

Reyntjens, Filip (2004) 'Rwanda, Ten Years On: From Genocide to Dictatorship', *African Affairs*, **103**(411), 177–210.

Reyntjens, Filip (2005) 'Burundi: A Peaceful Transition after a Decade of War?', *African Affairs*, **105**(418), 117–135.

Thomson, Jessie (2009) 'Durable Solutions for Burundian Refugees in Tanzania', *Forced Migration Review*, **33**(1), 35–36.

UNDP (United Nations Development Programme) (2018) *Human Development Report*, New York: UNDP.

UNHCR (United Nations High Commission for Refugees) (2018) *Global Trends: Forced Displacement in 2017*, https://www.unhcr.org/5b27be547.pdf, accessed October 7, 2019.

UNHCR (United Nations Human Rights Commission) (2019a) *Regional Overview of the Burundian Refugee Population as of 31 July 2019*, Geneva: UNHCR.

UNHCR (United Nations Human Rights Commission) (2019b) *Report of the Commission of Inquiry on Burundi*, https://undocs.org/en/A/HRC/42/49, accessed September 10, 2019.

Uvin, Peter (2010) 'Structural Causes, Development Co-operation and Conflict Prevention in Burundi and Rwanda', *Conflict, Security and Development*, **10**(1), 161–179.

Wilén, Nina (2016) 'The Rationales behind the EAC Members' Response to the Burundi Crisis', *Georgetown Journal of International Affairs*, **17**(1), 69–78.

World Bank (2019) *Migration and Remittances: Recent Developments and Outlook*, Washington: World Bank.

Young, Crawford (1988) 'The African Colonial State and its Political Legacy', in D. Rothchild and N. Chazan (eds), *The Precarious Balance: State and Society in Africa*, Boulder, CO: Westview, 25–66.

20. Blood, smoke and cocaine? Reflections on the governance of the Amazonian border in contemporary Brazil

José Miguel Nieto Olivar, Flávia Melo and Marco Tobón

1. INTRODUCTION

Taking as our empirical cut the region divided between Brazil, Peru, Colombia, and Venezuela in the Northwest Amazon, and flying over the cities of Novo Progresso and Altamira (in the Brazilian state of Pará), we seek to outline the problem of managing human (and non-human) insecurity and violence as a form of production, transformation, and governance in one of the most important transborder regions on the planet. We will initially reflect upon the frontier as a historically constructed empirical fact. This will permit us to think about some conceptual approaches that look at the Amazonian frontier as a plural object being disputed by capitalist extractive forces.

In dialogue with contemporary discussions regarding the *Anthropocene* (Latour, 2018; Haraway, 2016) and *Cosmopolitics* (Stengers, 2015, 2018; Cadena & Blaser, 2018), we conduct our analyses of the problem through the articulation of three axes through which the politics of violence, control, production, and destruction gain expression. The first of these is what we understand simply as the contemporary *intensification of civilizational reduction*. *Reduction* was the name of a territorial device much employed during the Portuguese and Spanish conquest and colonization of the Amazon. This consisted in concentrating large quantities of indigenous peoples of different ethnic and linguistic groups (usually enemies) into new and reduced territories under the control of colonial agents (Zárate, 2008; Wright, 2005). A cosmopolitical perspective highlights the need for understanding a multiplicity of worlds (human and non-human) and of differences in the composition of planetary politics for the present and the future. Thus, the *civilizatory* principle marking Amazonian colonization over the last two centuries (and which has become intensified in the Brazilian politics beginning in 2018) implies a strong policy of (bios-socio-cosmological) *reduction*. To *civilize* is to *reduce* differences, relations, bodies, territories, knowledge, and the ability for struggle.

The second axis concerns *necropolitical* forms (Mbembe, 2018) within the framework of a certain transnational neocolonialism. If it is true that *civilizational* processes have kept some traces of biopolitical interests (such as the promotion of health, education, and the maintenance of labor forces), it is also true that contemporary politics are sliding more and more towards the clearly necropolitical, with governance through technologies of assassination and death and their spectacularization. This new and localized *necropolitics* seems to be an ongoing device of a new rearrangement of two of the most important transborder and transnational businesses in neoliberal politics and late capitalism: cocaine trafficking and mining.

The third and final axis is the political and socio-technological intensification of nature and its destruction, perhaps as an effect or as a political–ontological principle of the other two axes.

We understand that the ongoing processes of civilization and necropolitical reduction do not affect only humans and do not intend to reduce and control only nature: it is an anachronistic reaffirmation of an androcentric and predatory human exceptionalism. It is necessary to insist on employing an *ecosophic* imagination (Guattari, 2015) in order to understand these forms of government and their effects on the constant redefinition of boundaries between humanity and non-humanity. It is precisely in this sense of understanding that we will proceed to analyze the fabric that all three axes co-constitute, rather than analyzing each axis separately, one by one.

Finally, we would like to invert the narrative device inside out that, in global and state-centered Northern perspectives, so readily connects borders, the Amazon, and violence. In order to do this, we want to think upon stories told from the point of view of the concepts and understandings of those who live and made life in the Amazon while dealing with the predatory and productive forces of the Anthropocene. Therefore, as Donna Haraway (2016) has suggested, this is a matter connecting alliances and stories in order to be able to construct histories that are different from those we have learned and which are still hegemonic. This allows us to think about the agency of Amazonian indigenous citizenship; of a collective subject that seeks to defend different forms of human and non-human life.

This chapter is the result of the intertwining of three trajectories of anthropological research and three very different lives lived in the Amazon along the triple border between Brazil, Peru and Colombia. The analyses and reflections presented here combine, on the one hand, data and results from specific research projects and, on the other, systematic and shared reflections from life and relationships in cross-border territories. Beyond expressing the trajectories of life and research (and their intertwining) in that part of the Amazonian frontier, the analyses presented here are also built on tremendously shifting and unstable territory that is threatened by the profound political transformations experienced by Brazil in recent years, which viscerally affect the human and non-human components of the Amazonian complexity described below (see Figure 20.1).

2. THE AMAZONIAN BORDER AS AN OBJECT MULTIPLE

The contemporary forms of government and production of/in the Amazon are intertwined in long-lasting historical and mytho-historical sequences. This does not mean, however, that Amazonian history can be read as a continuum in which everything is as it always has been and always will be. In the late twentieth century, for example, the Amazon was globally understood to be the "lung of humanity," a symbol of the struggle for conservation and cultural diversity. In the second decade of the twenty-first century, however, we now see the Pan-Amazon registered in fierce, brutal, and public disputes as an index of planetary destruction and an urgent source of national economic resources, as we have seen in presidential acts and statements in Ecuador, Peru, and Brazil. The Vatican is a very important actor in the invention and transnational governance of the Amazon. The region and its borders were a vehicle for the materialization, essentialization, and localization of Catholic fantasies about savagery and civilization. Today, it is a strategic symbol of the new eco-ecclesiastical politics enacted by the Pope and his allies.[1]

On the other hand, it is a mistake to think of the Amazon as a homogeneous unit, as a uniform entity or individual. Even while describing the Amazon as a biome, it is a highly complex

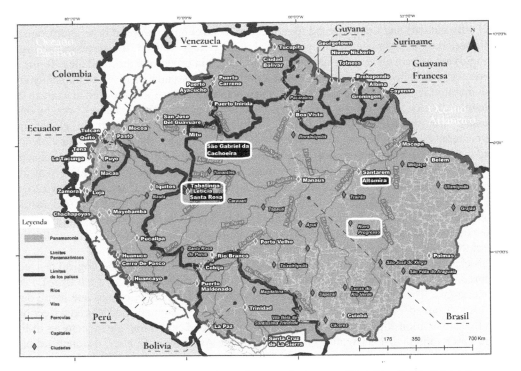

Note: The highlighted areas show Altamira and Novo Progresso in the state of Pará (Brazil), São Gabriel da Cachoeira in the state of Amazonas (Brazil) and the triple border between Tabatinga (Brazil), Leticia (Colombia) and Santa Rosa (Peru).
Source: Map based on the "Localización Pan-Amazonia" map, in Atlas Panamazónico (2019, p. 5).

Figure 20.1 Map of the Pan-Amazonian region and its national borders

system of multispecific symbiotic relations (Haraway, 2016). We must never forget that the plurality of its environmental, social, economic, and national characteristics is gigantic.

These Amazons are also, of course, a localized effect of government actions of nation-states that produce and differentiate them. The triple border between Brazil, Peru, and Colombia is a perfect example of this. The social and ecological life produced by nation-state intervention in the territory creates absolute inequalities. One can see the Brazilian Amazonian border policies, the abundant armies and federal "white," big security bodies – with the racializing processes they create, and the relatively abundant circulation of state resources in the last 20 years. Another image is revealed by the Colombian policies, crisscrossed by a history of internal warfare and drug trafficking, and committed to long-term processes of the "professionalization" of the National Police and to social development projects in border areas. Yet another coheres when we think of the eastern border of the Peruvian Amazon, relatively ignored by the national government and the regional government of Loreto.

So, it is enough to describe the Amazon as different Amazons?

In our case, Pan-Amazonia (Chaves & Del Cairo, 2010), the Amazonian border, is thus understood simultaneously as several borders. We are faced here with an object multiple, in the sense that Dutch philosopher and anthropologist Annemarie Mol (2002) understands the body in medical practice. The present chapter looks at the Amazon as a mytho-conceptual object (Serje, 2005) and a meta-frontier: a paradigmatic, ontological, imaginative border of modernity, which has extended from the European arrival and invasion of this land down to the present day. The Amazon is one of the last frontiers of great natural resource reserves. It is thus a frontier of monstrous and fierce capitalist expansion. It is a frontier for the *Gaia Intrusion* (Stengers, 2015) and one of the last immense "multispecies shelters" and, therefore, an expanse of what Donna Haraway (2016) has imagined as *Chthulucene*.[2]

On another scale, for the national governments of the countries that administratively share it, the Amazonian border is a symbol of multiple and contradictory riches and a huge problem of sovereignty, development, and integration (key words which show up repeatedly throughout this bionecropolitical economy). Thus, in the territory that is globally called "the Amazon", in its multiple hearts, one finds portions of nine national-states and, so, the borders of Peru, Ecuador, Colombia, Bolivia, Venezuela, Guyana, French Guyana, Suriname, and Brazil. This region contains some 33 million human inhabitants, including 1.5 million indigenous peoples from 385 different Native nations.[3] This, in turn, implies a heterogeneous series of governmental, military, and police provisions based on the protection and defense of national sovereignty in these territories, which include the huge intra-national technical, logistic, and economic human (mainly male) flows that these security policies demand. A whole tangle of border lines, areas, and strips, red points or roads of (in)security, mobility controls, practices, and customs check points make up the cartographic fantasies of national sovereignty of the states that divide the Amazon.

Since the beginning of the rubber trade (1880–1932), the Amazon has been exposed to massive and fierce predatory forces that have marked its experience in the Anthropocene. All manner of human and non-human beings who inhabit the region's forests and rivers in a non-destructive manner have suffered from the violence of this intervention, including the region's rivers, lagoons, feathered, furred, and scaled animals (to employ the Tikuna indigenous peoples' classification [Mr. León Macedo, Tikuna *knowledger*, to Tobón, personal communication]). In the practices of the elites of the region's several settler states, the Amazon appears to be the last frontier which must be tamed, a reserve open to agricultural activity (extensive cattle raising or soybean and palm monocultural plantations), to the clearing of forests that cover large mineral deposits mapped many years ago and already included in future plans for economic exploitation.[4] Through the acts of the transnational businessmen of South America's cities, the Amazon is understood as an uninhabited landscape, or as a prosperous land occupied by beings who are "obstacles to development":[5] forbidden characters, incomprehensible songs, wild Indians, cannibalistic creatures, and guerrillas. The Amazon is thus cast by these entrepreneurs and self-proclaimed "self-made men" as the place of godless fugitives, a territory in which the nightmares of the nation-state take refuge. This territory, therefore, must be civilized, sold, Christianized, and nationalized with all the weapons at the Fatherland's disposal. Hegemonic "western" society encounters multiple difficulties in fully asserting itself in the equatorial forests of America and along its borders, unable to consolidate the consent and obedience in these regions that it has wielded in other areas of national life.

These processes of environmental and social degradation and extermination are predicated upon the action of armed forces that exert violence against indigenous leaders and the defenders of territorial and environmental rights. Victoria Tauli-Corpuz, United Nations (UN) Special Rapporteur on the Rights of Indigenous Peoples, has warned the world about this situation in her report of September 2018.[6] She remarks that Brazil – together with Colombia,

Mexico, and the Philippines – causes some 80% of the deaths of indigenous rights' defenders in the world. She points out that of the 312 human rights defenders killed in 2017, 67% were indigenous people fighting to defend their territories and rights, often against extractive private sector projects. The Tauli-Corpuz report insists that Brazil and Colombia constitute the most dangerous and most lethal countries for human and indigenous rights defenders.

Finally, as paradoxical experience of *the end of the world* (Danowski & Viveiros de Castro, 2014), the Amazon is a huge cosmopolitical frontier (Stengers, 2018; Cadena & Blaser, 2018). That is, it is a dispersed and tentacular social space into which the processes of normative and ontological expansion of unification, homogenization, and control of late modernity have "failed", but still seek to effectively penetrate, or in which they take on very particular and monstrous shapes (in Haraway's sense of "monstrosity"). The Amazon is the region of the planet with one of the highest concentrations of cultural diversity, containing approximately 350 indigenous peoples (see note 6) who speak some 300 languages. As a cosmopolitical frontier, the experience of destruction and the end of the world is ancient and constituent in the Amazon, but so is the multiplicity of experiences, materialities and knowledges capable of resisting and blocking this process, or at least describing it in much more interesting ways (Danowski & Viveiros de Castro, 2014).

We thus understand the Amazon as an object multiple, dynamically composed of the actions, materialities, and decisions of an immense diversity of actors: the Amazon is all that these have made, at one and the same time. It is a gigantic cross-border territory, as a place of cosmopolitical and counter-border experimentation (Olivar, 2018) carried out mainly by and through the social networks of human and non-human, embodied and non-embodied, living and non-living beings that make the region their home.

3. A QUADRANGLE OF DESTRUCTION: THE INTENSIFICATION OF EXPLOITATION ALONG THE AMAZONIAN FRONTIER

In this section, our concern is to pay particular attention to contemporary forms of governmentality that point to the intensification of destruction as the principle of producing relations, socialities, and territories. Here, we will think through three interconnected axes: the first we understand to be simply the *intensification of civilizational reduction*; the second concerns *necropolitical forms* within the framework of certain transnational neocolonialisms; and the third is the political and socio-technological intensification of nature and its destruction.

It was still day when, suddenly, the skies over São Paulo darkened and day became night. The inhabitants of the state of São Paulo thus witnessed the result of what would later become known as "Fire Day" in early August 2019. The dense clouds that darkened the sky of the largest Brazilian metropolis came from afar. Smoke plumes originating in Bolivia, the Amazon, and Paraguay traveled southeast across Brazil. More than 2500 km away in Novo Progresso, a small southwestern city of the state of Pará with just over 25,000 inhabitants (IBGE, 2019), an arson agreement was allegedly made by a group of farmers and loggers. Between 9 and 12 August 2019, 1457 outbreaks of fire were detected in the Brazilian Amazon rainforest. The attack sought to garner support from the Brazilian government for deforestation for grazing and logging (Piran, 2019). A similar situation occurred in Colombia where, even with the declaration of the Amazon as a Subject of Rights by the Supreme Court of Justice in April 2018, environmental conflicts, deforestation, legal and illegal mining activity, and threats to indigenous peoples have appeared to intensify. In Colombia, 75% of the total loss of forest cover occurs in the Amazon region, which represents a loss of more than 177,000 hectares for the year of 2018 alone.[7] In Bolivia, deforestation affected more than 18.7 million hectares between 2005 and 2018. This reality has been dramatically reproduced in all Amazonian countries, where the economic model intervening in the region through predatory forces has materialized in interventions in transport infrastructure (roads), energy (hydroelectric projects), extractive industries (mining, oil, and gas) and the frequent burning and deforestation for soy and cattle plantations.[8] It is an important part of the Amazon-specific version of Anthropocene.

Near to Novo Progresso is Altamira, a city where 194 of the fire outbreaks in the Brazilian territory arose (Brum, 2019). Altamira is headquarters of one of the most ecologically damaging energy projects in Brazilian history, the Belo Monte Hydroelectric Power Plant. Built intrusively and catastrophically over the Xingu River basin, Belo Monte finally became a reality due to arbitrary decisions on the part of Brazil's federal government in 2010 during the moment of economic prosperity that Brazil experienced between 2004 and 2013.[9] The Belo Monte Hydroelectric Power Plant is a clear example of "internal colonialism" (González Casanova, 1963; Cardoso de Oliveira, 1966) due to its national insertion in global economies and its marginally profitable exploitation of natural resources. It has created the "anatomy of an ethnocide," mainly for the Kayapó, Arara, Arareute, Epidereula, Juruna, and Maracanã indigenous peoples (Brum, 2014).

According to data from independent monitoring sources in the Volta Grande of the Xingu River (ISA, 2018), the "consensus hydrograph" – the technical–political parameter imposed as a measure for "ecological and social sustainability" – which should guarantee free navigation along the river was heavily impacted by the project. The annual flooding of river margins and plains (a vital condition for maintaining the synchrony between the river and the riverside ecologies) in areas affected by the Belo Monte dam (2018, p. 17) was insufficient to fill even the region's lower plains. Riverside forestland used by aquatic fauna as a feeding and breeding refuge was damaged (ISA, 2018, p. 45). Low flow rates prevented spawning and feeding of fish and turtles, meaning that 2016 was the year of the end of the world for the Juruna peoples (ISA, 2018, p. 39). The waters trapped in the Belo Monte dams bore mute witness to the *ecocide* of Volta Grande do Xingu in 2016.

As is well known, the logic behind these great ventures that seek to "dominate nature" in the name of extraction of natural resources is nothing new. Amazonian history, specifically since the beginning of the twentieth century, already operative during the region's first republican regimes of government, has been thoroughly marked by these sorts of transnational economic initiatives. The 1970s signaled a brutal moment of expansion of the Brazilian agricultural frontier through the penetration and "ripping apart" of the forest with military Transamazon road construction projects (César, 2015). Here is where the contemporary history of Altamira began, for example, as well as that of another Amazonian city thousands of miles away: São Gabriel da Cachoeira. São Gabriel is yet another vertex in this partial overview of the territorial quadrilateral that we are presenting here, and which has been governed on the basis of smoke, blood, and cocaine, not to mention Bulls, Bullets, and Bibles (the political–economic–moral coalition in Brazil of agribusiness, the military and police, and the most conservative religious organizations).

We think of São Gabriel and from it because we know it well due to the research and collaborative work we have conducted there with indigenous and environmentalist organizations.

The city has a huge number of characteristics which make it useful to think about this Amazon as an object multiple, however. São Gabriel da Cachoeira is located in the region known as the Alto Rio Negro, in the northwestern Amazon. Most of the region is composed of continuously demarcated indigenous lands and the Pico da Neblina Natural Park (ISA, 2011). According to the 2010 Census, 29,017 of the 37,896 residents of the municipality declared themselves to be indigenous, some 76.57% of the total population, making the city the largest concentration of indigenous Brazilians in the country. The 2019 Census estimates that the city has a population of 45,564 people (IBGE, 2019). São Gabriel is typically presented as an indigenous city, and "urbanization" and the "community-city" relationship are central to anthropological production and indigenous political discussions (Lasmar, 2006; Andrello, 2006; FOIRN/ISA, 2005; Marques, 2015).

Federal Law 5449 of 1968 "framed" São Gabriel da Cachoeira as a national security area (César, 2015, p. 44). From there, it entered into the federal government's plans to build infrastructure and major roads in the Amazon. Between 1970 and 1980, the city's population almost quadrupled, going from 785 to 3,102 inhabitants, and, between 1974 and 1976, 6,000 people were registered as living in the city. Thousands of soldiers and workers arrived for the construction projects: mainly single and non-indigenous men. Long-standing merchant families have almost inherited local executive power, as well as several legislative positions. São Gabriel's economy profits from the salaries of civil servants, especially military personnel, and (following a tradition dating back to the seventeenth century [Wright, 2005; Andrello, 2006]) from the exploitation of indigenous bodies, products, needs, and money.

Within this framework, researchers have drawn attention to the fact that the income redistribution policies of previous Brazilian governments have created the greatest impact upon Amazonian indigenous groups, including those who live across national borders. These policies include social benefits such as the *Bolsa Família Program*.[10] This consists of a monthly payment made exclusively in the town (not in rural areas or indigenous communities) through ATS cards. Because of these payments, hundreds of indigenous families, who do not have any familiarity with money and cash, periodically leave their communities and head down the river to the city of São Gabriel to receive payments at banks and lottery agencies … and buy goods and some fuel just to come back. Without adequate conditions for lodging and food, they huddle precariously on the banks of the river in makeshift camps covered in blue plastic tarps.

The "new descents" (an evocative allusion to the old missionary practice of "descending" indigenous peoples as a means of arresting and enslaving indigenous labor [Bombardi, 2014]) towards the city of São Gabriel in search of social benefits has altered the dynamics of local commerce and upgraded old forms of exploitation, converting the old debt-bondage system (Meira, 2019) into an extensive magnetic card retention scheme (Melo, 2018). These dislocations also confront us with the precariousness of the blue-tarp covered camps scattered throughout the "Beiradão," near the port created in the 1970s by the Queiroz Galvão corporation, one of the construction companies that, decades later, worked to help construct the Belo Monte plant in Altamira (Figure 20.2). Known as the "Hup cemetery" (Marques, 2015, p. 39), the "Beiradão" is mainly occupied by Hupd'ah Indians who experience all kinds of disorders while there (including shamanic and spiritual) and suffer from hunger, drunkenness, and disease. As we saw in Belo Monte, the spectacular projects of the Anthropocene (in its developmental face) promote the destruction and disorder of material life, but also disorder the ontologies of Native peoples (Mantovanelli, 2016; Marques, 2015).

Source: Photo by Bruno Marques. Available at https://www.socioambiental.org/ (accessed 14 February 2020).

Figure 20.2   Encampment near Porto Queiroz Galvão, the "Beiradão"

The map of mourning and death created by these sorts of necropolitics focuses unevenly on certain types of bodies and dramatically reveals asymmetrical power relations centered on notions of ethnicity (allied with ideas regarding "progress," etc.). In recent years, abundant news reports and narratives have emerged regarding the sexual exploitation of indigenous girls, suicide, alcoholism, violent deaths, and drownings. These issues particularly impact upon the city's indigenous population and, in a different way, its young people and women. Along with these general events associated with violence come important collateral repercussions regarding life, death, and health conditions. Health care, in particular, is in a critical state, both in the city itself and in the surrounding indigenous lands.[11]

Three months before the "day of fire" in 2019, merchant Manuel Carneiro was honored by the city council of São Gabriel da Cachoeira for his work in the development of the region known as "the dog's head" (due to its resemblance to a dog's head on the region's maps). Carneiro and his two brothers control much of the food and beverage trade in the region as well as land ownership in the city itself. In addition, there are accusations and investigations that point to the brothers' participation (along with other major merchants in the city) in diverse crimes such as cocaine trafficking and the abusive control of *Bolsa Família* cards (particularly those associated with the Beiradão tragedy). Carneiro's honorable mention as the "Protector of the Dog's Head" came less than a year after he and his brothers were sentenced to 28 years in prison after more than five years of investigation for a series of sexual crimes against young indigenous women in São Gabriel. To complete the gendered necropolitical scenario and illuminate the forms of racism and the intensive and overt destruction carried out under it, we need to understand that Carneiro's award was presented by a military councilor and promoted by the Women's Rights Commission of the São Gabriel da Cachoeira City Council.[12]

Moving from this part of the Amazon border, following the line between Brazil and Colombia, we reach the last vertex of our quadrangle, on the highest part of the Brazilian

Amazon River (which Brazilians call the Solimões River), which forms the threefold Brazilian, Peruvian, and Colombian border. Here, we will focus on the *transborder urban complex* formed by Tabatinga (BR), Leticia (COL) and Santa Rosa Island (PE), which also connects other cities, countless riverside and indigenous communities within the three countries.

Occurring almost simultaneously with the military recolonization of the Amazon in Brazil, much of the expansion of the international cocaine trafficking has, since the 1970s, been crossing the Amazon and all of its borders in many different ways. Beginning with the gigantic and spectacular movements of the 1970s and 1980s, in the style of great *capos* like Pablo Escobar and proceeding through deforestation for the expansion coca crops (Bolivia, Peru, and Colombia), we are now witnessing the extreme capillarization of the cocaine trade in Brazil. Within this framework, Tabatinga (in the margins of the state of Amazonas) has turned into a red dot on Brazil's public security and national defense maps over the past ten years.

Here, as Candotti et al. (2017) have shown, smoke and blood mix with cocaine in a transnational "grand narrative" that provides the pillars for hegemonic interpretations of one of the largest prison massacres in Brazilian history, which resulted in the murder of 56 prisoners in the Anísio Jobim Penitentiary Complex in Manaus, capital of the State of Amazonas, on 1 January 2017. This "overarching Amazon narrative" creates a ubiquitous and potent enemy, "international drug trafficking", which disputes the international border of Brazil, commands the country's prisons, and has spread across the country from north to south. This threat materializes greed for Amazon territory not in terms of wood (felled and burned on Fire Day) or land (cleared for pastures), but in terms of cocaine and its relations with the dense and extensive hydrograph (not yet trapped by dams), where one can sail outside the reach of the watchful eyes of the state.

In March 2017, Brazilian TV broadcast the journalistic series *In the Veins of Trafficking* and introduced the world to the "pirates" of the Solimões River which, according to the report, was supposedly "the main artery of the cocaine route coming from Peru and Colombia to Manaus." Although already known for attacks on the boats and canoes that sail with all sorts of goods and valuables along the Amazon's rivers, said "pirates" are described in the series as a group of criminals vying for control of rivers with criminal factions that use Amazon hydrography to transport drugs produced on the triple border of Brazil, Peru, and Colombia. The "Solimões Pirates" attacked vessels carrying cocaine belonging to the Northern Family (NDF), an internationally known criminal faction, following the carnage in the Anísio Jobim Penitentiary Complex in January 2019.

These terrifying narratives aren't restricted to TV and movie screens. The main guidelines of the Brazilian Ministry of National Integration (2009) for border policies reiterates many elements such as the one described above. They can also be found in the content of the Report of the Interinstitutional Meeting on Justice along the Triple Brazil/Peru/Colombia Border (2011), published by the Amazonas State Public Prosecutor. Formulations such as these presuppose and naturalize "incipient regional development," the "low institutional density of the state," and the constant "threat from foreign enemies," concepts that decisively guide the policies of national integration, defense, and public security. Not surprisingly, such formulations easily and often become guidelines for military operations and logistical exercises that mobilize the Brazilian Armed Forces in an entire range of military expeditions designed to "safeguard and protect the Amazon and its vulnerable populations."

We must also note that the policy we are trying to describe here is still in the process of expansion and consolidation. Control over internal and international cocaine trafficking in

Brazil is in dispute and transformation. This has proven to be productive for the more necropolitical forms of "legal" developmentalism. Regional and national factions have recently gone to war for control of Brazil's cocaine business, producing – over the last three years – epic scenes of battle, death, and conquest in several Amazonian and border cities. There are records of public celebrations, massive declarations of victory, and ultimatums declared against the lives of the losers. The general feeling of researchers and inhabitants is that the dynamics of drug trafficking have changed substantially in the region. It is now much more capillary, pulverized, poorer, younger, and – following the model disseminated by the Brazilian Federal Government – more desirous of weapons, deaths, and violence. At the same time, the policies of killing, militarization, and incarceration followed by the Brazilian Federal Government continue to expand, limiting resources for the protection of the rights of traditional communities and for public, secular, and universal health and education, while expanding necropolitical action in terms of policing, militarization, evangelization, and imprisonment.

4. READING HISTORY IN THE ENTRAILS: OTHER HISTORIES TO RECOUNT OTHER STORIES

Multispecies biologist and speculative feminist Donna Haraway has engaged in the contemporary reflections about the Anthropocene and the *end of the world*. One of her strategies has been to improve the storytelling. Haraway, following the thinking of British anthropologist Marylin Strathern, noted that "it matters what stories we tell to tell other stories with" (Haraway, 2016, p. 12).

In this sense, we must keep sight of the fact that there are histories of the Amazon that are managed and promoted from within its own interior and the cultural lives of the Amazonian peoples, who reproduce ecological and political interrelationships with inhabited territories and the various botanical, hydrological, and phytochemical knowledges and subjects found therein. Here, we can find possible ways to escape exploitation and means to protect the multiplicity of worlds and defend collective rights. We mean the political powers contained in the reproduction of Amazonian lives: long and interspecific webs of care and raising children; people producing and exchanging food; performing ritual dances; tending gardens; producing solidarity; interacting wisely with the region's incredibly diverse plants and animals; extracting healing substances; appropriating the cities and their dangers; protecting the land and one another; and activating different forms of consciousness (though the use of tobacco, coca, ayahuasca, yopo, toé, timbó, peppers, and cassava, among other substances).

It is better to know the historically rooted set of Amazonian socio-technological and cosmo-political practices helps to materialize Haraway's idea of the Chthulucene as a monstrous resource against the Anthropocene in favor of the flourishing of a "world of many worlds" (Cadena & Blaser, 2018). It anchors the collective responses capable of facing and evading the ferocity of the predatory forces currently at work in the region. A clear example of the political potential of these practices are some indigenous ritual dances of the people of the Caquetá-Putumayo basin in the Colombia and Brazil borderland. The dances studied by Tobón (2015) mobilize the organization of social forces that produce and share food (substances derived from cassava, tobacco, coca, and peppers, among others), and are an expression of collective unity, autonomy, territorial defense, and the reaffirmation of the ways of life of the forest. These dances are conducted in order to transform external threats and dangers (produced by the presence of woodworkers, armed actors, drug traffickers, mining agents) into public opportunities for discussion, the ritual use of tobacco and coca, laughter, and collective protection. Dancing, the use of local substances, and wordplay (in storytelling and jokes) are some of the mechanisms for protection and transformation. In these public meetings, mutual protection is presented as a manifestation of indigenous citizenship, of a collective subject that participates in the construction of history. Many of the dances and celebrations of the Amazonian peoples therefore constitute forms of political agency, transforming hostility into festivity, adversaries and predators into guests, and bodies at war into bodies that join together.

Dialoguing with certain indigenous Amazonian concepts, such as the tension between animality and humanity, predation and socialization, it can be seen that, in the face of the advancement of destructive forces in the Amazonian regions, local, concrete, and humanizing actions often arise linked to reciprocal care, the exercise of "autonomy,"[13] and the public and collective mobilization of cultural ways of being. This highlights value-based social relations with strong ethical and political charges. Local scenario-builders can use the forces thus mobilized to escape the productivist, individualistic, anthropocentric, and mercantile frameworks in which human relations inevitably are marked by profit and oppression. It should be noted that we are not here implying any exoticizing idealization of the Amazonian peoples. Stressing their struggles and recognizing the common values of their ways of living does not mean losing sight of the contradictions created by mercantilism and the pressures of capital within their lives. We believe, however, that perhaps the Native Amazonian populations will be better able to cope with the insecurity, uncertainty, and confusion of the rising storms today through their accumulated history of common adversity and challenges.

On the other hand, the Amazon that is written from these other stories could be also profoundly and intensely urban. The borderlands thus reveal themselves as a social space saturated with creativity, intensity, social arrangements, and alliances of existence and resistance. For example, we have become interested in understanding how indigenous women – especially young women – deal with and resist the forms of violence directed at them and sexual exploitation of their bodies.

In the face of the diversified and massive sexual violence against young indigenous women in the city of São Gabriel da Cachoeira, ethnographic research conducted in this city, in dialogue with the international literature on *sexual economies* (Piscitelli, 2016), has revealed the situation in a new light (Olivar, 2018). We have seen how young indigenous women living on the outskirts of the city can, under certain circumstances, actively engage in the local (markedly racialized and intergenerational) sexual economies, especially with "white" men and not just be exploited by it/them. Mixing ancestral and urban resources, these women create bodies capable of managing male desire, alliances with night workers and with other women and boys, and forms of knowledge in order to better understand and manage "whites" (old and young, civil and military, desirable and depictable) who want and seek them. These bodies are also able to transit to and enjoy the city without fear (of rape and harassment), while building relational spaces for sexual enjoyment and learning. In São Gabriel and other Amazonian cities, one can see large numbers of foreign men in the networks of these young women, and boys, who circulate among the night clubs and other "white" nocturnal meeting spaces in order to strategically and carefully engage in processes of seduction, dance, drinking and money making. These youths, some of whom have grown up in rural communities or on the outskirts of the city, learn to move around downtown, walk in groups, which transportation can be taken and which should not, to think about sexuality in more relational (carefully, strategically) ways, and – finally – learn about money. Observing these processes, one must also pay attention to outcomes in terms of conjugal alliances with members of the white military, indigenous women's subsequent social ascension and the effect this has upon indigenous kinship networks (Lasmar, 2006).

In the face of a constantly solidifying system of colonization which has debt and sexual exploitation as its structural center, active participation in sexual markets becomes a translating mechanism for family histories and genealogies (often containing histories of rape or exploitation by white men). It is a social resource that allows these young women to, if not control, at least intervene and manipulate the historical forms of oppression and the possibilities of the context. It is a social knowledge which is intensely erotic, in a local sense indigenous, and which radically opposes joy and beauty to the programmatic imposition of pain and exploitation.

On the other hand, also within the framework of the Rio Negro Indigenous Organizations Federation (FOIRN, in Portuguese), socio-political agencies have pushed by indigenous women and their allies to understand and address the multiple violence to which these people are subject. The discussion regarding violence against women is now gaining space in the FOIRN agenda, as demonstrated at the XI Women's Meeting in the region, organized in April 2018 (FOIRN, 2018). This Federation, together with the Socio-Environmental Institute (ISA) and in partnership with the Faculty of Public Health of the University of São Paulo and the Observatory of Gender Violence in the Amazon, has been advancing in the understanding of these forms of violence and the ways in which they occur, as well as the manners in which indigenous women deal with or organize to confront them.

Finally, it is important to highlight the irreducible importance and comprehensiveness of indigenous social and political movements in terms of protecting lives (human and non-human) and ecosystems. These movements have been consolidated in the Pan-Amazon region for over 40 years and have produced important cross-border, regional and transnational connections. An example is the Kayapó Indian resistance against the Belo Monte Hydroelectric Power Plant, led by Raoní Metuktire, which for over 30 years now has been able to recruit international allies such as the British singer Sting. Another important example is the FOIRN, a political-administrative unit composed of dozens of Rio Negro indigenous organizations that has resulted in what is perhaps the largest continuous demarcation of land in Latin America and which has continuously struggled for Native rights and land for over 30 years. It is also important to mention in this context that, in partnership with several different allies, FOIRN has been carrying out its own Territorial and Environmental Management Plan (PGTA) since 2015. Because it is regional, participatory, and consensus-oriented, the PGTA has involved a tremendous amount of work by dozens of technicians and indigenous people, translating instrumentation systems across more than 20 indigenous languages, and creating exchange relationships with technicians and indigenous people on the Colombian side of the region's border.

5. FINAL CONSIDERATIONS

In this chapter, we have crossed only a small part of what is conventionally understood to be the territory of the Amazonian region, tracing the vertices of a quadrangle of destruction that connects four cities of the Brazilian Amazon: Novo Progresso and Altamira in the state of Pará, and São Gabriel da Cachoeira and Tabatinga in the state of Amazonas. These small Brazilian cities and the people who inhabit them have had their lives traversed by highly predatory "national defense," "regional development," "social," and "civilizational" policies based on the reckless exploitation of the much-coveted Amazonian "natural wealth" and upon the "need" to guarantee national sovereignty. We have also demonstrated how these processes of state formation and bordermaking/-keeping, observed in Brazil, transcend national boundaries and reveal modes of relationship (with humans and non-humans, with the environment and traditional populations) based upon "violence," both as a moral category of accusation and as a modern device of governance.

The effects of the processes we point out are leading not only to the destruction of the Amazon rainforest as a living and dynamic complex, as demonstrated by the widespread impacts of Fire Day in Novo Progresso or the "ecocide" caused by the construction of the Belo Monte plant in Altamira. The necropolitical devices upon which this destruction is conducted also marks bodies, especially those of indigenous people, youth, and women, such as the hungry and drunken Hupd'ah bodies scattered in the camps of the "Beiradão," or the abused and abandoned bodies of indigenous girls in the downtown of São Gabriel da Cachoeira. From the Venezuelan border to the Peruvian–Colombian border, blood and smoke mingle with cocaine and the device of violence as a form of government materializes in militarized bodies that act together, extensively, and intensively, on the territories of the upper Rio Solimões combating the "violence" of international drug trafficking with the "violence" of militarized forces.

These forms of governance continually produce differences and inequalities that undermine borders and borderline and marginal lives. It is precisely to these lives that we have sought to turn our attention to in the last part of the text and in our life and in our different research trajectories in the Amazon. In the face of the scant attention paid to these lives, moving beyond the perspectives guided by the sign of "violence," we approach these lives from a perspective centered on the inner Amazon in order to find, in these frontier zones, creativity, intensity, social arrangements, and alliances of existence and resistance that allow us to produce other maps of the Amazon and other ways of inhabiting it. Perhaps these histories from the forest have allowed us, in telling other stories, to map out other paths and forge other modes of relationship and resistance that counteract destruction and the sign of violence under which said destruction is conducted and condoned.

NOTES

1. Here we make reference to the recent Synod of Bishops of 2019, focused on the Amazon, available at https://www.vaticannews.va/ (accessed 25 June 2019).
2. "Chthulucene – past, present, and to come" is a collaborative and multispecies alternative constructed by Haraway (2016) to the hegemonic Anthropocene, According to the author, "'My' Chthulucene, even burdened with its problematic Greek-ish tendrils, entangles myriad temporalities and spatialities and myriad intra-active entities-in-assemblages – including the more-than-human, other-than-human, inhuman, and human-as-humus" (Haraway, 2015, p. 160). According to De Soto (2016, p. 28) "la proposición del Chthuluceno […] Es una llamada eco-tecnofeminista a la acción que invita a una exploración de la codependencia entre las especies como un proyecto cosmopolítico, construyendo otras formas de relacionalidad y parentescos, en simpoiesis."
3. Available at https://www.amazoniasocioambiental.org (accessed 12 May 2019).

4. As shown by the Amazon Georeferenced Socioenvironmental Information Network – RAISG (in 2019), throughout the Amazon there is a clear and directly proportional relationship between livestock activity and deforestation. This is confirmed by an increase in pastureland in the region of over 74% during the last three decades. It is estimated that 80% of the region's deforested areas are intended for livestock grazing. 2019 (a year that saw a huge burn off of the region's vegetation in recent decades, an act that created vast swaths of smoke over the South American continent) was the worst year for deforestation since 2016, according to the alert registered by the Deter B system of the INPE. This data shows that in the first nine months of 2019, the area being burned was some 7.853,91 km². This is almost twice the area of the same period during 2018, with a registered increase of 92.7%. Available at https://bit.ly/33PRbOK (accessed 12 May 2019).
5. According to Jair Messias Bolsonaro, the President of Brazil, reservations turn indigenous peoples into "poor landowners sitting atop rich lands." President Bolsonaro has promised to not demarcate "one more centimeter of indigenous land." Available at https://www.survivalbrasil.org/artigos/3543-Bolsonaro (accessed 12 May 2019).
6. Available at https://www.ohchr.org/Documents/Issues/IPeoples/SR/A.HRC.39.17.pdf (accessed 12 May 2019).
7. Available at https://infoamazonia.org/es/2019/03/espanol-la-amazonia-concentro-el-75-de-la-deforestacion-de-colombia/#!/map=49&story=post-19171 (accessed 12 May 2019).
8. Available at https://infoamazonia.org/es/2019/03/espanol-la-amazonia-concentro-el-75-de-la-deforestacion-de-colombia/#!/map=49&story=post-19171 (accessed 12 May 2019).
9. Available at http://g1.globo.com/brasil/noticia/2010/06/em-ato-no-para-lula-defende-construcao-de-belo-monte.html (accessed 12 May 2019).
10. *Bolsa Família* is a direct income transfer program for families considered to be poor or in extreme poverty, following the parameters of the UN Food and Agriculture Organization (FAO). Created in 2003 during the first presidential term of ex-president Lula da Silva, the program still exists today and benefits about 14 million Brazilian families, which represents more than 25% of the national population. The FAO parameter is the Malnutrition Prevalence Indicator (MPI), measured in 2002–2013 and 1990–2014. This calculation takes into consideration the availability of food per person, the population's energy needs by age group, and the population's access to food. Available at http://www.fao.org/ (accessed 20 September 2019).
11. This situation is aggravated by the departure of the Cuban doctors involved in the *Mais Médicos* program (and the lack of others to take their place) and also by the political threats that Brazilian indigenous policy has been facing at all levels. Available at https://www.socioambiental.org/pt-br/noticias-socioambientais/alto-rio-negro-am-vive-crise-na-saude-denuncia-organizacao-indigena (accessed 12 May 2019).
12. Available at https://amazoniareal.com.br/condenado-por-abusos-sexuais-contra-meninas-indigenas-recebe-homenagem-da-comissao-da-mulher-de-sao-gabriel/ (accessed 12 May 2019).
13. Roughly speaking, this "autonomy" can be locally understood as the capacity of a community to exercise its own cultural practices and its knowledge (Tobón, 2015).

REFERENCES

Amazonas State Public Prosecutor (2011). *AMAZONAS. Relatório do Encontro Interinstitucional sobre a Justiça na Tríplice Fronteira Brasil/Peru/Colômbia*. Manaus, AM: Ministério Público do Estado do Amazonas.

Andrello, Geraldo (2006). *Cidade do índio: transformações e cotidiano em Iauaretê*. São Paulo, Editora UNESP/ISA; Rio de Janeiro, NUTI.

Atlas Panamazónico (2019). *Aproximación a la realidad eclesial y socioambiental. Contribuciones al Sínodo de la Amazonia*. REPAM (Red Eclesial Panamazónica).

Bombardi, Fernanda (2014). *Pelos interstícios do olhar colonizador: descimentos de índios no Estado de Maranhão e Grão Pará (1680–1750)*. Masters dissertation in Social History, Universidade de São Paulo.

Brazilian Ministry of National Integration (2009). *Brasil. Programa de Promoção do Desenvolvimento da Faixa de Fronteira-PDFF*. Brazil: Ministério da Integração.

Brum, Eliane (2014). "Belo Monte: a anatomia de um etnocídio". Available at https://brasil.elpais.com/brasil/2014/12/01/opinion/1417437633_930086.html, accessed 12 July 2019.

Brum, Eliane (2019). "A notícia é esta: o Xingu vai morrer". *Opinium Column El País*, 12 September. Available at https://brasil.elpais.com/brasil/2019/09/12/opinion/1568300730_780955.html, accessed 12 July 2019.

Cadena, Marisol de la and Blaser, Mario (eds) (2018). *A world of many worlds*. London and Durham, NC, Duke University Press.

Candotti, Fabio, Melo, Flávia and Siqueira, Italo (2017). "A Grande Narrativa do Norte: considerações na fronteira entre crime e Estado". In Fabio Mallart and Rafael Godoi (eds), *BR 111: a rota das prisões brasileiras*. São Paulo, Editora Veneta, 21–31.

Cardoso de Oliveira, Roberto (1966). "A noção de colonialismo interno na etnologia". *Tempo Brasileiro*, 4(8): 105–112.

César, Edmar (2015). *São Gabriel da Cachoeira: sua saga, sua história*. Goiania, Kelps.

Chaves, Margarita and Del Cairo, Carlos (2010). "Introducción". In Margarita Chaves and Carlos Del Cairo (eds), *Perspectivas antropológicas sobre la Amazonia contemporánea*. Bogotá, ICANH – Editorial Pontificia Universidad Javeriana, 15–47.

Danowski, Débora and Viveiros de Castro, Eduardo (2014). *Há mundo por vir? Ensaio sobre os medos e os fins*. Florianópolis, Desterro, Cultura e Barbárie e Instituto Socioambiental.

DeSoto, Pablo (2016). *Antropoceno, Capitaloceno, Chthuluceno. Viviendo con el problema en Fukushima*. PhD Dissertation in Communication and Cultural Studies. Federal University of Rio de Janeiro. Rio de Janeiro: UFRJ/ECO.

FOIRN (2018). *Relatório do XI Encontro de Mulheres Indígenas do Rio Negro*. Departamento de Mulheres Indígenas do Rio Negro, FOIRN. São Gabriel da Cachoeira, FOIRN.

FOIRN/ISA (2005). *Levantamento socioeconômico, demográfico e sanitário da cidade de São Gabriel da Cachoeira (AM)*. São Gabriel da Cachoeira, FOIRN/ISA.

González Casanova, Pablo (1963). "Sociedad plural, colonialismo interno y desarrollo. América Latina". *Revista do Centro Latinoamericano de Ciencias Sociales* [S.l.], 6(3): 1963.

Guattari, Félix (2015). *¿Qué es la Ecosofía?: textos presentados y agenciados por Stéphane Nadaud*. Buenos Aires, Cactus.

Haraway, Donna (2015). "Anthropocene, Capitalocene, Plantationocene, Chthulucene: Making Kin". *Environmental Humanities*, (6): 159–165.

Haraway, Donna (2016). *Staying with the Trouble: Making Kin in the Chthulucene*. Durham, NC and London, Duke University Press.

IBGE (Brazilian Institute of Geography and Statistics) (2019). IBGE Cidades. Available at https://www.ibge.gov.br/cidades-e-estados, accessed 10 November 2020.

ISA (Instituto Socioambiental) (2011). *Povos indígenas do Brasil 2006/2010*. São Paulo, Instituto Socioambiental.

ISA (Instituto Socioambiental) (2018). *Xingú o rio que pulsa em nós. Monitoramento independente para registro de impactos da UHE Belo Monte no território e no modo de vida do povo Juruna (Yudjá) da Volta Grande do Xingu*. ISA, Altamira, Pará.

Lasmar, Cristiane (2006). *De volta ao lago do leite: gênero e transformação no Alto Rio Negro*. São Paulo, ISA/UNESP.

Latour, Bruno (2018). *Down to earth: Politics in the new climatic regime*. Cambridge, Polity Press.

Mantovanelli, Thais (2016). *Os Xikrin do Bacajá e a Usina Hidrelétrica de Belo Monte: uma crítica indígena à política dos brancos*. PhD Thesis in Social Anthropology. Federal University of São Carlos.

Marques, Bruno (2015). *Os Hupd'äh e seus mundos possíveis: transformações espaço-temporais do Alto Rio Negro*. Tese de Doutorado. Rio de Janeiro, Museu Nacional/UFRJ.

Mbembe, Achille (2018). *Necropolítica*. São Paulo, n-1 Edições.

Meira, Marcio (2019). A *persistência do aviamento: colonialismo e história indígena no noroeste Amazônico*. São Carlos, EDUFSCAR.

Melo, Flávia. (2018). "Pena e perigo no governo da fronteira: considerações para uma análise generificada da fronteira amazônica de Brasil, Peru e Colômbia". *Revista de Ciências Sociais*, 49(3): 201–242.

Mol, Annemarie (2002). *The body multiple: Ontology in medical practice*. Durham, NC, Duke University Press.

Olivar, José Miguel (2018). "Violence, the state and gendered indigenous agency in the Brazilian Amazon". *Third World Thematics: A TWQ Journal*, 3.

Piran, Adecio (2019). "Dia do Fogo: Produtores planejam data para queimada na região". *Jornal Folha do Progresso*. Available at http://www.folhadoprogresso.com.br/dia-do-fogo-produtores-planejam-data-para-queimada-na-regiao/, accessed 21 February 2020.

Piscitelli, Adriana (2016). "Sexual economies, love and human trafficking – new conceptual issues". *Cadernos Pagu*, (47): e16475.

Serje, Margarita (2005). *El revés de la nación: territories salvajes, fronteras y tierras de nadie*. Bogotá, Universidad de los Andes.

Stengers, Isabelle (2015). *No tempo das catástrofes: resistir à barbárie que se aproxima*. São Paulo, Cosac Naify.

Stengers, Isabelle (2018). "A proposição cosmopolítica". *Revista do Instituto de Estudos Brasileiros*, (69): 442–464.

Tobón, Marco (2015). "'La autonomía es como una planta que crece'. La cultura como continuación de la política por otros medios. Medio río Caquetá". *Revista de Antropología y Sociología: Virajes*, 17(1): 181–206.

Wright, Robin (2005). *História indígena e do indigenismo no Alto Rio Negro*. São Paolo, ISA/Mercado das Letras.

Zárate, Carlos (2008). *Silvícolas, Siringueros y Agentes estatales: El surgimiento de una sociedad transfronteriza en la Amazonia de Brasil, Perú y Colombia 1880–1932*. Leticia, Universidad Nacional de Colombia, Instituto Amazónico de investigaciones (IMANI).

21. The borders of Macau in a geohistorical perspective: political dispute, (non)definition of limits and migratory phenomena in an original *border-city*

Alfredo Gomes Dias and Jorge Macaísta Malheiros

1. INTRODUCTION

From its origins in the mid-sixteenth century to the founding of the Macao Special Administrative Region (MSAR) in 1999, the definition of the land and sea boundaries of Macau has always been an issue, assuming a specific character that can be analysed in different dimensions. Twenty-one years ago, when the administration of the territory passed from Portugal to the People's Republic of China (PRC), 450 years of tense colonial rule come to an end inaugurating a new period, which did not remove the border but made it change from international to "domestic" (although Macau kept an autonomous political and economic system different from China). Therefore its function of control and separation was maintained, but the level of porosity of the border gradually increased.

Historically, and from a diplomatic perspective, the question of the boundaries of Macao remained a matter of dispute. In its political dimension, the option assumed was to maintain the *status quo* defined in the late nineteenth century as a way of ensuring the economic vitality and preserving the socio-cultural characteristics of this simultaneously port-city and border-city, which benefitted from its geographical position in key Asian sea routes and from its close contact with China and the British possession of Hong Kong (established in 1841/42 and returned to China in 1997), located on the other side of the Pearl River Delta approximately 60 km away. At the social level, it has maintained its role as a port of entry and passage for various migratory movements, including not only commuting between Mainland China and Macao, but also the reception of refugees, Portuguese and Chinese, a particularly relevant phenomenon in the twentieth century. Since the creation of the MSAR, the deep transformations of the society and the economy of Macau, clearly dependent on gambling, leisure and tourism, have led to a very significant increase in both the number of visitors and the number of non-resident workers, assuming a preponderance of the people coming from Mainland China.

Taking this context into consideration, this chapter explores the original historical process behind the production of a specific Luso-Chinese port-city, separated from Mainland China by *de facto* limits that expanded in the mid-1850s, when Portugal, then a peripheral colonial power, benefitted from a context initially favourable to its interests that resulted from the British victory in the First Opium War (1839–1842) and the consequent imposition of European modern colonialism in the region. Particular attention is given to the systematic negotiations that took place over 450 years between a small and weak European maritime power and a large and strong Asian continental empire, which after the nineteenth century was constrained by the strength and expansion of European colonialism. Actually, Macau also had to reinvent itself after the mid-1800s due to the loss of its exclusive role in Sino-European relations and trade and the need to compete and simultaneously benefit from the presence of stronger European colonial powers in China, namely Britain, which through a "growing Hong Kong"[1] started to dominate the international relations in the region.

The negotiations with China, which involved the mediation of British authorities via Hong Kong, an example of which was the 1909 process, were not able to definitely formalize the limits of Macau. Nevertheless, the game of power, contacts and negotiations, bounded by the interests of merchants (including opium traders), navigators and some regional elites, created the dynamic conditions that produced a dense border-city with a mixed character, despite the very present Chinese element. The condition of the city as an intense space of social contact, where various populations interact, is precisely the other element explored in this text.

The uniqueness of the "Macau case" in its historical perspective, even when compared to Hong Kong, the nearby Special Administrative Region created in 1997 that was also a product of European – British – colonialism in Chinese territory, is crucial to understanding today's reality. This relatively small border-city with a special administrative status that depends on an increasing number of external visitors and a flexible regime of labour mobility, keeps its borders and flexible control mechanisms and has so far been able to preserve its identity (threatened by the expansion of gambling spaces and practices) in a specific political and economic context of progressive integration into the PRC.

2. MACAU: THE PRODUCTION OF A (NON)BORDER IN A PARADOXICAL COLONIAL CONTEXT OF CHECKS AND BALANCES

Since the formation of the "settlement of Macau" in the mid-sixteenth century, two issues have fed the history of Luso-Chinese relations: the exercise of Macau's sovereignty and the definition of its land and sea boundaries.

While hardly addressed separately, the analysis of these two issues focuses on the "limits" of Macao. The use of the word "limits", which the Portuguese authorities assumed as an alternative to the term "border", is a good starting point in order to acknowledge the specificities of Macau, its history and the dynamism of the interactions it maintained with neighbouring territories, defined mainly from the hinterland of its ports: the Inner Harbour, which kept Macau in permanent contact with the Chinese world; the Outer Harbour, serving foreign trade, which, until the beginning of the twentieth century, was the main source of income feeding the city and guaranteeing its survival.

The Macau peninsula, almost an island thwarted by a narrow tongue of land connecting it with neighbouring territories in the Pearl River Delta region, was home to a community of merchants, sailors and religious people who transformed that tiny territory into the main centre of diffusion of European culture in the vast Chinese civilizational context, dominant in East Asia.

> Each and every active port-city of international trade scale has a strong multilingual capacity. Macau, in the Ming period, is a pole of attraction for Chinese people from different origins and cultural backgrounds as well as for other Asians such as Japanese, Malays, Vietnamese, people from Siam, Indians and Koreans. It is also via merchants and missionaries, especially Jesuits, an international

European city, particularly Latin, where Portuguese, Italians, Spaniards pass or reside, but also and among others, English and Dutch. (Barreto, 2002: 127–128)

Being of Luso-Asian origin, many of the actors that led the process of founding the city pointed, right at the time of its birth, to one of its most important features: a port-city that was integrated into the different Asian trade routes, from India to Japan (Loureiro, 1997; Barreto, 2006). The construction of the city is associated with the formation of an intercultural social space, represented by the phenomena of ethnic–cultural miscegenation (in the case of the Macanese community), developing an urban reality marked by the image of cultural duality, the "Christian city" and the "Chinese city". This image is traditionally presented as a dichotomy that tends to hide the meeting spaces remaining between those "two cities": the formal communication channels between the political and administrative authorities of the city and the power of the Canton mandarins, and informal contacts between members of the two communities.

Over more than four centuries, Macau has developed through this socio-cultural and political dynamism of encounters and disagreements, revealing the ability to integrate diversity and adapt to the changes dictated by different political and economic circumstances that marked its history. Since the definition of Macau's limits was one of its structural issues, the profound changes that took place in East Asia after the First Opium War (1839–1842) gave this problem a new configuration (Dias, 1993, 1998; Saldanha, 1996).

Through the signing of the Sino-British treaty in Nanjing in 1842, Britain confirmed the occupation of the island of Hong Kong and affirmed its political–diplomatic, military and economic power in that region. Macau saw its exclusive place in Europe–China relations diluted in a new and complex geopolitical and economic reality, not only defined by the interests of the British imperial expansion, but also by those of the French, Russians and Japanese.

Immediately, Macau authorities began a negotiation process to guarantee the same conditions for their port as granted by the Chinese imperial power to a militarily victorious Britain.

In the first article of the document prepared by the Loyal Senate of Macau on 17 July 1843,[2] which was presented, on the 29 July of that year, to the delegate of the Imperial Commissioner, there was a demand for it to be:

> well specified so that it does not offer any doubt in the future that the land that rightfully belongs to the Portuguese is all that is surrounded between the Siege or Barrier and the sea on the one hand, and the river on the other hand, as well as Porto da Taipa, having the Portuguese to always keep a Military Post in place of Barrier Gate. (Representation of the Loyal Senate of 17 July 1843)

The answer of the imperial authorities reaffirming that "the established laws allow them to manufacture houses within the limits that mark the walls of Campo de St.°António"[3] (Figure 21.1) is a clear illustration of how the limits of the city had been redefined as a result of a negotiation dynamics seeking the accomplishment of a new *status quo* in function of the negotiating capacities of each of the parties, in each conjuncture.

The refusal to accept the Leal Senado's proposal to recognize the limit of Macau at the Barrier Gate was overcome shortly afterwards, during the rule of João Maria Ferreira do Amaral (1846–1849). Introducing deep reforms regarding the management of the City and modifying the forms of political relationship with the authorities in Canton, Ferreira do Amaral imposed a strategy of effective occupation of the territory (Silva, 2002). The construction of a road to the Barrier Gate was the formula found to open the old limits of Macau and extend

The borders of Macau in a geohistorical perspective 331

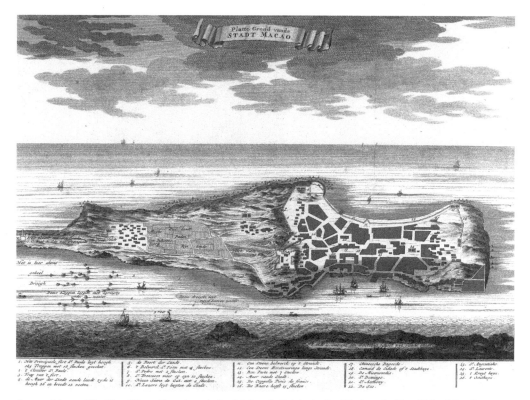

Source: Macau City Plan (*Platte Grond vande Stadt Macao*). Original print (black and white, 25.5 × 36 cm) published in the book *Oud ennieuw Oost-Indien, Vervattendeeen Naaukeurigeen Uitvoerigeverhandelinge van Nederlands Mogentheyd Indie gewesten* ... (1724–1726) (Jorge and Coelho, 2014: 134–135).

Figure 21.1   Macau walls (eighteenth century)

the sovereignty of the Portuguese administration to the entire peninsula. To this area was later joined the occupation of the islands of Taipa and Coloane, and the intention of also occupying the neighbouring islands of Lapa, D. João and Montanha (Figure 21.2) was maintained. The policies followed by Ferreira do Amaral and his assassination in Macau in 1849 started one of the rare periods of great political and military tension between the Portuguese authorities in Macau and the imperial power of Canton, but did not change the land boundaries that had been moved north, settling on the Barrier Gate.

Once again, it is opium and its trade that would extend the discussion about the limits of Macau to the waters surrounding the peninsula. The need for Chinese customs to control the opium trade between Hong Kong and Macau, most of which was clandestine, was not only an economic imperative, but also mirrored the claims to regain sovereignty over Macau. In a nutshell, the city's sovereignty was controlled by whoever controlled its trade. If the expulsion of Chinese customs carried out by Ferreira do Amaral guaranteed the full exercise of Portuguese sovereignty over the territory, the imperial authorities, in turn, recognized that they could only regain that same sovereignty by re-establishing their customs (Saldanha, 2006). Having refused this claim during the negotiations that continued during the 1860s to set Chinese

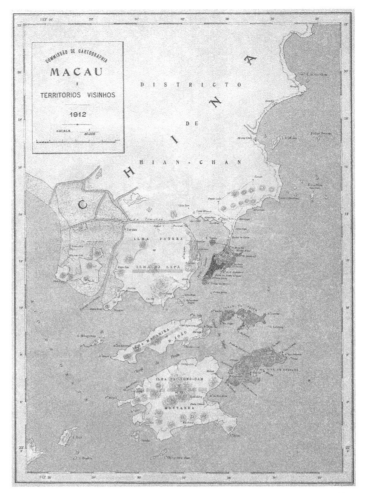

Source: Macau and neighbouring territories (1912). Cartographic Studies Mission. Macau Archive. MO/AM/CART/1/116.

Figure 21.2   Macau and adjacent islands (1912)

customs on the Macau peninsula, China opted to create a set of customs posts around Macau in 1868, a siege that triggered the discussion around maritime limits (Saldanha, 2006). On the one hand, with British support, China claimed its right to place its customs in its territory; on the other hand, Portugal demanded respect for commercial freedom and the principles defined in international law. Once again, without the affirmation of a formal treaty, a new reality was built due to the correlation of political and military forces, with the maritime limits to be designed according to Chinese and British maritime power.

Thus, the definition of the limits of Macau was a continuous process of successive negotiations, alternating with policies of "fait accompli" imposed by one or other party, depending on the strength assumed in each conjuncture. However, once the priority issue of the three countries – Great Britain, China and Portugal – was to control the opium trade it was necessary to affirm a *modus vivendi* that would guarantee the practice of that trade in a climate of regional stability. It is in this sense that Great Britain brought together the positions of Portugal and China with the aim of promoting the signing of a treaty between the two countries.

With the signing of the Luso-Chinese treaty of 1 December 1887, the opium issue was controlled and its stability was guaranteed until the beginning of the diplomatic process (the Shanghai Conference in 1909), which would lead to the prohibition of its international trade (Dias, 2004). However, the definition of the limits of Macau was, once again, postponed, leaving for the near future the holding of a conference between commissioners appointed by Portugal and China, with the specific objective of defining the maritime and land limits of Macau (Saldanha, 2006).

In 1909, the British colony of Hong Kong received the Royal Commissioner Joaquim José Machado and the Imperial Commissioner Gao Erqian. After four months of negotiation, they were unable to reach an agreement. In this way, the Portuguese Commissioner could not achieve a result that would offer the Portuguese monarchy an asset against republican aspirations (which resulted in the proclamation of the Portuguese Republic on 5 October 1910). On the other side, the Imperial Commissioner was clearly limited by the hostility of the Canton nationalist movements speaking out against the Portuguese presence in Macau.

Thus, the *status quo* defined in the 1887 treaty remained in force: "as long as the limits are not fixed, everything concerning them will be preserved as they are currently, without any increase, decrease or change by either party" (article II, *Treaty of Friendship and Trade between Portugal and China*, Beijing, 1 December 1887 (Negócios Externos, 1888)). Until 1999, the year the administration of Macao was transferred to the PRC and of the birth of the MSAR, the boundaries of the territory were preserved, even when regimes with the opposite political affiliation were installed, as was the case with the fascist-like dictatorial regime of the Estado Novo in Portugal and Chinese socialism in the figure of Mao Zedong and the Chinese Communist Party.

All through the twentieth century, this process continued with other episodes that illustrate the option of both countries of respecting the "no agreement" they defined. The joint and simultaneous landing, which occurred in the neighbouring islands of Macau (D. João and Montanha) in 1912, in pursuit of pirates persistently operating in the region of the Pearl River Delta, was the agreed formula so that the military expedition could not be used by either party in diplomatic negotiations on sovereignty on those islands, whose possession was being disputed in the diplomatic corridors of Portugal and China. Even so, the two countries continued to defend their own arguments favourable to the definition of the limits of Macau, namely with regard to the exercise of sovereignty over the neighbouring islands of Macau – Lapa, D. João and Montanha – which, according to a 1955 map of the Estado Novo, belonged to the Province of Macau (Figure 21.3).

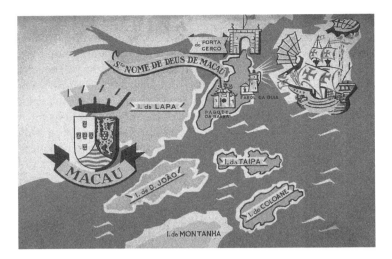

Figure 21.3   Map of the "Santo Nome de Deus de Macau" (1955)[4]

3. THE DEMISE OF THE COLONIAL REGIME AND THE CREATION OF THE MSAR WITHIN THE CHINESE FORMULA "ONE COUNTRY, TWO SYSTEMS": FROM AN INTERNATIONAL BORDER TO A "SPECIAL" INTERNAL BORDER

It was necessary to wait for the announcement of the end of the Portuguese administration for China and Portugal to sign an international agreement defining the limits of the territory of Macau. The Joint Declaration of the Government of the PRC and the Government of the Portuguese Republic on the Question of Macau, signed in Beijing on 13 April 1987, presents Macau as a region that included "the Macau peninsula, the island of Taipa and the island of Coloane". With regard to land tenure, the expression that Macau "is part of Chinese territory" is clear. This was the territory that the MSAR inherited from the Portuguese administration on 20 December 1999. Though the occupation of the Montanha, D. João and Lapa islands did not materialize in the past, the future has effectively led the territorial expansion of Macau to those neighbouring islands.

The transformation of the islands of Montanha and D. João on the island of Hengqin (similar to what the Portuguese administration has done on the islands of Taipa and Coloane creating, through landfills, the COTAI area), has given rise to the new special economic zone with the project to create an "island for international tourism" (Hengqin New Area), mobilizing capital from Hong Kong and Macau (Figure 21.4).

With the purpose of enhancing the consolidated dynamics in Macau around tourism and gambling, and because the MSAR is the only Chinese region authorized to economically exploit gaming, the PRC has started an expansion process from Macau to Hengqin. The first step was taken in 2009, with the renting of a vast area to build the new University of Macau facilities. The second step came in December 2019, when Xi Jinping visited Macau, on the occasion of the twentieth anniversary of the MSAR, with the Chinese president announcing in

The borders of Macau in a geohistorical perspective 335

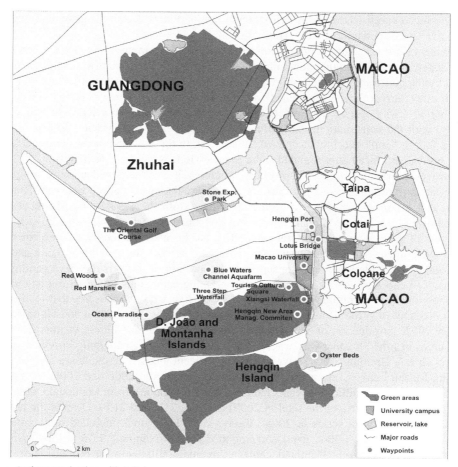

Source: Authors production with J. Seixas.

Figure 21.4 Hengqin, Taipa and Coloane

his speech that "you can focus on the exploration of Hengqin Island through cooperation with Zhuhai, to open space and inject a new long-term development force into Macau".[5]

This way, the MSAR extends its presence on the islands that it had always claimed, now as part of a Chinese strategic plan for the regional integration of the cities in the Pearl River Delta (the Great Bay), whose most relevant investment, with a significant impact in the national and international media, was the construction of the Hong Kong–Macau–Zhuhai bridge, opened in late 2019.

Despite the assumption of Macau as "Chinese territory" and the transfer of the territory administration in 1999, the existence of a formal land border (and a border control system) separating Macau from the Chinese Special Economic Zone of Zhuhai (Guangdong Province) remained. However, the nature of the border, which changed from international to internal (through separating spaces with different economic and political regimes) and become increasingly porous, experienced a meaningful transformation that reflected the growing integration of the two spaces (Edmonds, 2002; Breitung, 2009).

In terms of infrastructure, a process of renewal and enlargement of the checkpoints started immediately in 1999 with the inauguration of the Gongbei checkpoint (Mainland China) followed by the construction of a new enlarged and modernized border complex in 2004 on the Macau side (Barrier Gate checkpoint) (Breitung, 2009). In 2006, a new checkpoint (Industrial Transborder Park) opened and joined to the two existing ones (Barrier Gate and CoTai), Finally, with the construction of the aforementioned Hong Kong–Macau–Zhuhai bridge in 2019 a fourth "land" checkpoint opened. In addition to these checkpoints, there are international borders at Macau airport and also the Macau–Hong Kong ferry terminals.

However, more than changes in physical structures, it was the introduction of progressive simplification measures removing barriers to the circulation of people between China and Macau that led to an explosion in border crossings. Until the 1990s, only Macau residents were allowed to enter in Mainland China, but this situation started to change quickly in the first years of the new millennium transition. This has been stimulated by the implementation of a "development policy" geared towards attracting tourists supported by leisure and gambling, which benefitted from the special formal condition of this territory as a gaming zone (Yeung, Lee and Kee, 2010). In addition to marketing campaigns to attract tourists, the end of the monopoly of gambling in 2003 and the successive array of measures that facilitate the border crossing (e.g. the lifting of the tourist quota of Chinese to Macau and Hong Kong in January 2002; introduction of an individual traveller scheme for Chinese visitors from Pearl River cities in July 2003 that was progressively extended to all Guangdong Province and also to other cities – Breitung, 2009) have led to a significant increase in the movement of people crossing Macau borders. From less than 25 million visitors in 2008 and 2009, the numbers jumped to almost 40 million ten years later, almost 70% coming from Mainland China (these were approximately 50% of the total in 2009) (Figures 21.5 and 21.6). Despite the technical interruption of the data series in 2008,[6] figures for 2003 (which included more categories of visitors than the post-2008 data) corresponded to approximately 11.5 million visitors of whom only 37% were from Mainland China, a percentage still below the proportion of visitors coming from Hong Kong (about 44%).

All things considered, the porousness of the Macau border has increased substantially since the transfer of the administration to China and the creation of the Special Administrative Region (SAR) with a strong emphasis on leisure and tourism, despite some efforts to diversify the economy of the territory, especially after 2009 (Yeung, Lee and Kee, 2010). As a result, the historical condition of border-city, interacting with several Pearl River cities and Hong Kong as well as with other places in China, Asia and Europe, has actually increased. Just before the opening of the new checkpoint of Hong Kong–Macau–Zhuhai bridge, the Gongbei border between Zhuhai and Macau was the busiest in China and considered one of the busiest in the world with its 134 million crossings in 2018.[7] Despite the common elements shared by both sides of the border (e.g. the Cantonese language and culture and the "Chinese" element of identity) and the increasing territorial and economic integration of the Pearl River Delta spaces as well as the growing presence of visitors from Mainland China and the non-local Chinese population,[8] a "sense of cultural difference" still remains (Breitung, 2009). Thus, the specific economic features of the SAR and even the praise for the political autonomy somehow "naturalize" the presence of the old border, which seems porous enough to ensure contacts and protective enough to preserve the specificities of the maritime enclave.

The borders of Macau in a geohistorical perspective 337

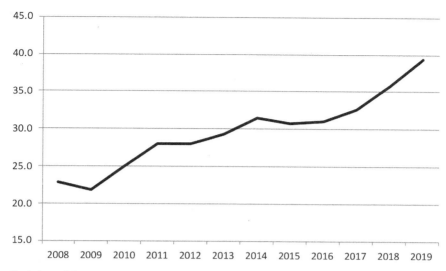

Source: Statistics and Census Service. Government of the Special Autonomous Region of Macau, https://www.dsec.gov.mo/ts/#!/step1/pt-PT (accessed 24 March 2020).

Figure 21.5   Evolution in the number of visitors in millions (2008–2019)

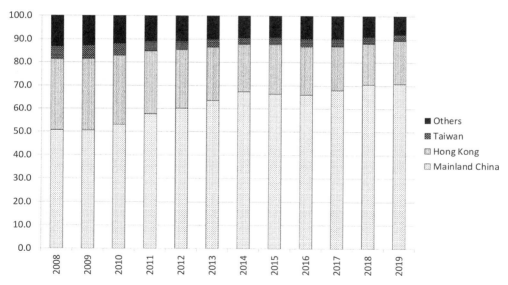

Source: Statistics and Census Service. Government of the Special Autonomous Region of Macau, https://www.dsec.gov.mo/ts/#!/step1/pt-PT (accessed 24 March 2020).

Figure 21.6   Main origins of the visitors (2008–2019)

4. MACAU: BORDERS AND MIGRATIONS

Analysing the formal (non)definition of Macau's borders implies extending its time–space framework, not only to the political–diplomatic dimension, but also to the economic and socio-cultural ones.

Macau emerged as a commercial warehouse that was strategic to the expansion of Portuguese trade in East Asia in the middle of the sixteenth century. The presence in India opened the horizons for a new East and, in 1511, the conquest of Malacca guaranteed the Portuguese merchants integration in the trade routes of East Asia, which extended to Southeast Asia, China and Japan.

After Malacca, the approach to China was carried out by navigators and private merchants who, ignoring the prohibitions of the Ming emperors, established the basis for the beginning of Luso-Chinese relations and the creation of a port, close to Canton, to consolidate the Portuguese commercial presence in the seas of East Asia (Chang, 2000).

Thus, the settlement of the first Portuguese community on the Macau peninsula, among some small fishing villages, took place in the 1550s. In the following decades, it went from a temporary installation to a permanent settlement, which housed adventurous sailors, merchants and missionaries: the payment of an annual rent (*foro do chão*) was formally established in 1571; the diocese of Macau was born in 1576; and the municipality of Macau was created in 1583, an institution with unique characteristics in the panorama of the Portuguese Empire of the East, the Loyal Senate of Macau (Loureiro, 1997; Souza, 2010; Vale, 2011). In the case of Macau, China chose to grant a circumscribed territory, where a foreign community settled, to more easily limit and control the impact of its activities. This formula was then repeated with other protagonists in other parts of the Chinese Empire.

In this way, the "desert island", as described by Fernão Mendes Pinto in his *Peregrinação* (*Pilgrimage* – see Alves, 2010), gave rise to an urban space that grew around the activity of its port. Thatched huts were progressively replaced by permanent dwellings, at the service of those who kept alive an intense trade that extended from Goa to Japan, passing through Malacca and many of the islands of Southeast Asia, benefitting from the proximity of Canton, port of access to the interior of China, and the products that came from it. "Macau's strategic position, at the centre of a vast merchant network, allowed it to conveniently serve all the routes that from the Chinese coast led to Zion, Cambodia, Cochinchina, Champá, Patane, Malacca, Sunde, Java, Timor", and also to the islands of Japan" (Loureiro, 1997: 42).

Around this commercial movement, which evolved over the centuries according to the different political and economic circumstances, the population of Macau grew, concentrating people who came from the different ports that the trade routes passed.

Its founding nucleus, according to Ptak (1982), originated in the transfer of the population that had already settled in Lampacau: "About 400 Portuguese and an unknown number of Indians, Malays, Timorese and Africans lived on Lang-pai-kang around 1555. These people, most of them merchants, seamen, craftsmen and servants, constituted the core of Macao's founding generation" (1982: 27).

Despite the fluctuations that occurred due to economic cycles, the population of Macau increased: the Chinese population constituted an overwhelming majority; the European and Luso-Asian population, experiencing slow and limited growth, became the minority that formally assumed the political and administrative management of the city; and the port of Macau, remaining at the centre of its economic activity, contributed to the formation of a third component of that human reality, with the constant movement but also settlement of people from the most diverse origins, from Europe to Asia.

Thus, the features of a port-city emerge, with characteristics of a maritime enclave, which, over four and a half centuries, has generated a complex migratory network, driven by the activity of its harbour and by its geostrategic location, both political and economic: a population of European origin travelling to Macau attracted by East Asian trade; a Chinese population, also of diverse origins, mainly from neighbouring provinces of Guangdong and Fujian; and a Macanese community, the result of a long relationship between European/Portuguese men and Asian/Chinese women.

Macau owes its universal character to the people who crossed it, some staying, others in transit to other destinations, many of whom have returned. In this way, the city became a bridge between Europe and Asia, between Portugal and China, between Southwest Asia and the State of India, attracting new commercial routes and getting involved in those that already existed in the Eastern Asia, but giving it new dynamics (Dias, 2016).

This convergence of different migratory flows in Macau would be the origin of the formation of a unique community – the Macanese, children of a long process of human and cultural encounters, resulting in a Portuguese–Asian community, which occupied a social space of interface between the two main communities present in Macau society.

Living close to the economic elites – whether Portuguese, Chinese or English – the Macanese community experienced a profound process of change due to the impact of the transformations that occurred in China and Eastern Asia following the birth of Hong Kong and the opening of several Chinese ports to international trade in the 1840s. The displacement of hundreds of migrants to the new British colony, beginning in 1842, started a long and intense migratory process, which lasted until 1999, involving almost all Macanese families (Dias, 2014, 2016).

Thus, in addition to the migratory movements that systematically converged in the city, Macau, through the role of the Macanese diaspora after the mid-1850s, has also assumed the condition of an origin space for emigration outflows which, at the beginning, targeted some Chinese cities (Hong Kong and Xanghai), diverging in the second half of the twentieth century to several countries on all continents (Dias, 2014, 2016).

Both through the Inner Harbour and the Outer Harbour, China and the rest of the world found in Macau a gateway almost always open to goods, ideas and people. Even the Barrier Gate, located on the Northern border tip between Macau and immense China, has not been narrow enough to prevent the daily entry and exit of Chinese who have their places of work in Macau.

This intense and diversified migratory reality was only possible in a city whose land and sea limits contracted and expanded due to political, economic and social circumstances, but never actually closed completely. The port franchise corresponded to a free movement tolerated by an economic and social system that included in its (Chinese) territory and under its (Portuguese) administration people who wished to work there daily, using both temporary and permanent settlement strategies.

Thus, this political and administrative reality that depended on a permanent reinvention of Portuguese–Chinese relations intersected with an economic reality that, from the middle of the nineteenth century, has been expressed through the opening of its port to international trade and in a social reality that that has been rebuilt in a daily life that generates intercultural relations.

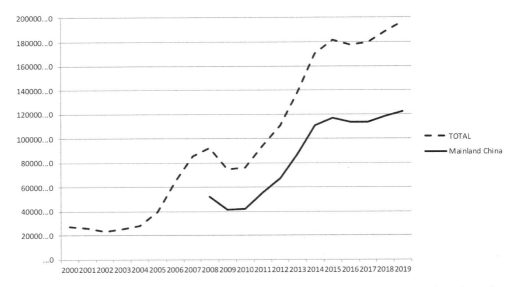

Source: Statistics and Census Service. Government of the Special Autonomous Region of Macau, https://www.dsec.gov.mo/ts/#!/step1/pt-PT (accessed 28 March 2020).

Figure 21.7   Non-resident workers established in Macau (2000–2019)

In addition to these structural migratory phenomena of Macao society, essentially marked by the pace of economic conjunctures, other examples of human mobility point to how the fluidity of the city's limits has been interpreted according to the needs imposed by the geopolitical role that Macau has assumed in the Pearl River Delta region.

The civil war in China that lasted through the 1920s and 1930s, the Japanese invasion that took place in 1937, the Second World War, the occupation of Hong Kong in December 1941 and the proclamation of the PRC on 1 October 1949 transformed Macau into a safe territory for the reception of Portuguese, Chinese and many other nationalities (Reis, 2003; Fernandes, 2000).

The Japanese invasion gave rise to the first major movement of refugees who sought Macau as a destination, leading the Portuguese authorities to take measures to guarantee the reception of many thousands of people (Reis, 2003). The first Portuguese began to arrive from Shanghai. However, it is in 1949, after the arrival of the People's Liberation Army of the Chinese Communist Party (CCP) on 25 May that the massive displacement of the "Portuguese from Shanghai" to Macau began (Dias, 2015). A few years earlier, in 1942, following the Japanese military forces' occupation of Hong Kong, Macau had already received some 1 200 Macanese escaping from that British colony.

To the "Portuguese of Shanghai" and Hong Kong we may add many men and women of other nationalities, as was the case with Germans living in Hong Kong and Canton, who took refuge in Macau in October 1939 (Reis, 2003). But, in addition to Europeans, the great social and financial impact results from the thousands of Chinese refugees who also sought in Macau the protection they needed to escape the scourge of the Japanese presence, the civil war and the economic and social instability that resulted from the installation of the new Chinese regime. The presence of these Chinese refugees lasted through the 1950s and 1960s.

The formal (non)definition of the boundaries of Macau, which even today, and despite the explicit presence of borders and border controls, incorporates potentially diffuse elements as evidenced by the possibility of the city expansion to Hengqin and the construction of the long Hong Kong–Macau–Zhuhai bridge, translates the permeability of Macao's social structures to the coexistence with the Other, currently present in the city in an increasing way, whether in the temporary form of the visitor or tourist, or in the most perennial way with holders of residence permits or non-resident workers. The latter have seen a significant increase since the beginning of this century, mainly involving Mainland Chinese (62.3% of this type of workers in 2019), but also a high number of other Asians, coming from countries such as the Philippines, Vietnam, Hong Kong and Indonesia (Figure 21.7). Living side by side with these aliens, or relating to them in an explicit or implicit way, the Chinese of Macau and the Macanese stand in this context of contact that prevails over the centuries and offers the city its hybrid and miscegenated character, marked by different ways of being and behaving socially and culturally.

5. CONCLUDING REMARKS

In summary, the various geopolitical and economic conjunctures that over four and a half centuries have characterized the history of Macau, the formation of the border-city and the formal (non)definition of its limits do not seem to result much from chance or from any incapacities on the part of the Chinese or Portuguese authorities. In fact, they result more from an effective interest in adjusting, in a flexible way, the area of the city and its characteristics to the economic cycles and to the (controlled) mobility of the populations. The result has been the production of an original port-city, whose specificities (e.g. the old and continued Portuguese presence that dates back to the sixteenth century, the autonomy in relation to the Chinese rule, the gambling rights after the establishment of Hong Kong) are beneficial for the surrounding regions and ensure a bridge between two civilizational worlds: China and Portugal; Asia and Europe.

In other words, there are clear signs of how the city's political, economic and social structures have adjusted to a definition of its land and sea boundaries: the integration of Macau in the commercial circuits of East Asia and Southeast Asia; Macau's dependence on neighbouring provinces of Guangdong and Fujian, which have guaranteed daily supplies of goods and workers who cross the Barrier Gate every day; the activity of the Inner and Outer Harbours, where people and products from China and the rest of the world come in and out; the mobility of migrants who enter and leave the city for economic or professional reasons; the existence of various movements of refugees, from different origins. To this, we must add the mobility of a workforce that enters and leaves daily through its gates, ensuring the functioning and subsistence of the city.

Far from being a traditional political border that marks the separation between two national spaces with their own identities, Macau's limits are the result of continuous negotiations in the political and diplomatic sphere, within different regional economic circumstances. Moreover, the boundaries of Macau are also a social construction, with marks of hybridity within the framework of a culturally diverse society, fuelled by the complementarity of migratory movements simultaneously converging in and diverging from Macau.

We may conclude by saying that the historical reading of both the tense political relations and the negotiations about the "assumed" (un)defined geographical limits of the border-city are crucial to understanding the present reality of the MSAR. Administrated by China since December 1999, Macau has so far kept a status of political and economic autonomy that justifies the existing border and border controls. This border, which is becoming progressively more porous, still assumes the symbolic (and effective) role of preserving differences and somehow protecting the original political and cultural elements still prevailing in Macau.

However, the signs of political tension (e.g. protests in Hong Kong and political pressure to eventually change the 50-year transition statuses that have been agreed with the UK and Portugal, respectively, about Hong Kong and Macau) and economic and structural change that are nowadays identifiable in the Pearl River Delta region may have important impacts on the future of the border-city. The economic dynamics of this entire space, which joins regions of Mainland China (Shenzhen, Zhuhai), Hong Kong and tiny Macau, have been crucial in the recent internationalization process of China and justified a planned strategy of integration, of which the 55 km[9] long Hong Kong–Zhuhai–Macau bridge, inaugurated in October 2019, is probably the best material example.

Geographically very close to the larger, highly internationalized and economically more advanced SAR of Hong Kong[10] (a distance of 60 km by sea at the Pearl River Delta), Macau has played a sort of complementary economic and social role due to its international specialization in the gambling industry and its function as a leisure destination that goes back to the second quarter of the nineteenth century (Vidal, 2016). If the changes that occurred in the early 2000s had the effect of stimulating the economy and multiplying the number of visitors and non-resident workers, they have also contributed to change Macau's scenery and to generate some concerns among residents about "crowdedness", corruption associated with gambling practices and unrest in public places (Breitung, 2009). So far, autonomous administration and specific and dynamic identity elements seem preserved with the contribution of the existing border and border controls. However, regional integration is moving forward and the border will probably be removed in 30 years (if not before), justifying the questioning about Macau's visibility and originality in the future.

NOTES

1. The growth of Hong Kong was political, economic and demographic but also spatial, because its territory expanded to the Kowloon Peninsula in 1861 and to the New Territories in 1899, following the formalization of the 100 years concession agreement with China. In fact, the area of Hong Kong (1 106 km^2) is almost 34 times the area of Macau (32.9 km^2) and its population, which in the beginning of the twentieth century was approximately 370 000 individuals (almost five times the population of Macau at the time), jumped to a value close to 7.5 million nowadays, now 11 times the population of the former Portuguese colony (Hong Kong Government Reports Online (1842–1941), http://sunzi.lib.hku.hk/hkgro/index.jsp, accessed 1 June 2020; Census and Statistics Department of Hong Kong and DSEC, MSAR, 2020).
2. Representation of the Loyal Senate of 17 July 1843, addressed to the Imperial Commissioner, attached to letter No. 304 of 31 July 1843 of the Governor of Macau, Adrião Acácio da Silveira Pinto, for the Minister of the Navy and Overseas. Overseas Historical Archive. MACAU/ACL/SEMU/DGU/005 Series, Box 0011, 1843.

3. Report of the decision for and against of the articles presented by the Portuguese to the Imperial High Commissioner, attached to letter no. 308 of 23 September 1843 of the Governor of Macau, Adrião Acácio da Silveira Pinto, for the Minister of the Navy and Overseas. Overseas Historical Archive. MACAU/ACL/SEMU/DGU/005 Series, Box 0011, 1843.
4. Pinto, Hermengarda Marques (1955). *Macau Terra de Lendas*. Lisbon: Companhia Nacional de Educação de Adultos, https://nenotavaiconta.wordpress.com/2013/07/05/mapa-de-macau-1955/, accessed 5 October 2019.
5. Visit Xi Jinping foi embora, mas deixou quatro tarefas para o Governo da RAEM. *Hoje Macau*, 21 de dezembro de 2019, https://hojemacau.com.mo/2019/12/21/visita-xi-jinping-foi-embora-mas-deixou-quatro-tarefas-para-o-governo-da-raem/, accessed 14 January 2020.
6. The statistical definition of *visitor* used by the Statistics and Census Service of the Government of the SAR of Macau (DSEC) was changed in 2008 and started to exclude certain categories such as non-resident workers. This prevents the inclusion of data prior to 2008 in Figures 21.5 and 21.6.
7. New Border between Macau and Zhuhai will Decrease Crossing Time. *Macau News*, 14 December 2019, https://macaunews.mo/new-border-between-macau-and-zhuhai-will-decrease-crossing-time/, accessed 28 March 2020.
8. According to DSEC, the non-local population includes non-resident workers and foreign students. These represented 13% of the total population in the 2011 Census, 17.4% in the 2016 Intercensus and more than 18% of the total population of the territory estimated for 2019.
9. It is considered the longest bridge in the world, comprising the 29 km of the main bridge system (22 km of bridge plus approximately 7 km of tunnel) and the remaining 26 km of secondary structures in Hong Kong and Zhuhai.
10. The SAR of Hong Kong has played a crucial role in the process of internationalization of China in the twenty-first century (Yeung, Lee and Kee, 2010), being one of the busiest ports in the world – particularly in container movement – and a world-level top financial market.

REFERENCES

Alves, J. S. (2010). *Fernão Mendes Pinto and the "Peregrinação"* (4 vols). Studies, restored Portuguese text, notes and indexes. Lisbon: Fundação Oriente and INCM.
Barreto, L. (2002). Macau: Fronteira intercultural no período Ming. *Clio*, 6, 121–142.
Barreto, L. (2006). *Macau: Poder e saber. Séculos XVI e XVII*. Lisbon: Presença.
Breitung, W. (2009). Macau residents as border people – A changing border regime from a sociocultural perspective. *Journal of Current Chinese Affairs*, 38, 1, 101–127.
Chang, S. (2000). The changing patterns of Portuguese outposts along the coast of China in the 16th century: A social-ecological perspective. In Jorge Santos Alves (ed.), *Portugal e a China. Conferências no III curso livre de história das relações entre Portugal e a China (séculos XVI e XIX)*. Lisbon: Fundação Oriente, 15–33.
Dias, A. (1993). *Macau e la I guerra do ópio*. Macau: IPOR.
Dias, A. (1998). *Sob o signo da transição. Macau no século XIX*. Macau: IPOR.
Dias, A. (2004). *Portugal, Macau e a questão da internacionalização do ópio (1909–1925)*. Macau: Livros do Oriente.
Dias, A. (2014). *Diáspora Macaense. Macau, Hong Kong, Xangai (1850–1952)*. Lisbon: Centro Científico e Cultural de Macau / Fundação Macau.
Dias, A. (2015). *Refugiados de Xangai. Macau 上海葡裔難民在澳門 (1937–1964)*. Macau: Instituto Cultural do Governo da Região Administrativa Especial de Macau/Arquivo Histórico de Macau (bilingual edition: Portuguese and Chinese).
Dias, A. (2016). *Diáspora Macaense. Territórios, Itinerários e Processos de Integração (1936–1995)*. Macau: Instituto Cultural da RAEM.
Edmonds, R. L. (2002). Macau in the Pearl River Delta and beyond. *China Perspectives*, 44, 18–28.
Fernandes, M. (2000). *Sinopse de Macau nas relações luso-chinesas. 1949–1995*. Cronologia e documentos. Lisbon: Fundação Oriente.

Jorge, C. and Coelho, R. B. (2014). *Viagem por Macau. (séculos XVII–XVIII)* (Vol. I). Macau: Livros do Oriente/Instituto Cultural de Macau do Governo da RAEM.
Loureiro, R. (1997). *Em busca das origens de Macau*. Macau: Museu Marítimo de Macau.
Negócios Externos (1888). *Documentos Apresentados às Cortes na Sessão Legislativa de 1887 pelo Ministro e Secretário de Estado dos Negócios Estrangeiros. Negociações com a China* (Vol. 1). Lisbon: Imprensa Nacional.
Ptak, R. (1982). The demography of old Macao, 1555–1640. *Ming Studies*, 15, 27–35.
Reis, C. (2003). Conjuntura e vida política. In A. H. Oliveira Marques (ed.), *História dos Portugueses no Extremo Oriente* (Vol. 4.º). Lisbon: Fundação Oriente, 13–176.
Saldanha, A. V. (1996). *Estudos sobre as relações luso-chinesas*. Lisbon: Instituto Superior de Ciências Sociais e Políticas, Instituto Cultural de Macau.
Saldanha, A. V. (2006). *O tratado impossível. Um exercício de diplomacia luso-chinesa num contexto internacional em mudança (1842–1887)*. Lisbon: Instituto Diplomático/Ministério dos Negócios Estrangeiros.
Silva, M. (2002). *Transição de Macau para a modernidade (1841–1853). Ferreira do Amaral e a construção da soberania portuguesa*. Lisbon: Fundação Oriente.
Souza, T. (2010). Bispado de Macau. In Maria Antónia Espadinha (ed.), *Dicionário Temático de Macau* (vol. I). Macau: Universidade de Macau, 189–191.
Vale, A. (2011). Leal Senado. In Maria Antónia Espadinha (ed.), *Dicionário Temático de Macau* (vol. III). Macau: Universidade de Macau, 844–846.
Vidal, F. (2016). Os primórdios do turismo em Macau e Cantão no século XIX: Do território de fronteira ao lugar urbano. *PLURAL, Revista do Programa de Pós-Graduação em Sociologia da Universidade de São Paulo*, 23.2, 17–32.
Yeung, Y.-M., Lee, J. and Kee, G. (2010). Macau in a globalising world: The challenges ahead. *Asian Geographer*, 27, 1–2, 75–92.

22. The Crimean borderscape: a changing landscape of political compassion and care
Greta Lynn Uehling

1. INTRODUCTION: NOT EXACTLY A BORDER AT ALL

This chapter is concerned with a border that is not an official international border at all. I am referring to the lines of demarcation across the narrow isthmus of land connecting Ukraine and its southern province of Crimea, now controlled by the Russian Federation. In February 2014, troops lacking military insignia invaded Crimea and rapidly took over key military and strategic sites. A referendum was quickly organized even though doing so violated Ukrainian law and international norms (Gregory 2014). Militarization of the peninsula followed as President Vladimir Putin revealed his intention to secure the territory against threats ostensibly posed by Ukraine (Klymenko 2015). The United Nations General Assembly passed a resolution condemning the action and a wide range of sanctions have followed, but no progress toward returning the territory to Ukraine has been made.

Maps of the region make the multiple political reimaginings of the region clear because the line of demarcation appears different depending on the internet server used. If searching from inside the Russian Federation, a solid line reflecting a clear international border appears.[1] When searching from inside Ukraine, the United States, or western Europe, by contrast, the border appears as a dotted line, communicating the disputed status of the territory. The reason that Google Maps displays the same location in two different ways is to avoid being an arbiter in the dispute, and to abide by the laws on the ground. The simultaneously solid and dotted lines underscore the made-up quality of the Crimean borderscape that has, somewhat paradoxically, taken tremendous work to establish and maintain. After the February 2014 occupation and *de facto* annexation, Russia and Ukraine each established customs and passport controls regulating entry and exit. Rotating cadres of officers monitor each of the boundaries. In between, there is a 2 km "no-man's land." Without any public transport, the majority of crossers walk this stretch of previously uncontested road. For those who traveled from continental Ukraine to Crimea freely in the past, the establishment of not one but two different national passport and customs control processes was an affront to their sensibilities. To study this area, I carried out ethnographic fieldwork between 2015 and 2017. "Border," however, was a word I quickly learned to avoid: it gave undue legitimacy to the unlawful state of affairs. United Nations organizations utilize a compromise term, the "ABL" or administrative boundary line to circumvent controversy over nomenclature.

This chapter theorizes the dynamics surrounding the administrative boundary line through the concept of borderscaping. The idea of a borderscape emerged from the notion of "scapes" that was introduced by Arjun Appadurai (1991) to capture the changing significance of borders under conditions of globalization. He used terms like mediascape, technoscape, and ethnoscape to capture the fluid, contested, and irregular nature of socio-spatial configurations as a result of intensified flows of information, goods, capital, and people (1991: 48). He was especially interested in the expanded role the human imagination plays when people can envision a different life for themselves. Indeed, how boundaries are imagined is crucial to how borderscapes take shape. Within critical border studies, the concept of a borderscape has been leveraged to overcome the limitations associated with placing state sovereignty at the center of border analyses (Brambilla 2015). Decentering the state brings the fluidity of borders into view, generating appreciation for how borders are in a continual process of being made and remade (Brambilla and Jones 2019). Paasi (1998) therefore used the term "bordering," and Rumford (2008) used the expression "border work" to capture how borders are constituted by social practices.

1.1 Organization of the Chapter

In what follows, I first explain how material for this study was gathered. Then, I discuss how politics of compassion were implicated in the *de facto* annexation of Crimea. Here, as might be predicted, compassion was directed toward some people more than others based on a selective interpretation of history. Considering the decline in the protection of human rights, especially for those with pro-Ukrainian sentiments, it is clear these particular politics contracted rather than expanding moral concern and compassion for the populations of the peninsula. A demographic reshuffling is one of the important outcomes, with forced migration propelling the most vulnerable individuals off the peninsula. Processes of militarization then brought Russian military personnel and military families in. The remainder of the chapter considers how the borderscape was variously constituted through social practices tethered to divergent political imaginations. Specifically, I focus on how activists who sought to resist the effects of the *de facto* annexation reimagined and reshaped the borderscape.

2. METHODOLOGY

The argument that follows is based on ethnographic fieldwork, semi-structured interviewing, and desk research. With regard to the fieldwork, I spent time near the administrative boundary line, in the armed compound established to resist Russian control of the peninsula. The interviewing carried out across the Ukraine comprised of 90 ethnographic interviews I conducted between 2015 and 2017. Two-thirds of these interviews were with people who had been displaced as a result of the *de facto* annexation of the Crimean peninsula. Through quota sampling with the assistance of three separate non-governmental organizations (NGOs) that help internally displaced persons, I selected respondents according to age, gender, ethnicity, and level of education to achieve a balance. I also used opportunistic sampling, inviting people I met at social, cultural, and political events over the three-year period to speak privately. Since people displaced from Crimea are dispersed across Ukraine, I based my research around four primary hubs where they had settled, and traveled to several villages to interview as broad a spectrum of people as possible. According to the terms of my funding, I did not travel to Crimea itself. Rather, I interviewed 15 people who continue to live in occupied Crimea at times when they were visiting Ukrainian-controlled territory. The chapter is also informed by previous research trips to Crimea, including a visit seven months prior to the Russian occupation.

3. UNEVEN POLITICS OF COMPASSION

Politics of compassion are concerned with how, and more importantly why compassion is extended to vulnerable members of a society. Exploring compassion provides insight into how some social groups come to be included in circles of concern and care whilst others remain excluded. Basically, politics of compassion manifest in the ability to perceive and feel another's suffering, accompanied by a willingness and desire to help (Murphy 2019: 6). As Nussbaum describes it, compassion is very much a moral sentiment that entails judgement and guides action (Nussbaum 2013). While some analysts argue compassion is crucial for democratic politics and essential to humanitarian assistance (Boltanski 1999; Fassin 2012; Nussbaum 2013, Smith 2002 [1759]), others are more skeptical, pointing out compassion has a tendency to be capricious, and often fails to deliver on its promises (Arendt 1963; Crisp 2008; Surriyeh 2017). In the Crimean case, expressions of compassion provided a smooth veneer for politics of a much more destructive nature.

Vladimir Putin justified the territorial claim in explicitly human rights and humanitarian terms: protecting the Russian community in Crimea. He alleged that Ukraine's language policies, anti-Semitism, crime, and corruption all posed threats to the members of the Russian-speaking population who saw themselves as part of *Russkiy Mir* or Russian World (Makarychev and Yatsyk 2018). Putin was in part responding to changes emanating from the 2013–2014 Ukrainian revolution, including changing laws on language. As the 2013–2014 revolution put Ukraine on an accelerated path toward political and economic integration with the European Union, the Russian government crafted the Putin Doctrine, which asserts that Moscow has the right and obligation to protect Russians anywhere in the world. For those familiar with humanitarian law, the Doctrine will sound a lot like the Responsibility to Protect. This is far from a coincidence. President Vladimir Putin cited the NATO bombing of Kosovo in 1999, carried out using the rhetoric of Responsibility to Protect, as precedent (Rieff 2000).

The Responsibility to Protect is a principle that was developed in the wake of the genocide in the Great Lakes Region of Africa when the international community was tragically slow in responding to genocide. Humanitarians, governments, and international organizations sought to change the decision-making calculus for cases in which outside intervention could make a difference. The 1999 US-led NATO bombing campaign in Kosovo and the *de facto* annexation of Crimea are two case studies for the way in which the rhetoric of compassion has provided a convenient cover for accomplishing what are primarily geostrategic objectives by labeling the action humanitarian. The territorial incursion into Crimea was framed in terms of compassion for an ostensibly vulnerable majority, but the objectives were much broader and more tactical in nature. Scholars of Ukraine tend to agree that, while the population of Crimea may have been persuaded they were under threat, the claims about "fascist" nationalists endangering the Russian population of Crimea (Wilson 2014; Kuzio 2017: 85) were exaggerated.

The political reimagining that was required to make the Crimean borderscape is particularly clear in publicity about the results of the 2016 referendum on the status of the peninsula. Data released by the President's Human Rights Council of Russia showed that only a small percentage of the population voted in favor of joining Russia (Gregory 2014). There was also a host of irregularities and the results have been widely challenged. The supposedly humanitarian intervention, then, is better summarized as a Trojan Horse for an army of policy objectives intended to strengthen Russia's power over Crimea.

4. AN HISTORICAL SLEIGHT OF HAND

Compassion for the Russian population was amplified by statements that Crimea is historically Russian made in speeches by President Vladimir Putin and others.[2] According to the last census in 2001, the majority of the population does claim Russian as their primary language.[3] Of the 2.2 million people living there, 1.5 million are Russians and 350,000 are Ukrainians, many of whom consider the Russian language their native tongue. About 290,000 are Crimean Tatars who, while disinclined to accept Russian authority for reasons that will be discussed below, also speak Russian.[4]

Crimea came under Russian control for the first time in 1783, when Empress Ekaterina II annexed the territory. At that time, Crimea was part of the Crimean khanate, which extended far beyond the borders of contemporary Crimea. Russian imperial policies had been aggressively Russifying the ethnically diverse area, where Crimean Tatar was widely spoken (Uehling 2004). When the Revolution of 1917 led to the disintegration of the Russian Empire, Crimean Tatars made a bid to reclaim some of the political power they had lost by declaring an independent and democratic republic (1918–1920) using the Crimean khanate as their model. In 1921, however, they lost that bid when the Red Army prevailed and Crimea was made part of the USSR.

One way to understand the *de facto* annexation, then, is as a historical sleight of hand. Whether it was the Russian imperial annexation of the territory of the Crimean khanate, the transfer of the territory from the jurisdiction of the Russian Soviet Socialist Republic to the Ukrainian Soviet Socialist Republic, or the deportation of the Crimean Tatars in 1944 for allegedly collaborating with the Third Reich, different parties have diametrically opposed views of what transpired. Contemporary Russian authorities have emphasized imperial history, downplaying both the centuries-long history of the Crimean Tatar khanate and the fact that, legally, Crimea is legally part of Ukraine. Crimea was legally transferred from the Russian to the Ukrainian Soviet Socialist Republic in 1954 according to a decree by the Presidium of the Supreme Soviet of the USSR. After the disintegration of the Soviet Union, the newly independent state of Ukraine retained its authority over Crimea. Unfortunately, Ukraine did not invest in developing the peninsula, which continued to offer the standard of living of a less-developed country. After Russia began to take control of the peninsula in 2014, the pro-Russian contingent embraced the prospects for development associated with becoming part of the Russian Federation.

The interpretation of history offered by the Crimean Tatars, who understand themselves as one of the indigenous peoples even though Russia does not recognize them as such, is understandably quite different. They see themselves as the rightful inhabitants of the area, and (as one of my interviewees put it) see Putin as an "emperor without clothes" who will eventually be defeated. These opposing views of history contribute to disenchantment over Russian territorial control on the part of Crimean Tatars in particular, and intensify the make-believe quality of the administrative line of demarcation.

5. HUMAN RIGHTS IN CRIMEA

To reinforce their *de facto* annexation in 2014, the Russian Federation militarized the peninsula and sought to crush resistance to their rule by circumscribing the human rights of the most vocal dissenters. The human rights picture in Crimea is dire: there have been physical attacks on Ukrainian media outlets; limitations placed on the freedom of the press; enforced disappearances; strict rules limiting peaceful assembly; politically motivated detentions, prosecutions, and disappearances (Crimea SOS 2020); limitations to freedom of movement; unlawful conscription into the armed services; and violations of the right to freedom of religion (Coynash 2017a; Coynash 2017b).

Those most affected are people seeking to contest the legitimacy of the *de facto* authorities, including academics, journalists, writers, and political activists as well as entire ethnic and religious groups that oppose or were at least believed to oppose the annexation. In particular, the Crimean Tatar community, which has historically been openly anti-Russian, was considered a threat. Followers of the Ukrainian Orthodox Church–Kyiv Patriarch, the autocephalous Orthodox Church of Ukraine (Coynash 2017a) and Jehovah's Witnesses have also been primary targets of the Russian-backed authorities (Coynash 2017b). In addition to violating Ukrainian sovereignty and international law, then, the Russian Federation has instituted what Prozorov calls a logic of *bespredel* (without limitations) in which authorities operate according to "tacit and informal norms that may themselves be illegal" (Prozorov 2012: 37).

The dubious legal status of Russian sovereignty over Crimea combined with the long list of human rights issues demonstrate that this peninsula has taken on the features of a "state of exception," Carl Schmitt and Giorgio Agamben's term for a political situation in which a sovereign power suspends the rule of law as a way of sustaining a political order in response to a perceived emergency or threat (Agamben 2005).

6. CHANGING DEMOGRAPHICS

Estimates of the number of people forcibly displaced by the *de facto* annexation of Crimea vary. The Migration Policy Institute estimates that of the 1.5 million internally displaced persons (IDPs) in Ukraine, some 50,000 are from Crimea (Jaroszewicz 2019). Because the data of the Ministry of Social Policy are not disaggregated by ethnicity, and because not all of the forcibly displaced register as such, this remains an estimate. What is certain is that there has been a demographic reshuffling: as people loyal to Ukraine fled, persons loyal to the Russian Federation were moved in. These individuals fill the Russian Federation's military and managerial apparatus in Crimea. By August 2015, 20,000 residents of Russia had already moved to the city of Sevastopol (Klymenko 2015: 2). Soldiers and their families made up the majority. These military are needed to operate the increasing numbers of tanks, combat aircraft, attack helicopters, submarines, and surface ships. Items of military hardware have at least doubled and in some cases tripled since the takeover.[5] This expansion of military capabilities on the peninsula is projected to continue. According to a United Nations report, if before the territorial incursion there were 12,500 soldiers, by 2020 there are expected to be at least 43,000 stationed on the Crimean peninsula.[6] The new S-400 "Triumph" surface-to-air system is intended to close Crimean airspace from any attack.[7] The prevalence of surveillance and helicopters flying low over urban areas has led people I interviewed to describe the peninsula as "a giant military base." Not all of the military hardware is real, however. The Russian armed forces have been purchasing inflatable tanks, fighter jets, tank turrets, etc. for about a decade and many of these items were deployed at the administrative line to bolster the image of Russian military might.[8] As with the Google maps, inflatables demonstrate there is a mix of material practices and make-believe constituting this borderscape.

7. THE CRIMEAN BORDERSCAPE

Borders are notoriously selective filters and the lines of demarcation between Russian-controlled Crimea and government-controlled Ukraine as a whole are no exception. If Bejarano and Hernandez argue in this volume that vulnerable communities challenge the blockades of the nation-state, this case presents a scenario that is somewhat the opposite because it was a vulnerable community that erected a blockade to challenge the weaknesses and indiscretions of the nation-state. Indeed, borders and their borderscapes providing fertile sites for resistant subjectivities to form and act. As Gaibazzi (2017) explains, borderscapes foster counter-hegemonic imaginaries, practices, and possibilities for agency. It is important to clarify here that borderscapes are not defined solely by a specific geographic location, and, like politics of compassion, include struggles over the terms of inclusion and exclusion (Rajaram Prem and Grundy-Warr 2007: xxviii). The concept of a borderscape is it invites serious consideration of the activities of non-state actors – both border-crossers and activists – as meaningful agents. I turn now to how these actors' ability to shape the way the border is experienced demonstrates they have been able to reimagine how the administrative lines of demarcation should work, exercising agency and taking a kind of control that is normally the exclusive purview of the state.

8. COMPASSIONATE RESISTANCE: THE *ASKERI*

One of the best examples of selective filtering – and reimagining the Crimean borderscape – can be found at the Ukrainian line of administrative control where numerous irregularities, to be described in more detail in a moment, were reported to occur. Crimean Tatar leaders therefore created a cadre of civilians to monitor the official Ukrainian border crossings where migrants had reported being fined, harassed, and having had their personal items arbitrarily confiscated. There were many cases of people being delayed at the border or being prohibited from crossing it. Lacking identity documents of their own, children were especially vulnerable to being denied entry or exit. The volunteer group formed for this activity, called *Askeri* after an elite military class under the Ottoman Empire, initially worked as observers. Eventually, however, they were recognized by the Ukrainian government as an official partner of the State Border Service of Ukraine. The *Askeri* demonstrate the importance of non-state actors in shaping how the border operates.

The *Askeri* also show how compassion can act in the way Adam Smith envisioned, which was as a second "invisible hand" softening the divisive effects of the market under capitalism. The *Askeri* offered their protection to individuals of any ethnicity or political view, and among those who benefitted the most were people trying to cross who did not see themselves as part of *Russkiy Mir* or Russian World at all. A crucial element of the *Askeri* success was the availability of a hotline established by Lenur Islyamov, the owner of the *ATR* television station. Islyamov and his associates counseled travelers with difficulties over the hotline and televised the process live, introducing a greater amount of transparency in a performance of power. This stripped the official border patrol of their ability to conceal their irregular practices from view. Further, the gap between the letter of Ukrainian law and how it was being practiced became more obvious to authorities in Kyiv. With the astute use of media, then, the compassionate actions of the *Askeri* mediated between travelers, border guards, and Kyiv, compassionately resisiting the legal irregularities.

9. NUMAN ÇELEBICIHAN BATTALION

The *Askeri* were not alone in providing compassionate resistance. Another concerted response to the *de facto* annexation was the one that was launched by a group of activists, the Numan Çelebicihan Battalion, led by Islyamov, that aimed to weaken the Russian Federation's control over Crimea with two main strategies. First, they stopped the illicit flow of products that had been moving from Ukrainian-controlled territory into occupied Crimea by the semi-trailer and changing hands before going to the Russian Federation. The value of the products in the first six months was calculated at approximately US $78 million.[9] In the first day alone, 241 semi-trailers were stopped.[10] For about 18 months previously, products had been traded without permits or taxes, with profits benefiting Russian and Ukrainian business people and oligarchs. The stoppage resulted in a rise in prices and shortages of consumer goods in Crimea. To the benefit of the Ukrainian government, the blockade helped reduce smuggling and reduced the corruption associated with the flow of products into Crimea as part of the gray economy (Bugriy 2015). Within this borderscape, the activists saw a need to restrict flows of goods and capital enriching the already wealthy oligarchs and perpetuating a corrupt political and economic system.

The second tactic was an energy blockade. In November 2015, electricity pylons supplying electricity to the peninsula (and located a short distance from the blockade itself) were blown up, cutting off the supply to the approximately 2 million inhabitants of Crimea.[11] The Russian Federation was forced to install generators and, as a result, energy became 30 times more expensive for the Russian-backed authorities in Crimea.[12] The Crimean *Procuror* or Public Prosecutor estimated that as of 2016, the blockade had caused US$2 billion worth of damage to the Russian economy.[13] The Crimean authorities were forced to institute rolling black-outs, which continued for several years. Unsurprisingly, this adversely affected health care, business, and daily routines in Crimea. In March 2019, two new power stations in Crimea were finally launched to full capacity.[14] The stations are expected to generate an equivalent amount of energy to the amount Crimea received from Ukraine prior to the annexation. The explosions led, rather remarkably, to the end of Crimean dependence on Ukrainian electricity.

The work of the battalion sharpens our appreciation of the hybrid nature of borderscapes, which are constituted by assemblages of diverse actors. In this regard, Islyamov likened himself to a Dudaev (the first President of the Chechen Republic of Ichkeria) hinting at his own potential as a first president of an independent Crimea by positioning himself, discursively at least, in a discussion of six centuries of first presidents. He compared his military philosophy to that of Publius Falvious Vegetius, a writer in the fourth century who wrote in his ancient manual that "if you want peace, get ready for war." Thus the political imagination behind the battalion and the blockade they maintained is almost as militaristic as that of the Russian Federation. Thinking about these dynamics surrounding Crimea as a *borderscape* is helpful because it emphasizes how this type of scape is created and maintained as much through political imagination (Rajaram and Grundy-Warr 2007) and contestation, as through material practices.

With regard to negotiation and contestation, crossing from Ukrainian- to Russian-controlled territory was both physically challenging and emotionally stressful. The situation was not, however, simply endured. Many people reported interactions with border guards and fellow border-crossers that underscore the significance of the ambiguous, shifting, and negotiated features of this borderscape. As a single woman in her mid-30s who currently resides in Crimea and crossed regularly between 2015 and 2017 described:

> Ukrainian border guards take advantage of the fact that the people don't know the law and they take bribes. I saw someone get out of a car at the border. They were bringing mushrooms from Ukraine to Crimea, and they took two crates and gave them to the border guards. Another car was carrying cucumbers, fresh ones. Again, they took a bag and brought it to the border guards.

Her description of the bribe, which was perhaps consumed or bartered for other goods, provides a window on the social transactions that contribute to making this border what it is. So much more than a solid or dotted line on the map, this is a place that is lived by a variety of actors in a variety of ways. One might expect this woman's story to have ended with her observation of the corruption, but she reported defiance saying, "you're doing pretty well for yourselves guys, you've got quite the cosmopolitan appetite." The quip is important to this analysis because it further demonstrates the political subjectivity that challenges authority, incited by the contested administrative lines. Another migrant reported Ukrainian border guards shaking down travelers by conflating migrants' rubles with dollars.

> So they ask a woman the question, "how much money are you carrying in cash?" She's like, 10 thousand rubles. And that's when they realize that she's, like, (knocks on the table to indicate naiveté) simple, and they're like, "oooh, you can only have up to 10 thousand on you. And you didn't declare the sum, lady."

The border guards were ready to take the woman's money on the false pretext that she had broken the law. In this instance, however, my interlocutor intervened by engaging with her fellow migrant. She explained to the woman that if she had 10,000 *rubles*, she could transit without declaring. If she had 10,000 dollars, on the other hand, she would be required to declare. The guards' ruse was revealed and as my interviewee opened her phone to report the incident to the hotline, the guards made a hasty retreat back to their car. Based on interactions like these, I suggest the borderscape was shaped not only by law and state institutions or empowered actors like those in the battalion, but also quotidian interactions between guards, observers, and migrants. Interactions like these are at the center of how a borderscape is constituted (Franck 2019: 20). Ultimately, the *Askeri*, the Numan Çelebicihan Battalion members, and the border-crossers were, together with the border services themselves, engaged in a process of negotiated borderscaping.

In the contemporary discourse on migration – including the discourse on borderscapes – descriptions of state control over borders using words like "enforcement", "policing," "spatial incarceration," "confinement," and "securitization" are common. These words are no less salient in the Crimean case. In this instance, however, members of the small numbered and politically less powerful groups, the *Askeri* and the members of the battalion are not policed but policers; and not securitized but securitizers. As an analytic tool, then, the notion of a borderscape helps illuminate the twists and turns in who really shapes the new administrative boundaries between Russia and Ukraine.

10. CONCLUSION

Although the Crimean case presents neither an official border, nor straightforward politics of compassion, it reveals what the editors of this volume refer to as a "crash site" of humanitarian projects and neoliberal political and economic logics. And while the governments of Russia and Ukraine had been willing to tolerate the consolidation of oligarchic wealth through the illicit flows of products, the activists at the blockade put a stop to the unfettered flow of semi-trailers. While the Russian Federation launched an ambitious economic development program, the activists altered the balance sheet by forcing the flow of energy to change. Their actions demonstrate how borderscapes are crafted through both material practices and the use of political imagination, and how that imagination is not singular, but multiple.

The Russian Federation used a rhetoric of compassion for the Russian community to justify taking control of Ukrainian territory. The egregious human rights violations suffered by the pro-Ukrainian residents suggest these politics of compassion ultimately contracted rather than expanding the circle of care and concern. While *Askeri* efforts could not improve the situation inside Crimea, they were, at the very least, able to extend compassion to border-crossers.

The features of the Crimean borderscape are worth close consideration in part because it was members of an historically marginalized group, the Crimean Tatars, and not law enforcement authorities, that took the lead in imposing better filters. Further, the Numan Çelebicihan Battalion's activists responded to the intimidation tactics of the Russian military discussed above – such as home searches and amassing inflatable military hardware near the border – with spectacles of their own, like setting up the barricade and taking credit for the explosion of the electricity pylons supplying Crimea. Thus the activists' work exposes not only the performative aspect of borderscaping, which has been well established (Plonski 2018; Franck 2019), but a reversal of roles. This reversal of roles demonstrates, moreover, just how improvisational was the Crimean borderscape at the time the research was carried out, https://www.kroger.com/p/wheat-thins-hint-of-salt-low-sodium-crackers/0004400003038. The notion of a borderscape therefore helps open up important analytic space for taking into account multiple political imaginings and appreciating the counter-hegemonic potential of marginalized groups. Thinking in terms of a borderscape creates an opportunity to acknowledge the significance of political subjectivities that not only resist but mirror the performance of power. My discussion does not seek to valorize the activities, but rather highlight their theoretical and empirical significance.

NOTES

1. See npr.org/sections/thetwo-way/2014/04/12/302337754/google-maps-displays-crimean-border-differently-in-russia-u-s (accessed November 16, 2019).
2. See http://en.kremlin.ru/events/president/news/20603 (accessed November 16, 2019).
3. 'Regions of Ukraine/Autonomous Republic of Crimea'. 2001 Ukrainian Census. http://2001.ukrcensus.gov.ua/results/general/nationality/ (accessed December 22, 2019).

4. 'Regions of Ukraine/Autonomous Republic of Crimea'. 2001 Ukrainian Census. http://2001.ukrcensus.gov.ua/results/general/nationality/ (accessed December 22, 2019).
5. See http://ukraineun.org/en/press-center/121-russian-military-capacities-in-crimea/ (accessed December 22, 2019).
6. See http://ukraineun.org/en/press-center/121-russian-military-capacities-in-crimea/ (accessed December 22, 2019).
7. See http://uatoday.tv/politics/russian-militarization-of-crimea-air-defense-missile-system-delivered-to-peninsula-718137.html (accessed November 22, 2019).
8. See http://bi.gale.com.proxy.lib.umich.edu/essentials/article/GALE%7CA249702717?u=umuser (accessed November 23, 2020).
9. See http://news.allcrimea.net/spets/blokada-kryma/ (accessed November 22, 2019).
10. See http://news.allcrimea.net/spets/blokada-kryma (accessed November 22, 2019).
11. See https://www.aljazeera.com/indepth/features/2015/12/alliances-crumble-crimean-border-151219110155013.html (accessed August 10, 2019).
12. This is according to an analysis of kilowatt hours before and after the action on the part of the leader of the blockade.
13. See http://gordonua.com/news/crimea/poklonskaya-zayavila-chto-ushcherb-ot-energoblokady-kryma-sostavil-2-mlrd-rubley-124475.html (accessed August 10, 2019).
14. See https://www.themoscowtimes.com/2019/03/18/putin-in-crimea-for-annexation-anniversary-launches-power-stations-a64844 (accessed August 10, 2019).

REFERENCES

Agamben, Giorgio (2005), *State of Exception*. Translated by Kevin Attell. Chicago: University of Chicago Press.
Appadurai, Arjun (1991), *Modernity at Large: Cultural Dimensions of Globalization*. Minneapolis: University of Minnesota Press.
Arendt, Hannah (1963), *On Revolution*. London: Penguin.
Boltanski, Luc (1999), *Distant Suffering: Morality, Media, and Politics*. Cambridge, UK: Cambridge University Press.
Brambilla, Chiara (2015), 'Navigating the Euro/African border and migration nexus through the borderscapes lens: Insights from the Lampedusan Festival', pp. 111–122. In: Brambilla, C., Laine, J., Scott, J.W., et al. (eds) *Borderscaping: Imaginations and Practices of Border Making*. Farnham: Ashgate Publishing.
Brambilla, Chiara and Reece Jones (2019), 'Rethinking borders, violence and conflict: From sovereign power to borderscapes as sites of struggles.' *Society and Space* 38(2): 1–19.
Bugriy, Maksym (2015), 'Ukraine's uneasy blockade of Russian-occupied Crimea.' *Newsweek*, October 16.
Charron, Austin (2018), 'In our country, but outside our homeland: Identity and diaspora among Ukraine's internally displaced Crimeans.' PhD dissertation, University of Kansas.
Coynash, Halya (2015), 'Crimean Tatar TV silenced, searches and arrests continue.' Kharkiv Human Rights Protection Group, April 1. http://khpg.org/index.php?id=1427847775. Accessed April 29, 2020.
Coynash, Halya (2017a), 'Cross and icons seized, archbishop assaulted in barbaric new attack on Ukrainian cathedral in Russian-occupied Crimea.' Kharkiv Human Rights Protection Group, September 1. http://khpg.org/en/index.php?id=1504187187. Accessed April 29, 2020.
Coynash, Halya (2017b), 'Crimean Jehovah's Witnesses told to renounce their faith or serve in Occupiers' Army.' Kharkiv Human Rights Protection Group, June 20. http://khpg.org/en/index.php?id=1497831415. Accessed February 28, 2020.
Crimea SOS (2020), 'Enforced disappearances: Problems of search and responsibility.' April 27, 2020. https://krymsos.com/en/news/nasilnitski-zniknennya-problemi-poshuku-ta-vidpovidalnosti/#:~:text=Enforced%20disappearances%20are%20one%20of,of%20them%20still%20remains%20unknown. Accessed November 11, 2020.
Crisp, Roger (2008), 'Compassion and beyond.' *Ethical Theory and Moral Practice* 11: 233–246.

Fassin, Didier (2012), *Humanitarian Reason: A Moral History of the Present*. Berkeley and Los Angeles, CA: University of California Press.

Franck, Anya (2019), 'The street politics of migrant il/legality: Navigating Malaysia's urban borderscape.' *Asia Pacific Viewpoint* 60(1): 14–23.

Freedom House (2015), 'Crimea*.'*Freedom of the Press 2015*. Accessed February 28, 2020. https://freedomhouse.org/report/freedom-press/2015/crimea.

Gaibazzi, Paolo (2017), 'Frontiers of exodus: Activists, border regimes and Euro-Mediterranean encounters after the Arab Spring', pp. 197–217. In: Gaibazzi, P., Bellagamba, A. and Dunnwald, S. (eds.) *EurAfrican Borders and Migration Management: Political Cultures, Contested Spaces, and Ordinary Lives*. New York: Palgrave Macmillan.

Gregory, Paul Rodrick (2014), 'Russia's Human Rights Council accidentally posts real Crimean election results.' Forbes, May 5. Accessed May 3, 2020. http://www.forbes.com/sites/paulroderickgregory/2014/05/05/putins-human-rights-council-accidentally-posts-real-crimean-election-results-only-15-voted-for-annexation/#7e0c4a8910ff.

Human Rights Council (2019), 'Report on the situation of human rights in the temporarily occupied Autonomous Republic of Crimea and the city of Sevastopol Ukraine 13 September 2017 to 30 June 2018.' A/HRC/39/CRP.4.

Jaroszewicz, Marta (2019), 'Years after Crimea's annexation, integration of Ukraine's internally displaced population remains uneven.' Migration Information Source Accessed November 11, 2020. https://www.migrationpolicy.org/article/fyears-after-crimea-annexation-integration-ukraine-internally-displaced-population.

Klymenko, Andrii (2015), 'The militarization of Crimea under Russian occupation,' Atlantic Council Dinu Patriciu Eurasia Center Issue Brief, October.

Kuzio, Taras (2017), *Putin's War against Ukraine: Revolution, Nationalism, and Crime*. Toronto: Chair of Ukrainian Studies, University of Toronto.

Makarychev, Andrey, and Aleksandra Yatsyk (2018), 'Illiberal geographies: Popular geopolitics and Russian biopolitical regionalism.' *Eurasian Geography and Economics* (59): 51–72.

Murphy, Edward U. (2019), *The Politics of Compassion: The Challenge to Care for the Stranger*. London: Rowman and Littlefield International.

Nussbaum, Martha (2013), *Political Emotions: Why Love Matters for Justice*. Cambridge, MA and London: The Belknap Press of Harvard University Press.

OHCHR (2016), 'Report on the human rights situation in Ukraine 16 August to 15 November 2016.' Accessed November 11, 2020. https://www.ohchr.org/Documents/Countries/UA/12thOHCHRreportUkraine.pdf.

Paasi, Anssi (1998), 'Boundaries as social processes: Territoriality in the world of flows.' *Geopolitics* 3(1): 69–88.

Plonski, Sharri (2018), 'Material footprints: The struggle for borders by Bedouin-Palestinians in Israel.' *Antipode* 50(5): 1349–1375.

Prozorov, Sergei (2012), 'The management of anomie: The state of exception in postcommunist Russia', pp. 32–51. In: Svirsky, M. and Bignall, S. *Agamben and Colonialism*. Edinburgh: Edinburgh University Press.

Rajaram Prem, Kumar and Carl Grundy-Warr (2007), 'Introduction', pp. ix–xxxix. In: Rajaram Prem, K. and Grundy-Warr, C. (eds.) *Borderscapes: Hidden Geographies and Politics at Territory's Edge*. Minneapolis, MN: University of Minnesota Press.

Rieff, David (2000), 'Kosovo's humanitarian circus.' *World Policy Journal* 17(3): 25–32.

Rumford, Chris (2008), 'Introduction: Citizens and borderwork in Europe.' *Space and Polity* 12(1): 1–12.

Smith, Adam (2002 [1759]), *The Theory of Moral Sentiments*. Boston, MA: Wells and Lilly.

Surriyeh, Ala (2017), *The Politics of Compassion: Immigration and Asylum Policy*. Bristol, UK: Bristol University Press.

Uehling, Greta (2004), *Beyond Memory: The Deportation and Repatriation of the Crimean Tatars*. New York: Palgrave Macmillan.

United States Mission to the Organization for Security and Cooperation in Europe (2019), 'Five years after: Human rights situation in the autonomous Republic of Crimea.' Accessed May 5, 2020. https://osce.usmission.gov/the-human-rights-situation-in-crimea/.
Wilson, Andrew (2014), *Ukraine Crisis: What it Means for the West*. New Haven, CT: Yale University Press.

23. The Irish border as sign and source of British–Irish tensions

Katy Hayward, Peter Leary and Milena Komarova

1. INTRODUCTION

Over a century ago, in December 1919, British Prime Minister, David Lloyd George introduced a series of recommendations concerning the governance of Ireland to the House of Commons. 'Sometimes', he remarked, 'when both Britain and Ireland seem to be approaching towards friendship, some untoward incident sweeps them apart and the quarrel begins again' (Fanning 2013: 15). Those proposals would lead to the partition of Ireland and the creation of a border that for 100 years has reflected the history and state of British–Irish relations and profoundly shaped the lives of communities living along the border. A century on from partition, as a consequence of the 2016 UK referendum vote to leave the European Union (EU) ('Brexit'), the border was once again thrust to the centre of events.

2. A CENTURY'S LEGACY OF COMPLEX BRITISH–IRISH RELATIONS

2.1 Ireland before Partition

The Irish border was created by the Government of Ireland Act 1920 and confirmed by the Anglo-Irish Treaty of 1921. It delineates the six counties that make up Northern Ireland from the remaining 26 counties of what was originally designated 'Southern Ireland', a territory that soon became the Irish Free State and, after April 1949, the Republic of Ireland. Partition arose from a centuries-long history of entanglement between the two islands of Ireland and Britain. It followed an extended political dispute and a short but intense period of military conflict over the extent of constitutional ties between them. That connection dates from the distant twelfth century, but the seeds of partition were sown in the seventeenth, when all of Ireland was brought under British control.

Long before partition, large parts of the future borderlands were a site of cultural encounter and a contested frontier zone. In 1607, following the defeat of Gaelic resistance to English rule and the flight of its leaders to continental Europe, James I of England (who was also James VI of Scotland) embarked upon a 'plantation' of Ulster – Ireland's most northerly and hitherto recalcitrant province. This settlement project augmented earlier plantation schemes and sought to secure the paramountcy of the recently united British Crown through the large-scale importation of loyal and dependant Protestants from Britain (Ó Ciardha and Ó Siochrú 2012). The venture was only partially successful. In many parts of Ulster, Protestants did not become a majority and, where they did, Catholic minorities endured. Nevertheless, the existence of a large, successful and comparatively pan-class colony in that province would continue to distinguish it from most other parts of Ireland. To the south and west, despite the establishment of a British or pro-British and Protestant elite, Catholic preponderance among the lower classes remained substantial (Heslinga [1962] 1979).

The last quarter of the nineteenth century and the first quarter of the twentieth were characterised by growing demands for self-government in Ireland. Under leaders including Charles Stewart Parnell and John Redmond – and riding the wave of expanding male suffrage – Irish nationalists secured election to the British parliament at Westminster and pressed the case for a limited form of Home Rule. But despite substantial changes in the intervening time – not least the emergence of Belfast as Ireland's preeminent industrial city – the religious differences that had once marked incomer from native remained the motive force in Ulster politics. There, the mobilisation of the Protestant population along confessional lines made Unionism – support for an unaltered link with Britain – into a formidable regional force.

2.2   The 'Reasoning' behind Partition

The decade of crisis that led to the establishment of a border on the island of Ireland had begun in earnest in 1912 with the passing of the third Home Rule Bill by the British House of Commons. Encouraged by elite interests including within the British Conservative Party, more than 200,000 Ulstermen responded to the Bill by signing a 'Solemn League and Covenant' pledging to resist a Dublin-based parliament by 'all means' with many thousands joining the paramilitary Ulster Volunteer Force (UVF). A similar number of women put their names to an equivalent 'Declaration'.[1] The outbreak of the First World War in 1914 saw Home Rule placed in legal storage until it was concluded but, by the time it ended four years later, the fallout from the 1916 Easter Rising had profoundly altered Irish politics, while, internationally, boundary-making had very much come into vogue.

Outside the north-east of Ireland, the post-War election delivered a landslide victory for the separatist Sinn Féin and was followed by the conflict now known as the War of Independence as well as large-scale sectarian violence in the north (particularly in Belfast). The Government of Ireland Act 1920 was Britain's response. Underpinned by a high level of tension, intense politicking and compromise, Home Rule would finally come to Ireland; but, instead of one, two parliaments were now provided for. Consenting to the demands of Ulster Unionists, Northern Ireland was comprised of six of the nine Ulster counties including the cities of Derry/Londonderry and Belfast. Its putative counterpart, Southern Ireland, would include three of the five Ulster counties that had Catholic majorities – Cavan, Donegal, and Monaghan – but not Fermanagh or Tyrone, both of which were in 'the north' (see Figure 23.1 for a map).

2.3   The Hardening Border

Unionists immediately accepted the new dispensation, establishing a Home Rule parliament in Belfast by June 1921, and thereafter imposing the new border through armed force. A Protestant militia, the Ulster Special Constabulary, was established and within a year roughly one in six adult male Protestants in Northern Ireland had enlisted in its part-time 'B Specials' element alone (Wilson 2010). Meanwhile, republicans rejected the arrangements and continued their own armed campaign to completely sever the entire island from any element of British rule. Eventually, the Anglo-Irish Treaty, struck in negotiations held in London, replaced what was known as Southern Ireland with an Irish Free State. Territorially identical, it would possess

The Irish border as sign and source of British–Irish tensions 359

Source: The Irish Borderlands project, http://www.irishborderlands.com/irishborder/index.html (accessed 24 February 2020).

Figure 23.1   A map of the Irish border and the counties of Northern Ireland and the Republic of Ireland

a greater degree of sovereignty but the provisions of the Treaty allowed for partition to remain. A short but bloody civil war between pro- and anti-Treaty factions was won, with British help, by the former and, by 1923, the Irish border was firmly in place.

Speaking of the transformation he had witnessed over recent years, in 1925 one borderland clergyman remarked, 'We never thought about the difference between one county and another before that change was made.'[2] Based on the old district boundaries, the new border cut through some 1,400 landholdings (Harvey et al. 2005) and even individual buildings including a spade factory and more than one house (Leary 2018). It divided villages, parishes and communities, and separated market towns from their traditional hinterlands. Approximately 200 roads ran across the border, as did many more informal crossings (Johnson 1979).

Eric Hobsbawm attributed the post-First World War remapping of Europe to a principle of national self-determination 'more easily held by those far from the ethnic and linguistic realities of the regions which were to be divided' (Hobsbawm 1995: 30). What went for Central and Eastern Europe was true of Ireland too. In both territories, partition left substantial minorities on the 'wrong' side of the border. At the time of partition, Catholics constituted over a third of the total population and more than half in the four counties adjacent to the boundary (Heslinga [1962] 1979).

Influenced both by imperial cartography and by the ideals of the Paris Peace Conference (Rankin 2007), the 1921 Anglo-Irish Treaty contained a clause for the establishment of a Boundary Commission to redraw the border, in line 'with the wishes of the inhabitants, so far as may be compatible with economic and geographic conditions'. Rejecting the option of plebiscite in contrast to several European counterparts, and despite the presence of large majority-Catholic areas inside Northern Ireland, the Irish Boundary Commission under British chairman, Richard Feetham, chose to preserve the basic outline of partition focusing only on the possible rectification of small anomalies (O'Callaghan 1999). Following the infamous leaking of its proposals, the Irish Boundary Commission collapsed in December 1925 without any changes being made to the erratic 300 mile (475 km) border line.

2.4 The Economic Border

As a result of partition, a number of borderland communities were separated from their historical economic hinterlands (McCall 2011; Hayward 2018). Protestant and Catholic borderland communities alike were affected deeply by this separation. For example, a town like Clones (on the southern side of the border) which had enjoyed relative affluence before partition went into a decline that saw it hold an official status of 'disadvantaged' in the 1950s (Dooley 1994). Within these border areas and small towns, the severing of 'ties of economic relationships and kinship [that] had run freely' across the county boundary before its status changed demonstrated the consequences of poor planning and implementation (Harris [1972] 1986: 19–20). Ever since it was created, in what many expected to be a temporary measure, the region along the border suffered from the multiple disadvantages of peripherality, rurality, low population and poor infrastructure. Research shows that unemployment rates in the border region have traditionally been higher than the state averages (on both sides) and this remains the case today, while 'GVA [gross value added] and GDP [gross domestic product] per capita within the border region is already significantly below the averages for both Northern Ireland and the Republic of Ireland' (Magennis et al. 2017: 43).

The general rise of economic protectionism following the 1929 financial crisis provided the backdrop to the first major wave of cross-border smuggling. During the so-called Anglo-Irish 'Economic War' beginning in 1932 this context, combined with the Irish government's decision to withhold 'land annuities' claimed by Britain under the provisions of the Treaty, saw the latter impose punitive tariffs on imports of livestock from the Irish Free State (Johnson 1979). Global conflict, too, produced a second great smuggling outbreak, during the Second World War, characterised this time by butter, bacon, white flour and tea, concealed about the persons of the women who then dominated the trade. Efforts to tackle smuggling centred on the strengthening of customs controls. This in turn had a knock-on effect of pushing communities either side of the border further apart.

By the time that its location was confirmed, the customs barrier that defined the lived experience of the border for many local residents had already been in place for more than two years. Reflecting Dublin's desire to utilise the autonomy afforded by the Treaty and fiscally diverge from London, customs posts appeared along the border in April 1923. Just 16 border crossings were equipped with customs facilities and 'approved' for bringing dutiable goods – including motor vehicles – across. The remainder were restricted to those not carrying taxable items and travelling 'by foot, cycle or horse drawn vehicle.'[3] As a consequence, those not using 'approved' roads were immediately subject to some suspicion – making the very act of crossing the border potentially disruptive and rebellious.

2.5 Border Violence

Most Irish nationalists, north and south, and official Dublin government thinking, remained unreconciled to partition. Customs posts were targeted by republicans from the early 1920s, and many were burnt down in 1937. Also targeted were British soldiers and other members of the security services, in a series of armed raids in the later 1950s. This 'border campaign' included high profile attacks on military and police targets in Northern Ireland conducted by the Irish Republican Army (IRA) (Leary 2016; Hayward 2017). With the onset of 'the Troubles' after 1969, however, violence erupted on a wider basis and although most of the literature relating to the conflict has focused on the 'urban epicentres of violence' (Patterson 2013), 'the Troubles' profoundly impacted on the border. Indeed, in both symbolic and practical terms, much of the conflict centred on the border region. In exploring the geography of conflict-related deaths during 'the Troubles', for instance, Gregory et al. (2013) suggest that while Belfast was perhaps the largest single theatre of violence during the period, the border areas of south Armagh and Londonderry/Derry, plus rural areas such as east Tyrone and north Armagh also became epicentres of violence. A reading of statistics from Sutton's *Index of Deaths from the Conflict in Ireland* (2001) similarly suggests that nearly 44% of these occurred in Belfast, followed by the second largest concentration of nearly 36% in the border counties of Armagh, Derry, Fermanagh and Tyrone (including Londonderry/Derry city).

Much research has documented the extent to which the creation of an international border and the violence that ensued in the intervening years affected border communities socially, as well as economically. The border region had long been woven by thick familial, social and economic networks. There was religious segregation in some villages on both sides of the border, but in other cases communities of different political and religious persuasion were deeply interconnected. The Irish Borderlands project showed how these connections were 'dramatically distorted or destroyed' by the re-emergence of conflict in the late 1960s. Old connections, friendships, 'patterns of sociability' and cross-community contact were seriously affected, not only as the security situation and political climate became extremely tense but as roads and physical connections in the border region were blocked and interrupted.[4] In some border towns extensive segregation of schools, sports and social infrastructure developed (Adams 1995), with Protestants and Catholics finding ways to systemically avoid interaction with each other (Larsen 1982).

Part of the British state's response to what they characterised as paramilitary incursions from a republican base across the southern side of the border was heavy securitisation that included the setting up of army checkpoints, the positioning of multiple military bases and watchtowers along the border itself, and the physical blocking, 'cratering' or 'spiking' of many of the 270+ border crossings and roads, carried out by the army (Mulroe 2017). This form of border management caused great inconvenience to daily life in the region, provoking anger at the demonstration of British state power. In response, nationalist border communities themselves would refill road craters or remove the spikes. A process of repetitive closing and re-opening of roads ensued until the British army moved to close roads on a more permanent basis (Buttazzoni 2016; Bardon 2011).

Far from removing the security threat, such road closures led to an increase in violent incidences at the border (Mulroe 2017), to further ratcheting up of political tensions between the two governments, and to a deepening alienation between communities within Northern Ireland and across the border. While unionists often saw the border as a vital means of preserving British culture in Northern Ireland and a form of protection against republican violence, Irish nationalists detested it as a lingering manifestation of British colonialism, and a reminder of their role in the 'northern state' as 'second class citizens'. Much harm was also caused to local businesses by violence, disinvestment, and 'back to back development' (as businesses avoided cross-border trade even with their close neighbours). Altogether, the entire border region suffered some of the worst social and economic consequences of violent conflict.

2.6 The Slow Transformation of the Border

Despite what was to follow, the decade up to the late 1960s had generally been one of reform and tentative reconciliation. Although unsuccessful on the first attempt, both Britain and Ireland applied to join the European Economic Community (EEC) in 1961 and hoped to smooth the path to entry through bilateral tariff reductions and improved intergovernmental relations. Under Irish Taoiseach, Seán Lemass, and Northern Ireland Prime Minister, Captain Terence O'Neill, a new tone was struck in cross-border affairs. To boost tourism and trade, in 1964 and 1965, several new crossings were approved for customs purposes while subsequent changes to the regulations made it easier for vehicles to go across. By 1967 the border was more porous than at any time since 1923 (Leary 2016). Much happened over the subsequent half century. By the time of the Brexit vote, just a decade and a half after the last remnants of the military watchtowers were removed, the Irish border was one of the most open borders in the world. This was a result of two key processes that fundamentally changed the relationship between the UK and Ireland, just as similar processes were taking place elsewhere in Europe (Sahlins 1991).

First, both countries joined the then EEC in 1973. This common membership opened both states to the processes and practices of European integration, particularly in terms of economic integration and of cross-border cooperation. The introduction of EEC regulations on customs declarations in 1987 had an immediate effect on the ease with which goods could be transported between north and south. Later, the creation of the Single Market (with its official entry into operation on 1 January 1993) erased many obstacles to cross-border trade and economic development, and customs posts on the border were immediately made redundant (Kowalsky 2010). In such a very practical way, the EU context successfully enabled change in cross-border economic relationships in Ireland, structurally impacting on the significance of the border as an economic and customs divide. As such, the border region became a site of growing economic cooperation, with plans for its further expansion through the Belfast–Dublin 'border corridor' and north-west city region (Hayward and Murphy 2018).

Cross-border trade, furthermore, is disproportionately significant to the smaller economy in the north, with a third of all goods exported from Northern Ireland going across the border to the Republic of Ireland (Phinnemore and Hayward 2017). The majority of cross-border transactions are made by micro and small businesses, although the value of such trade is concentrated in larger companies, especially in the agri-food sector. Much north-to-south trade is comprised of trade in 'intermediate' goods and, including market-ready agri-food products, two-thirds of it is part of supply chain activity. The 177,000 trucks that cross the Irish border per month carry mixed loads for destinations across the UK and the wider EU (Leheny 2018). Because it is frequently time-sensitive, the benefits of the practical disappearance of the border as an economic divide and as an international customs and trade outpost are most felt precisely in the movement of such products.

Until the peace process itself bore fruit however, the above-described benefits of economic cooperation in the Irish border region could not be properly felt. It was the 1998 Good Friday (Belfast) Agreement that would form the foundations for the Northern Ireland peace process, remaining to this day the lynchpin to good relationships between Britain and Ireland and on the island of Ireland. It was concluded by the British and Irish governments and negotiated through multi-party talks, in which each major party in Northern Ireland (bar the Democratic Unionist Party, who opted out) participated. Politically, the 1998 Agreement not only brought about the removal of the border security installations, it also created institutions and mechanisms for cross-border cooperation in a wide range of policy areas such as health, environment and transport. Such cross-border integration and cooperation has brought direct and tangible benefits. A 'mapping exercise' of north–south connections conducted to inform the Brexit negotiations revealed around 150 areas of solid cross-border cooperation – covering such spheres as health, education, transport and environment – that both governments acknowledged to be in need of preservation given their real benefit to residents on both sides of the border (HM Government 2018a). Additionally, the 1998 Agreement was enormously significant in lessening social tensions on the ground. While border communities on either side had long defended the permeability of the Irish border, 'the Troubles' had undoubtedly damaged long-standing cross-border and cross-community social and cultural relationships. The way towards their repair was now re-opened by the political Agreement.

2.7 Brexit and Northern Ireland's Borders

The UK's decision to leave the EU centred on a campaign to 'take back control' of its borders (HM Government 2018b). This objective was largely assumed to mean controls on the movement of people through British sea- and airports. The movement of goods and services across the UK's land border with the EU in Ireland, as well as the significance of any necessary controls over such movement that would arise from the border becoming an EU external frontier, was given scant consideration prior to the 2016 Referendum. The potential for social, political, economic and symbolic damage arising from the likely hardening of this border after Brexit was underplayed and misunderstood in the main political discourse in Britain. Indeed, the Irish border proved to be the most complicated challenge and a long-time stumbling block for the Brexit process.

First, this was a border whose existence was still contested, and whose openness was seen as a litmus test for the health of a peace process. Low level paramilitary activity has continued, fuelled by organised criminality (including by smuggling across the Irish border to avoid excise duties); and there have been organised groups on both sides who see the 1998 Agreement as a sell-out and who would gladly exploit circumstances to justify a return to 'war'. For this reason, policing in the border region continues to be far from normal. Experience of military surveillance and paramilitary intimidation, plus suspicion of state activity (both British and Irish), has meant that there is great sensitivity among local communities in the region to any form of surveillance, tracking or monitoring as well as – more generally – to any change in the status of the border, both in symbolic and real terms.

In recognition of the unique complexity of movement across the Irish border, the UK and EU promised to avoid a 'hard' border on the island of Ireland after Brexit and, in particular, putting 'physical infrastructure' at the border itself fearing that, as in the past, it could alienate local people and become a target for violence. However, neither have either wanted to turn a blind eye to this border, knowing that a porous boundary could rapidly become a gateway for illegal activity that may pose a risk to the integrity of their respective internal markets. Moreover, a clear tension has lain in the fact that for the UK to pursue its main ambitions from Brexit (e.g. an independent commercial and trade policy), it must seek to become increasingly distant from the EU, and thus more checks and controls would be needed at UK/EU borders. Whether these restrictions should be placed at the land border between the two states or the sea border between the two islands has been a matter that touches on the very core of the political conflict in Northern Ireland. A 2018 representative survey among 1,000 people in Northern Ireland recorded 'substantial and intense opposition to possible North–South border checks between Northern Ireland and the Republic of Ireland and to East–West border checks between Northern Ireland and Great Britain', with 61% of respondents preferring for the UK as a whole to remain in the Customs Union and Single Market (Garry et al. 2018: 9). Another research of over 500 people living and working in the central border region of Ireland north and south (Hayward and Komarova 2019) showed an overwhelming sense of uncertainty, fear and concern about the impact of Brexit and of potential border checks. The tension, as well as frustration with uncertainty generated by the negotiation of the UK's withdrawal, has of course been stoked by the lack of clear popular support for the UK (and thus Northern Ireland) leaving the EU, as demonstrated by the result of the 2016 Brexit Referendum where 56% of Northern Ireland's population voted to remain and 44% to leave (The Electoral Commission 2016).

3. CONFLICT, PEACE AND BREXIT IN A BORDER VILLAGE: A CASE STUDY

3.1 The Partition of Pettigo

Close to the western seaboard and the northern shores of Lough Erne, the village of Pettigo had fewer than 400 inhabitants recorded in the 1911 census (the last census to be conducted on an all-Ireland basis). Of the 365 residents listed that year, 140 were Catholics while the majority belonged to various Protestant denominations. Running through the settlement, the Termon River, little more than a stream during the summer, marks the line between Counties Donegal (in the Republic of Ireland) and Fermanagh (in Northern Ireland). Partition transformed the county boundary and the Termon into a border between two states (see Figure 23.1).

Pettigo's early experience of partition was a bloody and dramatic one. In the spring of 1922 the British army withdrew from the Irish Free State, with pro- and anti-Treaty IRA units taking over its former positions, including the barracks in the Donegal portion of the village and a fort strategically overlooking nearby Belleek. These two points commanded the gateways to a 'triangle' of County Fermanagh to which, at that time, there was no overland access from the rest of Northern Ireland except through Donegal. An attempt by forces loyal to the Belfast government to establish a presence in the area, travelling by boat across the waters of Lough

Erne, was abandoned following a series of violent clashes that included cross-border sniper fire. In June, under orders from Winston Churchill, Secretary of State for the Colonies, a large convoy of regular British troops was dispatched to support the locally recruited Ulster Special Constabulary. Aided by heavy artillery shells, the British forces occupied both sides of the village in violation of the provisions of the Treaty. Three local IRA members were killed in the fighting, with another dying shortly after (Ó Duibhir 2011; Cunningham 1982).[5]

As with other points along the border, these and related events 'left massive bitterness behind', but in many respects local people quickly learned to live with the boundary (Wright 1992). While the British army pulled out of the Southern side of Pettigo by January 1923, April the same year saw the erection of a hard border in the form of a customs barrier. The larger part of the village itself was in Donegal but most of its agricultural hinterland was in Fermanagh. Obtaining access to goods or services available just a short distance away entailed delays, searches and payment of customs charges, or a longer journey to an alternative town. The imposition of duties as well as price differences on either side soon gave rise to a popular smuggling trade. Mocked by outsiders as a 'farce' or a 'constitutional freak',[6] the two parts of the small village of Pettigo each had a police station, a post office, a medical dispensary and, of course, customs station of its own.[7]

3.2 The Troubled Border

The onset of 'the Troubles' and the growing violence in Northern Ireland in particular had direct effects on the border communities. Alongside customs posts came the infrastructure and paraphernalia and restrictions associated with securitisation. The experience of border life through conflict and peace was examined in The Border into Brexit project (Hayward and Komarova 2019). As part of the project, we conducted a focus group of eight participants (five men and three women, ranging from early 20s to late 60s in age) in Pettigo village in November 2019. Participants were volunteers from among those who had responded to an earlier online survey involving 475 self-selected respondents living in the central border region of Ireland/Northern Ireland, conducted as a part of the bigger research project. It is interesting to look at what was said in this group as illustrative of border experience of people on both sides of the border in the area. One middle-aged participant described his memories of 'the Troubles' from an early age in the village of Pettigo:

> During 'the Troubles', the helicopters used to fly up and down the [Termon] river at night with the big search lights ... we used to be sitting up in the attic window looking out at them. That was the border from four years old, or whatever.

One woman agreed with this description, as an indication of how childhood experiences adapted to an extraordinary and sometimes frightening context:

> My husband [who grew up in the village] was told that Santa Claus comes in a helicopter!

The hardening of the border that accompanied the military and security response to 'the Troubles' had physical effects of putting many off crossing the border altogether. For those in the border region whose lives were already very much cross-border, they could not help but also be affected in very practical and also in psychological ways by the rising tensions.

> People [nowadays] socialise together in a way that we didn't. [Before peace] it was a psychological iron curtain. We would go up [across the border] to visit family ... but there was a psychological dimension to it, that you avoided [crossing the border] otherwise. But that's gone now.

People in the focus group were at pains to try to explain why the border is viewed not simply in terms of practicalities but also as a social and cultural effect:

> I don't want to see it come back in any form, even psychologically. I saw the border, as we were growing up doing so much harm. It pushed people into corners and made people take sides.

The discussion also demonstrated that 'the border' itself has a political and psychological effect that affects the behaviour of individuals on a daily basis as well as the broadest, biggest political matters that shape identity and community relations:

> There's a line in the sand and ... that line says that first of all it's a different jurisdiction and second it's a different religion and it's different this and different that. It creates division and we got rid of that division over the years.

In an unusual way, the border has seen the creation of a unique identity and experience in the border region. This has gradually, and in the context of EU integration and the peace process, moved from being an experience of division to one of additional diversity, and is something cherished by many living in close proximity to the border. Few take the change for granted or see it as irrevocable:

> Kids today, they don't care who their neighbour is – race, creed or religion. They just socialise together, play football together, interact from different towns and different villages. If there is anything going on [in terms of social tensions], it's just rivalry between football teams or whatever it might be. We cannot go back to anything that is more serious than that.

This sense that the 1998 Good Friday Agreement initiated a fundamental, positive change in the ways in which people interact and move across the border is something that has been repeated in the research in the border region over the past 20 years (e.g. Harvey et al. 2005; McCall 2011; Hayward and Komarova 2019).

3.3 Cross-Border Symbiosis

It is important to recognise that, just as British–Irish relations could never be completely rendered asunder, so partition was far from a clean break. In many ways the border always remained permeable. For decades after partition, for example, the whole of Pettigo continued to receive its water supply from a single reservoir in Northern Ireland that was still serviced by Donegal County Council, to whom local people on both sides paid their water rates.[8] Throughout the summer, between 10,000 and 20,000 faithful Catholics continued to arrive in Pettigo by train – a journey that for most involved crossing the border twice – to reach Saint Patrick's Purgatory, the famous site of pilgrimage at Lough Derg less than five miles away.[9] Protestant children from Fermanagh still crossed the river into Donegal to get to school while, according to some accounts at least, thirsty drinkers travelled into Northern Ireland at night, because closing time in public houses was later there.[10]

The reality for residents of Pettigo, just as much as for those of other border towns and villages, is that of a border which has had enormous symbolic and practical significance. The border's presence is felt very physically and immediately in everyday life, yet is also one etched in generational memory and shaping a particular 'order of the mind'.

> For us here, the border is there on the other side of the street. It's part of our culture: it's who we are, it's who we always were. You have sterling in one pocket and euro in the other. You have to have a foot each side all the time, it's just the way life is.

Another participant said:

> It's in our bones that the border is here and what it means. The fact that it disappeared to all intents and purposes was fantastic and now it appears to be creeping back in again which is why we're so concerned. We spent so long trying to get rid of it.

The fact, thus, that the border is a matter of identity and a way of life makes fears of return to a harder border (albeit in different forms) more live and more deeply felt. Because it will have an effect on what happens between the UK–EU, and thus what happens across borders, Brexit will mean something far more for the Irish border region than for any other part of these islands.

Related to this, another theme in the focus group is an awareness of how exposed life at the border is to any change in the nature of the border:

> I cross the border six times on the way to work and six on the way back. So, there's a complete misunderstanding of the day-to-day commute, use of crossing the border that the political class [outside the border region] have. It's our day-to-day reality.

The sense of vulnerability is exacerbated by the significance of border crossing to people in the border region, especially in places such as Pettigo and – at the same time – by the fact that changes to daily life can come about as a result of the decisions being made by the 'political class' so far away from the border itself, in London or in Brussels. A sense of being so acutely affected by political vagaries has bred a mentality of mistrust and scepticism of politicians and the political establishment at large. This sense of political wariness is exacerbated by the logic of Brexit and – because the 'other' is in such close proximity in the border region – there are fears that the high level UK/EU, British/Irish tensions from Brexit take a micro-level, personal form in the border region:

> This whole [Brexit] thing is alienating people. ... now these questions are coming up. It's making people turn around and say 'who are my friends anymore? Who can I rely on?' ... It is forcing people into corners that I don't think they should be ... it's got really dangerous for us here.

The serious consequences of this melding of practical and psychological effects of Brexit were spelled out by one focus group participant from the business community. Although there has been overriding emphasis and focus on the needs of business, this participant noted that – much more than tariffs and customs declarations – the risks for peace and stability lie in the re-emergence of distrust and uncooperativeness.

> I'm in business and there's a lot of risks in business ... The greater danger for me [however] is if the fabric of society gets damaged. Because ... the businesses will eventually solve their own problems, but society is a different animal. When it's damaged, it takes a long, long time to solve.

What has been achieved after a century of conflict and cooperation is something that people in the border region want to preserve. As a woman living in Pettigo described it:

> We don't want to look like some sectarian dug-out little hole. We all want to move on for the betterment of our communities and our children. I know before the peace process, your Catholic or your Protestant neighbour mightn't have lent you a shovel, but from the peace process, that all changed. All of that broke down. People weren't afraid of orange and green [political differences] any more.

Local residents cherish the fact that they are no longer afraid of difference among themselves; and this is something that they are particularly keen to preserve given that the border region is one in which political, economic, social and cultural difference has been so damaging and divisive. Partition added new forms of division ad difference to those on which it had been banned. The peace process since 1998 has helped soothe and defuse these divides. Following the UK–EU Withdrawal Agreement reached at the end of 2019, the immediate effects of any new customs and regulatory procedures will now be seen and experienced through checks and controls for goods crossing the Irish Sea, not at the land border. However, as clearly demonstrated by our research participants, the border's significance and modus operandi has always been an intricate mesh of the practical, the legal, the psychological and the symbolic. Thus, despite the agreement reached it will remain a challenge to maintain hard-won levels of trust and goodwill as the British–Irish relationship underpinning the legal and symbolic border becomes inevitably more distant after Brexit. The Irish border is now an external frontier of the European Union. We can see from the history of a century of its existence that the impact of legal and regulatory change to the status of the Irish border will be felt most acutely and most personally in the border region.

4. CONCLUSION

A revised Withdrawal Agreement was reached between the UK and the EU on 17 October 2019, containing a Protocol on Ireland/Northern Ireland which had direct implications for the experience of Brexit and for avoiding a hard border on the island of Ireland. In summary, the Protocol avoided a hard border by treating Northern Ireland differently from the rest of the UK. This will apply to areas such as technical regulation of goods, agricultural and environmental production and regulation, state aid and other areas of north–south cooperation between Northern Ireland and the Republic of Ireland, including the Single Electricity Market. Its subsequent ratification by the UK parliament in January 2020 means that the openness of the Irish land border for the movement of goods will be largely maintained irrespective of the changing nature of the UK–EU relationship. In principle, there should be no need for checks and controls for customs or product standards at the land border, and thus no need for new physical infrastructure, procedures or resources for the movement of goods across the border. However, this is not indefinitely secured. These conditions will depend on the deals that the UK negotiates not only with the EU but also with other states, on the willingness of Northern Ireland regional elected representatives to sustain these conditions (as per the 'democratic consent mechanism' in the Protocol in the Withdrawal Agreement), and on the successful implementation of the Withdrawal Agreement itself. The Irish land border will remain a tender spot and a testing ground for both high-political and on-the-ground social relationships in the region.

While for Pettigo this means no return to the border of 'the Troubles' or to the accompanying everyday life disruption, more subtle changes will depend on the extent of the potential gradual distancing between laws and regulations (including price differences) on each side of the border. Just like partition or the peace process, Brexit does not constitute a one-off event or a 'clean break' from the past. The consequences of Brexit will be long felt in the border region. In the first instance, for example, this means that those residents of Pettigo who are British and not Irish citizens will lose the rights associated with EU membership – bringing a new layer of difference among citizens in the border region and it remains to be seen what role such divisions will play in stoking the ever-present shadow of 'the border of the mind'.

The new relationship between the UK and the EU will not only affect the practical significance of the Irish land border, it will also change relations between Northern Ireland and the Republic of Ireland and between Britain and Northern Ireland. Borders all around Northern Ireland are going to be under pressure, with the general trend being towards a hardening effect. In light of this, trust-building and cooperation, north–south and east–west, will be more important than ever. Indeed, our research clearly articulates the fears among border residents of losing precisely those hard-won accomplishments. Border communities have a long history of defending, maintaining and exploiting any permeability of the border in the face of attempts to impose various forms of a 'hard' border; this history has continued on into the Brexit debates. Thus, the models and examples of relationship-building and communication in border communities should be ones to inspire and to build upon at a time of immense economic uncertainty and political flux.

NOTES

1. In total 237,368 men signed the Covenant and 234,046 women signed the corresponding women's Declaration. 'About the Ulster Covenant', Public Records Office of Northern Ireland (www.nidirect.gov.uk/articles/about-ulster-covenant) (accessed 16 December 2019).
2. Evidence of Rev. J. R. Meara, 4 May 1925 (TNA, IBC, CAB 61/56, p. 5).
3. W. F. Stout to S. H. E. Burley, 20 November 1962 (P.R.O.N.I., Closing of cross-border roads: miscellaneous correspondence and incident reports, 1957–71, Cabinet Secretariat, CAB/9/G/73/11).
4. See the Irish Borderlands project, http://www.irishborderlands.com/perspectives/social/index.html (accessed 24 February 2020).
5. Account of John Travers, James Scollan, Nicholas Smyth, Denis Monaghan and Felix McCabe (BMH, WS 711) (http://www.militaryarchives.ie/collections/online-collections/bureau-of-military-history-1913-1921/reels/bmh/BMH.WS0711.pdf) (accessed 11 December 2019).
6. *Irish Press*, 11 January 1949.
7. *Munster Express*, 4 February 1949.
8. *Irish Press*, 11 January 1949.
9. *Irish Independent*, 2 July 1941.
10. *Irish Press*, 11 January 1949.

BIBLIOGRAPHY

Adams, L. (1995), *Cashel: A Case Study in Community Harmony*, Cashel: Cashel Community Development Association.

Bardon, J. (2011), *The Plantation of Ulster*, Dublin: Gill and Macmillan.

Buttazzoni, M. (2016), 'Brexit and the Northern Irish borderlands: Fragile progress moving towards disintegration', Borders in Globalization Research Project, No. 49, accessed 22 August 2019 at: https://biglobalization.org/sites/default/files/uploads/files/big_research_project_49_international_buttazzoni.pdf.

Cunningham, J. B. (1982), 'The struggle for the Belleek–Pettigo salient 1922', *Donegal Annual*, 34, 38–59.

Dooley, T. (1994), 'From Belfast boycott to Boundary Commission – fears and hopes in Co Monaghan, 1920–6', *Clogher Historical Record*, XV, #1.

Fanning, R. (2013), *Fatal Path: British Government and the Irish Revolution*, London: Faber and Faber.

Farrell, M. (1980), *Northern Ireland: the Orange State*, 2nd edition, London: Pluto Press.

Garry, J., K. McNicholl, B. O'Leary and J. Pow (2018), 'Northern Ireland and the UK's exit from the EU. What do people think?', Evidence from Two Investigations: A Survey and a Deliberative Forum. The UK in a Changing Europe Report, accessed 12 February 2020 at: https://ukandeu.ac.uk/wp-content/uploads/2018/05/Northern-Ireland-and-the-UK%E2%80%99s-Exit-from-the-EU.pdf.

Gregory, I. N., N. A. Cunningham, C. D. Lloyd, I. G. Shuttleworth and P. S. Ell (2013), *Troubled Geographies: A Spatial History of Religion and Society in Ireland*, Bloomington: Indiana University Press.

Harris, R. [1972] (1986), *Prejudice and Tolerance in Ulster: A Study of Neighbours and Strangers in a Border Community*, Manchester: Manchester University Press.

Harvey, B., A. Kelly, S. McGearty and S. Murray (2005), *The Emerald Curtain: The Social Impact of the Irish Border*, Carrickmacross: Triskele Community Training and Development.

Hayward, K. (2017), 'The origins of the Irish border', The UK in a Changing Europe, accessed 22 August 2019 at: https://ukandeu.ac.uk/explainers/the-origins-of-the-irish-border/.

Hayward, K. (2018), 'The future of the Irish border', *Renewal: A Journal of Social Democracy*, 26 (4), 12–22.

Hayward, K. and M. Komarova (2019), 'The Border into Brexit: Perspectives from local communities in the central border region of Ireland/Northern Ireland'. A report prepared for the Irish Central Border Area Network (ICBAN), accessed 17 January 2020 at: https://ukandeu.ac.uk/wp-content/uploads/2019/12/The-Border-into-Brexit-perspectives-from-local-communities-in-the-central-border-region-of-Ireland-and-Northern-Ireland.pdf.

Hayward, K. and C. M. Murphy (2018), 'The EU's influence on the Peace Process and Agreement in Northern Ireland in light of Brexit', *Ethnopolitics*, 17 (3), 276–91.

Heslinga, M. [1962] (1979), *The Irish Border as a Cultural Divide: A Contribution to the Study of Regionalism in the British Isles*, 3rd unrevised edition, Assen: Van Gorcum.

HM Government (2018a), 'Technical explanatory note: North–South cooperation mapping exercise', accessed 17 February 2020 at: https://www.gov.uk/government/publications/technical-explanatory-note-north-south-cooperation-mapping-exercise.

HM Government (2018b), 'EU exit: Taking back control of our borders, money and laws while protecting our economy, security and Union', accessed 15 February 2020 at: https://assets.publishing.service.gov.uk/government/uploads/system/uploads/attachment_data/file/759792/28_November_EU_Exit_-_Taking_back_control_of_our_borders__money_and_laws_while_protecting_our_economy__security_and_Union__1_.pdf.

Hobsbawm, E. (1995), *Age of Extremes: The Short Twentieth Century, 1914–91*, London: Abacus.

Johnson, D. S. (1979), 'Cattle smuggling on the Irish border, 1932–8', *Irish Economic and Social History*, 6, 41–63.

Kowalsky, W. (2010), 'Past and future of the EU single market', *European Review of Labour & Research*, 16 (3), 437–41.

Larsen, S. S. (1982), 'The two sides of the house: Identity and social organisation in Kilbroney, Northern Ireland', in Cohen, Anthony P. (ed.), *Belonging: Identity and Social Organisation in British Rural Cultures*, Manchester: Manchester University Press, 131–64.

Leary, P. (2016), *Unapproved Routes: Histories of the Irish Border, 1922–72*, Oxford: Oxford University Press.

Leary, P. (2018), 'A house divided: The Murrays of the border and the rise and decline of a small Irish house', *History Workshop Journal*, 86, 269–90.

Leheny, S. (2018), 'Making Northern Ireland a bridge between the UK and the EU', The UK in a Changing Europe, accessed 22 August 2019 at: https://ukandeu.ac.uk/making-northern-ireland-a-bridge-between-the-uk-and-the-eu/.

Magennis, E., A. Park and L. Heery (2017), 'Brexit and the border corridor on the island of Ireland: Risks, opportunities and issues to consider'. Report. East Border Region and Newry, Mourne and Down District Council.

McCall, C. (2011), 'Culture and the Irish border: Spaces for conflict transformation', *Cooperation and Conflict*, 46 (2), accessed 22 August 2019 at: https://journals.sagepub.com/doi/abs/10.1177/0010836711406406.

Mulroe, P. (2017), *Bombs, Bullets and the Border: Policing Ireland's Frontier: Irish Security Policy, 1969–1978*, Newbridge, Co. Kildare: Irish Academic Press.

O'Callaghan, M. (1999), 'Old parchment and water; the Boundary Commission of 1925 and the copper fastening of the Irish border', *Bullan; an Irish Studies Journal*, 4 (2), 27–55.

Ó Ciardha, É. and M. Ó Siochrú (eds.) (2012), *The Plantation of Ulster: Ideology and Practice*, Manchester: Manchester University Press.

Ó Duibhir, L. (2011), *Donegal and the Civil War: The Untold Story*, Cork: Mercier Press.

Patterson, H. (2013), *Ireland's Violent Frontier: The Border and Anglo-Irish Relations during the Troubles*, Basingstoke: Palgrave Macmillan.

Phinnemore, D. and K. Hayward (2017), 'UK withdrawal ("Brexit") and the Good Friday Agreement', Directorate General for Internal Policies, Policy Department for Citizens' Rights and Constitutional Affairs, European Parliament, accessed 22 August 2019 at: http://www.europarl.europa.eu/RegData/etudes/STUD/2017/596826/IPOL_STU%282017%29596826_EN.pdf.

Rankin, K. J. (2007), 'Deducing rationales and political tactics in the partitioning of Ireland, 1912–1925', *Political Geography*, 26 (8), 909–33.

Sahlins, P. (1991), *Boundaries: The Making of France and Spain in the Pyrenees*, Berkeley, CA: University of California Press.

Sutton, M. (2001), *Bear in Mind These Dead... An Index of Deaths from the Conflict in Ireland 1969–1993*, 3rd edition, Belfast: Beyond the Pale Publications.

Whyte, J. (1983), 'How much discrimination was there under the Unionist regime, 1921–1968?', in Gallagher, T. and O'Connell, J. (eds.), *Contemporary Irish Studies*, Manchester: Manchester University Press, 1–35.

Wilson, T. K. (2010), *Frontiers of Violence: Conflict and Identity in Ulster and Upper Silesia, 1918–1922*, Oxford: Oxford University Press.

Wright, F. (1992), *Northern Ireland: A Comparative Analysis*, Dublin: Gill and Macmillan.

PART V

VIOLENCE AND CONTAINMENT: APPROACHES TO YOUTH AND GENDER

24. African women on the road to Europe: violence and resilience in border zones
Kristin Kastner

1. INTRODUCTION

The same border means different things to different people. This simple statement holds especially true for the Strait of Gibraltar, the Mediterranean border between Morocco and Spain. The border between Africa and Europe is widely perceived as a boundary between Islam and Christianity, south and north, poor and rich. This common opinion does not just reflect a 'Western' point of view, since the same dichotomies apply within broad swaths of Morocco, except that the perceptions are reversed: Europe represents moral decay and impurity while Morocco stands for spiritual superiority and purity. Also, the perception of the permeability of borders largely depends on the legal status of the border-crossing subjects. While crossing the Moroccan–Spanish border may pose few problems for European passport holders, for those lacking the required documents, this border may represent an impregnable hurdle. Migrants from sub-Saharan Africa often perceive the Strait as a nearly invincible barrier that separates suffering and forced immobility from freedom, which is associated with physical mobility and what they assume to be 'a good life', also in the sense of social mobility. However, the route to reach this border has become increasingly difficult within the last two decades, and migrants on the road regularly face deportation – from Morocco to the Algerian border and from Algeria to the border with Mali or Niger. This 'open struggle between disciplining mobility and the desire for migratory self-determination' (Biemann 2013: 163) means that, while travelling north, the migrants do not simply cover a particular distance, but follow a way paved with various obstacles and detours, a 'fragmented journey' (Collyer 2010).

The present chapter is based on ethnographic fieldwork with Nigerian migrants and mainly conducted in the border zone of the Strait of Gibraltar in southern Spain and northern Morocco during a period of 15 months.[1] The undocumented migrants' high mobility had a considerable impact on the research itself, which was also marked by the border condition. During this multi-sited ethnography, complying with the ethical code of a transparent research was at times challenging and required situated approaches.[2]

The migration of women from southwest Nigeria, where most of my interlocutors came from, is not a recent phenomenon. Rather, the everyday life of many people in Africa is characterized more by different forms of movement and mobility than by sedentariness, which has a considerable impact on migration movements (see, among others, Hahn and Klute 2007). Joris Schapendonk also suggests viewing the movements of sub-Saharan migrants through a 'mobility lens' (Schapendonk 2012). In addition to commercial activities or a love of adventure, most of the young women currently leave their country primarily in order to support their family or, although rarely stated explicitly, to escape from strenuous social ties. The present international and intercontinental migration of Nigerian women can be considered an extension of already existing forms of autonomous female migration in Nigeria (Ikpe 2005). The

Nigerian women and men I encountered during fieldwork were mostly from the Bini group in Edo State, with its capital Benin City. They rarely used the terms 'migrant' and 'migrating' to refer to those who had left their country in search of greener pastures. Rather, most of them considered themselves 'travellers' or, for the Francophones, *aventuriers*.[3] This self-description as 'travellers' downplays or even ignores the existence of inhibiting national physical borders, illustrating a striking paradox when bearing in mind the rigid border regimes. This resolute attitude may be related to an understanding of migration as a horizon of action, of imagination and expectation, and not just the result of physical mobility (Graw and Schielke 2012: 13). The migrants' life-worlds can be grasped using Ghassan Hage's concept of 'existential mobility', which goes far beyond mere physical mobility and is associated with forward movement, viability and the future (Hage 2005). It also allows for integrating embodied ideas and imaginations that transgress physical borders and keep migrants alive, even when they find themselves immobilized.

Migration is a deeply bodily experience. This is not only true because migration, of course, entails the physical movement of bodies, but also because it involves crossing a range of borders and boundaries and may even shift the allegedly stable boundaries of the human body itself. The migrants' bodies play a significant role in various phases of the migration process: during the perilous overland journey from western to northern Africa, during the long phases of waiting while on the road, during the dangerous sea crossing between Africa and Europe, as well as the arrival on the other side and, finally, along the migrants' myriad routes and detours in Europe. Following Abdelmalek Sayad, the body can be seen as the place of condensation of the migratory experience (Sayad 2004). Although female and male migrants pass through the same places and often share similar experiences, their migration experience is highly gendered in the sense that women are exposed to multiple forms of violence while, at the same time, they make use of their body in order to proceed. Here, the pregnant body and the bodies of small children often gain particular relevance on both sides of the Mediterranean.

Although the body is frequently the target of suffering and gendered violence, it can be, at the same time, the ultimate resource and decisive capital. An analysis of extended, suffering, shadow, styled and disguised women's as well as children's bodies, therefore, illuminates the constant navigating of the migrants amidst the interplay of structural constraints and individual agency on the western route through Mali or Niger, Algeria and Morocco. I will elaborate on the gender-specific system of sponsoring within the migration of female Nigerians, before delving into the overland route to Europe, where women are exposed to multiple forms of violence while, at the same time, many of them develop specific tactics in order to continue the journey and to realize their migration project.

2. SPONSORING: EXTENDED BODIES

As it has become more and more difficult to legally cross the external frontier of the European Union, the organization of the journey has turned into a profitable business for various parties: for the members of the network that spans from Nigeria to different European countries, for cooperators on the road, and the migrants' families in Nigeria. Sponsoring is, in most cases, connected to high interest rates, and up to tens of thousands of euros, often earned through sex work, have to be paid back to the Nigerian madam who sponsored the journey. The system is highly gendered as Ifoma[4] explained:

Madam cannot sponsor boy, because [s]he know, boy cannot do prostitution here, you understand? Madam don't carry boy. (Ifoma, 9 June 2005, Spain)

After several years in Europe, once the migrant has repaid her debt, she becomes independent. While some women continue to work in prostitution after this point, most try to leave the business. Once the migrant possesses her own financial resources, she herself might take over the role of a madam, sponsoring the journies of female compatriots from Nigeria to Europe. Thus, this gender-specific system of sponsoring constantly reproduces itself.[5]

Within the context of sponsored migration, even one's own bodily boundaries can be transcended, ceasing to correspond to the physical shape of the female body. This is the case when certain parts of the body are occasionally removed from the women's sphere of action. By referring to the phenomenon of the 'extended body', I emphasize the deep embeddedness of embodied experience within the realm of the sociocultural, the meaning of which alters in the transnational context of Nigerian migration: migrants, whose journey to Europe is sponsored often undergo a ritual in Edo State. They leave a so-called *package* or *body*, comprised of different bodily substances like hair and nails, as well as, occasionally, a photo of themselves in Nigeria while they themselves set out for Europe. The pledge entailed in this act loses its power only when the debts related to the journey have been amortized. This has strong parallels to the *akpa*, the substitute corpse that is collected from a real corpse during mortuary rites amongst the Edo people (Bradbury 1973). As long as the migrant is on the road and her debts remain unpaid, she is 'in-between', in a liminal phase, seemingly dead. If the contract with the madam is not fulfilled, psychological and physical consequences provoked by the powers of the *juju* can result. Madness, illness or even death may not only strike the migrant herself, but also her family members back home in Nigeria.

Generally, the contract and the ritual are considered an accepted part of the travel arrangements by the majority of the sponsored women I encountered, with rights and duties for both parties. The ritual should protect the future migrant on her journey and help her to gain success and wealth once she arrives in Europe, while, at the same time, it strengthens her loyalty towards the madam.[6] The relationship between the migrant and the madam is very ambivalent. On the one hand, the women highly depend on their madam and therefore often are exposed to strong control, pressure and violence. On the other hand, the madam is, in most cases, viewed by the women as a respectable person and model. Despite frequent complaints about madams and the fear of possible sanctions, most women do not consider the sponsoring agreement as unfair per se; neither do they consider themselves victims. Moreover, the idea of human trafficking[7] is not familiar to most of them (see Skogseth 2006). Rather than behaving as mere individuals, the migrants act as social persons who are part of a tight network of dependencies and patronage. As daughters, wives or younger sisters, they act corresponding to a principle of seniority, which demands respect towards the elders. The pervasive system of patronage, which is part of the daily reality in Nigeria, has a long history. Originally defined as a mutual, though always asymmetrical relationship of exchange of resources meaning maintenance and protection in exchange for loyalty, this system has gradually been commercialized and corrupted in Nigeria, making the borderlines between voluntary migration, work and trafficking more and more diffuse.[8] Veronika Bilger's concept of 'bound migration' (Bilger 2001: 7) provides a useful addition to that of 'trafficking' since it makes it possible to analyse the complex network of dependencies and patronage from a perspective beyond simplifying dichotomies like victim and perpetrator.

3. VIOLENT BORDERS: SUFFERING BODIES

The migrants' experiences are marked by borders and various forms of border crossing. Due to tightened immigration laws and heavily guarded frontiers resulting from European migration policies, it has become very difficult to reach Europe, especially within the last two decades, and many migrants from sub-Saharan Africa spend several years in Morocco until they are able to cross one of the European borders. The Maghreb countries are considered European Union (EU) partners in the fight against so-called 'illegal immigration' and the border between Morocco and Spain, between Africa and Europe, is continuously moving southwards, even though this process is not visible on any map. Furthermore, in addition to the border shifting between the two continents, a multiplication of the border has developed as the border between Morocco and Spain has become omnipresent in the life of migrants. Although on a clear day in Tangier, one feels as if one could practically touch the other side of the Strait less than 15 kilometres away, it has become more and more difficult to cross this border of water due to heightened border surveillance.[9] Moreover, the border between the two continents seems to have multiplied within Morocco itself and the neighbouring countries as migrants regularly face deportation in regions quite far from the actual border zone.[10] As a consequence, migrants may find themselves unable to move forward along their route (see Brachet 2012) or may have to cross the same border various times. Especially near state borders, repressions are high and, as a consequence, deportations frequent. Sent into exile, without legal status and only limited contact with locals, for these migrants, improvised camps become exceedingly important. Far removed from national law and order, places like *Shoe Bridge* near the border between Mali and Algeria and *The Valley/Maghnia* near the Moroccan–Algerian border serve as informal junctions with their own laws and orders. Although the journey must be undertaken under clandestine circumstances, the migrants leave tracks, and the Saharan space and local economies of various desert towns undergo change and regain importance through the very presence of the migrants (Badi 2007; Bensaad 2005; Biemann and Holmes 2006; Scheele 2012). The raids and subsequent strenuous deportations that take migrants to their financial and physical limits are part of their daily reality. As in the Sonoran Desert in Arizona that straddles the border zone between Mexico and the United States, official death tolls are not reliable and the numbers are assumed to be far higher, since only migrant fatalities known to the authorities are counted (De León 2015: 36). Thus, also in the context of the migration from sub-Saharan Africa to Europe, the real number of people who have lost their lives while crossing the desert or the sea, will never be known. Those who do survive experience corporal deprivations like thirst, hunger, powerlessness and their own existential limits when faced with the death of travel companions while crossing the desert:

> Some die! Some die there. We leave them and go. It is because of the sun, no water, so we used to drink piss. We piss in a can and drink it. (Susan, 5 March 2006, Morocco)
>
> We drink piss, we eat rotten food. At the beginning you say 'I can't eat this!', but later, you don't even smell it. You have to eat spoilt food, it is the only way to survive. (Owens, 14 June 2006, Spain)

The migrants' narratives are often characterized by repetitive elements describing a suffering body: scars, changes in body weight and skin colour or the consequences of rape and abortions. The journey and migration biographies are inscribed on the migrants' bodies. Additionally, women may face forced relationships as Evelyn, for example, revealed when describing the relationship between Nigerian men and women in Morocco:

> You have to go out with men. Except if you have husband. [...] But if you are a free girl, you have to go out with somebody, whether you like it or you don't like it. (Evelyn, 9 May 2005, Spain)

Women frequently experience sexual violence committed by security forces on the road or their own compatriots and, as a result, may suffer from spontaneous or provoked abortions or births under extremely difficult circumstances that often lack basic sanitary conditions.[11] Especially in the *bush*, as the woods outside the cities of Tangier and the two Spanish exclaves of Ceuta and Melilla are named and where migrants had improvised informal camps, the situation is very delicate, particularly for women. As there is no official control of any type, an auto-government has been established over the years, mostly dominated by Nigerians. The fact that female Nigerian migrants need to enter into a relationship with a male compatriot to obtain minimal protection from other Nigerian migrants indicates another aspect of gender relations. Having a husband, a boyfriend or other 'protector' – a role in many cases taken on by the *patron* who organizes the journey to Europe and usually mediates between the female migrant and her madam – eases the daily lives of many women.

4. EMBODIED CLANDESTINITY: SHADOW BODIES AND STYLED BODIES

Migrants do not only passively endure the hardship of their journey and the markings on their bodies. They also actively engage in the appropriation of their environment. They build, for example, informal camps in peripheral areas and border zones denoted as no-man's lands and create their own distinctive vocabulary, which is unique to this form of travel and reflects the border condition and legal status of the migrants. Binary expressions such as 'hot and cool places' or 'uptown and downtown' refer to the creation and valuation of a migrant counter-topography, while expressions such as 'staying trankil' and 'beating' not only describe modes of mobility or immobility, but are the verbal articulation of embodied movement under clandestine circumstances (Kastner 2011). As Susan Coutin (2005) noted in her observation of migrants from Latin America on their way to the United States, migrants embody clandestinity when they try to move as invisibly as possible while travelling north. Coutin describes the migrants as being physically present and absent at the same time and understands migrants' deaths as 'the ultimate embodiment of illegality' (2005: 195, 199). That the embodiment of clandestinity may become, at least for the time being, a quasi-permanent condition, is also reflected in the children born on the way to Europe who do not run, but instead crawl and who do not talk freely, but whisper. Here, the embodiment of clandestinity, which implies a certain dynamic and flexibility, is reinforced over the years due to long transit stays and may, especially in the case of children, evolve into a clandestine habitus.

The constant hiding from Moroccan authorities becomes the rule, in Tangier as well, where migrants have to adapt their movements according to the situation. In times of police raids, migrants only leave their houses after dark. The routes they chose when moving around the city differed from mine, as they avoided certain places so as not to be picked up by the Moroccan police. During my visits to Tangier, every time I returned, the situation had changed: some migrants had been deported to the Algerian frontier, while others had moved to the big cities of Casablanca and Rabat, where life is easier thanks to metropolitan anonymity, and still others had managed to enter Spain.

Additionally, a temporal embodiment of freedom associated with mobility and free movement becomes obvious in the migrants' styling and conspicuous presence in those spaces where they can move around without police harassment, as in Casablanca and Rabat, where after decades of transit and settlement they have built up their own neighbourhoods and markets. Here, after a long period of deprivations, the migrants gain weight, their bodies become more shiny and, thus, from their point of view, much more beautiful. The remarkable care most of them take of their bodies becomes even more visible after they reach the Spanish coast, where styling becomes a means to remain human, despite all the hardship and a life that was frequently described to me as one of dogs or other animals. Styling, in this context, can be interpreted as the embodied expression and self-assurance of remaining human and of regaining one's dignity. The experience of suffering is opposed to the act of styling. In Morocco as well as later in Europe, Nigerian women most times do not correspond to the conventional image of the (poor) migrant since, for many of them, the act of styling, the expensive hair-extensions or wigs, sexy clothing, accessories like showy jewellery and extravagant sunglasses, handbags or make-up are the focus of attention. When they finally manage to reach Spain, they have the opportunity to dedicate themselves even more to styling, but even in Morocco, where they are faced with very difficult conditions, physical appearance is given priority. Through the act of styling, migrants transcend their harsh living conditions, at least for the moment. Practices of imagination seek to attenuate experiences of violence and structural power (Bakare-Yusuf 2002: 2). Bibi Bakare-Yusuf's concept of the 'imaginative stylization of the body' within a lived existential chaos advocates for a new approach, at least in the African context, in conceptualizing the relationship between suffering and creativity as well as between survival and imagination (Bakare-Yusuf 2002: 2, 5): survival is by no means to be reduced to the mere satisfaction of basic needs; it reveals the real and realistic aspects of the imagination and the way that imagination is intrinsically tied to being human.

5. A PROTECTIVE MASQUERADE: DISGUISED BODIES AND CHILDREN'S BODIES

For many migrants travelling overland, the European continent, once imagined as a place offering a 'sweet life', turns out to be very distant despite its physical proximity when the migrants reach Tangier. The daily reality on the road sharply contrasts with dreams of Europe. To manage this transitional phase, women in particular have developed a range of tactics designed to preserve a certain mobility. They adopt various roles, at times consciously and at times not. Identity fragments and assumed identities are accumulated that create a biographic tentativeness, where often no strict lines can be drawn between imagination and reality, truth or lie – a reality, that, of course, was reflected in my own research.

Despite living underground, migrants are often astonishingly visible, even during the extended liminal phase on the road. Migrants act according to the situation, as the following examples show. Dressing up or down constitutes one of the migrants' decisive tactics. Women – and particularly single women – confidently play different roles by dressing up to pass as 'legal' residents, tourists or as pregnant Muslim beggars to maintain their mobility.

Pregnancies are, for the reasons discussed below, also sometimes faked, as in the case of Rita, who described her arrival in Gourougou, an informal camp near Melilla with hundreds of migrants:

> My husband and I entered the bush with three other girls. The men told the girls: 'You go here with this, you go there!' My husband begged and begged for me and the other girls, who pretended to be pregnant one month, two month, to have their husbands soon come. I was small, small and pretended to have mental problem. I was looking like this [like a mad person], not wearing fine cloth. Finally they let us go. (Rita, 20 September 2005, Spain)

Rita's two female travel companions pretended to be pregnant to prevent sexual harassment by their compatriots as well as, in some cases, by the Maghrebian authorities; Rita herself dressed and acted like a mad person in order to make herself sexually unattractive to her compatriots. Here again, the manipulated body is the only means for the migrants to advance. In one case, styling increases the possibility of avoiding deportation, while, in the opposite case, the choice of non-styling or faking some kind of illness, whether mental or physical, is advantageous. Dressing up, particularly when combined with fair skin, also increases the chances for more mobility in Morocco. When I asked Jenny, a single girl, how she was able to manage to travel between Tangier and Casablanca without a baby or a pregnant belly, she answered: 'I dress like a student when I travel' (Jenny, 9 September 2005, Morocco). For Jenny, a styled body proved to be helpful when she had to face the Moroccan authorities. In contrast, non-styling or styling down, in addition to acting like a mad woman, helped Rita to escape from a delicate situation. Compared to their male compatriots, female migrants are able to expand the repertoire of possible identities. As the condition of being pregnant may help women to avoid deportation, pregnancies are sometimes faked. Stylish Nigerians transform their bodies into those of poor pregnant Muslim women ready for *salam aleikum*, as Nigerian migrants call begging in the street.

Many female migrants also make use of their children, who they carry as a kind of shield or 'papers' to enhance their mobility, since Moroccan law, at least on paper, prohibits the deportation of children. Although frequently a result of forced relationships or, at least, a lack of mutual consent, and despite the difficulties of raising a child in clandestine circumstances, children born on both sides of the Strait of Gibraltar play a crucial role. In Tangier, mothers sometimes sarcastically presented their babies to me: 'Look, this is my paper!' Nowadays, babies on both sides of the Strait of Gibraltar, whether born or unborn, literally function as 'visas' for their mothers. When it is 'hot' in Tangier, a time of frequent raids and deportations, pregnant women or young mothers are the only visible migrants in the streets of Tangier. Here, the conventional association of pregnancy with immobility is turned upside down, as it is due to their very pregnancy that women can move more freely. A baby in one's belly or on one's back not only enhances the mother's physical mobility but also her survival, since babies help to earn money through *salam aleikum*. As there are no job possibilities for Nigerian migrants in Morocco, many of them, especially female migrants, have to rely on begging as one way of surviving, and Moroccans are more generous when giving alms to pregnant women or young mothers. On the Spanish side, unborn children also protect their mothers from being deported; migrants who enter Spain pregnant or with small children are usually allowed to stay in the country. Although they are not given papers, young mothers have an advantage over male migrants or single girls, who regularly face deportation to their home country.

The children's importance for the mothers' lives, in addition to their experiences on the road, may be reflected in name-giving, which is often related to the situation and place of birth: babies born on the Moroccan side of the Strait of Gibraltar are frequently named Destiny or Hope, which emphasizes the current uncertainty, but at the same time, the prospects for a better future. Babies born shortly after their mothers' arrival in Spain are often given names like Success, Progress or Will, expressing an end to the suffering on the road and a positive view of the future.

6. OUTLOOK

While on a conceptual level, postcolonial and transnational perspectives regarding border zones have contributed to overcoming methodological nationalism to a remarkable extent, the impact of borders and boundaries on migrants' lives remains formidable. While travelling north from sub-Saharan Africa, migrants not only face cultural, linguistic and religious differences, which may be experienced as boundaries, but often also reach their financial and physical, and thus, existential limits. The same is true for issues of morality and ethics in the case of those women who have to survive through begging in the street or through sex work once they reach Europe. In the context of sponsoring, even the women's own bodily boundaries may be transcended.

Recent changes in the migration dynamics of Nigerian women show that these migrants are increasingly younger and, thus, less experienced and more vulnerable. Additionally, the rate of minors on the move is on the increase. Underage and mainly from rural areas, the educational level of these migrants is quite low, they have less access to information and anti-trafficking campaigns, like those produced by the Nigerian NAPTIP (National Agency for Prohibition of Trafficking in Persons), may not reach them.[12] Also, severe conditions at the borders have led to a prolongation and negative intensification of the journey to Europe. Moreover, beside the western route through Algeria and Morocco, which is the spatial focus of the present chapter, the eastern route through Libya has become more frequented (see Chapter 13). Here, inhumane conditions such as being imprisoned and tortured for months by security forces are a daily occurrence. Nevertheless, migrants – travellers or adventurers in their own terms – are often 'stubborn actors in search of a world where they can fulfill their life project' (Alioua 2006: 97) as they try, despite all obstacles, to realize their dreams of a good life. The immense diversity and existential limits of human embodied experience are condensed in women's migration accounts, which strongly epitomize the fact that their bodies are the lived and felt expression of their movements through time and space. A more thorough analysis of migrants' lives through approaches inspired from a bodily perspective is a promising approach to help to explain embodied experiences that are often fairly verbally communicable, as I have suggested by introducing concepts such as the 'extended body' and the 'clandestine habitus' as well as Bakare-Yusuf's notion of the 'imaginative stylization of the body'. The antithetical factors of deep suffering and styling both express the inherent ambivalences in many migrants' life-worlds. At the same time subjected to enormous constraints and limitations, the women are, nevertheless, actors who proceed with their journey and their dreams, who play their roles and shape their bodies, which are always a product of history and culture and are lived amidst structural political and economic power relations and asymmetries.

NOTES

1. Long-term field research started in 2005 and also included a few weeks' stay in Edo State, Nigeria. The main methods were participant observation, active listening, informal conversations and interviews as well as photography. Even though most of the material was collected more than ten years ago, I am still involved in the field through regular visits and try to follow and track its dynamics as well as the women's biographies. For the published Ph.D. thesis, see Kastner (2014).
2. For a discussion of methodological and ethical challenges related to research in the context of smuggling, 'trafficking' and different forms of 'illegality', see the contributions in van Liemp and Bilger (2009).
3. For the figure of the adventurer in the context of migration, see Bredeloup (2013).
4. All names are pseudonyms. The citations have not been changed; I cite their specific way of expressing themselves when talking to me in a mix of Nigerian Pidgin and Standard English.
5. For an excellent recent study on the economies of migration among Nigerian sex workers, see Plambech (2016).
6. Generally, the migrants were told not to talk about this preparatory phase; still, they often insinuated or made use of narrative tricks to be able to talk about what should remain unsaid. I also met some women who breached the contract for various reasons and were open to sharing their experiences.
7. I use 'trafficking' according to the UN definition as 'recruitment, transportation, transfer, harbouring or receipt of persons, by means of threat or use of force or other forms of coercion, of abduction, of fraud, of deception, of the abuse of power or of a position of vulnerability or of the giving or receiving of payments or benefits to achieve the consent of a person having control over another person, for the purpose of exploitation' (United Nations 2000: Article 3 (a)).
8. Other pervasive phenomena within the country, like foster parenthood and domestic service, reveal similar asymmetric relations.
9. For an in-depth study of African–European borderlands and the business of bordering Europe, see Andersson (2014).
10. Similar dynamics are observable at the US–Mexican border (De León 2015: 285); see also the chapters in this volume which deal with the US-Mexican border region (Part I); for a comparison between the two border zones (US–Mexican and Mediterranean), see the edited volume by Ribas-Mateos (2011).
11. For the life of migrant women in Morocco and abortions, see the report of Women's Link Worldwide (2011) in collaboration with the Tangier-based Spanish activist and journalist Helena Maleno.
12. For a recent report about the trafficking of Nigerian women and girls, see Women's Link Worldwide (2015).

REFERENCES

Alioua, Mehdi (2006), 'Silence! People are dying on the southern borders of Europe: Sub-Saharan transit migrants face the externalization of migration management to North Africa', in Ursula Biemann and Brian Holmes (eds), *The Maghreb Connection. Movements of Life across North Africa*, Barcelona: Actar, pp. 84–106.
Andersson, Ruben (2014), *Illegality, Inc.: Clandestine Migration and the Business of Bordering Europe*, Oakland: University of California Press.
Badi, Dida (2007), 'Le rôle des communautés sahéliennes dans l'économie locale d'une ville saharienne: Tamanrasset (Sahara algérien)', in Elisabeth Boesen and Laurence Marfaing (eds), *Les nouveaux urbains dans l'espace Sahara-Sahel. Un cosmopolitisme par le bas*, Paris: Karthala, pp. 259–277.
Bakare-Yusuf, Bibi (2002), 'The politics of the belly, the poetics of the belly: Practices of the self in the African world', conference paper presented at the 10th CODESRIA General Assembly: Africa in the New Millenium, Kampala, Uganda, 8–12 December.
Bensaad, Ali (2005), 'Les migrations transsahariennes, une mondialisation par la marge', *Maghreb-Machrek*, 185, 13–36.

Biemann, Ursula (2013), 'Counter-geographies in the Sahara', in Susanne Witzgall et al. (eds), *New Mobilities Regimes in Art and Social Sciences*, Farnham: Ashgate Publishing, pp. 163–174.
Biemann, Ursula and Brian Holmes (eds) (2006), *The Maghreb Connection. Movements of Life across North Africa*, Barcelona: Actar.
Bilger, Veronika (2001), 'Lucciole Nere', *Stichproben. Wiener Zeitschrift für kritische Afrikastudien*, 2 (1), 1–25.
Brachet, Julien (2012), 'Stuck in the desert: Hampered mobility among transit migrants in Northern Niger', in Jocelyne Streiff-Fénart and Aurelia Segatti (eds), *The Challenge of the Threshold: Border Closures and Migration Movements in Africa*, Lanham, MD, USA and Plymouth, UK: Lexington Books, pp. 73–88.
Bradbury, R. E. (1973), *Benin Studies*, London: Oxford University Press.
Bredeloup, Sylvie (2013), 'The figure of the adventurer as an African migrant', *Journal of African Cultural Studies*, 25 (2), 170–182.
Collyer, Michael (2010), 'Stranded migrants and the fragmented journey', *Journal of Refugee Studies*, 23 (3), 273–293.
Coutin, Susan Bibler (2005), 'Being on route', *American Anthropologist*, 107 (2), 195–206.
De Léon, Jason (2015), *The Land of Open Graves. Living and Dying on the Migrant Trail*, Oakland: University of California Press.
Graw, Knut and Samuli Schielke (eds) (2012), *The Global Horizon: Expectations of Migration in Africa and the Middle East*, Leuven: Leuven University Press.
Hage, Ghassan (2005), 'A not so multi-sited ethnography of a not so imagined community', *Anthropological Theory*, 5 (4), 463–475.
Hahn, Hans Peter and Georg Klute (eds) (2007), *Cultures of Migration: African Perspectives*, Berlin: LIT.
Ikpe, Eno (2005), 'Nigerian women and international migration: The historical record and its implications', unpublished paper presented at the Colloque International Mobilités au féminin, Laboratoire Méditarranéen de Sociologie, Tangier, 15–19 November 2005.
Kastner, Kristin (2011), 'Vivir con la frontera a cuestas: migrantes nigerianas de camino hacia Europa. El impacto de las zonas fronterizas en el cuerpo y la lengua', in: Natalia Ribas-Mateos (ed.), *El Río Bravo Mediterráneo. Las Regiones Fronterizas en la época de la Globalización*, Barcelona: Editorial Bellaterra, pp. 512–528.
Kastner, Kristin (2014), *Zwischen Suffering und Styling: Die lange Reise nigerianischer Migrantinnen nach Europa*, Berlin: LIT.
Plambech, Sine (2016), 'Between "victims" and "criminals": Rescue, deportation, and everyday violence among Nigerian migrants', *Social Politics*, 21 (3), 382–402.
Ribas-Mateos, Natalia (2011) (ed.), *El Río Bravo Mediterráneo. Las Regiones Fronterizas en la época de la Globalización*, Barcelona: Editorial Bellaterra.
Sayad, Abdelmalek (2004), *The Suffering of the Immigrant*, Cambridge: Polity Press.
Schapendonk, Joris (2012), 'Beyond departure and arrival: Analyzing migration trajectories of Sub-Saharan African migrants from a mobilities perspective', in Jocelyne Streiff-Fénart and Aurelia Segatti (eds), *The Challenge of the Threshold: Border Closures and Migration Movements in Africa*, Lanham, MD, USA and Plymouth, UK: Lexington Books, pp. 105–120.
Scheele, Judith (2012), *Smugglers and Saints of the Sahara: Regional Connectivity in the Twentieth Century*, New York: Cambridge University Press.
Skogseth, Geir (2006), 'Report. Fact-finding trip to Nigeria (Abuja, Lagos and Benin City), 12–26 March 2006', accessed 10 October 2019 at https://www.refworld.org/pdfid/4980858915.pdf.
United Nations (2000), *Protocol to Prevent, Suppress and Punish Trafficking in Persons Especially Women and Children, Supplementing the United Nations Convention against Transnational Organized Crime*, accessed 12 November 2019 at https://www.ohchr.org/en/professionalinterest/pages/protocoltraffickinginpersons.aspx.
van Liemp, Ilse and Veronika Bilger (eds) (2009), *The Ethics of Migration Research Methodology. Dealing with Vulnerable Immigrants*, Portland: Sussex Academic Press.
Women's Link Worldwide (2011), *Mujeres migrantes en la clandestinidad. El aborto en Marruecos*, accessed 10 November 2019 at https://www.womenslinkworldwide.org/files/1358/mujeres-migrantes-en-la-clandestinidad-aborto-en-marruecos.pdf.

Women's Link Worldwide (2015), *Trafficking of Nigerian Women and Girls: Slavery across Borders and Prejudices*, accessed 10 November 2019 at https://www.womenslinkworldwide.org/en/files/1355/trafficking-of-nigerian-women-and-girls-slavery-across-borders-and-prejudices.pdf.

25. Impact of the permanent crisis in the Central African Republic on Cameroonian return migrants[1]

Henri Yambene Bomono

1. INTRODUCTION

Since the 1960s the history of Central African Republic (CAR) has been marked by political insecurity. Recurrent episodes of violence, banditry, rebellion and successive overthrow of government can be observed. Today, the country is mostly controlled by criminal armed groups struggling among themselves to appropriate the country's resources (Escoffier et al., 2014). This insecurity mainly affects the frontal areas and therefore neighbouring countries. Cameroon shares a 797 kilometres border with the CAR, stretching from eastern Cameroon and western CAR. Historical and geographical links unite the two countries. On both sides of the Cameroonian–CAR border, societal composition is almost identical. The two dominant ethnic groups are the Fulani and Gbaya. This means that, in this neighbouring region, inhabitants share the challenges of security and humanitarian crises due to the CAR's troubled history. Because of countless government overthrows, rebellions and mutinies in the CAR, many CAR nationals and Cameroonian citizens have lost their lives and property. The 2013–14 crisis is an illustrious example of this loss. The March 2013 putsch of Michel Djotodia, supported by the Muslim Séléka militia, first led population flows to Cameroon, composed mostly of Gbaya that were suspected of being pro-Bozize, the deposed president. In December 2013, the situation reversed beginning with the intervention of French forces, known as "Sangaris", and later led to the resignation of Michel Djotodia and provoked atrocities against Muslims of majority Fulani ethnicity (de Waal, 2013; Escoffier et al., 2014). Anti-Balaka, a predominantly Christian militia has directed many people to Cameroon, particularly Muslims fleeing reprisals (Mehler, 2011; Einsporn, 2014; Mayneri, 2014).

This chapter highlights the experiences of Cameroonian returning migrants during and after the CAR crisis of 2013–14 with a focus on key actors that participated in the facilitation of evacuation, return and reintegration assistance as well as contributed to returnees' reintegration experiences in Cameroon. As a case study, the chapter demonstrates how the repeated crises in the CAR endanger the lives of many people on the border of this country (Lombard, 2016, 2014). Insecurity along the border is a long-term, complex issue and evolves according to the political context. Our main finding demonstrates concrete ways in which returnees have adopted a range of strategies to flee the CAR and additionally that crises have long-lasting implications for the mental health of those affected, in particular returning migrants who were subject to injustices where reports of discrimination, xenophobia, violence, harassment, beatings and horrific cutlass butchering, rape and torture, among others, were prevalent.

Data collection for this chapter consisted of a literature review (mainly newspapers both physical or online reports), field observations and interviews. Along with my research assistant, I conducted 41 semi-structured interviews with six stakeholder groups:[2] returnees, family members of returnees, government authorities, experts in migration policy, civil society organisations and intergovernmental organisations.[3] For returnees and family members, in order to identify appropriate interviewees, we adopted as recommended an approach of purposive sampling using the snowball technique. In an effort to diversify testimonies, we chose to interview return migrants independently of their family members. For other stakeholder groups we submitted, as prescribed, official letters to organisations in order to identify the most appropriate interviewees within an organisation, and organise interviews. The development of this chapter is based on data collected both at the level of documentation and during the fieldwork. To analyse the data we used categorisation and contextual analysis.

2. CONTEXTUAL AND STRUCTURAL FACTORS

2.1 Migration History, Demography and Human Capital Factors

Cameroon and CAR share a 797 kilometre border where communities sharing blood ties live in peace on both sides. The indigenous Cameroonian Gbaya and Fulani of the eastern region are also found in the CAR because they are cross-border communities (Amadou, 2015). Gbaya are considered indigenous to the eastern region along with two other ethnic minorities, the Baka and Kako, while the Fulani Muslims and semi-nomadic pastoralists arrived in this region as early as the late eighteenth century. The history of cohabitation between these groups shows a symbiotic relationship founded on blood ties and is further cultivated by a cultural mix and exchange of goods and services (Gourdin, 2013; Amadou, 2015). In addition, except for the Gbaya, the Cameroonian diaspora in the CAR is also made up of Cameroonians from other ethnicities (Arabs-Choa, Bamileke, Eton) and regions (Adamawa, West, Centre, North and Far-North) of Cameroon.

Historically, many Cameroonians settled in Bangui and other CAR towns but it is difficult to ascertain the quantity including students and teachers in secondary and higher education, civil servants working in international organisations, including the Commission Economique et Monétaire d'Afrique Centrale (CEMAC – Economic and Monetary Commission of Central Africa) headquartered in Bangui and others.

Because of the porosity of the border, there is constant movement of traders and pastoralists on both sides of the border, raising circular movements between the two (Gourdin, 2013). Some returned Cameroonian migrants (among our respondents), especially those living in close proximity to the border, frequently came to source manufactured goods, including drinks, candy, oil, soap, cement, and so on to Garoua-Boulaï and resell them in the CAR. As for pastoralists, they graze their herds in the CAR. Cattle breeders who were interviewed as a part of this study believe that the Central African savannah is more adequate for breeding as compared to that of Cameroon.

In addition to their voluntary migration patterns, CAR nationals have been displaced due to political instability in their country since the 1960s (Chauvin and Seignobos, 2013; Amadou, 2015). Many Central African refugees have established lives in Cameroonian territories, mainly in the Adamawa and eastern regions. The population of the East Region, estimated at 1 million, consists of approximately 20 per cent (200 000) CAR refugees (Mvongo, 2016; UNHCR, 2016).

The Douala–Bangui corridor, first dedicated to transporting goods, serves as a conduit for human mobility. Many migrants climb aboard trucks from Douala to Bangui and vice versa in order to improve their living conditions. This has been the case since 1962 when Cameroon joined the Union Douanière Equatoriale (Equatorial Customs Union – UDE), then consisting of the CAR, Congo, Gabon and Chad, which became the Union Douanière et Economique de l'Afrique Centrale (UDEAC – Economic and Customs Union of Central Africa) in December 1964 and finally CEMAC in 1998. Since its creation, this organisation has promoted the free movement of goods and people.

Cameroonian returnees who resided in the CAR did so for long periods of time, averaging ten years. Despite its instability, the CAR offers many economic opportunities for migrant communities, including in gold and diamond mining operations. Endowed with rich subsoil and evergreen pastures, the CAR has always been an attractive site for employment for many Cameroonians. In 2007 formally registered Cameroonian migrants in the CAR were estimated at 5103.[4] Most of them were long-term migrants (IOM, 2009).

In our sample of 23 returnees, 40 per cent of our respondents (nine out of 23 respondents) have spent between five and nine years in the CAR; 30 per cent (seven out of 23 respondents) between ten and 14 years and 17.5 per cent (four out of 23 respondents) between 30 and 34 years. This last group includes some aged over 60 years old and some born in the CAR, while others emigrated to the CAR at a very young age.

2.2 Legal Situation and Relevance for Migrant Status

As mentioned previously, migration patterns between Cameroon and the CAR have been established over time. Travel is constant across the border. For more than ten years Cameroon and the CAR have instituted a free movement of people and goods protocol within the CEMAC that allows their citizens to travel without being forced to obtain a visa for a stay that does not exceed three months. This implies that, beyond the trial period, all Cameroonians residing in the CAR have to obtain a residence card and be identified by the consular authorities of Cameroon.

Obtaining CAR visas and residence permits is usually pursued by migrants engaged in contracting/formal employment activities in the CAR. Generally, most migrants take advantage of lineage solidarity to cross the border. Once in the CAR jurisdiction, they use different informal connections to obtain a CAR legal identity document (identity card or passport), thus enabling them to stay and "operate" in the country.[5]

Intensive and irregular checks of foreigners are not compliant with CEMAC community legislation. Whether a migrant has a legal document or not, as a foreigner, he or she could be subject to harassment, which is contrary to CEMAC community agreements.[6] Six returnees out of the 23 (27 per cent) hid their Cameroonian nationality during their stay in the CAR in order to avoid harassment and possible xenophobic attacks. Nine returnees out of 23 (40 per cent) admitted leaving their Cameroonian identification documents in Cameroon to avoid stigma and blackmail because, during regular checks in towns and at home by CAR authorities, Cameroonian identity cards could be confiscated and held for ransom. All the 23 returnees interviewed stated that, having a CAR national identity could enable someone to avoid paying residence permit fees.[7] For those engaged in commercial activities (48 per cent, 11 out of 23 returnees), this tactic successfully helped to avoid harassment and pressures to pay taxes.

Because Cameroonian migrants sometimes hide their Cameroonian identity, the crisis in the CAR has generated confusion in regard to census and official statistics pertaining to the number of migrants in the country. Many returnees that had administrative tasks at the Cameroonian Embassy in Bangui and at the Cameroon/CAR border encountered difficulties proving their nationality due to lack of documentation, which was typically hidden, or left in Cameroon during their migration to the CAR.

2.3 The Socio-economic Position of Return Migrants in Comparison to Host Population

Interviewed return Cameroonian migrants succeeded in self-employment in the CAR before the crisis. Their jobs reflect some of the major causes for their departures to the CAR. Those interviewed mainly worked in two major business sectors, namely trade in manufactured goods (48 per cent, 11 out of 23 respondents) and breeding of cattle (27 per cent, six out of 23 respondents). Other jobs were minimally represented in the respondent pool: farmer, artist/dancer, fortune teller, etc. As for the five women returnee migrants we interviewed, we had a farmer (widow and owner of a big farm with farm workers), a shop owner, a cattle breeder and two housewives.

However, it is important to note that incomes generated by these activities also offered the opportunity to buy and resell precious stones (gold and diamonds). Some returned migrants (six out of 23 respondents) were used to buying gold from traditional miners and selling them at higher prices to authorised operators.[8]

The purchase and resale of these precious stones by Cameroonian migrants in the CAR is cited in articles, reports, books and web pages about the CAR, which also indicate that a large quantity of gold and diamonds sold on the world markets pass through Cameroon (Guion, 2013; Charbonneau, 2015; AFP, 2016). It should be noted that Cameroonian migrants participate in this activity, where 20 per cent of the diamond production would illegally leave the CAR for Cameroon (Guion, 2013).

Cameroonian returned migrants made easy profits from their various business ventures, which gave them financial stability to cover their daily needs, and at the same time support their families in Cameroon.

Approximately 65.2 per cent of the returned migrants interviewed (15 out of 23 respondents) sent remittances or items of monetary value back to their families. Among them three women out of five. According to family members we interviewed (four out of five respondents), this money would help send their children to school, assist family during funerals or meet their daily needs. Considerable amounts of money were sent through informal channels such as friends and relatives. Another informal channel was the practice of exchanging money for phone credit. This is valid in the border towns of Garoua-Boulaï, Kentzou or Ngaoui, which are covered by the networks of Central African telephone operators and telecommunications services.

3. RETURN MIGRANTS' RESPONSES TO THE CRISIS

3.1 Perception of Impact

Broadly, return migrants reported that both the war between the Séléka and the Anti-Balaka as well as the violence to which Muslims were subjected were the main reasons for their return. The CAR crisis caused distress in the ranks of the Cameroonian Muslim community in particular, where there are many cases in which people left all their belongings and just carried important documentation with them. Many of our respondents (17 out of 23) testified that they were just able to recover their Koran and prayer papers.

In 82.6 per cent of cases (19 out of 23 respondents), the decision to return was made by the migrant and in 17.4 per cent of cases (four out of 23 respondents) by the family in Cameroon. Indeed, some returnees, especially those having experienced previous crises in the CAR, simply called their relatives and insisted on their immediate return home.

Return migrants used several strategies to escape from the atrocities in the CAR and back to Cameroon. Among those strategies, the first was to hide or take refuge in various places, including Christian churches, until they could guarantee their safe return across the border back to Cameroon. This strategy was mostly employed by return migrants residing in suburban localities outside Bangui.

In the capital city, return migrants took refuge in the KM5[9] Muslim neighbourhood, in various buildings or houses or even inside the Cameroon Embassy in Bangui. At their own risk, migrants returned to Cameroon by air, road, or on foot through dense forests.

Up to 4000 Cameroonian returnees through a total number of 12 flights organised by the state of Cameroon were airlifted along the route Douala–Bangu–Douala from early December 2013 to February 2014. To get access to the airlift facility, return migrants had to show documents indicating Cameroonian nationality, which included their national identity card, birth certificate or passport. The absence of any of these documents was a hindrance for many Cameroonians or presumed Cameroonians expected to leave the CAR by air, causing significant confusion and congestion. In our sample, only three returnees (one of whom was a woman) succeeded in coming back by that means; seven failed.

Cameroonian returnees also travelled by road, borrowing trucks filled with goods and even travelling in containers. Others escaped on foot through dense, patchy forests. Most Cameroonian returnees did not organise collectively, but rather individually with the assistance of relatives to whom they returned.

In the case of large families in the CAR, in many cases, initially the head of household chose to send their family to Cameroon and stayed behind to protect assets and then subsequently meet the family at a later date. As for breeders' families, some family members travelled by car while others made the trip with their animals.

With 57 per cent of our sample, (13, among them three women) about 7000 other Cameroonians were able to reach the country through successful border crossings in Garoua-Boulaï, Kentzou, Kette, Gari Gombo and Ngaoui.[10] Other respondents (a woman and six men) travelled on foot through dense, patchy forests. They were among the significant number of about 5000 migrants who returned home by that means.[11]

Despite their modes of travel, all respondents interviewed for this study showed great psychological distress upon their arrival in Cameroon because of abuses experienced in the CAR and on the long journey to reach safety on the Cameroonian border.

3.2 Responses from Return Migrants' Family Members and Other Informal Social Networks

With the expansion of the crisis, migrant families became increasingly affected on several levels. First, they played a role in motivating the return of migrants. Indeed, those that had experienced previous crises in the CAR simply called their relatives and insisted on their need to return home immediately.

Family members also remitted money to their stranded relatives in the CAR, during departure from the CAR, or at a specific step along the way back to Cameroon. Return migrants who were traders reported that they came to Cameroon to supply their shops and did not return to the CAR; they had to organise the return trip of their families from the CAR to Cameroon while in Cameroon.

Three return migrants out of 23 interviewed for this study turned to their family members to regain possession of their national identity cards and passports previously left in Cameroon. In order to send the migrants their identification documents, family members had to get in touch with rare and courageous drivers with shipping routes from Cameroon to the capital city of Bangui. This process would take one to two weeks and its success was not guaranteed. If achieved, once the migrants were in possession of their identity documentation, they could go to the embassy or consular services in Bangui to benefit from the official protection and evacuation methods provided and ensured to citizens by the Cameroonian state.

3.3 Long-term Impact of Decisions

Following the CAR crisis, many returnees were left destitute and disillusioned. In addition to significant financial and material losses incurred as a result of the journey back to Cameroon, there was also an increase in household expenses, psychological problems and reintegration challenges experienced upon return.

3.3.1 Loss of property
Respondents reported losing important property and material belongings in the CAR, including valuable assets such as abandoned houses (some migrants reported losing up to two properties), storefronts, plots of land, other real estate and money. Out of 23 respondents, only three did not report losses and stated they had not owned property in the CAR (the two housewives and the student).

Migrant returnees reported financial losses, but the exact amount was not disclosed. Return migrants interviewed did not keep their savings in banks, whereas significant sums of money were held in cash and stored at home. This finding can be explained by the lack of a consolidated banking culture for those living in small towns, villages or in the savannah pastures. As for nomadic breeders, they kept their earnings invested in their ventures, acquiring animals and occasionally storing extra money by them.

Return migrants also reported losing documentation such as official diplomas or certificates. Although some had time to recover these important documents, others did not.

As for breeders, many of them lost some livestock during the journey back to Cameroon. Respondents accused the Anti-Balaka of taking or killing their animals. One household reported having abandoned their flock.

3.3.2 High expenses for family members

As already mentioned, return migrants' families provided many different kinds of support to their relatives to ensure a safe return. Some return migrants were housed by relatives, which placed an added financial burden on the household. Indeed, the budgets of these households sometimes doubled or even tripled due to this practice. Today, some family members continue to pay back debts incurred due to the high expenses of accommodating returnees. Some families allowed returned migrants to use homes that they owned, which caused a reduction in family incomes because these houses or real estate were formerly rental properties and contributed to the families' income.

The return has created many difficulties in migrant households, affecting families and contributing to a rise in broken families due to divorce or death. If partners had not already divorced, some have since separated due to psychological damage incurred during this stressful and highly tense migration. Indeed, in some cases, the separations occurred due to family members moving in with in-laws because of the lack of means to gather the entire family under the same roof.

3.3.3 Increase of psychological problems

For some return migrants, the loss of self-sufficiency in the CAR and having to be assisted in Cameroon resulted in increased feelings of humiliation, especially for those who were forced to abandon houses and other assets. Others complained of losing their powerful positions in marital unions, with wives complaining of having to rely on family assistance and an overall loss of autonomy.

Survivors testified to having witnessed horrific scenes of people butchered with cutlasses, rapes or being tortured during the crisis. These traumas generate feelings of grief, fear and helplessness, etc. Furthermore, given their experiences in the CAR, some migrants are still traumatised to this day.

3.3.4 Reintegration problems

The reintegration of returned migrants in their homeland is discussed within several theoretical frameworks. Quantitative approaches focus on the reintegration of migrants in their homeland at a professional level. As Gaillard (1994) emphasised, when migrants returned home, their first concern was reintegration into professional lives established in the CAR. Cameroonian returned migrants from the CAR are emblematic of this trend as they were sometimes forced to leave prosperous professions during their return.

Accustomed to the conditions and standard of living in the CAR, migrants had difficulties adapting to Cameroon after years spent abroad. According to theories of neoclassical economics, the reintegration of migrants upon return to their countries of origin is difficult because they are neither prepared nor expected (Cassarino, 2004; Nkenne, 2016). Professional downgrades of respondents highlighted the reality of the situation, where some were only able to take on roles that they considered subordinate (such as night watchman, motorcycle chauffeur, firewood merchant, plank seller, shop assistant or employee) to the positions they held in the CAR (such as shop owner, breeder, vehicle sales prospector or farmer).

In the sample, 39.13 per cent of migrants (nine out of 23 respondents) were former store owners and/or suppliers in the CAR with very well stocked shops. Another 30.43 per cent (seven out of 23 respondents) were former cattle breeders in the CAR and disclosed a large livestock holding. They testified that, in their reintegration in Cameroon, they were reduced to marginal activities which generate incomes below what they previously earned in the CAR.

This reduction in professional status can point to why some expressed a desire to return to the CAR after reintegration in Cameroon. It is also apparent that returning to Cameroon also meant a professional downgrade for women (corresponding to three out of five). Of the female respondents, a farm owner became a non-governmental organisation (NGO) employee, the cattle breeder became a firewood merchant and the shop owner now became a full-time housewife. The two remaining female respondents continued their roles as housewives in Cameroon as they had previously done in the CAR.

Reintegration, which appears difficult at any level, often requires a new start, signifying an increased and alarming vulnerability for Cameroonian returnees. These migrants paid the heavy price of the Central African crisis. Impoverished and ruined, most of them had become burdens on their relatives and friends. Thus, reintegration has neither been smooth nor easy for them or their families. Most, if not all, of our 23 returnees regret their past life in the CAR and attest that the CAR is a country full of opportunities, such as in the exploitation of precious stones that can allow almost anyone to make money easily and effectively. For this reason, they stated their intention to return once the situation subsided or died down. Indeed, the failure of reintegration entices about 30 per cent[12] of respondents to show intent to move back to the CAR, despite the atrocities and other traumas from their migration that continue to haunt them.

4. ACTORS AND INSTITUTIONS

4.1 Civil Society

Civil society organisations were at the frontline of the reception of migrants in Cameroon. Often lacking financial resources (ECHO, 2014), they provided moral support to the hordes of refugees and returnees returning to Cameroon from the CAR.

At the Kentzou, Ngaoui and Garoua-Boulaï entry points, the Cameroon Red Cross gave practical advice to newcomers, including information on reception, orientation, hygiene and sanitation services. The Cameroon Red Cross (CRC) assisted the United Nations High Commissioner for Refugees (UNHCR) and the International Organisation for Migration (IOM) when they deployed at the border to facilitate registration processes. First aid was provided by a local health facility, the Africa Humanitarian Action (AHA).

The Association of Youth Muslim Volunteers of Briqueterie collected food, financial and clothing donations from Muslims and distributed them to returned migrants mainly in Yaoundé and Garoua-Boulaï. Their actions were motivated and guided by the Islamic tradition of charity through the pillar of *zakat*, which is alms giving that every Muslim with sufficient wealth provides in solidarity with the Muslim community.

The civil society organisation, "Yes Cameroon" trained some CAR refugees and eight Cameroonian returnees on various aspects of entrepreneurship and commercial management of small businesses.

4.2 Intergovernmental Organisations

Returning Cameroonian migrants and refugees benefited from registration and assistance, including food, water, medical assistance provided by intergovernmental organisations. Alongside the CAR crisis, UNHCR set up registration checkpoints for returned migrants and CAR refugees, together with volunteers from the CRC. UNHCR worked with two types of partners, the implementing partners (AHA, FAIRMED, Catholic Relief Services (CRS)) and operational partners (World Food Program (WFP), United Nations International Children's Emergency Fund (UNICEF), United Nations Fund for Populations Activities (UNFPA) and World Health Organisation (WHO)).[13] Alongside Médecins Sans Frontières (MSF – Doctors Without Borders), the UNHCR supplied water and provided health care services to returned migrants and CAR refugees. When the first wave came from the CAR in December 2013, there were consultations between UNHCR, MSF and the sub-divisional offices at Garoua-Boulaï on how to organise the reception of people crossing the border in large numbers.

Notably, some organisations did not support Cameroonian returned migrants affected by the crisis, including the EU delegation in Cameroon. Instead, the European Commission Humanitarian Aid and Civil Protection (ECHO) has taken charge of CAR refugees in its place. Historically, the EU intervention is more related to prevention of crises rather than providing services to those affected by current crises. As such, various programmes contained in the European Development Fund (EDF), including the Regional Indicative Programme (RIP) and the National Indicative Programme (NIP), aim to prevent crises by promoting good governance and rural development in states.[14]

4.3 Private Sector

In the towns of Kentzou and Garoua-Boulaï, some businesses and donors provided returnees with blankets, clothes, food and water in addition to notable donations made by Muslim dignitaries (ECHO, 2014). Muslim families with sufficient space and real estate sometimes received more than 100 Cameroonian returnees and other refugees in their homes (ECHO, 2014). At Kentzou, according to the sub-divisional officer, Muslim traders gave 900 000 Central African francs (€1350) as well as bags of rice to returning migrants.

In Douala, government authorities refused the proposal made by some businessmen to give returnees food and items such as clothes and blankets, arguing that, in the absence of a transit camp, it would not be necessary for returnees to receive support since distribution would be difficult. The Cameroon government created an ad-hoc committee and did not deem the creation of a transit camp necessary since the target was to bring migrants back to their families.

4.4 State

The evacuation service has been the main response given to a certain number of returnees by the government of Cameroon. But in the longer term, to facilitate (re)integration and recovery after the crisis, state responses have been less robust for a number of reasons, primary among which is a lack of policy framework migration. Consequently, even the wealthiest returnees have become destitute and dependent on relatives.

As previously mentioned, an airlift was organised on the instructions of the President of the Republic of Cameroon. The ad-hoc committee was established on 13 December 2013 to facilitate the reception and integration of the evacuated migrants. By December 2013, more than 300 Cameroonian nationals were evacuated from Bangui in a special flight, with more than 1000 Cameroonian citizens resident in CAR pleading with their embassy's officials to shield them from the violence (Kindzeka, 2013). Planes from the national airline Cameroon Airlines Corporation (Camair-Co) and some military aircraft were chartered to bring back Cameroonian citizens in distress and willing to return home. By February 2014, the airlift had brought approximately 4000 evacuees back to Cameroon.

At the Cameroon Embassy in Bangui, Cameroonians were received after presenting their identity documents. Those who returned to Cameroon through the airlift organised by the state of Cameroon had to comply with the official documentation requirement, which, as previously mentioned, was difficult for most migrants. While not all citizens were able to present this, the majority had to show proof of their citizenship. After completion, they were then transported to the airport in preparation to be airlifted to Douala.

Upon arrival at Douala airport, evacuees benefited from a reception by the ad-hoc committee and were provided with the following services:

- a lunch ration, comprising a sandwich and a bottle of water;
- medical care for sick return migrants;[15]
- psychological care for all migrants provided by mobile psychologists hired by the ad-hoc committee;
- registration of migrants according to destination in Cameroon – this task was delegated to the police in charge of reception services;
- travel arrangements for return to their families – all arrangements were made by the ad-hoc committee.

After each airlift arrival, migrants were welcomed, grouped according to their final destinations in Cameroon and sent on their way. Since there was no transit camp to accommodate them, only evacuees with medical conditions were retained for appropriate care.

The ad-hoc committee rented buses from a travel agency to transport return migrants to their destinations. In Douala, the ad-hoc committee allocated different amounts of money to migrants depending on the distance they were travelling within the country. This was just transportation assistance and not an allocation for the reintegration.

The assistance provided by the government of Cameroon was carried out based on the sovereign funds[16] guaranteed by the Presidency of the Republic of Cameroon and released by order of the head of state. The final amounts allocated were not stated, since they were included in state budgeting due to the lack of a genuine migration policy and programme for returning migrants in Cameroon. Nevertheless, return migrants who arrived by air were given some support, though this only corresponds to a minority of respondents. Once airlifted by the state of Cameroon, evacuees left for their final destinations without an official follow-up to ensure that they actually joined their respective families.

For the migrants arriving by road in Garoua-Boulaï and Kentzou, sub-divisional officers organised the reception of migrants and refugees. They issued special permits to all those identified as Cameroonians who did not have identification documents. People who reported Cameroonian citizenship and were not in possession of identification documents were required to give the phone number of a close relative who was then called upon to confirm the citizenship of the migrant in question. After this confirmation, the migrant received a special permit, valid for one week, allowing them to join their family. Other migrants had to wait for their identification documentation at the border.

This courtesy was extended only to migrants who returned by road, for which the identification checks had not been completed before departing the CAR, unlike those who benefited from the government-sponsored airlift programme who had been subject to identification verification at the Cameroon Embassy in Bangui.

Despite integration with their respective families, Cameroonian return migrants currently receive no special attention. They are not registered and do not receive any funding assistance from the government of Cameroon or other stakeholders. The "Reception Committee of Returned Migrants from the CAR" was essentially an ad-hoc institution created for the management of returnees who were airlifted from Bangui to Douala. The committee was dissolved in March 2014. From an institutional perspective, no policy or programme concerning the reintegration of returned migrants has been put in place so far.

5. CONCLUSION

The aim of this chapter was to assess the impact of the 2013–14 crisis in the CAR on Cameroonian returned migrants and to analyse the responses from various actors to meet the migrants' needs. The impact of the Central African crisis on Cameroonian returnees and members of their families was negative in all aspects and areas. Not having prepared for their return, they came back in a state of vulnerability and were left to endure the psychological externalities of a forced migration and due to the extreme nature of their journey back to Cameroon.

In many cases migrants acted on their own, without support of other stakeholders, to escape the dire situation. Some travelled by road, borrowing trucks filled with goods and even travelling in containers. Others escaped on foot through dense, patchy forests.

Although the government of Cameroon does not have a policy framework on migration, it allocated funds to evacuate by air and repatriate up to 4000 Cameroonian returnees, who benefited from the provision of basic social services such as medical care, psycho-social counselling and transportation assistance to their desired destinations. Nevertheless, the considerable number of migrants who travelled by road did not benefit from these services, and this disparity in treatment represents a gap in policy and practice that must be addressed in the case of any future crises.

Civil society organisations served as the first interface of support for migrant returnees. They provided support to returnees, assisting the UNHCR and IOM in registration processes. Other actors like business owners and local community leaders have been involved in responding to the needs of returnees.

Although there was short-term emergency relief and repatriation support from families, government authorities, intergovernmental organisations, civil society, and private sector actors during the CAR crisis, medium- to longer-term socio-economic reintegration has not materialised for return migrants. The crisis exposed the need to strengthen the capacities of the Cameroonian government and its intergovernmental and civil society counterparts to manage long-term mass returns of migrants ensnared in humanitarian emergencies abroad (Pailey et al., 2017).

Most of our respondents found it difficult to adapt and this complicated reintegration efforts. Following the CAR crisis many returnees have been left destitute and disillusioned. On their return, they have been reduced to employment activities which generate incomes below what they used to earn in the CAR. As such, their socio-economic positioning has been altered significantly. From a policy standpoint, the lack of sustainable reintegration has left many returnees vulnerable to exploitation and possible re-migration to the CAR, where, despite the region's instability, Cameroonian return migrants have found considerable economic opportunity.

NOTES

1. I obtained the data for this chapter from the MICIC (Migrants in Countries in Crisis) project funded by the European Union (EU) and implemented by the International Centre for Migration Policy Development (ICMPD) in partnership with Oxford University's International Migration Studies (IMI). I acted as Cameroon's local research partner. Thanks are due to Robtel Neajai Paley, coordinator of the CAR case study for her input and to Jean-Marie Nkenne, research assistant, geographer and assistant lecturer at the University of Dschang, Cameroon.
2. The six interview guidelines and the six stakeholder groups were defined by the *Data collection manual* of the MICIC (Migrants in Countries in Crisis Initiative) project (https://micicinitiative.iom.int/sites/default/files/General_Background%20Paper.pdf). Due to the qualitative nature of the MICIC subject matter, interviews were not expected to be statistically representative but sufficient to enable the drawing of generalisable outcomes. The number of stakeholders to be approached depended on any fieldwork context and were finalised between the local research partner and the case study coordinator. Our fieldwork took five months (from April to August 2016).
3. We met 23 returned Cameroonian migrants (18 males and five females), five migrants' family members, three experts in migration policy (a University lecturer, an officer of the Central Bureau of Census and Population Studies of Cameroon and the Programme Coordinator of CEMAC in charge of migrations), three intergovernmental organisations' representatives in Cameroon (an officer of the International Organisation for Migration (IOM), the Programme officer of the United Nations High Commissioner for Refugees (UNHCR) and the Programme officer of the Delegation of European Union (EU)), three civil society organisations' representatives (among them the Cameroon Red Cross's Coordinator of operations) and four representatives of the Cameroonian government administration (an officer in the division of demographic analysis and migration, an officer in the service of the governor of the Littoral region and two sub-divisional officers).
4. In 2007, Cameroonian emigrants were estimated at 170 363. France – with 38 530 migrants – is the preferred destination of Cameroonians, followed by Gabon (30 216), Nigeria (16 980), the United States (12 835), Germany (9252), Chad (5135) and the CAR (5103), among others.
5. It is possible through informal corrupt means for a foreigner to be granted legal CAR identity documents (birth certificate, identity card) by the CAR officials (Scharbatke-Church et al., 2017).
6. This kind of situation is experienced by foreigners in the CAR, including Cameroonians. We can read about this in the tale of travel from Douala to Bangui described by Lakosso (2012).
7. The establishment of the residence permit, which has a validity of two years, is subject to payment of an amount of 200 000 CFA Francs (€305), with bribes of unspecified amounts often demanded from government officials (Scharbatke-Church et al., 2017).
8. In the CAR, it is possible to buy a carat diamond at US$160 (€150) from a digger or miner and resell it between US$400 and US$600 (between €376 and €565) at an authorised purchasing office (Guion, 2013).
9. KM5 (read as "Kilometre five"), is the name of a Muslim neighbourhood in Bangui.
10. Compiled data from newspapers and field investigations.
11. Ibid.

12. These are opinions expressed during interviews with returning migrants, which are difficult to verify. However, despite the return to constitutional order, the security situation in the CAR is still subject to many concerns.
13. We cannot elaborate more on how tasks were divided and on what various stakeholders decided, since the interviewees did not give detailed answers, pointing to the fact that some information was confidential or internal. The same goes for the UNHCR partners, namely the AHA, FAIRMED, CRS, WFP, UNICEF, UNFPA and WHO.
14. We obtained this information from an interview with the Programme Officer, Economy, Trade and Governance section of the EU Delegation in Cameroon.
15. After the health checks, patients were admitted to hospitals and received full support including a per diem of 10 000 Central African francs (€15) for food and nutrition. The ad-hoc committee agreed to pay for the medical costs of over 30 people, including those suffering from severe diarrhoea or malaria.
16. The practice of financing emergency operations by the Presidency of the Republic of Cameroon is not subject to any disclosure about how much funds are allocated and the manner in which funds are used. Therefore, it is difficult to ascertain what the funds could have been allocated for in the absence of the CAR crisis.

BIBLIOGRAPHY

AFP (2016). "Cameroon, the main transit country for the diamond trade of Central Africa", accessed 2 December 2016 at http://www.lexpress.fr.
Agence France-Presse (2013, 14 September). "CAR's Djotodia dissolves Séléka rebel group", *Agence France-Presse*, accessed 15 July 2016 at http://www.france24.com/en/20130913-central-african-republicdjotodia-dissolves-seleka-rebel-group.
Amadou, A. (2015). "WD CAR: The repercussions of the Central African Republic crisis in Cameroon: Tensions already perceptible", accessed 15 July 2016 at http://www.connecting-in-times-of-duress.nl/wd.
Cassarino, J.P. (2004). "Theorising return migration: The conceptual approach to return migrants revisited", *International Journal on Multicultural Societies*, 6, 2, 253–279.
Charbonneau, L. (2015). "Cameroon involved in Central Africa 'blood diamond' trade: UN experts", accessed 15 July 2016 at http://www.reuters.com.
Chauvin, E. and C. Seignobos (2013). "The Central African Republic's imbroglio: State territories, rebels and bandits", *Contemporary Africa*, 248, 119–148.
de Waal, A. (2013, 18 December). "Opinion: Playing the genocide card", *New York Times*, accessed 25 July 2020 at http://www.nytimes.com/2013/12/19/opinion/playing-the-genocide-card.html.
Denzin, N. and Y. Lincoln (eds) (1994). *Handbook of qualitative research*. Thousand Oaks, CA: Sage.
ECHO (2014, February). *Central African Republic, regional impacts* (Crisis Report No. 15). Brussels: ECHO.
ECHO (2016). *ECHO factsheet – Cameroon* (April). Brussels: ECHO.
Einsporn, H.M. (2014, 19 June). "A forgotten crisis: Displacement in the Central African Republic" [Web log message], accessed 25 July 2020 at http://www.migrationpolicy.org/article/forgotten-crisisdisplacement-central-african-republic.
Escoffier, S., E. Ferrier, M.M. Olsen, M. Shusterman, and M. Norkute (2014). "Nature and forms of violence, causes of the conflict in CAR", accessed 25 July 2020 at http://www.irenees.net/bdf_fiche-analyse-1022_fr.html.
Gaillard, A.M. (1994). "Migration return: A bibliographical overview", Occasional Paper, Center for Migration Studies, Staten Island.
Gourdin, P. (2013). "Central African Republic: Geopolitics of a forgotten country", accessed 15 July 2016 at http://www.diploweb.com/Republique-centrafricaine.html.
Guion, A. (2013). "In Central African Republic, diamonds are eternal", accessed 29 November 2016 at www.lavie.fr/actualite/monde.
INS (2014). "Statistical yearbook of Cameroon", accessed 20 November 2016 at http://www.statistics-cameroon.org.

International Crisis Group (2014). "The Central African Republic's hidden conflict" (Briefing No. 105/Africa), accessed 29 November 2016 at http://www.crisisgroup.org/africa/central-africa/central-africanrepublic/central-african-republic-s-hidden-conflict.
International Crisis Group (2015). "Central African Republic: The roots of violence" (Report No. 230/Africa), accessed 29 November 2016 at http://www.crisisgroup.org/africa/central-africa/central-africanrepublic/central-african-republic-roots-violence.
IOM (2009). *Migration in Cameroon: National profile*. New York: IOM.
IOM (2014). *Migration dimensions of the crisis in the Central African Republic: Short, medium and long-term considerations*. New York: IOM.
IOM (2016). *MIDA project Cameroon. Guide for the capitalization of the potential of the Cameroonian Diaspora, Dakar, OIM, MINREX*. New York: IOM.
Kindzeka, M.E. (2013). "Cameroonians stream home from troubled CAR", *Voice of America*, accessed 29 November 2016 at http://www.voanews.com/content/cameroonians-stream-home-fromtroubled-central-african-republic/1811339.html.
Lakosso, G. (2012). "The road is approaching, Police and Gendarmes disintegrate", accessed 3 November 2016 at http://www.base.afrique-gouvernance.net/fr.
Lombard, L. (2014). "Genocide-mongering does nothing to help us understand the messy dynamics of conflict in the CAR" (African Arguments blog), accessed 29 November 2016 at http://africanarguments.org/2014/01/24/genocide-mongering-does-nothing-to-help-usunderstand-the-messy-dynamics-of-conflict-in-the-car-by-louisa-lombard/.
Lombard, L. (2016). *State of rebellion: Violence and intervention in the Central African Republic*. London, UK: Zed.
Loubière, T. (2013). "Six keys to understand the conflict in CAR", *Le Monde Afrique*, accessed 29 November 2016 at http://www.lemonde.fr/afrique/article/2013/12/05/republique-centrafricaine-leconflit-en-six-points_3526169_3212.html#4zIP2lKfu2XxzyIt.99.
Mayneri, A.C. (2014). "The Central African Republic, from the Séléka rebellion to Anti-Balaka groups (2012–2014): Uses of violence, persecutory patterns and media perspectives on the conflict", *African Politics*, 134, 179–193.
Mehler, A. (2011). "Rebels and parties: The impact of armed insurgency on representation in the Central African Republic", *Journal of Modern African Studies*, 49, 115–139.
MICIC (2016). "Guidelines to protect migrants in countries experiencing conflict or natural disaster", accessed 22 April 2016 at https://micicinitiative.iom.int/sites/default/files/document/micic_guidelines_english_web_13_09_2 016.pdf.
Mvongo, G. (2016). "'Security in East Region', redoubled vigilance", *Cameroon Tribune*, 18 July.
Nkenne, J.M. (2016). "International migration and spatial changes in habitat: The case of the Cameroonian Diaspora in Yaoundé", PhD thesis in Geography, International Migration and Local Development option, Université de Poitiers, France.
OCHA (2014). *The crisis in the Central African Republic and its regional humanitarian impact. An overview of needs and required funds: Central African Republic, Chad, Cameroon, Democratic Republic of Congo and Congo*. Geneva: OCHA.
Pailey, R.N., H. Yambene Bomono, and R. Hoinathy (2017). "Central African Republic at a crossroads – socio-economic development implications of crisis-induced returns to Cameroon and Chad", accessed 30 September 2018 at https://www.micicinitiative.iom.int/sites/default/files.
Scharbatke-Church, S., L. de Coster, and K. Barnard-Webster, with K.M. Ekomo-Soignet, P. Woodrow, and A. Sende (2017). *Pity the man who is alone: Corruption in the criminal justice system in Bangui, Central African Republic*. Cambridge, MA: CDA Collaborative Learning Projects.
Sindjoun, L. (2004). *State, individuals and networks in African migration*. Paris: Khartala.
UNHCR (2016). *Cameroon factsheet, August*. Geneva: UNHCR.
Yambene Bomono, H. (2017, 23–24 January). "MICIC Central African Republic case: Cameroon fieldwork emerging findings", paper presented at the "Migrants in countries in crisis" workshop, Centre for Migration Studies, University of Ghana.
Yambene Bomono, H. (2018, 19–21 September), "Mobility of Cameroonians in Central African Republic: Integration under the prism of differentiated strategies", paper presented at the International conference "The Nordic Africa days", Uppsala University, Sweden.

Zourkaleini, Y., S. Nouetagni, K. Seke, N. Kouam Chouapi, S. Hamadou, and J. P. L. Tjomb (2013). *Towards the South: Migrants' profile and the impact of migration on human development in Cameroon*, Yaoundé: ACP.

26. From Afghanistan border to Iranian cities: the case of migrant children in Tehran

Pooya Alaedini and Ameneh Mirzaei

1. INTRODUCTION

Iran and Afghanistan share substantial history and culture, including the Persian language which is official in the former and co-official in the latter. The two countries have been separated by an extended border in the modern period—running for more than 900 kilometers from Dahaneh-ye Zolfaghar or the tripoint with Turkmenistan in the north to Malek-Syah Mountain or the tripoint with Pakistan in the south. Until the late 1970s, all was relatively quiet at this boundary—barring occasional cross-border movements by the related locals of the two sides (Ruhzendeh 2005: 32–35). This changed after 1979 as a result of the Iranian Revolution and direct Soviet military involvement in Afghanistan. In the 1980s, Iran's post-revolutionary Islamist ideology was largely welcoming of Afghans[1] who escaped the civil war ravaging their homeland. The flight of Afghans, particularly to Iran and Pakistan, continued unabated through the 1990s amid the rise of the Taliban, while the post-September 11 US military-security operations in the country have made but a modest dent in the trend. At certain points during the last four decades, upward of 4 million Afghan citizens were estimated to reside in Iran, placing the country among the top-ranked refugee hosts. According to the most recent information, more than 950,000 Afghans are in possession of refugee cards in Iran, while another 450,000 have valid visas and an estimated 1–1.5 million are undocumented (UNHCR 2018).[2] The last census (SCI 2016) counted 1,583,979 documented Afghans in the country.

Shifting policies of the Iranian government—from an open-door stance to calling for repatriation, with ebbs and flows (Rajaee 2000)—have influenced the options faced by Afghan migrants in crossing the border between the two countries and settling in their destinations. For example, in the 1980s, Afghan colonies were allowed to settle in Iran's border towns and other areas en masse. In contrast, since 2002, some territories in Iran have been declared no-go for Afghan migrants (Government Cabinet 2002; Baharnews 2012). Yet, restrictions placed at one point on the education of Afghan children in Iran were overturned in 2015 by the Supreme Leader of Islamic Republic—who called for the provision of access to free education for all Afghan children regardless of their documentation. According to UNHCR (2018), 97 percent of Afghan migrants in Iran reside in urban areas. Given their population and extensive economic activities that dwarf those of other regions, the province of Tehran and especially the capital city have been important destinations for Afghan migrants. According to the last census (SCI 2016), around one third of all documented Afghans in Iran reside in the province of Tehran. The number of undocumented Afghan migrants is also estimated to be large or perhaps the largest in this province.

Poverty and lack of security in Afghanistan together with employment, educational, and further migration prospects in Iran have given impetus to the presence of a large number of Afghan children in Iranian cities. Although many of these children were born in the country, others have come to Iranian cities either with their families or even unaccompanied. A significant number of migrant children are benefiting from available educational opportunities. This is not limited to those who are documented. For example, 103,000 undocumented Afghan children were reported to have registered in the two middle school levels of the Iranian educational system in 2018 (UNHCR 2018). At the same time, many Afghan adolescents have become active in various occupations available in Iran's informal labor market.

This chapter investigates the case of Afghan children in the city of Tehran. Its focus is especially on those who are engaged in various occupations in the city or are working on the streets—some of whom are likely to have come to or reside in Iran unaccompanied. The study probes their socioeconomic and occupational circumstances together with their journeys from Afghanistan. It also briefly discusses Afghan children's further migration attempts to Europe. Given the difficulties associated with conducting systematic field research on undocumented migrants and those working in the informal sector, this study has relied on a number of sources—semi-structured interviews, non-participant observation, public-sector documents, reports and other types of resources made available by non-governmental organizations (NGOs) and private researchers, and news reports. The interviews were conducted in September and October of 2019 with Afghan children and adults, community leaders, and experts from various institutions.[3] Non-participant observations focused on children involved in solid waste recycling in the Harandi neighborhood.

2. FROM AFGHANISTAN TO IRANIAN CITIES

Of the 37.2 million population of Afghanistan, 42.6 percent are under 14 years of age (World Bank 2019). Yet, 58 percent of those under 18 in Afghanistan are reported to suffer from multi-dimensional poverty (National Statistics and Information Authority 2019). Additionally, 14,000 cases of rights violations committed against Afghanistan's children were reported by the United Nations (2019) in the 2015–2018 period—as a result of which 12,600 persons either lost their lives or sustained serious injuries. These circumstances have arguably given impetus to the continued large presence of Afghan children in Iran not only as part of migrant families, but also unaccompanied.

3. THE JOURNEY

Obtaining an Iranian visa, which is usually granted for air travel, is not easy in Afghanistan and together with the cost of the journey may amount to US$1000. Given this high cost, illegal border-crossing remains a preferred option for many Afghans coming to Iran. This is especially true for Afghan children, who may not even understand the concept of citizenship or illegal border-crossing. In fact, they are more likely to think of such journeys as regular business of survival with which they are already quite familiar. The Iranian government at times—particularly in association with Arba'in Shia ceremonies—encourages surface travel via Iranian territory to Karbala in Iraq, which can be used as an opportunity for some Afghans to stay in Iran.[4] Notwithstanding the more-or-less open-door situation prevailing during such occasions, it appears that most other cross-border journeys by Afghan children are now made illegally (as compared to earlier times). The number of Afghan children residing in Iran may be increasing as a result of not only migration by families as well as births, but also a rise in the number of unaccompanied child migrants. Of note is that around 4 percent of Afghans deported across the border in 2017 and 2018 were reported to have been unaccompanied and undocumented children (IOM/UNHCR 2019). Many are likely to have at least tried to return to Iran. Although most unaccompanied children are boys, there is also anecdotal evidence of some girls.

It appears that, in many cases, parents entrust their children to the hands of the known smugglers in their areas—who enjoy social standing and well-established networks—believing that a better life would be secured for them. Yet, some children have been sold into what practically amounts to bondage as a result of the extreme poverty and indebtedness of their families. Most such children would likely be forced into begging on the streets, drug-trafficking, or sex work in Afghanistan. Some of these children might also be trafficked across the border to Iran, although this does not appear to constitute the dominant mode for the presence of unaccompanied Afghan children in Iranian cities. Notwithstanding, many stories about the children's journeys are similar for recent arrivals and those who came to Iran decades ago—many via the tripoint area bordering Afghanistan, Iran, and Pakistan. Border-crossing takes place in stages via a sequence of smugglers. Apparently, the trip from Afghanistan to Pakistan is much easier than from Pakistan to Iran. The tripoint area is mostly settled by Baluch families with relatives in the other two countries. Tight kinship networks across the three countries makes the borders meaningless for the local residents and difficult to control for the authorities despite their extreme surveillance measures. As the area is poverty-stricken, smuggling goods (especially fuel) and people (mostly Afghans) remains significant for the locals among their few viable subsistence options.[5] Our interviews have indicated two major routes. One runs through Quetta in Pakistan to Sistan-Baluchestan—especially Taftan and apparently Mir-Javeh and Saravan in the recent period. The other travel route originating in Nimruz can avoid Pakistan by using rough trails.[6] Uninvolved locals, including religious figures, dislike the smuggling operations as high-speed vehicle journeys have made the area unsafe and insecure.

Some of the children interviewed for this study intimated the extreme difficulties experienced during their journeys—which is corroborated by other sources (e.g. Salam Watandar 2019). In some (earlier) cases, smugglers bringing migrants from Pakistan to Iran did not agree to take unaccompanied children across the border until some adult assumed the responsibility for them—in particular to make sure the costs of their journeys would be covered. This might take a while, during which time the children would stay in certain dormitories and work for meager wages in bondage-type relations. Anecdotal evidence in our interviews suggests that, under these circumstances, some adults, in particular pedophiles, might find an opportunity to abuse them by covering their expenses. Apparently, in the more recent period, smugglers have readily brought unaccompanied children to Iran, who may then work in various occupations to pay back the cost of their journeys.

Human smuggling routes running through mountain terrain and valleys are difficult and dangerous for everyone, and certainly more so for the children. Although under the surveillance of border security personnel, they are to a large extent no-man's lands where life and security are treated differently. Needless to say, the operations are controlled through tight networks. While bribes must be paid, they cannot always guarantee a safe passage or at least one without significant hassle. Migrants may be mugged or even taken hostage for ransom—which perhaps suggests that the robbers and smugglers are working in cahoots in certain instances. Under these circumstances, children are likely to be preyed upon for sexual abuse. Once in

Iran, Afghan migrants are transported first in pick-up trucks and then in sedans that may carry 15–20 passengers (given the derogatory name of *Afghanikash* or Afghan-carriers). Migrants must usually change vehicles a few times before reaching their destinations. The over-packed vehicles drive at dangerously high speeds and have been reported in collisions with very high number of casualties (Mehrnews 2016, 2019). According to those interviewed for this study, the journeys may take between two weeks and two months, with the latter including intermittent stays at some villages in border areas. The price given for a few years ago was 2–2.5 million rials, estimated to indicate a turnover of 600 billion rials a year (Zand-Razavi 2016).[7] Payments for the journeys are made at the destination. They are usually covered for the children by family members or relatives. Yet, there are also cases of children working in Iran toward compensating the smugglers.

The governments of both countries have called for the control of smuggling operations and have taken a few steps in this regard. For example, the High Commission to Combat Human Trafficking and Migrant Smuggling was established in Afghanistan in the early 2010s (Ministry of Justice 2019). More recently, a meeting on human smuggling was convened with the participation of the countries of the region (IRNA 2019). Furthermore, some members of the Afghan civil society have expressed their concerns about human smuggling (Salam Watandar 2019). Yet, not enough attention has been given to the smuggling of Afghan children. Nor has there been any attempt by NGOs focusing on Afghans to operate out of border towns on the issue of children.

4. IN TEHRAN

Many Afghans have found residence in the poor neighborhoods and slums of Tehran (major destinations for domestic migrants as well), given the lower costs of housing and living (Alaedini 2020). Networks established by earlier migrants continue to attract newcomers to these areas. For example, in the recent period, a significant number of undocumented Afghan migrants appear to have chosen to reside in Harandi next to Shush. This area is well-served by a number of NGOs, providing services to Afghan migrants, including children. A number of employment opportunities are also accessible in or from Harandi (Alaedini 2020). Many such migrants may have accumulated debts during their journeys, which must be paid back through hard work. All members of the family are thus likely to try to engage in some type of work from the very first days of their arrivals. This includes the children, who may only get a chance to think about educational opportunities once their families' financial circumstances improve. Our interviews with the children are highly indicative of their mindsets focused more on work and their families' economic situation than on education.

Formal barriers to the education of Afghan migrants at primary and secondary levels have now been removed by the government[8]—notwithstanding the earlier ups and downs as well as persisting practical issues. However, registration at Iranian public schools for Afghan children is not without challenges. This is especially true for older Afghan children who have lost many years of potential education. Furthermore, some Afghan children may prefer to study at self-managed Afghan schools to avoid any real or perceived discrimination or bullying. According to a staff member of one of the schools, Afghan children are still considered as the "other," a situation which does not appear to be improving any time soon. Furthermore, according to the same person, of the 198 students, 60–70 work on the side and after school hours. In this vein, flexible types of occupation are more suitable for them, and in fact many are engaged in work on Tehran's streets. This does not mean those children who work on the streets necessarily go to school. Furthermore, whether Afghan children are in Tehran accompanied by their families or unaccompanied naturally affects their educational, employment, and shelter prospects. Yet, some children who have come to Tehran unaccompanied have been able to earn enough money to bring their families to Iran. According to the interviewed NGO staff, while many Afghan families shun the work of women outside home, they readily accept the work of children. In fact, these circumstances appear to be a common attitude in Afghanistan.[9]

Some Afghan families have been able to collect enough money through selling their assets in Afghanistan or working hard in Iran to start a business—for example repair or retail shops. Their children are often active in these businesses and may sometimes establish side-activities of their own. These businesses usually have informal permits, secured through under-the-table payments. The children working in such shops enjoy relative safety and security, which allows them to potentially benefit from educational opportunities.

Other children, who have been in Tehran for a longer period, may work in brick furnaces, crystal-making, construction, or various types of small-scale manufacturing workshops. More often than not they are deprived of any benefit stipulated in the Iranian Labor Code. They are likely to lack work permits while micro and small workshops are exempt from providing many such benefits according to Article 191 of the revised Labor Code (Ministry of Cooperatives, Labor, and Social Welfare 2019a). This means that many employers prefer to hire inexpensive Afghan labor, which they may consider a hassle-free situation. Yet, Afghan teenagers (and even younger children) working in such workshops must accept the difficult working conditions, possible sexual abuse, and exploitation—including occasional non-payment or delayed payment of wages—over the fear of being deported. Most may have dropped out of school to be able to work. Yet, some Afghans have entered into partnership with their Iranian employers—as they have worked for and built trust with them since childhood.

5. CHILDREN WORKING ON STREETS

Children working on the streets—as young as toddlers and both boys and girls—may sell fortune poetry or other small items, burn wild rue, clean windshields, or engage in other seasonal activities. Usually, a few families come together to hire a car for the transfer of the children to the chosen locations on the streets, as they may start work early and continue until quite late at night. The working children on the streets of Tehran are not only Afghans but also Iranians—among whom turf wars may sometimes break out.

NGOs have been able to carry out a number of programs to provide educational opportunities for working and street children—including Afghans—and also to offer services to Afghan families. According to the head of the management board of the Child Assistance Network (*Shabakeh-ye yari-ye kudak*), in Tehran, Rey, and the nearby Karaj, 12,000 working children are covered by their services. Three quarters are Afghans and the rest Iranian. It is claimed that they have succeeded in reducing child labor in the recent period, by providing the children schooling for half of the day. Some children have stopped working the streets altogether, according to the network. Yet, increasing poverty, especially as a result of the internationally imposed sanctions on the Iranian economy, means that many of the children must work. The work of the NGOs cannot stop this.

In 2015, the Iranian government adopted the Convention on the Rights of the Child (United Nations 1989). A dedicated institution has also been created for this, which now operates under the Ministry of Justice. However, according to activists, this office has not taken any meaningful step or sought the collaboration of civil society institutions to address the issue. Earlier public-sector initiatives in Iran have also treated street and working children (Ministry of Cooperatives, Labor, and Social Welfare 2019b). In 2005, some guidelines on street and working children were formulated by the government. Since then there have been occasional attempts by the public sector to remove the children from the streets—despite opposition from civil society institutions. According to our interviewees, a number of NGOs have complained that some children under their auspices had been picked up by the authorities from the streets more than five times and sometimes ten times. Despite the obvious futility of such attempts, similar actions were carried out in June 2019. There is a great deal of opposition to such activities, voiced by both public-sector and civil society institutions.

According to some of our interviewees, relaying the experiences of NGOs, as well as news reports (e.g. Khabaronline 2019a), during previous attempts to remove children from the streets, they were placed in quarantine. The children were cut off from contact with their families and in effect were imprisoned. They may have been humiliated (for example by shaving the boys' heads). Although the children may not be kept in quarantine for more than 21 days, in practice some of them were held for much longer. Many of the children picked up from the streets were Afghans, some undocumented. The authorities have said their cases were referred to the Foreign Ministry to be addressed in collaboration with the Afghan Embassy (Khabaronline 2019b). It is not clear how they have been dealt with by the authorities, but fears have been expressed about attempts to deport them. Deportation of unaccompanied child migrants from Iran has been mentioned in IOM (2019) as well as some foreign news reports (e.g. BBC 2018). Such action would be in violation of Article 22 of Convention on the Rights of the Child (United Nations 1989) as well as Articles 3 and 9.

In any case, picking up the children from the streets has not had much effect, because it has been carried out with no other plan in mind. Most children return to the streets, while those who do not (because they are afraid of being taken away) shift their work to places that are even less supervised. Critics of such plans point out that alternative activities are more promising. These include the project on supporting children and their families as well as Tehran Municipality's initiative to establish 20 Partow Centers with the help of NGOs, which provide educational services to children not in school (Mizan 2019a). Overall, opinions are divided on how to deal with the street and working children in Iran. While some believe that supporting them may inadvertently encourage further child labor on the streets and migration of Afghan children, others believe that the project to pick up the children from the streets is an utterly futile exercise.

6. CHILDREN WORKING IN SOLID WASTE RECYCLING

A large number of Afghans are involved in activities related to municipal work (see Alaedini 2020). These are mostly adults but some teenagers under 18 may also be engaged in street cleaning or gardening activities. Yet, a relatively large number of Afghan children are involved in solid waste recycling in Tehran. Some have reached Tehran accompanied by a family member while others live in the city unaccompanied. Many must pay back the cost of their journeys or send money back home. Tehran Municipality has outsourced many of its activities to private-sector contractors. Activities related to municipal waste recycling and disposal are awarded to contractors through a bidding process, which has increased the municipality's revenues several-fold over the last few years (Farsnews 2019; Association for the Protection of Children's Rights 2019). Given the size of Tehran's growing solid waste (Waste Management Organization 2019) and the increasing value of what can be recycled out of it (Farsnews 2019; Association for the Protection of Children's Rights 2019), this is apparently a lucrative business for the contractors—so many of them try to win a contract.

Yet, recycling is actually carried out via two sectors—formal and informal. In the formal sector, contractors hire young workers wearing uniforms—some of whom, nevertheless, appear to be young teenagers. In the informal sector, the contractors act as middlemen. A number of waste recycling workshops (garages) are located on the outskirts of Tehran. The contractors enter into agreements with these workshops—which may be controlled by either Iranians or Afghans—for the work of recycling. That is, the contractor gets paid by the workshop-owner based on the estimated size of the recycling operation. The majority of workers at these workshops are Afghan boys, some as young as five. They are mostly sent from places like Zamanabad, Qarchak, Pasgah-e Ne'matabad, Yaftabad, Malekabad, or Pakdasht to various parts of Tehran to collect recyclable materials especially from dumpsters. They work from around noon until late at night—sometimes 2 or 3 in the morning. The children are brought back to the garages in pick-up trucks or vans—which have also been reported in accidents (Etemad 2017). There are no safety measures—such as gloves—and there have been reports of children losing their life due to fires at the workshops (Fararu 2017). Other children work in the garages to separate the recyclable materials. If caught on the streets, the children's collected items are confiscated—sometimes by use of force. Thus, they may end up paying bribes to public-sector agents. Since many of them are considered illegal (and can be deported), they must accept all kinds of hardship and keep silent. This is probably why they almost always use large bags rather than carts to collect the materials—so that they can escape at any time. Yet, carrying these bags, which can get heavy, most likely has lasting negative impacts on their bodies.

It has been reported (Farsnews 2019) that around 14,000 persons work in Tehran's solid waste recycling, of whom close to 5,000 are children—mostly Afghans. The approximate breakdown of the takings has been given as: less than 2.5 percent for the children, nearly 10 percent for the municipality, more than 20 percent for contractors, and upward of 50 percent for the garage owners (Association for the Protection of Children's Rights 2019). Needless to say, these workers enjoy very little of their childhood and have very little educational opportunity (being mostly illiterate). The children live in the garages alongside some adults and are likely to be sexually abused. They are prone to a variety of diseases—including hepatitis, HIV/AIDS, tuberculosis, and all kinds of dermatological ailments as well as insect and rat bites. Only two NGOs have probed the issue, but they have not attempted to address it. While the NGOs have difficulty in reaching these children—given where they work and live—the children may also be reluctant to reach out to seek help. There is also the opinion that working with these children requires special skills on the part of the public sector or NGOs—which has not been forthcoming.

Municipal contracts for solid waste collection and recycling contain clauses on supervision over the activities. In practice, however, there is little supervision concerning the work of garbage recycling or child labor. The most severe action taken is to fine the employers—which is actually a source of revenue for the municipal administration, but has no effect on the living or working condition of the children. Yet, there is some anecdotal evidence, based on NGO experiences, of the deportation of such children, as relayed to us during interviews.

7. ON THE WAY TO THE WEST

For many Afghan residents of Tehran—including poverty-stricken children whose circumstances were discussed above—migration to Europe and beyond remains an unrealistic goal given its costs. However, over the past few years—and especially in connection with the recent migration wave toward the West—a relatively large number of Afghan teenagers and younger children have been able to reach Europe and seek asylum.[10] Many of those who have succeeded in reaching their destinations had been in Tehran or elsewhere in Iran as long-term residents, accumulating financial resources. In fact, straight attempts to cross Iran for Europe seem to have been rare. One reason for their migration has been the fact that they had remained in a limbo state in Iran—especially those born or raised in the country. They could neither get Iranian citizenship nor go to Afghanistan (Dimitriadi 2013: 13).[11] Once such children reach Western Europe—which is not an easy task—they are likely to benefit from prevailing legal frameworks concerning children. Some families are likely to encourage such journeys—especially given the situation of Iran's sanction-hit economy—in the hope that the children will eventually be able to bring them over as well. Yet, while the earlier successful migration attempts of some Afghan children fueled a wave, many attempts have ended in failure and some children have fallen into the hands of criminals and abusers. This means that the stories of the journeys can both encourage and discourage further migration. In practice, the number of children actually reaching individual European countries is a fraction of those who come to Iran or Tehran—despite public-sector panic and rising xenophobia in the former destinations, which is partly fueled by media hype.

The children's demanding and dangerous journeys to Europe have been described in a few reports (see Dimitriadi 2013; Donini et al. 2016). The smuggling caravans may be shot at by border guards, or their members may be taken hostage for ransom. The first stage of the journey is made from the Iranian borders usually to Van and then Istanbul in Turkey. Once payments are settled, migrants may take dilapidated boats to Greece (Subhekabul 2019). The rest of the journey to countries like France, Germany, or the UK may take years—which means that some of the children are likely to be older once they reach their destinations and not accepted as child refugees. Facing asylum hurdles at their European destinations, others may fall into despair (Reuters 2016).

8. CONCLUSION

Notwithstanding the significant historical precedence, the onset of large-scale migration from Afghanistan to Iran in the modern era is traceable to four decades ago. Specifically, the population of Afghanistan was subjected to devastating political and military circumstances in the 1980s, resulting in significant internal displacements and the exodus of a large number of people to neighboring countries—particularly Iran and Pakistan. Against the background of linguistic and cultural affinities between the Iranian and Afghan populations, a large number of Afghan citizens have continued to migrate to and reside in Iran—both as a result of the ongoing political instability in Afghanistan and for economic/employment reasons. Included are Afghan children, whose numbers appear to be on the rise due to the circumstances not only prevailing in Afghanistan but also in Iran. Accompanying their parents, attempting to transit to Europe, or seeking educational opportunities may comprise some of the reasons for the presence of a large number of Afghan children in Iran. Yet, particular employment niches have also become available in Iran that attract Afghan child labor, especially in light of the widespread poverty suffered by the children in Afghanistan.

This chapter has probed the circumstances of Afghan children in Tehran—focusing especially on those working in difficult manual jobs or on the streets. In many cases, these children have come to Iran unaccompanied, undocumented, and relatively recently. The study has traced their arduous journeys through the Afghanistan–Iran border to Tehran, which also entails relatively significant costs. The expenses are either covered by their families or must be earned in Iran. Afghan children constitute a large share of those working on the streets or in solid waste recycling operations carried out as part of municipal activities.

A number of NGOs have been providing various types of services to Afghan residents of Tehran. A few others have worked with street children in the city. Furthermore, educational opportunities at the primary and secondary levels have now become available for all Afghan children regardless of their documentation. While many working Afghan children, including street children, have benefited from the services, their poverty and reliance on their work limits the effects of these initiatives. Indeed, Afghan children toiling in solid waste recycling operations under deplorable circumstances, who are also likely to live in Iran unaccompanied and undocumented, are hardly able to access such services.

The legal framework more-or-less exists for the Iranian public sector to provide some protection to the working and street children, including Afghans. However, the main public-sector initiatives on the issue have become misguided—notwithstanding lukewarm support given to NGOs and a few small projects backed by the urban management. Some street children have been picked up by the authorities and kept for long periods of time without any follow-up plans. Similarly, children working in solid waste recycling could be penalized for their activities, whereas no attempt has been made to change their circumstances. If from Afghanistan, children belonging to either group are likely to fear being deported. This may push them to seek employment in activities that are less observable by the authorities but likely to be more difficult or dangerous.

No workable solution appears to have been put forward concerning Afghan street and working children. Indeed, any forthcoming solution or set of solutions must address several issues—the circumstances of Afghan migrants, the rights of migrant children, child labor, and the plight of street children. To this we should certainly add the complex issue of illegal border-crossing or even the larger issue of significant Afghan migration into Iran—which must be addressed by the governments of both countries, taking into account the economic and security conditions at migrants' places of origin, the demand for child labor and the legal framework at the destinations, and the circumstances prevailing in terms of legal as well as illegal cross-border journeys. Notwithstanding, few paths to citizenship for documented Afghan migrants or for regularizing the residence of undocumented individuals are currently stipulated in the Iranian legal system. This, however, places significant limitation on their upward mobility and condemns many of them to a life of poverty—while many Afghan children have in fact been born or raised in Iran and are likely to stay in the country. The government should therefore take a more realistic stance toward these circumstances and reconsider the legal framework governing the lives of migrants in Iran. Furthermore, more efforts should be made to protect the rights of migrant children in accordance with the Convention on the Rights of the Child. The same goes for the rights of street and working children—who are also subject to the provisions of the Iranian Labor Code. Yet, addressing the plight of street and working children in Tehran, including Afghans, necessitates a change of public-sector attitudes and approaches together with clear policies that prioritize the welfare of the children above other considerations. With the collaboration of the central government, municipal authorities, NGOs, social services organizations, Afghan and Iranian communities, and other domestic and international stakeholders, these should lead to concerted interim and long-term programs that can actually address the issue. The programs must be integrated and comprehensive but also flexible and suitable for a variety of individual circumstances. A few small initiatives focusing on educational opportunities have been carried out in Tehran in this direction. These should be improved and expanded upon by leveraging successful international experiences and best practices as well as through active participation of various stakeholders. Additionally, more in-depth research into the situation of Afghan street and working children in Iran, and certainly not just in Tehran, is needed to help guide such initiatives.

ACKNOWLEDGMENTS

Appreciation is extended to Dr. Ghasemzadeh, Dr. Mirzayi, Mowlavi Hafez, Mr. Musavi, Ms. Jafari, Ms. Abdodallahi, Mr. Sarabi, Mr. Rezazadeh, Ms. Mazyarfar, Ms. Afrafaraz, Mr. Haghigattalab, and other interviewees. Needless to say, the authors are solely responsible for any possible error.

NOTES

1. Some citizens of Afghanistan prefer to be called Afghanistani, rather than Afghan, which more correctly refers to the Pashtun population of the country. However, in keeping with the international nomenclature, the term Afghan is used here.
2. Afghan migrants entering Iran prior to 2003, as well as their children, were considered UNHCR-type refugees and could obtain residency cards, known as *kart-e amayesh*, which have been renewed on 13 occasions so far. Others have renewable valid visas. Since the two types of documentation have different sets of privileges and limitations, some Afghans have tried to switch between them. Yet, among the large number of undocumented Afghans in Iran, some might have lost their legal status due to various circumstances.
3. The interviews included: telephone interviews with two adult informants, one in Iran and one in Afghanistan, who had extensive knowledge about the subject; interviews with five children who had experienced illegal border-crossing; a telephone interview with a religious leader active in Sistan-Baluchestan Province's border areas; an interview with an academic, who had intimate knowledge of border-crossing from Afghanistan to Iran and from Iran toward Europe; an interview with a cyclist with significant experience in Iranian areas bordering Afghanistan; an interview with board director of the Child Assistance Network representing 39 NGOs; interviews with two experts from Emam Ali Society (an NGO with significant experience on the subject); interviews with the

principal and assistant principal of the Farhang School (a self-reliant institution dedicated to the education of Afghan children); an (unofficial) interview with an officer of Iran's State Welfare Organization; an interview with an expert from the Dyaran Institute with knowledge about Afghan migrants. Results of previous field research conducted in 2017/18 in Tehran for another study (Alaedini 2020), which included interviews with five Afghan teenagers, were also leveraged. Additionally, audio files containing the experiences of two interpreters—one in Germany and one in French Calais—were used.
4. As evidenced by the rise in the number of children in some Afghan schools right after Arba'in ceremonies.
5. The local population also suffers from security and surveillance operations being continuously carried out in the area.
6. The entry points to Iran have naturally changed over time, while there are probably many routes (including the less traveled ones) between Afghanistan and Iran at any given time.
7. One US dollar equaled approximately 3,000 Iranian rials at the time.
8. Domestic advocacy for universal education as well as active participation of some Afghan fighters at the front against ISIS in Syria and Iraq is speculated to have influenced this initiative.
9. Child labor is reported to be common in Afghanistan, for example in Herat (Mizan 2019b).
10. According to Reuters (2019), there has been a spike in the number of Afghans seeking asylum in Europe, partly attributed to the effect of international sanctions imposed on the Iranian economy.
11. The issue of citizenship has only recently been addressed for those who have Afghan fathers and Iranian mothers, whereas the children of Iranian fathers and Afghan mothers were automatically given Iranian citizenship (see UNHCR 2019).

REFERENCES

Alaedini, Pooya (2020), 'Afghan migrants in Tehran: Toward formal integration', in Zahra Babar (ed.), *Mobility and Forced Displacement in the Middle East*, London, UK: Hurst, 103–132.
Association for the Protection of Children's Rights (2019), 'Yaghma-ye kudaki: pajuheshi baraye shenakht, pishgiri va kontrol-e padideh-ye zobaleh-gardi dar Tehran' ['Lost childhood: A study for understanding, preventing, and controlling the phenomenon of trash-turning in Tehran'], institutional report.
Baharnews (2012), 'No-go cities for residence and education of Afghans', accessed 11 October 2019 at http://www.baharnews.ir/news/2756 (in Persian).
BBC [Persian service] (2018), 'During the last five months, 2,000 Afghan children and teenagers have been deported from Iran', accessed 18 November 2019 at http://www.bbc.com/persian/iran-42608880 (in Persian).
Dimitriadi, Angeliki (2013), 'Migration from Afghanistan to third countries and Greece', Hellenic Foundation for European and Foreign Policy, accessed 10 September 2019 at http://www.ec.europa.eu/migrant-integration/index.cfm?action=media.download&uuid=FC2FEB61-A69C-758E-4BBB990D8936BF04.
Donini, A., A. Monsutti and G. Scalettaris (2016), 'Afghans on the move: Seeking protection and refuge in Europe', Global Migration Center of the Graduate School Geneva, accessed 25 December 2019 at https://repository.graduateinstitute.ch//record/293919?ln=en.
Etemad (2017), 'Report of Etemad newspaper on the work of the children in depots and recycling places', accessed 7 October 2019 at http://www.etemadnewspaper.ir/fa/main/detail/82685 (in Persian).
Fararu (2017), 'Loss of Samad and Ahad in heavy fire', accessed 8 October 2019 at http://www.fararu.com/fa/news/303235 (in Persian).
Farsnews (2019), 'Loss of childhood amid garbage: Walk of 14,000 garbage-turners in Tehran', accessed 8 October 2019 at http://www.farsnews.com/news/13980322000795 (in Persian).
Government Cabinet (2002), 'Act approved by member ministers of the Implementation Coordination Council for Foreign Citizens concerning inclusion of new regions', accessed 15 November 2019 at http://rc.majlis.ir/fa/law/show/121961 (in Persian).

IOM (2019), 'Return of undocumented Afghans', Weekly Situation Report, accessed 21 September 2019 at https://afghanistan.iom.int/sites/default/files/Reports/iom_afghanistan-return_of_undocumented_afghans-_situation_report_15-21_september_2019.pdf.
IOM/UNHCR (2019), 'Returns to Afghanistan 2018', accessed 15 October 2019 at https://afghanistan.iom.int/sites/default/files/Reports/iom_unhcr_2018_joint_return_report_final_24jun_2019english.pdf.
IRNA (2019), 'Meeting on combating human smuggling in Islamabad with the participation of an Iranian delegation', accessed 16 September 2019 at http://www.irna.ir/news/83477243 (in Persian).
Khabaronline (2019a), 'Strange case of the project on addressing child labor: Deportation of 50 migrant children', accessed 23 September 2019 at http://www.khabaronline.ir/news/1279695 (in Persian).
Khabaronline (2019b), 'What is the story of the deportation of Afghanistani working and street children', accessed 23 September 2019 at http://www.khabaronline.ir/news/1280946 (in Persian).
Mehrnews (2016), 'Illegal transport of foreign subjects in Kerman took the lives of 100 individuals', accessed 16 November 2019 at http://www.mehrnews.com/news/3681933 (in Persian).
Mehrnews (2019), 'Human smuggling created disaster/5 children lost their lives', accessed 16 November 2019 at http://www.mehrnews.com/news/4719720 (in Persian).
Ministry of Cooperatives, Labor, and Social Welfare (2019a), 'Labor code', accessed 25 December 2019 at https://www.mcls.gov.ir/fa/law/276/.
Ministry of Cooperatives, Labor, and Social Welfare (2019b), 'A brief look at the phenomenon of street children in Iran', Bureau for Social Pathologies, accessed 25 December 2019 at https://asibha.mcls.gov.ir/fa/ghorop/stieetchildren/intro (in Persian).
Ministry of Justice [of Afghanistan] (2019), 'Report of the High Commission to Combat Human Trafficking and Migrants Smuggling—2018', accessed 21 November 2019 at https://moj.gov.af/en/report-high-commission-combat-human-trafficking-and-migrants-smuggling-2018.
Mizan (2019a), 'Skill-training on starting small businesses for the families of 500 working children', accessed 27 December 2019 at http://www.mizanonline.com/fa/news/536481 (in Persian).
Mizan (2019b), 'Existence of 9,000 working children in Herat', accessed 27 December 2019 at http://www.mizanonline.com/fa/news/544389 (in Persian).
National Statistics and Information Authority [of Afghanistan] (2019), 'Afghanistan multi-dimensional poverty index—2016–2017: Analysis and report', accessed 26 December 2019 at http://www.mppn.org/wp-content/uploads/2019/03/AFG_2019_vs9_online.pdf.
Rajaee, B. (2000), 'The politics of refugee policy in post-revolutionary Iran', *Middle East Journal*, **54** (1), 44–63.
Reuters [written by S. Nordenstam and B. Lesser] (2016), 'For one Afghan boy, hopes of a new life in Europe end in suicide', accessed 15 October 2019 at http://www.reuters.com/investigates/special-report/europe-migrants-sweden.
Reuters [written by F. Guarascio] (2019), 'EU sees spike in Afghan migrants as many leave sanctions-stricken Iran', accessed 28 December 2019 at http://www.reuters.com/article/us-europe-migrants-afghanistan-iran/eu-sees-spike-in-afghan-migrants-as-many-leave-sanctions-stricken-iran-idUSKBN1WU14C.
Ruhzendeh, Jamileh (2005), *Gozari bar tarikh-e ravabet-e syasi-ye Iran va Afghanestan (az avayel-e Qajar ta zohur-e Taleban) va digar havades va bohranha-ye nashi az an* [*A glance at Iran–Afghanistan relations (from early Qajar until advent of Taliban) and other associated incidents and crises*], Tehran, Iran: Sobhdam.
Salam Watandar (2019), 'Those who did not have money had to clean the toilets', accessed 28 December 2019 at https://swn.af/article.aspx?a=44287 (in Persian).
SCI [Statistical Center of Iran] (2016), Census results.
Subhekabul [written by M. Arjang] (2019), 'Afghanistani migrants: Human smuggling mafia', accessed 25 December 2019 at https://subhekabul.com/%D8%B3%D8%AA%D9%88%D9%86%E2%80%8C%D9%87%D8%A7/%D9%81%D8%B1%D8%B2%D9%86%D8%AF%D8%A7%D9%86-%D8%B2%D9%85%DB%8C%D9%86/afghan-migrant-human-smugglers/ (in Persian).
UNHCR (2018), 'Operation: Islamic Republic of Iran', accessed 8 October 2019 at http://reporting.unhcr.org/node/2527?y=2019#year.
UNHCR (2019), 'UNHCR welcomes Iran's new nationality law addressing statelessness', accessed 15 October 2019 at https://www.unhcr.org/ir/2019/10/08/unhcr-welcomes-irans-new-nationality-law-addressing-statelessness/.

United Nations (1989), 'Convention on the Right of the Child', accessed 15 October 2019 at http://www.unicef.org/sites/default/files/2019-04/UN-Convention-Rights-Child-text.pdf.

United Nations (2019), 'Children and armed conflict in Afghanistan', Report of the Secretary-General, accessed 18 September 2019 at https://childrenandarmedconflict.un.org/document/2018-annual-report-of-the-secretary-general-on-children-and-armed-conflict/.

Waste Management Organization (2019), 'Statistics on Tehran city's waste', accessed 5 December 2019 at http://pasmand.tehran.ir/Default.aspx?tabid=481 (in Persian).

World Bank (2019), 'Data on Afghanistan', accessed 18 September 2019 at https://data.worldbank.org/country/afghanistan?view=chart.

Zand-Razavi, Siamak (2016), 'Jabejayi-e niru-ye kar: Afghankashi' ['Labor force relocation: Moving Afghans'], accessed 7 December 2019 at http://academicstaff.uk.ac.ir/sizand (in Persian).

27. Adolescent mobilities and border regimes in the western Mediterranean[1]

Mercedes G. Jiménez-Álvarez

1. INTRODUCTION

In the western Mediterranean context, migration involving minor children and adolescents who have left their families behind to migrate autonomously has captured the attention of academics, crafters of policies to protect children and foreigners, international organizations and groups advocating for the rights of migrants and child protection. According to UNICEF (2017), approximately 50 million children are migrants or displaced in the world. The mobility of young boys and girls and adolescents on the move without their parents or an adult responsible for them has been a constant in modern migration. Since the early 1990s, boys, girls and adolescents travelling without their families and referred to as 'unaccompanied foreign minors'[2] have become a visible part of global migration flows. In the current European migration context, child protection systems in northern and southern Europe are receiving unaccompanied migrant minors who have travelled from other continents in search of better living conditions. Some apply for asylum and some do not, but minors in both situations merit the protection provided for under the Geneva Convention of 1951 and each individual country's protection legislation. According to Eurostat (2019), the number of unaccompanied minors amongst asylum seekers in Europe increased from 10,610 in 2010 to 95,208 in 2015, and then decreased to 63,280 in 2016, 31,400 in 2017 and 19,700 in 2018.[3] Most unaccompanied minors were males (86 per cent), with females comprising a little over 10 per cent of the total. Girls have always been present, but often invisibilized, and subsequently exposed to forms of exploitation and precarious situations.

This chapter adopts a agentive perspective (Jiménez-Álvarez and Trujillo, 2019) to analyse the presence of foreign children and adolescents under the age of 18 who are legally constructed as unaccompanied foreign minors, both within and outside European protection systems, and the interactions generated by their presence in the last 20 years. Amongst other questions, the article explores child and youth migration as a form of circulation, provides reflections from the viewpoint of agency, looks at the concept of autonomous migration, critiques the extensive use of the legal concept of 'unaccompanied foreign minor', analyses the processes of institutional abuse and racism and examines border regimes and biopower. The chapter ends with some conclusions regarding the presence of foreign boys and girls who have migrated autonomously in host societies.

The author of this chapter has carried out several research projects related to the profiles, contexts and mobilities of Moroccan boys and girls on the move, specifically between Spain and Morocco, work that had formed the basis of her doctoral thesis. Based on many years of working directly with these boys and girls, their families and professionals from different disciplines and institutions (Jiménez-Álvarez, 2011, 2015a, 2015b, 2015c; Jiménez-Álvarez and

Trujillo, 2019), the author presents a synthetic perspective of child and adolescent mobilities in a European context.

2. MIGRATION AS A FORM OF CIRCULATION

The boys, girls and adolescents under the age of 18 who move autonomously without legal guardians or families have been and continue to be an active part of modern and contemporary migration processes throughout the world (Klapper, 2007; Werner, 2009; Ribas-Mateos and Laiz, 2014). Over the course of these migrations, minors have been found both moving alone and as part of domestic groups. A historical reading of contemporary child and youth mobilities reveals how childhood and child protection have been considered and constructed. Although there is currently a consensus regarding the construction of minors as subjects of rights entitled to a specific form of protection, throughout history, a variety of constructions of childhood, adolescence and youth have been offered (Feixa, 1996). However, it is possible to speak of the migration of minors with some continuity with regard to these studies of child circulation and mobility. Child mobility, in short, can be defined as the circulation of boys and girls connected to work, education, care, adoption or shelter (Lallemand, 1993).

The circulation of minors is a multifaceted, polysemic phenomenon that has been subject to three predominant interpretations. The first economically based interpretation explains the circulation of boys and girls in terms of burden-sharing, with respect to child rearing and education. The second interpretation views the exchange of minors as a way to reinforce ties in an extended family, while the third understands circulation as a type of social promotion (Jacquemin, 2009). The migration of minors, then, is a form of circulation in a globalized context characterized by the migration of adults with a polysemic significance (promotion, burden-sharing, crises in protection and dependency systems, the reinforcement of ties) (Jiménez-Álvarez, 2011, 2015b).

3. FROM THE PERSPECTIVE OF AGENCY

Traditionally, the migration of boys and girls has been analysed within the family orbit and trapped between two antithetical perspectives: protectionist or criminalizing. Analysing the agential capacity of children and adolescents in migration requires delving into the meanings and potentialities in the transnational migration network. Often, the academic focus is on the migration processes of adults, which eclipses the experience of children. However, over time various authors have begun to highlight the key role played by children in family migration processes. This chapter aims to be bolder, going further in considering the autonomous migration of these children and adolescents from an agential perspective, separately from the family, although in relation to and interacting with it. Minors are not, then, understood only within the logic of dependency on the domestic group. Rather, age – in addition to gender – is used to illuminate power relations within the family, making it possible to subjectivize its members and create the basis for autonomy.

4. AUTONOMOUS MIGRATIONS

In socio-anthropological terms, these adolescent mobilities (Ribas-Mateos and Laiz, 2014) contain a dimension that makes it possible to separate the interests of the domestic group from the interests of these age groups, and define power relations and interactions, thus underscoring how boys and girls in migration processes are the protagonists and take their own decisions, accepting risks and establishing strategies. These autonomous decisions are conditioned by their own circumstances, resources and individual objectives, not just those of their families, which may be more or less influential (ranging from an amicable agreement to a complete break with the family). First, the circumstances that concern them are related to the specific context that constructs their subjectivity, such as their schooling, first work experience, sexual orientation, relationship with their family, relationships with friends, a desire for advancement, structural or domestic violence, their life story and so forth. Second, their individual, non-transferable resources include, most notably, their peer networks, background, resilience and social capital. Finally, their distinguishable objectives refer to the subjects' own goals or aims, which may or may not differ from family decisions.

These three factors are the basic keys in the construction of this form of autonomous mobility (Jiménez-Álvarez, 2011, 2015b). The perspective of agency understands that minors who migrate outside their domestic group are creating a new form of movement. Their mobility evinces a social transgression that, on the one hand, questions gender and generational relations within the family and, on the other, challenges the territoriality of protection systems in Europe, putting international legal mandates to protect children and adolescents to the test. The question of agency also makes it possible to reformulate perspectives regarding the family through the viewpoint of the autonomous mobility of minors. Analysing the family situation based on the decisions taken by minor children provides an interesting contrast to the traditional approach, which looks at migrating minors within the sphere of family decisions. The standard bibliography establishes the categories for migrating minors: as minors 'left behind', so to speak, when one of their parents emigrates; minors who migrate with one of their parents; or unaccompanied minors. The epistemological field needs to be broadened, underscoring the key role that these children can play in family processes. This requires incorporating situations in which boys and girls migrate, while the families are left behind (Jiménez-Álvarez, 2015b)

> My family did not agree and my father was always cross with me when I returned from the harbour. But I was a very stubborn boy and it was very clear to me that I wanted to cross. However with time I never did imagine that I would miss my family so much [...] Imagine! I was able to cross when I was 17 and it took me two full years to see them again, and actually I was lucky enough, I have friends who have spent five years without seeing their families [...]. I have friends that do not see their families since five years ago [...[. (Mohamed)

> I have never told anyone that I have crossed with a patera [small wooden boat]. Actually, this is the first time that I am telling someone. I am not afraid to talk about my family any more. My father got the money for my trip with the patera, but he made me swear that I would not tell anyone. I use to have many problems at school, and in my village, I only wanted to leave. My mother used to cry and cried for a long time, every time I called her [...]. (Fatima)

> The worse moments, now, that I look at them in retrospective, is the time I spent in the streets of Ceuta. I could no call my family during months ... I could not call my mother ..., who is the only one in my family because I never got to know my father. My mother has never told me but I know that she had spent night after night without sleep. The day that I was able to reach her and tell her that

I was fine, that I was in Spain, was very exciting. During the time I was in the streets in Ceuta I had nothing, no mobile phone, no clothes, nor food. We were like animals ... I have never told my mother and I will never tell her. (Abdu)

5. CHALLENGING THE TERM 'UNACCOMPANIED FOREIGN MINOR'

This discussion of autonomous migration also aims to debunk the terms seized by epistemological and methodological nationalisms, such as the legal category of 'unaccompanied foreign minor', which distort the social complexity of this mobility. As an appropriate legal concept for the description of rights and duties, the extensive use of the term to describe the mobilities of autonomously migrating minors imposes an ethnocentric construction of childhood, adolescence and protection.

In its resolution of 26 June 1997, the European Council defined the legal subject of 'unaccompanied minor' and its use because it was widespread in European legislation on aliens. Endowed with legal potential – defining the vulnerable situation that entitles them to protection as both minors unaccompanied by adults and as foreigners in a country – the term began to be used widely. Social intervention disciplines started to employ it and, in the face of the need to name the potentially threatening unknown, many other terms were invented at the same time. The categorical use of 'unaccompanied minor' to describe the complex life processes of migrating boys, girls and adolescents reveals an epistemological and methodological nationalism that cannot be overlooked. Focus is placed on the point in the migration process that corresponds to access to European territory, as if nothing worthy of being named and/or considered before (or after) existed. The subjects' past and history are forgotten and they are constructed as a homogenous group to be handled as a uniform whole. Moreover, the territorial logic of child protection constructs a territorial and partial analysis and perception of these boys and girls. Action is only taken with regard to occurrences in areas where the social services have jurisdiction. However, when the only resource available to 'users' to counter standardized institutional responses is their mobility, protection falls short. Consequently, the use of the term 'unaccompanied minor' outside the legal sphere simplifies the complexity of the lives of these protagonists.

6. RACISM AND INSTITUTIONAL ABUSE

I arrived at Algeciras, after many attempts to cross from the new harbour in Tangiers, the big port. I hid with a friend and we arrived at Algeciras, they did not believe that we were under age. They did the bone test on us, and even so they repeated that we were not minors. I did cry and did swear to them that I was not yet 18, but it was useless to them. I was one of the most awful moments I remember. I felt I had to keep on the run, that Spain was not my dream anymore [...]. (Mohamed)

Of course, after having the experience of having lived in the streets in Ceuta you tend to think that you have seen it all, that nothing can be worse than that, but no, things can really be worse than that. Because Spain is like a obstacle course race, there is always a problem even if you do not believe it could be that way. In order to study, in order to have the documents [*los papeles*], in order to get a job ... I had never imagined that my life was going to be so hard. Look, I went then up to France, then up to Belgium, and then I went back to Spain, because as you move up from country to country, the situations gets much more complicated. They do not want us, you know? (Abdu)

These boys and girls are unique in that they are minors entitled to protection, according to international law, and, in turn, foreigners to be controlled, according to legislation on aliens. Since the mid-twentieth century, a consensus has formed about the construction of childhood as a subject of law deserving of a specific form of protection under international law. This consensus has led to the development of forms of government, legislation and international institutions that focus on protection. However, when the subject to be protected is a 'foreign minor' who has entered the territory in an irregular way, various forms of institutional abuse can occur. The roots of this abuse are found in the pre-eminence of border control in global migration policies and the fact that the migration and movement of these boys and girls challenges migration control systems. In short, the rights of minors are constantly called into question because of their dual status as both minors and foreigners. Child and adolescent protection systems are hijacked by their incapacity to ensure that the protection mandate prevails in this dual status.

The legislative framework regarding childhood is constructed around protection, while the legislative framework for immigration is predominantly focused on security. In general, the essence of childhood protection is aimed at defending children's rights and providing support, accompaniment, shelter, guardianship, defence, assistance and care. On the other hand, legislation on aliens restricts rights, focusing on control, expulsion, observation, detention and the quantification of foreigners. In other words, the two sets of regulations are at the opposite ends of any body of legislation. This is the scenario in which institutional abuse can occur. The image of trembling children disembarking on European coasts after highly dangerous sea voyages perpetuates a mediatized and racist view of the complexity of their motivations, a view that is, moreover, hijacked by the so-called compassion industry (Jiménez-Álvarez, 2015c, where I go beyond the migration industry adding the aspect of the oscillation between control and compassion). Europeans regularly witness extreme right-wing political groups attacking foreign boys and girls who have arrived without an adult responsible for them, and who are simultaneously within and outside protection systems. Their discourses and actions have incited racism and hatred, and distort the complexity of the migration processes led by these boys and girls and their subjectivities, fuelling false ideas and generating prejudice.

7. BIOPOWER, BORDERS AND EUROPEAN BORDER REGIMES

Although these unaccompanied foreign minors are entitled to a wide range of rights, in practice they are treated as 'infrasubjects' (De Lucas, 1996). Administrative practices create governed subjects with differentiated access to rights. In this respect, foreign minors are constructed as outsiders undeserving of protection and abusers of the public system. Some amount of laxity is allowed in the application of the law, and certain forms of institutional abuse are applied as a way for the government to control the migration of foreign minors, a form of biopower or intervention into the lives of people and the resistances they put up (Foucault, 2009 [2004]). On occasion, the rights of migrant minors are profoundly challenged by administrative actions, as they are deprived of guardianship, schooling and documentation (UNICEF, 2019). It is possible to violate the rights of foreign unaccompanied minors in various ways and for a number of different reasons: the rights of effective legal guardianship are impossible to exercise; the right to be heard is limited or non-existent; authorization for residency or work permits is slow, unreasonably delayed or stalled in paperwork; age determination processes are invasive or abusive; health care and education are provided with a lack of diligence; coordination between administrations is lacking to the point of institutional abuse; and the processing of repatriations and/or family reunifications is less than ideal.

Moroccan adolescents moving around Europe provide a window into how to look at these borders. The example of these adolescents reveals that borders must be analysed using a dynamic and transnational perspective. These young boys and girls and adolescents demonstrate the capillarity of power and its ways of governing mobility. The children have shown that borders are processes that are implemented in countries, and these processes trigger mechanisms of classification that determine access to rights. These children speak through their bodies, of how they are x-rayed and touched to determine their age; they speak about biopower and the forms of control and discipline that exist to ensure that they will be 'good users' of protection systems. These adolescents demonstrate that borders are legalized because laws on foreigners yield to child protection laws, which must prevail. Borders are politicized because attempts are made to control the mobility of these adolescents through cooperation projects with their countries to expel them, without considering the individual project of each person. Borders are material elements and technologies of control, because these minors' bodies are detained, harmed, weighed, touched, x-rayed and locked up without giving them a say, without letting them express what they think, without explaining to them what is happening in their own language. Borders are a way of thinking, because for many people, these are not 'first-rate minors'; rather, they are seen as 'the other', not 'the desired ones'. In short, borders are not only physical, but also legislative, executive, technological and ideological (Jiménez-Álvarez, 2015a). Young boys and girls and adolescents who migrate and move autonomously represent a group where the dynamics of control and foreignization crystallize with the most ferocity. They are intruders, even though they are children, even though they come from war zones, even though they are fleeing violence.

8. CONCLUSIONS

This chapter has focused on agential capacity in the field of migration and borders and human security. These are not good times for children and adolescents to be moving on their own. The zeal to control the border seems to be much stronger than the laws to protect children. However, the arrival of these 'unaccompanied' foreign boys and girls in European societies has provided an opportunity to both update and put child protection laws to the test on the continent. This chapter has offered some theoretical reflections on the concept of agency with regard to the meanings of these child and adolescent mobilities in a transnational context and their subjectivities in host societies. Providing support for new narratives and epistemological tools and practices that incorporate the complexity of human processes is one way to fight institutional abuse and racism.

The chapter has demonstrated how, by broadening the analytical angle of epistemological constructions related to boys and girls migrating autonomously, the specific subjectivities of their presence in host societies becomes recognized. The chapter (in addition to earlier research work, e.g. Jiménez-Álvarez and Trujillo, 2019) has also shown at least three ways of exploring such agential capacity with regard to three different contemporary changes.

8.1 The Protection Systems

The existence of Moroccan children and adolescents has created an opportunity to reformulate the way in which cultural diversity is managed and to intervene using networking, interdisciplinarity and a perspective that goes beyond territory. Because of the presence of foreign minors, various child protection systems in Europe are beginning to focus on cultural diversity and how to manage it. Generally speaking, the various child protection systems in Europe differ in their legal definition, pedagogical approach, intervention methodology and resources. At first, the presence of foreign minors who had migrated without a responsible adult and who needed protection from the public authority produced dysfunctions. Child protection systems were originally designed for minors with family in the same area. For the protection systems, beginning to work with foreign minors who had no family where the protection systems were operating led to a fundamental reformulation in the forms of protection and how to relate to the families. From being seen as a problematic reality, over time other initiatives consolidated that were committed to a new way of thinking about the family (with transnational social mediation being among the most important), attention to diversity, the need to learn other languages, and the incorporation of a perspective of inclusion and respect for difference. Although it is true that foreign minors in protection systems often experience the tension between being subjects of protection and control at the same time, it is also important to highlight the functional practices that have been constructed from a respectful perspective regarding their rights. Indeed, new professional profiles have emerged that make it possible to meet the needs of minors and ensure their rights. These new perspectives are beginning to look at aspects related to cultural diversity, question ethnocentrism in social intervention, and consider the importance of the children's language, their cultural and religious conceptions and the importance of training and supervising teams and professionals.

8.2 The Emergence of New Ways to Defend Children's Rights

A movement to defend the rights of foreign boys and girls has emerged and produced important legal achievements that benefit children and adolescents as a group. This has involved the creation of new ways to defend children's rights. In the case of Spain, the violation of the rights of foreign minors by the state led to the mobilization of a series of political actions to defend them, which have also had an impact on the way that the protection of Spanish children and adolescents is viewed. The quintessential example of this institutional abuse was the handling of 30 family reunifications to Morocco between 2007 and 2009, as data from my own fieldwork showed. In the face of this abuse, the Fundación Raíces (Roots Foundation) and lawyer Juan Ignacio de la Mata directed a defence network with the support of other organizations, lawyers, individuals and institutions in Spain and Morocco (SOS Racismo, Al-Khaima Association, General Council of Spanish Lawyers, Spanish Refugee Aid Commission, Coordinadora de Barrios Organization). This network carried out a group of actions aimed at effectively defending fundamental rights, challenging repatriations and aliens' legislation in the interest of safeguarding children through effective legal protection and the right to be heard. The way in which foreign minors have been defended has helped to reformulate the strict legal limits defining them and promoted legal actions that recognize their progressive capacity to exercise their rights.

8.3 The Emergence of New Forms of Social Intervention

Finally, the presence of these boys and girls has generated new forms of social intervention, such as transnational social mediation, that are making moves to accompany the mobility of these minors and rethink the territoriality of protection systems, which has been shown to be insufficient. Child mobility in the globalized world presents a window of opportunity to consider transnational social work. As I have shown, understanding the processes in which children migrating autonomously participate is circumscribed by the territoriality of the protection system. For this reason, it is necessary to deterritorialize how child protection is understood. These boys and girls are socialized in two systems, the contexts of the origin and host social systems. They are visibilized in a fragmented way, and their reference contexts are either not taken into consideration at all when protection actions are planned and carried out or, if they are considered, it is done from an ethnocentric, stereotyped perspective. Perhaps this reality is best represented by the legal term applied to them in the host countries: 'unaccompanied foreign minors', a designation shaped by a methodological and epistemological nationalism that fragments the way these children are viewed. Transnational social mediation is a methodology that consists of mediating by building a psychosocial and educational context between the family, association networks, public institutions and the migrating minors. It seeks to create a frame of reference for foreign minors and hold the family, public institutions and associations responsible for their part in the functional protection of foreign adolescents and children. The formulation of transnational social mediation advocates for a holistic view of the migration process, and for intervention that incorporates the life process and does not segment people according to a political construction of them. Moreover, it supports an inclusive dimension of intervention with foreign minors from the general perspective of protecting the rights of them all. This involves simultaneous actions in the origin and host contexts aimed at producing changes that foster individual development, making it easier to understand life projects. Here, the frameworks of belonging in which minors participate interact, strengthening the emotional ties between boys and girls, families and their contexts.

NOTES

1. This article was made possible by a postdoctoral contract with the Department of Applied Sociology, Faculty of Sociology and Political Sciences, Universidad Complutense de Madrid (UCM – BOUC, 24.07. 2017). For the ethnographic part of the chapter my research base is sustained by three life stories (2019) of two young adults and one female young adult in the frame of my postdoctoral research: Mohamed (A1), aged 20 living in Madrid; Abdu (A2), aged 20, living in Cádiz; and Fatima (A3), aged 22, living in Sevilla. They are all from Morocco.
2. Council Resolution of 26 June 1997 on unaccompanied minors who are nationals of third countries (97/C 221/03). The Resolution concerns third-country nationals below the age of 18, who arrive on the territory of Member States unaccompanied by an adult responsible for them whether by law or custom, and for as long as they are not effectively in the care of such a person. This Resolution can also be applied to minors who are nationals of third countries and who are left unaccompanied after they have entered the territory of the Member State. The persons covered by the previous two sentences are here in referred to as 'unaccompanied minors'.
3. The increase in 2015 was due to the migration crisis in the Mediterranean and the restrictive refugee policy in Europe.

BIBLIOGRAPHY

De Lucas, Javier (1996), *Puertas que se cierran. Europa como fortaleza*, Barcelona: Icaria.
Eurostat (2019), 'Asylum applicants considered to be unaccompanied minors', accessed 4 November 2019 at https://ec.europa.eu/eurostat/documents/2995521/9751525/3-26042019-BP-EN.pdf/291c8e87-45b5-4108-920d-7d702c1d6990.
Feixa, Carles (1996), 'Antropología de las edades', in Prat, Joan and Martínez, Ángel (eds), *Ensayos de antropología cultural*, Barcelona: Ariel, pp. 72–81.
Foucault, Michel (2009 [2004]), *Nacimiento de la biopolítica. Curso del Collège de France (1978–1979)* (Horacio Pons, trans.), Madrid: Akal.
Jacquemin, Mélanie (2009), *Urbanisation, changement social et protection des enfants en Afrique de l'Ouest et du Centre. Une revue documentaire*, Dakar (Senegal): UNICEF WCARO (Bureau de l'Afrique de l'Ouest et du Centre).
Jiménez-Álvarez, Mercedes G. (2011), 'Intrusos en la Fortaleza. Menores extranjeros marroquíes en la Frontera Sur de Europa'. PhD. Departamento de Antropología Social y Pensamiento Filosófico Español de la Facultad Autónoma de Madrid de la Universidad Autónoma de Madrid. Madrid.
Jiménez-Álvarez, Mercedes G. (2015a), ' Trasnacionalismo y régimen fronterizo: de lo jurídico, procedimental, institucional y conceptual', in *Actas del XIII Congreso de Antropología de la Federación de Asociaciones de Antropología del Estado español*, pp. 3869–3893, accessed 13 November 2020 at http://digital.publicacionsurv.cat/index.php/%20purv/catalog/book/123.
Jiménez-Álvarez, Mercedes G. (2015b), 'Autonomous child migration in southern European border', in NíLaoire, C. and White, A. (eds), *Movement, Im/Mobilities and Journeys*, Geographies of Children and Young People, Singapore: Springer, pp. 1–23.
Jiménez-Alvarez, Mercedes G. (2015c), 'Border externalization in the western Mediterranean: Mobilities, violence and the politics of compassion', *Revista de Dialectología y Tradiciones Populares*, vol. LXX, no. 2, 307–314.
Jiménez-Álvarez, Mercedes G. and Trujillo, María A. (2019), 'Infancia, adolescencia y juventud extranjeras que migran de forma autónoma. Entre la agencia, las movilidades y las fronteras', *Arxiu d'Etnografia de Catalunya*, no. 20, 183–204.
Klapper, Melissa (2007), *Small Strangers: The Experiences of Immigrant Children in America, 1880–1925*, American Childhoods, Chicago: Ivan R. Dee.
Lallemand, Suzanne (1993), *La circulation des enfants en société traditionnelle. Prêt. Don. Échange*, París: L'Harmattan.
Ribas-Mateos, Natalia and Laiz, Sofía (eds) (2014), *Movilidades Adolescentes. Elementos teóricos emergentes en la ruta entre Marruecos y Europa*, Barcelona: Bellaterra.
UNICEF (2017), 'A child is a child: Protecting children on the move from violence, abuse and exploitation', accessed 4 November 2019 at https://www.unicef.org/publications/index_95956.html.
UNICEF (2019), 'Los derechos de los niños y niñas migrantes no acompañados en la Frontera Sur Española', accessed 24 October 2019 at https://www.unicef.es/ninos-migrantes-no-acompanados.
Werner, Emma (2009), *Passages to America: Oral Histories of Child Immigrants from Ellis Island and Angel Island*, Washington, DC: Potomac Books.

Afterword: a brief mapping on borders

Marcos Correia

Maps give shape to the world and, often, maps shape the world where we live. The importance of maps grew along the evolution of their precision and accuracy. Beginning with the European Renaissance and along with the first globalization in the world's history, maps were used as an effective tool to travel, reclaim, conquer and divide the immense known and unknown territory. In 1494, the Treaty of Tordesillas, between Portugal and Spain, with (comprehensively) incomplete cartography divided the world into two spheres of influence; in the nineteenth century, it was used to quarter every square metre of Africa; and today it is such a common good that one cannot perceive how important cartography and maps are to our life through a myriad of apps and software.

Ultimately, a map is still a powerful tool that influences how one perceives the world by compartmentalizing original and artificial societies inside borders. Borders are often imaginary drawn lines created by multiple purposes and events: identity, natural resources, war, imperialism, geography. In the end, imaginary or not, they create a real division between people and societies. Nevertheless, their impact can be diminished, nulled or overcome through treaties and policies: the Schengen Space is a perfect example how a sense of intercommunity may overcome the traditional purpose of borders, especially in a continent where geopolitics had had such an important role over centuries.

The power of borders transcends representation beyond their physical and bureaucratic obstacles, feeding a collective and individual imaginary in many different ways. One does not need much time to remember a movie, book, music, painting, and other forms of art related with the thematic of borders, especially if one lives in a country marked by great events emanated from borders. In Europe, the famous film *Before Sunrise* is set aboard a train crossing an almost borderless territory; in USA the *Border Trilogy* novels of Cormac McCarthy explore the exemplary life on the border with Mexico; the band U2 sings about "Bloody Sunday" in a divided Ireland. These are some (Western illustrations and quick) examples of the materialization of the border beyond their objective reality.

However, the present book deals with much more important impacts of borders. There are 27 chapters from different authors who are able to demonstrate the effect of borders on people's daily and ritual life, in their life transitions and travels, in their aspirations for a better life and in their experience of violence and forms of compassion. They fundamentally show the interactions between migrants and borders (here represented by policies, politics, law enforcement agencies, society) in different areas of the world and between and in different countries and regions: the USA, Canada, Mexico, South America, Europe, North and Central Africa and Asia.

The maps created in this book followed a non-traditional format. Still, they are accurate enough for one to easily understand where each chapter takes place (the numbers on each map indicate the corresponding chapter numbers). The style used was drawn from the abstract and fragment pieces from geography that are usually in our mind. Many times, when trying to remember a specific route or country, a fragment that I had already seen on Google Maps or, in this case, Mapbox, came to my mind.

The maps I present here do not follow a contemporary format in other ways. They do not completely show what the geometry of occupation means within the practices that appear to be a global contagion. They do not completely show the conflicts in a global mapping, they do not show the "security algorithms" as a form of mapping and monitoring movements. They do not display how territories and territoriality are negotiated, how spatial technologies and practices are applied to the global shaping. Of course, borders are dynamic and are continuously evolving. Even if shown by basic lines they are not homogenous; they often tighten and loosen. Such maps neither show the reticular dimension of human and material movements, nor do they show the temporality of circulation. They do not show the geo-visualization which flattens technicity and web support and often become a superficial image of what we want to display, many times reproducing the dehumanization of border tragedies. They do not show the "encampment of the world" or a dynamic thought of migrants' and refugees' constantly changing routes.

In the end, it may be astonishing to realize that even the representation of maps in our head has evolved and, probably, our navigation skills too. Let us hope that, in the same way, we are able to create a more borderless world, in reality and in our minds.

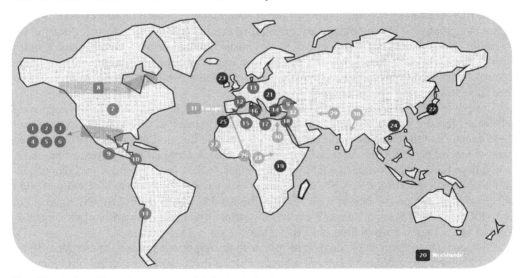

Note: The circles with numbers correspond to the book chapters.

Figure A.1 Location of the borders discussed in the book (general overview)

Afterword: a brief mapping on borders 423

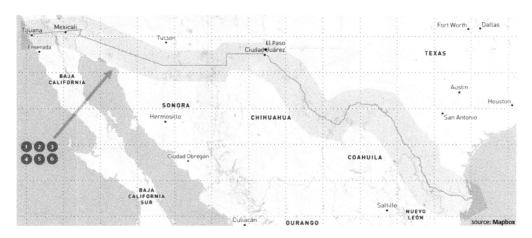

Figure A.2   USA–Mexico border

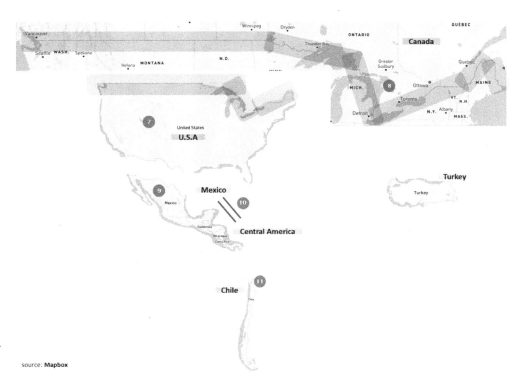

Figure A.3   Cases in the American continent and Turkey

424 *Handbook on human security, borders and migration*

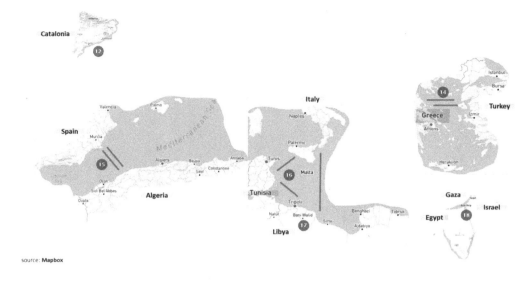

Figure A.4   Mediterranean border spaces

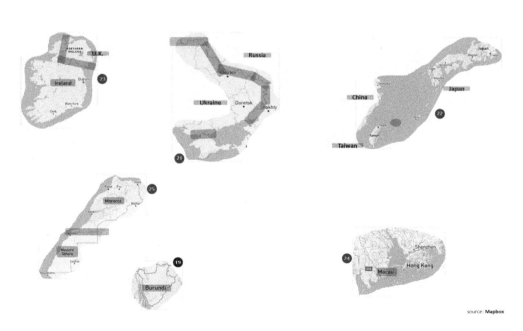

Figure A.5   Disputed borders and tense spaces – Africa, Asia and Europe

Afterword: a brief mapping on borders 425

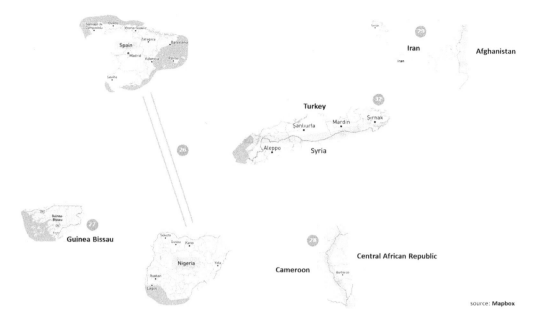

Figure A.6   Borders and migration links involving the Global South

Index

abortion 376–7
accountability 18, 36, 45, 47, 57, 63, 65, 112, 117, 134, 139, 144, 211, 215, 221, 291, 303
action research 10, 18, 210
activism 1–2, 8, 13, 25, 45, 55, 57, 96, 107, 202, 212, 234, 275
Adey, P. 12
Adra 217
advocacy 18, 25, 60, 74–5, 142, 144, 153, 190, 202–3, 211, 214–15, 217–18, 221
Aegean Sea 197–200
Afghanistan 25, 111, 192, 262, 399–403, 405–6, 425
Africa 13, 106, 182, 189, 213, 253, 255–6, 261, 266, 269, 273, 286, 288–9, 291, 301, 306–8, 347, 373, 376, 380, 421, 424
  see also individual countries
  African women on the road to Europe 373–80
Africa Humanitarian Action 391
African Development Fund 289
Agamben, G. 166, 232, 349
agency 1–2, 5, 12–13, 22–3, 25, 36, 47, 66, 75–6, 81, 113, 190, 197, 212–13, 221, 300, 306, 313, 350, 374, 412–14, 417
agentic approach 272
agriculture 18, 96, 103, 131, 149, 165, 169, 180, 244–5, 286–9, 315, 317, 365, 368
Ahmed, S. 232
AIDS 156, 180, 405
Alaedini, P. 23
alarmist portrayals 43, 45, 76
al-Baghdadi, A.B. 137, 139
Algeria 253–66, 373–4, 376, 378, 380, 424
Allende massacre 65
Alliance for Prosperity 149
Alonso, G. 93
Al-Qaeda 249, 260
Álvarez, R. 153–4
Amazon 24, 312–24
American Civil Liberties Union 59, 127
American Public Health Association 45
Andreas, P. 126
Anguiano-Téllez, M.E. 94
Anthropocene 21, 312–13, 315, 317–18, 321
anthropology 11, 215
anti-Latin@ policing 24, 125–35
Appadurai, A. 76, 92–4, 345–6
Arab Spring 13, 213

Arendt, H. 8, 195, 212
Argentina 145
Arias, G. 97
Ariztía, T. 94
Askeri 350–53
Associated Press 151
asylum seekers 3, 12, 24, 41, 44, 47, 55, 57–9, 61, 74, 78, 81, 84, 86, 181, 184, 406
Aucthter, J. 138
audio-visual 190–92, 96–7, 200–204
Aung San, S.K. 292
austerity 225–6, 228
Australia 303
Austria 180, 229
authoritarianism 5, 47, 57, 64, 73, 114, 139, 143, 227, 229, 231, 256, 302
autoasilados 71, 80, 82, 85–6
autonomous migration 6, 76, 211, 322, 412–15
Aznar, J.M. 260

Bakare-Yusuf, B. 378, 380
Balibar, E. 190, 194
Balkans 4
Bank of America 63
Bannon, S. 62
Barr, W. 134–5
basurización 15, 73, 81–2, 85–6
Beck, G. 132
Beck, U. 92
begging 378–80, 401
Bejarano, C. 9, 14–15
Belgium 301, 303
Belize 149
Bella, A.B. 256
Bello, C. 75
belonging 19, 75, 81, 93, 96–8, 226, 230, 232, 269–70, 272–80, 419
Bendjedid, C. 257–8
Bensakhira, M. 260
Berda, Y. 114
Berlin Wall 114, 118
Bilger, V. 375
Bin Laden, O. 141
Binational Front of Indigenous Organizations 96
biopolitics 18, 114, 120, 141, 165–73, 177–8, 182, 185–6, 232, 312
biopower 17, 166, 412, 416–17
Black Lives Matter 143
blackmail 386

427

body 22, 71, 83, 142, 315, 374–80
Boeing 37, 127
Bolivia 167–8, 315–17, 320
Bolsonaro, J. 229
Boltanski, L. 6
Bonito, M. 171
border
    economies 244–9
    enforcement 1, 3, 7, 9, 12–13, 26, 352
    external 227
    filters 12–13
    law enforcement agencies 26, 35, 39, 46, 129–31, 133
    militarization *see* militarization
    multiplicity 9
    practices 93, 114, 253
    strategy and tactics 38–41
    zones, violence in *see* violence
Border Patrol 14, 17, 35–46, 58, 62, 114, 125–35, 140, 192, 194, 351
Border Tuner 72, 75, 82–4, 86
Border Violence Monitoring Network 197, 200
borderism 93
borders *see individual borders*
    activism at 1–2, 8, 13, 25, 45, 55, 57, 96, 107, 202, 212, 234, 275
    approaches to fieldwork 10–11
    changing role of 1, 7–8
    disputed 21, 241, 345, 424
    humanitarian intervention at 1, 3, 5–6, 12–13, 18, 25, 45–6, 156, 170, 190, 202, 211–12, 215–17, 221, 232, 307, 347
    impact of globalization on *see* globalization
    militarization of *see* militarization
    new *spatialization* of 19
    porosity of 26, 96, 328, 336, 342, 362, 364, 385
    securitization of 2, 4–6, 8, 11, 23, 26, 112–13, 115–18, 171, 194, 211, 214, 216, 221, 255–6, 260, 262, 352, 361, 365
    violence at *see* violence
borderscaping 353
Borja, J. 92
Bosnia-Herzegovina 200
Boumédiène, H. 256
Bourdieu, P. 93, 270, 272
Bourgois, P. 139, 240
Bouteflika, A. 262
Bowling, B. 226
Boyce, G. 17, 128
Braidotti, R. 232
Brandariz-García, J. 226
Brazil 145, 229, 312–24
Breckenridge, K. 119
Brexit 12, 22, 233, 357, 362–5, 367–9
bribery 58, 63, 352, 401, 405

Bringas, N.L. 95
Brookings Institute 306
Brubaker, R. 230
Buckland, B.S. 116
Burgoon, B. 230–31
Burin, D. 75
Burundi 300–309, 424
Bush administration 36–41, 43, 46, 233
Buzan, B. 113–14
Buzatu, A.-M. 116

Cabezón-Fernández, M.-J. 19
Calderón, F. 64
Cambodia 182, 338
Cameroon 24, 384–95, 425
Cameroon Red Cross 391–2
Camp David agreements 239
Campos, A. 93–6
camps *see* refugee camps; tent cities/settlements
Camps-Febrer, B. 16
Canada 24, 90, 135, 157, 303, 421, 423
    see also US–Canada border
Canary Islands 4, 260–61
Candotti, F. 320
capitalism 10–11, 16, 20–21, 25, 55, 57, 63, 73, 79, 90–91, 102, 104–5, 111, 118, 166, 177, 179, 185–6, 212–13, 249, 285, 287, 289, 312, 315, 350
caravans 43, 71, 76–7, 151, 160, 253, 406
Care International 306
Caritas 158, 306
Carneiro, M. 319
cartels 38, 40, 62, 64–5, 79–80, 113, 143, 184
    see also drug trafficking
Carter, J.A. Jr. 16
Castells, M. 92
Castillo, D. 73
Catalonia 24, 228, 269–80, 424
Catholic Relief Services 153
Cayuco Crisis 260–61
Centers for Disease Control 135
Central African Republic 25, 384–95
Central America 9, 15–17, 20, 27, 35–6, 41–6, 54–9, 61, 64–6, 71–2, 76–8, 80, 82, 85, 96, 103–4, 106–8, 143–4, 180, 291, 425
    see also individual countries
    government responses to deported nationals 148–61
Centre for Returned Migrants 153–4, 156–7
Chad 386
chain migration 286
Chalfen, R. 197
checkpoints 17, 93–4, 126, 128, 134, 139–40, 144, 248, 336, 361, 392
Chicago Boys 166

child protection systems 195, 412–13, 415, 417–19
children 3, 6, 25, 41, 44, 71, 76, 81, 84, 180–81, 211–13, 217, 219, 221, 290, 304, 319, 324, 374, 379–80, 387
    adolescent mobilities in the western Mediterranean 412–19
    deaths during migration/detention 44, 60
    detention of 6, 44
    separation from parents/family separation 9, 43–4, 47, 59–60, 84, 95–6, 304
        see also unaccompanied minors
    street/working children 25, 403–4, 407–8
    in Tehran 399–408
    unaccompanied minors 6, 9, 42, 59, 106–8, 156, 181, 193, 200–201, 234, 401, 403–4, 412–19
Chile 24, 145, 165–73, 423
China 179, 182, 288, 293–4, 328–42, 424
Chthulucene 315, 321, 324
Churchill, W. 365
circular migration 49, 91, 165, 255
citizenship 1, 36, 47, 71, 75, 81, 85, 132, 134, 139, 226–8, 240, 269–70, 275, 305, 313, 322, 393, 400, 406
Ciudad Juárez 15, 63, 65–6, 71–4, 76–86, 94–6, 243
civil society organizations 25, 71, 84, 94, 140, 385, 391, 394
class 3, 8, 24, 71, 82, 139, 180, 212, 265, 269, 273, 288–9
climate change 109, 113, 177, 183–5, 286, 291
climate wars 179, 185
Coast Guard
    European Border and Coast Guard 195
    Greek 192
    Italian 217
    Libyan 14, 213, 216–17
Colombia 262, 312–17, 319–20
colonialism 11, 21–2, 24, 73, 111, 114–15, 139, 186, 257, 306–7, 312, 317, 328–9, 362
Commission Economique et Monétaire d'Afrique Centrale 385–6
Common Foreign and Security Policy 257
community security 2
compassion *see* politics of compassion
Concern International 306
concertina wire 62, 79
Consequence Delivery System 38–9
consular cards 153
Contreras, J. 132
Convention on the Rights of the Child 404, 408
coronavirus *see* Covid-19 pandemic
Correia, M. 24
corruption 57, 63–4, 86, 157, 288, 302, 342, 347, 351–2, 375

Cosmopolitics 21, 312
Couldry, N. 191, 201, 204
Coutin, S. 377
Covid-19 pandemic 5, 18, 24, 26, 134, 179–81, 186
Crimea 345–53
criminal organizations 38–9, 42, 56–8, 62–4, 66, 115, 150, 168, 320
criminalization of migrants 23, 36, 41–6, 114–15, 143, 226–7
critical race theory 79
CSI Aviation Services Inc. 158
cultural coding 16, 113
Curtis, D. 302
Customs and Border Protection 37, 41–2, 59–60, 62, 74, 78, 107, 125–7, 132, 134
Czernel, K. 127

Danish Refugee Council 181
de Genova, N. 158
De Giorgi, A. 226
de la Mata, J.I. 418
de Wilde, J. 113
deaths during migration 4, 38, 42, 44–5, 58, 60, 139–40, 144, 177, 182, 194, 213, 225, 232, 246, 376
    shipwrecks 4, 13–14, 197–200, 202, 213, 218, 225
debordering 15, 24, 72–4, 78, 82–6, 90, 92
debt 64, 106, 287–90, 318, 323, 375, 390, 401–2
deforestation 316–17, 320, 325
dehumanization 73, 86, 135, 138, 142–4, 170, 216, 221, 230, 233, 240, 422
Della Ratta, D. 203
democracy 64, 131, 143, 166, 190, 194, 228–9, 234, 256, 302
Democracy Now 140
Democratic Republic of the Congo 185, 192, 285, 304, 307, 386
Denaro, C. 18
Department of Defense 39, 134
Department of Homeland Security 37, 41, 43, 60, 125, 127–8, 133–4, 158
Department of Justice 127
Deported to Death 62
detention centres 44, 59, 143, 202, 213, 216–17, 219
detention conditions 44, 47, 59–60, 143, 193, 211, 304, 380
dignity 5, 15, 47–8, 81, 156, 173, 177, 198, 378
Dilla, H. 168
displaced pláticas 74, 85–6
displacement 9–10, 13, 15–16, 20, 23–4, 54–5, 60–61, 65–6, 71–9, 82–6, 94, 102–4, 107, 109, 139, 149, 157, 167, 212, 216–17, 244, 293, 300–305, 308, 339–40, 346, 349, 385, 407, 412

disposability 15, 71–4, 80–81, 84–5, 185–6, 221
disputed borders 21, 241, 345, 424
distant suffering 6, 18, 211, 215
Djotodia, M. 384
Doctors Without Borders 181
domestic violence 76, 304, 414
drones 37, 118, 127, 183
drug trafficking 38–40, 42, 46, 55, 58, 62–4, 72, 107, 115, 127, 150, 165, 168, 171, 247, 269, 312, 319–22, 324, 329, 331, 401
   see also cartels
Dublin Regulation 196
Dunn, T.J. 3, 12, 14–15, 54, 80

East India Company 111
economic development 20, 106, 108, 178, 181, 186, 244, 286–8, 291, 294, 353, 362
economic growth 104, 106, 150, 171, 178, 290, 293–4
economic security 2
economy, criminal 249
Ecuador 313, 315
Edensor, T. 276
Egypt 239–50, 424
Ekaterina II 348
El Fandango Fronterizo 96
El Paso 5, 9, 15, 38–9, 44–5, 54, 59–60, 65, 71–2, 79–84, 86, 95, 126, 243
El Salvador 57, 61–2, 76–7, 107
   government responses to deported nationals 148–61
Elbit 37, 42
elites 3, 56, 64, 106, 113, 117, 138, 177–9, 184, 186, 230, 257, 287, 290, 300, 302, 315, 329, 339, 350, 358
Emirates 181–2
empathy 75, 225, 233, 235, 306
encampments *see* refugee camps; tent cities/settlements
environmental security 2
Erdoğan, R.T. 137–9, 180
Erqian, G. 333
Escobar, P. 320
ethnic profiling 3, 12, 15, 17, 24, 45
ethnocentrism 3, 418
ethnography 7, 10–13, 15, 17, 19, 22, 25, 62, 74, 85, 191, 204, 215, 241, 246, 250, 274, 276, 280, 322, 345–6, 373
ethnoscapes 93–4, 97, 345
European Border and Coast Guard 195
European Border Surveillance System 195
European Central Bank 182
European Commission 182, 210
European Convention on Human Rights 193, 203
European Council 195, 210, 415

European Court of Human Rights 193–5
European Development Fund 392
European Economic Community 361
   see also European Union
European Parliament 195, 210
European Union 2, 4, 13–14, 118–19, 189, 191, 194, 202–3, 210, 213, 216–17, 225–7, 230, 253, 255, 257, 260–61, 269, 308, 347, 357, 363–4, 366–9, 376
   Brexit 12, 22, 233, 357, 362–5, 367–9
   EU–Turkey deal 189, 191, 193
Eurostat 412
existential mobility 374
expulsions 16, 20, 23, 25–6, 56, 60, 79, 86, 96, 102, 104–8, 167, 170, 179–81, 195, 198, 227, 232, 234, 242, 256, 259, 285–95, 331, 416
extreme violence 4–5, 8–9, 14, 109, 210–15, 221, 240–41, 286, 294, 384, 390
   see also torture
extremism 255, 261, 269

fabrication of corpses 8, 212
Facebook 190, 192, 200, 204
fake news 218
Falcón-Orta, V. 95
Families for Freedom 130
Family Network of Missing Migrants 153
family separation 9, 43–4, 47, 59–60, 84, 95–6, 304
   see also unaccompanied minors
fascism 181, 183, 229, 333, 347
Fassin, D. 5, 270
Félix, H. 92, 95
feminism 5, 9–10, 74, 96, 232, 321
Fernandez, M. 139
Fernández-Bessa, C. 226
Fernández-Suárez, B. 19
Ferrajoli, L. 219
Ferreira do Amaral, J.M. 330–31
fieldwork, approaches to 10–11
financial crisis (2008) 138, 228, 255, 262, 265–6
Floyd, et al. v. City of New York, et al. (2013) 134
FONAMIH 153, 156, 159
food security 2, 76, 301, 303
force, use of 16, 26, 111, 115, 117–20, 189, 194–5, 405
foreign direct investment 103
foreign policy 2, 13, 257
Forensic Architecture 144–5
Forensic Oceanography 203
Fortress Europe 4, 227, 266
Foucaldian approach 17, 26, 165–6, 177
France 178, 180, 229, 231, 255–8, 262, 303, 330, 406
Fraser, N. 280
free movement 102–3, 227, 232, 269, 349, 378

Freedom of Information Act 125, 128, 134
French Guyana 315
Frontex 192, 195

Gabon 386
Gaddafi, M. 219
Gaibazzi, P. 350
Gaillard, A.M. 390
Gambia, the 216, 271
gambling 328–9, 334, 336, 341–2
gangs 36, 40, 46, 57, 76, 150, 183, 219
Gaynor, N. 20, 302
Gaza Strip 239–50, 424
gender 3, 5–6, 8, 14, 25, 71, 76, 103, 139, 180, 210–17, 219–21, 230–32, 234, 269, 275, 290, 319, 322–4, 346, 387, 391, 403, 413–14
  African women on the road to Europe 373–80
gender-based violence 4, 96, 118, 214, 216, 218, 221, 234, 304, 323–4, 374
  see also sexual violence
Geneva Convention 203, 412
genocide 8, 212, 214, 218–21, 304, 347
Germany 166, 217, 229, 287, 406
Ghana 289–90
Ghertner, J.L. 126
Gilbert, E. 126
global economy 16, 102–9, 290
Global Legal Action Network 203
Global North 1, 102, 177–9, 182, 184, 213, 286, 290, 306–9
Global South 1, 3, 20, 24, 109, 119, 177–9, 182–4, 213, 285, 287–91, 294, 306–8, 425
global warming *see* climate change
globalization 1, 4, 7–8, 11, 16, 90–92, 96, 103, 115, 119, 168, 181–2, 215, 226, 230, 269, 285–6, 300, 306–9, 345, 413, 421
glocalization 92
Gomes Dias, A. 21
Gonzales, A. 227
Good Friday (Belfast) Agreement (1998) 363, 366
Google Maps 345, 350, 422
Goytisolo, J. 276
GPS 202–3
Grauvogel, J. 302
Greece 4, 180–81, 189, 191–8, 200–201, 204, 255, 424
  Coast Guard 192
Greek Refugee Council 193–4
Gregory, I.N. 361
Gros, F. 179
gross domestic product 104, 288, 308, 360
gross national income 300, 307
gross national product 256–7, 262, 289

gross value added 360
grounded theory 10–11
Guaido, J. 171
Guatemala 61, 76–7, 107, 126, 142, 144
  government responses to deported nationals 148–61
Guatemalan Repatriates Project 156
Guevara, E. 141
guns 54–5, 57, 62–3, 76, 128, 200
Guyana 315

Habermas, J. 91
Haesbaert, R. 92
Haftar, K. 216
Hage, G. 270, 272–4, 276, 278–9, 374
Haiti 9, 170, 308
Hamas 239, 243, 247, 250
Haraway, D. 313, 315–16, 321
hard borders 183–4, 364–5, 368–9
Hasan, A. 202
hate speech 226, 229–31
Hayward, K. 22
health care 106, 228, 290, 304, 319, 351, 392, 417
  see also medical attention
health security 2
Heavily Indebted Poor Country initiative 289–90
Help Refugees UK 201
Hernández, A. 93
Hernandez, E. 36, 39
Hernández Sánchez, M.E. 9, 14–15, 72, 79
Herrada, E. 131–2
Heyman, J. 3, 9, 11–12, 15, 172, 183–4
Hirschman, A.O. 201
HIV/AIDS 156, 180, 405
Hobsbawm, E. 359
homicides 15, 54, 57, 63–5, 80, 107, 113, 150–51
Honduras 57, 61, 76–7, 107, 271
  government responses to deported nationals 148–61
Hong Kong 328–30, 333–7, 339–42, 424
Hope Border Institute 80
horrorism *see* necropolitics
human agency *see* agency
Human Development Index 300
human rights 1–10, 13–15, 18, 21–3, 25, 35–6, 44–7, 55, 57, 59, 75–6, 83, 86, 97, 102, 107, 114, 117, 138–42, 144, 151, 153, 155, 158, 169, 171, 181, 186, 190–93, 195–7, 200–201, 203–4, 210–14, 219–21, 225–6, 228, 231–5, 301, 307, 316, 346–9, 353, 400
Human Rights Watch 181, 301
human trafficking 6, 12, 14, 26, 38–9, 42, 58, 113, 115, 157, 213, 217, 219, 375, 380, 401–2

humanitarian action 1, 3, 5–6, 12–13, 18, 25, 45–6, 156, 170, 190, 202, 211–12, 215–17, 221, 232, 307, 347
  transnational humanitarianism 210–21
Humanitarian Asylum Review Process 61, 78
humanity in excess 19, 181, 242
Hungary 229
hurricanes 149, 157

identification documents 128, 130–31, 386, 388–9, 393–4
  see also passports
Identification for Development 119
Iglesias, N. 93, 97
Immigration and Customs Enforcement 59, 126, 132, 143, 154, 158
Immigration and Nationality Act 127
immigration legislation 6, 40, 55–6, 58, 61, 77, 134, 144, 225, 227, 232, 257, 376
Imo 196
imprisonment 16, 59–61, 66, 103–4, 153, 180, 321, 380, 404
impunity 17, 54, 63, 137, 139–40, 144, 214, 220, 302
India 106, 262, 272, 330, 338–9
indigenous peoples 21, 96, 107, 170, 276, 291, 312–13, 315–24, 348, 385
Indonesia 292, 341
inequality 5, 8, 26–7, 64, 79, 103–4, 135, 157, 178, 212, 215, 225–6, 234, 275, 280, 285, 302, 306
institutional abuse 23, 412, 415–18
institutional violence 134–45
Integrated System of External Vigilance 260–61
intelligence 29, 39–40, 43, 116, 129
intergovernmental organizations 148, 151, 385, 392
internally displaced persons 65, 71–2, 76, 78, 85, 217, 304–5, 346, 349, 407
international law 6, 142, 194, 203, 211, 234, 416
International Monetary Fund 106, 182, 288–91
International Organization for Migration 151, 156, 181, 210–11, 214, 217, 220, 304, 391, 394
international relations 111–13
International Rescue Committee 181
Iran 4, 25, 399–408, 425
Iraq 111, 118, 192, 261
Ireland 24, 357–69, 421, 424
  Irish Republican Army 361–2, 364–5
  Troubles 361–3, 365–6, 369
Irish Republican Army 361–2, 364–5
irregular migration 3, 6, 80, 115, 205, 211, 227, 256, 265
Isacson, A. 84
ISIS 137, 139, 249
Islamic Relief 217

Islyamov, L. 350–51
Israel 239–50, 424
Italy 4, 7, 196, 201, 210–11, 216–17, 220–21, 228, 231, 255, 265, 424
  Coast Guard 217
  Covid-19 pandemic 180–81
Iturra Valenzuela, L. 17–18

James I 357
Japan 182, 330, 338, 340, 424
Jehovah's Witnesses 349
Jiménez, M. 6–7, 23
Joint Task Force–North (JTF–N) 39–40, 43, 49
Jones, R. 56, 93, 98, 194
Juergensmeyer, M. 65

Kaak and Others v. Greece 193
Kastner, K. 22
Kennedy, J.F. 142
Khader, B. 257
kidnapping 15, 57, 62, 66
Komarova, M. 22
Krischner, R. 142
Kuch, A. 305
Kurdistan 4

La Ceremonia del Abrazo 96
Laddaga, R. 75
land grabs 20, 102, 108, 286, 288, 290–94
Latin America 4, 8–9, 11–12, 17, 20, 56, 66, 80, 106, 117, 125, 130–31, 133, 150, 169–71, 180, 182, 289–90, 323, 377
  see also individual countries
Latin American Studies Student Organization 95
Leahy, P. 128
Leary, P. 22
Lemass, S. 362
LGBTI+ 143, 230–31, 414
Libya 4, 7, 14, 185, 203, 210–21, 261, 380, 424
  Coast Guard 14, 213, 216–17
lifestyle migration 255, 262–3, 265
living conditions 180–81, 193–4, 196, 200–201, 204, 247, 254, 304, 378, 386, 390, 412
Lloyd George, D. 357–69
Low, S.M. 277
Low Intensity Conflict Doctrine 80
Lukunka, B. 304
Luna, G.G. 64
Lundsteen, M. 19

Maastricht Principles 220
Macaísta Malheiros, J. 21
Macau 328–42, 424
Macedonia 200

Machado, J.J. 333
Madrid bombings (2004) 260
Maduro, N. 169, 171
Mahecic, A. 181
Maigman, W. 170
Malaysia 292–3
Maleno, H. 202
Mali 373–4, 376
Malta 4
Mann, M. 111
manufacture of corpses 8, 212
Mao, Z. 333
maps 314, 334–5, 359, 421–5
    see also Google Maps
maquila 12, 29, 67
Mare Nostrum Operation 7, 211
Martínez, O. 97
Marxism 118, 256
Massey, D.A. 41
Mauss, M. 178
May, L. 194
Mazouni, A. 19
Mbembe, A. 26, 139
McCarthy, C. 421
McMahon, S. 192
media 4, 43, 46, 157, 196, 200, 204, 219, 292, 351
mediascape 345
medical attention 45, 60, 211, 393
    see also health care
Medici Senza Frontiere 181
medicolegal gaze 17, 137–45
Mediterranean 1–4, 6–9, 11–14, 18–19
    adolescent mobilities in the western Mediterranean 412–19
    African women on the road to Europe 373–80
    blurred boundaries in Libya 210–21
    Catalonia bordering practices 269–80
    Egypt/Israel/Gaza Strip border 239–50
    hate discourse and policies of compassion 225–35
    migration/border changes following liberalism 177–86
    shipwrecks 4, 13–14, 197–200, 202, 213, 218, 225
    Spanish borders in Southern Europe 225–35
    Spanish–Algerian border relations 253–66
    violence at eastern European borders 189–204
Melo, F. 21
Mendoza, J. 95
mental health 54, 58, 201, 379, 390
metering 58, 78–9
#MeToo movement 221
Metuktire, R. 323

Mexico 25, 56–7, 107, 316, 421
    see also US–Mexico border
    Ciudad Juárez 15, 63, 65–6, 71–4, 76–86, 94–6, 243
    Covid-19 pandemic 135
    necropopulism in 144–5, 302
    Tijuana 65, 77, 94–6
Mezzadra, S. 90
Middle East 4, 189, 253, 255
Migrant Protection Protocol 61, 73, 76–80, 83, 85
'migrant trash' 73, 148, 160–61
migration flows 17–18, 105, 108, 150, 158, 189, 192, 195, 198, 204, 226, 254–5, 257, 286–7, 412
Migration Policy Institute 349
migration routes 18, 189–91, 196, 202
militarization 3, 14, 21, 26, 35–48, 54, 57, 78–80, 82, 85, 112, 114–16, 125, 133, 135, 183–5, 232–3, 240, 321, 324, 345–6, 348
militia groups 4, 13, 23, 40–41, 44–5, 74, 111, 183, 185, 212, 215, 301, 358, 384
Miller, C. 127
Miller, T. 17
mining 20, 104, 106–8, 286–94, 312, 317, 322, 386–7
Minnesota Protocol 142
Mirzaei, A. 23
mobility 1–7, 9, 12–13, 26, 72–3, 76, 78, 93, 114–15, 139, 159, 195, 211, 221, 253–5, 259, 262–4, 266, 269, 280, 329, 340–41, 373–4, 377–9, 408, 412–19
    existential 374
    paradox of 24–5
Mohanty, C.T. 75
Mol, A. 314–15
money laundering 63, 65
Monje, A.M. 75
Montenegro 200
Morales, M.C. 95
morality 5, 14, 25, 112, 232, 276, 308, 347, 380
Morawiecki, M. 229
Morocco 6, 9, 11, 25, 111, 255, 258, 260–61, 271–2, 373–4, 376–80, 412, 417–18, 424
MSS v. Belgium and Greece 193
Müller, J.-W. 138
multiculturalism 7, 11, 225, 233–4
Multilateral Debt Relief Initiative 289–90
multinational corporations 179, 288, 307
multi-territoriality 16, 90–92, 98
munitions 55, 63, 115
    see also guns
Myanmar 106, 287, 291–4

National Forum for Migration 157
National Guard 39–40, 43–4, 46–7, 60, 77, 80

nationalism 22, 24–5, 54, 62, 92–3, 97, 120, 138, 230–31, 274–5, 277, 333, 347, 358, 361–2, 380, 415, 419
nation-states 2, 7, 14–17, 36, 47, 71–2, 74–6, 79, 81, 84, 91–3, 97–8, 111–12, 135, 138, 182, 185, 227, 230, 232, 234, 255, 270, 276–7, 285, 314–15, 350
  see also sovereignty
natural disasters 149, 157–8
Navone, L. 19
Nazism 166
necropolitics 19, 21, 26, 115, 120, 139, 232, 234, 241, 312–13, 315–16, 319–21, 324
necropopulism 17, 137–45
Negri, A. 166
Neilson, B. 90
Neocleous, M. 119
neocolonialism 178, 183, 185, 312
neoliberalism 2, 10, 18–19, 23, 26, 92, 102, 112, 116, 119, 165–6, 172–3, 177–86, 216, 225–8, 230, 232–4, 312, 353
Nepal 308
Nestlé 106, 291
Netherlands 229
new security 26, 111–20
New York Civil Liberties Union 130
Nicaragua 158
Nicol, H. 126
Nieto, E.P. 64
Nieto Olivar, J. M. 21
Niger 220, 373–4
Nigeria 216, 373–5, 377, 379–80, 425
Niven case 203
Nkurunziza, P. 300–301, 305
Noda, E. 91
non-governmental organizations 4, 13–14, 148, 151, 153, 155, 158, 160, 181, 185, 190–91, 195, 200–201, 210, 212–19, 221, 228, 231, 233, 242, 275, 306, 346, 400, 402–4, 406–7
  see also individual organizations
non-refoulement 14, 79, 192, 194, 198, 203, 213, 218, 220
normalized violence 54–66
North American Free Trade Agreement 90–91
North Atlantic Treaty Organization 183, 347
North Korea 113
Northern Triangle of Central America 148–61
  see also individual countries
Nussbaum, M. 225, 233, 347

Obama administration 36–41, 43–4, 46
Oberreit, S. 181
Obrador, A.M.L. 92
Ocean Viking 181
Odgers, O. 94–6

Oglesby, E. 128
oil crisis (1973) 182
Oil Producing Export Countries 287
O'Neill, T. 362
Open Arms 218, 233
Operation Cast Lead 247
Operation Faithful Patriot 43
Operation Jumpstart 39–40
Operation Phalanx 39–40
Operation Rainbow 246
Operation Sophia 14, 213
Orbán, V. 229
Organisation for Economic Co-operation and Development 182
organized crime see criminal organizations
Orraca-Romano, P.P. 94
Orta-Falcón, A. 95
Oslo-II Accord 240
Ottoman Empire 141, 251, 350

Paasi, A. 346
Pakistan 202, 401, 407
Palestine 13, 192, 212, 239–50
Palidda, S. 18
pandemics 179–82
  see also Covid-19 pandemic
paradox 24–7
Paraguay 316
paramilitary 35, 46
Paris Peace Conference 360
Parnell, C.S. 358
Pasha, H. 141
Pasha, M. 141
passports 129, 168, 181, 242, 248, 255, 292, 345, 373, 386, 388–9
Patel, N. 306
paternalism 7, 232
peace process (1998) 22, 363, 366, 368–9
peacebuilding 300–303
Peraldi, M. 265
performance violence 65
personal security 2
Peru 145, 167–9, 258, 312–15, 320
Pettigo case study 22, 364–9
Peutz, N. 158
Philippines 316, 341
physical abuse 45, 47, 62, 211
Piché, G. 126
Piñera, S. 165–6, 168–72
Pinochet, A. 166, 168
Pinto, F.M. 338
Plan for the Alliance for Prosperity 76–7
Plan Frontera Norte 165, 168, 172
Plan Frontera Segura 17–18, 165, 172

plantations 20, 106–8, 285–8, 291–2, 294, 315, 317, 357
Poguisch, T. 211–12
Poland 229
police 35, 38, 43, 57, 64, 84, 111, 114, 118, 127–8, 133–4, 177, 179, 182–4, 200, 248, 261, 314, 321
  anti-Latin@ policing 24, 125–35
  Revolution in Military (and police) Affairs 178, 182–3
police violence 37, 47, 56–7, 118, 143
political security 2
politics of compassion 1–2, 4–7, 9, 13, 20, 211–12, 217, 346–8, 350–51
politics of responsibility 306–9
politics of violence 21, 312
population growth 179, 184
populism 19, 24, 137–8, 142–4, 225–6, 229–31, 233–5
  see also necropopulism
porosity of borders 26, 96, 328, 336, 342, 362, 364, 385
ports of entry 21, 38, 58, 62–3, 65, 71–2, 75, 78, 80, 91, 112, 133, 328
Portugal 182, 255, 265, 273, 312, 328–9, 331, 333–4, 338–42, 421
postcolonialism 25, 120, 380
post-Fordism 226, 253
poverty 3–4, 16, 54, 76, 103–5, 150, 157, 165, 178, 182, 184, 215, 286–7, 290, 294, 306–9, 399–401, 403–4, 406–8
power relations 97, 178, 221, 247, 250, 272–3, 319, 380, 413–14
pregnancy 376–9
'prevention through deterrence' 38–9, 42, 45
Pries, L. 96
privacy 114, 135
private security 16, 112, 116, 118–20
privatization of security 16, 111–20, 158
privilege 3, 12, 114, 232, 302
Proactiva Open Arms 228
Prompt Asylum Claim Review 61
prostitution see sex work
protests 47, 196
Ptak, R. 338
Puente, D. 218
Puguisch, T. 7
Purdeková, A. 303
pushbacks 189, 191–2, 195, 197–8, 200, 203–4, 213–14
Putin, V. 345, 347–8

Qatar Charity 217

Rachik, H. 11

racial profiling 3, 12, 15, 17, 24, 45, 115, 178, 232, 269, 314
racism 6, 8, 11, 15, 18, 36, 41, 45–7, 54–7, 65–6, 71, 74, 76, 79, 126, 130, 139, 143–4, 170, 172, 177, 180–81, 185, 211, 215, 226, 273, 275, 277, 279, 319, 412, 415–17
  see also anti-Latin@ policing
Rafah Border Crossing 19, 239, 241–3, 245–50
Rancière, J. 8, 212
rape 214, 219–21, 322–3, 376, 384, 390
rape trees 214, 221
rebellion 22–3, 384
rebordering 15, 73–4, 81, 84, 90–92, 98, 285
recession 138, 225
re-displacement 20, 300–301, 303
Redmond, J. 358
refoulement 14, 79, 192, 194, 198, 203, 213, 218, 220
refugee camps 4, 13, 180–81, 193, 203, 212, 216–17, 232–3, 242, 304–5, 377
  see also tent cities/settlements
refugee crises 6, 234, 303, 305
refugees, Syrian 18, 190, 192, 196–7, 201–3
Remain in Mexico policy 73, 76–80, 83, 85
remittances 152, 159–61, 181, 258, 307–8, 387
residence permits 258, 341, 386, 395
resilience 22, 25, 86, 221, 249, 373–80, 414
resistance 1, 8–11, 14–16, 23, 55, 58, 73, 83, 92–3, 140–41, 143, 166, 172, 186, 190, 196–7, 212, 228–9, 241, 322–4, 348–51, 357, 416
Responsibility to Protect 347
returned migrants 387, 390–92, 394
Revolution in Military (and police) Affairs 178, 182–3
Reyes, L. 132–3
Ribas-Mateos, N. 3, 18, 183–4, 253
risk management 115–16
Road and Belt project 294
Robertson, R. 92
Rocha-Romero, D. 94
Rohingya 287, 292–5
Roitman, J. 249
Romania 180
Rooduijn, M. 230–31
Rosales Sandoval, I. 17
Ruiz, O. 95
rule of law 118, 142, 349
Rumford, C. 346
Russia 330, 345–53, 424
  see also USSR
Rwanda 221, 302–4, 307

Sadat, A. 244
Sahlins, M. 8, 272, 362

Salter, M.B. 126
Salvini, M. 181, 220, 228
same-sex marriage 231
Sánchez, A. 91
Sassen, S. 7, 16, 20, 79, 91, 104–5, 178, 182
Saudi Arabia 182, 245
Save the Children 221
Sayad, A. 374
Schapendonk, J. 373
Schengen Area 4, 115, 118, 196, 227, 255, 257, 261, 421
Scheper-Hughes, N. 240
Schmitt, C. 349
Scull, A.T. 118
Sea-Watch 216, 218, 233
Second World War 102, 105, 340, 360
Secure Border Initiative 37
securitization 2, 4–6, 8, 11, 23, 26, 112–13, 115–18, 171, 194, 211, 214, 216, 221, 255–6, 260, 262, 352, 361, 365
security fetishism 116
security governance 112, 116–19
Sempere-Souvannavong, J.-D. 19
Senegal 271
September 11 attacks 11, 38, 91, 126–7, 133, 232–3, 255, 260, 399
sex work 156, 374–5, 401
sexual violence 4, 214, 216, 220–21, 304, 319, 323, 376–7, 379–80, 390, 401, 403
  see also rape
shadow bodies 377–8
Shamir, R. 115
Sharifi and Others v. Italy and Greece 193
SHD and Others v. Greece et al. 193
shipwrecks 4, 13–14, 197–200, 202, 213, 218, 225
Sigona, N. 192
Silva Santisteban, R. 72–3
Single Market 22, 362, 364
Sjoberg, G. 212–13
Skull Tower of Nis 141
Slack, J. 54, 62
slavery 293
slums 20, 106, 286, 288, 290, 402
Snow, C. 142
social media 65, 125, 190–92, 197, 200, 202, 204, 218
socialism 231, 333
sociology 24–9, 191–4, 229–30, 269–80
Soler i Lecha, E. 264–5
solid waste recycling 404–7
solidarity 1, 5, 8–9, 13, 18, 36, 75, 81–4, 96, 196, 202–3, 212, 215, 225–6, 228–35, 275, 321, 386, 391
Solis, M. 15–16
Somalia 185

SOS calls 196–8, 202, 206
Soufi, N. 197–8, 200, 202
South Africa 113
Southeast Asia 21, 179, 182, 291–4, 338, 341
  see also individual countries
sovereignty 1–2, 5, 12, 47, 113–15, 143, 166, 171, 216, 220, 230, 270, 285–6, 315, 329, 331, 349, 359
space 3–29, 59–69, 71–87, 90–98, 103–8, 112–16, 165–72, 180–84, 189–205, 210–221, 239–49, 253–61, 270–80, 293–5, 302, 316–23, 329–42, 349–53, 376–80, 421–4
Spain 145, 312, 373, 376, 378, 380, 412, 415, 418, 421, 424–5
  Spanish borders in Southern Europe 225–35
  Spanish–Algerian border relations 253–66
special administrative status 21, 329
Spencer, D. 90
Spitzer, S. 349
sponsoring 374–5
Staudt, K. 90
Still I Rise 197, 201
Strait of Gibraltar 4, 373, 379–80
Strathern, M. 321
street children 403–4, 407–8
street vendors 81, 98, 133
structural adjustment programmes 288–9
structural violence 1, 15, 20, 25, 36, 45, 47, 54, 56–8, 61, 66, 139, 414
styled bodies 377–9
subcontracting 118, 158, 185, 263
sub-Saharan Africa 13, 213, 286, 301, 306, 308, 373, 376, 380
suffrage 358
Sümer, B. 17
Summers, L. 183
Suriname 315
surveillance 6, 26, 35–7, 39–40, 42–3, 46, 71, 76, 82, 114–15, 119–20, 127, 134, 178, 183, 192, 195, 211, 243, 249, 259, 269, 285, 349, 363–4, 376, 401
Sutton, M. 361
Sweden 303
Switzerland 273
Syria 192, 201–2, 261–2
Syrian refugees 18, 190, 192, 196–7, 201–3

Taba Agreement 240
Taiwan 337, 424
Tajikistan 308
Taliban 399
Tanzania 301, 304–7
tariffs 60, 80, 247, 360, 362, 367
Tarrius, A. 253–4, 265
Tauli-Corpuz, V. 315–16

tax havens 182
technological revolution 182
technoscape 345
Tellez, M. 221
tent cities/settlements 15, 24, 71–86
territoriality 92, 114, 274, 414, 419, 422
   see also multi-territoriality
terrorism 11, 36, 38–40, 42, 114–16, 126–7, 133, 186, 233, 255–6, 260–62, 269
Thailand 292–3
thanatopolitics 18, 177, 181, 185–6
Thompson, E.P. 278
threat landscape 26, 111–20
Ticktin, M. 6
Tijoux, M. 170
Tijuana 65, 77, 94–6
Tobón, M. 21, 321
Tonga 308
torture 23, 62–4, 211, 213, 219–20, 380, 384, 390
tourism 95, 169, 184, 242, 258, 262, 328, 336, 362, 378
trafficking
   drugs 38–40, 42, 46, 55, 58, 62–4, 72, 107, 115, 127, 150, 165, 168, 171, 247, 269, 312, 319–22, 324, 329, 331, 401
   human 6, 12, 14, 26, 38–9, 42, 58, 113, 115, 157, 213, 217, 219, 375, 380, 401–2
transborder 10, 21, 24, 71, 82, 90–98, 157, 219, 253–4, 312, 320
Transfortierizx Alliance Student Organization 95
transnational feminism 96
transnational humanitarianism 210–21
transnationalism 92
transparency 1, 117, 350
treaties 7, 75
TRICAMEX 149
trinity of threats 114–16
Trócaire 306
Troubles 361–3, 365–6, 369
Trump, D. 4, 6, 10, 36–7, 43, 45–7, 56, 62, 77, 90, 92, 137, 139, 185, 229–30
Trump administration 37, 40–45, 56–7, 77–8, 135
Tunisia 4, 210, 216, 219, 255, 261, 424
Turkey 4, 180, 189, 191–5, 197–8, 200, 204, 406, 423–5
   EU–Turkey deal 189, 191, 193
   necropopulism in 139, 143, 302
Turkmenistan 399

Uehling, G.L. 6, 21
Uganda 289–90, 304, 307
Ukraine 345–53, 424
unaccompanied minors 6, 9, 42, 59, 106–8, 156, 181, 193, 200–201, 234, 401, 403–4, 412–19

undocumented migration 11, 22, 46, 126, 133, 139, 149, 154, 157–8, 178, 180, 194, 227–8, 233, 243, 308, 373, 399–402, 404, 407
unemployment 16, 103–4, 106, 150, 157, 248, 265, 271, 273, 290, 360
United Kingdom 111, 113, 117, 229, 328–30, 332–3, 342, 406, 424
   Brexit 12, 22, 233, 357, 362–5, 367–9
   Irish border 357–69
United National High Commissioner for Refugees 394
United Nations 4, 116, 137, 151, 169, 210–11, 216–18, 245, 305, 308, 315, 345, 349, 400
   Convention on the Rights of the Child 404, 408
United Nations Commission of Enquiry on Burundi 301
United Nations Convention on the Law of the Sea 220
United Nations Fund for Populations Activities 392
United Nations High Commissioner for Human Rights 210
United Nations High Commissioner for Refugees 181, 192, 210, 216–17, 303–4, 307, 391–2, 399
United Nations Human Rights Committee 203
United Nations International Children's Emergency Fund 392
United Nations International Narcotics Control Board 168
United Nations Office on Drugs and Crime 150
United Nations Security Council 221
United Nations Support Mission in Libya 210
United States 13, 25, 106–7, 111, 113, 118, 178, 182–3, 185, 227, 229, 232–3, 255, 258, 288, 303, 399, 421
   see also US–Canada border; US–Mexico border
   Bush administration 36–41, 43, 46, 233
   Covid-19 pandemic 135, 180
   Customs and Border Protection 37, 41–2, 59–60, 62, 74, 78, 107, 125–7, 132, 134
   Department of Defense 39, 134
   Department of Homeland Security 37, 41, 43, 60, 125, 127–8, 133–4, 158
   Department of Justice 127
   Department of State 292
   El Paso 5, 9, 15, 38–9, 44–5, 54, 59–60, 65, 71–2, 79–84, 86, 95, 126, 243
   Freedom of Information Act 125, 128, 134
   Immigration and Nationality Act 127
   necropopulism in 139–44, 302
   Obama administration 36–41, 43–4, 46
   September 11 attacks 11, 38, 91, 126–7, 133, 232–3, 255, 260, 399

Trump administration 37, 40–45, 56–7, 77–8, 135
United States v. Brignano-Ponce (1975) 128
United States v. Martinez-Fuerte (1976) 128
United States v. Preciado-Robles (1992) 128
Universal Declaration of Human Rights 234
universal rights 10, 190
    see also human rights
urban spaces 270, 274–7, 338
urban violence 107
USAID 156, 160
US–Canada border 125–35
US–Mexico border 1–4, 6, 9, 11–12, 14–16, 26, 103–4, 140, 180–81, 194, 232, 243, 249, 376–7, 423
    along the Great Lakes and 49th Parallel 125–35
    border wall 9, 37, 41–2, 62
    deportation to NTCA 148–55
    militarization of 35–48, 79–80
    normalized violence since 2014 54–66
    tent city mantling/dismantling at 71–86
    undo/redo the violent wall 90–98
USSR 182, 348
Uvin, P. 302

Vásquez, P. 126
Vatican 313
Vegetius, P.F. 351
Venezuela 165, 169–72, 231, 273, 312, 315
Verdery, K. 138
Verduzco, B. 95
Vianello, V. 264–5
Viber 196, 203
victimization 6–7, 15, 54, 57, 61, 232
Vicuña, J.T. 170
Vietnam 182, 341
vigilantes 40, 44–5, 62, 74, 111
Vila, P. 11, 90, 98, 243
violence 1–2, 8–10, 13–14, 25, 36, 41, 47, 75–8, 80, 85–6, 97, 102, 113, 115, 143, 150, 157–8, 214–16, 240, 319, 324, 361–2, 384, 388, 393, 417
    in Burundi 300–309
    conditions of 219–20
    domestic 76, 304, 414
    at eastern European borders 189–204
    extreme 4–5, 8–9, 14, 109, 210–15, 221, 240–41, 286, 294, 384, 390
    gender-based 4, 96, 118, 214, 216, 218, 221, 234, 304, 323–4, 374
    homicides 15, 54, 57, 63–5, 80, 107, 113, 150–51
    institutional 134–45
    as a missing discourse 194–5

normalized 54–66
performance violence 65
police 37, 47, 56–7, 118, 143
sexual 4, 214, 216, 220–21, 304, 319, 323, 376–7, 379–80, 390, 401, 403
    see also rape
structural 1, 15, 20, 25, 36, 45, 47, 54, 56–8, 66, 139
systematic review of 57–65
torture 23, 62–4, 211, 213, 219–20, 380, 384, 390
urban 107
use of force 16, 26, 111, 115, 117–20, 189, 194–5, 405
violent wall 90–98
virtual wall 37, 42, 46, 119
    see also surveillance
visas 3, 12, 19, 41, 46, 58, 133, 170, 227, 243, 248, 254–66, 379, 386, 399–400
Vogt, W. 72, 82
volunteers 45–6, 59, 74, 132, 134, 153, 191, 200, 202–3, 218, 248, 350, 358, 365, 392
vulnerability 5, 7–9, 14, 61, 76, 81, 135, 211–13, 230, 320, 415

Wachovia Bank 63
Wæver, O. 113
Walicki, N. 73
wall, building a 9, 37, 41–2, 62
'war against migrants' 9
War of the Pacific 167–8
war on terror 114
Watch The Med Alarm Phone 197–8, 202
Weiss, R.P. 118
Weizman, E. 144
Welcome Home Programme 153
welfare chauvinism 19, 225–6, 229–31, 234
Westenra, S. 226
WhatsApp 196, 200, 203, 210
Wilén, N. 302
Willeman, V. 153–4, 156
Williams, R. 278
Wingard, J. 71
Witteborn, S. 196
women *see* gender
working children 25, 403–4, 407–8
World Bank 106, 119, 157, 182–3, 256–7, 288–91, 301, 306–8
World Food Program 392
World Health Organization 392
World Trade Organization 182, 288

xenophobia 11, 15, 19, 23, 36, 46, 55, 57–8, 60, 63, 172, 204, 234, 384, 386, 406
Xi, J. 334–5

Yambene Bomono, H. 22–3
Years and Years 233
Yes Cameroon 391
YouTube 210, 215

Zambia 285, 289–90
Zelaya, M. 158